The Collected Works of J. Krishnamurti

Volume XIII

1962–1963

A Psychological Revolution

COLLECTED WORKS VOLUME 13

Photo: J. Krishnamurti, ca 1963 by Cecil Beaton

P.O Box 1560, Ojai, CA 93024

Website: www.kfa.org

Printed in the United States of America

ISBN 13: 9781934989463
ISBN: 1934989460

Contents

Preface

Jiddu Krishnamurti was born in 1895 of Brahmin parents in south India. At the age of fourteen he was proclaimed the coming World Teacher by Annie Besant, then president of the Theosophical Society, an international organization that emphasized the unity of world religions. Mrs. Besant adopted the boy and took him to England, where he was educated and prepared for his coming role. In 1911 a new worldwide organization was formed with Krishnamurti as its head, solely to prepare its members for his advent as World Teacher. In 1929, after many years of questioning himself and the destiny imposed upon him, Krishnamurti disbanded this organization, saying:

Truth is a pathless land, and you cannot approach it by any path whatsoever, by any religion, by any sect. Truth, being limitless, unconditioned, unapproachable by any path whatsoever, cannot be organized; nor should any organization be forced to lead or to coerce people along any particular path. My only concern is to set men absolutely, unconditionally free.

Until the end of his life at the age of ninety, Krishnamurti traveled the world speaking as a private person. The rejection of all spiritual and psychological authority, including his own, is a fundamental theme. A major concern is the social structure and how it conditions the individual. The emphasis in his talks and writings is on the psychological barriers that prevent clarity of perception. In the mirror of relationship, each of us can come to understand the content of his own consciousness, which is common to all humanity. We can do this, not analytically, but directly in a manner Krishnamurti describes at length. In observing this content we discover within ourselves the division of the observer and what is observed. He points out that this division, which prevents direct perception, is the root of human conflict.

His central vision did not waver after 1929, but Krishnamurti strove for the rest of his life to make his language even more simple and clear. There is a development in his exposition. From year to year he used new terms and new approaches to his subject, with different nuances.

Because his subject is all-embracing, the *Collected Works* are of compelling interest. Within his talks in any one year, Krishnamurti was not able to cover the whole range of his vision, but broad applications of particular themes are found throughout these volumes. In them he lays the foundations of many of the concepts he used in later years.

The *Collected Works* contain Krishnamurti's previously published talks, discussions, answers to specific questions, and writings for the years 1933 through 1967. They are an authentic record of his teachings, taken from transcripts of verbatim shorthand reports and tape recordings.

The Krishnamurti Foundation of America, a California charitable trust, has among its purposes the publication and distribution of Krishnamurti books, videocassettes, films and tape recordings. The production of the *Collected Works* is one of these activities.

Banaras, India, 1962

First Talk at Rajghat

I think most of us regard individual action as important. While there is so much collective action necessary, for most of us, the individual action is generally opposed to the collective action. Most of us regard that collective action is much more important and has greater significance for society than individual action. For us, individual action leads nowhere. It is not sufficiently significant, or creative enough, to bring about a definite change of order, a definite revolution in society. So we regard collective action as much more impressive, much more urgent than individual action. Especially technologically, mechanistically, in a world that is becoming more and more technically minded and mechanically minded, individual action has very little place. So, gradually, the importance of the individual diminishes, and the collective becomes all-important.

One can observe this taking place when the mind of man is being taken over, is being collectivized—if I may use that word—is being forced to conform much more than ever before. The mind is no longer free. It is being shaped by politics, by education, by religious organized belief and dogma. Everywhere throughout the world freedom is becoming less and less, and the individual is becoming less and less significant. You must have observed this, not only in your lives, but also generally, that freedom has withered away—freedom to think quite independently; freedom to stand up against something which you think is right, freedom to say no to established order, freedom to discover, to question, to find out for yourself. More and more, leadership is becoming important because we want to be told, we want to be guided; and unfortunately, when this takes place, corruption is inevitable; there is deterioration of the mind—not the technical mind, not the capacity to build bridges, atomic reactors, and so on, but deterioration of the quality of the mind that is creative. I am using that word *creative* in quite a different way. I do not mean creative in the sense of writing a poem or building a bridge or putting down, in marble or in stone, a vision that is being caught—those are mere expressions of what one feels or what one thinks. But we are talking of a creative mind in quite a different sense: a mind that is free is creative. A mind that is not bound by dogmas, by beliefs; a mind that has not taken shelter within the limits of experience; a mind that breaks through the barriers of tradition, of authority, of ambition, that is no longer within the net of envy—such a mind is a creative mind. And it seems to me that in a world where there is the threat of war, where there is general deterioration, not technologically, but in every other way, such a creative, free mind is necessary.

It is absolutely, urgently necessary to alter the whole course of human thought, of human existence, because it is becoming more and more mechanistic. And I do not see how this complete revolution can take place except in the individual. The collective cannot be revolutionary. The collective can only follow, can only adjust itself, can imitate, can conform. But it is only the individual, the 'you', that can break through, shattering all these conditionings, and be creative. It is the crisis in consciousness which demands this mind, this new mind. And apparently, from what one observes, one never thinks along these lines, but one is always thinking that more improvement—technological, mechanistic improvement—will bring about in some miraculous way the creative mind, the mind that is free from fear.

So in these talks—I believe there are going to be seven of them—we are going to concern ourselves not with the improvement of the technical processes which are necessary in the world of mechanistic action, which is collective, but rather how to bring about this creative mind, this new mind. Because in this country, as one sees, there is a general decline, except perhaps industrially, in making more money, in building railways, dredging canals, dredging rivers, iron works, manufacturing more goods—which are all necessary. But that is not going to bring about a new civilization. That will bring progress, but progress, as one observes, does not bring freedom to man. Things are necessary, goods are necessary; more shelter, more clothes, and more food are absolutely necessary; but there is the other thing also equally necessary—the individual who says no.

To say no is much more important than to say yes. We all say yes and we never say no and stand by no. It is very difficult to deny, and very easy to conform. Most of us do conform because it is the easiest way—to easily slip into conformity through fear, through desire for security, and thereby gradually to stagnate, disintegrate. But to say no requires the highest form of thinking, because to say no implies negative thinking—that is, to see what is false. The very perception of what is false, the clarity with which one sees what is false, that very perception is creative action. The denial of something, the questioning of something—however sacred, however powerful, however well-established—requires deep penetration, requires the shattering of one's own ideas, traditions. And such an individual is absolutely essential in the modern world where propaganda, where organized religion, the make-believe is taking over. So, I do not know if you also see the importance of this—not verbally, not theoretically, but actually.

You know there is a way of looking at things. Either we look at them directly, experience the thing which we see, or we examine what we see, verbally, intellectually; we spin theories about *what is* and find explanations for *what is*. But without finding explanations, without mere judgment, which we will also come to later, to perceive directly something as false requires attention, requires all your capacity. And apparently—especially in this unfortunate country where tradition, authority, and the ancient so-called wisdom rule and dominate—that energetic quality to see what is false, to deny it and to stand by it seems to be utterly lacking. But to inquire into what is false requires a free mind. You cannot ask if you have committed yourself to a particular form of belief, to a particular form of experience, to a certain course of action. If you have committed yourself to a particular pattern of government, you cannot question, you dare not question, because you lose your position, your influence, the things that you are afraid of losing. And also when you are committed to a particular form of religion as a Hindu, a Buddhist or what not, you dare not question, you dare not tear through, destroy everything to find out. But unfortunately, most of us are committed politically, economically, socially, or religiously; and from there, from that commitment, we never question the very center, the very thing to which we are committed. Therefore, we are always seeking freedom in ideas, in books, in a lot of words.

So I would suggest, if I may, that while you are listening, you are not only hearing the words which are only a means of communication, a symbol which needs to be interpreted by each one, but also, through the words, discovering your own state of mind, discovering the things to which you are committed yourself, discovering for yourself the things to which you are tied hand and foot, mind and heart—actually discovering it and seeing whether it is possible to break down the things to which you are committed, to find out what is true. Because, I do not see otherwise how a regeneration is to take place in the world. There will be social upheavals—whether communistic or otherwise—there will be more prosperity, more food, more factories, more fertilizers, more engines, and so on. But surely that is not all life, that is only a part of life. And to worship and live in the fragment does not solve our human problems. There is still sorrow, there is still death, there is still anxiety, guilt, the aches of many ideas, hopes, despairs—they are all there.

So, in listening, I would suggest that it should be rather the listening of a mind which is self-examining—examining its own processes rather than listening to words with which it agrees or disagrees, which is of very little importance. Because we deal only with facts—the fact that human beings are becoming more and more mechanical; the fact there is less and less freedom; the fact that when there is confusion, authority is resorted to; and the fact that there is conflict outwardly as war and inwardly as misery, despair, fear. These are all facts, and we have to deal with them, not theoretically, but actually. So, what we are concerned with is how to bring about a change, a radical revolution in the individual, in the listener, because he is the only one that can be creative—not the politician, not the leader, not the important man; they have committed themselves, and they have settled down in a groove, and they want fame, they want power, position. You also may want them, but you are still feeling your way towards them; so, there is still some hope because you are not completely committed, you are not the big men of the land. You are still small people, you are not leaders, you have no tremendous organizations over which you are the bosses, you are just ordinary average men, and being fairly uncommitted, you have still some hope.

Therefore, it may be possible, though at the eleventh hour, to bring about this change in ourselves. And so, that is the only thing with which we are concerned: how to bring about this tremendous revolution within ourselves?

Most of us change through compulsion, through some outside influence, through fear, through punishment, or through reward—that is the only thing that will make us change. Do follow this, sirs, observe all this. We never change voluntarily; we always change with a motive, and a change through a motive is no change at all. And to be aware of the motives, of the influences, of the compulsions that force us to change, to be aware of them and to deny them is to bring about change. Circumstances make us change; the family, the law, our ambitions, our fears bring about a change. But that change is a reaction and therefore, really, it is a resistance, a psychological resistance to a compulsion; and that resistance creates its own modification, change; and therefore, it is no change at all. If I change or if I adjust myself to society because I expect something from society, is that a change? Or, does mutation take place only when I see the things that are compelling me to change, and see their falseness? Because, all influences, whether good or bad, condition the mind, and merely to accept such conditioning is inwardly to resist any form of change, any radical change.

So, seeing the world situation, not only in this country, but throughout the world—where progress is denying freedom, where prosperity is making the mind more and more secure in things and therefore there is less and less freedom, where religious organizations are taking over more and more the formula of belief which will make man believe in God or in no God—seeing that the mind is becoming more and more mechanistic, and also observing that the electronic brains and the modern technological knowledge are giving man more and more leisure—not in this country because we are fifty years or a hundred years behind, but it will come—seeing all this, we have to find out what is freedom, what is reality.

These questions cannot be answered by a mechanical mind. One has to put the questions to oneself fundamentally, deeply, inwardly, and find the answers for oneself, if there are answers—which means really questioning all authority. Apparently, that is one of the most difficult things to do. We never regard society as the enemy. We regard society as something with which we have to live, conform, and adjust ourselves; we never think it is really the enemy of man, the enemy of freedom, the enemy of righteousness. Do think about it, look at it. Environment, which is society, is destroying freedom. It does not want a man who is free. It wants the saints, the reformers who would modify, bolster up, uphold the social institutions. But religion is something entirely different. The religious man is the enemy of society. The religious man is not a man who goes to church or goes to a temple, reads the Gita, does puja every day—he is not really religious at all. A really religious man has got rid of all ambition, envy, greed, fear, so that he has a mind that is young, fresh, new, so as to investigate, to find out what is beyond all the things that man has put together and which he calls religion. But all this requires a great deal of self-inquiry, an inquiry into oneself, self-knowing; and without that foundation, you cannot go very far.

So, a mutation, a complete revolution, not a modified change, but a complete mutation in the mind is necessary. How to bring this about is the problem. We see it is necessary. Any man who has thought at all, who has observed the world conditions, who is sensitive to what is going on within himself and outside of himself, must demand this mutation. But how is one to bring it about?

Now, first of all, is there a "how"—the "how" being the method, the system, the way, the practice? If there is a way, if there is a method, if there is a system, and if you practice it in order to bring about a mutation, your mind is merely a slave to that system; your mind is shaped by that system, by that method, by that practice, and therefore can never be free. It is like saying, "I will discipline myself in order to be free." Freedom and discipline do not go together—which does not mean that you have become undisciplined. The very "seeking freedom" brings its own discipline. But the mind that has disciplined itself in a system, in a formula, in a belief, in ideas—such a mind can never be free. So, one has to see from the very beginning that the "how," which implies practice, discipline, the following of a formula, prevents mutation from taking place. That is the first thing that one has to see because practice, method, or system becomes the authority which denies freedom and therefore mutation. One has really to see that fact, see the truth of that. I mean by "seeing" not seeing intellectually, verbally, but being emotionally in contact with that fact. We are emotionally in contact with the fact when we see a snake; there is no question about it; there is a direct challenge and a direct response. In the same way one has to see that any system, however well thought out—it does not matter by whom—does deeply destroy freedom, does deeply pervert creation—not pervert, but stop creation—because system implies gaining, an achievement, arriving somewhere, a reward, and therefore the very denial of freedom. That is why you will follow somebody: because you pursue the medium through which you gain—the medium being some kind of discipline.

But one must see this fact that the mind must be absolutely free—whether it is possible or not, that is quite a different matter—that there must be freedom; otherwise, you become merely mechanical like any glorified machine. One has to see very clearly that freedom is essential. And it is only when there is freedom that you can discover if there is, or if there is not, God or something immense, beyond the measure of man. Then you will begin to question every system, every authority, every structure of society. And the crisis demands this mind. Surely, only such a mind can find out what is true. It is only such a mind that can find out if there is, or if there is not, something beyond time, beyond the things that man has put together in his thought.

All this requires immense energy, and the essence of energy is the denial of conflict. A mind that is lost in conflict has no energy, whether the conflict is within oneself or outside with the world. All this requires immense investigation and understanding. And I hope that we can do this in the next six meetings: to be aware of the fact and to pursue the fact to its end and see whether the mind, our mind, your mind, can be really free.

Question: How is one to know if one has changed at all?

KRISHNAMURTI: The gentleman wants to know: "How does one know if one has changed at all?" Even if it is a healthy change brought about by outward events, should it not be encouraged? How do you know anything? "How do you know you have changed?" is an important question—the gentleman says so. We will go into it. How do you know it? Either by direct experience, or you have been told about it. There are only two ways—someone tells you or informs you, or you have experienced yourself.

Now, is experience a criterion by which you know? Will your experience tell you what is true? Your experience is the response to a challenge, and that experience is according to your background. Surely, you respond according to your background—to every challenge; and your background is the result of innumerable influences, of a thousand years of propaganda, and that propaganda may be good or may be bad. That background is the result of your conditioning; that background is your conditioning, and according to that conditioning, you respond to every challenge, however small. Is that the criterion of good and bad, or is the good, the really healthy, outside the conditioning? You follow? This country is now beginning to worship flags, is becoming nationally conscious, and that is the new kind of conditioning that is going on.

Nationalism obviously is a poison because it is going to separate man and man. In the name of the flag, we are going to destroy people, not only in this country, but also in other countries as well. We think that it will be the rallying point which will bring unity to man, and that is the latest influence, the latest pressure, the latest propaganda. Now, without questioning that—merely accepting the influence of the daily newspaper or of the political leaders without questioning it—how will you find out whether it is righteous, whether it is true or false, whether it is noble or ignoble? There is no influence which is good; every influence can be bad. So, your mind has to be like a razor to cut through this to find out, to be sane in a mad world where false things are worshiped.

So, that is why you have to inquire into your own conditioning, and the inquiry is the beginning of self-knowing.

Question: Can we keep our mind free when we are in contact with nature?

KRISHNAMURTI: The gentleman asks: "Is it possible to be free when we are in contact with nature?" I do not quite understand this question. Perhaps he means that we are being constantly stimulated by outward events, by our senses, and every stimulus leaves a mark on the mind as memory; and how can we be free of this memory? That is—let me make the question clear to myself also—how can a human being who is receiving challenges all the time in the form of stimuli and is responding to them consciously or unconsciously from his background, from his memory—how can such a mind be free? And is it possible for such a mind to be free?

Now, may I put the question in a different way? I am not avoiding the question. I am putting it in a different way. Every experience leaves a mark on the mind as memory; every conscious or unconscious experience leaves a scratch which we call memory, and as long as that memory is in operation, can the mind be free?

What is the need for memory? I need to know where I live; otherwise, I could not get back home. I need to know how to build a house. I need to know how to run a bicycle, a motor. So, memory becomes essential in mechanical things, and that is why we create habits. Once I have a habit, I function without thinking, and that becomes mechanical. So, our life is gradually made mechanical through habit, through memory, through these so-called experiences which leave their mark. So, let us differentiate between the necessity of memory as mechanical and that of memory which is detrimental to further understanding. I need to know how to write; that memory is good. The English I am speaking is the result of memory; that is essential for communication. The technical knowledge, the know-how, of the things I have learned is necessary to run an office, to function in a factory, and so on. But when society, through culture, through tradition, imposes on the mind a certain belief, and according to that belief I function mechanically, are not that belief and that mechanical pursuit according to that belief detrimental to the mind and therefore denying freedom? You are Hindus. You have been told so for centuries. You have been brought up from childhood in believing certain things, and that has become automatic, mechanical. You believe in God absolutely—that is mechanical. Must you not deny the whole of that to find out? If you observe, you can deny all that, wipe out all that memory as being a Hindu.

So, there is freedom when you see the things that have been imposed upon you in thought, as an idea, as a belief, as a dogma—and you deny them and go into the whole process of denial, why you deny. Then out of that comes freedom, though you are mechanically functioning in the daily events of life.

You may say man is merely the result of environment—which you are. It is no good pretending you are not, and saying you are paramatma—a kind of propaganda which you swallow, which you have been told. So, the fact is that you are the result of environment—the climate, the food, the newspapers, the magazines, the mother, the grandmother, the religion, the society, the social and moral values. You are that, and it is no good denying that. That again is merely propaganda. One has to admit that, to see the fact of that, and to break through it. Is it possible to break through it? It is not possible verbally, theoretically. But if you go into it factually, step by step, deny totally being a Hindu or an Indian or a Christian or what you will—which means to inquire into the whole question of fear, which we are not going into now because that involves a great deal—then you can find out whether man can be free of not. Merely speculating about freedom is utterly useless.

Question: Does not thought function in symbols?

KRISHNAMURTI: The lady says: "Thought functions in symbols; thought is word, and is it possible to wipe away symbols and the word, and therefore let a new thought come into being?" Symbols and words have been imposed upon us through centuries upon centuries. Now, is it possible to be aware of the symbols and the source of those symbols and to go beyond them?

First of all, we must inquire not only into the conscious mind but also into the unconscious. Otherwise, we will merely be dealing with words—again with merely symbols, and not with actuality. There is only consciousness. We divide our consciousness into the conscious and the unconscious for convenience, but there is no actual division as such. We are dividing it for convenience. There is no such division as the conscious mind and the unconscious mind. The conscious mind is the educated mind which has learned the new language, the new technique—how to go to the office, how to run an engine—it has recently been educated to live in this world. The unconscious, comprising the deeper layers of that mind, is the result of centuries of racial inheritance, of racial fears, of the residue of man's experience—collective as well as individual—the things that one has heard in boyhood, the things that one's great-grandmother told one, the influences that one has gathered by reading a newspaper, of which one is not absolutely conscious. So, the influences, the past—whether the immediate past or ten thousand years past—all those have taken root in the unconscious. You do not have to agree with me. It is a psychological fact. It is not a matter of my invention with which you agree or disagree. This is so. It is so only if you have gone into yourself—not reading books and saying it is so. If you have gone into yourself very deeply, you are bound to come across this. If you have merely read books and come to a conclusion, then you have to agree or disagree—it has no importance at all.

All thinking is symbolic. All thinking is the result of, is the response to, your memory. That memory is very deep, and that memory responds in words, in symbols. And the lady asks: "Is it possible to be free of these symbols? Is it possible for the Christian to be free of the symbol of Jesus and the cross? Is it possible for the Hindu to be free of the idea of Krishna, the Gita, and all that?" The lady also asks: "How did these symbols arise?" You know it is much easier to get excited about the symbol rather than about reality. The symbol is the means of propaganda in the hands of the propagandist. The symbol is the flag, and you can get terribly excited about the flag. Now the symbol of Krishna, the symbol of the cross, and all the rest of it—how does it arise? Obviously, to make man behave in a certain pattern, to make man conform to authority through fear, because this world is a deteriorating world, a messy world, a confused world; and the cross and Krishna are symbols with which to escape from this world. The authority says, "Look to that, and you will be happy. Cultivate that, and you will become noble," and all the rest of it. So, through fear, through the desire to be secure psychologically, inwardly, symbols come into being.

A mind that is not afraid inwardly, deeply, has no symbol. Why should it have a symbol of any kind? When the mind is no longer seeking security of any kind, why should it function in symbols? Then it is facing the fact and not an idea of the fact, which becomes the symbol. So, psychologically, inwardly, for most us, symbols become extraordinarily important. And the lady asks: "Is it possible not only to be aware of the symbols and their source but also of the fear?" I can say yes, but it will have no importance because it is my word against somebody else's word. But if you can go deeply into yourself, think and be aware of all the thought-process—why you think, how you think, and whether there is such a thing as going beyond form—and inquire into all this, it will be your direct experience. And it is only such a mind which knows the source of the symbol, and which is free of the symbol and of the word—it is only such a mind which is free.

Question: Can a mind be free and yet have faith?

KRISHNAMURTI: The gentleman asks: "Can a mind that is free have faith?"

Obviously not. Faith in what? Why should I have faith in a fact? I see a fact, I see I am jealous. Why should I have faith and say that one day I will not be jealous? I am dealing with the fact, and the fact is I am jealous; and I am going to wipe it out. To find out how to do it—that is more important for me than to have faith in not being jealous, faith in the idea.

So, a mind that is inquiring into freedom destroys everything to find out. Therefore, such a mind is a very dangerous mind. Therefore, society is an enemy to such a mind.

Question: How is one to stop one's mind from getting conditioned?

KRISHNAMURTI: The gentleman asks: "What is the concrete action that will arrest conditioning? What is the definite action that will stop a mind from being conditioned?"

It can only be stopped when you are aware of the conditioning processes. When you read the newspaper every day, as you do, in which nothing but politics is discussed, obviously that is being imprinted in your mind. But to read a newspaper and not be influenced, to see the world as it is and not to be influenced requires a very alert mind, a very sharp mind, a mind that can reason sanely, rationally, logically—which means a very sensitive mind.

Now, the question is how to bring about a sensitive mind. Sirs, there is no "how," there is no method. If there were a method, it would be like taking a tranquilizer—you know what it is; it is a pill that will tranquilize all your troubles, put you to sleep. To be aware of all the difficulties—which is to know them, to watch them, just to feel them, not verbally but actually, to know them as you know your hunger, your sexual appetites—that very knowing, that very contact with the fact, makes the mind sensitive. To know that you have no courage—not that you must develop courage—to know that you cannot stand by yourself, to know that you cannot stand up for what you think, to know the fact that you have not the capacity brings you the capacity. You do not have to search for capacity.

January 1, 1962

Second Talk at Rajghat

I think we all realize that there must be some kind of change. The more intelligent, the more penetrating we are, the more demanding, the more urgent is the necessity for change; but we think, do we not, of change generally at a superficial level—change of circumstances, change of jobs, a little more money, and so on.

We are talking of change which is total, completely radical and revolutionary. To bring about such a change, we must ask fundamental questions. It is important to find out how to ask a question. We can ask questions which spring from a reaction. I want to bring about a certain change in myself or in society, and that change may be a real reaction. The question I ask myself may either be the result of a reaction, or a question which is not put through any reaction. There are only two ways to ask a question: one through reaction, and the other which is no reaction. If we ask questions out of reaction, we will invariably find superficial answers. To ask questions which are not out of reaction is very difficult because, perhaps, there is no answer. It may be only that there is a questioning without an answer; and that, it seems to me, is far more significant than to put a question which has an answer.

I would like to discuss this evening a change that is absolutely necessary for a mind that seeks complete, total revolution, a mind that demands complete freedom, if there is such a thing as complete freedom. And to inquire into it, I think we must first find out the total significance of authority because most of our minds are ridden by authority—the authority of tradition, the authority of the family, the authority of a technique, the authority of knowledge, the authority laid down by law, the sanctions of government and religion and social morality. These are all the various forms of authority which shape our mind. How far can the mind be really free from them, and what does it mean to be free? I would like to go into that because I feel that authority which is not completely understood destroys all thinking, distorts all thought, and that a mind that merely functions mechanically in knowledge is really incapable of going beyond itself.

And so, it seems to me, one has to ask oneself, or inquire into, the whole question of authority: why and at what level we obey the physical laws or the psychological experiences which become knowledge and guide us. Why should there be obedience? All governments, especially tyrannical governments, wish their citizens never to criticize their leaders. We can see very simply why tyrannical governments demand such absolute obedience. Also we can see why, psychologically, we follow authority—the authority of the guru, the authority of tradition, the authority of experience—which invariably breeds habit, a good habit or a bad habit, the resistance against the bad and the shaping by the good. A habit also becomes authority, like the authority of knowledge, of the specialist, of the policeman, of the wife over the husband or of the husband over the wife.

How far can the mind be free from such authority? Is it possible to obey law, a government, the policeman, and to be inwardly completely free from authority, including the authority of experience with its knowledge and memory? Please, if I may suggest, it would be a thousand pities if you merely listened to the talk verbally, intellectually, and not actually experienced what is being said. That is, we have to question ourselves under what authority, under what compulsion, our mind functions and experience shapes our mind. And we have to be aware of all this because, after all, we are talking not to do any propaganda, not to convince you of anything, not to compel you into a particular course of action. It is only when we begin to question ourselves, partially or completely, that there can be true action; then only can all this travail and sorrow come to an end. To treat the talks merely verbally or intellectually, it seems to me, is an utter waste of time. It is not a matter of argument, agreement, or disagreement. But we have to observe all facts outwardly, and observe inwardly how our minds are slaves to authority and whether we can ever be free from authority—because obviously freedom implies freedom from authority—what the state of the mind is when it is actually free from authority, and whether such a state is possible.

To find out for oneself, one must put fundamental questions, and one of the fundamental questions is why we obey: why we obey the policeman, why we pay taxes—I am not saying you should not or you should, but we must ask this question, surely, to find out.

It may sound rather childish, immature; but if we can go very slowly into the matter step by step, perhaps we shall be able to understand whether it is possible or not to be utterly free from the past, which is authority. That is a fundamental question because the past shapes our mind all the time—the past experience, the past knowledge, the past incidents and accidents, the past flattery, the past insult, the thing that has been said and the thing that is going to be said from that which has been said. And so, the question arises whether it is at all possible to be free from this enormous network of the past, which is always translating the present, and so distorting the present which makes the future.

So, why is it we obey? The schoolboy obeys because the teacher is an authoritarian, a big man; there is an examination and all that. Then, there is the obedience to law, which is also very clear—we generally obey because we shall be punished for various reasons. So, there is an intelligent obedience to law. And is there any other form of obedience necessary? Why should the past—I am talking psychologically, inwardly—condition the mind and thereby impose certain restrictions, make it conform to the pattern of the past? We say that if we have no past as knowledge, all action is impossible. If there were no knowledge accumulated—which is science—then we could not do anything, we could not have a modern existence. So, scientific knowledge is essential, and you have to obey if you want to be a physicist. But if you want to be a creative physicist—really creative, not an inventor adding a few more gadgets—you must put aside knowledge and be in a state of such negation—if I can use that word—that the mind is very sensitive, very alert, and so capable of perceiving something new.

The mind is shaped by the past, by time, by every incident, every movement, every flutter of the past or thought. Can that past be wiped away, which is actually memory? Because, if we do not wipe it away—it is possible to wipe it away—we can never see something new, we can never experience something totally unforeseen, unknown. And yet, the past is always guiding us, always shaping us; every instinct, every thought, every feeling is guided by the past, the past being the memory; and memory insists that we should obey, follow. I hope you are watching yourself in action while listening to what is being said.

Where is memory necessary and essential, and where is it not? Because, memory is an authority for most of us. Memory is the accumulated experience of the past, of the race, of the person; and the reaction of that memory is thought. When you call yourself a

Hindu or a Christian or have committed yourself to a particular course of action, it is all the response of that memory. And so, it is only a man who has really understood the whole anatomy, the structure of authority, of memory, that can experience something totally new. Surely, if there is God—not that I am an atheist; it does not matter if I am—or if there is not can only be discovered when the mind is totally fresh, when the mind is no longer conditioned by the tradition of belief or nonbelief. So, can one wipe away memory which breeds authority, memory which breeds fear and from which there is the urge to obey? As most of us are seeking security in some form or other, physical security or psychological security, to be safe outwardly we must obey the structure of society, and to be inwardly secure we must obey the experience, the knowledge, the memory which has been stored up. Is it possible to wipe away all memory except the mechanical memory of daily existence which in no way interferes, creates, or engenders further memory? The older we get, the more we rely on authority, and so all our thinking becomes narrow, limited.

To bring about a complete mutation, we must question authority very fundamentally. For me, questioning is far more important than finding out how to be free from authority because in questioning, we shall find out the nature of authority, its significance, its value, its detriment, its poisonous nature. By questioning, you will find out what is true. Then the problem is solved; you do not have to ask yourself: How am I to be free from authority? But it is absolutely necessary to question everything, every form of belief, every form of tradition, to tear down the house. Otherwise, we remain mediocre people. It may be a calamity of this country that leadership—political authority, the authority of the guru, the authority of the sacred books—has really destroyed all thinking, and so there is no real inquiry. If all inquiries start with the acceptance of the authority of the Gita, the Bible, or whatever it is, how can you inquire any further? It is like a man who believes in God, or in a particular form of utopia, and hopes to inquire, to question. Such questioning, such inquiry, has no validity at all.

Most of us start with the acceptance of some kind of authority. It may be necessary for a child to accept some authority, but as the child begins to grow up, begins to reason, he can be encouraged, educated, to question the parents, question the teacher, question the society; but we have never so questioned. It does not naturally arise because, basically, there is fear, and a mind that is frightened, surely, can only create illusions. And from fear there arises authority. A man who is not at all afraid of anything has no authority, no belief, no ideal; and it is only such a man, obviously, that can discover if there is or if there is not the immeasurable.

So, authority is necessary in specialization. For a man who is seeking freedom—not freedom from something, which is a reaction and therefore not freedom—in order to find out, freedom is right at the beginning, not at the end. To discover what is true, to discover for oneself—not through what somebody tells you, however sacred the book or the person be; there is no sacred book at all, all books are the same—and to find out, the mind must be free. Otherwise, we only become mechanical, pass examinations, get a job, and follow the pattern set by society; and that pattern is always corrupting, always destructive.

Really, for a man who is seeking what is true, society is an enemy. He cannot reform society. It is one of our favorite ideas that good people are going to reform society. The good man is one who leaves society. I mean by "leaving" not leaving the house, clothes, and shelter, but leaving the things which society stands for—which are basically authority, ambition, greed, envy, acquisitiveness—leaving all these things which society has made respectable. It is only really by questioning very fundamentally, basically, that one begins to shatter the false, to shatter the house that thought has built for its own self-protection.

Question: Must we not have security in order to live?

KRISHNAMURTI: The gentleman says that there must be security as otherwise we cannot live. We have to be fed, we have to have shelter and clothing; and at the same time how can there be freedom? I wonder why he put the question as though the two are not possible together.

Is it impossible to be physically secure and not let that physical security interfere psychologically? Is such security made possible at all by wanting psychological security? Let us take a very simple example—I do not like to take examples, but we will. There is starvation in the world, in the whole of Asia—which you know well. There are scientific means for completely feeding all men, clothing them, and giving them shelter. Why is it not done? Practically, it can be done; there is no question about it, and yet we are not doing it—why? Surely, the reason is psychological, not physical—because we have separated ourselves as Hindus, Muslims, Christians, with sovereign governments, with separate religions, separate dogmas, beliefs, countries, nationalities, flags, and all the rest of it. It is that which is preventing fundamentally the feeding of man and giving him shelter and clothing. The communists say that they have a method, and so the method becomes all-important, and they are willing to fight for the method. For them, the method is more important than solving the problem of starvation. Every organizer identifies himself with the organization because that is another form of self-aggrandizement, of self-importance—which prevents the solution of starvation.

So, one can be physically secure—and must be—but why should one be psychologically secure? You understand? Why this demand to be psychologically secure? Is there such a thing as psychological security? We demand security in our relationship, as husband and wife, with our children; and when we demand such security, what happens? Love goes by the window. Can you be secure in any relationship? You can only be secure with something that is static, not with something which is living; and yet we demand, we insist that we must have security with something that is alive—which does not mean that we must seek insecurity; to seek insecurity will only lead to mental illness, and the hospitals and wards are full with mentally ill people who are so frightened of insecurity that they invent all forms of security.

So, why this insistence to be secure? Is there anything secure; can you ever be secure in anything? So, why not accept, why not see the fact that there is no such thing as psychological security—as belonging to India, to Russia, or whatever it is—and thereby create a world in which we all have physical security? You understand the question, sirs? Nobody is willing to give up intelligently, sanely, without being persuaded or driven to give up, his commitments to his nation, his particular pattern of action, his particular pattern of belief. Why should we be Hindus? Why should we belong to India? I know you will listen, but it does not mean a thing to you. You are settled down in your form of belief, in your security; you are born as Hindus, and you will die as Hindus. You are really not concerned about starvation. So, that gentleman's question is merely theoretical; it is not an actuality to him. If it were an actuality, a thing that has got to be faced and resolved, then he would inquire into the whole structure of security.

Why do we ask a question? Is it to find an answer? I can tell you the answer—which is an explanation. But does an explanation really answer the problem? Here is a problem: The world has divided itself into separate countries, sovereign states, and therefore prevents the solution of starvation and so on. That is a fact. And yet we go on being Hindus, Muslims, communists, socialists, capitalists; we are committed to various things. Now, when we do question, we are looking for an answer which will be generally satisfactory according to our conditioning. You follow? Therefore, such questioning is really immature. But you have to ask a question and not seek an answer because the answer will invariably be according to your conditioning, and to break down the conditioning, you must ask without seeking an answer.

If you want to be an engineer, you must have read books on mathematics. You cannot destroy all the accumulated knowledge—mathematics, biology—you must have all that. But why should you have the Gita? Why don't you treat the Gita as any other book? Because we seek security in that, we think that it is written by God himself.

Question: Will further inquiry into memory strengthen the center, or the 'me'?

KRISHNAMURTI: Is there a danger in inquiring further into memory? Is there a danger in digging out the past and thereby strengthening the center, which is the result of the past? Let us be clear what the question is, first. That digging into myself—the myself being the center of all experiences, of all knowledge, of all accumulated knowledge and frustrated desires and so on—does not that very inquiry into myself strengthen the self, the center?

It all depends on how you inquire. If you inquire and if your inquiry is based on condemnation or justification, a mere adjustment to the pattern, then such an inquiry is bound to strengthen. But if we do not condemn, if the mind merely observes *what is* without condemnation, without judgment, then there is no possibility of strengthening the center.

What do we mean by observing? Do we observe anything with words? Do we see things with words, with symbols—which is, the thought? Do I see the river, observe the river, by the associations connected with that river, with the name, with the tradition which has been handed over for centuries about that river, or do I merely observe the river without all that tradition? Therefore, I either observe with thought or observe without the word, which is thought. I observe, let us say, a flower. Do I observe the flower without the botanical association—its species and so on? Do I observe botanically, or do I observe nonbotanically? In that same way, do you observe jealousy with the word, which is already associated with condemnation and resistances, or with the justification of it? Or do you merely observe it without the word? Because, if you observe with the word, you are strengthening the word—the word being the symbol, the word being the thought, and the thought being the response to memory—and therefore strengthening the center. But, if you observe without the word—which requires a great deal of inquiry into the word, into the whole process of verbalization—then you can look, observe, see, without strengthening, enriching the center.

Question: Is the observer different from the questioner?

KRISHNAMURTI: "Is there a difference between the observer and the questioner?" I should not think so. Is there? That is why I said at the beginning, it is important to find out for yourself how you question. You understand? You must question this decaying society. I must tear down the society by questioning. How do I question? Do I question because I cannot become an important member of that society? I am frustrated as I cannot be somebody in that society; therefore, I question—which is a reaction. That questioning is the result of my frustrations and fears and all the rest of it. Therefore, I question to find out the truth about society, to find out what is true virtue—not the virtue of society, which is no virtue at all. Society is only concerned with sexual morality and nothing else. To find out what is real virtue, you must question the morality of society, and therefore you must tear down society, all the morality which society has established.

Is not the questioner the observer? He observes, and from that observation arises the questioning. But if the observer is merely the entity which comes into being through reaction, then his observation also will be a reaction and therefore no observation at all.

Question: Does observation imply cessation of memory?

KRISHNAMURTI: The gentleman asks: "Is observation the cessation of memory?" I do not know if you have experimented with yourself in seeing something, in observing something. You look at somebody; you look at him through all the impressions that you have received about him, and so you are really not looking at him at all. Most of you—but not the students—are married; do you ever look at your wife? You look at the picture, the image, the impressions that you have had about her, but you never look at her; and perhaps if you do look without all the impressions, the insults, the quarrels, the memories that you have accumulated, there must be something terrific happening; and therefore you keep the screen between you and her. To really look at something without memory—which is thought, which is accumulated reaction, and all the rest of it—to look at the fact without the word releases energy, because the fact itself produces the energy, not I looking. To look at the fact—not the explanations, not the theories, not why should it not or why must it be, and so on—to look at the whole structure of authority would bring about a tremendous revolution in your thinking. And we do not want to have a revolution because it disturbs—I may not go to the office; I may do something totally different, so I protect myself with the word and never face the fact. And for most of us, philosophy and religion and the enormous thing called life are just words. To free the mind from the word is really quite an extraordinary thing.

Question: Is it possible for the human mind to comprehend truth?

KRISHNAMURTI: "Can a human mind comprehend truth?" I do not think it can. What is the human mind at present? Is there a human mind, or is merely the instinctive response of the animal still continuing in us? It is not a sarcastic remark.

First of all, to comprehend anything in life, let alone truth—to comprehend my wife, my neighbor, my child—there must be a certain quietness of the mind, not a disciplined quietness; then it is not quiet, it is a dead mind. So, a mind in conflict prevents observing anything, observing myself. So, I am perpetually in conflict, perpetually in motion, moving, moving, talking, endlessly questioning, explaining; there is no observation possible here at all. That is what most of us are doing when we are face to face with *what is.*

So, one sees that there can be observation only when there is no conflict. To have no conflict, one can take a tranquilizer, a pill, to become tranquil, but it is not going to give you perception; it will put you to sleep, and that is probably what most of us want. So, to observe, there must be a certain tranquility of mind, and whether you see what is true depends on the quality of the mind.

Truth is not something that is static. Truth is not something that is fixed—which has no power. It is something which must be alive, must be tremendously sensitive, alive, dynamic, vital. And how can a putrid, puny mind which is in turmoil, everlastingly bitten with ambition—how can it understand that? It can say there is truth and keep on repeating it and putting itself to sleep.

So, the question is, really, not whether the human mind can perceive truth, but whether it is possible to break down the petty walls that man has built round himself which he calls the mind—that is really the issue. One of the walls which we all like so much is authority.

Question: Are love and truth one and the same thing?

KRISHNAMURTI: "Are love and truth one and the same thing?" You know all similarities should be distrusted, but there are similarities. Take that word *love*. The general who is about to kill, who is planning killing, talks about love of his country, love of his wife; and he also talks about love of God. The politicians also do the same thing; they talk of the inner voice, God, love. How does one find out what love is, what truth is? Not whether they are similar or dissimilar, but what is it to love, what does it mean? Obviously, we have not got the time to go into the whole of it.

To find out what love is, there must be sensitivity. For most of us love is sex, desire. Through tradition, through all the innumerable waves of saints that this poor unfortunate country has had, love has gone because love is associated with sex. They preach about love of God, love of man; but yet, they are terribly crude, utterly insensitive—these saints whom you worship. Beauty is denied—you must not look at a tree; you must not look at a woman; turn away, treat her like a leper, or ask her to shave her head; you know the tricks we all play when we are insensitive.

So, we have to be really sensitive, and then we will know what love is. To be really sensitive, one must break with the past, one must break away from all the heroes and saints. I really mean it. If you follow them, you are imitating, and a mind that is imitative is not sensitive.

I wonder at the end of an hour's talk and questions what actual effect all this has on your minds—actually—not theoretically, not ideationally, but factually? Are you any more sensitive at the end of it?

The girl says the whole mind is disturbed. I am very glad. Be disturbed for the rest of your life. Disturbance is only the beginning of it. But what actual effect has it when you are disturbed? It is only when you are young, you are disturbed. The old people are not disturbed because they are committed far too heavily—they have their puja, their saints, their gods, their ways of salvation, their ways of saving society, and so on; they are committed—there are too many duties and responsibilities, and therefore there is no love.

So, when we say we are disturbed, what does it mean? Disturbed at what depth? When the river is disturbed by a passing wind, you see the ripples; but deep down, there is no disturbance, it is deadly quiet. And perhaps it is the same with us—deep down there is no disturbance. Perhaps when you are young, you are disturbed; you will soon get married, pass examinations, get a job, and you are settled for life—not that you should not be married and get jobs. But when you do, your disturbance goes with it; you are disturbed about the job, you want a better job, more money. I am not talking of that kind of disturbance—that is too immature. I am talking of a mind that is really disturbed, disturbed and not finding an answer. The moment you find an answer, you think you have solved the problem. Life is not so cheap as that.

So, what actual effect has this, an hour's talk? A ripple on the water, or disturbance at a great depth, the uprooting of a tree? Have you ever seen a tree being uprooted? You know what it goes through? Everything is shaken. It dies to everything that it has known. I wonder how deeply a talk of this kind has taken root! You cannot answer; I am not seeking an answer.

The world needs human beings who are not mechanical. The world needs men who have really got a new brain, a new mind. There will be a thousand mechanical entities. But surely, a new mind is necessary to answer the innumerable problems which are multiplying, which are increasing. So, if I may so express it, find out whether the house is being torn down, or you are merely patching up the house.

January 3, 1962

Third Talk at Rajghat

I would like to talk to you of something this evening which I think would be worthwhile. I would like to talk about conflict and if it is at all possible to live in this world without conflict. But before I go into that, I would suggest that you look at it, that you listen to what is being said quite objectively, quite dispassionately—not whether it is not possible or it is possible, but merely look at it as one would look at the mechanical process of an engine; not to say it can be or cannot be; and not be on the defensive, not deny, not agree, but merely look as you would look at a marvelous machine which you have never seen before. To look at it you must be fairly attentive; you must give your attention; you must be interested in the machine, and then you can undo it and see if it is workable at all, whether it has any value for each one of us in life or not.

I would like to talk about conflict and the possibility of actually living, in life, without conflict. Most of our lives, from the moment we are born to the moment we die, is a series of conflicts, endless battles within and without. Our minds and our hearts are battlefields, and we are always trying to better ourselves, to achieve a result, to find the right activity, to effect various social reforms, ardently wishing, in ourselves, to bring about change. This constant, violent, unobtrusive, deep-down battle is going on within each one of us. We are either conscious or unconscious of it. If we are conscious of every conflict, in the sense we are directly in relationship with it, we try either to escape from it, or to suppress it, or to find a way of conquering it. All this implies, surely, a constant battle—a weary, unending process. And if we are unconscious of this conflict that is going on within ourselves and outwardly, we either become totally dead, insensitive, or various forms of psychosomatic diseases take place; and in our relationships, in our activities, in everything we do, this unconscious battle has its effect. That is our life—acquiring, losing, trying to be something and never succeeding, always hoping for deep final fulfillment, and always frustrated; and with it comes the sorrow and the aching jealousy of others who are fulfilling, and knowing that there is also frustration. And so we are always caught in this misery of an everlasting battle with ourselves and with society. That is a fact.

We can either deny it, or be blind to it, or reject it, or say, "What can be done about it?" We can find out the various causes of conflict, of the battle. Will the discovery of the cause free the mind from the battle, from the conflict? That is, if I discover why I am jealous, will I be free of jealousy? When I discover why I am in conflict and find the right explanation, will conflict come to an end? The mere discovery of the cause does not, if you observe very carefully, end the conflict of anything. Explanations have no value for a man who is very hungry. Words do not fill his stomach. But apparently, for most of us, explanations do strangely satisfy—the explanations of why we struggle, why it is inevitable to struggle, why we are brought up on it. We can also see the reasons—self-aggrandizement, self-pity, ambition, and various hidden causes which are fairly obvious when one examines them—we know them. And yet, our life is a battle, and we have accepted it as a way of life.

Now I would like to question that way. I mean by questioning, not as a reaction against it; the questioning is not born out of the reaction against conflict. I see there is a consciousness of conflict, I see most human beings are caught in it, and I want to find out why it is like that—not merely be satisfied with explanations or merely find the cause of the struggle—and to question deeply whether it is possible to live without conflict. That would be the real inquiry, because you can see that a mind which is in conflict all the time, endlessly, soon wears itself out, it becomes dull.

We think that conflict sharpens the mind; it does make the mind more cunning; it makes it more underhanded. But the mind in conflict is continually wearing itself out like any instrument that is being constantly used and is creating friction—that machine, that instrument is bound to wear out very soon.

So, is there a way of living without conflict, actually—not theoretically, not verbally, not as prescribed in some sacred book, but actually? Is there a way? Probably most of us have never put that question to ourselves because we have accepted conflict as inevitable, like death. When we do put that question to ourselves, we must find out at what level we put that question. Is it merely an intellectual questioning out of curiosity, or is it a questioning which opens the door to a new perception, to a new perfume? I do believe that in so questioning, which is not a reaction, we will find in the very act of questioning a life without conflict coming into being. Which is, there is no way to lead a life without conflict; there is no method, there is no system, no practice. If you do have a method, a system, a way, then questioning has stopped; you have accepted a system leading to that, and in the very practicing of that system, you are in conflict, and therefore, you are continually in conflict, hoping out of conflict to arrive at that state where there is no conflict—which is an utter impossibility. I do not know if I am making myself clear on that issue. We will discuss this after I have finished what I have to say this evening.

For me, the very act of seeing the total emptiness of conflict, the total falsity of conflict, the very perception is the ending of conflict. But to see the complete intricacy, the complete factual reality of conflict, the whole anatomy of conflict, you must have a very sharp mind—it is not like being a BSc—you must have a very acute mind, a heightened sensitivity; otherwise, you cannot see anything, let alone a most complex issue. You cannot see anything if you are not very alert; you cannot see the river, the fishermen, the light on the river, and the beauty of that green bank and the trees beyond if you are not intensely alive; you just look at it and pass it by.

So, to see something totally, there must be an intensity. That intensity is not mere concentration but an intensity which comes when there is energy, and that energy can only come when there is no conflict. So, the act of seeing something totally, the act of seeing a fact totally, liberates energy; and that energy is the way of living without conflict.

I see very clearly that conflict in any form inwardly and outwardly, at any level, conscious or unconscious, is destructive; it makes the mind dull, stupid, heavy. A mind in conflict is in an uncreative state. I see the whole of it, not verbally but actually, as I see a snake, as I see you sitting there. I see that conflict in every form is the most deteriorating factor in life—the conflict involved in trying to become something, in trying to reach God, in trying to become a super-executive, and so on. I see the whole pattern of it. The fact is far more important than my explanation of the fact, than to discover the cause of the fact. The fact is far more important than to escape from the fact—to go to gods and temples, to take tranquilizers, or to do various forms of futile meditation to dull the mind. So the fact and the seeing of the fact demand a total attention in which there is no escape. You cannot escape when you are attending to something.

Conflict breeds antagonism. I can give you the explanation because most of us want explanations, we are playing with explanations; explanations have no validity. Conflict makes the mind dull, cunning; conflict wears down the mind; conflict introduces various forms of psychosomatic diseases. Psychosomatic diseases are diseases produced by the inward state of conflict, of misery, of suffering, of pain inwardly, which brings about physiological disorders, bodily ills, and so on. I see conflict outwardly between people, between nations. I see conflict in all relationships in the family, between friends, between the big man and the small man, between the rich man and the poor man. I also see what conflict does actually, not theoretically but factually. So, I am aware totally of conflict, inwardly and outwardly, consciously and unconsciously, expressed in all relationships; I see the effect of conflict on the mind, on so-called affection; when I am alert, aware, observing, I see the whole map of it, the whole anatomy of it—I do not take time over it, I do not read all the books but see what is actually taking place.

To see totally you need energy, obviously. Now, observing the fact releases the energy, and that very act of seeing is the way of living without conflict. It is not a miracle or trick. From that I see every form of conflict is death. So, seeing totally every thought and every feeling that produces conflict is the very ending of that thought and the very ending of that feeling, without conflict, without suppression, without control, without discipline. So, I say definitely there is a way of living in this world without conflict. It is not reserved for those people who have inherited money, who live a luxurious life—it is all too silly; that is not the way of life in which there is no conflict. I am talking of a way of life of which one is aware and sees the whole implication of conflict, not theoretically or verbally, but actually, factually. The wars that are going on in the world, the divisions of people into classes and castes, into religions, into nations, all the absurd divisions man has built around himself—the very act of seeing all that opens the door to a life without conflict.

But what is important is not how to find a way of life without conflict but seeing totally the complete implication of conflict. The seeing is not intellectual, emotional, sentimental, or verbal. Seeing it totally—that is the real issue. To see totally that I am stupid, dull, without finding explanations, justification, and all the rest of it—as when I say I am afraid and I try to become clever—in that very perception, there is the breath of the new.

Comment: Observation is very taxing; it takes away energy.

KRISHNAMURTI: The gentleman says that with all of us observation is taxing, is trying, and that it takes away energy. Why is it taxing? Why do we find looking at a fact tiresome, wasting energy, demanding a great deal of energy? Let us discuss it. Do not accept a thing that I am talking about; I have no authority. It is a marvelous thing if you go into it. Why do we find it difficult, taxing, and wearying?

First of all, I think, we resist something new. Somebody comes and says there is a different way of living; and you do not listen, you do not try to find out, you immediately resist. Your resistance takes away your energy. Then you are afraid of the consequences of seeing, which may alter the course of your life—it may or may not, but you think it will. There is fear; there is also the uncertainty of what might happen: you have established your life in a certain way, in a certain direction, in a certain groove; and if you look at the fact very observantly, you might have to alter the whole process. Therefore you resist. Resistance, fear, and the disinclination to see something new obviously take away your energy and therefore prevent you from looking at the fact.

Take a very simple thing. We are violent—each one of us is violent in some way or other, to some degree or other. We know what it means. Do not ask me to analyze the meaning of the word. Now, we never face the fact that we are violent, but we say, "I am violent. What shall I do about it? How shall I get rid of it? Will an ideal help? Will pursuing a guru, will reading a book help?"—everything to take us away from the fact that we are violent. Do listen to this. You have to be completely aware that you are violent—which means you are no longer condemning it, you are no longer justifying it, you are no longer trying to introduce a new factor, which is the ideal, which becomes the contradiction of the fact. You have to be alive to that fact only and nothing else. That is rather a difficult and arduous thing to do—to look at something nakedly without any word. Do try it sometime.

Question: When I try to look at a problem, I am distracted. What am I to do?

KRISHNAMURTI: If I understand the gentleman rightly, he says he has a problem, and when he tries to look at the problem, other things, other ideas, other beliefs, impinge on the mind and so distract it; what is he to do?

What do we mean by a problem? We mean, don't we, something which is not resolved. Please follow. The very word *problem*—the word in itself, not the fact—has the connotation of conflict. When I say I have a problem, I have ceased to look at the fact, but I have introduced the word which is making it into a problem. The word is not the thing. So, in trying to understand a problem, I have already started condemning it. So, I am a slave to the word and not to the fact. But when I am aware of the fact, nothing will distract me. That is why one has to understand what deep significance words have in our lives—like the word *problem*, like the word *God*, like the word *communist*, like the word *Gita*. What amazing importance these words have for us! How symbols have become important—symbols, not the facts!

Now, there is a problem—that thing which we call a problem. Now, how do I regard that fact? I say, "I must find an answer, I must resolve it; it is annoying, it is disturbing; I do not like it." So, my concern is to resolve it, and I approach the fact with the feeling, with the idea that it must be resolved. So, what am I doing? I am coming to the fact with an opinion—which is, I want that fact to be something other than what it is. But whereas when I realize the falseness of words in all that, when I see that, the fact only remains. Then the fact begins to translate itself; I do not have to do a thing about the fact; the fact itself does something. I do not know if you have tried all these things.

We said that when one is aware of the fact, there is no distraction. Let us keep to that for the moment. Is there anything such as distraction? When I want to concentrate on something, then everything is distraction. You see this? I want to concentrate on that picture, and somebody comes along; and I say that is a distraction. My thought wanders off, and I say that is distraction. I question whether there is any such thing as distraction. Distraction arises only when there is the conflict which is involved in concentration. Therefore, concentration is a resistance which necessitates the building up of a wall against every form of distraction, every form of thought which wishes to wander off. So, concentration is the problem, not distraction. Therefore, I begin to question not distraction but concentration. By questioning we find that concentration is resistance, is narrowing down, compelling, imitating, forcing—which all create conflict. So, concentration is not the way to look at anything.

So, if concentration is not the way, then what is the way in which there is no contradiction and therefore no distraction? I do not know if you are following this. There is attention. To attend, to be attentive is always an active present, and therefore there is no distraction—to be attentive to who goes in, to be attentive to what is being said, to be attentive to somebody, to what is actually taking place, to somebody scratching himself, to be attentive to all this. When you are so attentive, then awareness is a way of looking without concentration.

Question: Does not attention imply concentration?

KRISHNAMURTI: The gentleman wants to know if attention does not imply concentration, or does not attention include concentration?

You see you are asking me as though I were an expert and you are going to learn from me. I refuse to be put in that position. I say: Learn from yourself, not from me. I am not your guru. I am not your teacher or leader. I won't be put into that position. It is a most vulgar position which has no meaning at all. It does not alter your life.

If you say to yourself, if you are asking yourself, not me, and if you say, "I do not quite understand what you mean by attention; I have followed you, and I see that life demands concentration," why do you say that? Or do you mean that in attention there is also concentration? Do not put me in the position of the oracle and thereby become weakened in your own investigation.

Now, let me explain what I mean by attention. To be attentive means you are listening, you are seeing, you are feeling, you are thinking; words have their limitation, and therefore your thinking has gone beyond the word; and therefore, there is no thought but mere observation with an intensity which includes and does not exclude. All concentration is an exclusive process.

Now, we begin to understand what it is to be attentive. I have to do a certain piece of work: I have to write, I have to keep account, and so on. Can I do that work in a state of attention, or do I have to put aside attention and merely become concentrated? I say: Be attentive, and you will do the work rightly without effort. The moment you introduce concentration, effort comes in. I do not know if you have ever learned. You cannot learn if you are concentrated. Concentration is resistance. It is like the schoolteacher saying to the boy, "Look at the book; do not look out of the window." The boy is not learning; he is acting up, he is memorizing;

and therefore he passes examinations and remains stupid for the rest of his life. But learning is a state of awareness: he can look out of the window, see the birds, see everything alive, moving, and yet read the book and learn. Therefore, you can learn only when your mind is at ease, when you are happy, when you are playing.

Question: How can a mind which is in a state of conflict be aware?

KRISHNAMURTI: The gentleman says, "How can a mind which is in a state of conflict be aware?" I shall put it differently. Is not awareness involved in the framework of conflict?

That is why I talked at the beginning about conflict. To understand conflict, you need total awareness—that is, you have to be aware consciously, unconsciously; you have to be aware with your body, with your mind, with your heart; you have to be aware totally. In that state of awareness, is there any conflict? It is only when we are not totally aware, attentive, that conflict arises. I took that example of violence. When I am aware totally of violence, there is no conflict—how to get rid of it, and so on—the mind ceases to be violent.

But the difficulty with most of us is to be so totally aware. First, we like violence; there is some fun in violence, in talking brutally about somebody, in making a brutal gesture, when you are an important leader, somebody big—which is the result of violence, obviously; and you like that position. So, deep down, you like it. Be aware that you like it, that you want it, that you pursue it, that you think it is right to go on with it; but do not pretend that you are seeking nonviolence, and all the rest of it. So, in awareness, when you are observing a fact totally, there is no conflict; conflict is not within its framework.

Question: We are not interested in mathematics. How are we to pay attention to it?

KRISHNAMURTI: Why are you not interested in mathematics or in geography or in the innumerable things that life has? Why? Either you are being taught wrongly or you do not like the teacher and his methods of teaching. There are innumerable reasons why we do not like something. Instead of tackling why we do not like it, we say we must learn mathematics. This is a question that for the moment should not be brought in by students. We will discuss this when we meet another time.

You see, there is such a thing as finding something that you love to do all your life—love to do, but not to do what will bring you reward. To love something that you want to do in your life—you are not educated for that. You are educated to do anything but to love what you are doing. When we love what we are doing, then everything is included in it, mathematics too.

You have heard about conflict and the way of living without conflict. How do you regard it? How have you listened to it? Are you going to go out of this room and make yourself into a battlefield? Will the very act of listening—which is really a miracle if you know how to listen—strip you of all conflict? Will that wipe away the whole of conflict? Otherwise, what is the point of attending these meetings? We are not dealing with words or intellectual theories; we are dealing with life, with the totality of life. Take, for instance, conflict. Conflict is ambition—the ambition of the saint, the ambition of the politician, the ambition of the teacher who wants more. You know what ambition means—the drive, the struggle to be, to become, and the enormous implication of conflict in it. Has that dropped away? Of course not. Then, if I may ask, what is the point of listening? It only helps to add another problem to you: that you can live without conflict and yet you are in conflict, and how are you to arrive at that way of living in which there is no conflict? That is, another problem is added to the already innumerable problems. Do think it out. I hope I have not paralyzed you from asking questions.

We have not, first of all, understood the whole structure of conflict. In understanding conflict and not resisting it, in seeing its depth, its width and its height and its various nuances, the very seeing gives an awareness. Sir, there is a way of looking at a flower botanically and a way of looking at a flower nonbotanically. When you look at the flower botanically, you are not seeing it in the sense of seeing totally. You see it botanically when you see the structure, the color, the perfume, the species, the petals, the pollen; but you do not see the totality of the flower. Now, to see the totality of the flower, you have to cease to be a botanist; though you may be a botanist, you cease to be a botanist, and you look. And that is where you find it difficult. We cannot put aside the knowledge which we have acquired and look; and therefore we maintain a conflict.

Is it possible to look without the word, without the symbol? Please try it some time—to look at a flower, to look at your son, to look at your wife, to look at the politicians, the leaders, the sannyasis, the saints, and all the rest of them; look at them—not whether you like them or do not like them, not whether you think they are right or wrong, not what their political inclinations are. That is all your personal opinion, which is based on your past experience, which is conditioned by the culture in which you have been brought up, and therefore it has no validity. But when you want to see, that very drive to see puts all that aside. Therefore that drive itself is the way of life in which there is no conflict.

Question: Instead of having a well-defined conflict, there is a sense of restlessness. What is one to do?

KRISHNAMURTI: Why is one restless? I have seen these gentlemen in front of me waggling their knees, twitching their fingers, doing something all the time—that is a part of restlessness. They are not aware of it. Why do they do this? Why do they not sit quietly? Why? First of all, it may be they are sitting uncomfortably, or it has become a habit and therefore they are unconscious of it, or it may be an indication that they have had a quarrel with their wives or husbands—whatever it is.

So, restlessness is an indication, is it not, of some deep-rooted cause which has not been discovered. You can deal with a definite conflict. Why do we not deal with restlessness? It may be that you are really lonely, deep down you are miserable, deep down you have not found the way of life, deep down you are frustrated, you do not love—there may be several reasons for restlessness which is the outward expression of this deep inward inquietude. The problem is also how to investigate, how to unravel, how to open up the thing that is making you restless.

Question: What is the purpose of life?

KRISHNAMURTI: That is the favorite jargon of every so-called seeker—what is the purpose of life? A person who puts that question is not living. He wants a purpose to live by. Therefore, for him living is not sufficient; it does not have its own beauty, its own depth; and he wants to impose on it a purpose invented or given to him—a purpose, an end. Does a happy man want a purpose? He is happy. A man who is intensely alive, living—does he want a purpose?

So, when we say I have not found a purpose, that may be a cause of restlessness. But you question, not the validity of seeking a purpose, but how to get rid of restlessness. Why is one restless? It may be that you have no purpose; it may be that you are lonely. Do not deny it, go into it. I mean by "lonely" a sense of self-isolation, having no relationship deep down. Though you may have innumerable relationships—husband, wife, children, and all the rest—deep down you have no contact, which is generally a sense of the self-isolating process of loneliness. Or it may be that you have not found your own way of living. It may be that one is married to a wrong person. It may be several things. I have not mentioned all—it may take too long to enumerate. Instead of trying to find out how to stop restlessness, how to get rid of restlessness, I say: Do not bother about restlessness, but find out, go into yourself deeply.

You know, gossip is one of the favorite forms of restlessness—to talk about somebody else. Why do we do it? You know it does not need an explanation. To stop gossip, one has to go deeply within oneself—which most of us are not willing to do.

So, have you answered the question to yourself? You have listened for an hour and ten minutes. We have discussed sufficiently and fairly deeply about conflict. Has it meant anything to you? Can you completely drop conflict? Or are you beginning to see that it can be dropped, and will you pursue that all the days of your lives? Or will you just treat this as one of the things that you have heard and let it go by? Please answer it to yourself.

To be really serious means to pursue a thing to the very end of it. Pursuing to the very end the whole implication of conflict, looking at it in different ways, day after day, never allowing it to go by, watching it, neither denying it nor accepting it, but watching it flower—then you begin to be a light to yourself. You do not have to read a single book; you do not need a single guru. And this brings its own illumination. But you have to set it going, you have to start; like getting hold of the tail of a comet, you have to get hold of it first and go with it.

January 5, 1962

Fourth Talk at Rajghat

We were talking the day before yesterday when we met here, about conflict and the ending of conflict. I would like to approach the same question differently.

One perceives throughout the world a general deterioration, perhaps not mechanically, but in every other way; there is no creative burst. And is it possible for individuals to break through this mechanical barrier of existence and explode dangerously into that creative mind which must of necessity be utterly free from all conflict, because creation cannot be the result of conflict? Any man, I am sure, who has invented or written a poem, who has caught something of the otherness, must have had a mind which is completely quiet, not made quiet, not disciplined, not ridden by problems and hopelessness and despair—but quiet in the sense of being normally a mind without any effort, but disciplined in freedom without control. Such a mind is not the result of time; it does not come about by putting various things together. It is there, or not there. This whole idea of change, which brings about conflict because of change, is a form of conflict. At least for us all, change is conflict because we refuse from the very beginning to search out and discover the fact or the truth of security.

So, for most of us, change implies conflict. We are driven by circumstances, by propaganda, by necessity, and we change; out of that change and compulsion there is obviously a certain modification. But this modification and the multiplication of modification do not bring about that mind which has the quality of newness, something totally unpremeditated, and which is not the outcome of detailed deliberation or of much deliberation. How is it possible to bring this about? What is the quality, what is the characteristic that is necessary completely to revolutionize all our thinking, not gradually, but immediately? Because through a gradual process, obviously, there is no mutation; the very word *mutation* implies immediacy. How am I, an individual living in this world, surrounded by so many problems, so many influences—how am I to see the totality of life? The enormous effort involved in conflict at any level does not bring about mutation. I think that is fairly clear. For it is obvious to any thinking man that a gradual process does not answer his immediate problems. And as we live in immediate problems, each problem dissociated from the other, how is it possible to see something totally? I think that is where the issue lies: to see that this quality of the mind is not brought about through any institution, through any education, through any religious practice or discipline, or through any effort. One has to see that totally because if one can see the thing totally, in that perceiving, in the very act of that perception, comes mutation. I would like to talk about that this evening a little bit.

We have relied on time as a means of bringing about a change. We have used time as a means of arriving somewhere in the changing process of our consciousness. We have used time as a steppingstone. And seeing not only the world situation but also that time in any form, at any level, does not bring about the new quality of the mind—if one sees that not only intellectually or verbally but also being in contact with it emotionally, sensitively, as one is when one sees a snake—then time has no validity except chronologically. Otherwise, there is no time; every other form of time is laziness, psychological laziness, psychological evasion, psychological postponement. If one realizes actually, not verbally, that time has no meaning any more, then in the realization of that, there is mutation.

Someone sees something very clearly; you see something very clearly, totally, and I do not. You see the whole implication of man's dependence on institutions—the whole implication, in which is implied authority, guidance, dependence, formal ideation—and I do not. It takes me many years to see what you see. Why does this take place, that you see and I do not see? You see something entirely, totally, with all your being. You see the evil of authority—if I can use that word *evil*—and you shun it completely, right through; and I do not; I come to it later, and even the coming to it later is only partial. I see authority is not right in that direction, but I see authority is necessary in another direction. My perception, my arrival at the denial of authority is still partial; it is not total as yours is. Why is this? You see and I do not see—why? You do not go through experience, you do not add, you see it immediately with a freshness; and I see it out of my barren mind. Why? I may ask such a question, and there may be no answer to it. I think there is, but there may be no answer. One must ask that question, and I think that is a fundamental question. Why are you not an artist and I am an artist, why are you clever and I am not clever?—these are very superficial, and not fundamental, questions. But the other is a fundamental question.

You see and I do not see—why does this happen? I think it happens because one is involved in time; you do not see things in time, I see it in time. Your seeing is an action of your whole being, and your whole being is not caught in time; you do not think of gradual arrival; you see something immediately, and that very perception acts. I do not see; I want to find out why I do not see. What is the thing that will make me see something totally so that I have understood the whole thing immediately? You see the whole structure of life: the beauty, the ugliness, the sorrow, the joy, the extraordinary sensitivity, the beauty—you see the whole thing, and I cannot. I see a part of it, but I do not see the whole of it. If the question is clear, and if you have really put it to yourself—not because I am putting it to you—if you are actually putting that and not finding an excuse or explanation and not seeking an answer—obviously, because you do not know—then you and I are in communion with regard to that questioning. I do not know if I am making myself clear. The man who sees something totally, who sees life totally, must obviously be out of time. Sirs, do listen to this, because this has something actually to do with our daily existence; it is not something spiritual, philosophical, out of daily existence. If we understand this, then we will understand our daily routine, boredom, and sorrows, the nauseating anxieties and fears. So do not brush it away by saying, "What has it to do with our daily existence?" It has. One can see—at least for me, it is very clear—that you can cut, like a surgeon, the whole cord of misery immediately. That is why I want to go into it with you.

Time is an extraordinary thing, and time is really only true mechanically. There has been a yesterday, there is a today, and there is a tomorrow—and there is no other time. It will take time to build a house, to educate the children; it will take time to go from here to your house. But actually, there is no other time. It is only thought that invents time—thought which says, "I must become something great, noble; I must arrive." And the process of thinking is conflict; and out of that conflict, out of that barrenness, time is born, psychologically, inwardly. If there were no time psychologically, if there were no tomorrow at all psychologically, the next moment you would be an entirely different being. If somebody were to tell you that you are going to die the next instant and not give you time to think, you would see the whole of life immediately because it is thought which interferes with perception. Thought is time; thought is the reaction of memory, of many thousands of years of man's inheritance, of a thousand memories, experience. But one has to step out of it; otherwise, there is no possibility of ever being free from sorrow, of being free from conflict. Do what you will—take any tranquilizer; do every form of tricky meditation to pacify your mind, to dull your mind; play with all the sacred books in the world—unless you understand the seed of sorrow, which is time, there is no end to sorrow; and you do not see something of that, totally.

All this implies the denial of experience, the denial of knowledge. Not mechanical knowledge, not scientific knowledge, not knowledge of mathematics—all such knowledge is essential, necessary, to exist, to survive physically; and to survive physically at the highest level, all that is necessary. But you have to see the whole significance of experience and be out of it, because when you are experienced, there is no freedom from sorrow, there is still sorrow, there is still effort, there is still a battle going on. You may know how to avoid, how to resist; it all implies further conflict, further deepening of the barren thought. So, there can be mutation only when the mind has denied time in the sense of every single thing that is involved in time—progress, arriving, self-fulfilling, becoming, achieving; you have to wipe away all that.

What is the thing that is necessary to bring this about? No words or symbols. Symbols have no meaning; they are used only to communicate. By themselves, they are not important. The thing is not the word. So, what brings about that timeless quality into life? I think there are only two things: affection and integrity.

By "integrity" I do not mean being true to something—that is merely conformity, that is merely an adjustment, imitation. To have an ideal and to conform, to have a belief and to conform, to have an experience or an idea and adjust to that, to be true to that—that is not integrity. I mean by the word *integrity* a mind which pursues the self, the 'me', and learns all about it. In the learning of all about it, there is an integrity which is not born out of knowledge but born out of learning. Learning about myself—which is endless—is not the same as acquiring knowledge about myself; the two things are entirely different. The more I am learning about myself—the conscious, the unconscious, the whole of the inward movement of myself—out of that, there is integrity. And if I am merely acquiring knowledge about myself, gathering information about myself and being true to that which I have gathered, then in that there is a dualistic conflict—to the thing I have learned, to that which I know, I must be true; and so there is the furthering of conflict. All knowledge does increase conflict about oneself, whereas learning about oneself does not. So, there has to be this learning, not only about myself, but about everything. And to learn, the mind must always be alert, always watching, always attending, testing, feeling, highly sensitive; and that is not possible when there is knowledge, when you are merely gathering.

So, there is an integrity which is not born of conflict, which is not imitative, which is not conforming but which comes into being by itself, without seeking, when there is learning about oneself. That integrity is necessary, and also affection. You know, the explosion of affection is not calculated, is not thought out. You know what I mean by affection? It is obviously the feeling, the sensitivity for beauty—whether a man, or a woman, or a child, or a bird, or a tree. And that is much more necessary, much more vital, than even integrity. Out of affection there comes the beauty of integrity. This affection cannot be analyzed and begotten; and no book will give it to you; neither your wife nor your husband will give it to you; of course, society can never bring it to you. I think this affection comes when you have denied everything totally—father, mother, society, virtue—not knowing what is tomorrow. You can deny knowing what is tomorrow, but that is not denial. When you deny totally everything, including yourself—first of all yourself, all the traditions and the values, totally—then out of this extraordinary sense of not knowing the next moment comes affection—not bitterness, not the sordid stuff of thought. So, affection and integrity are the two catalysts. If you notice, affection and integrity are not of time. You cannot have more integrity—that is mere political jargon. You cannot be more affectionate—you are affectionate, or you are not.

So, the perceiving of something totally is to deny. Please try it, and you will find how extraordinarily impossible it is for most of us to deny. Because we are yes-sayers, we have never said to ourselves no to anything. We are always compromising, always dodging—we say no to something not pleasurable; to pain we say no. But, to say no to pleasure also, to completely deny and to remain in that denial—I think that is the quality of timelessness, and out of that timelessness there is affection.

Comment: You always talk of time but never of space.

KRISHNAMURTI: The gentleman says, "You always talk of time and never of space."

Space is thought, from here to there, from here to the moon. To reach the moon, you need a mechanical means, a rocket; and for that you must have time to cover the space of two hundred and fifty thousand miles or whatever it is. Now, is there space between me—between this—and that which I want to be? We said there is space—"I want to be one day the saint, or the big business executive." From being what one is to arrive at saintliness, there is space which demands time—a gradual process. Through time will you become a saint? All the saints say so. They practice, they deny, they sacrifice, they control; they go through all the machinery of thought to become something. But if you saw directly now, for yourself, that there is no space, no time, except the time and the space which thought creates, what would happen?

Look, sirs, there is deterioration—no one will deny that—in this country; there is terrible decline—intellectual, moral, physical. In every way, there is deterioration. Perhaps I should not use the word *deterioration*, because when I use that word, it implies that one has reached the height and then declined. Probably it has never reached the height; it is going along the same path, then declining, getting worse—not reaching a point of declining. That is a fact. You see that in education; you see that in political morality; you see that in everything. It is going down, down, down. Don't you? There are more industries, more dams, more railways; but they are all mechanical. You know it. You see corruption—will time mend it, will a new government mend it? Will a new party—communist or socialist—change it? They may or may not. I question whether they can change it.

The individual has to change—not the individual on the periphery, on the outside, but the individual right in it. He has to explode. And will this explosion take time and space, time being from here to there? You follow? You know the fact that there is deterioration—the fact, not my assertion of the fact. It is there under your nose, you know it in detail and in bigness; everything is going down. And what do you do? Will you take time to change it? By the time you have taken to change, it has gone down further. So, you have to stop it. The action has to be immediate; it cannot be tomorrow because between now and tomorrow you are down further. It has got to be started immediately, and therefore there is no time; you cannot think in terms of past, future, or present. Deterioration has got to be completely stopped. And you can only stop it if you see the totality of the decline, not little bits of goodness, improvement, betterness here and there, this and that.

If you see this total disintegration, inwardly, totally, you do not have to do anything about it. The very perception will bring about a tremendous upheaval and explosion. That is why you must see this thing, not when you are eighty and down in the grave, but now. What will make you see it, what will induce you, influence you, what will be the offering, what will be the punishment that will make you see it totally? Obviously, no God, no institutions, no books, no promise, no reward, nothing. You have to see it yourself—completely.

Question: But how, sir?

KRISHNAMURTI: The lady asks, "How?" "How" implies time, "how" implies space between here and there, and how to arrive there. This demands a new mind, a new dimension, a new quality in the mind; and I say you can have it now, immediately, if you see this thing totally. Do not ask how to see. When you are asking for a method, a system, you are off in a wrong direction. Systems have been invented by man to postpone the moment of explosion.

Question: Is there a difference between struggle and conflict?

KRISHNAMURTI: They are the same.

Question: You have used the word affection. *Do you differentiate it from love?*

KRISHNAMURTI: Yes; as long as you understand, do not quibble over words. Let us talk more seriously.

Question: Perception is either voluntary or else we must wait for faith to bring it; what else is it?

KRISHNAMURTI: The gentleman says: "Either it must be voluntary, uninfluenced, or you must wait." That is what you are doing. The waiting is deterioration.

Question: How to perceive it?

KRISHNAMURTI: Leave it for the moment. I shall come back to this. When I say, "What shall I do in the meantime until the explosion takes place?" the interval between that moment and now, waiting for that explosion, is a deterioration. I do not know if you catch all this.

If there is no way, you do it immediately and voluntarily, completely; then you do not look to time, do you? You have to do it, and the urgency itself is its action.

Comment: This very thing is not perceived with that intensity which you wish.

KRISHNAMURTI: What are you going to do? Will you wait? If you deny time, if you deny the whole process of all the saints, of all the gods and all the books, of all tradition, you wipe it away as you have to.

Your problem arises only when you have not wiped it away. What will make you wipe it all away, to die to everything of the past? What will make you do it? Nothing. Only you have to see it, and you do not see it. Why? Why don't you see this thing?

Comment: It seems to be a paradox. Unless you see it, you are not able to perceive it totally; you see it verbally.

KRISHNAMURTI: Seeing verbally, seeing emotionally, seeing partially, you do not see it. Then what? Do pursue it, go to the very end of it.

Comment: It comes to the end, there is nothing there. I do not know what to do.

KRISHNAMURTI: Then, do not do anything. You laugh! I am saying something very seriously: Do not do anything except the mechanical things. But you are doing, all the time, something else. Do not do anything psychologically, inwardly; do nothing except what you have to do ordinarily in daily existence. Have you ever done it, and not gone off into a mental hospital? I do not mean that way, but actually do nothing, inwardly.

Comment: I beg to differ from your thesis. I may be excused. I beg to differ from you. It may appear that we are declining. If you take the things as they are, the moment we appear going down, actually the desires are gradually coming up and will get cleansed in due course.

KRISHNAMURTI: The gentleman says that because you have had freedom politically now, all the hidden suppressed desires and anxieties are coming up, and that they will disappear; and also that this process of giving up all the things that have been held back for centuries is not deterioration but is just cleansing. Is it so? Is bringing all this up cleansing? How long are you going to continue with this inward spitting out? If you say it will take time, then the very fact that you will take time is an indication that you are deteriorating.

If I may explain, I am not talking of a thesis, I am not making a talk just to get a PhD or to get your approval. We are dealing with facts, not with ideas. A man in sorrow does not talk about a thesis; he wants to know how to end sorrow. There are several ways to end it—drugging yourself, going to church, taking tranquilizers, chemicals, forgetting, escaping—but that does not solve the question; it is still there when you go back. One has to be aware of all this process and watch the escapes—drugs, drinking, women, and all the things that one does to avoid the real thing.

Comment: If I may interrupt you, there is a way, and that is to surrender to God. It is not theoretical but practical.

KRISHNAMURTI: The gentleman says there is one way: to surrender oneself to God.

How do you surrender yourself to God? What does it mean?

Comment: We should not be affected by the results of our action. We should have that attitude.

KRISHNAMURTI: What is my duty? Is it what society tells me?

Comment: It differs from person to person.

KRISHNAMURTI: It is what my guru tells me, what my family tells me. What is my duty? I refuse to have a duty.

Comment: That depends upon the person.

KRISHNAMURTI: You and I are talking at cross purposes. We have questioned the very existence of God to find out if there is God. We have questioned radically the whole idea of duty, responsibility, and who the entity is who is to surrender.

Comment: If we see a building, then naturally, the question arises: there is a person who has built it. When we see beauty, we appreciate the intelligence of the person who has built it. Our body can be compared to it. If there was no being that built it. . . .

KRISHNAMURTI: The gentleman says: "If there is no being, God, who built our physical body, then how do you explain this whole process?" The communists do not believe in God, they spit on that word; they have been brought up to live in that way. Like you who have been brought up logically, sanely, rationally, to believe in God, they have also been brought up logically, sanely, rationally, not to believe in God. What is the difference between them and you? You are conditioned one way and they the other way. You are conditioned by centuries of propaganda, and they by forty years of propaganda; what is the difference? The existence of life does not depend upon the idea of God; it depends on ourselves. You first postulate an idea that there is God and work it all out—which means you have stopped inquiry, you have stopped questioning. Don't you see that education, everything, has failed in this world? There have been two disastrous wars; there are monstrous things going on. It is no good saying everything is all right. We shall all be involved when the atom bomb comes, and we have to do something.

That is why you have to question everything, leave not a stone or leaf unturned in your questioning, even your logic which becomes so illogical when you are conditioned. When you remain a Hindu and reason from that background, your reasoning, your logic, your sanity is in question. You do not seem to see this. There must be a new world—not the Hindu world, not the Brahminical world, not somebody's pattern world. Something new must take place in each one of us, and the new cannot take place unless there is death, unless there is destruction, something which is a denial of all this and which is not a thesis.

Comment: I am not talking in terms of a Hindu or of a Buddhist when I say that there is a supernatural power which controls everything.

KRISHNAMURTI: When you say there is a supernatural power which controls everything, what does it mean? Controlling these tyrannies, controlling these disastrous wars, controlling our sorrow, controlling that poor villager who trudges along every day for two *annas* when you and I live comfortably and talk about God?

Question: Is denial different from condemnation?

KRISHNAMURTI: The gentleman says: "This denial of which we were talking earlier—is it different from condemnation?"

Obviously, condemnation is personal, like good taste; and to deny is like beauty which is not contaminated by personal taste. Do you realize what is happening in the world? People are denying all leadership; they are questioning all your superhuman gods, everything. It is not a matter of your belief; you are questioning your belief also. If you say—as the Catholics say—"Do not question my belief, that is a mystery, do not ask," then this is not a place for that. For me there is a reality, not the thing which we have been taught; there is something much more significant than all these things—that we have to find out. And you cannot find that out if you do not deny everything totally. Sir, you must die to everything to be born anew, you must die to find a new thing.

Your question is: What is the difference between denial and condemnation? Your condemnation is based on your conditioning. If you do not condemn, if you see the truth of it, you are out of conditioning. We have been raised from childhood to condemn, to justify, to accept, to believe—right through the world, the communist world and this world. It is easy to condemn, and we think by condemning we understand, as we think by comparing we understand—which is absurd. When you see the falseness of condemning and thereby deny condemning—not knowing how to evaluate, you say that this is false, not knowing what is true. When you see that condemnation is a conditioned response, and therefore deny it, you are no longer condemning, you are merely seeing facts.

I am not condemning that gentleman's "all-pervading spirit." The fact is that it is one of our favorite beliefs, imposed through centuries of man's endeavor. There is a cave in France in which about seventeen thousand years ago, the people who existed then painted pictures of extraordinary colors and vitality and breadth, of bulls fighting men. The bulls were the evil fighting the good. We are doing the same. I say I do not want to fight. That is a most irrational way, to fight, to struggle, to control, to be in conflict. You have to see something ugly as you see something beautiful. When you see the fact, that very fact will explode, will bring something new into being.

I say these are the facts: there is the threat of war; people are divided through religious, political division; a separation is going on, linguistically, nationally; and there is an inward decline also, psychologically. These are facts. There is a decline.

Question: How can you call it a decline?

KRISHNAMURTI: I take away that word *decline.* Decline implies reaching a height and then declining. I am merely stating facts. There is no peace in the world—peace implying brotherliness, etc.

Question: So, you have an ideal?

KRISHNAMURTI: I have no ideal. If I may say so, probably you are here for the first time, and that is why you ask that question. First of all, the difficulty is semantic—that is, the meaning of words—how I use certain words and how you use them. We have to be in communion with each other, not only at the verbal level, but also in the meaning level. You have to listen a little more.

Question: We are disintegrated, are we not?

KRISHNAMURTI: Yes, everything implies a standard, a judgment, a condemnation. For me, the way I look at it is not from an ideational point of view at all, not an emotional standpoint. I see the mere fact that I am in sorrow—which is a fact. I do not say, "I have been happy; how shall I get back to it?" The fact is that I am unhappy; if my wife has left me, that creates sorrow; if my son is dead, that creates sorrow. I speak of the fact of being in sorrow, and how to resolve that fact. That is why all communication is difficult. Especially, in these matters, words and symbols play such an important part, and one has to go beyond the word and the symbol—which is not something mystical, extraordinary.

If I want to communicate something to you, I have to communicate it not only verbally, but also I have to express it so that you and I meet somewhere which is not at the verbal level. For most of us, the verbal level is the communication and the meeting point; and the verbal implies what was, what is, and what will be.

Comment: Comparison by itself is not evil.

KRISHNAMURTI: When I say that waiting is deterioration, I am not comparing. I see the fact that when a man waits, obviously, something is happening to him—call it deterioration or what you like. When a man is not actively pursuing the fact that something must be done, when he waits—to that man who waits, something must be happening. And that state is deterioration. It is not because of comparison.

Comment: There is a certain affection associated with evil itself.

KRISHNAMURTI: All affection implies suffering?

Question: Where there is affection, a man suffers out of that also. Don't you suffer?

KRISHNAMURTI: I do not think so.

Question: To see somebody suffering?

KRISHNAMURTI: I know it sounds terribly brutal. I see my son suffering. What shall I do, what can I do, factually? I give him a few rupees. That is all I can do.

Comment: You cannot help suffering.

KRISHNAMURTI: Why? His wife has left him, or his son has died, or he cannot get a job—and he suffers.

Comment: Take something which is deeper.

KRISHNAMURTI: What is deeper?

Comment: Something, say a son's death.

KRISHNAMURTI: "The fact of love brings pain," we say, and we accept it. I question it. Is it self-pity? Is it identification with my son? Is it I am helpless, and I cannot do anything; therefore, I feel frustrated; therefore, in a roundabout way I feel sorry? Do I feel sorry because my son is dead and I am lonely? Without understanding all that, how can I say love and suffering go together?

Comment: I feel they do go together.

KRISHNAMURTI: All right.

Question: Are you denying suffering?

KRISHNAMURTI: I am not denying suffering.

Comment: Love we know, and also suffering.

KRISHNAMURTI: That gentleman says that suffering and love go together. I do say that they go together as long as you have not investigated what you call suffering, as long as love and suffering have not been understood totally. But do not insist on saying that they go together, as another person says love and jealousy go together.

Comment: I am not talking of my son; I am talking about suffering.

KRISHNAMURTI: Somebody says that he also suffers for the country which does something terribly wrong. Is that suffering?

Comment: Attachment is the cause of suffering, and not love.

KRISHNAMURTI: As things are, we suffer; we say we love. I am not questioning, please. Please question yourself whether love, what you call suffering, is not part of self-pity. It may be loneliness; it may be the feeling of frustration, a feeling of not being able to do anything. If you could do something, then you would not suffer. There may be ten explanations, one of which might explain your suffering. After explaining away everything, where are you at the end of it?

That gentleman says that attachment breeds sorrow. Yes, we all know that. We are all attached. Then why don't you break it, why don't you extricate yourself completely out of attachment?

January 7, 1962

Fifth Talk at Rajghat

We were talking the other day about conflict and how conflict invariably dulls the mind. I would like to approach the same problem from a different angle because, it seems to me, most of us have ideas which have much more importance and much more significance than the actuality.

We live in a world of ideas, totally divorced from the fact, and we always try to link the fact with the idea. And one of the causes of conflict is this attempt to approximate the fact to the idea. Why is it that ideas, concepts, formulas have become so extremely important? If you observe yourself, you will discover that ideas, the 'what should be', the intellectual concepts, the intellectual formulas are much more rigorous, much more important than the actual living, than the actual fact of what is taking place. If you observe yourself, you are bound to find out in what manner they have usurped the whole field of thought. We are not dealing with ideas because these talks are not at all concerned with ideas; we are concerned with the understanding of the fact which is life—with all its sorrow, misery, confusion, ambitions, fears; with its depths; and which has its discipline, corruption. We are trying to understand life, not in terms of ideas, but actually—to understand life and see if we cannot be free of those travails that give us such anxiety, make us feel so guilty, and if we cannot wipe away fear. That is what I would like to discuss this evening, if I may.

Why do ideas take root in our minds? Why do not facts become all-important—not ideas? Why do theories, ideas, become so significant rather than the fact? Is it that we cannot understand the fact, or have not the capacity, or are afraid of facing the fact? Therefore, ideas, speculations, theories are a means of escaping away from the fact. Do please apply this to yourself, not just listen to what is being said. What is being said has no value at all; but it has value—at least, it seems to me—when one can apply it to oneself and experience the things that are being said, by directly observing oneself. Otherwise, these talks will be utterly empty, without much meaning. So, do please give a little attention to that.

Is it that we are incapable of facing facts, and therefore ideas at all levels of existence offer an escape? The facts cannot alter; do what you will, the facts are there. You may run away, you may do all kinds of things; the facts are there—the fact that one is angry, the fact that one is ambitious, the fact that one is sexual, a dozen things. You may suppress them, you may transmute them, which is another form of suppression; you may control them, but they are all suppressed, controlled, disciplined with ideas. Is it possible not to live with ideas at all but with facts only? Do not ideas waste our energy? Do not ideas dull the mind? You may be clever in speculation, in quotations; but it is obviously a dull mind which quotes, that has read a lot and quotes.

Is it possible to live all the time, every minute, with facts? I do not know if you have ever tried to do that—to live with the fact of what actually is, and therefore to have no contradiction. You remove the conflict of the opposite at one stroke if you live with the fact and therefore liberate the energy to face the fact. For most of us, contradiction is an extraordinary field in which the mind is caught. I want to do this, and I do something entirely different; but if I face the fact of wanting to do this, there is no contradiction; and therefore, at one stroke I abolish altogether all sense of the opposite, and my mind then is completely concerned with *what is*, and with the understanding of *what is*.

Most of us have fear of some form or another. We are not concerned with what one is afraid of; we are not talking of that, but of fear itself—not fear of death, fear of your wife or husband, fear of losing a job, fear of so many things. We are talking of fear. Is it possible to live with the fact of fear without escaping from it, without creating the opposite and thereby making the mind dull in conflict? Has one the capacity to live with fear, and does capacity come through time? Is capacity to face the fact a matter of development, of time? I have to face the fact of fear. And when I face fear, I push aside all conflict of the opposite. Will the actual facing of fear develop its own capacity, rather than my developing the capacity to face it? I shall go into it a little bit.

Fear is an extraordinary thing. Most of us are afraid of something or other. Fear creates illusion; fear makes us suspicious, arrogant; fear makes us seek all kinds of refuge, all kinds of stupid virtues, moralities. And I want to face it, and not escape from it. Now, what is this "being aware of the fact"? The fact is fear; there is the awareness—what does awareness mean? All choice—I should not be afraid; this should not be; that should be; or any other choice—is denied the moment I face a fact. Awareness is a state of facing a fact, in which there is no choice. Awareness is that state of mind which observes something without any condemnation or acceptance, which merely faces the thing as it is. When you look at a flower nonbotanically, then you see the totality of the flower; but if your mind is completely taken up with the botanical knowledge of what the flower is, you are not totally looking at the flower. Though you may have knowledge of the flower, if that knowledge takes the whole ground of your mind, the whole field of your mind, then you are not looking totally at the flower.

So, to look at a fact is to be aware. In that awareness, there is no choice, no condemnation, no like or dislike. But most of us are incapable of doing this because traditionally, occupationally, in every way, we have been brought up to condemn, to approve, to justify; so, that is our background. To look at something without a background is to face the fact. But as we are not capable of facing the fact without the background, we have to be aware of the background. We have to be aware of our conditioning, and that conditioning shows itself when we observe a fact; and as you are concerned with the observation of the fact and not with the background, the background is pushed aside. When the main interest is to understand the fact only, and when you see that the background prevents you from understanding the fact, then the vital interest in the fact wipes away the background. If I am interested completely in fear, then I neither condemn it nor justify it; there is fear, and I want to go into it; no background, no ideation will interfere with it because my interest is in the understanding of fear.

Now, what is fear? We are not dealing with ideas, with words. We are dealing with life, with the things which are happening inside and outside, which needs a very clear, sharp mind, a precise mind; you cannot be sentimental, emotional, about all these things. To understand fear, you need clarity—clarity not of something that you will get, but the clarity that comes when you understand that the fact is infinitely more important than any idea. So, what is fear?—not fear of something. Is there such a thing as fear, per se, in itself, or is fear related always to something? And is there fear?

I will take death for the moment. You can supply your own example. Is there fear if there is no thought—that is, if there is no time? Most people are afraid of death. However much they might have rationalized it, whatever their beliefs may be, there is the fear of death. That fear is caused by time—not by death, but by time—time being the interval between now and what is going to happen, which is the process of thinking, which brings about the fear of the unknown. Is it the fear of the unknown or the fear of leaving the things that we know? We are afraid of death. We are not talking of death, what happens after death; we are talking of fear in relation to death. I say: Is that fear caused by the thing which I do not know? Obviously I do not know about death. I can know about it, but that is not the point now. I can investigate, discover the whole beauty or the ugliness or the terror, the extraordinary state death must be. If we have time, we can go into it later.

Is the fear in relation to death caused by death—which means facing the unknown? Or is it caused by the things which, I know, are going to be taken away from me? The fear is of the things being taken away from me, the 'me' disappearing into oblivion. And so I begin to protect myself with all the things that I know and live in them more strongly, cling to them much more than becoming aware of the unknown. What is it I am afraid of? Not facing the unknown, but facing something which may happen to me when I am taken away from all the things that are held dear, which are close to me—that is what I am afraid of, not of death. What is it that I have—factually, not theoretically? I do not know if you have ever asked yourself a fundamental question to find out what you are. Do not translate it into the terms of the Gita or of some guru—that is all nonsense.

Actually, what are you? Have you ever asked it, and have you found an answer? Is there an answer? If there is an answer, it is not in terms of what you already know. But what you know is the past, and the past is time, and the time is not 'you'. The 'you' is changing. I do not know if you are following all this. To find out what you are, if you say, "What am I?" possibly you are asking to find out the 'I' that is static. Therefore, you say, "I know I am this." You can only know of something which is static; you cannot know of something which is living. I do not know if you have ever thought about this. You can speculate about the living; you can have ideas about the living and approximate the living with the idea and, therefore, introduce conflict. But if you say, "I want to know what I am," is that question put in order to find out for yourself the static 'me', or is there a 'me' at all which is not static? This is not a philosophical lecture. When I put that question to find out what I am, that "what I am" is always in the past. The 'me' is always the past. I can only put the question and inquire into something static. And through the thing that is dead, that is static, the past, I have to find out what I am—and so fear never goes away. But fear goes away the moment I put that question and watch myself all the time, not direct my attention to the past, but actually to what is taking place, which is the 'me' that is alive. Therefore, the thing that is alive never engenders fear. It is the thing that is past, or the thing that should be, that breeds fear.

Let us look at fear in a different direction. There is the word, and there is the thing. The word *tree* is not the tree. We will keep it very simple. We will use only one symbol: the word tree is not the actual tree. But for us, the word is the tree. So, we must be able to see clearly that the word is not the thing. This is important to go into the question of fear.

Now, the word *fear* is not the actual state which is called fear. That is a different emotion, a sentiment, but the word is not it. The thing called fear is not the word, and yet we are caught in words. Why has the word become important and not the thing? Because the symbol, not the fact, is an idea which becomes much more important than the fact, because you can play with ideas, you cannot play with the fact. So, we are slaves to words like the *supreme being,* like *God.* If I want to find out if there is God, obviously, the word must go—and with it the authority of all the saints and such people. I must completely destroy the word; otherwise, I cannot find out. A man who says there is God or no God, a man who is caught in words, will never find. So, in understanding fear, there must be an awareness of the word and all the content of the word—which means, the mind has to be free of words. To be free of the word is an extraordinary state. Being aware of the symbol—the word, the name—then there is awareness of the fact at a different dimension, if I can use that word.

Now I am aware of the fact, of fear through the word, and I know why the word comes into being. It is an escape, it is tradition, it is the background in which I have been brought up, to deny fear and to develop courage—the opposite—and all the rest of it. And when I understand the whole implication of the word, then there is an awareness of the fact, which is entirely different. In that awareness, is there fear?

To unravel, which is really self-knowing, is the process of freeing the mind from everything except the fact; and that is a part of meditation. If you do not understand all the implications of fear or of ambition and try merely to meditate, only repeating some silly words which have no meaning, it is only an illusion; it is not rational, it is not sanity. So, facing the fact all the time without the idea is like the river. Into the river the city throws everything—all the chemicals, all the dirt of the sewer. Everything goes into the river as it passes by. And three miles away from there, the river has purified itself; the very movement of the river has cleansed it. In the same way, the mind cleanses itself all the time if it is facing the fact, if it lives with the fact and nothing else; and therefore, there is no contradiction and therefore no conflict of opposites. If I live with violence and completely understand it, what need is there for the opposite? As the river is always purifying itself, so am I when I face the fact all the time. And to face the fact, you need tremendous energy; and that energy is begotten when there is no conflict of the opposites, when there is no effort made to become something.

So, a mind that is facing a fact has no discipline because the very fact disciplines the mind; it does not impose it upon the mind. I do not know if you see all this, see the beauty of such living with facts, because otherwise you cannot go far; and one has to go very very far—farther than up to the moon—to go within oneself. You cannot go very far, straight as an arrow flies, if there is no right foundation. And the right foundation is the fact—not an idea. Then the mind can fly always high—not in illusion.

Question: When I look at a fact, my conditioning interferes. The conditioning is also a fact. What am I to do?

KRISHNAMURTI: The question is when you are looking at the fact, your background—your conditioning, your Hinduism, your Christianity, your scientific training, your education—interferes; and so, for you, the fact is the background and not the fact that you are trying to understand. You want to understand ambition. You are ambitious, and that is a fact. You want to look at it, but your whole background—your training, your society, your culture—says, "What would happen if you were not ambitious?" So, there is the fact that you are ambitious, and there is the other fact of your tradition, of your conditioning. Now the conflict is between these two facts. Fact A is an actuality, and fact B, which is your conditioning, is also an actuality. But if you want to understand A, you must understand B, surely; so your whole attention is not on A but on B.

How is one to understand the background? This is really a very complex question because it involves not only the modern educated conscious mind—the mind that has become that of a clerk, a governor, a bureaucrat, a moneymaker, and all the rest of it—but also the mind which is the unconscious mind, the hidden mind deep down. So the whole of that is the conditioned mind, which is the past. Our concern is with B, not with A; and to understand B, we must go into the whole question of consciousness. Consciousness is not something you discover in the books because what is in the books is merely an idea. Somebody says it is so, somebody asserts. Somebody's idea may be his actual experience; when he writes it down, it is an idea, and your following that idea or obeying that idea prevents you from discovering your own state of consciousness. So, you have to find out what you are, what your consciousness is, not according to somebody else, but actually. I am going to do it—not that you are going to listen to my ideas, but we are going to go into it—I am going into it verbally, but you are going into it actually. I am going to use words, but the word is not the thing. And the thing is for you to face the fact—the fact of your own consciousness, not of Shankara, Buddha, myself, or XYZ; that has no value at all. If that is clear, let us go into it.

Question: What I am is always in the past; why is it not in the present?

KRISHNAMURTI: I am answering your question exactly, if you kindly follow what I am saying. We are occupied with our own problems. Do follow this, your question will be answered.

We are dealing with life. There is consciousness, what is it? Please follow your own mind in operation—not my mind. We see obviously that there are certain levels of our consciousness which are of the modern educated mind, the mind that is caught in knowledge, in specialization, in technique, in understanding how to live in this world, to go to the office, to do business, with all the trickery, the corruption, the knavery—that is one level. And you have to do all that because otherwise you cannot live. Then, there is another level below that. First of all, there is no division between the conscious and the unconscious; we divide it only for convenience. In actuality, there is no such division; there is an interplay all the time going on between the conscious and the unconscious.

The unconscious mind and the conscious mind are receiving innumerable experiences all the time. But one segment of the mind says, "I must be educated," and has educated itself in order to live in the present world at the present time. There are other parts of the mind, other parts of the consciousness, which are the result of our race—the race being your traditions, the things that must be done and the things that must not be done, the ideas, the things that you have been taught—all that is the past, hidden in the unconscious. You are listening to my words, but actually you are seeing it in yourself. The unconscious is the mechanism of habit; the unconscious is the mechanism of motive; it is where all our experiences are stored away—the experiences of the race, of man; the experiences as a Hindu, as a Buddhist, as a Catholic, or what you will; the experiences that have been accumulated as knowledge, hidden deeply inside; the fears, into the details of which I will not go now, as it will take too long.

There is this consciousness. And the moment there is a past, it has boundaries, it has a framework, it is caught up in the past, and there is all that which we have now described. That whole background prevents you from looking at the fact. So, we have to look into that background and dissipate that background. Is it possible? Some psychologists, who think they are atheists, say that you cannot dissipate it at all; and those who think there is God, equally feel it cannot be dissolved—all that can be done is only to decorate the background, give it more education to modify it, to control it, to shape it. How is one to be rid of the past?—which is, the experiences of yesterday influencing today, obviously, and so conditioning tomorrow. I have had an experience yesterday of being insulted or praised, and that conditions my thinking now; and when I meet you tomorrow, that shapes my thinking with regard to you. So, the past uses the present and becomes the future.

Now, to understand the fact, I must look at it without the background, obviously. Is this possible? And the fact will not remain as a fact—it is moving, living. To understand it I must move with it; my mind must be as rapid, as swift, as sensitive as the fact. And my mind is not so if it has a background, if it is conditioned. Please follow. The background must be surgically operated on immediately, to follow the fact. So, there is no time to investigate the background.

Comment: There is only one more difficulty in between—that is, between the background and the fact. There is a tendency.

KRISHNAMURTI: Obviously.

Comment: At that time it is in a new dimension which has taken something of the color of the fact because it is in contact with the background.

KRISHNAMURTI: Let us get the ideas. You say that the background in relationship with the fact brings about a tendency—let us keep to that.

Comment: The background is very rich, very varied by the contact of the fact with the background.

KRISHNAMURTI: I do not quite understand. You are saying this, are you?—that the background has enormous history; the background is the story of all mankind, not only the mankind of India, but of all mankind of which India is a part; the Indian background is modified but has the background of humanity. You are saying that if that enormous history or story is wiped away, there is nothing left as one fact. There is this enormous history or story which gives color to the fact; otherwise, the fact is barren. Is that it? Let us take that.

As far as I understand, a part of the question is this. The background is our history; the background is all the mythology, the experiences of mankind; that is very rich, and being very rich, it is also crooked, just as every rich man is a crooked man; and that richness, however slightly perverse it is, distorts the fact.

I do not say that the background is not rich. Obviously, the background is very rich; and being rich, it must distort. There are ten thousand years of the Gita or more—the date does not matter—and that has conditioned your mind, your thinking, your belief in discipline. Someone has told you, or some guru has told you that you must discipline yourself; and millions of people have disciplined themselves, and it has left a tremendous history behind. Somebody like me comes along and says, "Look, discipline is not necessary. Live with the fact, and the fact will bring about discipline; you will not have to discipline yourself." Looking at the fact eliminates contradiction and therefore conflict, and therefore duality. Therefore, he says, "Look at the fact," but you say that is impossible. Shankara, Buddha, your guru, the Gita—everybody says discipline, discipline, discipline.

So you are not looking, nor are you listening to what another is saying. Whereas you have to see your background and see whether it is true or false. If it is false, cut it with a surgeon's knife; do not have a thing to do with it; wipe it away and see if this is so. But you cannot see if this is so if you still have a background, a discipline. That is very clear.

Your mind is the result of ten thousand years and more—a million years; I am not talking about reincarnation. As the mind is the result of man living on earth, the mind has a tremendous history of experience, and you cannot wipe that mind away; but when that mind interferes in the discovery of what is true, then that mind has no relationship with what you may discover. There is scientific knowledge. It would be absurd and silly to wipe away all that knowledge, but a scientist who wants to discover something new cannot be burdened with it. He knows that knowledge is there, but he is free to inquire. This is so simple. I do not know if you follow it.

In the same way, if I want to inquire into the whole process of fear, I have to cut away everything to find out the whole process, to inquire into it; because, what you have acquired apparently has not solved your problem of fear—you are still afraid.

Question: Is the fact different from the mind which interferes?

KRISHNAMURTI: The lady asks: "Is the fact different from the interference?" Now, do think it out. I am not a Delphic oracle.

Is the fact different from interference? Are they not all in the same field, on the same ground? Is not the fact a part of the mind? I am jealous—it is part of the mind. And also it is part of the mind that says, "Do not be jealous, be virtuous, whatever it is. Jealousy is hate, so you must love; therefore, wipe out jealousy." Do you follow? I am jealous, and a part of the interference is that I must not be jealous. They are both within the same field. No? The fact is not outside the field of the mind. It is still within the field of the mind, as interference is still within the field of the mind. But with us, the interferences have become tremendously strong and important, and they interfere with the fact. We have emphasized the interferences and not the fact.

Now, is it possible not to allow the interferences at all to come into play? I say it is possible, but only when you have understood the whole question of interference. The question is this: There is the fact, there is the interference, and there is the attempt to understand the interference. Now the fact, the interference, and the urge to understand the interference in order to face the fact—all these arise only when I want to face the fact. If I allow interferences to play all the time, as I do, then there is no fact, and I live with the interferences.

I have said: Face the fact; do not let interferences interfere, but be aware of the interferences. So, there are three problems—the fact, the interference, and being aware of the interference. All the three are in the same field. They are not in separate watertight compartments; they are all in the same field and on the same ground. Watch it. Please follow it carefully. Experiment with this—which is, be totally aware of all this, aware of the fact, aware of the interference, and aware that there is no understanding of the fact if there is interference. Be totally aware of all that, aware of the significance; then you are getting the meaning of all the three because in that total awareness there is no division. As I explained the other day, when there is attention, there is no distraction. It is only when there is concentration there is distraction, because concentration is exclusion; to be totally aware of these three is to be attentive without the borders.

So what happens psychologically, what takes place, when you are aware of the three as a whole, when there is an awareness of the total thing—the fact, the interference, and the understanding of the interference?

Question: Is fear something natural or acquired?

KRISHNAMURTI: When you meet a snake, you jump. That is a natural, self-protective fear; without that you would be run over by a car, by a bus, or be killed by a snake. But all the others are unnatural, psychological desires to be secure, and all the rest of it. When you are totally aware of the fact and the interferences and have understood them, and also the desire to understand those interferences—which will not interfere with the fact—when you are totally aware of all this, totally attentive to all this, what happens? Then is there the fact, does the fact remain—the fact that you are afraid? It would be absurd if you accepted my word.

We have come thus far by questioning. If I have questioned, and you are merely expecting, the result is absolutely worthless. It is like a hungry man being fed on words; he still remains hungry. But if you have really followed inwardly, you are bound to come to this position that there is a fact, an interference, and the urge to understand the interference in order to complete the fact. When you are totally aware of all these three and of their significance, and do not merely concentrate on the fact or on the interference or on understanding the interference, then is there the fact? Is there jealousy, envy? I say there is not; obviously, you have wiped away every form of envy and jealousy.

Now, sir, this is real meditation. Without the fact ceasing to be—the fact of jealousy, of envy completely ceasing to be—how can you go very far? How can you find something which is beyond time? It is for you to find out, not for Shankara or Buddha or XYZ—that has no meaning, to rely on somebody. If you want to find out if there is or if there is not, you must go through this. You must be totally free of fear, and to be totally, completely free of fear, you must face the fact—the fact that you are afraid, the fact also that you are conditioned, which interferes with the fact, and the urge to get rid of the background in order to understand the fact. To be totally aware of all this is the beginning of meditation—not sitting on the banks of the Ganga, repeating empty words, and all the rest of the nonsense going on in the name of meditation. You must lay the right foundation. Otherwise, your building will totter, it has no meaning, it cannot remain straight.

What we have done this evening is the inquiry into oneself in which there is no assumption of any kind, not saying this is permanent or impermanent—you should wipe away all that completely, and so you begin to understand yourself.

So self-knowing is the beginning of meditation. And you can go infinitely into this marvelous thing called meditation if you have the right foundation; otherwise, you get lost, you are caught in sensations, visions, and all kinds of absurdities which have no validity for a man who is seeking. Then you will find, if you have gone so far, that you are moving with the fact, and therefore there is the ending of the fact, all the time; and thereby your mind becomes astonishingly supple, extremely sensitive. That is an absolute basis for meditation.

Then you will find out, if you have gone into it, that your mind or brain becomes astonishingly sensitive, therefore very quiet. A brain that is sensitive is very quiet; it is like a most delicate instrument—quiet, sensitive. You must have a brain that is completely quiet, uncontrolled, because the moment you control it, sensitivity is lost. It is only when the brain is completely quiet, uninfluenced, unrubbed, not disciplined, not controlled—one cannot achieve a still brain; to think of achieving it is immature, utterly vain, and has no meaning—that you will find out whether there is, or whether there is not, a movement beyond that. There is a movement beyond that, and that movement is creation, is God, or whatever you like to call it—it is irrelevant what name you give it. It is that movement which is necessary in this world at the present moment, because we have become machines—scientific or technological or specialized machines. Do you think a mechanical brain is going to find out anything?

Comment: I find it difficult to separate the word from the thing and treat them as different.

KRISHNAMURTI: The gentleman says he finds it extremely difficult not to allow the word to be the thing.

Why is it difficult? Is the door which you see there the same as the word *door;* is that word not different from the thing? The gentleman says he has never forgotten the word; the word is never absent, it is always there. For most people it is so. The word is there, not the thing. Psychologically, the word becomes so important because the word is a means of escape from the fact.

Let us take the word *envy.* The word is not the thing, and the word envy becomes important to us. Psychologically, inwardly, we do not know what to do with envy. It is respectable. All our social structure is based on envy; our education from childhood up to whatever we have reached is still based on envy, and envy is the symbol of position, authority. Psychologically, we want all that, and the symbol has become respectable, popular; it means success, position, power, and all the rest of it; and so we avoid envy, and we worship the symbol, the word.

Comment: One does not know one is envious. One knows it only at a later stage.

KRISHNAMURTI: The gentleman says that there are two stages with regard to envy. One is completely oblivious of envy; one does not know one is envious, and if one lives in that state, obviously, it leads to insanity, ill health. If one is aware of it, is there envy then? If one is not aware that one functions in envy, that envy is the motive power; then that leads to mental illness. But when one becomes conscious of it, then the whole mechanism of thought is set going, and the mechanism of thought is verbal. Thought is the structure of words. So to one who wants to look at the thing without the word, all those are explanations. But explanations do not satisfy the hungry man. The hungry man says, "Give me food."

When a man is not conscious of his envy, it breeds illness. When he is conscious of his envy, he begins to verbalize and builds a structure of words, which becomes the thought and opposes the fact. Only when there is total awareness of all this, without any thought arising in the mind, will envy cease to be.

Question: Will you please say what is the purpose of your saying that there is no God?

KRISHNAMURTI: I did not say there is no God. I said very definitely: To find if there is God or no God, you must abolish, wipe away from your mind, all concept of God. To find if there is God or if there is no God, you must wipe away all the information that you have received about God. The people who have given you information might be mistaken; you will have to find out for yourself. And to find out for yourself, you must get rid of all authority, understand the whole structure, the anatomy of authority—whether it is the authority of the policeman, the authority of the government, the authority of the guru, or the authority of your own desires; they all play a part.

Without understanding all this, merely to seek what you call God has no meaning at all. God is something amazing, not to be imagined by some kind of belief. You have to find out. I do not say if there is or there is not. To find out, you must be free first. There is London; it is a fact, a physical fact.

It is the same thing with a physical fact which can be examined by a microscope. You believe in God because you have been brought up in that belief. The communist does not believe in God; he says there are only physical phenomena which are explicable.

January 10, 1962

Sixth Talk at Rajghat

As there are only two more talks, today and Sunday evening, and as there are so many things to talk about, perhaps we should inquire into the problem of leisure. Leisure does breed with most of us discontent, and so we occupy ourselves with so many things to keep our minds busy. We try various activities, and if they are successful, profitable, gratifying, then we settle in those. The rest of our lives is spent in furthering that particular cause or that particular thing to which we are committed, and so our days and our thoughts and our feelings are taken up with that. So there is very little leisure. I think leisure is very important—that period when you have nothing to do, that time when there is no thought, no occupation, when your mind is not asleep but very alert.

Most of us have very little time for leisure because our days are taken up with gaining and losing, going to the office, attending meetings or going to the club, or some form of amusement; or you read a great deal, and if you are so-called religiously inclined, you turn to sacred books—I do not know why those books should be more sacred than any other books, why they are called sacred books. So we spend our days and our whole life being thus occupied; no part of our mind is at leisure, is quiet; no part of our being comprehensively understands the work, the activity, the things that one has to do. And yet there is within the totality of it a certain repose, a certain quietness, a quality which is untouched, a quality which is constantly keeping itself clean like the river because its very activity, its very movement keeps it clean, untouched, uncorrupted.

Please, if I may point out, this is not an intellectual, verbal, ideational talk. We are here, as I take it, really to investigate into ourselves and thus to open the door and look through into ourselves and discover what is true and what is false. And perhaps in merely listening to the words, you might be able for yourself to see clearly without distortion the actual process of the mind, the ways of one's own thinking and the habits of one's own feelings.

Most of us are discontented. For most of us, discontent is a torturous thing. We try this and that, and we always want to commit ourselves to a course of action. And the action, invariably, if one is at all intellectually sensitive, is turned in the direction either of social work—to improve society—or of so-called religion, apart from life. One finds something in this process of wandering in action, some activity that is completely satisfactory, and there one remains solidified in that activity. But life will not leave us alone. There is always somebody saying something that is not quite right. So, you again begin to be discontented and keep going until you find; you are always avoiding leisure, the time when there is no occupation at all. When the mind is really very quiet, not harassed, not all the time occupied with problems, then perhaps out of that quietness some other quality can come into being.

I would like, if I may, this evening to inquire into that quality of mind which has leisure and has not committed itself to anything, which can see, act, and yet be uncontaminated. I would like, if I may, to go into that—but not how to acquire it. Let us be very clear from the beginning that such a mind is not come to by any method, by any system, by any work, by any sacrifice, through any virtue. That is the beauty of such a mind. But to understand such a mind really, for such a mind to come into being, we must inquire into the process of thought, what is thinking; not that it begets sorrow, not that it is complex, not that it creates problems—which it does.

I think it is necessary to understand the whole mechanism of thought. Unless we understand it, there is inevitably unreasoning, unbalanced thinking, which is not healthy thinking at all. And one needs to have clear reason, logic, precision in thought. One needs to have a great deal of understanding of the whole process of the mechanism of thought. Because, a mind, a brain, which is not capable of really dispassionately, objectively looking, observing, feeling, sensing, with great balance, with sanity—such a brain obviously cannot go very far. So, we must find out what is thinking and also, in the process of that inquiry, find out the contradiction that exists between the thinker and the thought. As long as there is that contradiction, there must be effort, and therefore conflict.

So, we have to understand the whole process of thinking. You know we have an extraordinary history, a story which is the past, an immense richness collected not only by the individual mind but also by the collective. I question if there is an individual mind. Probably there is no individual mind; until the mind is freed, it is only a collective mind. But the mind is the result of time; the brain with all its extraordinary capacities is the result of time, of many thousand yesterdays. Biologically, I believe the rear part of the brain is the result of all the animal instincts which are still retained, and the forepart of the brain is still to be developed. But, for us, the past is the background from which we think, the past is the experience, the knowledge, the innumerable incidents and influences which have been stored up. The culture, the civilization in which we have been brought up, all that is the past. And from that past, we think; that is the background, and that gives us the tone, the quality of thought. Every question, every challenge is answered and responded to from the past.

Thought is really, if one goes into it, if one observes it, the response of memory; and without memory there is no thought, no thinking. Whatever we are asked, whatever the challenge, whatever the response to that challenge—all that is still the recording, the response of the past, of the memory, of all the experiences that one has gathered. And that past has always a center from which we think; and that center is more emphasized in our life, has more importance; that center becomes profitable, that center assures security. From that center we think, we act. That center is more or less static; though its challenge takes a different form, a different shape, though things are added to it and taken away from it, it is still there. That center has become important for each one of us. That center might be the family; that center gives me comfort, gives me pleasure; that is the thing round which I have gathered so many things in order to protect myself. So, there is this center which is created by thought, thought being the mechanism of the past. Until we understand thought and the thinker, there must be duality, there must be conflict; and all conflict wastes energy, deteriorates the quality of the mind.

So, a man who would really understand this whole process of gathering energy must obviously comprehend totally this division between the thinker and the thought, and the conflict that exists between these two. We have a center, and that center is created by thought; that center is the background. That background is very extensive and historical and has also plenty of mythology and moral values of society. However extensive that background is, there is always a center in it, the 'me', which is more important than history. That 'me', that self, is created by thought, because if there is no thinking, there will be no 'me'. The 'me' is not created by some supernatural entity; the 'me' is created by everyday incident, by every accident, by every experience, by the innumerable assertions and denials and pursuits.

If I may suggest, listen to what is being said, do not take notes; taking notes is not important at all. It is like looking at the sunset and at the same time talking—you are paying attention neither to the sunset nor to what you are saying. If I may request you, do apply your mind to what is being said, and discover for yourself, directly experience what is being said, rather than vicariously, verbally, accept or deny.

Is it possible to remove this conflict between the censor and the thing that is censored? That is really a very important question if you ask yourself, because that removes all conflict, all contradiction. A mind in contradiction, in conflict, is a wasting mind, is a deteriorating mind; every problem which is given time deteriorates the mind unless the problem is solved immediately, instantly. And the problem which we are talking about is very important because that is the center from which all problems arise.

Is it possible to have no center at all? Do not translate this into your own language, into what you have read in the Gita or some other book; forget all that, and look at the issue. Do not interpret it in your own peculiar language—then you lose the vitality of perception.

Is it possible to think, to feel, to act, to do everything that we do, without the center? The things that we do, and the misery, the chaos, the confusion, the sorrow, the extraordinary despair that we have—will they exist if there is no center, if there is no entity that is committing itself and acting from a thing that has become merely a bundle of memory and which has assumed such importance? Surely, there is only thinking, and not a center which thinks. But thought has created the center for several reasons. One reason is that thought is insecure, thought is uncertain, thought can be changed, thought has no security, thought has no resting place, thought can be changed from day to day; but man is always seeking a place of security where he will not be disturbed under any circumstances, and so gradually the center becomes psychologically very important, and in that center there is security.

Is there such a thing as security in anything—in one's family, in one's job, in what one thinks, in what one feels? Is there security, is there any kind of permanency? And yet thought seeks permanency in everything, and the search for permanency is the breeding ground of the center. Just listen to it; you cannot do anything. Do not say, "How am I to get rid of the center?" It is too immature a question, there is no meaning; but if you observe, just see it, see the effects, then perhaps a new way opens out.

So thought is the response of memory, experience, the past; that is our mind, that is our consciousness; and in that consciousness, there is pain, joy, suffering, the things that one wants to do, to improve, to change—all starting from there. And not being satisfied with anything, unless one is utterly immature, one finds some stupid satisfaction, gratification, and there settles down for the rest of one's life; or being discontented, being dissatisfied, one wants to commit oneself to a particular course of action. As one begins to act in that field, one sees that it is not good; so, he goes to one thing after another, always pursuing.

For us, idea becomes extremely important, not action, and action is merely an approximation to the idea. Is it possible to act without idea and therefore no approximation at all at any time? This means really that one has to go into the question of why idea has taken the place of action. People talk about action: What is the right thing to do? The right thing to do is not an idea divorced from action, because then action becomes an approximation to the idea, and still the idea is important but not action. So, how are you to act so completely, so totally, that there is no approximation, that you are living all the time completely? Such a person has no need of an idea, of concepts, of formulas, of methods. Then there is no time but only action; time arises only when there is approximation between action and idea.

This may sound extravagant and absurd. But, if you have gone into the question of thought, into the question of idea, and as you cannot live without action, you ask, "Is it possible to live without idea, without word, but only with action?" It is only when the mechanism of thought is understood that there is action which is not an approximation. Surely, if you think about this yourself, you will see what an extraordinary thing it is.

We have separated action, knowledge, love, and kept them all apart; each has its own drive, its own intensity, its own pull, and each is in contradiction with the other; that is our daily existence, our lives. To see the significance of these separated activities, which are really ideational and not factual, and to discover for oneself—not to be told; not that one reads it in a book, but actually discovers for oneself—the state of action without idea, to do something totally—that can only happen when you have love, affection. Thought creates all the divisions that exist in life—godly love, human love, and all the rest of it. Is not the quality of the mind that has complete leisure—that has come into being through understanding, through observing—quietness, a sense of silence? For me, this whole process of investigation into oneself is meditation. Meditation is not the repetition of words and formulas, mesmerizing oneself into all kinds of fanciful states. If you take opium, a tranquilizer, it will give you marvelous visions, but that is not meditation.

Meditation is actually this process of investigation into oneself. If you go into it deeply yourself, you are bound to come across all this, where it is possible to think without the center, to see without the center, to act so completely without idea and approximation, to love without the center and therefore without thought and feeling. And, when you have gone through all that, you find out for yourself a mind that is completely free and has no borders, no frontiers—a mind that is free, which has no fear and which does not come about through discipline. And if one has gone that far, one begins to see—or rather, the mind itself begins to observe the thing itself which unfolds thought—that the quality of time, the quality that is yesterday, today, and tomorrow, has completely changed, and therefore action is not in terms of yesterday, today, and tomorrow. Such action has no motive—all motive has its root in the past, and any action born out of that motive is still an approximation.

So, meditation is the total awareness of every movement of thought and never denying thought—which means letting every thought flower in freedom; and it is only in freedom that every thought can flower and come to an end. So out of this labor—if it can be called labor, which is really out of this observation—the mind has understood all this. Such a mind is a quiet mind; such a mind knows what it is really to be quiet, to be really still. And in that stillness, there are various other forms of movement which can only be verbal to people who have not even thought about this.

Question: After a day's hard work, one's mind gets tired. What is one to do?

KRISHNAMURTI: The question is: "After a day's work with so many occupations, one finds the little time that one has is occupied; the mind is weary; what is one to do?"

You know, our whole social structure is all wrong; our education is absurd; our so-called education is merely repetition, memorizing, mugging up. How can a mind which has been struggling all day as a scientist, as a specialist, as this or that, which is so occupied for thirteen hours in something or other—how can it have a leisure which is fruitful? It cannot. How can you, after spending forty or fifty years as a scientist or a bureaucrat or a doctor or what you are—not that they are not necessary—have ten years when your mind is not conditioned, not incapable? So, the question is really: Is it possible to go to the office, to be an engineer, to be an expert in fertilizers, to be a good educator, and yet, all day, every minute, keep the mind astonishingly sharp, sensitive, alive? That is really the issue, not how to have quietness at the end of the day. You are committed to engineering, to some specialization; you cannot help it; society demands it, and you have to go to work. Is it possible, as you are working, never to get caught in the wheels of the monstrous thing called society? I cannot answer for you. I say it is possible, not theoretically but actually. It is possible only when there is no center; that is why I was talking about it. Think of a doctor who is a nose and throat specialist, who has practiced for fifty years. What is his heaven? His heaven is nose and throat, obviously. But is it possible to be a good first-class doctor and yet live, function, watch, be aware of the whole thing, of the whole process of thought? Surely, it is possible, but that requires extraordinary energy. And that energy is wasted in conflict, in effort; that energy is wasted when you are vain, ambitious, envious.

We think of energy in terms of doing something, in terms of the so-called religious idea that you must have tremendous energy to reach God, and therefore you must be a bachelor, you must do this and do that—you know all the tricks that the religious people play upon themselves and so end up half starved, empty, dull. God does not want dull people—the people who are insensitive. You can only go to God with complete aliveness, every part of you alive, vibrant; but you see, the difficulty is to live without falling into a groove, falling into habits of thought, of ideas, of action. If you apply your mind, you will find you can live in this ugly world—I am using the word *ugly* in the dictionary sense, without any emotional content behind that word—work and act, and at the same time keep the brain alert, like the river that purifies itself all the time.

Question: What is the kind of conflict you are referring to, that degenerates the mind?

KRISHNAMURTI: The gentleman wants to know what kind of conflict degenerates the mind.

Does not every conflict dull the mind?—not one series of conflicts, not one specific conflict. Does not every conflict, of any kind, at any depth, weaken the mind, deteriorate the mind, make the mind insensitive? If I and my wife quarrel all day, will that not dull, weaken, the mind?

Question: Does not conflict give us energy?

KRISHNAMURTI: The gentleman says that it is through conflict that we derive energy.

Any machine which functions in friction soon loses its speed, it wears itself out—does it not? Mechanically, it may not be possible to find a machine without friction. Anything that is being constantly used, in friction, must wear itself out; and you say that from that usage it derives energy; is that so? Do you derive energy through friction? You know how to resist. And resistance does give some sort of energy, but it is a very limited, narrow, petty energy. Is it a very difficult thing to see, or to understand, that every conflict—the wear and tear—between nations, between people, between two ideas, does make the mind dull? There is the theory of thesis and antithesis; there is a thesis, and the opposite of it, the antithesis, breeds friction; and out of that friction you have synthesis. First the idea, then the resistance to that idea, which will produce new ideas; and so this process of something and the opposite of it. We all know this. I am angry, and the opposite is "not to be angry"; and the synthesis of these two will be a state which will be neither anger nor non-anger, but something quite different. Do you create anything, do you do anything, out of friction? We do, that is our daily existence. Everything we do is out of resistance or out of friction. I am saying: Every form of friction, every form of conflict, dulls the mind. For you that is a new idea, and you say that you do not see in that way. Your first response is to resist it because you are used to the old system, or to the new system—thesis, antithesis, and synthesis—and so you resist. What happens out of that resistance?

Comment: Movement.

KRISHNAMURTI: When you resist, is there a movement? You are moving behind your own wall, and I am moving behind my wall, if I have one. We are trying to understand, to find out how to live in this world without conflict. When the politician talks about peace, what does he mean? And what do we mean when we talk about peace? It is the cessation of conflict, obviously.

Question: Is the quietness of the mind the same as inertia?

KRISHNAMURTI: The word *inertia* implies as far as I understand it—I am not talking in terms of the scientist—the idea of inertia, which is laziness, a sense of nonmovability, a thing that is completely inert.

Comment: The scientist says that the law of inertia is that a thing at rest continues to be at rest and a thing in motion continues to move in a straight line unless acted upon by an external force.

KRISHNAMURTI: That is precisely it. A thing which moves straight, if there is no impediment, if there is no conflict, which purifies itself, which keeps on moving always in a straight direction, and which therefore understands every impact, understands every influence, every experience which distorts this movement—that is the quality of the mind which I am talking about.

Question: Is it possible to move the center of our action?

KRISHNAMURTI: The gentleman asks: "Is it possible, by intensifying the center and expanding the center, to be free of conflict?" The center implies, does it not, just a periphery. That periphery may be very wide or very small; but a center implies always a border, always a limitation, however extensive the periphery is. When I am ambitious, when you are ambitious, when one is envious, it is the center trying to expand, is it not? And that expansion creates conflict. Is it possible to live without envy?

Comment: When I am aware of a thought, that thought ceases. Yet, there is the consciousness of the center.

KRISHNAMURTI: The gentleman says: "When one is aware of one's own thought, at that moment of awareness, thought stops; but yet there is a consciousness of the center." A certain thought arises—of fear, of ambition, or of envy. When you are aware, when you become conscious of that thought, for the moment it stops; and later on again it comes back because of the very simple reason that that particular thought born out of ambition has not been completely investigated, gone into thoroughly, understood. And you cannot go into it thoroughly because you condemn it or you justify it, because you say, "I cannot live in this world without ambition; therefore, I must be ambitious". You can only understand a thought completely when there is no condemnation or justification—which means that the thought must flower in freedom completely, and then end. But if the thought does not end, it is because you have condemned it or you have justified it—which is from the center, from the background. The gentleman says that thought can be encouraged, justified, or condemned only when it is moving, living, when it is acting; but when you observe it, it stops, and therefore it cannot be examined. You can examine thought only when it is alive, moving; but by condemning, encouraging, justifying, we stop thought, and so that thought recurs. So, we have to find out why we condemn; we have to investigate thought—the whole process of resistance and so on.

The gentleman says that when you observe, there is the observer and the observed, the seer and the thing seen; and in that there is duality and therefore conflict and all the rest of it. Is it possible to see something without this? Is it possible to see something without the word, the word being thought? Is it possible to look at anything—the flower, my neighbor, my wife, my child, my boss—without thought, without the word? Have you tried it? Try it sometime, and you will find out for yourself that you can look without the word—which does not mean that you have forgotten there is the past, which does not mean that you have obliterated all memory. It is like looking at a flower botanically and nonbotanically.

Question: Does not the conflict help to clarify our minds?

KRISHNAMURTI: The gentleman asks: "Are we not clarifying our minds in this sort of conflict?"

Is there conflict in investigation? There is conflict only when you resist or accept or approximate. I am not a propagandist. I say: Just watch your mind; do not try to change, to add or subtract, but just watch it. If you were to accept what I am saying, or if you were to resist when you have your own ideas, that would be a conflict. I say: Do not accept what I say, do not reject what I say, but listen to what I have to say. You are a Hindu, a Brahmin, a Christian, whatever you are—specialized in something, and you have your background. I say that your background—not my background, not what I say, but your background—is preventing you from seeing things as they are.

Take a very complex thing. There is starvation in this world about which you all know. There are the scientific means to prevent that. Science is capable of preventing starvation, feeding people, clothing them, housing them, and making the world an extraordinary place to live in. It is possible, but it is not made possible by the politicians, by the divisions, by the nationalities, by sovereign governments, by this and by that. Those are the reasons. But nobody will remove their frontiers. You want to remain a Hindu, and I want to remain a Muslim, and therefore we prevent feeding the people. Now you hear that. And you, being a Hindu, say, "How can I give up my religion? I will tolerate the Muslim, but I cannot give up my religion." And the Muslim says, "I will tolerate you, but I cannot give up my religion." But can't you and I give up our nationalities in order to feed the people? I say: Look at your own background; do not open your mind to me. Look at yourself, look at the way your mind is working; look at your own envies, your own ambition. And I am just pointing out how to look at it.

The gentleman says, "When I listen to you, I am receiving; and in that reception, there is a conflict going on. At that time, I observe my own mind in relation to what you are saying and thereby increase the conflict which will alter, which will bring about a heightened sensitivity." That is what I am trying to answer. You are obviously listening and therefore receiving, but is that reception something foreign to you, or is it that in what the speaker is saying, you really look at yourself, at your own mind, and discover what is happening to that mind? Do not accept in that reception what he is saying, but look at your own mind; in that, is there a conflict? There is conflict only when the reception insists that you look this way. But the speaker does not say this; he says to you to look at your own mind, to watch your mind; in this, where is the conflict?

The gentleman says it is only a verbal deadlock, but I am not at all sure it is. I do not think we have understood each other. You say, "My philosophy is conditioned, and your philosophy is conditioned; and when the two meet together, there must be a friction; and through that friction I put aside my conditioning, and that helps you to liberate your conditioning; and that liberation is a process of conflict." First of all, mine is not a philosophy, it is not a system, not a method; and you can wipe that out completely. I really mean it. I do not object to your calling it anything, but only as long as it is not a system to get somewhere. The gentleman says, "I hear you, you have something to say; and if you have something to say, I receive it, and in that very process of receiving, I am changing; in the process of listening to you, whatever things I held previously are loosening up; and this process of loosening up is conflict, and it comes about through the conflict between the two."

Why is there a friction, whatever you may mean by that word? Why should there be a conflict when you see something different? Why should my seeing, if I see something new, bring about a resistance or a friction between what is being seen and what is seeing? Why should there be a conflict? I will tell you why conflict arises. Because, I am conditioned one way, and when something new is put to me, I reject it, I resist it; or I try to see how it can approximate to my conditioning, how my conditioning prevents me from seeing totally what he is trying to say; or, when I listen to him, I do not listen with all my being but with my conditioned being to assimilate what is being said. How can I assimilate what is being said if I am incapable of digesting? I cannot digest it; I can digest it when I have no conditioning, when I can absorb it completely. I say that in the process of absorption the digestion becomes indigestion when there is a conditioning. I am a communist, a Catholic, or what you will. You say something new to me. I listen to you; I either resist you, or I say that there is something new and that I must assimilate it. I take it in completely because I have understood it completely. Or I cannot take it in completely because of my background, my habits, my fears, which prevent me from assimilating. The conflict arises when I try to assimilate the new and yet not break down my conditioning. The speaker says: Do not bother to accept the new—there is nothing new—but break down your conditioning, and in the breaking down of your conditioning, you will find yourself anew.

All conflict, whether it is between ideas and ideals, between husband and wife, between society and the individual—all conflict at all levels dulls, stupefies, makes the mind insensitive. And I say: Do not accept what I say; do not create a conflict between what I say and yourself; and if you do, then you will lose, you will become more dull, you will create problems. Watch yourself, be aware of yourself, and to be aware of yourself, do not let the word become important, and all the rest of it. The speaker is not introducing something new; he is not saying, "This is the way to look"; on the contrary, he negates everything and says that in the process of negation there is no resistance, and therefore you can look. But if you say, "No, I cannot break down my background, the knowledge which I have, the things which I have experienced," then there arises friction. You are conditioned and I am conditioned—let us assume we are. I try to impose on you and you resist; that inevitably creates a conflict. I try to push into you, and I say, "You must break down and accept my ideas, look at the way I look," and that creates conflict. Or I say to you, "I have nothing to say at all, I have no ideas, I do not deal with ideas because for me an idea is nonexistent, it is a contradiction. So look, watch yourself, watch your own mind, watch the way you think, why you think as a Hindu, why you think as a Muslim, why you feel this way and that way"—which is all a negative form of asking you to look, not a positive way of saying to you to look this way.

So, through negation you uncondition yourself, not through resistance and therefore not through conflict. The gentleman says positively, "If I love you, there can be no conflict." But he has added the word *if*, which is conditional thinking, and conditional thinking is an idea. You say that if you love, there is no conflict. Then, sir, love. But is that your state? Is that actually your state, not an ideational state? An ideational state is a conditional state—which means you do not love. When you say that when you really love there is no conflict, are you saying this from the fact, or are you saying it from an idea? Is it not a proposition? The man who is hungry says, "Give me food"; he does not want ideas about food, he has no concept of food, he wants the actual material which will satisfy his hunger. That man is entirely different from the man who thinks he is hungry and who says, "If I am hungry, I will do this and this and this."

January 12, 1962

Seventh Talk at Rajghat

This is the last talk. Since we have been meeting here, we have been considering how to bring about a new mind, a mind that is religious—not in the sense of orthodox—a mind that has no roots in beliefs or in dogmas or in ideation. Such a mind not only is necessary at all times, but also is essential at the present period of great crisis in the world. Is it possible, not theoretically, but actually, to bring about a new mind, or to transform the present, confused, dull, insensitive mind into something totally different? Is it to be done through practice, through discipline, through some form of exercise, forcing the mind to conform to a pattern? Or has the mind the capacity to see directly and immediately what is false, and thereby through negation see what is true?

I think we ought to be clear what we mean by negation and what is positive thinking. Most of us start thinking from a basis, from a conclusion, from an experience. We take a position that we believe in something—believe, because of experience, of knowledge, of tradition—and from there we think, from there we act. That position is generally that of psychologically being secure. That security is either in relationship or in an idea. Mostly, it is in an idea, which we call belief, an ideal, an example—still an idea—an idea being a word. We take refuge in words, and that is our platform; and from that we act, and from that basis we think. I think that is untenable; and all our judgment, evaluation, all our consideration and inquiry start from that—from a position, from an idea, from a conclusion, which prevents us from investigating what is true and what is false, or from seeing directly, immediately, what is true.

Now, is it possible to inquire, to wipe away belief, wipe away our conditioning as a Hindu, a Christian, or what you will, and investigate? That is what a scientist obviously does; he does not start from a conclusion; he has knowledge, but he will not allow that knowledge to interfere with his investigation. But our human existence is not so definite as that because we are afraid, we want security, we want so many things in life; we want a name, a position and power, freedom, and many other things; and these form the basis of our platform, and from these we try to investigate. All investigation is denied the moment you take a position from which you are looking. Whereas negative investigation, if I may so use that word, is to be free from conclusions, from dogmas, from beliefs, from conditioning, and then inquire. Such inquiry, you may think, prevents action; you may ask, "How can one live, act, and be with a mind that is constantly inquiring?"

All action is the result of an idea, of an experience, of knowledge; and from that we act, and we think action will be denied if we are only in a state of constant inquiry. Is our action, whether it is a little one or a most complex one, a most unselfish one and all the rest of it—is our action denied unless it is already foreseen, controlled, shaped? Is not all action free and therefore must always be the result of inquiry? So, from negative inquiry—that is, not seeking a positive result, but denying all positive positions which the mind takes, and inquiring from that denial—is there not action which is more significant, much more effective than action which springs from conclusions? All life is action, is it not? Our coming here, our listening to the talk, my talking, your listening, anything that we do is action; and we base that action on a conclusion. Our actions are confined or limited by the idea which we have, and the idea is the result of experience. The idea is born out of knowledge; and with this background, which is fixed, which is more or less confined, limited, conditioned, we proceed to act upon life; and life is always moving, always changing; and so there is a contradiction, and out of that contradiction there is sorrow; and we try to escape from sorrow through different means.

Look, sirs, if I may put it differently, most of you here are probably Hindus, or committed to a particular course of action or belief; and with that background, with those ideas, with that conditioned thinking, you face life, you face the modern world which is so tremendously changing; and so between the world which is changing and the mind which refuses to change, there is a contradiction. You have taken a stand, a position—as a Hindu, as a Catholic, or what not—and with that tradition, you meet life, and so there is a contradiction. Is it possible to meet life without taking a stand of any kind?

There are enormous changes going on outwardly, but the outer always influences the inner, and we have divided the outer and the inner as two separate things. After all, the inner life, the inner psychological state, is of the same movement as the outer; it is like a tide that goes out and comes in. And to understand the tide that is coming in, you must understand the tide that is going out; you must understand the world, and without the understanding of the outer, the inner pursuit has no value at all. So, the thing is not to divide life as the outer world and the inner world but to understand the totality of this movement. You cannot understand the totality of this movement if you take a stand of any kind.

The religious mind is the noncommitted mind because it is only such a mind that can discover what is true and what is false. It is only such a mind that can find out if there is or is not a reality, God, a timeless thing—but not the committed mind, not a mind that believes or does not believe. Obviously, the religious mind is not the mind that goes to the temple, that does puja and all kinds of tricks. The religious mind sees the falseness of all that totally, completely; and therefore being free and not having a platform from which to proceed to inquire, it begins all inquiry from freedom. Therefore, such a mind is dispassionate, objective, sane, rational, capable of reasoning—which is, after all, the scientific mind. The scientific mind is not a religious mind. The scientific mind is committed to examine a certain part of existence, a segment of life; so the scientific mind cannot understand the totality which the religious mind can understand.

To have such a religious mind, there must be a revolution—not economic or social, but a psychological revolution—a revolution in the psyche, in the very process of our thinking. Now, how is such a mind to be brought about? We see the necessity of such a mind—a new mind that has no frontier, a new mind that is not committed to any group, race, family, or culture or civilization, a new mind that is not the result of social morality. Social morality is no morality at all; it is only concerned with sexual morality; you can be as ambitious, as ruthless, as vain and envious as you like. And social morality is the enemy of the religious mind.

So, how is the religious mind or the new mind to come into being? How would you set about it? It is not a rhetorical question. We are all faced with this problem: to have a fresh, young mind, a new mind—because, the old mind has not solved a thing; it has multiplied problems. How would you get it; how would you set about to realize this mind? Will you have a system, a method? Please see the importance of the question which I am asking, and see the significance of it. We do require a new mind; it is essential, and how do you come by it? Through a method—a method being a system, a practice, a repetitive thing day after day? Will a method produce a new mind? Please find out, inquire into it with me; do not just merely listen, and go back to thinking that you must have a practice, a method, whereby to acquire a new mind.

Surely, a method implies, does it not, a continuity of a practice, directed along a certain line towards a certain result—which is, to acquire a mechanical habit, and through that mechanical habit to realize a mind which is not mechanical. Essentially, that is what is implied in a method. When you say, "discipline," all discipline is based on a method according to a certain pattern; and the pattern promises you a result which is predetermined by a mind which has already a belief, which has already taken a position. So, will a method, in the widest or the narrowest sense of that word, bring about this new mind? If it does not, then method as habit must go completely because it is false. Whether it is Shankara, Buddha, or the latest saint who has said that you must have a method, such a method is utterly false because method only conditions the mind according to the result which is desired. But do you know what the new mind is—a fresh, young mind, an innocent mind? How can you know? You cannot know it, you have to discover it. So you have to discard all the mechanical processes of the mind. Just listen to this. It does not matter if you do anything about it or not—it is up to you. Please do follow this. The mind must discard all the mechanical processes of thought. So, the idea that a method, a system, a discipline, a continuity of habit will bring about this mind is not true. So, all that is to be discarded totally as being mechanical. A mind that is mechanical is a traditional mind; it cannot meet life which is nonmechanical; so, the method is to be put aside. Then, how will you approach it?

Will knowledge give you the new mind, knowledge being experience? Experience is the response to a challenge, and the response is according to your memory, surely, according to your conditioning. So, will knowledge—that is, experience—help you to the new mind? Must not the new mind be in a state of nonexperience? If I may, I will go into it a little bit, and perhaps we shall be able to understand afterwards by questioning. There is challenge and response. We live that way. Every moment life challenges, and we respond. We respond according to our conditioning, our conditioning being as a Hindu, a Muslim, and all the rest of it. If you reject the outer challenge—which very few do—then you create your own challenge inwardly, psychologically; and again there is the inward questioning and to that you respond; and all that, both the outer and the inner questioning, is based on experience. And that experience is always accumulating as knowledge, as time. Please, what we are talking about is not difficult. All that you have to do is to watch yourself, and you will see that we are only talking about facts, not about theories. Time being experience as knowledge, will that bring the new mind? Obviously not, because the very words *the new mind* imply something new, totally new, not to be brought about by experience. Experience is always the past—which is time. So, one realizes, if one has followed this, that neither habit nor experience as knowledge will produce the new mind, nor will one get the new mind through time.

When you deny all this—as you are bound to if you have gone into yourself and examined—then you will see that the total denial of everything that you know, of every experience, of every tradition, of every movement born of time, is the beginning of the new mind. To deny totally, you must have energy. We generally derive energy by resistance—do I need to explain that? We derive energy by escape; we derive energy through envy, through ambition, through greed, through brutality, through the desire for power. But such energy creates its own contradiction, and the contradiction wastes that energy. So, most of us have no energy to deny and to remain in that state of denial which is the highest form of thinking. But that denial gives energy because in that denial there is no contradiction.

So, the religious mind, or the new mind, is the revolutionary mind. Because, it is no longer ambitious, envious; it has seen the significance of envy, ambition, authority, and therefore is free of it—not eventually, but actually, immediately. And this denial is the way of meditation. Meditation is not the silly thing of repeating words, sitting in front of a picture and trying to get visions and all the sensations, but meditation is this constant awareness of seeing the false and denying it totally. That denial gives energy—not the energy brought about through conflict, not the energy that is prescribed by the so-called religious people, of being a bachelor and all the rest of it; those are all forms of resistance and therefore contradiction. You can see factually the totality of all this process, understand it completely, only when you have not a platform, a perch, an idea, from which you are examining. It is only the religious mind that can go very far; it is only the religious mind that can discover what is beyond the measure of the mind.

Question: Is not denial and rejection a method?

KRISHNAMURTI: Have you ever denied anything, and in that denial was there a motive? If there was a motive, is that a denial? And then if there is a motive and if there is the denial which is born out of that motive, then it is a method. But we are talking of denial without a motive—to renounce, to give up doing something, without a motive. Don't you know that? Have you done anything—acted, given up, put aside, renounced, denied, whatever you would like—without motive; have you ever done it? And when you do, does that bring about a method? Does that constitute a method?

You see, the difficulty lies in using words. For us, words are extraordinarily significant—we live by words, like the word *India.* We are now inquiring into a mind that is not a slave to words. Do we love out of a motive? Is there love when there is a motive? You will very easily say, "Of course not"—at least probably you would. How is it possible to love without a motive?—"how" as a question mark, not as a method. First, you must discover if you have a motive and understand that motive, go into it; and the very going into it is the very denial of the motive. Then perhaps, you will understand what love is.

Question: Sometimes, a challenge is such that it paralyzes one, and there is no proper response. Is it possible not to feel paralyzed but respond immediately to the challenge?

KRISHNAMURTI: The gentleman says: "One is overwhelmed by the reaction to a challenge. My son dies, and there is an immediate reaction; and that reaction is so overwhelming, so shocking that I am paralyzed. It may take me a year, two years, or a day." The question is, if I understand the gentleman rightly: "Is it possible to respond immediately without being overwhelmed by the response? My son dies, and it is a shock; it is an unexpected, unfortunate, not-wanted incident in my life; it leaves me in a paralyzed condition." And the question is: "Need I be paralyzed, need I be overwhelmed by the reaction?" Surely, one cannot lay down a general principle on this. It depends on the sensitivity, on the dullness, on the so-called affection, on many interrelated reasons for this extraordinary sense of being paralyzed, overwhelmed; but we do not have such extraordinary incidents all the time of our lives. There are one or two challenges which really overwhelm us, but there are minor challenges all the time, of which we are conscious or unconscious—minor, not of an extraordinarily major kind. Most of us do not know that they are taking place; we are so dull, we are so immune; we live in a world of our own making. And for such a mind "response and challenge" is nonexistent—and that is what most of the sannyasis, saints, and monks do—they live behind a wall of ideas. So, they have rejected the world and live in a world of their own, in a world of ideas; they do not want to be disturbed, they have no challenge; they have found an asylum, an abode which will always be satisfactory, and so they have no response and challenge. Most of us would like to be in that position where nothing touches us. Most of us want that—that is our idea of God, having peace of mind and all the rest of it—where nothing will touch us. But life won't leave you alone. My son dies, my wife turns to somebody else, I lose a job, I lose my money, there is disease, there is death—everything is a challenge. And I have always relied on a conclusion, the things which I have learned, tradition, and all the rest of it. So, my response is weak.

If I may go further into it, the question really is: Is it possible for the mind to be so attentive all the time, so sensitive that every challenge is answered completely and immediately, and to come to a state when there is no challenge and no response, when it is no longer in a state of experiencing? Do think about it. You may deny it; you may say it is a very nice theory, but do look at it. When you understand something totally, say for instance, when you understand authority totally—all its peculiarities, its tendency—when you have completely read the whole book of authority, which is yourself, in yourself, when you have completely understood authority, then there is no problem any more about authority, no experiences of authority can ever touch you. In the same manner, if you regard the totality of life with all its intricacies, and therefore be free of envy, greed, jealousy, ambition, authority, then is there a need for experiencing? I say: It is only such a mind that can understand what is true, what is false, and if there is something beyond time; it is only such a mind that is free from the known and therefore not in a world of experience, challenge and response, and knowledge—it is only such a mind that can discover the timeless.

Question: Will the new mind be of the nature of life?

KRISHNAMURTI: I do not quite understand the meaning of that question. It is a theoretical question, is it not? I am not belittling your question, when you ask, "Will not the new mind be of the nature of life?" We are not talking of ideas, of symbols, of comparisons; either you have the new mind or you do not have it. If you have it, there is nothing more to be said; if you have not got it, how will you have it—not, what it is like?

Question: Is it possible not to have any psychological experience?

KRISHNAMURTI: Psychologically speaking, the questioner asks: "Is it possible to have no experience psychologically?" Mechanically, you can add, you can improve the engine from the piston type to the jet type and harness the power in the atom—you can improve mechanically. The question is: "Is it possible at all psychologically to be free of experience?" If you ask that question, what do you expect me to reply? Yes or no? If I say yes, what value has it to you? If I say no, you will say it shows that we cannot do it. At the end of the question, where are you? Have you found out whether, psychologically, it is possible to be free of experience or not—for yourself, but not because somebody else says so? To find out the truth of that question, you have to dig into yourself tremendously, have you not? You have to inquire, burn everything to find out.

You know death is a strange thing; you cannot argue with death. You cannot compromise with death; you cannot postpone death. It is absolute and final, and it is the most destructive thing. To find out what death is, you must die to everything. Similarly, to find out if it is possible to live in this world without authority, you have to dig very deeply into yourself, have you not?—which means, you must deny totally the authority of the guru, the authority of the family, the authority of the state; you must find out where the authority of the state holds, and where it does not hold, where you have to obey the policeman, and where the policeman cannot possibly enter.

Question: You have talked about denial and contradiction. Is not contradiction a denial?

KRISHNAMURTI: The question is: "You have talked about denial and contradiction; is not contradiction a denial?"

Let us keep it very simple. Is not denial contradiction? What do we mean by a contradiction? When different desires pull in different directions—when I want to do that but do something else, when I want to be kind but I am unkind—there is contradiction, and that contradiction saps the energy. Is denial contradiction? I say no. Denial is not a contradiction because denial is not a reaction. I have understood the whole significance of authority at all its levels; I have seen the whole totality of authority or envy, and I deny it; it is not a contradiction, it is not a reaction.

When you deny something, either you deny through a motive—then it becomes an assertion—or you deny because you see it as false. It is a very complex thing. You all believe in God because you have been told, you have been brought up, you have been conditioned to believe in God. But to find out if there is God, you must deny the God which you believe in, but that denial becomes a reaction if that denial is born out of discontent with the God which you hope will give you something. But that denial is not a reaction when the mind says, "Look, as long as I have a belief of any kind—either belief in God or belief in no God—I cannot find out; to find out if there is such a thing, I must put aside all this." Surely, that is very clear.

Question: You say that denial without reaction brings energy. What is the source of that energy?

KRISHNAMURTI: The denial which has a motive, the denial which is the outcome of what is to be in the future, the denial born of knowledge—all such denial does not bring the energy we have been talking about. On the contrary, the denial without reaction brings that energy. The gentleman wants to know from what source that energy comes into being. You need energy to deny. Most of our energy we derive from escapes, from repression, from resistance; but that energy is not the same energy that you need in order to deny. I said that and I stick to it. I am not challenging it. You can see how you derive energy by resisting. That is very simple. Is that not clear?

I resist, and in the process of resistance, I have energy. I have energy when I think of nationalism, of the Indian flag; I feel emotionally stirred up, and I derive a certain form of energy. When I hate, that brings a form of energy. All those breed contradictions, and thereby that energy which is engendered through resistance is dissipated. But the energy of which I am talking, the energy that comes through denial, is different. The gentleman asks, "What is the source of that energy?" First of all, motive of any kind gives energy. I want money, and that produces energy; I feel a sexual urge, a biological urge, and that produces energy. So motive, as far as we know, produces certain forms of energy which become contradictory; and if you deny with a motive, then that energy is dissipated. But if you deny because you understand totally, then that energy is necessary to go further into the whole process of the mind. From where does that energy come? Where do you think it comes from? Don't wait for the answer. It is only a question. There is no answer. If you put a question without wanting an answer, you will find the answer. But if you put the question hoping to find the answer, your answer will then be according to your conditioning. But if you put the question without any motive, that very questioning is the source of energy.

I want to know what is that timeless state which everybody talks about. What is the source of that urge to know? Is it to escape from the world of sorrow, from my nagging wife, from my brutal husband, from death, from disease? Then such an urge, productive of energy, creates a contradiction and thereby dissipates energy. If I put the question without a motive, why do I put the question without a motive? I put it because I have understood very clearly, completely, that a question with a motive is like thought anchored to a belief; it cannot go very far.

Question: What is all this for, sir?

KRISHNAMURTI: I have nothing to offer. I do not take your escapes away. I point out your escapes; you can have them, or worship them, or do what you like; but it is for you. I have pointed out something much more significant.

Question: Can one live in this world without any contradiction, psychologically?

KRISHNAMURTI: "Is it possible to live in this world in a state in which, psychologically, there is no contradiction? I want to experience that state. It must be there. How do I proceed?" That is too difficult. Let me take something simpler.

You know what death is? You have seen death being carried away to be burned, and the burning of death is the continuity of death. I want to know what it is to die while I am living—not when I am old, diseased. I want to know what it is to die while living with my faculties fully alive and while my brain can reason, while it is not diseased. I want to know the state, the feeling of dying, of being dead. I want to know it, not because I am frightened, but because I have said a motive cannot take me very far—then the motive dictates the journey.

Therefore, I see that a mind that wishes to know what is death must be free from fear. So, I must inquire into the whole question of fear. Is it possible to live in this world without fear? So, I inquire, I see, I cross-examine, I am aware of every movement of thought. And it is only then, when there is no fear and therefore no motive, that I can find out what death is. That means I must totally abandon everything I know. I must die to everything known—to my family, to my tradition, to my virtue, to everything. Is it possible to die? I say it is possible, but it has no validity for you; it has validity only when you die to all the known. When you die to the known, every day, never accumulating, then you will find out what death is. And the discovery of what death is comes with the understanding of the totality of fear and therefore being free of fear; and the freedom from fear is the source of energy.

Question: Is love a feeling?

KRISHNAMURTI: The gentleman asks: "Is the love that you talk about a feeling?" What is feeling? Feeling is like thought. Feeling is a sensation. I see a flower, and I respond to that flower; I like it or dislike it. The like or the dislike is dictated by my thought, and the thought is the response of the background of memory. So, I say, "I like that flower," or "I do not like that flower"; "I like this feeling," or "I do not like that feeling." Now, is love related to feeling? What is your answer? Look at what my question is. Listen to it. Is love a feeling? Feeling is sensation, obviously—sensation of like and dislike, of good and bad, of good taste, and all the rest of it. Is that feeling related to love? That is the question, and what does love mean to you?

Do you associate love with women or men; do you associate love with sex? You must, because you have denied beauty; all your saints have denied beauty. And beauty is associated with women. So, you have said,

"No feeling," and so you have cultivated rough personalities, crude egos, which deny beauty. Have you watched your street, have you watched the way you live in your houses, the way you sit, the way you talk? And have you noticed all your saints whom you worship? For them passion is sex, and therefore they deny passion, therefore they deny beauty—deny in the sense of putting those aside. So, with sensation you have put away love because you say, "Sensation will make me a prisoner; I will be a slave to sex-desire; therefore, I must cut it out." Therefore you have made sex into an immense problem. Sex is a problem to all of you; and all your gods whom you want to reach say that you must be without feeling, you must never look at a woman, never look at a man, never look at the tree, at the river, at the beauty of the earth. So is love a feeling? When you have understood feeling completely, not partially, when you have really understood the totality of feeling, then you will know what love is. When you can see the beauty of a tree, when you can see the beauty of a smile, when you can see the sun setting behind the walls of your town—see totally—then you will know what love is.

Question: You talk about being free from experience. But is it right to be indifferent to a person who is suffering because someone is dead?

KRISHNAMURTI: You see, sirs, what do we mean by being indifferent? Are you not all indifferent to what is happening in this country which is rapidly declining? Are you not all indifferent to the dirt, the squalor, the sordidness of life about you? Please listen to this. Are you not indifferent to love, are you not indifferent to your neighbor, to the village which is hungry? Being indifferent, you say you want to act; being insensitive, you force yourself to do something.

Indifference and insensitivity go together. But a sensitive mind, which is not blunted through experiences, can give sympathy, love, affection to somebody. But the thing is to be sensitive, not blunted, not made dull by experience, by tradition, by authority, by all the gods that man has invented. You need a sensitive mind to go into everything.

Question: Have you not set up an authority to liberate yourself from all authority including itself?

KRISHNAMURTI: The gentleman says that I have an authority which liberates me from all authorities including itself. Should I accept such an authority? If I met an authority which destroys all previous authorities including itself, should I accept such authority? Authority can never liberate you from any other authority, and if it does, that new authority has taken root in you; it has not destroyed authority; you have only replaced old authority by a new one. If that authority has denied all authority and helped you to be free of all authority including itself, where is the need of acceptance of any authority? I see authority is pernicious. I have gone into it. Do not ask me about the authority of policemen, of government, etc.; I won't go into it now.

The understanding of authority is absolutely essential for a free mind, and it is only a free mind that can find—not a crippled mind. If you understand the full significance of authority—not because somebody else tells you to look, or somebody else tells you that you are free only when you are free from authority, but through your own examination, through your own questioning, from your own inquiry, every day of your life—then you will find there is no authority. You have got to accept no authority of any kind, including my own; but that requires a tremendous understanding, that requires your seeing facts.

The question is: Is the religious mind an individual mind or the collective mind? Or, is it something else? Sir, is your mind, the mind that you use, an individual mind—individual being unique? Is your mind unique? Or is it merely the collective and the interaction of the collective modified in the present by various experiences and incidents and accidents? Is yours an individual mind? You may have a technical job, a mechanical functioning; is it an individual mind? Are you not of the collective? You are all Hindus, Christians, Catholics, Buddhists, communists, Indians, or Russians—you are the collective. To see that you are the collective and to see the fact of it and to free the mind from the collective—that can only be done through self-inquiry, through self-knowing. And the freeing of the mind from its conditioning through self-knowing brings about a new mind which is neither individual nor collective; that mind is something totally new.

May I say something, sirs? First of all, it is very kind of you to have come and listened to these talks. And these talks would be utterly useless, absolutely worthless, would be empty ashes, if you merely lived by the word, if you merely treated it as an idea, as a theory which is added to the old theories which you already have. But if you have listened so that the very listening is an act of self-inquiry, self-knowing, then these talks will have real significance—then they will take you infinitely far.

January 14, 1962

New Delhi, India, 1962

First Talk in New Delhi

I think it would be good if we could, verbally at least, establish a communication between us because for most of us language is the only means of communication. We cannot communicate in any other way, and therefore language plays an important part in all communion and communication. Of course it would be very good if two or three of us could get together quietly and discuss these matters very deeply, but unfortunately that is not possible. So, we have to establish from the very beginning, it seems to me, a right relationship between the speaker and yourself.

These talks are in no way meant to be propaganda. Nor are they to tell you what you should do, or in what manner you should think, or to direct you to a particular course of action, or to a series of ideas. Ideas are merely thought verbalized, and ideas in themselves have very little significance. They do not bring about a radical change; they do not transform the mind totally. And those who depend on ideas as a means of stimulation to bring about a change in themselves will invariably leave this *shamiana* empty-handed, because we are not dealing with ideas at all. We are dealing with something much more profound, much more enduring, whose import is deep revolution in the quality of the mind itself. And such a revolution cannot be brought about by words, nor by ideas. Words have a meaning. Words are not the thing, and ideas, if you observe very closely, conform to a pattern of thought. And ideas and words do not play a deep significant part in our lives—at least in the lives of those who are very thoughtful and serious. So we must at the very beginning understand each other.

This is not a gathering to convert you to any particular idea, to a particular way of thinking. On the contrary, we shall go into matters to which you will have to apply your whole being, and you will not merely intellectually accept or deny certain words. You will also have to bear in mind that we are not speaking as an authority. There is no authority in spiritual matters; there is no following, no leader, no guru. One has to find the light for oneself. And what we are going to try throughout these talks is not only to establish clearly for ourselves the impediments imposed upon us by society but also to discover the bondages the mind is held to.

And so we are going to discuss primarily in what way to bring about a new mind, a totally different mind, a different way of thinking, a different attitude, a different evaluation. And for that you need very clear, precise thinking; for that you need also the capacity to face life totally alone. And it is not possible, surely, is it, with the collective mind, which is never capable of revolution. It is only the individual mind, the mind that is not caught up in society, in the morality of society, in the tradition of society, in the ways of society, that is capable of revolution. There must be individuality to bring about a radical revolution and not conform to a pattern laid down by society. Such a mind can possibly do what it will to bring about a lasting, a revolutionary change in the world.

So we must differentiate between the collective action and the individual action. We are not individuals at all; we are the result of the collective. You are the result of your society, of the religion, the education, the climate, the food, the clothes, the tradition in which you have been brought up—you are all that. And to think that you are an individual is really quite absurd if you go very deeply into the matter. You may have a name, a different body, a bank account, certain superficial qualities; but essentially, deep down, the whole totality of the mind is conditioned by the society in which it has been brought up. And to be aware of such a condition and to break through that, break through the encrustation of centuries of the past—it is that quality, that intensity, that understanding that brings about an individuality. And it is only the individual that can find out what is real, not the collective. It is only the individual that can find out if there is, or if there is not, what you call God, not the collective mind. The collective mind can only repeat the word, but the word *God* is not God. The collective mind can read the Gita, quote the Upanishads and all the religious authorities, but such a mind can never find out what is true. It is only the mind that has broken through tradition, shattered the values imposed upon it by society, broken away from the past—it is only such a mind that can find out.

And we are concerned with discovery and not with assertions, agreements, or disagreements. We have to find out for ourselves. But it is almost impossible to find out what is true, to find out if there is such a thing as the timeless, as something beyond the measure of the mind, if you belong to a religion—if you are a Hindu, a Parsi, a Sikh, a Christian—if you belong to any organized religion, because belief and dogma are essentially in the way of discovery. It is only a mind that perceives all the falseness, the conditioning influences, the propaganda which is called religion—it is only such a mind that breaks through, that can find out.

But that requires a great deal of insight, a great deal of inquiry, an alertness, awareness of things as they are, but not mere intellectual denial or acceptance. Because, to accept or to deny is a matter of mere verbal exchange. But if one really sets about to find out—because we must find out—we must question everything that has been established. Because, everybody must be aware of the world situation, everybody must be aware of the deterioration. Religions have failed totally. Education has not brought peace to the world—though it was once thought that, having given information to man, man will be so civilized that there would be no war, that there would be no nationality. But all that has gone overboard because with every means of communication an extraordinary change is taking place. The rapidity of the change is far more significant than the change itself. And there is no peace in the world, and no politician of any kind will ever bring peace into the world. Because, the politicians, like most people in the world who are also partially politicians, are concerned with the immediate—with the immediate well-being, with the immediate action—and are not concerned with the long view. As you observe your own life, you will see you are not concerned with the totality of living; you are only concerned with the immediate, your job, your position, your family, this and that—which is all in terms of the immediate. And the person who is concerned with the immediate is obviously the politician. And the so-called social and religious leaders are also concerned with the immediate.

It is necessary to bring about a radical revolution. One may not be aware of the actual deterioration in the quality of the mind. But if you observe, there is less and less freedom in the world. Democracies talk about freedom, but you must comply with the party rules, you must conform either to the party or to tradition. And conformity to tradition is obviously a deadly thing because it does not help man to see clearly, to discern radically. And seeing not only the state of the world but also its misery and its confusion, those who are thinking fairly intelligently deny leadership, deny authority; and therefore there is more confusion, more conflict, and therefore greater deterioration.

I am sure you must have asked yourself the question: What is to be done in a world that is rapidly on the decline; what can one do about war, about the threat of the bomb, about tyranny and the lessening of freedom; and what can one individual do about this appalling starvation in the whole of the East, the poverty, the degradation, the inhumanity of it all? What can you and I do? Or is it the action of the government, and it has nothing to do with individual action at all? And also you must have asked yourself: Seeing what the world is, is there actually a reality, something which can be experienced, which can be uncovered? And one can only ask these questions when one is very deeply dissatisfied, when there is deep discontent. But most of us, when we are discontented, find easy channels for contentment, easy ways to be satisfied. And I do not know if you have not noticed that the more there is of confusion, the more there is of uncertainty; the greater the search for authority, the greater is the reliance on that which has been the past. And observing all these things, observing the facts that are actually taking place—the facts, not the opinions about the facts, not your agreement or the translation of the facts according to your own background—surely, you must have a new mind to confront these facts, to understand them and to bring about a different way of life.

Surely, sir, the problem is this, is it not?—that there is the immense knowledge from centuries of the past, the weight of the past which confronts the future which is unknown, a blank wall of which you know nothing but which you translate in terms of the past, and therefore you think you know. But you don't actually know. And that, it seems to me, is the central issue for a man who has really felt and deeply asked himself questions that are not answerable, because most of us ask questions in order to find an answer.

May I say here that there is a way of listening and there is a way of merely hearing words. The capacity to listen is an art because if you listen, you listen without translation, without interpretation. You listen to find out, not to agree or to disagree—which is quite immature—but to really find out. And so you have to listen. But you cannot listen if you are all the time translating what you hear in terms of what you know, in terms of what you are acquainted with. Perhaps you do not know what is being said; therefore, you have to listen and not interpret it according to your background—while you are interpreting according to your background, you have stopped listening. I wonder if we have ever listened at all to anything! Most of us do not want to listen because it is too dangerous—it would shatter the things that we hold dear, the things that we are accustomed to. And so we hear words and intellectually agree or disagree. And then we say, "How am I to bridge action with what I think? I intellectually agree with what you are saying, but how am I to carry it out?" There is no such thing as intellectual understanding; you only mean really that you hear the words, that the words have some meaning similar to your own, and that similarity you call understanding, intellectual agreement. There is no such thing as intellectual agreement. Either you understand or you do not understand.

And to understand deeply, really, with all your being, you have to listen. Have you ever listened to your wife, to your husband, to your child, or even to your boss? We dare not listen. And when you do try—perhaps you will another time, perhaps you will, here also, listen actually—then you will find out in the very act of listening a deep change is going on. The very act of listening, not agreement with an idea, produces that change. When you do so listen, when you listen with all your being—with all your senses, with your mind, with your heart—to what you hear, to what you feel, to everything totally, you are able to discern what is true and what is false. And as you listen, you will find out for yourself what is true. And the act of listening is the act of discovery of the fact. But we always avoid the fact, whatever the fact, as we have opinions about the fact. We never look at the fact as we want to do something about the fact, as we try to organize so as to act upon the fact.

Take a very simple thing that is going on in this unfortunate country—this disease of nationalism. The politicians are inflaming it. And if you observe, the fact is that nationalities are always at war with each other; they are responsible for wars. The worship of the flag is a symbol. And the symbol is supposed to bring about unity. But it does not bring about unity to the world at all. On the contrary, flags are separating people, as religions have done. That is a fact. Whether you acknowledge it or not, it is a fact. It is actually taking place in this country; the poison which never existed before is being injected into the mind to bring about unity. And unity cannot be brought about through a flag. Unity cannot be brought about by a symbol. A symbol is merely a word; it is not the actual. And to face that fact, to discover what is true, you require all your capacity, all your intelligence. And that means you have to dissociate yourself totally from the collective. And that is very difficult to do because you might lose your job, you might turn against your family—there may be innumerable unconscious difficulties that prevent you from looking at the fact.

Take a simple fact again. You call yourselves Hindus, Sikhs, Muslims, and God knows what else. And you have been made to think, through propaganda for centuries, that you are this and that. But that does not make you a religious person. That does not give you the quality of a real mind which is religious. You conform to the pattern of organized religion—which is so-called religion—which has religious doctrines, beliefs, and dogmas. And now to face that fact, you have to listen to the whole quality of the mind that is religious. And to so listen implies that you yourself are beginning to dissociate yourself totally from the propaganda which is called a religion.

So, sirs, to bring about a change within oneself and thereby in the world, the change must come, not through compulsion, not through agreement, not through intellectual words and arguments, but by discovering what is true for yourself—which nobody can tell you—by being alive to oneself—which nobody can give you. You say you agree for the moment, intellectually probably; but after you leave here, you will still be a Hindu, you will still be a Christian, a Sikh, a Muslim, or whatever else may be your names and labels. But if you really listen to yourself, to the process of your own thinking; if you actually observe, then you will see that you are no longer part of the collective; you are no longer part of the tradition that is already breaking away. And the breaking away comes not through conscious effort because the conscious effort is merely a reaction, and every reaction produces its own further reactions.

So, you are listening to what is being said—which is, actually listening to yourself, not to the speaker. The speaker is merely pointing out in words. And if you merely follow the words and their meaning, they have no significance at all. But if you listen, you face the fact that there is deterioration in the world, perhaps more rapid than before, that the world is being taken over by the politicians, by the tyrants, by reactionary people. I mean by that word *reactionary* those who call themselves revolutionaries, who are really tyrannical because of their reaction, because they base their activity and their thought upon reaction—communism is a reaction in opposition to capitalism. And reaction is merely the further encouragement of what has been, only modified.

So observing all these things—that religion has lost completely its meaning, that education is training technicians, not human beings, that modern existence is so utterly superficial—what is one to do? How is one to find a way out of this wilderness, this chaos? It all depends on how you ask this question. You can ask this question either as a reaction, and therefore find an answer which will still be a reaction and not an action in itself, or you can ask the question which has no answer. When you ask a question which has no answer, because it has no answer, you are thrown back upon yourself. Therefore you have to inquire within yourself, and not ask a question outside.

One asks questions because one always wants answers. I have a problem, and I want to solve that problem; therefore, I ask a question. I do not want to find the truth of that problem; I do not want to go fully, deeply, irrevocably into that problem, but I irredeemably want to find an answer because I am disturbed by the problem; I want a satisfactory, convenient, comforting answer—which will be a reaction. And therefore such a questioning which produces a reaction will only further produce more reactions and therefore more problems. Please, you can apply this to yourself; you can see for yourself the logical sequence of such a questioning. Or you can question, not seeking, not wanting an answer; then when you question, you will be thrown back upon yourself, and therefore you have to inquire within yourself how your mind thinks, what you think and why you think—because what you think, why you think, what you feel and why you feel create the problem. Without understanding yourself, merely to ask a question which will give you a satisfactory answer is avoiding the fact—which is: you are the creator of the problem, and not society, not the religion in the present actual state.

So it matters a great deal how you ask the question—and you must ask the question. If you ask the question because you want to find a way out of this misery, out of this confusion in the world, then you will find some guru, some prophet, some leader who will momentarily satisfy your discontent, your misery. But where are you at the end of it? You are still where you were because you have not understood that you are still the maker of problems. But if you question and not try to seek an answer, your question is only to find out; and you can only find out through your own thinking, the quality of your own feeling, the emotional nature of your own being.

So what we are going to do throughout these talks is not to give answers to problems—that is too cheap and too trivial—but to learn how to look at problems, how to question every problem that life presents, so that you will find out by questioning rightly. I mean by "rightly," never seeking the answer from anybody, from any book, from any authority—but questioning in order to understand the whole content of the problem. And for that you need to have a mind that is very clear, sharp, logical, sane, that is capable of facing facts. Then you will see how your mind is completely held in the past, in tradition, in memory, in the experience of many thousand yesterdays, and with that you look at life—the life which is constantly moving, changing, which is never still. So, the mind is the result of time, time being the past, which shapes every thought, every feeling. With that mind, which is the past, which is the result of centuries of time—I will not go into all that now; I will deal with the problem of time and all that during the talks that will follow—we are trying to understand this extraordinary change that is going on in the world, we are trying to understand sorrow. With that mind we are trying to understand the future, the unknown.

So, one has to realize for oneself by questioning the state of one's own mind—not how to resolve the state of the mind, but to understand it. One has to understand it. I mean by that word *understand*, to look at something without condemnation, to look at something without evaluation—which is extraordinarily difficult for most people, practically for all people—to look, to see, to listen, without bringing in opinions, judgments, condemnations and justifications, just to look. I do not know if you have ever done it—to look without thought, to look at a flower without bringing in all the botanical knowledge, but merely to look. You will find how difficult it is because the mind is a slave to words. The word is far more significant for most of us than the fact. And as long as the mind is a slave to words, to conclusions, to ideas, it is utterly incapable of looking and understanding.

So understanding a fact is not to have an opinion about the fact but to have the capacity to look—to look without judgment, to look without the word. I do not know if you have ever looked at a bird or a tree, or looked at the squalor or the filth of the streets; I am using the words *squalor* and *filth* in the dictionary sense, without any emotional content behind those words. Because, you see, when you are capable of looking, fear is gone. There is no fear when you can look, when you can look at yourself. And it is necessary to look at yourself in that way, and that is the only way that you can know yourself. Without knowing yourself, you have no reason to think at all; you have no foundation for any thought; you are merely an automatic machine thinking what you are being told. But if you are able to observe yourself, your ways, your thinking, your activities, or how you look at people, what you see, what you do, how you talk—the whole of it—then you will find that observation, that seeing, that total perception is energy, is the flame that burns out the past.

And then you will see for yourself that the mind has penetrated deeply within itself. The mind has to penetrate deeply within itself because more and more of education, progress, and industrialization is making us more and more superficial. And life is not just industry, going to the office, earning money, and begetting children. Life is something much greater than all this; it includes all this. But the lesser does not include the greater; the greater includes the lesser. But we are apparently contented with the lesser, and therefore we are concerned with the immediate. And life is becoming extraordinarily superficial. You think that going to some weekly or daily puja or this or that makes you extraordinarily direct; you think you are clever because you have read some books—all this is still very superficial. Depth is not in any book, whether it is the Gita or the Upanishads. It does not live with any guru; it is not in any temple or church. It is to be found within oneself. You have to dig very deeply; you have to go into it profoundly, step by step, watching every movement of that, watching every action, every feeling. Then you will find there is no limit, no bottom, to the thing that you see.

Surely, it is only such a mind which has completely dissociated itself from society, from tradition, from its morality, and which is able to stand completely alone, that can find out whether there is the unnameable, the unknowable. There is. I say there is, but it has no value to you, no value at all, because you have to find out for yourself. The laboratory is you; you have to tear down, to destroy everything to find out. And that is the only revolution that is worthwhile, that has deep meaning; that is not the economic, not the social, not the industrial revolution that is taking place in this country.

There is only one revolution—that is the revolution in the mind, in consciousness—and that revolution is not brought about by argument, by words, by putting two and two together and making various conclusions. That revolution comes deeply, lastingly, precisely, when you go into yourself—never accepting a thing, therefore questioning everything. And by that very questioning, which is not the seeking for an answer, you will find that there is an extraordinary revolution taking place without an effort. And it is only such a mind that can discover for itself if there is or if there is not the timeless.

January 21, 1962

Second Talk in New Delhi

We were saying the last time when we met here—it was on Sunday—how important it is that there should be a total revolution—not reformation, not the reforming of society, but a complete inward revolution of the mind. We said that a new mind is necessary to meet not only the present crisis, which is always expanding and growing worse, but a new mind is necessary also to discover for ourselves what is true and if there is a state of creativity beyond time. For that, a new mind is necessary, a new mind that is not a slave to obedience to authority, that comprehends totally that state of humility in which alone there can be learning.

And as I said last Sunday: Is it possible for the individual to break away from society? It is only in breaking away from society that the individual comes into existence. And is it possible for that individual to bring about a new mind? We said that society is the past, and each one of us is the result of the past. Each one of us is the result of his environment, of the society he lives in, of the culture in which he has been brought up, of the religious propaganda with which he has been inculcated through centuries. He is the result of all that which is the past. Is it possible to break away from the past totally—the past being not only yesterday but the many thousand yesterdays, the past which is the atomic bomb as well as the tradition of the Hindu, the Christian, the Buddhist, or of all the other religions, or of the social revolutionary who is the communist?

The past is not only the tradition but also the result of that tradition in conjunction with the present which creates the future. Because for most of us tradition is very important, we have to understand tradition. There is the tradition of the weaver, there is the tradition of the scientist, there is the tradition of the scholar, there is the tradition of the so-called religious person, the tradition of the technician. Where is one to draw the line between the various kinds of tradition, and when is technical knowledge essential to live in this world, and when is it a total detriment to the creative mind?

I think each one of us should comprehend this problem of tradition because tradition is, after all, habit seasoned in time. And that habit shapes our thought, shapes all our existence, forces you to go to the office, forces you to maintain a family, which evokes responsibility, duty, and morality, in which is included obedience. All these are surely tradition: they compose tradition, they make up tradition.

Does tradition help to bring about a creative mind that is the new mind? Or does habit prevent the total comprehension of that which is beyond time? There is no good habit and bad habit—all habit is the same. But to free the mind from habit is, surely, extraordinarily important because habit is merely a technique, an easy way of living in which no deep thinking is necessary. That is why most of us cultivate habits which become almost automatic, and thereby we need not exert too much vitality or thought. So we cultivate habits which gradually, through time, become tradition.

Now, the whole of that is the past; the past including the ideas, the gods, the various conscious and unconscious influences, the various compulsions and urges, the various accumulations to which we are attached. All that is the past—not only the accumulated memories of the individual, of the person, but also the accumulated knowledge of humanity which has been gathered, accumulated through centuries. There is the accumulation in the unconscious, and there is the accumulation in the conscious. The accumulation in the conscious is the present technological education, the environmental and social influences in the present. There is also in the unconscious the residue of thousands of years of man's endeavor—his knowledge, his hopes, his frustrations, his unexpected demands. All that is the past. The past is you, and there is nothing else but the past. And I think it is very important to understand this.

I mean by understanding, not intellectually, not verbally. If you merely assent to what has been said, agree or disagree and add more in detail to what has been said, verbally, intellectually, then you are not understanding, because anybody can agree with anything or can be persuaded not to agree. But understanding is something entirely different, surely. Understanding comes into being when you give your whole attention, not only to the word and to the meaning of the word, but also to your reaction to those words and the reaction, which is the response of your memory, which is the past; the whole, total process of that brings about understanding.

These talks are not verbal, are not meant to be merely a series of ideas with which you can play. They are meant for those people who are serious, earnest, who are willing or wishing to go to the very end to find out—to the very end, not to the intellectual barren end of words and theories, but to the very end of an idea, of a thought like the past—to inquire very deeply into it, and to pursue it logically, sanely, rationally to the very end. Such a person is a serious person who will not be thwarted by any formula.

This evening we are proposing to do that, and that is not only to inquire verbally but also emotionally to be in contact with the word. You know, there is a difference between these two. Mere verbalization is not connected with our emotions, with our feelings; there is a division between the idea and the feeling which brings about action. When we divide the idea, we separate it from the feeling; then there is the contradiction between the feeling and the idea. And most of us spend our time in trying to find out how to bridge the gap between the idea and the action. The idea is merely the word; the idea is merely a series of thoughts verbalized.

Ideas have no value at all. As you must have observed, every politician throughout the world talks of peace. That is double talk. They talk of peace and prepare for war. They talk of not having position, power, prestige; and they are craving, burning after it. So it is an idea. But we are not dealing with ideas; we are dealing with the fact that action can only come about when there is an emotional contact with the fact.

I feel that the past can be completely dissolved. The future, the unknown, is just beyond the wall of the past. But to go beyond, to break through that wall, one has to go very deeply into the question of the past. One cannot go deeply into the whole process of consciousness verbally. One cannot inquire through thought. Thought is not capable of inquiry because thought is born of reaction. Thought is the reaction of memory, and memory is the result of experience, and that experience is the conditioning in which we have been brought up. So thought is not the way to inquire; thought is not the instrument of questioning, of demanding.

So, when one realizes very clearly, sharply, that thought is not the instrument of inquiry, then how is one to inquire, how is one to understand? As I am talking, please listen to find out the state of your own mind. Do not merely hear the words, but use the words to open the door into your own mind. Because, really, what we are doing this evening is the process which opens the door into yourself. We are taking a pilgrimage inwardly, taking a journey together into the whole process of the mind. If you are merely listening to words, then it will have no value. But if you are journeying together—not merely listening to me, but journeying together with me—then you will discover for yourself the truth or falseness of what is being said.

And if the intellect is not the instrument of inquiry, and the intellect is not the way that opens the door, then what is the way? I am using the word *way* not as a method, not as a system, not as a practice, not as a discipline—those are all too immature and childish; it does not matter who says so. A mind that follows a system is a narrow mind, it is a limited mind. And a mind that is disciplined, shaped, controlled, ceases to think. So I am using the word way in the sense if this is not it, then what is? If thought is not the way to inquire into how to dissolve the past—because thought itself is the past, is the result of the past, and therefore it is incapable of dissolving the past—then what is? How is the past to be dissolved? I hope I am making myself perfectly clear.

The hand that gives cannot at the same time take away. Thought wants to dissolve the past, but yet thought is the result of the past. No action, no projection, no desire, no volition from the past can dissolve it because all that is still of the past. Do what you will, every action, every sacrifice, every movement of the mind is of the past; and thought, do what it will, cannot resolve it. If this is very clear, not merely in agreement—not merely that you agree with what is being said, which is not important at all—then what is important is to find out if you can dissolve the past. The past can give the technique of daily existence; the past is the machinery of daily existence; it can offer, it can facilitate, but it cannot take you very far. And we have to take a journey beyond the past, beyond time, and it is necessary because the only revolution that matters is the religious revolution. And such a revolution only can bring about an extraordinary order out of this disorder. I will explain that presently. It is not a contradiction.

So, thought under no circumstances offers a way out of the past. The past is necessary; otherwise, you would not know where you live, you would not be able to know what your name is, or to go to the office, or to recognize your wife, husband, your friends, your children, or to speak. The past is memory, and memory is essential. You cannot put it aside. But the cultivation of memory, which is knowledge, which is the expansion of thought, cannot possibly break down the wall of the past. And therefore the mind is never new, never fresh, never young, never innocent. But it is only such a young, fresh, innocent mind that knows humility—not the mind that is burdened with the past.

So how is one to break through the past? There is an act which comes into being with seeing. Please pay a little attention to what is being said. Because of its very simplicity, you will find it difficult to understand; our minds are so complicated, so immature, with a lot of information which has no value, so frightened, so insecure. Being insecure, the mind seeks security and therefore furthers insecurity, and such a mind is incapable of seeing something very simple and therefore acting very simply.

And I am going to talk a little bit about the act of seeing, which like listening is an extraordinary act. To listen without judgment, without thought, without the word, without interpretation, without condemning or accepting; just to listen, which is an extremely attentive state of mind; to listen to somebody, it does not matter who it is, whether it is your child, your husband, your boss, your bus conductor; to listen completely—it requires a great deal of attention, not concentration, but just attention. And seeing and listening involve this attention. There is the past—which nobody can deny. It is there, solid, brutalizing, crippling, destroying the young mind that must be totally alive. That is a fact—not only an outward fact, but also a psychological fact. One must see the fact without condemnation, without any judgment—merely see the fact what the past is.

Now, let me go into the question of seeing in a different way. For most of us authority is very important—the authority of the books, the so-called sacred books; the authority of the policeman, the law; the authority of the boss, the tradition; authority as domination of the husband over the wife or the wife over the husband and of the parent over the child; the authority that makes you obey; the authority that has created such disorder in this world. For through obedience you do not create order but you bring disorder—as all tyrannies do bring disorder. This again is a fact, both an outward and an inward fact, that you obey. And your constant demand is to find an assuring, comforting, enduring authority that will give you great, immense satisfaction which you call peace.

Do please listen to this and apply it to yourself. You are not listening to words; you are listening to yourself. You are not listening to ideas; you are observing yourself in a mirror. You may turn your back; you may not look at the mirror, but it is there if you look, if you want it. As you are here, do look at the mirror which is yourself. So there is authority—the authority that makes you do things, the authority of right conduct, the authority that says that you must not and that you must, the authority that destroys all creativity—which is shown in the soldier. The soldier is not allowed to think. He is only allowed to obey. The more completely he obeys the authority without hesitation, the more is he the complete soldier. Then for him he has no responsibility; his superiors take the responsibility, and that is why war is popular. That is what most of us want: the authority of the guru who tells you what to do—and you don't have to think, you don't have to feel, you don't have to question; you just follow.

And so obedience becomes almost second nature. And a nation brought up on obedience is a nation that ceases to be. That is what is happening in this unfortunate country. There is no questioning; you don't break down authority—I do not mean the authority of the government and the authority of the law. If you do break that down, if you do not pay taxes, you will go to prison; that is very simple—I don't mean breaking down that kind of authority; that would be too stupid and immature. When I speak of breaking down authority, I mean the breaking down of the psychological authority, the authority that one has built up within oneself, which is to obey—to obey the guru, to obey tradition, to obey what you have been told, to bend your knee to the so-called religion, which is nothing else but propaganda. We will go into the whole question of religion later. So authority cripples all that and brings about deterioration; you are never free, there is always fear.

And how can a mind which is ridden by authority of every kind, from the little authority to the great authority of the highest guru, Shankara and all the saints—how can such a mind ever find out what is true for itself? Surely, it has to find out what is true for itself. It need not be told by a thousand gurus what is true, for all of them may be wrong—they probably are. But you have to find out, and to find out you have to destroy every authority that you have created within yourself. That very denial brings what you may call disorder, because that disorder is really fear which arises when you begin to question this inward authority and so tear down the house that one has built up through centuries, especially in this country which is in a state of deterioration. You see this fact of authority and follow it; you say, "What would happen if there were no inward authority?" Probably, if there were no inward authority, you would be disturbed for a few days, but soon you would find another authority to replace the old. And in the meantime there is disorder, and you are frightened by that disorder.

Surely, sirs, you must tear down everything to create; you must question everything. And in that very questioning, the individual comes into being; otherwise, we remain the mass. And, surely, that is what is necessary at the present time—to question everything, to question, not to find out the answer. If you question with a motive, it is no longer questioning; then you are merely seeking a result. But if you question without a motive—which is quite an extraordinary thing to do—then your mind is completely capable of seeing what is true.

So it is important, is it not, that there should be a new mind, a fresh mind. And such a mind is not possible if it is burdened with authority. Authority is not only the authority of the guru, the authority of the book, the authority of the wife and the husband and all the rest, the authority or the will to dominate, but also there is a much deeper significance in authority—which is experience. Because most of us live by experience, experience becomes authority. There is the experience of the scientist who has accumulated for centuries knowledge, which is authority; and also, there is the experience which each one of us has gathered as knowledge, and that becomes our authority, which again is the past: the authority of which the conscious mind is aware, and also the authority which is the accumulated experience in the unconscious. Experience is the reaction to challenge. I ask you something. The very asking is a challenge to which you respond, and the responding is the experiencing. And that experiencing is the result of your previous experiences, which become the authority.

Please see, it is quite simple. It may sound very complicated, but it is not. All experience is of the past. And any response of experience, which is of the past, will not break down the wall of the past. So authority of any kind, inward or outward, will not free the mind from the past. And you can never be a master of the future, except in mechanical things, because the future is the unknown. But we look at the future, the tomorrow, with the eyes of the past, and therefore we think we can control it. And we do control it mechanically—tomorrow you are going to the office; tomorrow you are going to have certain results in your activities, and so on. Mechanically you will do all kinds of things; therefore, you think you are the master of the future, but you are not. Psychologically you are not the master of the future, which is tomorrow. Because, how can you be the master of something which you don't know? How can you be the master of a mind which is—which must be—young, fresh, innocent? So when you see—I am using the word *see* in the way I have talked about seeing—that certain outward forms of authority are necessary, like the authority of the engineer, the doctor, the government, the law, the policeman, but every other form of authority is destructive and prevents the mind from being free, then the mind can be free. And it is only the free mind that can go beyond.

So we are the result of the past. We are the past. And any projection of the past is not the future, except mechanically, except in time. All projections into the future—such as "I shall be this, psychologically; I shall arrive," or "I shall find the truth"—are born of the past and therefore are productive of conflict.

Now, if you are able to see this totally—that is, as I explained seeing something totally, with your mind, with your heart, with your senses, with your eyes, nose, ears, with all your senses, as well as mentally, emotionally, completely; seeing something without contradiction, without effort—then you will find that the past can be broken down completely, not bit by bit, but totally, immediately, because seeing prevents the gap from action. There is no gap between seeing and acting. I hope I am making myself clear.

You see, sir, it is very important to remove contradiction, to be free of contradiction, because contradiction brings about conflict. I am talking of the inward, psychological contradiction, the double talk of the politician—and most of us indulge in that double talk. And if one is really going to the very end of any thought, to introduce contradiction prevents further journey; you are caught in contradiction. So what we are pointing out is seeing something totally, without contradiction.

Sir, to see that you are angry, what is involved in that seeing? The fact is that you are angry. And when you see that fact without denying it, without justifying, without saying, "It is right" or "It is wrong"; when you are just aware choicelessly of the fact that you are angry, then that very fact that you are angry will bring about an action which is not contradictory. Then you do not pretend, or persuade yourself, or discipline yourself not to be angry, because in that very act of seeing, there is no contradiction. And this fact of seeing is very important to understand, because on that point I am going to talk all the time, because that is the only liberating factor—the act of seeing, the act of listening—then you do not have to do a thing.

But to see so completely, you must be attentive, and attention denies contradiction. You cannot attend if you are condemning. You cannot give your whole attention if you are trying not to be jealous. It is only when you are completely aware that you are jealous or envious, completely, then that fact brings its own energy. And you need tremendous energy to have this attention. And the act of seeing is attention. I am not talking of something mystical, something of a special process, a new particular way of thinking—

all that is absurdity. We are moving from fact to fact.

And the act of seeing without condemnation, judgment, evaluation, without the word, which is thought; the act of looking, observing every movement, every feeling, when you pay your total attention to everything that you see and feel—that act of seeing brings about a new mind, a fresh mind. That fresh mind is not created by thought, by modern education, by going to the temple, reading the Gita or the Koran or the Bible everlastingly. That mind comes into being only through seeing; and to see, you must question desperately. The very act of seeing is very destructive because it destroys the society in which you have been brought up. You are no longer concerned with the reformation of that society. You cannot reform society because society is the result of the past. And if you will reform it, you are still in the past. But a man who has broken down the past completely—and such breaking down is possible—he, being alone, may affect society; that is irrelevant.

So what is important and essential is to see that a new mind is necessary. And a new mind cannot be brought about by the tricks of the mind—which is thought. The new mind can only come into being when there is a questioning of the society in which we have been brought up. And you cannot question if you have a motive. And so seeing authority, seeing obedience frees the mind from obedience. After all, what prevents you from seeing is your condemnation, your justification, which is the past. So when you look, when you see, when you listen, without condemnation, you are free of the past. You can look, and to so look you need to have attention, and attention is the essence of energy. And that energy only comes into being when you are constantly looking, watching, observing, seeing, questioning.

So out of this extraordinary listening and seeing, the mind has lost its mooring, its connection with the past. The mind has its anchor in the past; the mind is the past, but when the mind gives complete attention to seeing, it has broken down the past. And it is only such a fresh, young, innocent mind that can go beyond the limitations which the mind has placed upon itself. It is only then that it is possible to discover for oneself—as an individual who is no longer a part of society—to find out if there is, or if there is not, the immeasurable.

January 24, 1962

Third Talk in New Delhi

If I may, I would like to continue with what we were talking about when we met here last Wednesday. We were saying that it was highly important to have a new way of thinking, and that a new way of living is absolutely necessary in a world that has become so utterly superficial, that has problems multiplying, and that constantly faces enormous danger. I do not think we realize, especially in this country, how serious the issue is. We are fairly safe here; perhaps we are very corrupt but safe. We have our problems: nationalism is increasing while other countries have discarded it; we still have leaders when other countries deny leadership; we still have authority in position when in other countries authority is being questioned. We have in this country talked a great deal on religion, but we are really not religious at all; we are like anybody else, superficially interested in getting money, success, making progress, and having amusement, like everybody else in the world, though we may talk loudly about God and all the rest of it.

So, it seems to me, a different kind of mind is absolutely essential. You will see that the demand is urgent when you observe the state of the world: its superficiality, the mechanical success, the technological progress, the immense pressures that are operating. When one observes closely and has gone into this fairly deeply, one must see that a new quality of the mind is necessary, is essential. And that quality cannot be brought about by, or through, any technological progress. I think we must see this very clearly. And if I may, I would like to talk a little bit more about what we were saying last Wednesday.

You see, you are the result of the past, of all the yesterdays that lie behind you. You are the result of your environment, of the society in which you have been brought up, of the propaganda which is called religion and which has been instilled into you for centuries. You can glibly talk about religious ideas and the Western impact on the Oriental mind, on your mind, but all that is still very superficial. Seeing all this, one must, if one is at all serious, demand and ask oneself: Where is all this leading to; what is it all about? When you put that question earnestly, you may return to your conditioning and reply that everything will be all right, that this is only a periodical change through which man goes, and through turmoil everything will come out right because there is God, there is justice, there is beauty, there is love. But those are all words; they have not much meaning. The hungry man is not fed by words; he wants food. When you put that question seriously to yourself, you will see, as we pointed out last week, that you are the result of the past—actually the result—and that there is nothing new.

Any attempt at the new is really a reaction of the old, is a projection of some part of the old—the old being the religion in which you have been brought up, the culture, the family influence, tradition, and all the rest of it. So, there is really nothing new. And yet the circumstances of life—the present crisis, the confusion, the misery, the sorrow, the immense dearth—demand that a new mind shall come into being; not a new state of ideas, not ideation, not ideals, but a totally different approach to life. And this approach is not a matter of time. That is, there must be a mutation; there must be an immediate change, a change in the quality of the mind, a mutation that would bring about a different kind of action, different values.

And how is this mutation to take place? That is what we were trying to talk about last Wednesday, and I would like to go on with it. We were saying that what is important is to understand a fact: the fact that one is imitating, the fact that one seeks success, the fact that one is ambitious—to see that fact. Because, seeing that fact in itself brings about the mutation. The very seeing of something as a fact, without an opinion, without judgment, without condemning, brings about the necessary impetus, the energy which brings about mutation. Perhaps most of you do not understand the implication of this seeing, of this listening. And I would like to go into that because for me the act of seeing, the act of listening is the only medium, the only instrument that brings about a revolution, a transformation in the mind.

Most of us want success. I am going to talk about this in order to help you to see the fact—not to deny it, not to accept it, but just to see the fact. Most of us worship success, success in this world; or psychologically, we want to become successful. And to be successful there must be imitation, there must be copying, there must be the continuity of what has been. And if you observe yourself, you will see that is what you want: you want success, not only here, but inwardly, you want to achieve a result. And this desire to achieve a result implies, does it not, that you must have a pattern to follow. And when you have a pattern to follow, no fundamental change can be brought about. Any departure from the pattern creates fear. And in order to avoid fear, you follow the lines laid down by authority, and you pursue that authority—whether it is the Gita, whether it is the political leader, whether it is your guru, or whatever it is—in order to be successful, in order not to have any trouble, in order to avoid any conflict, always bearing in mind that you want a result which will be satisfactory, which is success.

Please, if I may deviate a little—if it is a deviation at all—let me again say that we are not dealing with words or phrases, we are not coining new ideas. We are really concerned with bringing about a mutation of the mind. And in bringing about such a revolutionary change within yourself, you have to listen—not accept, not deny, not compare, but just listen—which is quite a difficult thing to do because most of us, whenever we listen to something, are either justifying it or comparing it with what we know, or referring to some authority which we have established for ourselves. When you do that, you are not actually listening; you have deviated, you have gone away. So I suggest that you listen without comparing, just listen without judgment, because you do not know what I am going to say. And in order to understand what the speaker has to say, you have to listen; but you cannot listen to what is being said if all the time you are interpreting what he is saying.

So the act of listening is the act of perceiving the activity of your own mind. Through the act of listening you are learning about yourself—what prevents you from seeing, what prevents you from listening. And you will find that you are not listening; therefore, you feel you must force yourself to listen. And the compulsion to listen is also a distraction. So it is very difficult to listen, not only to the speaker, but to everything in life—to listen to your wife, your husband, to listen to a political speech, to listen to all that is being said on the radio if you do listen to the radio, to listen to what you read in the newspaper—to see that clearly without any prejudice, without any judgment.

And I hope that you will do this while I talk because that listening is an act of humility. It is only the mind that is really humble that can learn. It cannot cultivate humility because then it is vanity clothed in humility. But there is humility when you listen, not comparing, not judging, not saying: "He is right, he is wrong; this is right, this is true, or this is false." We are not trying to do any propaganda; we are not trying to force you to think in any particular direction; what we are trying to do is to see facts. And to see a fact requires enormous energy, enormous attention. And you cannot pay attention, you cannot attend, if your mind is evaluating what is being said. Please do see the importance of this—not only see now the importance of what is being said, but also see throughout life the importance of everything you hear. Then you will find that out of this seeing, out of this listening, there comes an energy which is necessary to see a fact that is constantly changing.

So I keep on repeating this: the importance of seeing, the importance of listening. You know, when there is attention, goodness flowers; when there is no attention, every form of evil comes into being. So attention is the only virtue. And you cannot attend if you are all the time in conflict with yourself. And I want to deal this evening with that conflict.

Why is it that all of us have taken conflict as a part of existence? Why have we accepted conflict as essential to living? If you observe your own life, you are in conflict, not only with your neighbor and with the world, but also psychologically; inwardly, you are much more in conflict. You do not know what to do. Or if you know what to do, you do it, and out of that comes a problem—there is misery, there is strife, there is struggle. All that we know is conflict, and we are always trying to avoid it, to escape from that conflict. This is a fact. I am not trying to tell you how not to be in conflict—the way, the escape. The escape, the thing to which you escape, becomes much more important than the conflict itself. Then the thing to which you escape becomes important—it may be drink, it may be your church, your gods, sex, power, ambition; all these are escapes from the fact that you are in conflict. That is a fact. Please see that fact—see in the sense that I am using the word *see;* don't deny, don't say, "What am I to do with it; how shall I escape from it?" but see the fact that you are in conflict and that there is this urge to escape from that conflict. And after escaping, the thing to which you have escaped becomes all-important. Your religion, your nationalism, your guru, the ideals, the saints—all are escapes from the central issue that you are in conflict, that you are in misery.

Now, how does conflict arise—not only the little conflicts of everyday living, but the deep, inward conflicts, the unconscious and conscious conflicts that are unresolved? How does this conflict come into being? Again, please, neither accept nor reject it, but please find out if the speaker is telling the truth, find out—not agree—why you are in conflict. If you are at all aware of your own condition, you are bound to be conscious of being in conflict. You are in conflict, why? There is conflict because there is contradiction. You want to do something, and you also want to do something opposite—a contradiction like love and hate, wanting to be ambitious and at the same time pretending not to be ambitious, wanting to be rich and at the same time trying to play the game of politics, of being a poor man. There is the fact of what you are and there is the idea of what you should be; the fact of 'what actually is' and the idea of 'what should be'—a contradiction. So you are brought up on what you should be, and not to face the fact. You are brought up to be nonviolent, and never to face the fact that you are violent. That is what this country has been told for umpteen years—that you must be nonviolent, that you must be idealistic. And ideals are far more important than *what is.* So between *what is* and 'what should be' there is a gap, and the bridging of that gap brings about conflict. Please observe yourself. I am only putting into words what is the actual fact.

So contradiction arises; conflict arises when there is contradiction, and then there is effort. We like making efforts. For us effort is very important. Everything that we do is the result of effort. That is a fact. That is what you are used to. Why should we make an effort?

Is it not possible to live in this world without any effort? And that question can only be answered if you can understand this whole process of conflict, not only the conflict outwardly, but conflict inwardly—conflict between nations, between people outwardly; and conflict within, deep anxiety. And when there is conflict, there is this effort to conquer the conflict. So conflict arises through contradiction. And when there is contradiction, with its misery, with its turmoil, with its anxiety, then there is the urge to make an effort to overcome that conflict; in this circle we are caught. And all our concern is to escape from this fact, and therefore there arises further effort—further effort in religious practices, to discipline, to control, to shape, to comply, to alienate, to obey. So our mind is never quiet, is never capable of looking at anything, listening to anything fully, completely. It is always in turmoil.

And how can such a mind that is in turmoil understand anything? Life is an immense thing to understand. Life is not just merely going to the office; life is not merely begetting children; life is not merely sex, life is not merely prosperity, life is not a series of successes, life is not the fulfillment of ambitions—life is something much more than all this. Life is also an inquiry: to find out whether there is, or whether there is not, God or something beyond all words; what is love; how to face and understand despair, the sense of guilt, the enormous sorrow, the anxiety that is in the heart of man. All that is life. And to understand all that you must have a very quiet mind, not a mind torn in conflict, in travail.

And so what happens when we are faced with all this? We turn to the past, or to some book, or to some authority; and we think we have understood all this enormous complexity by following some absurd formula, or the Gita, or following a guru, or some book or other. But to understand this immensity, there must be a revolution in your mind—not an economic, social revolution, but a mutation in the quality of the mind. And this mutation cannot be brought about through volition because the more you bring in the past, the more conditioning there is, and therefore there is no longer mutation. So just see the fact of all this—how mechanical we have become.

You see, sirs, virtue has lost its meaning because by taking some chemicals, you can become very virtuous. I do not know if you have seen all that is happening in the world. You can take a pill and become tranquil. So tranquillity has lost its meaning. You can take a pill, some chemical, to become less angry, less jealous, less hateful, and all the rest of it. If you are passionate sexually, you can take a pill and quieten love. So all virtue has lost its meaning. And the computers, the mechanical brains, those extraordinary electronic machines are taking over all thinking; they can do far better than man. And automation—a machine running other machines—is also coming into being. We are becoming—not only in India but over the rest of the world—very superficial because we are becoming mechanical. So seeing these, which are facts and which are not my inventions, gods have no meaning any more, religions have lost their significance; and you are faced with immediate danger. The future is unknown; all that you have is the past and nothing else—the past of what you know, the past of what you have learned, the past of the atomic bomb, the past of your tradition, and all that. That is all that you have, nothing else. That is your mind and nothing else.

Now, how to bring about a tremendous mutation, a radical revolution out of this? That is the real issue. I hope you understand the question—not what to do. But first we must understand the question and the significance of the question. Look, sirs, you read the Gita; you are Christians, Buddhists, or Muslims, or whatever you are. What makes the difference is not what the Gita says but what you actually are; not your turbans and your coats and your learning and your knowledge, but what you are. When you are stripped of all this, what you are is merely the past, something that has existed, the thing that you have known, the machinery of the past. And whatever you do from the past will condition the future and is therefore still of the past.

Do please see the importance of what is being said. If you make an effort to bring about a mutation—that mutation is absolutely necessary in this world at the present time—that urge is from the past and therefore conditions mutation, and therefore it is no longer mutation; it is merely a continuation of the past. We are concerned with mutation, with a new mind that can see the whole of the totality of existence, not just a part of it. It is a strange thing that at one time in this country, you were told that you must not be provincial, you must not separate yourself from the rest of the country; and now you are becoming nationalists, still in parts. You are concerned with the whole of life, not of India, not of Hindus, or of Buddhists, but of man, and with what is going to happen to man, to the mind of man, of which you are a part. So when you see this fact, the seeing of the fact must make you question most fundamentally. But if you try to find an answer to that question, that answer will be from the background, so you must put the question without seeking an answer. And that is very difficult to do, merely to put the question and inquire.

So our problem is this: that a radical revolution is necessary within the mind, within consciousness. When that revolution takes place, it will act socially, economically, and quite differently. Now, how is this revolution to be brought about? I am using the word *how* not to suggest a method, a system—if you have a method and a system, it is still of the past—but merely as a means of inquiry, not as a means of offering a system. How is this revolution to be brought about?

First of all, to live fully, to see anything very clearly, there must be no conflict of any kind, and therefore there must be the understanding of the whole problem of contradiction—which means inquiring, observing the operations of your own mind, and seeing that every form of ambition, outwardly or inwardly, brings about a contradiction. Wherever there is self-fulfillment, wherever there is the urge to fulfill—to become this or not to be that—in that very desire to fulfill there is a contradiction which is frustration. So ambition, success, fulfillment implies frustration, and from that frustration there is conflict. These are all psychological facts; these are not my inventions. If you observe yourself, you will see that these are the facts that take place.

So a mind that is seeking to understand what is implied in mutation has completely ceased to have ambition. And then you will ask: How can such a mind live in this world—this world made up of conflict, ambition, ruthlessness, each one for himself—how can a mind which is not ambitious live in this world? It cannot. Therefore, when you understand ambition and have denied ambition totally, then you will find you can live, not in the terms of the old society; you will create a new world. Do you understand, sirs, what it is we are talking about? A new world has to come into being. And you cannot create a new world by merely saying, "I must conform and live in this world." You must destroy this society and create a new world. I am talking not of the destruction of buildings but of the destruction of social values. And you do not want to do that because you are afraid; therefore, you are caught again in conflict.

So you have to see very clearly for yourself that where there is ambition of any kind, there is conflict, there is sorrow. But, you see, we are brought up on ambition, on competition. Every schoolboy is taught to compete. Every schoolboy is taught to worship success. And how can you deny this whole pattern, the pattern in which you have been brought up? You will deny it when you see its importance, when you are faced with a crisis. And the crisis now is that there should be a new mind. That is the crisis—not how to reform the old pattern. So when you are aware of the crisis, when you are aware of all the implications of ambition, when you have gone into yourself very deeply to find out the source of ambition—why you are ambitious, why this competition, this travail, this ruthless search for position, prestige for oneself—when you understand this whole anatomy of ambition, then you are either with ambition with all its ruthlessness or you are out of it. And the man who is out of it brings about a new mind, a new quality of thinking.

So what we are concerned with is to see the importance of this deep inward revolution and to find out whether such a revolution is possible or not for each one of us. Time demands it, circumstances demand it, your own life demands it; and the strange part of it is that there is no time. You cannot say, "I will eventually change through time; I will gather the energy to bring about this change." Time does not give you energy. Time takes away your energy; you are old, you wither away. What gives you energy to pursue deeply is facing the fact, just to face the fact, whatever that fact may be. And you will see that, as you face it, out of that comes energy. Not the denial of the fact—that never gives you energy. And you need tremendous energy because not only are there all the trivialities of life which one has to face and understand, but also one has to go beyond them. There is also something else much more significant which demands all your attention. And that is to find out for yourself, not through words but actually, if there is something beyond the measure of the mind, if there is something called the immeasurable, something which is beyond death, beyond words, beyond thought. Unless you find that out, life becomes very shallow, life becomes mechanical; then life is full of sorrow and travail. And to find that out, you need immense energy.

And this energy can only come when you have understood the quality of seeing, the quality of listening, when you can look at facts, look at your jealousy, look at your ambition, look at your passions and all the absurdities that you have built around yourself and which you call religion. And when you can face them and not react, then out of that confrontation comes energy. And it is this quality of energy that brings about mutation. And only then does the mind become something extraordinary; it is no longer the thing of environment; it is no longer the thing of experience. Then it is capable of renewing itself everlastingly; then it has the quality of youth, of innocency. And it must have that quality of innocency, of complete humility, to find out that which is beyond words, beyond thought, beyond time.

January 28, 1962

Fourth Talk in New Delhi

I want to talk this evening about discipline, knowledge, and sorrow. But before I go into it, I think we must be clear that we are not dealing with ideas, theories, or abstractions, because they have no value at all. When you are concerned with actual life, with everyday facts, mere theories, abstractions, and ideations have little or no meaning at all. And we must be very clear that what we are going to talk about is not merely translated into ideation, formulated into some kind of vague abstractions, because we are dealing with the whole problem of life—the life that is lived every day, the life that is great pain, great travail, in which there is such agony, despair, frustration.

We are not dealing with words. A man who really understands, who is really serious and learning, must go through beyond words. Words generally are a hindrance because we take the symbol for the actual, we take the word for the thing. But the thing is not the word. The word *tree* is not the actual tree. But the word tree becomes all important when we are dealing with words, with ideations. But when we are dealing with facts, the tree, apart from the word, has an immense significance. Similarly, we are not concerned with words, nor with ideas, nor with abstractions. We are concerned with the actual daily life with its miseries, little successes and joys and constant anxiety with norms of hard work. So we are dealing with life and not with words.

For most of us discipline is merely imposed by circumstances—going to the office, passing examinations, leading a certain kind of life, following certain ideas, imposing a certain discipline. And most of us, not merely the so-called religious people, do this constant discipline. The man who goes to the office has to get up at a certain time; he has to be there in the office punctually, and the boy who wants to pass an examination has to study; he is forcing himself to conform to a pattern—as most of us do—and that pattern is either imposed by society or self-imposed.

And if you observe closely, you will see that this imposition of a pattern implies every form of suppression, conscious and unconscious—not only suppression, but resistance. When you suppress, you cultivate resistance. If you are angry, you discipline yourself not to be angry. If you are lustful, you discipline, control yourself not to be lustful—that is to resist. Or if resistance is not possible, you find a substitution, you cultivate some form of resistance—to resist anger by an idea. If you observe yourself closely, you will see that is what you are doing all day. You want to do something spontaneously, naturally, freely; but society—with its norms of established order, with its regard for respectability, which is a horror—is all the time controlling, shaping you. And so gradually discipline becomes a form of suppression, resistance, or a substitution—and escape from the fact.

Please, you are not merely listening to the speaker, you are observing yourself. Because, it is much more interesting, much more alive, much more significant when you are watching yourself through the words which the speaker is using so that you get to know yourself. And the knowledge of oneself—what actually is taking place—is far more important than merely to follow a verbal discourse. So if you observe yourself not only at the conscious level but also at the deep, unconscious level—which is perhaps much more significant than the mere conscious pursuit of an idea—you will find that discipline is a resistance, a suppression. And the moment you suppress, you resist what is taking place psychologically, inwardly. Outwardly one can see suppression as it is. But inwardly, when you are forcing, compelling, controlling, shaping, suppressing what is actually taking place, that is called discipline.

You will find, if you go sufficiently deeply into yourself, that there is a contradiction between the fact of *what is* and the idea of 'what should be'. The fact is that you are angry, and the nonfact is the idea that you should not be angry, so the adjustment to the pattern which is not the fact is called discipline. The adjustment to an ideation is discipline—that is, if you are violent, you have an idea, an ideal, a belief in nonviolence, and you are adjusting yourself to that. This adjustment, this constant process of trying to bridge the gap between the fact of *what is* and the ideal of 'what should be' is called discipline. In that process of disciplining oneself to an idea, to a pattern, to a belief, one invariably develops psychological contradictions, and therefore there is a continuity of more conflict, not less conflict. A mind in conflict is a dull mind; a mind in conflict soon wears itself out, like any machine which is in constant friction, and loses all its power.

So discipline is really, if you observe very carefully, the process not only of creating a contradiction within oneself but also of dissipating that energy which is necessary to learn. After all, learning is far more important than discipline; if you learn about something, in the very act of learning there is a discipline which is not imposed. I mean by learning not an additive process. Learning is not adding to something all the time; in that there is no learning; that is merely accumulating. Adding to what is already known, which is knowledge, is not learning. Learning is a constant living process; observing, being aware of things actually as they are taking place. And from that your mind becomes alert, learning, watching. If you are merely accumulating knowledge and translating, if you are interpreting or translating or comparing what you already know with what is actually taking place, then you are merely accumulating from the fact of *what is,* adding to that which you already know. And that process is not learning.

To learn one must have humility; to learn the mind must be in a state of not-knowing. Not-knowing is the essence of humility. A mind which has accumulated knowledge, which knows, has no humility. It is only the mind that has the essence of humility that learns, and therefore that humility never accumulates. If you observe yourself sometimes, you will see that the moment you use learning as a means of accumulating, from that accumulative acting, there is invariably psychological contradiction because that learning is a static process; that knowledge is static, and from that staticity you are trying to understand or control or shape a thing which is alive, and therefore there is a contradiction; therefore, there is a conflict. Learning is never a conflict. If your mind is very alert, very sharp, watching, learning, that very learning brings about its own extraordinarily subtle discipline which is not controlled; therefore, the mind is always young, innocent, fresh.

So, there is discipline when one controls the fact by what one has already known. Do please listen to what the speaker wants to say. I mean by listening not listening with what already you know. If you are listening from a center of knowledge, from your book, from your learning, from your experience, from the Gita, from your environmental experience and all the rest of it, from a center which you already know—if you are listening from all that, you are not actually listening. All that is the screen through which you are listening to the words of the speaker. But if you are actually listening, you have no screen; you are not starting from something which you already know. Therefore, your mind has become extraordinarily alert; therefore, the mind is in a state of humility—not in terms of only disciplining, but in terms of learning, trying to understand, seeing what is true—not in terms of what has been.

So, you see, discipline is now practiced by the so-called religious people—who are not at all religious—trying to conform to the pattern of a religious life which has been laid down. Discipline is also practiced by the office worker or by the laborer, getting out, going every morning to his work—which must be utterly boring. And this practice of discipline is out of a desire to succeed, to arrive, and therefore it brings about conflict; and being in conflict leads to suppression, resistance. All this is called discipline, either for a religious life or for a successful life through ambition.

So a disciplined mind, as it is understood now, is incapable of learning; it is incapable of understanding; it is not sufficiently subtle, free, young. But if you begin to understand this whole process, then you will see that knowledge has quite a different meaning; it has quite a different place. Knowledge is necessary. A good bureaucrat or a good scientist or a good mechanic or a good professor must have knowledge. And his learning is merely an addition to what he already knows; it is a new way of looking at something; it is a new scientific discovery, and he adds to what he has already known; his learning is accumulated. But such a mind, which is accumulating knowledge and from that knowledge experiences and gathers more knowledge in order to add more to itself, is not a creative mind. So knowledge is never creative.

Let us look at it a little more. The world is growing more and more; it is superficially acquiring more information, more knowledge, and knowledge is expanding more and more and more. And most of the minds are being trained either scientifically, mechanically, or to function in a factory. Such knowledge is obviously necessary; otherwise, the affairs of the world cannot be run properly, efficiently—anyway, it is not done properly, so it does not matter one way or the other. But efficiency implies knowledge, and an efficient person is concerned with accumulating knowledge to be more efficient. And that is what most of us are concerned with—becoming more and more efficient, which mechanically makes the man more and more ruthless.

Do watch your own mind. You are not listening to me. That is not important. What is important is your own life; watch it. But when knowledge becomes all-important, learning ceases. It is only the mind that is capable of learning that begins to have the feeling of what it is to be creative because in a sense, it has humility. So a mind that is not acquiring knowledge, and therefore not disciplining itself according to the desire to acquire, is capable of learning. But most of us are practicing discipline—the ambitious politician is disciplining himself, in his crooked way; the man who wants to be rich is disciplining himself in his crookedness. But we are not talking of such disciplines. We are talking of a much more radical discipline that comes when there is the essence of learning without accumulation—which demands a mind that is very alert and very sharp, that watches.

The more you accumulate anything, the more you become dull. Have you not noticed it? The moment you have a secure job, the moment you have a family—secure, made respectable by man, by law, by children, family, everything—you have become dull. You may smile, but the actual fact is your sharpness is gone; your watching, your looking, seeing, learning is completely gone because you have established yourself in respectability. A mind that is being made respectable by society, by a discipline which is in conformity to the pattern established by society—such a mind obviously can never find what is true, can never find if there is such a thing as God or no God.

To inquire, to learn about sorrow is a very extraordinary thing. We have to learn about sorrow because for most of us there is sorrow—sorrow of not having a good job, sorrow caused by death, sorrow through disease, sorrow brought about by self-pity. We are not talking about the cause of sorrow; we are trying to understand the whole problem of sorrow. But to understand the problem of sorrow, there must be no escape from sorrow. To understand something you must look at it; you must know all the content, all the beauty, all its significance, its depth, its height, its violence—everything you must know. But you cannot know if you are trying to avoid it. You cannot know, you cannot understand the depth of sorrow, if you are trying merely to cover it up with a lot of belief, if you are trying to run away, if you are merely using abstractions, beliefs, ideations as screens between yourself and the fact. And most of us have sorrow of some kind or other—through death, frustration, injustice in this world, the husband leaving the wife or the wife leaving the husband, realizing the incapacity of oneself, living in darkness, in anxiety, in fear, in loneliness, living with a petty little mind everlastingly comparing itself with something else. These are all the symptoms, these are all the causes, but there is sorrow.

But how is one to understand sorrow? Because, unless you understand sorrow, you cannot be free of it. You can deny it, you can rationalize and think it out and push it away from you, go to the temple, or pick up a book, or tune in the radio, or take a drink; do what you will, it is always there like a shadow. You may read all the sacred books, study everlastingly the Upanishads, the Bible, the Koran, or what you will; sorrow is always there like a festering sore. But how are you to understand it?

Now, why do you make a problem of sorrow, why should sorrow be a problem for man, something that is not resolved, that is not understood? For most of us sorrow is a problem; you don't know how to break it, how to be free of it, how to put it aside. A dull mind will never resolve it; it will only be in deterioration, and every person is caught in it and, being caught in it, makes of it a problem. Why? I mean by a problem something that is not resolved, something which has a continuity as memory.

First of all, sorrow is an indication of a dull mind. Please listen to it; do not accept, do not deny; just listen. Sorrow is an indication that a mind has gone to sleep. Sorrow is an indication that there is self-pity—that is, pitying oneself. Sorrow is an indication of the strength of your memory, which is the past. You want things as they were, or things as they should be; or you want a continuity, a fulfillment of your ambition which makes you frustrated; or you have felt the death of someone. We are not talking of death; we will talk about it another time. We are talking about sorrow, to know that it is in our minds, in our hearts, deep down, suppressed, never revealing it to ourselves. We may become occasionally aware of it. But we want to forget it; we want to escape from it as quickly as possible; we want to get rid of it.

Neither the altar nor the chemist can ever solve sorrow. Sorrow has to be understood. It has got to be completely exposed. And you cannot expose it if you are running away from it, if you are only giving an explanation—because it is so easy to give an explanation, and that explanation becomes a cover behind which you lurk, behind which you take shelter. Please watch all this in yourself. We are exposing ourselves. So the essence of sorrow is self-pity, memory of what has been and of what should be, and the hope that you will gain what should be. The essence of sorrow is this knowing, self-pitying, comparing always yourself with what has been or what should be, comparing yourself with others—always the others who are more powerful, more rich, more happy, more this, and more that. And comparison is psychological, is based on self-pity. So you have to look at this fact of sorrow, and not try to interpret sorrow, not try to explain it away—you cannot, it is there—not try to take shelter in a temple, in a book, in the family, in pictures, in drink, or anything else; you have to see it, to feel it.

It is very difficult to see the fact of sorrow because the word *sorrow* interferes with the fact. If you want to know, to learn and understand if there is or if there is not that extraordinary thing called God, you must go beyond the word *God*. The word is not the reality, surely. So, if a man wants to discover, he must go to the very end, he must discard the word, he must discard everything that he has known about God—all the doctrines, all the beliefs, all the dogmas—he must totally discard them to find out. Similarly, the word *sorrow* itself has an extraordinary weight, has an extraordinary significance. We have made it respectable; we have made it into something great. "The man of sorrow"—how the Christians have made that an extraordinary thing! They worship sorrow. Yet sorrow is too emotional to be disregarded; it has to be understood and pushed aside completely.

So can sorrow be put aside completely, so that the mind is never oppressed with the weight of sorrow? Otherwise life will become so empty, so shallow. Have you not noticed your own mind in sorrow; have you not noticed other people's minds in sorrow? How shallow they are—how empty and incapable of depth! They can discuss very cleverly, but sorrow slowly makes the mind small, dull.

Now, is it possible to be free of sorrow? All that you can find out is not that it is or that it is not possible, but you can learn about it. Please follow what I am going to say—follow, not in the sense of disciples listening to some guru—follow it step by step in yourself, inch by inch. Observing the facts, you will find that we are being trained—through education, through religions, through environmental influences—never to view a thing directly. We are all sidestepping, always avoiding the fact. Is that how one suffers? One can give a thousand explanations why there is sorrow in this world—like ignorance. I mean by ignorance, not lack of knowledge, but the ignorance of what psychologically is going on inwardly; that is real ignorance—not to be aware of the total process of what is going on in the consciousness in yourself, inside the skin. So there can be a thousand explanations, but at the end of it, you will still be in sorrow.

Now, how is one to be free of sorrow? Or, is that a wrong question? If you say, "How am I to be free of it?" the "how" then becomes a problem. And a mind that has a problem is in sorrow because it is in a state of contradiction, of trying to conform in order to avoid sorrow. Please follow this. The moment you say "how," you have introduced a problem. And a mind ridden with problems is a sorrowful mind; a mind that has no problems has no sorrow. There is such a mind which has no problem, and it can meet problems. But if you begin to ask, "How am I to be free from sorrow?" you have already introduced a problem, which will prevent you from understanding. This is not logic. Do not be intellectually caught by the logical sequence of it. It is not so.

To put a wrong question—how to be free?—invariably brings you a wrong answer. But to look at the fact that the mind is in sorrow, to look without interpretation, without an opinion, without a conclusion, merely to observe—that looking, that observation, demands attention. And the moment you attend, the moment you give your whole attention, then there is no problem. It is only the mind that does not give total attention that creates the problem. When you give attention with your body, with your mind, with your heart, with all your senses, totally—in that there is no problem.

But we never give to anything our complete attention because we have been trained to think with a motive. You pay attention because you want to be a big man, or you want a little more money or a better job. You want to be a greater partner, a greater poet, a well-known person; therefore, you give attention. That is not attention. When you have a motive behind it, which makes you attend, then the motive is much more important than the attention; so there is a contradiction; so there is conflict; and therefore you will never give complete attention to anything. And when you give your complete attention to something, you have no problem, and therefore your mind is capable of paying complete attention to the fact of sorrow.

You will find, if you so pay attention, from that attention there is energy. You know, only in attention there is virtue, only in attention there is goodness; there is no other virtue or goodness. The incomplete attention that one gives when one tries to cultivate virtue is immorality; it is not virtue. But the mind that gives complete attention—I mean by that attention, it not only observes, sees, listens but also feels with all its organs highly awakened, not dull—has sensitivity; attention implies sensitivity. You cannot be attentive if you are insensitive—insensitive to the squalor, insensitive to your children, to your clothes, to the food you eat, to the manner of your sitting, walking, talking, insensitive to the birds, to the trees, to all the things about you.

If you are insensitive, you cannot possibly give your whole attention. Just listen to all this, do not say, "How am I to become sensitive?" That is a wrong question. You have to know, to be aware, to recognize that you are not sensitive—not find an explanation. The fact is that you are insensitive; otherwise, this poor and unfortunate country would not be in this appalling state, a country ruled by politicians. And this insensitivity will be there only when you are not aware. There must be the recognition of the fact, the seeing of the fact—not the accepting—because the moment you accept something, there is a dual process, there is a contradiction and therefore a conflict.

So, similarly, when you observe, when you see that there is sorrow, when you see the fact that in that sorrow is implied self-pity, the misery of self-pity, the loneliness of self-pity, and the weight of memory that gives rise to sorrow—when you observe all this, see all this, then you will see that you are completely, totally, out of sorrow. Sorrow is, surely, a problem, and if the problem takes root in the mind, the greater is the sorrow. But as the thing is presented to you, if immediately you meet it, if immediately you see it completely with all your being, then the mind becomes entirely different.

A sorrowful mind has no love. It may have sympathy; it may show kindliness, tenderness for others, but it has no love because it is concerned with itself and has the problem of sorrow. It is only when the mind is free from sorrow that there is love. When it is gripped with sorrow, do what it will, there is no love—not the love of God and love of ideas; all that is not love; that is just ideation, that has no meaning at all. Love is not something abstractive. It is that extraordinary vitality, extraordinary energy with extraordinary depth, which comes when you have understood sorrow.

You cannot understand sorrow and the vast immense thing called life if there is no humility. And knowledge prevents humility. A mind that is learning, watching, seeing, never accumulating—such a mind is in a state of humility—not the humility of the saints, not the humility of the politicians, not the humility of the very learned man trying to pretend that he is very humble, but that humility that has never climbed the ladder of success, that humility that has never acquired, that humility that has never strengthened itself in knowledge.

It is only when there is freedom from the known that there is the unknown.

January 31, 1962

Fifth Talk in New Delhi

We have been talking about the necessity of having a new mind, a mind that is capable of meeting all the innumerable problems of life at all levels and also at the depth of one's consciousness. We have been talking of the necessity of a revolution, not an economic or social revolution, but a religious revolution. I would like, if I may, this evening, to talk about the religious mind. But before I go into that, I would like to point out—I think it is relevant—that there must be a denial of thought. We never deny; we are all yes-sayers. We accept according to our tendencies, idiosyncracies. When we do deny, that denial is a reaction and therefore not a denial at all.

I would like to talk a little about denial, for it is important to understand that in order to pursue and find out for oneself what is the religious mind. We never deny. If you have observed yourself sufficiently carefully and seriously, you will see that we have always found an easy path, accepted the easiest solution. We have accepted tradition and various cultural, economic, social influences. We have never stood against them, or if we have stood, we have stood against them by force, not willingly, not comprehendingly. And so our denial is always tinged with fear. It has always come about through a form of acceptance in which there is a hope. It is never a denial of not knowing what is to come; it is a denial with an acceptance of a regulated orderly future.

Please do listen to what I am saying, because when we talk about the religious mind, we are going to deny the whole structure of religion as it is, totally, because it is utterly false, because it has no meaning whatsoever. And to understand what we are going to say a little later, you must, if I may point out, comprehend deeply this act of denial.

You can be forced to deny; circumstances can force you or compel you to say no. All circumstances such as lack of money, environmental influences, some trouble or the other can force you to say no. But to say no with clarity, without any motive, without wanting a reward, or not for fear of punishment; deliberately to say no to something to which you have given your thought completely, uncompromisingly; to say no when you have thought out the problem completely, seriously—that is quite a different matter. To say no seriously means to go into a problem to the very end, not romantically, not emotionally, not according to your particular idiosyncrasy of vanity, of pleasure or desire, but to go to the very end of the thing, putting aside your personal fancies, myths, likes, and dislikes. To go to the very end of a thought, of an idea, of a feeling is to be serious.

I would like this evening to go into this question of religion because I feel that if we could walk out of this tent with a very clear, strong, religious mind, we would solve our problems. Religion is something that includes everything, it is not exclusive. A religious mind has no nationality. It is not provincial; it does not belong to any particular organized group. It is not the result of ten thousand years of propaganda or two thousand years of propaganda. It has no dogma, no belief. It is a mind that moves from fact to fact. It is a mind that understands the total quality of thought—not only the obvious, superficial thought, the educated thought, but also the uneducated thought, the deep-down unconscious thought and motives. When a mind inquires into the totality of something, when it realizes through that inquiry what is false and denies it because it is false, then the totality of that denial brings about a new quality in that mind, which is religious, which is revolutionary. But for most of us religion is not merely the word, the symbol, but it is the result of our conditioning. You are a Hindu because you have been told from your childhood that you are a Hindu with all the superstitions, beliefs, dogmas, traditions of Hinduism, and you have all accepted what you have been told. The same thing applies when you are a Muslim or a Christian or what you will. As the communist accepts in his youth that there is no God, you accept that there is God. There is not much difference between you and the person who denies God; both are the result of a conditioned mind. Please, I am not attacking you; therefore, there is no need to defend yourself; you do not have to resist. We are dealing with facts, and it would be utterly unwise to resist a fact; it has no meaning. The world is in such a chaos that even if you deliberately set about to make the world more chaotic than it is, you could not succeed—in spite of the politicians. And it needs a very sharp, clear, decisive, sane mind to resolve such a chaotic condition. I do not think such a mind can come about except through religious perception.

Please follow the operations of your own mind—not the word, not the speaker, agreeing or disagreeing with the speaker. If you watch your own conditioning—not because I tell you, but because it is a fact—when you look at that fact, when you become aware of that fact, then you can proceed to dissolve that fact, that conditioning. But first you must be aware of the fact that your mind is conditioned. When it says it is a Hindu, it is conditioned; it is shaped by the past, by centuries of culture; it is the result of a historical process and a mythological process. The religions that you have are the result of other people's experiences. Your religion is not your own direct experience; it is what you have been told either in some book or by some teacher or by some philosopher; it is not something which you experience. It is only when your mind is completely unconditioned that you can experience or discover if there is something real or not.

But before you uncondition your mind, to say that you are religious, that you are a Hindu, a Muslim, a Buddhist, or a Christian has no meaning whatsoever. That is pure romanticism, which is exploited by the priest, by an organized group, political or religious, because they have a vested interest in it. These are all facts, whether you like them or not. I am merely describing the fact. These divisions into religious groups, believing in this and that, accepting this dogma and denying that dogma, going from prison to prison, from temple to temple, doing endless puja—all that is not a religious mind at all; it is merely a traditional mind bound by fear. And surely a mind that is afraid can never find out if there is, or if there is not, something beyond the word, beyond the measure of the mind.

Do please listen—not only listen to what the speaker is saying, but also listen to the operations of your own mind. When I use the word *listen,* it is not a command. I use that word listen with a special significance. Listening is an art, because we do never listen. We listen halfheartedly, with our thoughts elsewhere. We listen with condemnation or comparison. We listen with likes and dislikes. We listen either to agree or disagree. We listen by comparing what we hear with what we already know. So there is always distraction; there is never an act of listening. And it would be worthwhile if you could listen without any of these distractions of thought, so that the very act of listening is the breaking down of that condition.

When I use the word *religion,* all kinds of images come to your minds, all kinds of symbols. The Christian has his own symbols, dogmas, and belief. The Hindu, the Muslim, all the people who call themselves religious—they have a peculiar approach, an idiosyncratic approach, a traditional approach; so they can never think clearly about the matter. They are first Hindus or Muslims, and then they begin to seek. So to find out if there is, or if there is not, something which is beyond thought, which is not measurable by the mind, the mind must first be free. Surely that is logic. You see, another peculiarity with religious people is that they are totally illogical. Psychologically they have no sanity. They accept without inquiry, and their inquiry is motivated by fear, by the desire for security which prevents their thought; they become romantic because it pleases them. They become devotional—it gives them a sense of joy, happiness. But that is not a religious mind at all; it is a fanciful mind; it has no reality.

If you observe your own mind, you will see how cluttered up and burdened it is with belief, and you think that belief is necessary. You use belief as a hypothesis—which is sheer nonsense. When a man is inquiring, he does not start out with a hypothesis, he has a free mind. He is not attached to any dogma and he is not bound by any fear. He starts out denying all that and then begins to seek. But you never deny for various reasons. You never deny because it would not be respectable in a respectable society—though that society is really rotten. You never deny because you might lose your job or position. You never deny because of your family; you have to marry off your daughter, your son, to do this and that. Therefore, you are bound consciously or unconsciously, through fear, to the dogma, to the tradition in which you have been brought up. Again this is a fact; this is not my fancy. This is a psychological, everyday fact.

So a mind which is bound to a belief, to a dogma, however ancient or however modern, like the communist—such a mind is incapable of bringing about an orderly world, a sane world. Such a mind is incapable of being free from sorrow, from conflict. Surely it is only the mind that is free from conflict, free from problems, free from sorrow that can find out. And you must find out because that is the only way out of this misery, this confusion that we have created in this world—the way out is not by joining innumerable groups, or by going back to the old tradition which is dead, or by following a new leader. I do not know if you have not observed that when you follow somebody, you have destroyed your own thought, you have lost your own independence, you have lost your freedom—not only politically but, much more, psychologically, not only outwardly but, much more, inwardly.

So where there is a following and where there is a leader in matters that are really spiritual, really psychological, there is bound to be confusion, because in that there is a psychological contradiction between your own deep-down urges and compulsions and the imposition upon them by the leader, by what you think you should do; and that contradiction leads to conflict; and where there is conflict, there is effort; and where there is effort, there is distortion. The religious mind has no conflict. The religious mind does not follow anyone.

The religious mind has no authority. Authority implies imitation, authority implies conformity. And there is conformity because you want success; you want to achieve, and therefore there is fear. Without dissolving fear completely, how can you proceed to inquire, how can you proceed to find out? These are not rhetorical questions. If I am frightened, I am bound to seek comfort, shelter, security in whatever form comes along, because fear dictates—not sanity, not clarity. Fear dictates conformity; fear dictates that I must imitate, that I must follow somebody in the hope I shall find comfort. The religious mind has no authority of any kind, and that is very difficult for people to accept because we have been bred in authority. The Gita, the Upanishads, the Bible, the Koran, and all the innumerable so-called sacred books have taken the place of our own thinking, of our own suffering; they give us comfort in illusion; they are not real at all. You make them into reality because in them, in the dead words of others, you find comfort; in the authority of another you find light. How absurd it is really if you examine it, and yet you are so-called educated, sane, rational people!

Where religious matters are concerned, we become totally irrational, insane; and all these build the walls of our conditioning. Again this is a fact, a psychological, undeniable fact. You are going to the temple; you are reading the Gita and muttering a lot of words which have lost their meaning. That is not a religious mind at all. Such reading, such repetition, makes the mind dull, insensitive. There is a contradiction between daily living and what you think is real. There is no living a religious life. You have divorced life from religion; you have divorced ethics from religion. And a mind that lives in this duality, in this contradiction, in this cleavage—such a mind is creating the world at the present time; it is bringing into the world more and more chaos. We see all this. Where there is confusion, where there is misery, people turn to authority, to tyranny—not only politically, but also religiously. Gurus, teachers, ideas, beliefs, dogmas multiply and flourish because we have never looked into ourselves deeply to find out for ourselves what is true.

The beginning of the religious mind is self-knowledge—not the knowledge of the supreme self; that is sheer nonsense. How can a petty mind, a narrow mind, a nationalistic mind, a mind that is begotten through fear, through compulsion, through imitation, through authority—how can that petty, shallow mind try to find out what is the supreme self? To seek the supreme self is an escape; it is pure unadulterated romanticism. The fact is: You have to understand yourself first. How can a thought which is the result of fear inquire? How can a thought which is the result of contradiction, of sorrow, of pain, of ambition, of envy—how can that thought search out the unsearchable? Obviously, it cannot, but that is what we are doing all the time.

So, beginning to understand yourself as you are is the beginning of wisdom, and also the beginning of meditation is to see without distortion the fact of what you are, not what you think you should be. When you think, as most of you do, that you are the supreme self, that there is a spiritual entity in you, all that idea is the result of your past conditioning. You have to be aware of that fact and not accept that you are the supreme self. The idea has no meaning. What has meaning and significance is the fact of what you are every day, not what you should be. Again the idea, the ideation, the ideal is a piece of mythology; it has no significance. The fact has significance. The fact that you are envious has significance, but not the idea that you should be in a state of nonenvy.

Another peculiarity of the religious mind is that it is rid of ideas, rid of ideals. You are all idealists—that is, you are concerned with what you should be, not with what you are. But the religious mind is concerned with the fact and moves with the fact. The scientist is concerned with the fact. He is investigating matter, investigating life as matter in his laboratory. He is investigating it under the microscope. He has no fear; he moves from fact to fact, and he builds up knowledge; and that knowledge helps him to investigate further, only along a particular, narrow, restricted line which is science. But we are concerned with the totality of life, not with science only; not only with buildings, but with anger, with ambition, with quarrels, with what we are—the totality of life. Science does not include the totality of life, but a religious mind does.

When the economists or the sociologists try to solve human problems, they are dealing only partially and therefore bringing about more chaos, more misery. But the religious mind is not concerned with the partial. It is concerned with the total development of man; it is concerned with the total entity of man—that is, the outward movement of life is the same as the inward movement. The outward movement is like the ebb, the tide that goes out; and the inward movement is like the flow, the same tide that then comes in. If the two—the outer and the inner are divorced, if the two are separated, then you have conflict, you have misery.

The so-called religious people have divided this life into the outer and the inner. They do not regard it as one unitary process. They avoid the outer by retreating to a monastery or by putting on a sannyasi's robe. They deny the outer world, but they do not deny the world of tradition, of their knowledge, of their conditioning. They separate the two, and therefore there is a contradiction. But the religious mind does not separate the two. For the religious mind the outward movement of life and the inward movement of life form one unitary movement, like the movement of the tide that goes out and then comes in.

Do please listen to all this, neither accepting nor denying. I am not attacking you, so you do not have to take refuge or resist. Nor am I doing propaganda. I am just pointing out. If you can, you may accept it. You can see it or reject it, but first, intellectually or verbally even, look at it. You may not want to go the whole way completely, totally, to the very end. But at least you can look at it verbally, intellectually, and find out; and out of that intellectual comprehension, which is not full comprehension at all, you will perhaps see the whole significance.

Knowing yourself is the beginning of meditation. Knowing yourself psychologically as you are is the beginning of the religious mind. But you cannot know yourself if you deny what you see, if you try to interpret what you see. Please follow this. If you deny psychologically what you see in yourself, or if you want to change it into something else, then you are not understanding the fact of *what is*. If you are vain, and if you try to change it and cultivate humility, then there is a contradiction. If you are vain, and if you try to cultivate the ideal of humility, there is a contradiction between the two; and that contradiction dulls the mind, it brings about a conflict. You have to look at the fact that you are vain; you have to see that fact completely and not introduce a contradictory ideal. But to see that you are vain, you cannot say, "I must not be vain." Obviously that is fairly simple because to see something, you must give your attention totally to it. When you say that you must not be vain, your mind has gone away from the fact, and the going away from the fact creates a problem—not the fact; the fact never creates the problem. It is only the avoidance of the fact, the running away from the fact, trying to change the fact, trying to make it conform or approximate to the ideal, that creates a problem—never the fact of *what is*.

So, when you observe yourself very clearly, when you are aware choicelessly of every thought, of every feeling, then you will come upon something—which is that there is a thinker and there is the thought; that there is an experiencer, an observer, and there is the experience, the observed. This is a fact, is it not?—there is a censor, an entity which judges, evaluates, which thinks, which observes; and there is the thing which is observed.

Please search your own minds; you are not to listen to my words. Words have no meaning. Watch your own mind in operation as I am talking. Then you will go away from here with clarity, with a mind that is clear, sharp, and sane.

So there is a thinker, and there is the thought. There is a division between the thinker and the thought—the thinker trying to dominate the thought, trying to change the thought, trying to modify the thought, trying to control it, trying to force it, trying to imitate, and so on. This division between the thinker and the thought creates conflict because the thinker is always the censor, the entity that judges, that evaluates. That entity is a conditioned entity because it has arisen as a reaction to thought, which is itself merely the reaction of conditioning, of memory. You understand, sirs? That is a very simple thing to find out for yourself.

Thought is the reaction of memory. I ask you something, and you respond according to your memory. The interval between the question and the answer is time, and during that time you think it out and then you reply. If you are familiar with the answer, your answer is immediate; and if the question is very complicated, you need a longer time, a lag, a greater distance between the answer and the question. During that lag, your memory is responding, is reacting, and then you answer. So thought is the response of memory, of association with the past. So there is the thinker and there is thought; the thinker is conditioned, and his thought also becomes conditioned. When there is a gap between the thinker and the thought, there is a contradiction; and as long as there is a division between the thinker and the thought, there is endless conflict and misery. Is it possible to remove this contradiction, this conflict—which means there is no thinker as the central entity which is acting, but there is only thinking? This is a very complex question. You have to find out for yourself the whole implication of this problem.

One can see the implication that where there is division between the thinker and the thought, there must be contradiction. And contradiction implies conflict, and conflict dulls the mind, makes the mind stupid, insensitive. Conflict of any kind, whether it is a conflict between your wife and yourself, between you and society, between you and your boss, between you and anybody—every kind of conflict dulls the mind. If one would understand the central conflict, one must inquire into this question—not accept it—whether there is a thinker first and thought afterwards. If you say that it is so, you again resort to your tradition, to your conditioning. You have to find out through your thought how your memory responds. As long as that memory, which is conditioned by every movement of thought, by every influence, responds, there must be conflict and misery.

If you go very deeply into it, you will find out for yourself that action based on an idea, which is thought, breeds discord because you are approximating what action should be according to the idea. So you will find if you have gone deeply into yourself that action is not idea. There is action without motive. And it is only the religious mind that has gone very deeply into itself, that has inquired profoundly within itself, that can act without an idea, without motive, because it has no center, no entity as the thinker who is directing action. Such an action is not a chaotic action.

So self-knowledge, or the learning about yourself every day, brings about psychologically, inwardly, a new mind—because you have denied the old mind. Through self-knowledge you have denied your conditioning totally. The conditioning of the mind can be denied totally only when the mind is aware of its own operations—how it works, what it thinks, what it says, what are the motives.

There is another factor involved in this. We think that it is a gradual process, that it will take time, to free the mind from conditioning. Please, follow this. We think that it will take many days or many years to uncondition our conditioned mind—which means that we will do it gradually, day after day. What does that imply? Surely, it implies acquiring knowledge in order to dissipate this conditioning—which means that you are not learning but acquiring. A mind that is acquiring is never learning. But the mind that uses knowledge in order to arrive, in order to succeed, in order to achieve a sense of liberation—such a mind must have time. Such a mind says, "I must have time to free myself from my conditioning"—which means it is going to acquire knowledge, and as the knowledge expands, it will become freer and freer; this is utterly false.

Through time, through the multiplication of many tomorrows, there is no liberation. There is freedom only in the denial of the thing which is seen immediately. You react immediately when you see a poisonous snake—there is no thought, there is immediate action. That action is the result of fear and of the knowledge that you have acquired about the snake. That demands time. So, there is the quality of seeing through knowledge, which demands time. There is also a quality of seeing something which does not demand time. I am talking of the mind that sees without time, that sees without thought, because the mind is the result of many yesterdays; the mind is the result of time. Again this is a fact. We are dealing not with a supposition, not with a theory. Your mind is the result of many yesterdays; your mind is the result of the past. And without being free of the past totally, it is not possible to have a new mind, a religious mind. Now to see that past totally, completely, to see it immediately, is to break down the past immediately.

But you cannot break down the past immediately if your mind is in the grip of knowledge which says, "I will gradually accumulate knowledge and eventually break the conditioning." The mind must see the conditioning immediately. For instance, if you see the absurdity of nationalism, the poison of nationalism, if you see it, if you comprehend it completely—which you can do if you give your attention to it completely—then the moment you comprehend it, you are free of nationalism; nationalism will never touch you again. But you do not see the poisonous nature of nationalism because it is very popular, because you feel you are united around a flag—which is absurd. You feel a sense of unity, a sense of being together, about nothing; a flag is merely an idea, a symbol which has no reality, which the politicians and others exploit. But when you see that fact—you can see it if you can give your whole attention and not justify it, saying that you will lose your job, and all the rest of it—when you give your whole attention to that fact of nationalism, it will go away, and it will never touch you again. But that requires attention. Attention is the total denial of the past, the total denial of this division between the thinker and the thought.

So a religious mind is a mind that has no belief, that has no dogma, that has no fear, that has absolutely no authority of any kind. It is a light to itself. Such a mind, being free, can go very far. But that freedom must begin very close, very near; it is the freedom is in yourself, in the understanding of yourself—and then you can go very far. Then you will find out for yourself that extraordinary stillness of the mind—it is not an idea but an actual fact. A mind that is completely still without any distraction, a still mind, but not the romantic mind, a mind that is not begotten through conflict or through contradiction or through misery—it is only such a mind that is completely quiet and therefore completely alive, totally sensitive; it is only such a mind that can receive that which is immeasurable.

February 4, 1962

Sixth Talk in New Delhi

I would like this evening, if I may, to go into the question of meditation, because I feel that without understanding and knowing the full implication of meditation, the religious mind about which we have been talking is not possible. As we said the other day, the religious mind contains the scientific spirit, but the scientific mind does not include the religious spirit. The scientific mind is partial; it is concerned with the superficial, but the religious mind is concerned with the totality of life. Without understanding and knowing the deep implication of meditation, it is not at all possible to have that quality of mind which can go above and beyond time. But before I go into that, I think it is important to understand the nature of mediocrity.

Mediocrity is of the petty mind, of the narrow, limited mind. The petty mind may be, and is, generally concerned with the immediate; and the immediate may be projected into the future, but it is still the immediate. The politicians, though they may be concerned about the future, are concerned with the immediate in relation to the future. Most of us are also concerned with the immediate—the short view instead of the long view—and all our life is hedged about with immediate concerns. Not that the immediate is not important, but if the immediate becomes all-important and the long view has been totally forgotten, then the immediate concern of bread and butter—the way to live, the job, the husband and wife, the petty thoughts, the shallow attempts—this limited, narrow, short view with which most people are concerned, does lead to misery, does lead to sorrow and to strife. And this mediocrity of the petty mind invariably commits itself to some course of action, to some form of belief, to some dogma. It is the nature of the petty mind to belong to something. It is the nature of this mediocrity, which is rampant in the world at the present time, to be concerned out of proportion with society.

And if I may point out, as I have done throughout all these talks, we are not discussing ideas, we are not verbalizing, we are not indulging in theory. We are dealing with actual facts, and the understanding of the facts is the only problem. As we said the other day, any escape or running away from the facts creates the problem. When we talk about mediocrity and the shallow mind, we are not discussing it as an idea—something to be broken down and to be replaced by a very clever mind that is extraordinarily active and has immense width and depth. We are just showing that a mediocre mind is the soil in which sorrow grows; and as most of us are in sorrow of some kind or another, without breaking down the walls of pettiness, sorrow will invariably continue.

As we have pointed out before, listening is an art—to listen not only to what is being said but also to everything in life, to the birds, to the incessant chatter of children, to the sound of a flute in the early morning; to listen without interpretation, without comparison, without condemnation; just to listen. In that listening you will discover for yourself, if you do so listen attentively, how your mind is working; though the speaker is describing, you are observing the actual state of your mind, of your own thought and feeling.

We are not indulging in ideas, in ideation and ideals. A man who is concerned with facts has no ideals, and we are concerned with facts. The fact is that there is mediocrity, pettiness—not that someone else is petty, but each one of us is petty. So one has to be aware of it oneself, apply it to oneself. The highest form of criticism is self-criticism, but we do not criticize; we merely see and avoid. The critical capacity is to be aware of the total implication. As we are talking about mediocrity, pettiness, shallowness, please be aware of it in yourself. Merely to be verbally aware of it is of no value at all. Verbally being aware of mediocrity does not bring about a change in the mediocre mind.

The petty mind commits itself to some course of action—social action, economic action, political action, so-called religious action, or the acquisition of knowledge. The petty mind is always committing itself; it is always belonging to something—and the desire to belong is a psychological phenomenon of an intellectual mind. It belongs to the communist party and then denies it later; it belongs to some kind of dogmatic religious activity which, later, it denies. You will observe, if you have taken note of it in the world, that the so-called intellectual people subscribe, either in groups or singly, to some form of theory, to some form of utopia, to some committed religiosity. The desire to belong is the desire for permanency.

Please follow all this, because we are inquiring into the process of meditation, and this is part of that meditation. You all belong to something. You are not an entity alone, but integrated. You are put together by society, by the environmental influences which compel you to belong. If one is anxious to bring about a change in the world, one belongs to something. All of us do belong to various forms of beliefs, dogmas, and activities because in belonging we not only explain ourselves, but by identifying ourselves with the thing to which we are committed, we feel—intellectually, physically, emotionally—acting as a total entity in a world that is disintegrating. Without understanding the urge to commit oneself to a particular course of action—whatever it be, a particular thought, a particular idea, a particular aspect of technological knowledge, or to belong to something—is surely an indication of pettiness.

A petty mind then proceeds to inquire into the immensity of life. Having committed itself to something, it proceeds to inquire from that commitment into what it is all about. Now, we have to find out what is meditation, which is really a most marvelous thing, which has nothing to do with romanticism, ideation, speculation, seeing visions, or having all kinds of sensations—which are utterly immature. So, this urge to belong, to commit oneself to a method, to a system, must be understood.

Most of us, if you will permit me to say so without any disrespect, are mediocre; even the most talented are mediocre because their talent is partial, limited, narrow. A gift does not lift you out of mediocrity. A painter may paint the most beautiful pictures, but he is still a mediocre person when he hungers after fame, recognition by society. He wants to be rich, known, famous—which all indicate a petty, shallow, mediocre mind though gifted with a talent. Most of us, unfortunately, have neither great talents nor great capacity of thought. Perhaps it is just as well, because when we are eager to find out, to search out, to inquire, the man who has committed himself to something refuses to inquire into anything except to proceed along the lines he has chosen.

So, to find out what is the meditative mind, there must be no commitment—which is quite a difficult thing because you may be committed either to prayer, to a repetition of words, or to contemplate upon something, or because you may be committed to a symbol. Most of us are committed to symbols—not to reality because reality is much too dangerous, much too destructive. The petty mind cannot contain reality; therefore, it seeks symbols and has committed itself to symbols—the symbol of the church, of Christianity; the symbol of the Hindu; the symbol of the Muslim, and so on. The petty mind has committed itself to the symbol, the word, the shadow, the unreal—not to the fact but to the image, graven by the mind or by the hand, in the temple or in the mosque or in the church. Please observe this for yourself, see it yourself. Being committed, then you proceed to meditate; and then you want to seek methods, systems, to arrive at what you think is the permanent, what you think is God, what you think is a most extraordinary vision. What you think is conditioned by your past, by the society in which you live. Of course, if you are a Christian, you have extraordinary visions of the Christ, and you project those visions. If you are a Hindu, you have your own images, your own visions. When you get a vision, an image, projected, that gives you a certain sensation, and you call that meditation. If you examine this, you will find it is utterly immature because it is your own desire seeking fulfillment in an unreality which has no basis except your own thought; it is conditioned by the past, by the society in which you live, by the experience which you have gathered through that condition.

So meditation is not seeking visions or indulging in prayer. Prayer implies supplication, begging, asking, demanding. When do you demand? When do you seek? When do you search out? You do all this when you are in trouble, when you are in pain, when you are in misery, when you are in conflict. That means you want comfort—not the comfort which you get at home—you want psychological comfort. So you pray, and unfortunately, psychologically the prayer is answered, because you do find comfort. That comfort is awakened, has formed itself, in an idea which you have projected, in an idea or in a belief or in a dogma in which you take shelter, comfort. It is like a person taking shelter in a storm—in a shelter made up of words, ideas. By sticking to that, by holding on to that, by having committed himself to that, he hopes to find shelter; but that shelter is merely in words, not in reality, not in something that has substance. And with that most of us are satisfied.

So, meditation is not prayer, nor the desire to find truth. A petty mind seeking God will find a god of its own pettiness. Do you understand, sirs? If I have a petty mind, a small, narrow, shallow mind full of ambition, greed, envy, jealousy of another, and I think about God, my god is equally petty, stupid; and with that stupidity we are satisfied.

Now, we are inquiring into the process of meditation. To inquire you must first deny, you must negatively approach it—that is, you must be aware of something which has no reality except a projected reality of one's own desire, one's own fancy; you must put away what is false. So, through negative thinking we are going to find out what is the positive. But negative thinking is essential because that is the highest form of thinking—not positive thinking. Positive thinking is an imitative process, moving from the known to the known. We will never find the unknown if we merely proceed from the known to the known, which is the so-called positive process. That way, you will never find out for yourself what is real meditation. The things that have been put forward as meditation are so utterly immature and have no psychological basis at all. So, if you are serious enough, if you want to go into the question of meditation right to the end—not just play with it—you must meditate as you go to the office, as you breed families, as you beget children. There must be meditation because it breaks down the wall of pettiness, it breaks down the wall of respectability and imitation. An absolutely free mind is necessary right at the beginning, not at the end.

So, negatively we are thinking out what is meditation. Meditation is not contemplation—to contemplate is to think about an idea, to contemplate upon something, generally on a symbol or on a phrase which one has read in the so-called sacred books—which are not sacred at all but are just books like any others. You pick a phrase and you think about it, and that you call contemplation. You do not inquire into the entity that contemplates. That entity is conditioned; that entity is petty, narrow, jealous. And that entity inquires, contemplates upon something!

So meditation is not prayer. Meditation is not contemplation. Meditation is not the pursuit of a particular method or system. The method or the system conditions the mind. And what the method or system offers, you will get, but what you get will be a dead thing. It is like having a dull, stupid mind that is disciplined through a system and refuses to think any more; it has lost all pliability, all sensitivity; it is no longer fresh. So, meditation is not a system to be practiced. Meditation is not a process of disciplining the mind. Please follow all this intellectually if you cannot do it actually. If you do it actually, then you can go very far. I am going to go very far into it this evening with those who have the capacity to travel light, far, freely.

So, meditation is none of these things, nor is it discipline. What does discipline imply?

Discipline implies conformity, imitation, adjustment to a pattern, to an idea, to an ideal; and therefore control, which implies suppression—this does not mean that you indulge in what you want to do. You are going into the entire machinery of discipline. Where there is suppression, there is contradiction; where there is contradiction, there is conflict and effort. A mind that makes an effort to achieve, except in mechanical things—to achieve what it calls God, to achieve a purpose, an end—is a dead mind. For meditation you want an extraordinarily pliable mind, a highly sensitive mind. And you cannot be sensitive if you are committed, if you are caught in a system invented by man through his fear.

Meditation then is none of these things. But you must lay a foundation for meditation. As meditation is none of these things, it is too immature even to think about the obviously psychological tricks that we have played upon ourselves through the centuries. You must lay the right foundation. The right foundation for meditation is not to be ambitious, not to have envy, not to accept any form of authority. The laying of the foundation is of the highest importance because without that, you cannot build. A house cannot be built without a foundation; it topples over. To be without ambition, without authority, without envy, without fear, jealousy, and all that, must be a thing that must be seen immediately, and not cultivated as an ideal—this is where the difficulty lies.

The importance of laying the foundation for meditation has to be seen immediately. If you say, "I will lay the foundation," you introduce the factor of time. Just taking one brick for laying the foundation—envy—you may say, "I will not be envious," because intellectually you have seen that it is not profitable and that it involves strain, struggle, pain. But mere intellectual acceptance does not absolve you from envy, nor your saying, "I will use an ideal in order to get rid of envy; that is to say, I will not be envious," because that "I will not" implies time. When you say, "I shall not be envious," you have introduced the factor of time—that is, you think it will take you time to get rid of envy, and you say that in a few years, or sometime later, you will get rid of envy. And when you introduce time, the continuity of envy goes on; you do not get rid of it; you are still envious when you say, "Envy should not be." Please understand this. Envy has to be cut immediately, and it can be cut immediately only when you "see" the thing, when you "see" envy.

As I said, we do not "see," nor do we listen. We never see because we have opinions about what we see. When you are envious and when you consider envy, you justify it because the whole structure of society is based on envy, and you are educated to be envious; and you say, "How am I to live in this world without envy?" So you approach the fact, which is envy, by having an opinion about it already. The word *envy* is already condemnatory, and so you approach it with condemnation. So, to see envy, you have to be free of the word.

What I am talking about is not complicated; it is very simple. It is really extraordinarily simple if you listen, if you try even intellectually to listen. The word is not the thing. The word is the symbol. We are brought up in symbols and not brought up in actualities, not brought up with what is the fact. Envy is not a thing to be postponed. Either you are envious or you are not envious. A man who wants to meditate, who wants to go into this question of meditation very profoundly, has no time to postpone envy. Envy has to cease completely, totally. So also ambition has to cease totally because a man who is ambitious has no love. Those people who out of ambition seek position, prestige, and power, have no love, though they may talk about peace, about brotherhood. They may have sympathy, pity, organizing capacity for social action, but they have no love.

A mind which is envious, which is comparing, which is wanting, seeking power, position, authority has no love. One may read about love in the Gita, in the Upanishads, and in other books, but love does not come through books. Love comes only when you are no longer envious, when you are no longer ambitious, when you are no longer seeking power, when you are no longer a slave to the morality of society. The morality of society is concerned only with one thing—which is success. Society is not concerned with greed, ambition, envy, nor with following this or that.

To meditate you must lay the foundation, not during the days to come, but immediately. This is very difficult—that is the real crux of this matter—because we want to be ambitious, we want to be envious, and we also talk about God, truth, and all the rest of it. Your gods or your truths have no value as long as there is no foundation. When you are no longer caught in the machinery of society and its morality—which means when your mind is free from ambition, greed, envy, power, and all the things that man seeks and which society has encouraged from your childhood—then there is freedom; not tomorrow, not at the end of your life, but right at the beginning, now.

That is the beginning of meditation. That implies self-knowing, not knowing the supreme self. There is no supreme self for a petty mind, except the thing which it has invented and which it calls the supreme self. So when the mind is free—not tomorrow, but actually immediately, on the instant—of envy, greed, acquisitiveness, of the search for fame and power, then you begin to meditate. For such a mind seeking stops. When you say you are seeking, what are you seeking? You are seeking something you already know; otherwise, you won't seek. You cannot seek something you do not know; you can seek something which is recognizable, and recognition is of the past. Recognition is part and parcel of knowledge—that is, of the known. So when you deny totally ambition, greed, envy, authority, through self-knowing, you have become a light to yourself; then the mind, being free and uncommitted, is not seeking because it has nothing to seek, it is still.

How can a petty mind seek the immense? It can only translate the immense in terms of its own shallow pettiness. Therefore the mind must be completely free of all these. When the mind is completely free of all these, then the mind becomes quiet; it has not to seek peace of mind—which is an absurdity; it is like people talking about corruption but keeping their hands in another man's pockets. There must be complete dissociation from society. This does not mean that you leave society, go to a forest, or become a hermit—that is merely a change of clothes, a change of habitation. You must completely dissociate yourself from society so that you become alone; your mind then is uninfluenced by society.

When your mind is uninfluenced by society, it is capable of standing completely alone. Then you proceed to meditation. You will then notice that the brain—which is the result of time; which is the result of all animal instincts, biological instincts; which is the result of the accumulated knowledge of society, of the nation, the race, the group, the family—becomes extraordinarily quiet because it is no longer seeking. The brain is no longer frightened; it is no longer pursuing an idea; it is no longer craving for comfort, for security, for permanency. Therefore, the brain becomes extraordinarily quiet, and it must be quiet because any movement of the brain which is compelled by the past, if it projects, creates illusion. Therefore the brain is completely still.

The stillness of the brain is not acquired. You cannot acquire stillness; you cannot practice stillness, because a brain that practices stillness is a dead brain. How can you force the brain which is extraordinarily active—and it must be sensitive—to become quiet? You can destroy it—and you do destroy it—by denying the world and escaping to some form of other world, by destroying beauty and thinking that God is something else. A sensitive mind cannot be destroyed; it must be sensitive. If you understand the whole significance of discipline, then there is an extraordinary discipline which is the outcome of freedom, which is not controlled. When you practice a discipline, the discipline that you practice is out of fear of punishment, or for reward, or for gaining something which you want. Such a discipline makes the brain dull, insensitive.

Life does not belong to the hermit or to the sannyasi or to the politician, or even to the saintly politician. Life is something extraordinarily vast, immense, immeasurable. A petty mind cannot possibly understand it. A petty mind is essentially an ambitious mind, a greedy mind, an acquisitive mind. And the moment you cease to be ambitious in every form—even the ambition to find out God—the moment you have broken off from ambition, your brain becomes astonishingly quiet. The brain then is quiet without any movement of desire because desire has been understood. When you have understood the imaginary visions, belonging to this and that, when all that has been set aside, forgotten, then you are no longer caught by the known. Most of us move from the known to the known; that is our daily activity. All your life is spent in the office or in some technical work, from the known to the known. Your mind thinks in terms of the known and therefore is never free from the known.

A meditative mind is free from the known—that means free from the word, the symbol, the idea, the belief, the dogma, the projections from the past. When the brain is free from the past, or rather when the brain is quiet, the totality of the whole consciousness becomes completely still—the totality of consciousness, not just one part—because it is completely alone, uninfluenced. It no longer belongs to any society, any group, any caste, any religion, any dogma; it has finished with all these. Therefore there is complete stillness of the mind, and in that stillness there is neither the observer nor the observed—because the observer, as I explained, is the result of the reaction of thought; the observer, the thinker, is the reaction of thought. You can yourself think all this out if you are interested, afterwards.

So there is no state of experiencing—which is very important to understand. Experience—I will put it very quickly and briefly—is that state when there is response to a challenge. Every response to a challenge produces an experience, and that experience is the result of your conditioning. If you are a Hindu, with your background you respond to a challenge, even to the smallest challenge. Even to a petty challenge of every day you respond from the background of your Hinduism, of your conditioning, and that reaction is experience. So a mind that is experiencing is reacting, and therefore it is never a free mind.

A still mind is not seeking experience of any kind. And if it is not seeking and therefore is completely still, without any movement from the past and therefore free from the known, then you will find, if you have gone that far, that there is a movement of the unknown which is not recognized, which is not translatable, which cannot be put into words—then you will find that there is a movement which is of the immense. That movement is of the timeless because in that there is no time, nor is there space, nor something in which to experience, nor something to gain, to achieve. Such a mind knows what is creation—not the creation of the painter, the poet, the verbalizer, but that creation which has no motive, which has no expression. That creation is love and death.

This whole thing from the beginning to the end is the way of meditation. A man who would meditate must understand himself. Without knowing yourself, you cannot go far. However much you may attempt to go far, you can go only so far as your own projection; and your own projection is very near, is very close, and does not lead you anywhere. Meditation is that process of laying the foundation instantly, immediately, and bringing about—naturally, without any effort—that state of stillness. And only then is there a mind which is beyond time, beyond experience, and beyond knowing.

February 7, 1962

Seventh Talk in New Delhi

If I may, I am going to talk about death this evening; but before we go into that immense question, I think we ought to understand the capacity to investigate, the capacity to inquire, to find out, because that is very important in the understanding of this whole question of what is death. If we have that capacity to inquire, to investigate, to ask, to find out, then we shall be free from fear. Without freedom from fear of every kind, outward as well as inward, without the understanding of the outward fears as well as of psychological fears, we shall never be able to understand the immense question of death.

What is this capacity to investigate? How does it come about? What are the necessary requirements, if I may use that word, so as to have that directive, understanding capacity that will open the door to find out? First of all, it seems to me, there must be no motive in inquiring. The search must not be motivated by any personal idiosyncrasy or for any utilitarian purposes, or colored by a peculiar desire for safety. Those are absolutely essential for all inquiry, whether it is a scientific inquiry or a psychological inquiry.

We are this evening going to investigate psychologically into the whole question of death, and to do that the mind must be free of motive. It is one of the most psychologically difficult things to be free of motive—a purpose, an end, which is sought unconsciously or consciously. If one wishes to be free from the agony that fear causes with regard to death, one must surely be free of motive—a motive being not only the cause but also the search for an end. To overcome fear, one must find out what is the cause of fear, and also of the desire to be free of it, which will prevent investigation.

I do hope that you will listen so as to investigate into your own mind, into your own heart, and not merely verbally accept or deny or bring an argument to refute—because this will be of no avail; at the end you will be nowhere, and fear will continue. Is it possible to be totally free of fear—psychologically inwardly—and to investigate into that question not intellectually, not verbally, but actually? To walk out of this tent without fear would be a marvelous thing; then you would be free of society and the agony of relationship which is society; then you would not be caught in the neck by the innumerable conflicts, problems, anxieties, griefs that exist in the mind and heart of every human being.

And to investigate into this question, as I said, the mind must be entirely free from motive. Can it be free, and does it take time? If you see the necessity of being absolutely free from fear, then that very perception eliminates the motive—because your intention, your urge, your insistence is to be free from fear; and you see that the investigation into the question of fear is prevented if there is a motive. Therefore, when you understand the necessity of being free from fear, the motive disappears. This is a psychological fact: Where there is something of greater importance, the less important ceases—as in everything else.

So, in inquiring into this question of fear, we must understand first of all what it means and what is implied in the process of investigation, not of fear yet, but of the mind that is capable of inquiring into fear. We are only concerned for the moment with the capacity to inquire—not the capacity to inquire into death, into love, into beauty, into ambition, or into any of those things in particular. The capacity to inquire is denied if the mind is seeking to get rid of the problem. Most of us are concerned to be free of fear, and therefore we avoid it; and the moment the mind seeks avoidance, you stop investigating. So, in investigation there must be no escape. And it is extremely difficult not to escape. One has to be aware of the implication of motive and also of escape because if one desires to escape, to avoid, to run away, then the whole process of investigation completely ceases. And there is no investigation if you bring in your personal opinion or your particular idiosyncrasy or the things that you have learned. As I was saying, investigation into any problem, especially a psychological problem, ceases if you bring in your personal opinion, or the knowledge that you have acquired from others, or if you project your own experiences based on your own conditioning.

So, please see all the implications and the difficulties involved in investigation. As we are talking of very serious matters and of things that are very urgent, you have to pay attention. Attention has no distraction because it is a part of the process of investigation—and opinion, judgment, or evaluation, is a distraction which prevents investigation. We are going to investigate into the whole question of fear. So, your mind must be prepared for investigation; mere acceptance or denial of what is being said or not said is of no value.

You are concerned with living—everyday living, with all the misery, the anxiety, the sorrow, the pain, the passing joy. When you are concerned with all that, the mere acceptance of verbal explanations, or the mere assertion of some knowledge that you have acquired from some book, does not solve your problems. The problems are solved only through investigation, through a complete understanding of the problems. This problem of fear is an extraordinarily urgent problem. There is the fear of death. It does not matter whether it is for the old or for the young, because death faces everyone of us, the young and the aged. And to understand, to investigate, to go into this whole problem of what it is to die requires a mind that is capable of investigating.

Investigation, as I pointed out, is impeded, is denied, when there is a motive. When there is a search for an end, when you project into your investigation a personal opinion or knowledge that you have acquired, all investigation ceases. So, when you are investigating, you must be aware of these facts—the motives, the urge to seek an end and to escape, and the subtle forms of opinions, evaluations, and judgments.

If that is very clear for each listener, we can proceed into the investigation of fear. What is fear? What is it that fears, and how does fear arise? Fear distorts perception, distorts clarity. A mind that is afraid lives always in illusion, whether it is the illusion of God or the illusion of adjusting oneself to society, or the illusion of trying to make oneself perfect. As long as there is any form of psychological fear at any level, conscious or unconscious, there must be distortion of thought, distortion of perception. Therefore it is very important for sanity, for sensitive living, that the mind should not only understand the whole process of fear but also find out if it is possible to live without fear.

The essence of fear is nonexistence because we all want to live, we all want to continue in some form or another even though our life is miserable, petty, narrow, shortsighted, and not rich, not full. However shallow it is, we want to live, we want to express ourselves, we want to be in relationship with something. And this desire to be in relationship with another, with nature, with ideas, is the very essence of the desire to live, to love, and to be loved, to express and to fulfill, with all its anxieties, frustrations. Fear surely exists only in relationship to something; fear does not exist in abstraction, by itself. Fear exists in the desire to continue, and to search out, to find, to establish a permanency.

Please, as I have said, you are listening not to me, nor to my words nor to certain ideas; but you are listening to, you are observing, your own mind and your own heart. You are watching your own processes in your own life. The words are merely a mirror, but the mirror is not the life. The mirror shows what is in your heart, in your mind; but if you merely listen to words, accepting or denying those words, then you are not watching your own mind and heart. All these talks are not meant to add more ideas and ideations, but rather to point out to you the operation, the working of your own mind and heart. So, please, if I may point out, observe your own mind.

And also, as I have said often, listening is an art. If you know how to listen rightly, there is an immediate perception and understanding—to listen to something totally with all your being, that is, with all your senses, with your heart, with your mind, with your body, completely. Then you will see that in that very act of listening, the thing of which you are afraid, the thing that causes fear has completely gone away. But you do not listen; you never do listen because you are tired; you have your own problems, and when you do hear, you compare what is being said with what you already know.

So, your mind is never quiet to listen; it is always agitated in listening. And a mind that is agitated can neither understand nor listen. And this is a problem of understanding immediately. Understanding does not come about through time, through comparison. Understanding comes when your mind is clear, sharp, and rational. Then you understand immediately, and the immediacy of understanding is essential. As you know, the world and yourself are in travail, in great anxiety and misery. Anxiety and misery are not just words, are not slogans. You have to understand them; you have to go to the very root and then tear it out to find out. So, if you know how to listen, and if you do listen attentively, completely, then you will find, as you are listening, that the very thing of which you are afraid, conscious or unconscious, is being revealed; and you will wipe it away completely, totally, forever.

A mind that has fear is a corrupt mind. It may occupy a high place; it may go to a church or to a temple and repeat endlessly some sacred words—these have no meaning because the heart and the mind are corrupt in fear. To understand fear is quite a difficult problem. But it is very important to understand it. Fear exists—not only of little things, but also of great things. You are afraid of your wife or husband, you are afraid of losing the job, you are afraid of public opinion, you are afraid of not having anything permanent in your life. Everybody in fear seeks some form of permanency. There is no permanency in this world; there is no permanency in any relationship: between your wife and yourself, your husband and yourself, between yourself and society, between yourself and your boss and your occupation. There is nothing permanent in this world, and so the mind seeks something much more permanent, which it calls God—an idea. And having established that idea, the mind holds that idea tight to its heart.

Is there anything permanent, psychologically? You know, outwardly there is nothing permanent. Inwardly, we want permanence, and there is nothing permanent—even your wife or your husband, your children, your ideas, your beliefs, your dogmas. Nothing is permanent. But you refuse—the mind refuses—to see that because all our society, all our virtues, all our principles are based on this idea of permanency. Your fear comes into being when that permanency is questioned. In that permanency we establish our being. We identify ourselves with an idea which we say is permanent, as the supreme God and all the rest of the ideological jargon. And when that permanency is questioned, the whole structure of fear arises.

There is fear of immediacy and of the future. The future that is tomorrow is the projection of time, which is thought. I am talking very simply of a very complicated problem. It is only when you approach very simply a problem which is complicated that you begin to see it clearly. Thought is the response of time. Thought is the response of memory, which is the past. Thought, which is the present, which was the past, creates the future. We have to understand the process of thinking in order to understand fear, and to understand fear, we must understand time.

So let us first inquire into the question of thought. What is thinking? I am asking you a question: What is thinking? And your immediate response, if you are aware of your response, is the awakening of memory, which seeks to find an answer. Please follow this. It is very simple. Let me put it differently. I ask you: Where do you live? And your response is immediate because you are very familiar with that. There is no interval between the question and the answer; you know it instantly because you are familiar with it. I ask you something a little more complex; then there is an interval of silence, an interval of time; and during that interval your memory is in operation, and then you answer. So during the question and the answer, the time interval is the process in which memory comes into operation, and thought comes out expressed in words. So thought is the response of memory. And memory is the multiplication of a thousand yesterdays with all its experiences and knowledge. The culture in which one is brought up, the education one has had, conscious or unconscious—from this background of knowledge and memory every challenge is answered, and the answering is an action previous to thought. Thought comes and acts. That is the whole mechanism of memory. So unless you have understood this mechanism of memory, of thought, you will not be able to understand what time is.

There is the chronological time by the watch, time as twenty-four hours, time as yesterday, today, and tomorrow. When we talk about time, we are not talking of that time; we are talking of psychological time. The time that builds up tomorrow, the time thought has invested in hope, the time as the future where you will be something, time as achievement, time as arriving, time as gaining—all that time is psychological; it is not chronological. So a mind that wishes to understand and comprehend the whole problem of fear has to understand the process of thinking—in itself, not in some book—the process of its own thought and how thought fabricates time.

If there is no thought, there is no time. If there is no time, there is no fear. If you are told that you will die on the instant now, there is no fear because you are dead already. Fear comes in only when there is an interval between the fact and what you hope should not be. So thought is fear; thought is time, and the ending of thought is the ending of fear. Just listen to this. Do not ask how to end thought. Just listen to what is being said. If you are able to listen to it, you will understand. So in investigating fear, one has to understand thought. Thought is the reaction of memory, and memory is the past—the past being not only the past of a thousand years but also the past of yesterday, the past in which you have been educated in English, in technology.

All the reaction of the past is time, which is thought. And fear arises when thought is conscious of itself in contradiction. If there is no contradiction, if there is no conflict, if there is no urge to fulfill, then there is no consciousness of the border of time. Thinking is the response of memory, and that memory is the center from which all action takes place—the me, my family, my country, my job, my virtue—it is the center from which all thought as reaction takes place. As long as that center exists, there must be fear. That center is nothing extraordinary, nothing spiritual. It is just the machinery of memory. It is a bundle of memories. There is fear when that center is questioned, when that center is made to feel uncertain, when that center feels it cannot achieve, when that center feels itself frustrated, when that center feels utterly lonely.

We are going to examine this question of loneliness, because that is the very essence of fear. I do not know if you have ever been aware how lonely you are. I do not mean solitude, I do not mean aloneness; I mean loneliness. You feel this loneliness when someone whom you love dies, or someone whom you love turns away from you. When that person turns away from you, you are jealous, and that jealousy is the response of this loneliness, which is the questioning of the very center that demands permanency. I do not know if you have ever been aware of this loneliness, the ache of loneliness, complete isolation without having any relationship to anything. You must have felt it. Every person who is at all sensitive, thoughtful, aware, obviously feels it; and then feeling this loneliness, from which arises fear, he runs away from it; he takes to drink, women, church, God, rituals—anything in order to escape from this feeling of loneliness to something more satisfactory. For those who call themselves religious, God becomes an extraordinary escape; for those who are worldly, intellectual rationalization is an escape; and if they have money, drink or sex is an escape. One thousand and one things are there to escape from this loneliness. And these escapes become all-important because they give you a sense of permanency. When that permanency is questioned, you are back again to the problem of loneliness and fear; and you try to fill this loneliness with knowledge, with education, with sex, with virtue. But nothing can fill it. If you have gone into yourself and observed this whole process, you will see that nothing can fill it. All that you have to do with loneliness is to face loneliness. All that you have to do with fear is to face fear. That is, the word is not the thing.

Please follow this. The word is not the thing. The word *fear* is not fear. But for most of us the word has become important, not only with regard to fear, but also with regard to God, with regard to sex, with regard to communism, with regard to politics. With regard to everything, words or symbols have become important, and not the fact—which means that the mind is a slave to words. You are slaves to words like *communism* or *congress* or *Hindu* or *Buddhist* or *Muslim.* So if you want to understand fear, the mind must be free of the word. The word contains condemnation, and therefore you cannot approach the fact if the mind is a slave to the word. I will put it very simply. Take the word *jealousy;* in that word itself there is a condemnatory implication. Likewise is the word *anger;* in that word there is the significance which involves that you must not be angry. And if you would go behind the word and understand the feeling that is involved in jealousy, you must be free of the word. Surely, that is simple.

So when you are investigating into fear, you must be free of the word—not only of that word *fear* but of the whole system of words and symbols to which the mind has become a slave. Please follow this, because if you do not understand this, you will miss totally what I am going to explain further. The word *God* is not God. But to be free of that word, it is extraordinarily important to find out what God is or if there is God. Similarly, fear is a word, an opinion, an escape from the fact. If you are confronted with that fact immediately, there is no fear. You have to look at it. So is thought; there is no thinking if it is not verbalized. But the word implies time which is thought; and when there is thought, there is an interval between the fact and the process of thinking; so you never see the fact.

There is death, an undeniable fact. You see it every day. Every house has it. Every human being knows it. It is an end, an absolute, final, irrevocable end. You may spin a lot of theories around it—that there is continuity, that there is a hereafter, that there is a future life, and all that. But the fact is a fact. If you understand the fact, you will find out what is beyond. But without understanding the fact, without facing the fact, you cannot go beyond. The fact is that there is death, and there is no argument about that. You cannot argue with death. You cannot say to it, "Come tomorrow." So what is this dying? There is certainly the physiological dying, the body coming to an end. Death will inevitably come to the body because the body is a machine; it is an organism that is worn out by misuse, by conflict, by pressures, by various struggles, by bad diet, and so on—and the whole process comes to an end. That we can accept very easily and very readily. But is that all?

I have lived, I have struggled, I have acquired experience, I have built up tremendous power—what for? If I die, will all that go or will there be a continuity? How are you to find it out? You understand, sirs? You are not listening to me to accept ideas. I am not giving you arguments; I am not refuting what you believe and substituting my particular form of belief. I have no belief in this matter; I have only facts. I want to know what death is, and I cannot find it out if I do not know how to die. Physically your body continues—you know it—until you come to an end, that is, until the machine dies.

Now, is it possible to die psychologically? Do you know what it means to die, to end? You understand my question? Am I making my question clear? Look here, sirs. There is death, something you do not know. And what you do not know, you are afraid of. At least you think you are afraid of something you do not know. Is that not so? How can you be frightened of something you do not know? You are frightened of losing something which you already know. That is the real cause of fear; the fear is not of the unknown. You are afraid of losing something which you have stored up. You are afraid of losing the known, not of the unknown.

So can you die to the known? Can you die to yesterday's memory, to all your achievements, to all the things that you have gathered? Can you die freely, easily, happily, to the things that you have held dear? You may love your family—I wonder if you do love your family; if you did love your family, this rotting society would not be like this. Can you die to your pleasures, to your vanities, to your ambitions, to your greed, on the instant? Because, that is what is going to happen when you do die. To die to yesterday, to die to every minute, to all the things that you have gathered, is death. This means: Can you live always in a state of not-knowing, and therefore always young, fresh, innocent? You know, death is an extraordinary thing. Death is the unknown. You cannot come to it with the known; you cannot come to it with all your burdens. Death is going to strip you of everything—your family, your sons, your character, your ambitions. So why not strip yourself of all that now? When you do it, then you will know what death means. And I assure you that when you do know it, you know great beauty. Then you know what love is because death, love, and beauty always go together. The thing that we call love is not love; it is mere memory. What you love is your personal investment. Your family is the continuity of yourself; your family is your own. And you know, when you die there is no family; nothing exists.

So is it possible to die to everything that you have known? This is not annihilation; this is not denial; this is not nothingness. There is an immensity, there is a vastness, there is something beyond words when you know how to deny the whole ground, deny all that you have known. So to die to every thing that you have known, every moment, means never to gather, never to accumulate, and therefore never to have the conflict of detachment.

Death is a state when the mind has lost its recognition of itself as consciousness and of the borders of time. Where there is continuity of thought—which is what most of us want, which is all that we know—it breeds sorrow, anxiety, guilt, and all the travail of life; that thought has a continuity of its own, but thought is bound by time. When thought dies to itself, when the machinery of memory as thought comes to an end—it is psychological thought, not the mechanical thought of knowledge—then you will find that the thing that you are afraid of is not there. Fear ceases altogether. Then you are living completely, integrally, wholly, from moment to moment—and that is creation.

You know, for us beauty is a thing that is put together by the mind. For us, beauty is woman or man, service, a building, a picture, a piece of pottery, or an idea. But there is a beauty beyond thought and feeling which is not put together by the mind. And that beauty is love. Without that love, life becomes utterly empty—as most peoples' lives are; though they have families, though they have virtues, though they have jobs, their life is petty, shallow, empty.

But when you have died to everything psychologically, when you have gone that far, you will find that out of dying, there is a living—a living which has no meaning as compared to this living. That living is the state of creation, and that creation has no time. That is the immense, the immeasurable, the unknowable. And only that mind that has died to itself and to everything that it has known will know the unknowable.

February 11, 1962

Eighth Talk in New Delhi

This is the last talk. I would like this evening, if I may, to talk about freedom and the quality of energy that is necessary to find a new way of living. We have been talking about a great many subjects concerning everyday life. We have not been talking about abstractions, about ideas; nor have we indulged in scholastic or theological conceptions and formulations. We have been dealing with facts. And it would be a thousand pities if those of you who have listened should translate all that has been said into mere ideas, conclusions; formulate certain sanctions, and follow them as a method in order to arrive at what you think is the ultimate reality.

We have not laid down any path because there is no path, there is no way, no system. We are concerned with the whole, the totality of life, not with one segment, not with one part, one idea, or a series of ideas. We are concerned with living, with the totality of life. And as we observe in our daily activities, in our troubles and sorrows, our life is getting more and more complex. There is greater and greater division and contradiction in ourselves and in society, in ourselves as individuals and in society as collective human beings.

More and more freedom is being denied in the name of religion, or of organized spiritual thought and belief, or of institutionalized political action. If you observe—and it does not demand a great deal of intelligence—you will find that politics has become extraordinarily important, and the political leaders seem to usurp the whole of the world by their thought, by their activities, by what they say, or by what they do not say. We are being conditioned by them. At one time the priests of religions shaped our minds; now the politicians and the newspapers mold our thought; they are becoming the priests. And it shows how extraordinarily superficial, how on the surface we are living. We talk about freedom from a superficial level. We talk of freedom from something. Is freedom from something real freedom, or is it merely a reaction and therefore not at all freedom?

We must have freedom, not verbal freedom, not mere political freedom, nor freedom from organized religions. I think that most people who are aware of the world situation have gone away from these institutionalized ways of life; though these have had a superficial effect on our life, deeply they have not had much effect. If one has to find out what is freedom, one must question everything, question every institution—the family, religion, marriage, tradition, the values that society has imposed upon us, education, the whole structure of social and moral organization. But we question not to discover what is true but to find a way out, and therefore we are never psychologically free. We are concerned more with resistance, and not with freedom. I think it is important to understand this.

All our life is built on resistance, on defense. A mind that has taken shelter behind defense can never be free, and we need freedom—complete, absolute freedom. But to understand the quality and the depth of freedom, one must first be aware in what manner, at what depth we have built defenses and resistances psychologically, and how on these defenses and resistances we depend. From behind these walls we look upon life; from behind these resistances we look at and translate life. So before we can inquire and find out what is freedom, we must understand the resistances that we have built, and also never build again any form of resistance. These two must be understood before there can be freedom. We have built up resistances ideologically, verbally, traditionally, because psychologically we take shelter behind these resistances. If you observe yourself, you will see this to be a fact. And we are not discussing, we are not talking as a communication merely of words, but we are concerned with the understanding of ourselves. You cannot go very far without knowing yourself as you are—not as the supreme self and the divine self and all that kind of theological nonsense and ideas, but actually what you are from moment to moment, not ideas, not what you want to be, but the fact of what you are, which fact is undergoing change all the time and is never still. And one has to understand that. That is, there must be self-knowing, knowing oneself. Without knowing oneself, it is absolutely impossible not to live in illusion.

So we are inquiring not into ideas, not into new formulas or new speculative theories, but we are actually looking at ourselves, as it were, in a mirror, and from that observation discovering for ourselves what it is to be free. If we have the capacity to look at ourselves without distortion, to see actually what we are, then every form of resistance, every form of dependence ceases. And that is what we are going to do. As I was saying, we have built resistances because we are always in conflict. We have never a moment when we are not in a struggle, in travail, in sorrow, in conflict, in some form of confusion. And to escape from this confusion, from this sorrow, from this insufficiency, from this poverty of being, we have built walls, and behind these walls we seek security. And these walls are ideas; they have no value at all; they are just ideas, they are just verbal structures. You call yourself a Hindu or a Muslim or a Christian or what you will—they are merely ideas, words having no reality; they are just symbols. The symbol has no reality; it is merely a shadow. But to find out what is beyond the shadow, one must see through the shelter, the refuges, the resistances. You have during the course of your life built walls of resistance—resistance as an idea, as an ideal. The more so-called spiritual you are, the more ideals you have. And ideals are resistances; they are not facts. The fact that you are violent is real, but the ideal of nonviolence is pure theory; it has no value at all. That ideal is a form of resistance which prevents you from looking at the fact that you are violent.

There must be freedom—I will go into it presently, and you will see the real significance of it. A mind that is inquiring into freedom must be completely free of romantic ideas because they are unreal. The ideals which the churches have built up, the religions have built up, the saints have built up, are all different forms of resistance, and they have no validity. What has validity is the fact—which is that you are violent, that you are ambitious, greedy, envious, creating enmity. And a mind that is ridden—as most minds are—with ideals derived from books, derived from gurus, derived from society, can never be free because we are dealing with actuality, with facts, and not with ideals, not with theories, not with speculations. As I pointed out earlier, a religious mind is concerned with facts; as the scientific mind is concerned with observable facts under the microscope, we are concerned with psychological facts. And when we are examining those psychological facts, it is only in freedom from resistances that there is mutation.

Change implies resistance to the present, a continuity of the present modified—but still the continuity of *what is,* only modified; that is not mutation. When we are concerned with freedom, we must also inquire into the question of change. A mind that is concerned with changing gradually, through time over a long period, through a process, is only undergoing a modified change but continuing the same old pattern. Mutation is not gradual change. The idea that you will gradually change is another form of resistance. Either you change immediately or you do not change at all. You do not change because the very process of change implies revolution, and there is fear of what might happen.

So through fear you resist every form of change. And a mind that resists change can never understand what mutation implies. You are angry and you say, "I will get over it; I will become nonangry." So you have introduced another problem, which is the ideal, and therefore there is a conflict between what you are and what you should be. The idea then becomes the means of gradual change. Therefore you do not really change at all. There is mutation only when you see anger immediately and not build up the defense of an idea. Please observe this, think it over, look at it. As I am explaining, please look at yourself. Do not accept what we are talking about. There is no authority in the world in spiritual matters; if you have authority, you are dead. So when you introduce the time element, when you say, "I will change gradually," you do not change at all. The gradual process is a form of resistance because you have introduced an idea which has no reality. What has reality is that you are angry, you are vicious, you are ambitious, envious, acquisitive. Those are facts. Now to look at them and to be free of them immediately is all-important. And you can change them immediately when you have no ideas, when you have no ideals, but when you are capable of looking at them.

So freedom is the capacity to look at a psychological fact without distortion, and that freedom is at the beginning, not at the end. You must understand that time is a process of evasion and not a fact—except chronological time, which is a fact. But the psychological time that we have introduced—that of gradually bringing about a change in ourselves—has no validity. Because, when you are angry, when you are ambitious, when you are envious, you take pleasure in it, you want it; and the idea that you will gradually change has no depth behind it at all. So one removes psychological resistances by observing the fact and not allowing the mind to be caught in unreal, ideational, theoretical issues. When you are confronted with a fact, there is no possibility of resistance; the fact is there.

So freedom is to look at a fact without any idea, to look at a fact without thought. I will go into that later; you will see what I mean. Either you look at a fact with words, which is thought, or with conclusions, which again is thought and words, or with knowledge which you have acquired previously, which again is words based on experience—that is, the result of memory conditioning every form of experience. So you have to look at something without thought—which does not mean looking at something blankly, emptily, but looking at it through the understanding of the whole significance of thought.

Sirs, may I suggest something? There are several people taking notes. Please do not take notes, if I may suggest. This is not a lecture for you to take home and consider. You are considering it right now. You are listening now, not tomorrow, not after the meeting is over. And you cannot listen while you are taking notes. Listening implies attention, and you cannot attend doing various other things and paying verbal attention. Attention means complete, not concentrated, listening—listening with all your being, with your heart and mind—because our lives are concerned. We feel that everything must come to us on a silver platter, that we have got to do nothing. But we have to work tremendously hard to salvage ourselves out of this confusing misery of this political world, of this religious world, of society; otherwise—we are being destroyed. This is not a rhetorical statement but an actual fact.

So, if you are at all serious—and you must be somewhat serious to come and stay here for a whole hour—do please pay attention. Do not write, do not fiddle about; give your whole mind. Your whole life is at stake.

When you are confronting a fact, every thought is a form of resistance. Why should you have thought at all? Can you not look at something without thought? Can you look at a flower, a tree, a woman, a man, a child, an animal without thought? That is, can you look at a flower nonbotanically—though you may have knowledge concerning the flower: what species it belongs to, what kind of flower it is, and so on? The color, the perfume, the beauty—all that interferes with your looking at the flower; that is, the thought process prevents you from looking. Just understand this. Do not say, "How am I to get to that stage?" or, "When can I look without thought?" There is no system; there is no power. But if you understand that you do not see anything clearly, definitely, sanely if thought interferes, then you stop thinking; then you look.

So freedom is that state of mind that comes into being when it is concerned only with a fact and not with an opinion. And if you look at yourself in that mirror of freedom, whatever you are, without the distorting effect of thought, there is immediate, instant mutation. If you can look at yourself—when you are angry, if you know the fact that you are angry, envious, acquisitive, and that envy, acquisitiveness, ambition, and so on form the whole structure on which society is built; if you can look at the morality of society which is yourself in relationship with another; then as you see yourself actually as you are, without the interference of thought, there is absolute mutation; then you are no longer ambitious.

If you take pleasure, if you derive benefit from being envious, from being ambitious—as most politicians do—then you will not listen to what is being said. But a man who is inquiring into the whole process of freedom must come to this point when mutation takes place without time. And that can only happen when thought is not interfering with the fact; then there is no resistance. You will see that most of us are in conflict, live a life of contradiction, not only outwardly, but also inwardly. Contradiction implies effort. Watch yourself, please. I am explaining, but I am explaining you. Where there is effort, there is wastage—there is waste of energy. Where there is contradiction, there is conflict. Where there is conflict, there is effort to get over that conflict—which is another form of resistance. And where you resist, there is also a certain form of energy engendered—you know that when you resist something, that very resistance creates energy. I resist what you are saying; to resist what you are saying is a form of energy, and that energy prevents me from being free from contradiction. Now, through resistance you can create energy; through contradiction you can create energy—as most people do. You know, there are people who have contradictory selves, opposing selves—wanting to do this and not wanting to do that. The two elements, the good and the bad, when they are in friction, make us act.

All action is based on this friction that I must and I must not. And this form of resistance, this form of conflict, does breed energy; but that energy, if you observe very closely, is very destructive; it is not creative. I mean by that word *creation* something entirely different, which you will understand as I go into it. Most people are in contradiction. And if they have a gift, a talent to write or to paint or to do this or that, the tension of that contradiction gives them the energy to express, to create, to write, to be. The more the tension, the greater the conflict, the greater is the output, and that is what we call creation. But it is not at all creation. It is the result of conflict. To face the fact that you are in conflict, that you are in contradiction, will bring that quality of energy which is not the outcome of resistance.

Please understand this. Look, most of you probably go to your office every morning. Probably you have done this for the last ten or twenty or thirty years. It must be a terribly boring and agonizing effort, unless you have become so completely mechanical that you go through it as a machine moves. Now, observe the fact that you are bored, that you are being destroyed by this machine; merely observe it, watch it; do not say, "I must or must not," or "What am I to do, or how am I to stop being bored?" but merely observe the fact. Then through that observation of the fact, you will see how mechanical your mind has become and how the office, the job has taken the place of life, of living—which does not mean you give up the job but you begin to understand the whole significance of action.

Let me put it in a different way. For most of us action is based on an idea. I must be good; India is a nation; and, therefore, I must resist, I must build up—an idea and then action. Therefore, if you observe, you will see that in that there is contradiction, and to get over that contradiction, you create more ideas. You change ideas, but always action is based on an idea. Now, if you observe that your action is based on an idea, then you will see that the idea is a form of resistance to complete action. Look, sirs, as long as you are acquisitive, envious, ambitious, seeking power, position, prestige, society approves of it; and on that you base your action. That action is considered respectable, moral. But it is not moral at all. Power in any form is evil—the power of the husband over the wife or the wife over the husband, the power of the politicians. The more tyrannical, the more bigoted, the more religious the power, the more evil it is. That is a fact, a provable, observable fact, but society approves of it. You all worship the man in power, and you base your action on that power. So if you observe that your action is based on acquisitiveness of power, on the desire to succeed, on the desire to be somebody in this rotten world, then facing the fact will bring about a totally different action, and that is true action—not the action which society has imposed upon the individual. So, social morality is not morality at all; it is immoral; it is another form of defending ourselves, and therefore we are being gradually destroyed by society. A man who would understand freedom must be ruthlessly free of society—psychologically, not physically. You cannot be free of society physically because for everything, you do depend on society—the clothes that you wear, money, and so on. Outwardly, nonpsychologically, you depend on society. But to be free of society implies psychological freedom—that is, to be totally free from ambition, from envy, greed, power, position, prestige. But unfortunately we have translated freedom from society most absurdly. We think freedom from society is to change clothes—you put on sannyasi robes and you think you are free from the world, or you become a monk and you think you have somehow destroyed the world or society. Far from it—you may put on a loincloth, but inwardly you are psychologically bound by society because you are still ambitious, still envious, still seeking power. So, a mind that is inquiring into freedom must be totally free from society psychologically, and also from dependence on the family.

You know, the family is the most convenient form of resistance because that resistance is made highly respectable by society; and if you observe, you will see how entangled the mind is in the family. The family has become the means to your fulfillment; the family has become the means of your immortality, through the name, through the idea, through tradition. I do not say the family must be destroyed; every revolution has tried it; the family cannot be destroyed. But one must be psychologically free of the family, inwardly not depend on the family. Why does one depend?

Have you ever gone into the question of psychological dependence? If you have gone into it very deeply, you will find that most of us are terribly lonely. Most of us have such shallow, empty minds. Most of us do not know what love means. So, out of that loneliness, out of that insufficiency, out of the privation of life, we are attached to something, attached to the family—we depend upon it. And when the wife or the husband turns away from us, we are jealous. Jealousy is not love, but the love which society acknowledges in the family is made respectable. That is another form of defense, another form of escape from ourselves. So every form of resistance breeds dependence. And a mind that is dependent can never be free.

You need to be free, because you will see that a mind that is free has the essence of humility. Such a mind, which is free and therefore has humility, can learn—not a mind that resists. Learning is an extraordinary thing—to learn, not to accumulate knowledge. Accumulating knowledge is quite a different thing. What we call knowledge is comparatively easy because that is a movement from the known to the known. But to learn is a movement from the known to the unknown—you learn only like that, do you not? Please observe yourself. The moment you know something and you say, "I will learn," you are adding to the knowledge which you already have. So you are never learning. You are merely acquiring, adding; it is an additive process. But learning is freedom. You can only learn in freedom, not in acquiring. A mind that is free is learning and therefore is capable of that extraordinary energy which can never be corrupted.

A mind has energy through resistance, through conflict, through contradiction. We all know that form of energy. But there is an energy which comes when there is no conflict of any kind, and which is therefore completely incorruptible. I am going to explain presently. I mean by the mind, the totality of consciousness and more. The brain is one thing and the mind is another. The brain, which is the result of time, which is sensation, which has accumulated knowledge through centuries of experience—that brain is conditioned, as also the total consciousness is conditioned. These words, *consciousness* and *conditioning,* are very simple. What you are—the educated, the unconscious, the accumulated mind, the accumulated consciousness of time—all that is you. What you think, what you feel when you call yourself a Hindu, when you call yourself a Muslim, a Christian, or this or that—all this story about yourself is the total consciousness. Whether you think you are the supreme self or the greatest atma or this or that—it is still within the field of consciousness, within the field of thought. And thought is conditioned.

Now, in that state of condition—resistance to life—you do create energy. The more the resistance, the more the conflict, the more energy you have, and that energy is of the most destructive kind. This is what is actually going on in the world. That energy dissipates itself. It is always corrupting. It always needs stimulation, always needs some form of attachment through which it can derive power, energy, growth. Please follow all this. When one realizes that fact and sees that fact—that our energy comes into being through resistance—and when you have understood the whole story of contradiction within yourself, then out of your so seeing the fact, there comes a different kind of energy.

The energy I am talking about is not the energy preached by religion, it is not the energy of the *bramacharya,* the bachelor who refuses sex because he wants to have the supreme experience. Because his whole process of living, the sannyasi life or the monk life, is a form of resistance, and that does give you energy—a very limited, narrow, destructive energy, which is what most religions offer. But what we are talking about is a totally different kind of energy. That energy is born out of freedom, not out of resistance, not out of self-denial, not out of ideational pursuits and discussions.

If you understand all this which I have been talking about, and face these facts, then out of that comes an energy which is incorruptible—because that energy is passion. Not the passion of sex, or identifying yourself with the country, with an idea—which passion is destructive—that gives you also a peculiar kind of energy. Have you not noticed that people who have identified themselves with their nation, with their country, with their job, have a peculiar energy? So also most politicians, most so-called missionaries, or those who have identified themselves with an idea, with a belief, with a dogma, as the communists do—they have a peculiar energy which is most destructive. But the energy which is the most creative energy has no identification; it comes with freedom, and that energy is creation.

Man throughout the ages has sought God, either denied it or accepted it. He has denied it, as those do who are brought up as atheists or communists; or he has accepted, as you Hindus do because you have been brought up in the belief. But you are no more religious than the man who is being brought up in nonbelief. You are all around the same. It suits you to believe in God, and it does not suit him to believe in God. It is a matter of your education, of your environmental, cultural influence. But man has sought this thing throughout the centuries. There is something immense, not measurable by man, not understandable by a mind that is caught in resistance, ambition, envy, greed. Such a mind can never understand this creative energy.

There is this energy which is completely incorruptible. It can live in this world and function. Every day it can function in your offices, in your family, because that energy is love—not the love of your wife and children which is not love at all. That creation, that energy is destructive. Look what you have done to find out that energy! You have destroyed everything around you psychologically; inwardly you have completely broken down everything that society, religion, the politicians have built.

So, that energy is death. Death is completely destructive. That energy is love, and therefore love is destructive—not the tame thing which the family is made up of, not the tame thing which religions have nurtured. So, that energy is creation—not the poem that you write, nor the thing put in marble; that is merely a capacity or a gift to express something which you feel. But the thing we are talking about is beyond feeling, beyond all thought. A mind that has not completely freed itself from society psychologically—society being ambition, envy, greed, acquisitiveness, power—such a mind, do what it will, will never find that. And we must find that because that is the only salvation for man, because in that only is there real action; and that itself, when it acts, is action.

February 14, 1962

Bombay, India, 1962

First Talk in Bombay

It must be fairly obvious to most people that there must be throughout the world a tremendous revolution—a revolution not of words, not of ideas, not the exchange of beliefs or dogmas, but a change, a total mutation in thought. Because, in the world, which is our world—the world we live in, the world that you and I inhabit—the companions, the relationships, the work, the ideas, and the beliefs and the dogmas that we hold have produced a monstrous world, a world of conflict, misery, and perpetual sorrow. There is no denying it. Though every one of us is aware of this extraordinary state of things in the world, we accept it as a normal condition, we put up with it day after day, we never inquire into the necessity, the urgency of a revolution that is neither economical nor political but much more fundamental. And it is that we are going to discuss, we are going to talk about together, to explore together, during these three weeks.

But to explore, there must be freedom. To explore really, deeply, lastingly, you must leave your books, your ideas, your traditions, because without freedom, no exploration is possible. No inquiry is ever possible when the mind is tethered to any kind of dogma, to a tradition, to a belief, and so on. The difficulty with most of us is not that we are not capable of inquiring, not that we are incapable of investigating, but we are apparently totally incapable of letting things go, putting things aside, and therefore with a fresh mind, with a young mind, with an innocent mind, looking at the world and all the appalling things that are taking place in it.

To investigate, to inquire into all the questions that touch our lives—death, birth, marriage, sex, relationship, if there is or if there is not something beyond the measure of the mind, what is virtue?—that requires freedom to pull down, because it is only when you can destroy completely everything that you have held sacred or right or virtuous that you can find out what is truth. We are going to inquire into everything, question everything, tear down the house that man has built through the centuries to find out what is truth. And that requires freedom, a mind capable of inquiring, a mind which is serious. I mean by "seriousness" a quality of pursuing a thought to the very end, a questioning that is not afraid to face the consequences. Otherwise, there is no inquiry; otherwise, there is no investigation. We remain merely on the surface and play with words, with ideas. And if one has observed sufficiently the things that are happening—not only mechanically, technically, but also in our relationships between people—when one observes that progress throughout the world is denying freedom, when one observes the strength of society in which the individual has completely ceased to be, and when one observes how nationalities are dividing themselves more and more, especially in this unfortunate country, one will see that some kind of deep revolt must come about.

It seems to me that the first thing to inquire into is "society"—what is the structure, and what is the nature of society—because we are social beings. You cannot live by yourself; even if you withdraw into the Himalayas, or become a hermit or a sannyasi, you cannot live by yourself; you are in relationship with another, and relationship with another creates the structure which we call "society." That structure controls relationship—that is, you and I have relationship, we are in communion with each other; in that communion, in that relationship, we create, we build a structure called society. That society controls our minds, shapes our hearts, shapes our actions—whether you live in a communist society or a Hindu society or a Christian world. Society with its structure shapes the mind of every human being, consciously or unconsciously. The culture in which we live, the traditions, the religions, the politics, the education—all that, the past as well as the present, shapes our thought. And to bring about a complete revolution—there must be a revolution, a crisis in consciousness—you must question the structure of society.

If I may add here, words lose their significance if you merely use them as symbols and do not go beyond the words. Most of us are slaves to words; whether we call ourselves Hindus, Parsis, or Muslims, we are slaves to words. And as long as words remain important, we cannot go beyond the words. When we talk about society, its culture, its structure, they are merely words; and to go beyond these words, one must see oneself in relation to the structure, in relation to what is actually taking place in the world, and in relation to what is actually taking place in one's own life. Words are merely a means to communicate, but if we stop merely at words, all communication ceases, except verbal communication.

We are not dealing with ideas; we are not dealing with various beliefs or dogmas. We are concerned with bringing about a different action, a different mind, a different entity as a human being; and to go into that really, profoundly, we must not be slaves to words. This is very important to understand right from the very beginning because the word is never the thing. The word *bird* is not the bird. They are two different things. But most of us are satisfied with the word, and not with seeing beyond the word. We are satisfied to call ourselves individuals and talk of society and the structure of society, but is there an individual at all? Because we are the result of environmental influence, we are the society, we are the result of that structure which we call society. It is only when you completely, totally, break away from society that you are an individual, but you are not now an "individual" at all; you are the result of your environmental influence. You are being brought up as a Hindu, as a Buddhist, or what you will; you are the result of the influence of a particular society. So we must be greatly aware of the influence of words and discover for ourselves to what extent, to what depth, we are slaves to words.

These meetings, these gatherings, are not entertainment; they are not propaganda; they are not for an exchange of ideas. But what we are concerned with, essentially and deeply, is to bring about a radical, religious revolution. And that requires a tremendous investigation into oneself; that requires a questioning of everything that man has built—every attitude, every value, every tradition, every relationship—and we are going to do that; we are not going to leave one stone unturned. There is nothing holy, there is nothing sacred. And therefore, to investigate, you need a very sharp, clear, precise mind—not a mind befogged with ideas, with words, with sentiments. And to think very clearly, there must be freedom; otherwise, you cannot think freely. If you are a Hindu or a Parsi or what you will, if that is the basis of your thought—or from that you begin to think—it is absolutely impossible to think because you are not free. So the first essential necessity of inquiry is freedom because then you can begin to question.

There are two ways of questioning. One is to question with a motive and therefore try to find an answer to the question. The other is to question without a motive, and therefore seek no answer. It is really important, if you would follow what is being said, to understand the difference between these two questionings.

Most of us do question, and our questioning is a reaction. I do not like something, and I question and reject it, or modify it; my questioning is according to the urge or the demand of what I want. So, that kind of questioning has a motive behind it, and that questioning is a reaction. We know what a reaction is: I do not like something and I revolt against it. That revolt is merely a reaction, a response to something which I do not like. But there is a different questioning which is without a motive, which is not a reaction, which is to observe, to question the thing which is a fact.

I do not like to take any examples because examples do not get us very far. Similes are dangerous things, but they might be somewhat helpful in order to explain the difference between the two kinds of questioning—the questioning which seeks an answer, and the questioning that has no answer but is merely questioning. You take the fact of what is happening in this country: nationalism and caste prejudices are prevalent. That is a fact. The worship of the flag is an abomination because it separates people, it brings war. This worship of the flag with a nationalistic spirit is a fact; it is actually going on in this country. Now, you can question it to find out why it is happening, the truth of it, without a motive and therefore without defense, without attacking it, but merely questioning it sharply to find out. Or, you can question it having accepted the nationalism—which is accepting the division of people as castes, as classes, as groups—and when you so question, there is a motive behind it, and that questioning does not reveal the truth of that matter.

There are two ways of questioning the whole process of living. One is questioning with a motive, which seeks a result, which is a response, which is a reaction—therefore you will not find the truth of that questioning. The other is questioning without a motive, without seeking an answer—and that is what we are going to do. The moment you seek an answer, it will invariably be a conclusion of words but not of facts.

We are going to question the whole structure of society. We are going to question the whole relationship of man and man, his relationship with ideas, with his conceptual existence, his abstractions, his everyday conduct. And out of this questioning, we shall discover for ourselves what we actually are. Because, without knowing yourself, you cannot go very far; without knowing what you are, consciously or unconsciously, what you think, what you feel, every movement of ideas, every feeling; without uncovering, without discovering and understanding the processes, the motives, the impulses, the compulsions, the frustrations, the failures, the hopeless loneliness, despairs, anxieties, guilt, you cannot go very far. That is the foundation and that requires freedom.

Freedom is not at the end but at the beginning, so as to be capable of looking at yourselves actually as you are, what you are in your relationship—and that relationship is the structure of society. There must be a complete change in our relationship because all relationship is action. Relationship is action, and your relationship is mostly based on an idea. Your relationship with your wife is not an idea, but your relationship with your neighbor, with your country, with your gods, is an idea. Your relationship with your wife, with your children may be based on an idea, what you want your wife and children to be; but the fact is you are actually related to the person through your feelings, through your sexual, protective demands.

So, society is relationship. And that social structure, as it is now, is based on ambition, greed, envy, seeking power, position, prestige and all the things that man has set up as extraordinarily significant in life. That is the actual fact—not your gods, not the Gita, not your guru, not your saints and saviors; but the daily life in which you are, which is your ambition, your greed, your envy, your pursuit of power and wealth and position which you want. And without altering that radically, without breaking down the whole system, you cannot have a religious revolution. A religious revolution is the only revolution that has significance because every other revolution has failed. The French and the communist revolutions have completely, totally failed because those revolutions were reactionary revolutions; they were a reaction against *what is*. The communist revolution was the reaction to capitalism—the actual reaction. And when you react, it produces the same pattern in a different form. A religious revolution is not concerned with reaction at all. It is concerned with dealing with a fact and destroying that fact—that is, being aware that our relationship, that our social structure is based on this extraordinary sense of values, on ambition, greed, envy; and destroying that completely in ourselves, totally, wholly eradicating it. That is the beginning of a religious revolution—not the pursuit of an idea, which you call God.

Without laying the foundation, how can you go far, how can you find out if there is something beyond words, beyond divisions, beyond the conditioning of man? Surely, sirs, this thing which we call the morality of society—which admits that you can be ambitious, envious, greedy, powerful, and all the rest of it, which it calls moral—you pursue; and how can you, with that morality, with that virtue, find something which is beyond all virtue, which is beyond all time?

There is something beyond all time; there is something immeasurable, timeless; but to find that, to uncover that, you must lay the foundation; and to lay the foundation, you must shatter society. I mean by society not the outward structure, not blowing up buildings, not discarding clothes and putting on a sannyasi's robe or becoming a hermit—that does not break down society. When I talk about society, I mean the psychological structure, the inward structure of our minds, of our brain, the psychological processes of our thinking; those need to be completely destroyed to find out, to create a new mind. You need a new mind because if you observe what is taking place in the world, you will see more and more that freedom is being denied by the politicians, by progress, by organized religions, by mechanical, technical processes. More and more the computers are taking over the function of man, and they are quite right to do that. Virtue is being brought about by chemicals: by taking a certain chemical, you can be free of anger, irritability, vanity; you can make your mind quiet by taking a tranquilizer, and you can become very peaceful. So, your virtue is being changed by chemicals; you don't have to go through all the tyranny of discipline in order to be virtuous. All that is going on in the world. And so, to bring about a new world, not chemically, not industrially, not politically, but spiritually—if I may use that word *spiritually*, so hackneyed, so spoiled by the politicians, by the religious beings. You cannot be spiritual if you belong to any religion, to any nationality. If you call yourself a Hindu, a Buddhist, a Parsi, a Muslim, or a Christian, you can never be spiritual. You can only be spiritual when you destroy the social structure of your being—which is the world in which you live, the world of ambition, greed, envy, seeking power. For most of us, that world is reality, and nothing else; it is that which we all want; from the highest politician to the lowest person in the street, from the biggest saint to the daily worshipper—that is what everybody wants. And without breaking that, do what you will, you will have no love, you will be no nearer happiness, you will always have conflict, misery.

So, as I said, we are going to inquire into the structure of society. The structure of society is brought about through thought; the structure of society has resulted in the brain which we now have—the brain which is now used to acquire, to compete, to become powerful, to gain money crookedly or rightly. The brain is the result of the society in which we live, the culture in which we are being brought up, the religious prejudices, dogmas, beliefs, traditions; all that is the brain, which is the result of the past. Please examine yourself, please do not merely listen to what is being said.

You know, there are two ways of listening. One way is: you merely hear the words and pursue the meaning of words—which is to listen, to hear comparatively, which is to compare, which is to condemn, translate, interpret what is being said. That is what most people do; that is how we listen. When something is said, your brain immediately translates it as a reaction into your own terminology, into your own experiences; and you either accept what pleases or reject what does not please. You are merely reacting, you don't listen. And then there is the other way of listening, and that requires immense attention because in that listening there is no translation, there is no interpretation, no condemning, no comparison; you are just listening with all your being. A mind that is capable of so attentively listening understands immediately; it is free of time and of the brain which is the result of the social structure in which we have been brought up. As long as that brain has not become completely still but is intensely alive, active, every thought, every experience is translated by that brain according to its conditioning, and therefore every thought, every feeling prevents total inquiry, total investigation.

Look, sirs, the majority of people who are listening here are either Parsis, Hindus, or Christians. You have been told you are a Hindu, from your childhood; that memory is held through association in the brain cells; and every experience, every thought is translated according to that conditioning; and that conditioning prevents your total understanding of life. Life is not the life of a Hindu or of a Christian; life is something much more vast, much more significant—which a conditioned mind cannot possibly understand. Life is going to the office; life is sorrow; life is pleasure; life is this extraordinary sense of beauty; life is love; life is grief, anxiety, guilt—the totality of all that. And without understanding that, you cannot find. There is no way out of sorrow. And to understand the totality of life, the brain has to be completely quiet—the brain which is conditioned by the culture in which you have been brought up, by every thought which is the reaction to your memory, by every experience which is the response to a challenge, the response of the past, which is all centered in the brain. Without understanding this whole process, the brain can never be quiet. And to bring about a new mind, it is absolutely essential for the brain to understand itself, to be aware of its own responses, to be aware of its own dullness, stupidity, conditioned influence. The brain must be aware of itself, and therefore it must question itself without seeking an answer because every answer will be projected from its own past. And therefore when you question seeking an answer, the answer is still within the boundaries of the conditioned mind, the conditioned brain. Therefore when you question—that is, when you are aware of yourself, of your activities, of your ways of thinking, feeling, of the way you talk, of the way you move, of everything else—don't seek an answer, but look at it, observe it. And then out of that observation you will see that the brain begins to lose its conditioned state. And when you do that, then you are out of society. So, inquiry, investigation, is into yourself, first and foremost—not into what Shankara, Buddha, or your guru has told you, but inquiry into yourself, into the ways of your mind, of your brain, into the ways of your thought.

And mutation is different from change. Please listen, give your attention. Change implies time, change implies gradualness, change implies a continuity of what has been, but mutation implies a complete breaking and something new taking place. Change implies time, effort, continuity; a modified change that implies time. In mutation there is no time, it is immediate. We are concerned with mutation and not with change. We are concerned with a complete cessation of ambition immediately, and the immediacy of breaking down ambition is mutation—immediately, not admitting time.

We will discuss this further as we go on. But just capture the significance of this: we have so far lived through centuries of time, gradually changing, gradually shaping our minds, our hearts, our thoughts, our feelings; in that process we have lived constantly in sorrow, constantly in conflict; there has never been a day, there has never been a moment of complete freedom from sorrow, and sorrow has always been there, hidden, suppressed. And now what we are talking about is complete ending and therefore total mutation, and that mutation is the religious revolution. We are going to explain it a little this evening.

What is important to understand is the quality of seeing, the quality of listening. There are two ways of seeing—only two ways. Either you see with knowledge, with thought, or you see directly without knowledge, without thought. When you see with knowledge, with thought, what is actually taking place is that you are not seeing but you are merely interpreting, giving opinions, preventing yourself from seeing. But when you see without thought, without knowledge—which does not mean that when you see, your mind becomes blank; on the contrary, you see completely—that seeing is the ending of time, and therefore there is immediate mutation. For instance, if you are ambitious, you say you will gradually change—that has been the habit which society approves; society has invented all kinds of ways and means to get rid of your ambition slowly—and yet at the end of your life you are still ambitious, you are still in conflict—which is so utterly infantile, immature. What is maturity is to face the fact and end it immediately. And you can end it immediately when you observe the fact without thought, without knowledge.

Knowledge is the accumulation of the past, from which thought springs, and therefore thought is not the way to bring about mutation; thought prevents mutation. Please, you have to go into this very carefully, not just accept it or deny it. I am going into it during these talks, but first just capture the significance, the perfume of it. Because, for me there is only mutation, no change. Either you are or you are not—not that when you are ambitious, you are trying to become less ambitious; it is like the politicians who talk about the ending of politics and power and continue to be in politics. That is double talk. What we are concerned with is immediate ending so that a new mind can come into being.

And you need a new mind because a new world has to be created—not by the politicians, not by the religious people, not by the technicians, but by you and me who are just ordinary average persons, because it is we that have to change completely, it is we that have to bring about a mutation in our minds and hearts. That can be brought about immediately only when you can see the fact and remain with the fact—not try to find excuses, dogmas, ideals, escapes; but remain with the fact totally, completely. Then you will see that complete seeing ends the conflict. Conflict must end. It is only when the mind is completely quiet, and not in a state of conflict—it is only then that the mind can go very far into the realms that are beyond time, beyond thought, beyond feeling.

February 21, 1962

Second Talk in Bombay

We were saying the last time that we met here, how important it is that, out of this chaotic society, the individual should emerge. It is only the individual that can find reality, and he must find it, he must discover it for himself. And to find it, to uncover the reality, demands that we should understand the structure of society and be free of society, for the essence of individuality is freedom. Freedom is not for one to do what one wants to do. One is not to be compelled to conform, to adjust, to obey. But one has to understand the whole structure of society, and in the very process of understanding the whole structure of society, from that understanding, emerges the individual. If we do not so emerge, our lives will be very shallow, empty, dull, as the lives of most people are. You may have plenty, you may belong to any type of absurd political group; you may belong to any kind of organized religion, do puja every day, follow a guru. But unless you understand and are free from the psychological structure of society, there is no hope for you, for man, because the world is denying individuality; the world through its education, through propaganda, through its government, through organized religions, through the family, is denying individuality. And if there is to be a new mind, a new way of life, a new generation, the individual must emerge; and he can only emerge in total freedom from the psychological structure of society. That is what we were talking about the last time that we met here.

I would like, if I may, this evening, to talk about the need psychologically to break down the structure of society, which has not only molded our conduct and our ways of thinking but has imposed on the mind a series of "musts" and "must-nots," a series of assertive dogmas, conclusions, ideas. And an individual who will emerge from this psychological structure of society must be totally uncertain. There is no certainty in anything—neither in your senses nor in your ideas, nor in your family, nor in the nation, nor in the books. There is only a continuity of ideas in thought, thought in relationship with words; and ideas create a continuity which is time, and that continuity has been established through the centuries, through psychological processes. And the individual who will emerge must be free, and therefore he must not accept any psychological form of society.

Please, I would like to point out that we are not discussing ideas, theories; we are stating facts, and about facts you can neither agree nor disagree; you have only to look at them. And you can refuse to look at them—that is perfectly right—but to deny the fact, to obstruct the fact, to force yourself to see or not to see, prevents clarity. What we are concerned with is clarity, understanding; and there can only be understanding when there is perception of the fact, and that understanding is denied when you agree or disagree.

So, it is important to think out the problem together, and not think that the problem is of one person who is imposing the problem on you. We are not doing propaganda, we are not trying to convince you of anything, because a mind that is convinced, that has come to a conclusion, is a dead mind. But the fact is there is nothing that you can trust, and that is a terrible fact, whether you like it or not. Psychologically there is nothing in the world that you can put your faith, your trust, or your belief in. Neither your gods nor your science can save you, can bring you psychological certainty, and you have to accept that you can trust in absolutely nothing. That is a scientific fact as well as a psychological fact. Because, your leaders—religious and political—and your books—sacred and profane—have all failed, and you are still confused, in misery, in conflict. So, that is an absolute, undeniable fact.

We are going to examine one of the major psychological aspects of the social structure, which is "authority", and if there is time, we are going to find out for ourselves what it is to love.

Possessiveness in any form breeds authority—authority of the family, authority of the books, authority of the belief, authority of the law. So we must be able to discern for ourselves psychological authority. The authority of law is fairly clear—the policeman, the taxes, the government. You cannot disobey the authority of law. You may want to disobey it; you may not want to pay taxes, and probably many rich people—those who are corrupt are generally rich people—may dodge taxes. We have to discern intelligently, freely, this question of obedience to law and psychological authority. Obedience to law is necessary, but psychological obedience to anything—to the family, to the father, to the mother, to the parents, to society—is evil, as power is evil in any form, whether it is the power of a politician, of a dictator, or of a guru.

So, obedience to a family, the psychological acceptance of authority, is evil. I will explain why. You don't have to accept my word. Only I would beg of you to listen. You may be terribly attached to your family, but attachment is not love. You may be terribly anxious to see that your son and daughter are well educated, are married safely. But that attachment to the son and daughter is indicative of evil, for it breeds authority, it indicates possessiveness. Because, as I said in my previous talk, to find out what is truth, we are going to tear down every structure that the human mind has built through the centuries. We are going to question without a motive, for motive only leads to reaction, and not to action. We are going to question without a motive this whole structure of authority and obedience. You may not want to listen, but since you are here to listen and you have taken the trouble to come, do please listen.

I mean by listening not accepting, not denying, but listening to find out, to explore, to uncover, to investigate. For centuries we have had authority; every saint, every guru, every dictator, the father, the mother—they have shaped your mind psychologically. And we are going to question, tear down to find out what is truth, so that when you discover for yourself what is truth, out of that discovery there is freedom. And from that freedom, in that freedom, emerges the individual. In that freedom, there is a discipline without control. And it is only the individual that can find out the eternal—if there is an eternal. I do not say there is no eternal—the eternal may be; for the speaker there is, but not for you. You have to find out, you have to search your mind and heart, you have to break down all the walls that you have built; every stone must be upturned psychologically so that out of that you emerge with a clean, healthy, fearless mind, not with an obedient mind.

To listen to what is being said, you need attention, and attention is not possible when there is distraction. I do not mean by "distraction" the cawing of the crows, or the movement of the palm tree in the breeze, or the man next to you who is scratching his arm or his head—those are not distractions, they are part of this extraordinary total awareness. What I mean by distraction is that which prevents you from listening. When you have opinions, conclusions, comparisons, these prevent you from listening. When you have an idea, when you judge what is being said, when you approach with an opinion that which is being said—those are distractions. When you are comparing what you hear with what you already know, with what you have read, that is distraction. So, to listen attentively, such distractions must come to an end. You must listen totally. And if you so listen attentively, you will see what is really a miracle: in that act of listening, you will find there is freedom, because what is truth liberates without effort. But unfortunately, we are not capable of seeing, we are not capable of attending, because all our life is a distraction. To be able to see, to listen, to observe, is to have a mind which has no distraction but which only observes the fact in solitude.

As I have said, where there is possession, where there is the desire to be secure psychologically, there comes into being authority. The rich man seeks the authority of the policeman because he wants to be secure with his money; he maintains the status quo of a particular society; he does not want a revolution; he does not want a change; he wants to continue in the traditional psychological state which society has built for him, and so he insists on authority—the authority of the father, the authority of the family, the authority of the family possession over the individual person, the daughter, the son—and he educates his son to obey, to conform, to imitate. And in that conformity to the pattern there is security, but for a mind that is seeking security, there is always sorrow. Only a mind that is free has no sorrow. And such a mind that is free from sorrow has to understand this whole immense structure of authority. When we seek security in any form—physiological or psychological, inward or outward—there must be fear, which breeds authority, obedience. Most of us want security, and we find that security in possession—in possessing knowledge, technique, a family, money, power, position, prestige. Even that prestige, power, family may endure for a few years; in that, we seek security. And our whole marriage system is based on this security, which is to possess the wife, the husband; and that possession is called love. Please listen. I am not attacking your system. Life is breaking it down anyhow. Only an intelligent man looks at it, understands it, educates his son and his daughters differently and therefore brings into being a new state, a new world, a new human being, a new mind.

Every form of possessiveness, attachment, indicates the urge to dominate. That is what the family is—domination over the wife or husband, and that is called love; domination over your children and getting them married off to richer persons; and that is all you are concerned with: to find security for yourself and for your children, and that you call love.

So the process and the structure of authority begin with the family, and the family is the basis of this desire for security. There is nothing secure in the world—not your ideas, not your books, not your gods, not your puja—there is nothing that you can trust—not even your family, not your money that you put away in your bank, because communism may come, socialism may come, there may be a revolution, there may be an earthquake, anything might happen, and it is going to happen. If a man who is aware of all this would realize that reality is not for the rich man or the poor man, he must understand the structure of authority, which is based on security, which is established in the family. And a man who is seeking reality has to break down the family psychologically. Do think about it. That is why the sannyasis and the monks leave the family, but they do not leave the psychological structure; they leave a family, a name, but they take on a new name, and they are still psychologically conditioned; they still obey, they still follow a particular pattern of thought, which is the result of society, the culture in which they have been brought up. The Christian monks and the Hindu sannyasis are not free human beings; they have left the so-called outer world and changed their clothes; that is all. Changing clothes does not give you freedom, nor does having one meal or a loincloth. What brings freedom is the understanding of authority.

There is also the freedom from knowledge. For most of us there is security in knowledge. Knowledge has become the security now—not the gods, not the books, perhaps not the family either, but knowledge, technique. What is knowledge, and why does the mind give such extraordinary importance to knowledge?—which you do. You consider your books—the so-called sacred books: the Gita, the Upanishads, the Bible, and all the rest of it—enormously important because they are full of wisdom. Words do not make wisdom; books don't carry wisdom. A mind must be free to be wise. The essence of wisdom is the denial of experience, and the denial of experience is the denial of knowledge, because experience has become our authority. Technologically knowledge is right; the more knowledge you have how to run a motor, an office, a rocket, the computer, the more capable you are. That you must have, but the psychological experience which accumulates knowledge—that is what we are questioning.

Please understand this a little bit. This may be rather difficult because we are going to question experience. A mind that is seeking an experience—mechanical, technological—is still an immature mind; it can add, it can take off, but as a human being, it is not a mature, full, rich human being—technological knowledge does not give that, nor does experience give that. What is experience based on? What is experience? Experience is the response to a challenge—however little, however great. When you see those crows flying, that is an experience. When the world is in a crisis and you respond to that crisis, that response is experience. When you quarrel with your wife or husband, that is an experience. When you see a palm tree, that is an experience. Everything is an experience, and we question that experience. I say a mind that merely experiences and accumulates is an immature mind, and the mind that is beyond and above experience is the free mind, is the new mind, is the young mind.

So, experience is the translation of every challenge and response, and that translation of the challenge and response is based on your conditioning, on your previous knowledge, on the past, on tradition. You don't experience something new, you can't. You are always translating something new in terms of something old, in terms of your tradition, in terms of what you already know, of what you have gathered, of what you have accumulated, of what you have stored up in the past. The past dictates, shapes the responses. I insult you or I flatter you; that you remember, and when you meet me the next time, you respond according to that insult or flattery. That is an experience that is based on knowledge, and that knowledge, that past becomes the authority; and according to that experience, according to that knowledge, you shape your life, your thought, your conduct. And when you question that experience, that authority based on experience, then you have nothing left. When you question every experience of a religious man—whether he is a Christian saint, or a Hindu monk, or any other religious man—you will find that what he says, his visions, his ideas, are the result of his culture, of his past; that they are worthless, they have no meaning; that they are merely the projection from the past of what he has learned; and you will also see how his mind has been shaped by society.

So, knowledge—except technological knowledge, knowledge of how to read and write, and knowledge of that kind—is a hindrance to freedom. There is psychological knowledge, and every form of psychological knowledge prevents freedom, and therefore there is no individuality; there is a continuity of what has been and it may be modified, but it is still the structure of what has been—which is society. Please follow all this: you can't trust what you see, what you experience, what you know psychologically. So, obedience has lost its meaning; authority has no longer any significance, except the authority of law—which is denied by the politicians when it suits them; they go to war when it suits them, they obey that law when it suits them; one moment they are pacifists, the next moment they are warmongers. So you can't rely on, you can't trust, authority.

And in the very process of investigating authority, as we are doing now, you don't revolt against the authority of the father or mother, or the psychological structure. By the very process of investigating, through that very inquiry, your mind begins to be disciplined because to inquire, to investigate, you need a very sharp mind, a fearless mind. When the mind is no longer afraid, no longer anxious, no longer seeking security, then out of that comes an extraordinary discipline—not the disipline imposed by authority; not the discipline imposed by society, by your guru, by your teachers; not the discipline which you have imposed upon yourself, thinking that you are free, which is really the continuity of the psychological enforcement by society.

Please follow all this. When you say, "I will discipline myself according to a pattern not set by anybody but by my own experience," please see that your own experience is the result of your past, your conditioning. You can't trust your discipline because that discipline narrows the mind, destroys the mind, makes the mind, the brain, inadequate, dull, insensitive. So by questioning, inquiring, out of that comes an extraordinary discipline in which there is no enforcement, in which there is no imitation, no conformity, because there is no pattern to conform to, because there is no security.

When you see this, when you understand this, then out of this understanding there is love, because authority and love can never go together, nor can attachment and love abide together. But you are attached, aren't you?—to your families, to your ideas, to your gurus, to your visions, to your pujas, to money; ten different things you are attached to. And yet you talk of love! For you, love is security. And how can a mind that is enforcing obedience, that is educating the whole world to conform, that is merely concerned with the acquisition of outward technological knowledge—how can such a mind love? All that you want is security for yourself and for your children. That is all you are interested in, and to see that they conform. Now, love is not attachment. Love has no motive, and it is very arduous, it requires enormous work, psychological work—not sitting under a tree, or doing puja, or disciplining yourself; that is not work, that is immature childishness. But deeply to inquire into yourself, you have to go to the very end of that inquiry. Then out of that freedom there is love. But, you see, most of us are satisfied with loving superficially; most of us are satisfied with earning a livelihood, if we can get a little job and rot; most of us are satisfied with our bank account if we are rich; and we prattle about God, puja, and all the rest of it. But our hearts are empty, made empty by a dull, stupid mind which only thinks in terms of authority and obedience. So the breaking down of the psychological structure of society, which is your brain, which is you—that is absolutely necessary for a man who is really bent on finding out the immeasurable, if there is such a thing as the immeasurable.

So, authority, which breeds power, is evil. The man in power, in position, with prestige, is as evil as the snake, as deadly poisonous. A religious mind has nothing to do with such people. No rich man can come to know what love is if his God is still his money. And unfortunately, in this country, the people in power and the rich people are shaping the mind. There is nobody who breaks through all this structure. They are all conformists, "yes-sayers"; not one says no. And saying no is not a revolt but the psychological understanding of this whole structure which has built the present society.

So, a man who would be free, who would understand what is real, must break through the psychological structure of society; that is the first thing to do—not the pujas, not going to the temples, to the churches, and all the rest of it—they have lost their value completely; you can't put your trust in any one of them. You must stand completely alone. There is beauty in that aloneness, for that aloneness is love. And only in that aloneness is there the possibility of uncovering that which is not nameable, that which is not measurable.

February 25, 1962

Third Talk in Bombay

We have been talking about the necessity for the emergence of the individual. Society with all its complex influences and conditioning shapes thought, and if an individual is to emerge—and it is only the individual that can find the immense—it seems to me that this social influence, its morality, its corrupting ideations must be understood. Is it possible for the mind which has been so conditioned—every thought which has been so shaped, molded by every kind of influence—to emerge totally, uncorrupted, without a mark, completely free? Because it is only such a mind which is an uncorrupted mind—not a shaped mind, not a mind that is molded by circumstances, by influences—that can go very far in the discovery of what is truth, that can find out if there is a reality which is beyond the measure of the mind. And as we were pointing out the other day when we met here, power, position in every form, breeds authority.

This evening I think we should go into the question of desire, ambition, and fulfillment, and inquire if the mind can come out of all this without a scratch.

As we have pointed out at every talk, it is important to understand what "listening" is—just to listen completely, easily, without effort. Because it is effort, struggle, that prevents clarity. It is effort that perverts, that induces every form of distortion. And is it possible to listen to anything without a struggle, without a distortion? To see a flower, not botanically, not horticulturally, but to see it actually—what is it? It is quite arduous to see your friend, your wife, your children without distortion, without giving an opinion, without bringing in innumerable ideations—just to observe. From that observation and from that listening there is an action which itself brings about clarity without any form of effort.

And it seems to me that if each one could so listen, could so see, easily, without effort, then the whole process of living would miraculously, without a struggle, change. And it is possible because man can do anything with his mind, with his brain. He has gone, or he is going, to the moon; he has built computers; he has done the most extraordinary things outwardly, but he has not gone very far deeply within himself. The journey to the moon is very near compared to the journey within, and very few are willing to take the journey within because it requires attention and nothing else. It requires total attention to listen, to see exactly, every minute, without distortion, every thought, every feeling. I do ask most earnestly that you should so listen.

Most of us are ambitious; most of us are ridden by the desire for success, for fame, or by the desire to be known, and it is an everlasting struggle and effort. Struggle is apparently accepted by each one as a necessity—in learning, in getting educated, in going to the office, in climbing the ladder of success, in understanding what is truth; everything has become a question of struggle, effort. To think, to love, to be kind, to have humility—all this has been reduced to a formula of struggle and effort, control and discipline. For me such a life of discipline, control, struggle, subjugation, conformity, is destruction of the individual who must emerge, and it is only the individual that can find out the eternal, if there is such a thing as the eternal.

So we must understand struggle. I am using the word *understand* in the sense not intellectually, not verbally, but actually observing the fact of what you are—the fact that you struggle from morning till night, from the moment you are born until the moment you die, fighting, quarreling, making incessant effort without end. Surely, there must be a different way of living. But we have accepted the way of struggle. The schoolboy accepts it; the older generations have accepted it, and every saint, every philosopher, every teacher has asserted that you must struggle, that you must make an effort. I am pointing out, if you will listen, that there is a way of living without effort—which does not mean that you become sluggish, that you become dormant, stagnant; on the contrary. That effort, that struggle, is a waste; and when effort, struggle, entirely, totally ceases, there is a way of living completely with such energy. And to find out such a way we must inquire diligently, wisely, and intelligently into this problem of struggle.

We are investigating; we are not accepting what is being said because it is not a question of accepting or rejecting. We are not doing propaganda; we will leave that to the politicians, to the others. Propaganda is the continuity of nonfact, and a man who would understand a fact must approach it without distortion, see clearly what are the problems involved in ambition, in desire, in struggle. And we are going to investigate together. Therefore, you are going to journey into yourself, and not merely listen to what is being said.

Why do we struggle? What is the essence of struggle, what is the essence of ambition? Surely, conflict is the essence of ambition. Why are we so everlastingly ambitious at all levels of our existence? The so-called spiritual man, the sannyasi, the man with a beard, the politicians, the merchant, the man who is acquiring knowledge—they are all ambitious. Why? Why this conflict and struggle? Conflict exists because there is contradiction. If there were no contradiction, there would be no struggle.

Please follow this, not the words, but actually observe yourself as it were in a mirror. If there is no contradiction, there need be no effort. And we are a mass of contradiction. Why does this contradiction exist? Why does desire tear in different directions? Being torn in different directions, we say to ourselves, "I must be without desire," or "I must control the desire." Psychologically it is impossible to control desire; you have to understand it, you have to unravel it, you have to go to the full length, not in its expression, not in its fulfillment, but understand the whole significance of desire which breeds contradiction. Because it breeds contradiction, we resist desire, we suppress desire, we say to ourselves, "We must be desireless"—which is to destroy the whole immensity of life. For desire is part of life, and merely to suppress it, deny it, control it, is to shut off the immensity of life.

So, struggle exists because there is contradiction outwardly and inwardly. Outwardly there is the attraction of power, position, or prestige, which is offered to a man who seeks status. There is a living with function. We have to function as human beings; we have to go to the office, we have to learn, we have to do things—a function. But with that function goes the desire to be more than a functionary because you use that function as a means to acquire power, position, prestige; and so, there is contradiction. Function produces contradiction when there is the desire to use function to arrive, to achieve success, to achieve power. Please observe this. This is a fact. Cooking is treated by people not as a function but as a position, as a status, and therefore with contempt; and so there is a contradiction. The minister, the man of power, the man of position, the man of wealth—you treat him with respect, with tremendous consideration, because he will give you, or can offer, patronage. So, he uses his function to achieve status—which you also want—and therefore there is contradiction. So, where there is function which gives status, there must be a contradiction. And society is based on this—that the function is not important, but the status is important, status being power. And that contradiction is sustained by society. Whether it is the function of a minister or of a saint, with it goes prestige. And what you want is not the function, what you respect is not the function but the status, and therefore you have contradiction.

A man who uses function to achieve status can never be efficient. And we need to be efficient in this world because function matters enormously. The rocket that goes to the moon has a million parts, literally a million parts, and if even one of those parts does not function properly, it cannot go. And the man who designs it cannot seek, through that design, status; he must love what he is doing; otherwise, he cannot make the thing perfect. It is only the man who loves what he is doing—whatever it be: design, construction, structure—and is not deriving a psychological status, a psychological position; such an entity alone can be efficient and not be ruthless. It is the man who is using function for status who becomes ruthless.

So, struggle is not necessary to learn a technique. But through your education, the society in which you are brought up forces you not to love what you are doing but to pursue the necessity of a particular demand of the society. Society now demands engineers or scientists, and everybody becomes an engineer or a scientist because it is more profitable. But very few are real scientists, real engineers; they are using science and engineering as a means of acquiring money, position, prestige. So they are breeding contradiction. And outwardly there is all the expression of society with its wealth, comfort, progress. We all want wealth; we all are caught in this mania to achieve success in the world, to derive fame.

Why is there this intense desire on the part of each one, almost everyone, to achieve fame? Why is there this desire? I do not know if you have gone very far into that question. Let us look at it. Let us find out why you want to fulfill, why you want success, why there is this incessant battle with yourself. Surely, for most of us, we are aware at some time or other, consciously or unconsciously, that there is a great emptiness, loneliness in us. You know what that phrase means: "to be lonely"? It means to have no relationship with anything, to be completely cut off, to be in solitude, suddenly to find oneself alone, inwardly. And we are all the time struggling psychologically to fill that loneliness, to escape from it. I do not know if you are aware of your own loneliness, if you have ever come across it. And because we are so frightened of that loneliness, we run away from it, so there is a contradiction. We try to escape from that loneliness through knowledge, through success, through money, through sex, through religion, through every form. But the fact is that you are lonely—which you don't want to face—and you are escaping from it, and so there is contradiction, which breeds conflict.

We are concerned with conflict. A man who has no conflict is not ambitious. And a man who is ambitious can never love; he does not know what it means to love because he is concerned with himself and with his own ideas and his own achievements. A man who seeks fame—how can he love, how can he have kindliness, generosity? And this sense of achievement can only come about when there is an escape from the fact that you are lonely. Do what you will, until you understand that extraordinary loneliness, your gods, your knowledge, your power or your position have no value, nor does virtue have any value.

Now how does this loneliness come about? You understand what I mean by that word *loneliness?* Perhaps many of you have not felt that because you have never been alone, because you are always surrounded by your friends, family; you are always doing something, going to a cinema or to a temple, doing puja, being active all the time and therefore never aware of yourself or of what is going on within yourself. So, very few know this sense of complete loneliness. You must have come across it; perhaps when you are sitting alone in a bus, or suddenly when you are talking to your husband or your wife, and when you are surrounded by your friends, you are aware that you are completely alone, lonely. And it is a very frightening thing suddenly to come upon it; and being frightened and not being able to do anything about it, you run away from it and thereby you create a contradiction. And where there is contradiction there is conflict.

So, all our life, wherever we go, whatever we touch is conflict. Is there a way of living without conflict? There is a way of living without conflict, without struggle—it does not mean becoming lazy, the mind going stagnant, dull. That way of living without effort can only come about if we understand this whole process of contradiction. Contradiction exists where there is an ideal. The ideal of nobility, the ideal of goodness, the ideal of nonviolence—that, you must be; this, you must not be—all this breeds contradiction.

Please listen to this, because if you can listen, you can walk away from here without conflict for the rest of your life. Then ambition, struggle, and the brutality of ambition and the ruthlessness of ambition—all that will go away. You will have a simple, clear, unspotted mind. And it is only that unspotted mind that can function clearly, design without seeking perversion, without seeking position, and therefore love what it is doing. And it is only love that has no contradiction, and to understand that extraordinary state, you must understand the contradiction in yourself.

So, this contradiction exists when there is an avoidance of the fact—the fact that you are lonely, the fact that you are angry, the fact that you are violent. You are violent, you are angry, or you are ambitious—that is a fact. You should not be angry, you should not be violent, or you should not be ambitious—that is an idea, that is a nonfact. Therefore ideals, which have no reality, no substance, breed contradiction. The man who faces the fact of every day, of every minute, without distortion—such a man has no conflict. And to live without conflict demands tremendous energy. Not that the man who has conflict has no energy; he is dissipating energy. Not that the man who is ambitious has no energy; he has the energy which comes about through resistance, but that is destructive energy. There is that energy which comes when there is no conflict, when you are facing the fact every minute—I mean by "the fact" the psychological fact, what you are inwardly.

Now, to understand the psychological fact, you must understand the outward movement also—the outward movement of expression, of design, of color, of structure, of function. You cannot come to the inner without understanding the outer. They are both interrelated. You cannot understand the inner world without understanding the outer world—that is, without understanding society, which is relationship. Relationship between two people is society. And that relation has built the social structure, which is ambition, greed, envy, ruthlessness, cruelty, war, corruption—which is what is going on at the present moment in India, which you know very well. Without understanding that whole outward movement of life, you cannot understand the inward movement. They are interrelated; it is like a tide that goes out and comes in. You cannot separate the tide as the outer and the inner; it is one movement, and it is only the uncorrupted mind that rides that movement.

So, that is the fact, and one has to understand the fact. We do not understand the fact because consciousness is the result of influences. We cannot see the fact because of the influence that has shaped thought, the influence which is shaping the conscious mind as well as the unconscious mind. Do you understand? The newspapers, the speeches, the books, the cinema, the food, the clothes, the environment, the buildings, the air—all that influences you, your mind, consciously or unconsciously. Every form of propaganda, political or religious, the so-called gods that have become the tradition—everything influences and shapes thought. You are listening to what is being said, and you are not being influenced. You are not being influenced because there is no direction, there is no compulsion, there is no pressure. The speaker only says, "Look, observe, listen, watch"; and therefore what the speaker says does not influence you at all, consciously or unconsciously. But you have to understand the social influence.

Is it possible for the mind to be free of influence? You understand, sir, influence?—the word, the family, your wife, your husband, the books you read, and the things that unconsciously impinge on you. Can you be aware of every influence—be aware without choice, just be aware of every influence that is going on around you? Is that possible? Because, if you are free, if you can observe influence, your mind is already sharpened and therefore capable of freeing itself from influence. This is a complex subject; it needs attention, it needs all your thought to find out, because you are the result of influence. When you believe that you are the higher self, and all the rest of it, when you say there is in you God, divinity, the atma—all that is influence. When the communist does not believe in God, he is also influenced.

So all life is influenced. And is it possible to be free of influence totally? Otherwise, whatever you think, whatever you deny, whatever may be your action, is the result of the past, is the result of your conditioning; and therefore such a mind cannot possibly be free to discover if there is reality. So, is it possible to be free of influence? Which means, really, is it possible to be free of experience? We will come to that presently. Surely, you cannot be free of all influences. You can only be free of those of which you are conscious. But you can only be conscious of a very few influences; there is the whole unconscious which is receiving influences all the time.

Please listen to this. Is it possible to be free of all influences? Otherwise you cannot proceed to inquire into the question of freedom and be free. As I said, you can never be free of influence, but you can always be watching every influence that you meet. That means watching every minute what you are doing, what you are thinking, what you are feeling; and in that watching, not to allow any form of distortion, self-opinion, evaluation to take place, which is the result of influence. All influence is evil, as authority is evil. There is no good influence or bad influence, as all influence shapes the mind, corrupts the mind.

So, if one understands the fact that every form of influence—it does not matter whether it is good or bad—distorts, cripples, corrupts the mind, if one understands that fact, sees that fact, then one will be aware, totally, of every influence that impinges on the mind. That is, in denying, in negation, there is the emergence of the fact, of truth. When you deny, when you say no, you do so either with a motive or without a motive. Probably you have never said no. Because, most of us are yes-sayers; we accept, we never say no to anything without a motive—which means that when you say no without a motive, you are out of influence.

Please do understand this. It is a very simple thing once you understand this. When you say no to power, to fame, to ambition, to authority, you do so because you don't happen to have authority, power, position, but you would like to have it; apparently you can't get it, and therefore you say, "No, I can't have it." That is what most people do, but give them position, offer them authority, they will take it. So, there is denial with a motive, saying no with a motive. There is also denial or saying no without a motive—which is to see the fact that ambition in any form—spiritual or otherwise, outward or inward—destroys, corrupts. If you see that as the truth, then you will be aware of every form of influence, positive as well as negative. Then you are concerned with the fact only.

So, negation is the ending of influence, not the positive mind. I mean by "positive mind" the mind that conforms, the mind that imitates, the mind that obeys, the mind that is made respectable by society—that is merely a mind which has accepted and pursued a definite pattern of social, environmental, cultural living. That mind is called a positive mind, but it is not a positive mind at all; it is a dead mind. I mean by a "negative mind," a mind that denies without a motive. When you deny the attitude of the politician who thinks he will change the course of the world or he will alter man, when you deny the whole attitude of the politician, you are out of that particular influence, totally. The politician is concerned with the immediate, projected into the future—which he thinks is the long-term, is the long view, but that long view is still the short view. That is, the politician, like all the technicians, is not concerned with the total man; he is only concerned with the outer. And when you deny the outer, which is the short view, without a motive, then you are out of that field altogether; then you are concerned with the total being of man. So it is important to understand a mind that faces facts through denial, through negation, and only remains with the fact.

I hope we are not making it very difficult. It is not difficult—what we are saying. For instance, if I am angry, it is a fact that I am angry. Then to deny that I am angry, to find reasons why I am angry, to substitute, to alter, to condemn that, to pursue the ideal—all those are negations of the fact, distractions from the fact. And when I deny totally all evasion, all distractions, only then is my mind empty of all influence and therefore capable of looking at the fact; then I look at the fact.

Please do this as you are listening. Most of you are ambitious; most of you lead a contradictory life, and you know the pain of contradiction. You are trying to fulfill either through the family, through the name, through writing a book, through your children, or trying to become a big man—you are all the time trying to fulfill. And where there is this urge to fulfill, there is also frustration with its misery. You try to fulfill, as you are lonely, empty inwardly. That is a fact. Now, look at the fact that you are ambitious and do not find excuses; do not say, "What am I going to do to live in this rotten society which is built on acquisition, power, and ambition?" When you deny that society, you are out of that society; therefore, you may live a different kind of life and yet be in society. So, you have to look at the fact that you are ambitious, that you are envious, that you are acquisitive, and be aware of the influences that prevent you from looking at it—which are the ideals and all the rest of it. When you deny the influences, you are moving from fact to fact. So, out of that denial, out of that negation, there is energy to look at the fact—you need tremendous energy and not friction.

Where there is conflict, there is the dissipation of energy. Where there is fulfillment, self-fulfillment in any direction—in God, in a book, in a woman, in your children—there is the dissipation of energy because it breeds frustration, contradiction. And to deny it is to face the fact that you are ambitious. And that fact reveals why you are ambitious. You don't have to do anything; you merely observe that fact, and that fact reveals. All that you have to do is to observe without comparison, without judgment, without evaluation; then you will see how extraordinarily empty one is. You have a job, you have a wife, you have a husband, you have money, you have knowledge—outwardly. But inwardly, there is immense poverty, an emptiness, a loneliness that nothing can fill, and running away from that is the essence of contradiction. Now, you have to look at that loneliness. I am going to go into it a little bit, how to look at it.

First, the fact is that you are lonely; the fact is that your mind is completely distorted by society; the fact is that you are trying to escape from the reality of what you are—which is absolutely nothing. You are absolutely nothing—which does not mean despair, disgust; but that is a fact. Now, to observe the fact means denial, as I have pointed out, without comparison, judgment, evaluation. But also, to look at a fact demands the understanding of the word. You understand?

The word *anger,* the word *God,* the word *communist,* the word, *congress,* the word *India*—we are slaves to these words. And a mind that is a slave to a word cannot see the fact. When we think of India, we get emotionally stirred up—the ancient land and all the rest of it—and that prevents you from looking. To deny all the past and see the fact—that you cannot do because of the word, because of the meaning which the word India gives you, an extraordinary sense of emotional gratification, with which—the word, not the reality—you have identified yourself. What is the reality that is not related to the word? In the same way, how do you look at anger? The word anger in itself is condemnatory. Is it not? As the word anger is in itself condemnatory, how is one to be free from the word and look at what is called anger?

So, you begin to discover for yourself how extraordinarily slavish thought is to a word. And you will find, if you will go into it very deeply, that there is no thought without a word. And you will find, if you go still deeper, that where there is a thinker and a thought, there is a contradiction, and every form of experience only divides and strengthens the thinker and the thought as a separate process. So, it is only when this whole process, which I have explained from the beginning until now, is understood, examined, watched, that the mind comes out of this social, environmental, verbal structure as an uncorrupted, clear, sane, rational mind. It is only then that the mind is no longer influenced; it is completely empty. It is only such a mind that can go beyond time, and beyond all space. It is only then the immeasurable, the unknowable, can come into being.

February 28, 1962

Fourth Talk in Bombay

I would like to talk this evening about fear. And I would like to talk about it so that we, both of us, leave this place free of fear, not temporarily, but totally. It is possible.

But before I go into that, I would like to establish the quality of humility, because there is so little of it. Without humility you can't learn, and learning is not a matter of accumulation—when accumulated, it becomes merely knowledge. There is a vast difference between accumulated information as knowledge, and learning without the center of accumulation. And this is important to understand, because then when we talk about fear—the whole issue involved in fear—we are going to learn. Without humility you will never be free from that extraordinary thing called fear.

So we must understand what is learning. Learning demands a mind that has clarity and compassion with precision. Without these two there is no humility. That is, a mind that is capable of thinking very clearly, rationally, sanely, without any perversion; and a heart that is precise—these two must exist where there is humility, and humility implies learning. Humility is not a quality to be cultivated. The moment you cultivate humility, it ceases to be what it is. It is not a virtue. Virtue is merely order. To have order is necessary. Order in the room, order in your mind, order in your life, order in your speech, dress, and so on, order in your behavior—all that implies virtue. But humility is not virtue. It exists from moment to moment. It exists when the mind is aware, learning, searching, absorbing. And humility is that quality which is essentially of the nature of affection, because without affection, without the sense of deep love, you can't learn.

So learning is important—learning which is not a process of accumulation. You can learn from your wife, your husband, from your children, from your office. You can learn from your behavior—how you behave, what you say, what you do. You can learn how deeply you are vain, how frustrated you are. And this process of learning is in flashes, from moment to moment. Do please understand this: learning cannot be continuous; the moment it has a continuity, it is accumulative and therefore it ceases to be learning. You can only learn when the mind is fresh, eager, innocent, and that can only happen when it is from moment to moment, when there is no accumulation, when there is no gathering, no storing up at a center from which you learn. If there is a center from which you learn, it is merely an additive process, and therefore it ceases to be learning.

We are going to learn about the problem of fear. But to learn about fear is to have the capacity to investigate and to learn from that investigation—but not to be permanently free of fear. We are going to learn, but the moment you say, "I must be permanently free from fear," you have already established the knowledge of continuity, and therefore you will never be free of fear. So we are going to learn. And to learn there must be clarity of mind and the precision of compassion. Without these two, learning is not possible and there is no humility.

We have inherited from society many problems. We are born with problems, and we die with them. We have thousands of them; everything we touch, everything we think about becomes a problem, and we are never free, even for a single day, an hour, without problems. Even in sleep we are bedeviled with problems. To continue in a problem makes the mind dull, corrupts the mind. The problem you carry over from yesterday has already distorted the mind, the clarity of thought. But we go from day to day, year after year, with problems, unsolved, not understood; and they become a burden which distorts, which corrupts, which dulls the mind.

There are not only the conscious problems but the unconscious problems, which express themselves through dreams which need interpretation. And so, whether we are awake or whether we are asleep, there are problems, multiple problems. A problem is something which has not been resolved, which has not been understood, and we have inherited from society many problems to which our existence has added. The first thing, it seems to me, to realize is that a problem must be ended immediately, not carried over, whatever the problem is. Because, if it is not immediately ended, you get used to it, it becomes a habit; and a mind that is functioning in habit cannot think clearly, it has no compassion.

So there needs to be a precision of thought which ends a problem immediately as it arises—whatever the problem may be, a physical or psychological problem. If you are ill, do not let that illness take root in the mind because then it becomes psychosomatic—having a psychological problem, which distorts thought and therefore affects the body physically. So, it is essential to end every problem instantly as it arises, so that the problem does not take root in the mind.

It is possible to live without problems at all—which does not mean that you avoid society, or that you withdraw and disappear into the mountains, into an asylum. Every minute there is a problem. I am posing a problem to you. I am saying that it is possible to live without a problem by ending the problem immediately, and that becomes a problem to you. You say, "How?" You have already many other problems, and you add this problem. There is no "how". But you have to understand the importance of ending a problem immediately as it arises; you have to see that when a mind has a problem and continues to live with a problem of whatever kind it may be—the problem of husband, wife, sex, God, drink, earning a livelihood, whatever that problem may be—if the problem is not immediately resolved, it makes the mind dull, it corrupts the mind, and such a mind is incapable of learning. When you have problems, you cannot be affectionate; you are self-centered, you become hard, cynical. So one has to meet a problem—which is a conflict, which is an unsolved issue—as it arises and, as it arises, to learn all about it.

And you can't learn if you approach it with past knowledge. That is why it is important to understand what it is to learn. For most of us, learning is an additive process.

You will say, "I will learn, I will experience, I will add; and from that I will be able to lead a better life, I will be able to understand better." Is understanding the result of an accumulative process as knowledge? Or is understanding an immediate action? That is, when a mind has no problem, it can look, observe, watch, listen instantly. And that is only possible if each one realizes the necessity and the tremendous importance of resolving every problem as it arises, not allowing it to take root in the soil of the mind.

In the next four or five talks—I do not know how many more there are—I am going to talk about a great many other things, like death, religion, meditation. But without understanding all that has been said now, you will never be able to follow deeply the question of death and meditation. And that is why it is important to understand what it is to learn about your problem. And you can't learn about the problem swiftly if you get accustomed to the problem, so it is very important not to get used to the problem. But that is what happens with most of us: we quarrel with our wives, our children, our neighbors; we walk on the filthy road, sit in the dirty buses; we never notice all this, we have got used to it. You will never notice a beautiful tree, the palm that stands by your house, because you have got used to it. You have got used to the way you talk to your servants, and the tremendous respect that you show to the man from whom you are going to get something—to that too you have got used. So the moment you get used to something, to whatever problem, corruption has set in, and dullness has begun.

I am stating all these facts because when we are going to investigate into the question of fear and learn about it and not make a problem of it, we have to understand very deeply the implication of learning. Because, you see, love demands a free mind, an unspotted mind. But our minds are spotted. We are not free; we do not know what love means. We know what lust means, we know what the acquisitive attachment to a family means, but it is not love. And a mind that is full of problems, torn with unsolved, unresolved issues can never love. Our feelings are dead. And it is the problems that have killed all our beauty, weighed down our instinctive, natural, spontaneous, free response, the quickness of the heart.

If you will listen this evening—not intellectually, not verbally, not with the idea that you are going to resolve your problems by listening, but just listen—then you and I will be able to communicate at that level where there is compassion, which is precise, which brings clarity to the mind. It is only when you are emotionally—not sentimentally, not romantically, but emotionally—in contact with a problem that the problem will be resolved. But we are never in such contact; we are intellectually or verbally in contact with the problem but not emotionally, not vitally, because, we have got used to life, we have got used to the way we are living; we get used to our wives and our children, to our jobs, to the dirty city, to organized religions. You never see the restless sea and the beauty of a sunset because you have problems. And the mind that has a problem is never an adventurous mind, is never a young mind; and to learn, you need a young mind, an uncommitted mind, a mind not committed to any belief, to any church, to any organization, political or religious, or to the family. It is only then that you will learn. There is beauty in learning, not in acquiring knowledge that becomes tedious; where there is acquisitiveness, a piling up of knowledge, there is vanity; and vanity, which is the essence of fulfillment, becomes bitter, cynical.

So, we are going to learn about fear. We are not resolving fear, but through learning about fear we are going to resolve it totally, so that there is an ending to fear. But if you start out with the intention, conscious or unconscious, saying what a marvelous thing it would be to be free of fear, then you will never be free of fear, then you will never learn. And we are going to learn. Fear is never constant; it is there because of thought. Fear is there because of thought which projects that anxiety into the future, or which derives from its knowledge of the past what it has been "to be afraid," and therefore wants to avoid. Please follow this, not verbally but actually, in yourself. You know you are afraid of so many things, aren't you?—afraid of your wife, your husband, afraid of your neighbor, afraid of your job, afraid of not reaching heaven, afraid of death, afraid of public opinion, afraid with a thousand fears. Take one of them with which you are ridden and with which you are familiar, and examine it as I talk about it; examine it, investigate it, observe it, watch it. Don't try to get rid of it or say, "I am going to watch it in order to get rid of it." That way you are never going to get rid of it. But you are going to learn about it, and you will learn about it only when you see that it is not possible to get rid of it. You are going to learn about it, and therefore you are going to understand it; and if you approach it that way, you will be totally free of it.

Thought is the origin of fear. If there were no thought, there would be no fear. If you had no thought about death—such as, "What would happen if I died?"—if death took place immediately, there would not be fear. It is thinking about it that breeds fear derived from past experience and projected into the future. Please, what I am saying is very simple, not complicated. Observe it yourself. Thought is the result of time; time is memory. I am not talking about time; I am talking about thought as time. We are talking about thought and not time. Thought has built up, through experience, self-protective responses, physiological as well as psychological. When you meet a snake, there is the instinctive response of self-protection. That kind of fear, which is self-protective, must exist; otherwise, you will be destroyed; otherwise, you will not pay your attention to the bus and you will rush into it, or you will walk into a pit. So there is the self-protective instinct, the physiological self-protective instinct built through time, through experience as memory, which responds when you meet a snake, when you meet an animal, when you see the bus. That response must exist for a sane, healthy mind. But every other form of fear is unhealthy because it is brought about through thought, through the response of memory, which has been accumulated through centuries of experience, and which thought projects. So, you have to understand the process of thinking if you want to understand fear—which means you have to understand the thinker and the thought.

Please, what I am saying is simple; really, I mean it, it is really simple. But if you are going to approach what I am saying with your conditioning, that is what makes it difficult. You don't come to it, you don't listen to what I am saying, with a freshness. You are coming to it with what you know already, with what Shankara, Buddha, or XYZ has said about the thinker and the thought; and therefore you will approach what is being said with a conclusion, with memory, with previous knowledge; and that is what makes it difficult. Please see that. So, if you are to learn about what is being said, you have to put all that aside, and you can only put all that aside when you are emotionally in contact with what is being said.

You know, to hold somebody's hand is not an intellectual fact; when you are emotionally in contact with that person, there is a rapport, there is a communication, a feeling between the two people. In the same way, to commune with each other, we must emotionally hold our hands together, not intellectually. And you must have this emotional, compassionate, affectionate contact with the fact of fear, with the fact of thought, which we are going to examine. Unless you are emotionally in contact with it, vitally, immediately, you won't go beyond the first few words. As long as there is a division between the thinker and the thought, fear is inevitable. Please see why. Because there is a contradiction between thought and the thinker. The thinker is trying to guide, control, shape, discipline thought; but out of this division there is conflict, there is contradiction; and where there is contradiction, there is the urge to conquer it, to go beyond it—which indicates the essence of fear. So you have to understand the process, how this division has arisen between the thinker and the thought, and not accept what somebody else has said—it does not matter who it is, the most ancient, enlightened, or the most recent. Don't accept a thing from anybody, but question. Don't follow anybody; when you follow, you are incapable of learning. And you can only learn when you are questioning without a motive. If you are questioning with a motive, you are only adding, you are trying to resolve something which can't be resolved. So, don't follow what is being said and accept it as gospel truth—it is not. What another says is not gospel truth; you have to find out for yourself, without any restriction. And that can come about only when you are free, when the mind is unspotted and compassionate.

There is the thinker and there is the thought. We know this. This is what we do every day—the division. The thinker is the censor; the thinker is the judge; the thinker is the center which accumulates knowledge, psychological experience, and so on. It is the thinker that responds to any challenge, and his communication, his contact with something is through thought, which he has created. But thought has created the thinker; there is no entity as the thinker, except what thought has created—if you don't think, there will be no thinker. All this division, the conflict, breeds fear. The center, the observer, the experiencer, the thinker is established; and thought is vagrant, moving, changing. This center never changes; it adjusts itself, it modifies itself, it puts on new clothes, a new varnish, new characteristics; but it is always there. And that center breeds fear because it is always responding from a fixed point, however flexible.

So thought establishes the thinker—it is not the thinker who establishes the thought—because if there is no thought, there is no thinker. It is possible not to think at all, not to have a single thought—it is that extraordinary state of mind which is empty and therefore contains all space. That can only come about through meditation; that we will see when we discuss meditation. But don't say, "I will wait until that day when you talk about meditation; then I will find out." Then you won't. You must lay the foundation; and to lay the foundation, you must be in contact, and you can't be in contact if you are merely intellectually and sentimentally in contact—you must be in contact totally, with all your being, with your body, with your senses, with your heart, with everything that you have.

So, you have to understand the process of thinking. Thinking is the response to a challenge, whether great or little. The response is the result of memory which you have accumulated. When I ask you if you are a Hindu, you will say yes. The response is immediate because you have been brought up in that society, in that culture which says it is Hindu, Parsi, or whatever it is. All thinking is the response of memory. And memory is association. Memory is the result of innumerable conscious and unconscious experiences. Please, sirs, this is nothing new—what I am saying. Any psychologist, any person who has thought a little bit about this, will tell you this; but to understand the process of thinking and to eliminate totally the center as the thinker which breeds fear—for that, you need clarity, you need to have an intellectual knife to cut everything that you can't completely understand.

Therefore what is demanded is not to have any authority—the authority of memory even, or the authority of your experience, which has been conditioned through centuries, which has created the 'me', the 'I', the self, the ego. As long as that center exists—and that center creates the division between itself and thought—there must be fear. So, the question is how to bridge, how to put away the center. Do not translate it as the ego and get all kinds of ideas about it; merely keep to the fact that there is a center from which you judge, you evaluate, you censor. That center of accumulated experiences creates a division between itself and action, between itself and thought. And trying to overcome that division, and not being able to overcome it—that breeds fear. If you can bring these two together, there is no fear, but you can't bring the two together because there is only one fact, which is thought, and not the thinker.

There is no reality when you say the "thinker." The 'I' is a bundle of memories, nothing permanent; it is no more permanent than thought is permanent. But the mind wants, thought wants, security; thought wants permanency; therefore, thought establishes itself as a center, and that center speaks of the permanent high self, the cosmic self, the super-self and God, and all the rest of it—but still it is in the process of thought. So unless you have completely understood the whole mechanism of thinking, fear will always exist. You know, they have now all kinds of chemicals, drugs that will get rid of your fear; you can take a pill and become very tranquilized, very quiet, very peaceful. Anxiety, guilt, envy, and all those things that man has battled with through the centuries can be got rid of through a pill. This is a fact. But you see, taking a pill does not absolve you from having a petty mind, a narrow mind, a limited mind, a stupid mind. It is still there; you have only drugged it, you have put it aside into abeyance. What we are concerned with is not giving or taking pills but wiping away the pettiness of the mind, which means the pettiness of thought; thought is always petty because thought is never free, because thought is the response of what has been in terms of what will be.

So the question is: In understanding fear, is it possible for thought to end—which is for thought not to project into the future, and therefore for the mind to see the fact every minute, as it arises, without any projection? You understand? The fact is: One is afraid of death. We are not talking about death; we will talk about it at another time; we are now talking about fear.

Now thought projects itself into the future. It does not want to die; it does not know what it will be in the future; it knows what it is in the present with all the turmoil, the ache, the anxiety, the sorrow, the misery that it lives in; and it projects itself into the future and is afraid. Because it is confused, uncertain, not clear, it projects an idea of permanency, and therefore it is afraid that it may not reach permanency. It is afraid of public opinion because it wants to be respectable; because respectability is a very paying thing, society recognizes it; it is a noble thing, and so it is afraid of what society may say; therefore, it guards itself. It is afraid of the dark; it is afraid of all the unconscious, uncovered issues. Still it is a process of thinking. So one has to meet each fact as it arises, without thought, merely to observe it as each fact arises in a flash.

Now, sir, I am going to explain it a little more because I see you will not be able to follow quickly. There is the fact that I am afraid of my wife. Thought has created it, my action has created it, and I am afraid. I am taking that as an example—really I am not afraid because I am not married. You can take something of which you are afraid. I am afraid of my wife. I have done something which I am ashamed of or which I want her not to know. Or she nags me, and I do not want all that; I will rather get used to it, and so I have got used to it—which is, my mind has accepted it, and the acceptance has become a habit; I don't pay attention any more to whatever she says. So, my mind has formed a habit. Acceptance—therefore taking on what she is saying, casually—has corrupted my mind; I have become dull to it; it has become a habit, and I dare not break from that habit because breaking away from that habit implies change, and I do not want change. So I am afraid. And that is a fact.

How is it possible to understand that fact of fear without introducing thought? Because, thought either wants to reject it or accept it or change it or modify it according to its convenience. You understand what I am saying? How to meet this fact that I am afraid, without the background of fear, of thought? Because, thought will translate it, will interpret it, will shape it, will deny it, will want to get over it, will try to conquer it. Thought will not understand it because thought is the result of memory; it only can respond to what it already knows, and therefore it is incapable of meeting fear. Fear always comes and goes; it is not constant. Though fear may be in the unconscious permanently, it expresses itself not continuously but in flashes. How is one to meet those flashes of fear without thought?

Those who have permanent fear become neurotic; they have other problems. But those who are more or less rational have not any constant fear; they meet fear occasionally, or they meet it often when they meet their wife. So when you meet that fact, you have to meet that without thought, to meet it completely—which means having understood the whole process of thinking intellectually, verbally, and with compassion, which gives precision, and which gives immediate contact with the fact. To meet the fact totally implies meeting it not only intellectually but emotionally. And this process of learning of the fact is not possible when you approach it with thought, which already has known, thought being the outcome of the known.

Can you meet fear without the known? Then you will see, if you can so meet it, that there is no fear, because it is the projection of the known that creates fear. The projection of thought, which is the result of the response of the known, creates fear. Thought as time creates fear. And when you have understood the whole process of thought and are able to look at the fact, when you are able to see the fact, are able to be emotionally in contact, totally, with the fact, then you are not approaching with thought, which is the result of the known; therefore, you are approaching it anew. A new mind is not afraid; a new mind is inquiring.

So, as I said at the beginning of this talk, there must be humility. Humility never accepts and never denies. It is arrogance to accept or deny. Humility is that extraordinary capacity to learn, to find out, to investigate. But if you have already the accumulation of your investigation, then you are not learning; therefore, you cease to be humble. And it is very important to have humility because it is that essential quality which has affection. Without humility there is no love, and love is not a thing that has roots in the mind, roots in thought. So it is only from this extraordinary sense of humility, there comes the sense of precision with compassion and clarity of mind. It is only then that fear ceases. And where there is the cessation of fear, the ending of fear, there is no sorrow.

March 2, 1962

Fifth Talk in Bombay

I would like to talk this evening, if I may, about laziness, sorrow, and action and, if there is time, about beauty.

Ideas or theories do not actually change the mind or the heart. No amount of persuasion, no punishment or reward prevents the cunningness of the mind and the cruelty of the heart. No belief or dogma can dissuade the mind from its course to achieve what it desires. And it would be a pity if each one of us were to go away from these meetings with a cupful of ashes which are merely ideas and words—they don't change. And mutation can only take place when one deeply perceives or sees the actual fact.

We have often discussed, analyzed, quoted, had innumerable arguments for and against, but we still remain as we were—dull, insufficient, insensitive, completely absorbed in one's own commitments and problems. And no amount of thought, anxiety, or fear will dissolve the pain. I am going to talk about these problems, as we have already talked about fear, power, position, and authority. We are not dealing with ideas; propaganda does not reveal the fact, and you have to understand the fact. Neither the temple nor the book nor the guru will show you how to look, but you have to look yourself, you have to be a light to yourself. And to be a light to yourself, you must not follow anybody; you have no authority when you are a light to yourself—you have no guru, you are not a follower. When you are a light to yourself, you are a creative entity, and creation cannot take place if there is any form of laziness.

Laziness is the essence of self-pity. We are lazy, indolent, given to slipshod thought with no precision. Our minds are as confused as our hearts, and equally dull. And to understand laziness—not how to get rid of laziness—one has to learn about it.

As we pointed out at the last meeting, learning is far more important than merely to resolve a problem. If you can learn about a problem, you have already resolved it. We are going to learn about laziness, this extraordinary indolence of the mind—not accumulate knowledge about laziness, which becomes merely verbal. Learning implies investigation. And to investigate, the mind must be free to find out, and there is no freedom if you merely acquiesce, agree or deny or defend yourself behind the barrier of words and conclusions. These are distractions, which prevent the clarity in which learning can take place. So, please, we are going to learn together about laziness, especially with people who live in this climate, who have lived under various forms of tyranny and authority and who easily slip into mental lethargy, into indolence, into an easily accepted attitude and value. So, one has to be aware that to learn, there must be freedom to inquire.

We are going to learn about this quality, this thing called laziness. As I said, the essence of laziness is self-pity. I am going to go into that statement because if we do not understand this problem, this question of self-pity, we shall not understand what is to follow—which is sorrow. It is right to be lazy, it is good to be lazy—lazy in the sense of not being incessantly active like an ant, or like a monkey everlastingly doing something. Most of our minds are everlastingly occupied with something—words, problems, ideas, issues; it is always chattering to itself, it is never lazy, it is never quiet, it is always under a tension. And a mind that is not indolent, not lazy, but has that quietude, in its very gentleness perceives in a flash what is true. That laziness, that indolence, that sense of infinite leisure is not to be confused with comfort. A mind that has leisure is an extraordinary mind because then it is not caught up in the net of action; it is not everlastingly chattering with itself or about something.

So there is a quality of leisure, of quietude, a sense of indifference which is necessary. But that sense of quietness, that sense of indefinite emptiness, in which a flash of the real can take place, is only possible if we understand the laziness, not only of the body, but also the laziness of accepting ideas, thoughts, assertions, and conclusions, along which, like a tram car, we run along the same grooves. And we do not know, we are not even conscious, that we are running in grooves. That is laziness—not to know, not to be aware that your thought, your feeling, and your activities are perpetually along the same lines, along the same grooves. What you thought about a thing when you were twenty or thirty, you are still thinking the same about it; there is no change, there is no breaking away, there is nothing new, there is no freshness.

And the laziness of the body, the indolence which most people have—they feel they can arouse it to activity by disciplining the body, forcing it, driving it, compelling it. Every form of compulsion creates conflict, and a mind in conflict with the body does not give energy to the body, to the organism, but creates conflict, and that conflict is not the energizing quality which makes the body active.

So discipline, control, forcing the organism to conform, to get up from bed, to do various things to assert its activity, only creates resistance. And where there is resistance there is contradiction, and it is this contradiction which is not understood that breeds laziness. If you have studied your own body, watched it, observed it, then you will know when it should rest and when it should not rest. Then you will know that you need no compulsion, no enforcement, no driving the body to do something; the body will do it naturally, spontaneously, easily. For that, you must understand the whole process of your own mental indolence. When a man overeats, indulges himself in various forms, all those indicate an extraordinary sense of lassitude; because his mind is asleep, he merely follows an appetite which has become a habit, and that habit is merely a thoughtless continuity of what has been.

So, it is important to understand the process of the mind that has become lazy. There is laziness as long as there is conformity, settling down in the little corner that you have carved out for yourself and your family, feeling safe emotionally and mentally; feeling that you have achieved a certain result; patting yourself on the back, which indicates that you have come to a point where you feel pretty secure, that nothing can disturb you—then begins laziness. And it is that laziness which is the essence of self-pity.

You know what I mean by self-pity? Self-pity means to feel for oneself that one has no one to rely on, to feel for oneself that one is left out, neglected, that one is not loved though one may love, that one is a failure, that one must make a success, that one is this, or that one is that—the everlasting assertion of oneself. In your tears, in your happiness, in your frustration, in your misery, there is this thread, an unbreakable thread, of self-pity running right through life—and that is laziness. There, you have begun to conform, to settle down, to go fat mentally. And everyone seeks security in that laziness. And having established that sense of security psychologically, from that center one acts, one is, one's life is.

Please, as I said, don't merely listen to the words but observe your own mind, your own state of consciousness; see how closely the words represent your own state; watch your own mind in operation. Then what is being said will have significance, but if you are merely relying on words, then you are empty, and your cups will never be full, though you may search everlastingly. So, listening is really the observation of your own mind; seeing is really watching the movement of your own thought. For it is thought, it is the word, that prevents you from listening, from seeing. And if you would understand the whole problem of sorrow, the problem of action, you have to understand this self-pity.

Sorrow is both the action and the interaction of self-pity and memory. You are in sorrow because you have lost somebody; you are in sorrow because somebody does not love you; you are in sorrow because you cannot get a better job; you are in sorrow because somebody else is more beautiful, clever, alive, sensitive; and you are jealous, you are envious, greedy. Those are all the signs of conflict and sorrow. Sorrow is not a tremendous crisis of something uncontrollable, or of something which cannot be understood. You can change your mind completely; you can be completely free of sorrow so that it will never touch you again.

If you listen this evening—I mean, really listen without effort, without wanting to be free of sorrow—if you can listen with an enchantment, with ease, with pleasure, as you see the sunset, the flutter of a bird or a leaf, as though it were not related to you, then you will see that this burden of sorrow is taken away from you—not for a moment, not for the day, but you are free from sorrow.

If you could understand sorrow, the actual fact of it—not the ideation, not the idea about sorrow, but the actual fact of sorrow—then you would have the clue to the ending of sorrow. There is the idea of sorrow, and there is the actual fact of sorrow; these are two different things. Most of us have the idea of sorrow. If my son dies, if I lose my wife, if somebody does not love me, if I am not so intelligent as you are—the idea is more important than the fact. We do not know how to face the fact that there is sorrow—not the idea about sorrow.

Please do understand the difference between the two. Because we look at sorrow with the idea, with ideation, we do not look at sorrow. The ideation about sorrow is self-pity. The ideation about sorrow is the response of memory and therefore is not sorrow. The idea about food is not food. But most of us live on ideas, inherited or acquired, and that is our mental food; with that we are satisfied. So, our minds become dull, insensitive, unaware, empty.

To see the fact of sorrow is to be out of self-pity, to be free of self-pity. Self-pity is an idea about oneself. Why should it happen to me and not to you; why should I not be as powerful, big, noisy, vulgar as you are; why should I be deprived of my son, of my wife; why should my wife turn away from me; why am I not loved?—these are all the ideas of self-pity, the response of memory. And with that self-pity, with that response of memory, one looks at what one considers to be sorrow. Therefore it is not sorrow; it is self-pity in motion. It may sound very harsh, but that is the fact, the psychological fact. If you say to a person who has lost his father, his wife, his brother, whoever it may be, "Look at the fact; don't get lost in your self-pity," he will think that you are very cruel, that you have no heart, no sympathy, no love.

The fact is that no man is out of sorrow. When you observe yourself in sorrow, you will see that only when you understand the whole process of sorrow, you are out of sorrow. When you observe your own sorrow, you will see how extraordinarily closely it is related to self-pity and to all the remembrances of the things that have been. It is the things that have been, and the remembrance of those things, that breed self-pity and the sense of loneliness. So sorrow continues day after day, month after month, until you die. You have built around yourself a wall of self-pity, a wall of frustrated remembrances.

You are living in a house of death, which has lost its meaning. From there you investigate sorrow, from there you read books, you try to find out how to run away from sorrow.

So you have your gods, your books, your cinemas, your drinks, your women, your men, your amusements; they are all on the same level. Whether you take to a drink or go to the temple, it is the same thing. They are all escapes born of a lazy mind, which is the very essence of self-pity. You can't get rid of self-pity; don't say, "How am I to be free from self-pity?" That is another form of self-concern, which is self-pity. All that you can do is to learn about what prevents you from looking at the fact of sorrow—the fact: the anguish, the agony, the confusion, the misery in which one is caught.

How do you look at the fact of sorrow? When you do look at that fact without self-pity, without remembrance of the things that have been, then is there sorrow? If there were no remembrance of my son, how nice he was, how playful, what he would have been; if I am not immolating myself in him; if I have not, through him, immortalized myself; if I have not put everything into him, myself, my ideas, my hopes, my fears, my frustrations, which are all remembrances, the things that have been; and if self-pity (the very essence of this self-pity is sorrow) and the remembrance of things that have been do not exist—is there sorrow then? Can I not look then at an event with a totally different mind? That mind is not lazy; that mind is free of those causes that bring it indolence, laziness, slothfulness. That is, self-pity and remembrance are the causes that make the mind dull; these are the things that prevent the complete seeing of the fact instantly.

So, a mind that would understand sorrow must understand this whole process of self-centered thought, self-centered expansive action and the mechanism of habit, the mechanism of memory. You are what you are, a battlefield of memory and nothing else. Remove those memories of infancy, of youth, of all the things that you have acquired, of all the things that you have experienced, suffered, the things that you think you are; then, what are you? It is the sense of loneliness, emptiness, insufficiency that causes self-pity, and it is that thought that breeds infinite sorrow and travail. You are listening to me so that you understand yourself. And when you understand this, you can instantly wipe away this process of self-pity.

You do not want time. Time is not the way of mutation; time never brings about change; time brings acceptance, time brings habit. You get accustomed, grow weary, dull, stupid. But to break from the continuity of self-pity, which engenders sorrow, you have to see it instantly. And you can see it instantly. You may add more details to it—the details do not matter, reasons do not matter, conclusions about it do not matter. But the fact is you are incapable of facing the fact—the fact that I have lost my son, the fact that I cannot be as intelligent, as vital as you are; when I do face that fact, without self-pity, without consolation, without escapes, then I am free of you, then I am not in a state of comparison.

So a mind is concerned with itself, as most people are. You have to be concerned with yourselves at one level, physiologically—earning a job. But the self-concern at a deeper level, at the deep psychological level, breeds inaction, which is laziness. Psychologically, inwardly, if you have observed yourself and the world about you, you see that your action is merely a reaction, all your activities are a reaction, are a response to likes or dislikes.

Please follow this a little bit, because I want to show that there is an activity which is not the result of reaction or the result of an idea. I want to show that there is an action which is the outcome of total negation of reaction, and therefore such action is creative action. To understand that, to go into that question—which is really not complex but is an extraordinary state of mind—you have to understand your reactions from which your daily action springs. We react, we revolt, we accumulate, we defend, we resist, we acquire, we submit—all these are reactions.

I say something to you; you don't like it, and you do something in response to that which you don't like to accept. At that level we are acting all the time. You have been brought up, conditioned to a particular pattern of life; that is your daily life, pattern of life, inwardly and outwardly. And when that is questioned, you revolt, you react according to your conditioning, according to your habits; from that reaction there is another action. So we move from reaction to reaction all the time, and therefore we never are free. That is one of the origins of sorrow. Please understand this.

There must be reaction. When you see something ugly, it must react; when you see something beautiful, it must react; when you see a poisonous snake, it must react; otherwise, you are dead, you are insensitive, you are not alive, you are dull. But that reaction is different from the reaction which society and yourself through experiences have built up, which has become your conditioning. When you see a tree, when you see a sunset, if you do not react, you are paralyzed. But when you react according to self-pity, according to your conclusions, according to your habits, according to your failures, successes, hopes, despairs, such reaction leads to incomplete action and therefore to the continuity of more conflict, more misery.

I hope you see the difference between the two kinds of reaction. The reaction which sees and does not translate what it sees in terms of its own conditioning—that is one kind of reaction; that is the real action. And the other kind of reaction is that which sees and says, "That is beautiful, I must have it"; that reaction is the response of its own conditioning, memory, of its own self-pity, of its own desires, and all the rest of it. So, please see the difference between these two. The response born of idea is one thing, and the response without idea is another. Response born of ideation, of conclusions, of habits, of traditions leads to bondage, to misery. And the response without idea, merely observing, leads to freedom; that is freedom—it does not lead; freedom does not lead you anywhere.

It is only a free mind which is in a state of negation, negation of the positive reactions of a conditioned mind. And only a mind that is in negation, in that state of negation, can see in a flash what is true. Please, I am not saying something which is very complex; it is not complex, it is very simple. But because of its very simplicity, you are going to miss it; your minds are so complicated—you want to find various things—and what is being said is very simple. Your reactions are the outcome of your conditioning as a Hindu, a rich man, a poor man, a woman, a man, or whatever you are, with all your experiences, with your hopes, with your gods, with your anxieties, with your attachments—the conditioning is there, and from that you react; and the more you react, the more those reactions take you deeply into yourself; and you are still within the bondage of your own reactions, your own limitations. That is very simple. It does not need great psychological investigation. But what does demand energy and attention is to deny totally this positive reaction of a conditioned mind. When you deny, then you observe without any ideation, without any thought; then you look.

Surely, sirs, when you want to understand your unfortunate child—the child is unfortunate because you don't know how to educate him—you hand him over to a school, and that is the end of it; the child becomes a machine. This is not a discussion on education. If you have a child, you have to observe him, to watch him. When you want to learn about him, you don't say that he must be this or that, you don't compel him to do this or that; you observe, you learn, because your heart has to respond—not your ugly, little mind of possession.

So you have to learn about your child. And you can't learn if you respond, if you react, as a parent, with your authority, with your extraordinary sense of importance, as though you have produced a marvelous world. So, if you want to understand a child, you look at him without thought, to find out what he feels, what he thinks. Now if you look at him that way, your mind at that moment is empty because you are concerned about him. You don't clothe him with your ideas and your hopes and your fears, but you want to see what he is.

So if I can look at sorrow—the incident, the death of my son—if I can look at it, look at that fact, then I look without reaction; self-pity and remembrances have been put aside. But most of us indulge in self-pity. We have nothing else to live on; therefore, self-pity becomes our nourishment. The older we grow, the more important are the remembrances of the things that have been.

So, action which is born of reaction breeds sorrow. Most of our thoughts are the result of the past, of time. A mind that is not built on the past, that has totally understood this whole process of reaction, can act every minute totally, completely, wholly.

Please do listen. What I am going to say will probably be rather difficult. So, listen as though you were far away. I am going to talk about something which you will come to if you have gone through all this sweetly, with pleasure. When you have gone through the whole process of action born of reaction, and denied it with enchantment, with joy—not with pain—then you will see that you will come naturally, easily to a state of mind that is the very essence of beauty.

You must understand beauty. A mind that is not beautiful, that is not enchanted by a tree, by a flower, by a lovely face, by a smile; which does not stand by the sea and watch the restless waves; which has no sense of beauty—such a mind can never find love or truth. And you have been denied that beauty because that beauty demands passion, that beauty demands all your energy, a complete, undivided attention, and that complete undivided attention is negation, is a state of negation.

It is only out of nothingness that creation takes place; out of that emptiness there is that creation which is the summation of all energy. And you cannot come to it. You must leave yourself far away; you must lose yourself far away, forget yourself; you must come to it unspotted, without a remembrance, without thought, without a memory. Because, there is nothing you can experience, there is no experiencing; if you are seeking experience, then you are still caught in the known, in the things of yesterday.

I am talking of a mind that is not lazy, that has no self-pity, that has no memory except the mechanical memory of living—where it lives, going to the office, and doing the mechanical things of life. Such a mind has no psychological memory, and therefore no experiencing; therefore, there is no challenge. And it is only that mind which is itself the reality, which is itself creation—and that is beauty.

Beauty is not in the face, however refined it is. Beauty is something which is not put together by man. Beauty is not the result of thought, of feeling. Beauty is that communion with everything without reaction, communion with the ugly and with the so-called beautiful. And that communion is out of nothingness, and in that state there is that beauty, which is love.

March 4, 1962

Sixth Talk in Bombay

I want to go this evening into the question of death. I would like to talk about it as age and maturity, time and negation, which is love. But before I go into that, I think we should be very clear and have deeply understood that fear in any form perverts and breeds illusion, and that sorrow dulls the mind. A dull mind, a mind caught in illusion of any kind, cannot possibly understand the extraordinary question of death. We take shelter in illusion, in fancy, in myth, in various forms of story. And a mind so crippled cannot possibly understand this thing that we call death, nor can a mind understand which has been made dull by sorrow, as we explained in a previous talk.

The question of fear and sorrow is not a thing that you can philosophize about or put away from you through an escape. It is there as your shadow, and one has to deal with it directly and immediately. We cannot carry it over from day to day, however deep we may consider the sorrow or the fear; whether it is conscious or unconscious, it has to be understood immediately. Understanding is immediate; understanding does not come through time. It is not a result of continuous searching, seeking, asking, demanding. Either you see it totally, completely in a flash, or you don't see it at all. I have dealt with that sufficiently in the two previous talks, when we considered fear and sorrow.

This evening I would like to go into this thing called death with which we are all so familiar. We have observed it, we have seen it, but we have never experienced it; it has never been our lot to go through the portals of death. It must be an extraordinary state. I would like to go into it, not sentimentally, not romantically, not with a series of built-up structural beliefs, but actually, as a fact, to comprehend it as I would comprehend that crow cawing on that mango tree—as factually as that. But to understand something factually, you must give your attention as you listen to that bird on the tree—you don't strain, you listen; you don't say, "It is the crow. What a nuisance it is! I want to listen to somebody," but you are listening to that as well as to what is being said. But when you want to listen only to the speaker and resist the bird and the noise it is making, you will hear neither the bird nor the speaker. And I am afraid that is what most of you are doing when you are listening to a complex and profound problem.

Most of us have not given our minds totally, completely. You have never taken a journey of thought towards its end. You have never played with an idea, and seen the whole implication of an idea, and gone beyond it. So it is going to be very difficult if you don't pay, if you don't give, your attention—that is, if you don't listen easily, pleasantly, with a grace, with a playfulness in which there is no restraint, there is no effort. That is a very difficult thing for most of us to do—to listen. Because, we are always translating what is being said, and we never listen to what is being said.

I want to go into this question of death as a fact, not your death or my death or somebody's death—somebody whom you like, or somebody whom you don't like—but death as a problem. You know, we are so ridden with images, with symbols; for us symbols have an extraordinary importance, more factual than the reality. When I talk about death, you will instantly think of someone whom you have lost, and that is going to prevent you from looking at the fact. I am going to approach it through diverse ways, different ways—not just what is death and what is the hereafter after death; those are utterly immature questions. When you understand the extraordinary thing implied in death, you don't ask that question: What is hereafter? We have to consider maturity. A mature mind will never ask the question:

What is hereafter, is there a life hereafter, is there a continuity? So we have to understand what is mature thinking, what is maturity, and what is age.

Most of us know what age is because we do grow old, whether we like it or not. Age is not maturity. Maturity has nothing to do with knowledge. Age can contain knowledge but not maturity. But age can continue with all the knowledge, with all the traditions it has acquired. Age is a mechanical process of an organism growing old, being used constantly. A body that is constantly being used, in strife, in travail, in sorrow, in fear—an organism that is driven—soon ages, like any machine. But an organism that has aged is not a mature mind. So we have to understand the difference between age and maturity.

Most of us are born young, but the generation that has aged soon brings old age to the young. The past generation, which has aged in knowledge, in decrepitude, in ugliness, in sorrow, in fear, impinges that on the young. They are already old in age, and they die. That is the lot of every generation caught in the previous structure of society. And society does not want a new person, a new entity; it wants him to be respectable, it molds him, shapes him, and so destroys the freshness, the innocence of youth. This is what we are doing to all the children around here and in the world. And that child, when he grows into manhood, is already aged; he will never mature.

Maturity is the destruction of society, of the psychological structure of society. Unless you are totally ruthless with yourself, and unless you are completely free from society, you will never be mature. The social structure, the psychological structure of greed, envy, power, position, obeying—if you are not free of all that psychologically, then you will never mature. And you need a mature mind. A mind that is alone in its maturity, a mind that is not being crippled, not being spotted, that has no burden whatsoever—it is only such a mind that is a mature mind.

And you have to understand this: Maturity is not a matter of time. If you see very clearly, without any distortion, the psychological structure of the society in which you are being born, brought up, educated, then the instant you see, you are out of it. Therefore there is maturity on the instant, not in time. You cannot mature gradually; maturity is not like the fruit on the tree. The fruit on the tree needs time, darkness, fresh air, sunlight, rain, and in that process it ripens, ready to fall. But maturity cannot ripen; maturity is on the instant—either you are mature or you are not mature. That is why it is very important psychologically to see how your mind is caught in the structure of the society in which you are being brought up—the society that has made you respectable, the society that has made you conform, that has driven you in the pattern of its activities.

I think one can see totally, immediately, the poisonous nature of society as one sees a bottle marked "Poison." When you see it that way, you will never touch it; you know it is dangerous. But you don't know that society is a danger, that it is the deadliest thing for a man who is mature. Because, maturity is that state of mind which is alone, whereas this psychological social structure never leaves you alone, but is always shaping you, consciously or unconsciously. A mature mind is a mind which is completely alone because it has understood, it is free. And this freedom is on the instant. You cannot work for it, you cannot seek it, you cannot discipline yourself in order to get it—and that is the beauty of freedom. Freedom is not the result of thought; thought is never free, can never be free.

So, if we understand the nature of maturity, then we can look into time and continuity. For most of us, time is an actual reality. The time by the watch is an actual reality—we have to stop this meeting at seven o'clock or a quarter past seven; it takes time to go to your house, it takes time to acquire knowledge, it takes time to learn a technique. But is there any other time, except that time? Is there psychological time? We have built up psychological time, the time which is covered by the distance, the space, between 'me' and what I want to be, between 'me' and what I should be, between the past which was the 'me', through the present which is the 'me', to the future which is the 'me'. So thought builds psychological time. But is there such time? So to find out for yourself, you have to consider continuity.

What do we mean by that word *continuity?* And what is the inward significance of that word which is so common on our lips? You know, if you think about something—such as the pleasure that you have had—constantly, day after day, every minute, that gives to the past pleasure a continuity. If you think about something that is painful, either in the past or in the future, that gives it continuity. It is very simple. I like something and I think about it; the thinking about it establishes a relationship between what has been, the thought which thinks about it, and the fact that I would like to have it again. Please, this is a very simple thing if you give your mind to it; it is not a complex thing. If you don't understand what is continuity, you will not understand what I am going to say about death. You have to understand what has been expressed by me, not as a theory or a belief, but as an actuality which you see for yourself.

If you think about your wife, about your house, about your children, or about your job all the time, you have established a continuity, have you not? If you have a grudge, a fear, a sense of guilt, and if you think about it off and on, recall, remember, bring it out of the past, you have established a continuity. And our minds function in that continuity, all our thinking is that continuity. Psychologically you are violent, and you think about not being violent, the ideal, so through your thinking about not being violent, you have established the continuity of being violent. Please, this is important to understand; it is very simple once you see this thing—that thought, thinking about something, gives it continuity, whether it is pleasant or unpleasant, whether it gives you joy or gives you pain, whether it is something past or something that is going to take place tomorrow or next week.

So it is thought that establishes continuity in action—as going to the office day after day, month after month, for thirty years until your mind is a dead mind. And you equally establish a continuity with your family. You say, "It is my family"; you think about it; you try to protect it; you try to build a structure, a psychological protection on it and around yourself. And so the family becomes extraordinarily important, and you are destroyed. The family destroys; it is a deadly thing because it is a part of the social structure which holds the individual. So having established continuity, psychologically as well as physically, then time becomes very important—time, not by the watch, but time as a means of arriving, time as a means of psychologically achieving, gaining, succeeding. You can't succeed, you can't gain, unless you think about it, until you give your mind to it. So psychologically, inwardly, the desire for continuity is the way of time, and time breeds fear, and thought as time dreads death.

If you have no time at all inwardly, then death is in an instant; it is not something to be frightened of. That is, if every minute of the day thought does not give continuity to either pleasure or pain, to fulfillment or to lack of fulfillment, to insult, to praise, to everything to which thought gives attention, then there is death every minute. One must die every minute—not theoretically. That is why it is important to understand this machinery of thought. Thought is merely a response, a reflex of the past; it has no validity, as the tree has which you see actually.

So, to understand the extraordinary significance of death—there is a significance of death, which I shall go into presently—you must understand this question of continuity, see the truth of it, see the mechanism of thought which creates continuity.

I like your face; I think about it, and I have established a relationship with you in continuity. I do not like you; I think about it, and I establish it. Now, if you don't think about what gives you pleasure or pain, or of tomorrow, or of what you are going to get—whether you are going to succeed, whether you are going to achieve fame, notoriety, and all the rest of it—if you don't think at all about your virtue, about your respectability, about what people say or do not say; if you are totally, completely indifferent; then there is no continuity.

I do not know if you are at all indifferent to anything—I do not mean getting used to things. You have got used to the ugliness of Bombay, the filth of the streets, the way you live. You have got used to it; that does not mean you are indifferent. Getting used to something as habit dulls the mind, makes the mind insensitive. But being indifferent is something entirely different. Indifference comes into being when you deny, negate a habit. When you see the ugly and are aware of it, when you see the beautiful sky on an evening and are aware of it—neither wanting nor denying, neither accepting nor pushing it away, never closing the door to anything—and so, being completely, inwardly sensitive to everything around you, then out of that comes an indifference which has an extraordinary strength. And what is strong is vulnerable because there is no resistance. But the mind that only resists is caught in habit, and therefore it is a dull, stupid, insensitive mind.

A mind that is indifferent is aware of the shoddiness of our civilization, the shoddiness of our thought, the ugly relationships; it is aware of the street, of the beauty of a tree, or of a lovely face, a smile; and it neither denies it nor accepts it, but merely observes—not intellectually, not coldly, but with that warm, affectionate indifference. Observation is not detachment because there is no attachment. It is only when the mind is attached—to your house, to the family, to some job—that you talk about detachment. But, you know, when you are indifferent, there is a sweetness to it, there is a perfume to it, there is a quality of tremendous life-energy—this may not be the meaning of that word in the dictionary. One has to be indifferent—to health, to loneliness, to what people say or do not say—indifferent whether you succeed or do not succeed; indifferent to authority.

Now, if you observe, you hear somebody is shooting, making a lot of noise with a gun, you can very easily get used to it, probably you have already got used to it, and you turn a deaf ear—that is not indifference. Indifference comes into being when you listen to that noise with no resistance, go with that noise, ride on that noise infinitely. Then that noise does not affect you, does not pervert you, does not make you indifferent. Then you listen to every noise in the world—the noise of your children, of your wife, of the birds, the noise of the chatter the politicians make—you listen to it completely with indifference and therefore with understanding.

A mind that would understand time and continuity must be indifferent to time and not seek to fill that space which you call time with amusement, with worship, with noise, with reading, with going to the film, by every means that you are doing now. And by filling it with thought, with action, with amusement, with excitement, with drink, with woman, with man, with God, with your knowledge, you have given it continuity—and so you will never know what it is to die.

You see, death is destruction, it is final; you can't argue with it, you can't say, "Nay, wait a few days more." You can't discuss, you can't plead; it is final, it is absolute. We never face anything final, absolute; we always go around it, and that is why we dread death. We can invent ideas, hopes, fears and have beliefs, like "We are going to be resurrected, be born again"—those are all the cunning ways of the mind, hoping for a continuity, which is of time, which is not a fact, which is merely of thought. You know, when I talk about death, I am not talking about your death or my death—I am talking about death, that extraordinary phenomenon.

For you a river means the river with which you are familiar, the Ganga, or the river around your village. Immediately when the word *river* is mentioned, the image of a particular river comes into your mind. But you will never know the real nature of all the rivers, what a real river is, if the symbol of a particular river arises in your mind. The river is the sparkling water, the lovely banks, the trees on the bank—not any particular river, but the "riverness" of all the rivers, the beauty of all rivers, the lovely curve of every stream, every flush of water. A man that sees only a particular river has a petty, shallow mind. But the mind that sees the river as a movement, as water—not of any country, not of any time, not of any village, but its beauty—that mind is out of the particular.

If you think of a mountain, you will probably visualize, being an Indian brought up with all the so-called religious books and all the rest of it, that a mountain means the Himalayas to you. So you have an image of it immediately, but the mountain is not the Himalayas. The mountain is that height in the blue sky, of no country, covered with whiteness, shaped by the wind, by earthquakes.

When a mind thinks of mountains vastly, or of rivers of no country, then such a mind is not a petty mind, it is not caught by littleness. If you think of a family, you think immediately of your family, and so the family becomes a deadly thing. And you can never discuss the whole issue of a family in general because you are always relating, through continuity of thought, to the particular family to which you belong.

So, when we talk about death, we are not talking about your death or my death. It does not really very much matter if you die or I die; we are going to die, happily or in misery—die happily having lived fully, completely, with every sense, with all our being, fully alive, in full health; or die like miserable, crippled people with age, frustrated, in sorrow, never knowing a day happy, rich, never having a moment in which we have seen the sublime. So, I am talking about death, not of the death of a particular person.

Death is the ending. And what we are frightened about, what we dread, is the ending—the ending of your job, the putting away, the going away, the ending of your family, of the person whom you think you love, the ending of a continuous thing which you have thought about for years. What you dread is the ending. I do not know if you have ever deliberately, consciously, purposely thought of ending something—your smoking, your drinking, your going to the temple, your desire for power—ending it completely, on the instant, as a surgeon's knife cuts cancer. Have you ever tried to cut the thing that is most pleasurable to you? It is easy to cut something that is painful, but it is not easy deliberately to cut with a surgical precision and with compassionate precision something pleasurable, not knowing what is going to happen tomorrow, not knowing what is going to happen in the next instant, after you cut; if you cut, knowing what is going to happen, then you are not operating. If you have done it, you will know what it means to die.

If you have cut everything around you, every psychological root—hope, despair, guilt, anxiety, success, attachment—then out of this operation, this denial of this whole structure of society, not knowing what will happen to you when you are operating completely, out of this total denial, there is the energy to face that which you call death. The very dying to everything that you have known, deliberately to cut away everything that you have known, is dying. You try it some time—not as a conscious, deliberate, virtuous act to find out—just try it, play with it, for you learn more out of play than out of deliberate conscious effort. When you so deny, you have destroyed, and you must destroy; for, surely, out of destruction purity can come—an unspotted mind.

There is nothing psychological which the past generation has built that is worth keeping. Look at the society, the world, which the past generation has brought about. If one tried to make the world more confused, more miserable, one could not do it. You have to wipe all that away instantly, sweep it down the gutter. And to cut it, to sweep it away, to destroy it, you need understanding and also something much more than understanding. A part of that understanding is this compassion.

You see, we do not love. Love comes only when there is nothing, when you have denied the whole world—not an enormous thing called the world, but just your world, the little world you live in—the family, the attachment, the quarrels, the domination, your success, your hopes, your guilt, your obedience, your gods, and your myths. When you deny all that world, when there is absolutely nothing left, no gods, no hopes, no despairs, when there is no seeking—then out of that great emptiness comes love, which is an extraordinary reality, which is an extraordinary fact not conjured up by the mind that has a continuity with the family through sex, through desire.

And if you have no love—which is really the unknown—do what you will, the world will be in chaos. Only when you deny totally the known—what you know, your experiences, your knowledge, not the technological knowledge, but the knowledge of your ambitions, your experiences, your family—when you deny the known completely, when you wipe it away, when you die to all that, you will see that there is an extraordinary emptiness, an extraordinary space in the mind. And it is only that space that knows what it is to love. And it is only in that space there is creation—not the creation of children or putting a painting on the canvas, but that creation which is the total energy, the unknowable. But to come to that, you must die to everything that you have known. And in that dying, there is great beauty, there is inexhaustible life-energy.

March 7, 1962

Seventh Talk in Bombay

I am going to talk this evening about several things, but the central point of this talk is meditation. But to comprehend it fully and to go into the meaning, not only of the word, but of the activity of a mind that is meditative, demands a certain intensity of thought and clarity of perception. It is a very complex subject and what I am going to say, what I am going to explore, will not at all be traditional. So, if you would journey with me into the question of what is meditation and the meditative mind, you have to be attentive—attentive not in the sense of making a tremendous effort to concentrate or to learn a few phrases, or to get a few ideas, but attentive in the wide, large sense of that word, not only to what is about you as you are sitting—to the trees, to the light on the tree, to the cawing of the birds, to the breeze—but also to the operation of your own mind, how it is functioning. All this demands a certain clarity of attention in which there is no concentration, in which there is no effort.

But for a mind that is sharply, eagerly, intensely inquiring, searching, seeking, and going into the question of what is meditation, there must be also the art of listening. I mean by that word to listen without any form of denial or acceptance, to listen without comparing, to find out. If you compare, if you merely hear a series of words and ideas, then you are not listening. Listening is quite an extraordinary fact. And we very rarely so listen with a freedom, with an enchantment, with a smile, to find out.

We are going to talk about something which needs a mind that can penetrate very profoundly. We must begin very near because we cannot go very far if we do not know how to begin very close, if we do not know how to take the first step. The flowering of meditation is goodness, and the generosity of the heart is the beginning of meditation. We have talked about many things concerning life, authority, ambition, fear, greed, envy, death, time; we have talked about many things. If you observe, if you have gone into it, if you have listened rightly, those are all the foundation for a mind that is capable of meditating. You cannot meditate if you are ambitious—you may play with the idea of meditation. If your mind is authority-ridden, bound by tradition, accepting, following, you will never know what it is to meditate on this extraordinary beauty. And as we have gone into all that, I would like to go this evening into the question of goodness and generosity.

Pride in any form prevents generosity of the mind and heart, because pride is self-centered activity—pride in achievement, pride in knowledge, pride in an aim, pride in the race. We are all very proud, consciously or unconsciously. And a mind that is proud can never be generous, can never have the excellence of heart, can never have humility—as we talked about the other day—which is the beginning of learning, which is wisdom. The flowering of generosity cannot take place in the arid soil of the mind. The mind can never be generous, but only the heart and the hand. The mind can imagine what the qualities of generosity are and try to cultivate generosity, but the cultivation of generosity is not to be generous.

It is the pursuit of its own fulfillment through time that prevents generosity. And you need a generous mind—not only a wide mind, a mind that is full of space, but also a heart that gives without thought, without a motive, and that does not seek any reward in return. But to give whatever little one has or however much one has—that quality of spontaneity of outgoing, without any restriction, without any withholding, is necessary. There can be no meditation without generosity, without goodness—which is to be free from pride, never to climb the ladder of success, never to know what it is to be famous; which is to die to whatever has been achieved, every minute of the day. It is only in such fertile ground that goodness can grow, can flower. And meditation is the flowering of goodness.

Please listen to this, not in order to achieve goodness—you won't be able to achieve it. You can't practice goodness. Goodness is a flower that bursts overnight; it comes into being without your wanting, without your seeking, without your cultivating. It can only come through listening. It will take place suddenly, in full blossom. Goodness is never the repetition of what has been; you cannot be good if you remember the past, either the pleasure or the pain, or the insult or the flattery. In that soil it will never grow. It will never grow in the ground of time, but it comes into being without your knowing. This goodness cannot be when there is pride, and this goodness is the very essence of never accumulating and therefore never forgiving—there is no forgiveness; there is only forgiveness when you have accumulated. But a mind that is constantly moving, flowing, never having a resting place, never looking back to its memories, to its knowledge, to all the things that it has experienced—it is only in such a mind that goodness can grow and generosity be.

You have to find out what meditation is. It is a most extraordinary thing to know what meditation is—not how to meditate, not the system, not the practice, but the content of meditation. To be in the meditative mood and to go into that meditation requires a very generous mind, a mind that has no border, a mind that is not caught in the process of time. A mind that has not committed itself to anything, to any activity, to any thought, to any dogma, to any family, to a name—it is only such a mind that can be generous, and it is only such a mind that can begin to understand the depth, the beauty, and the extraordinary loveliness of meditation.

I am going to go into that this evening, not only verbally—which is the only means of communication that you and I have—but also nonverbally. And to understand the nonverbal pursuit of meditation, the mind must be free of the word. The word is the symbol, and the symbol is never the truth. So the man who is bound by a word can never pursue that form of meditation which is beyond and above the word, beyond the symbol, beyond the vision. But to go into that we will begin very close, very near, and we will proceed step by step. Meditation is a part of life, just as your going to your office, or your eating your meal, or your speaking, or your acting is a part of life. And meditation, being a part of life, is not to be neglected any more than you neglect to clean your teeth, to bathe, to go to your office; but most of us neglect this side because it is much more arduous, demanding much greater energy, and of greater insistency.

Meditation is the beginning of self-knowledge. To know oneself and nothing else is meditation. To know what you are thinking, what you are feeling, what your motives are, to be choicelessly aware of them, to face them as facts without an opinion, without judgment—that is just the beginning of meditation. If you have not done that in your life ever, but have pursued the traditional meditation of sitting down in a quiet corner and trying to focus your attention on something, then you can sit for ten thousand years and go on repeating words, mantras; you can hypnotize yourself by the repetition of words, which quietens the mind. But that quietness leads nowhere but to death, decay, and withering.

Please listen to it. We are not condemning, so you don't have to resist. We are merely pointing it out for you to take it or not to take it. But you must observe it. The beginning of meditation is self-inquiry, self-critical awareness, just to know what you are, and from that very simplicity grows the immense, which is beyond words, beyond time, beyond thought. But you must begin at that very simple, immediate step.

Most of us do not want to know what we are. We invent the higher self, the supreme self, the atma, and all the innumerable ideas, to escape from the reality of what we are—the actual everyday, every-minute reality of what we are. And we do not know what we are from day to day, and on that we impose something which thought has bred as the atma, which tradition has handed over as the higher self. With all that, we cover ourselves and try to reach the thing invented by the mind, and then if you do reach it, it is empty, it is ashes, it has no meaning.

So to meditate, you must destroy everything totally, completely deny everything that is being imposed. You must deny nationality; you must deny the Gita, the Bible, the Koran—everything. And that is a very difficult thing to do because we need them as a means of security, as something to lean on in time of trouble, in time of pain, in sorrow. They are merely escapes—your Krishna, your saviors, and all those people. What is of importance and of the greatest significance is your daily, everyday existence—what you think and what you feel. And you can't understand what you think and what you feel if you are encumbered, if you are weighed down by the knowledge of the past, of what the books have said.

So, the beginning of meditation is the knowing of yourself—not what you think you should be, not what Shankara thinks you should be—just as you are, as when you look at yourself in a mirror. So, if you pursue self-knowing, you begin to inquire into what you are—your daily activities, the way you talk to your servant, the way you treat your wife, your husband, the way you play up to important people, the everlasting desire to be "somebody." Without knowing the whole field of the conscious and the unconscious of your being, do what you will, you will never know what meditation is.

So, the beginning of meditation is the denial of every form of authority, because you have to be a light to yourself. And a man who is a light to himself has no authority at any time, either at the beginning or at the end. But to be a light to oneself implies a great many things, and from the beginning you must be a light to yourself, not at the end. To be a light to yourself implies no fear—we have gone into it. To be a light to yourself implies no attachment of any kind, neither to your wife nor to your husband nor to your knowledge nor to your experience, because these cast a shadow and prevent you from being a light to yourself. But more than that, to be a light to yourself you must inquire into experience.

Experience is the essence of time, experience builds time as knowledge, experience conditions the mind. If you are a Hindu or a Christian or a Buddhist, you are being brought up in a particular culture, which is in the religion, in the education, in the family, in the tradition of that particular culture; your mind is shaped, molded according to that culture, according to that tradition. You either believe in Krishna or Christ or whatever you believe in, and that is your conditioning, and according to that conditioning you will experience. A mind that experiences according to that conditioning cannot possibly ever know the immense significance of meditation.

We are inquiring into meditation. I hope you are listening—not merely verbally following, but actually living the thing that is being explained—so that when you leave this place, you will know the immensity, the beauty, the ecstasy of meditation—not the toil, not the struggle to achieve a state or a vision. Because, the vision which you want, which you crave for, which you desire, is the result of your conditioning. When you see Krishna or Rama or any other person, it is your background that has projected it there. Your background has been built through centuries of time, through fear, through agony, through sorrow; and whatever vision may be born of that is utterly empty, has no meaning; and a mind caught in that can never know the freedom of meditation.

So you have to understand the meaning of the word *experience.* We all want more experience, more and more—more wealth, more property, more love, greater success, more fame, more beauty; and we also want more experience as knowledge. Please do follow this. A mind that is experiencing is dependent on experience; and experience is, after all, the response to a challenge. I do hope you are following this—this is not very complex. The mind that is athirst for more, wanting more experience, more knowledge, more thrills, more ecstasy, is a mind that is dependent. And a mind that is dependent, leaning upon something—that can only indicate that it is asleep. Therefore every challenge to it is an experience of waking up for a moment, to go to sleep again. So every challenge and response is an indication of a mind that is asleep.

There are innumerable challenges all our life. There are influences all the time, impregnating our minds and hearts all the time, whether we are conscious or unconscious of them. The cawing of the crow has already gone into your unconscious, it is there; the color of that sari, whether you see it or not, has already given its impression; the sunset, the cloud caught in the light of an evening—that has left its mark. So the conscious or unconscious mind is full of these impressions, and from these impressions all experiences arise. These are psychological facts; you don't have to dispute or agree or disagree. And a mind that is dependent on experience as a means of advancement, as a means of growing, as a means of maturity, as a means of unfoldment—such a mind which is dependent on time, on experience, can never obviously penetrate that which is beyond time, beyond experience. Therefore, you will have to understand very profoundly the significance of experience.

Experience dulls the mind. It does not enlighten the mind because that experience is the result of a response to a challenge, and that response is from the background of what you have already known. So every experience only strengthens what you have known, and therefore there is no freedom from what you have known.

Meditation is the very beginning of the freedom from the known. You must meditate, not because somebody says so, not because a man talks about meditation and enchants you. You must meditate because it is the most natural thing to do. Meditation gives you an astonishing sensitivity, a sensitivity that is very strong and yet vulnerable; though it may sound contradictory, it is not. A mind that is put together by time, by experience, by knowledge, by conflict, by assertion, by aggression, or by ambition—such a mind is not a strong mind; it is only capable of resisting. I am talking of strength of quite a different kind, a strength that is vulnerable, that has no resistance, and therefore it is a mind that is beyond experience.

You must understand the meaning, the depth, and the quality of experience that you all want. To see Rama, Krishna, Christ, this or that—that you call meditation. It is not meditation; it is only a projection from the past, a projection of what you have been brought up on. A Christian sees the Christ and glories in what he sees. But the man who is never brought up to worship Christ as the Savior, or whatever it is, will never see Christ any more than you who have been brought up to believe in Krishna. You will never see other gods; you will see your own gods, and when you are caught in your own gods, you are caught in your own illusion. A mind that is caught in an experience can never, do what it will, go into the depth, into the complete silence of emptiness of space—which is part of meditation.

So, through understanding the whole process of experience, you will be able to deny the known completely. There are various forms of drugs that make the mind very sensitive. They have them now in Europe and America; probably they will come to this country also. They give you a great capacity to see color, shape, light, intensely, vividly; and by taking those, you have extraordinary experiences. But what you see through the drugs—the visions, the experiences, the sensations, the clarity, the beauty of the trunk of a tree, or the leg of a table—they are still within the field of the known. Those drugs will never free the mind from the known, and therefore there is no possibility for the unknown to be.

So, you begin to see for yourself, if you are listening, that every form of repetitive thought, practice, discipline, every form of experience only engenders the demand, the urge for further experience; you are never satisfied with one experience; you want more, more and more. So, you begin to see that there is no method. A method is the practice, the tradition, of doing something over and over again, following some thought, some action—which only dulls the mind. Therefore there is no method, there is no path.

Please follow all this. There is no path to enlightenment. You begin to see that every form of experience is to be denied through understanding because you understand that every experience dulls the mind, every experience is a translation of the known, of the past. A mind caught in time can never go beyond time. So, when you deny authority, when you deny discipline as the known, as practiced by a method, then you will also have understood and put aside experience completely.

Most of us are brought up on concentration. From childhood you are told to concentrate on your book; when you want to look out of the window and see the birds on the wing, or see a leaf on the tree, see a bullock cart passing by, your teacher says, "Concentrate, pay attention to your work." Do you know what that does to you? It builds up a new conflict, a contradiction. A child absorbed in a toy is concentrated. You must have noticed your children—when they have a toy, they are completely absorbed in that toy, the toy takes them, and you call that concentration. You concentrate on an idea; when your mind wanders all over the place, you want to fix it on one thing, and your mind goes off again; you pull it back and it goes off again, so you have the conflict—you call this meditation—it is so immature, so infantile.

But you have to follow every thought, understand every thought that arises, and not say that any thought which is not concentrated becomes a distraction. If you don't say that but examine every thought, follow it to the end, then there is no distraction. Because, then there is no concentration, then you are understanding every movement of thought, every movement of the mind. When you follow every movement of the mind, in such following, there is no distraction. There is no distraction when you listen to that crow. There is no distraction when you listen to that noise of the traffic. But there is distraction when you say, "I want to concentrate on one thing and deny everything else"; then everything else becomes a distraction.

So a mind that has learned to concentrate has become a narrow, dull mind. I am not denying concentration; I am going to go into it. But when you understand the whole significance of concentration—which is to resist, to cut away and focus your mind on one thing—you see that such a focusing narrows the mind, dulls the mind. That focusing is a resistance and therefore creates conflict, and a mind in conflict can never pursue the depth, the ecstasy found in meditation.

When you understand the whole significance of concentration, then there is an attention, awareness. Attention is not focused but inclusive—you can listen to the birds, you can listen to that traffic, you can listen to the speaker, you can watch the movement of the leaf in the breeze, you can see the sunset, you can see the light on the building. In this awareness there are no borders; it is inclusive, it includes everything. And such a mind which is attentive, which is completely taking everything, can concentrate; and such concentration is not resistance, such concentration has no conflict. Look at what is actually taking place now, if you are observing. The speaker is talking, expressing, and at the same time there is listening to the birds, to the traffic, to the light, seeing the quietness of the leaf, seeing the stars, taking everything in, and therefore denying nothing.

So a mind that has gone through and has understood concentration, experience, has realized that there is no method, no system, no practice. Such a mind is in a state of attention. Such a mind then understands what is stillness. The brain, the actual brain, is constantly active. The brain is the result of time; the brain is the result of the animal instincts, animal demands, animal urges. The understanding of this whole process of the brain is really self-understanding because it is the brain that has the impulses of ambition, greed, envy. The brain has association; it works on the same principle as an electronic brain.

So, one has to understand the process of the brain, which is built up through society, which is the result of society. The instincts, the pursuits, the fears, the ambitions, the greed, the envy—all that is contained in the brain. The brain can be completely, extraordinarily still—not by force, not by compulsion, not by discipline, but by understanding and being free of ambition, greed, envy, success, fear, including fear of public opinion, the righteous immorality of society, by putting all those aside, completely. And you must have that stillness; otherwise, you can't proceed. A mind that is seeking peace, as most people are, is only seeking darkness. But when you begin to understand the whole process of the psychological structure of society, which has put into the brain all the memories, associations, results; when you understand that, out of that comes the quietness of the brain. If you have not understood it, if the brain is not completely quiet—quiet, not drugged, not hypnotized—then there is no space in the mind.

You must have space in the mind. Space cannot exist if there is not complete quietness. Space is not imagined, is not romantic, is not brought about by stupid ideas of achievement, but it comes through when the brain has understood and has become completely quiet; then there is space within the mind.

There must be space within the mind, and it is that space that is innocency. No society, no thought, no feeling, no experience can enter into that space which is the unknown. That space is not the space which the rockets discover, the space above us. That space cannot be discovered, you cannot seek it, there is no way to it, but there will be that space when you have understood the whole psychological structure, conscious as well as unconscious, of your being. You can understand it instantly, in a moment, without going through all the rigmarole of analysis, inquiry; you can come to it immediately, and when you do come, there is that space. That space is completely empty, and no thought, no feeling can enter it. Thought and feeling are the reactions of the known, and the brain has associations built up through the social influences as the 'me'. And therefore the freedom from the known is the quietening of the brain.

Now what I am going to say about that space will have no meaning for you; it will be a theory. It will have no value for you, except as repetition, and what you repeat will have no meaning at all. But I am talking about it for you to see that there is such a thing—just to see it casually; not for you to get it and hold it; you can't hold it any more then you can hold the wind in your fist. But you must know the poesy of something beautiful. To see that space there must be an extraordinary sense of sensitivity. Now, in that space there is nothing, as the mind is empty—the mind has no thought, no feeling. And because that space is empty, there is energy, not the energy brought about through resistance. Because it is empty, because there is space, there is that energy which is creation.

That creation is also destruction. Everything created is the known. And because that creation is innocency, it is destructive of everything known; the known cannot enter. And because it is creation and also is destruction, there is love—not the love of remembrance, not the love of your husband or wife, not the love of your children; all that is merely the response of various desires, pursuits, and ambitions and fulfillments. In this love, there is no division; it is love. And that mind can love the one or many because in that, there is no division.

So, meditation is the beginning of the flowering of goodness. When that goodness flowers deeply, without a root in the mind as the self and self-pity and memory, from that little beginning grows the immensity which is not of time, which has no beginning and no end. And that is the everlasting and the immeasurable.

March 11, 1962

Eighth Talk in Bombay

This is the last talk. I am going to talk this evening about the religious mind and the new mind. And to go into it, as I would like to go rather deeply, we must understand, I think, the significance of words.

Words are used for communication, but words become barriers to communication when we accept the common meaning of a word—which becomes the pattern of our thinking. I am going to use the word *religious* in quite a different sense. The religious mind has the capacity to act totally, not in fragments, not in divisions. A mind that is capable of seeing, in the immediate, the whole and not merely the particular, a mind that is capable of comprehending the totality of existence in the immediate now—such a mind essentially has beauty and that sense of love which alone binds action to the whole. And one has to understand this quality of the religious mind, whose action is not divided, broken up, fragmentary, but is total. Such a mind is essentially free from ideation as memory, the self. I think one knows, perhaps at rare moments, this quality of action that is not tinged by the self, the 'me'. It is the self, the 'me' that breaks up action into fragmentation; it is the self, the 'me', that drives to acquire. And that sense of attachment can never comprehend the totality of action which is of the religious mind.

So, I am using the words *religious mind* as a state of action which binds all the various activities of life; it is not divided in itself as the world and the not-world, as the outside and the inside. There is no outside world and inside world. There is only a movement as the outer and as the inner, like the tide that goes out and then comes in. The religious mind has the quality of comprehending the outer, and through the comprehension of the outer comes to the inner naturally, easily, without dividing the world as the "outer" and the "inner."

But to comprehend this totality of the religious mind, one must begin to inquire into the various complex processes of living. Our daily living is so confused; it is in conflict, it has innumerable sorrows, it is in contradiction, it is always striving—and that is our life. We only know that. We do not know any action apart from reaction. And it is this reaction that breeds sorrow, and from that sorrow there is further division as the outer and the inner, as something illusory and something real. There is only one world—not the outer and the inner, not that world divided as the outer and the inner. And without understanding the totality of action of the religious mind—do what you will, have every kind of revolution, economic or social, plan what you will—prosperity becomes merely a means of destroying freedom; and though we must have prosperity, prosperity then becomes a means of psychological security. And a mind that is psychologically secure is not a religious mind.

So, to inquire into the nature of the religious mind, into that state of mind which is free from this conflict of the self, we must inquire into simplicity, to find out what it is to be simple—not the idea of simplicity, not the ideal of simplicity, not the symbol of simplicity, but the actual state of a mind that is really simple. I mean by that word *simple* to face every fact of everyday and every minute without the complexity, to look at facts without the complex process of thought, to look at facts without ideation, without ideals. And such simplicity is not in mere clothes, not in the loincloth and one meal a day, not in a long beard or a clean-shaven face; but it is the simplicity that has precision when it has to think, that has no conflict, that has no illusion, that has no future, that faces the fact and only the fact, nothing else but the fact.

Such a mind, such an approach to life, does bring about an extraordinary sense of joy. Very few of us are happy naturally, easily, spontaneously. We are so complex, we have so many problems; everything we touch either by the hand or by the mind becomes ugly. And when something becomes ugly, crude, vulgar, there is no sensitivity, and therefore there is no appreciation of things as they are. It is only in the understanding of the things as they are, actually facing things as they are—out of that comprehension, there is revolution.

Revolution is not brought about according to a pattern of someone else—of the economist, of the reformer, of the politician. The revolution of which we are talking comes into being when you can see the fact and act according to that fact, from moment to moment. In so acting, you will find, out of that simplicity, not only there is an extraordinary sense of relief, a sense of unburdening, but out of that comes a deep joy. And without joy, without the spark, without a song in one's heart, life becomes so utterly empty. You may be very clever, you may have big houses, you may occupy very important positions, you may influence thousands of people through newspapers; but behind that façade of words, position, prestige, and power, there is a hollowness—such a mind is not a creative mind.

And it is important for the individual, for each one of us, to have this sense of unending joy. It does come, not because you have a job, not because you are happily married, or unhappily married; it has no reason. And there is that joy; you can only come to it darkly, unknowingly, when you understand the simplicity of virtue. Virtue is not something to be striven after—then it ceases to be virtue. When a man who is vain practices humility, then that humility is the essence of vanity. But virtue is order: just to have order in one's mind. And you can't have order if it is merely a pattern after the sanction of society, if it is merely a practice, a habit—then the mind is made dull. And a dull mind is not a virtuous mind; it may have excellent habits, it may never get angry, it may be self-righteous and comply with the commands of society; but such a mind is not a sensitive mind and therefore not a virtuous mind.

Do please listen to this, not that you are suddenly going to become virtuous. You will, suddenly on the instant, be virtuous, which is not after the pattern of an ugly, corrupting society; but you will have order, and space in that order. That order brings about efficiency. It is the mind that is efficient in thought and that has no conflict that is a virtuous mind, that lives virtuously. When virtue is the result of conflict, is the result of constant striving, which is the battle of opposites, such a mind not only becomes insensitive but is incapable of swift flight. It is only the efficient mind that is capable of rapidity, that sees things in a flash. For truth is perceived only in a flash; truth has no continuity. What has continuity is of time, and what has time has no space. And it is only a mind that has space that can see in a flash what is truth. It is only the virtuous mind that has space, and therefore only such a mind can, in a flash, see immensity—that which is eternal. Virtue is not the outcome of memory. If virtue is the outcome of memory, then virtue is a reaction to memory; reaction is a reflex of memory. Such virtue as is recognized by society, by religious orders, by groups, does breed conflict, and therefore such a mind is not a simple mind.

You know, the world is becoming more and more complex. Your relationship with another is getting more and more complex, not simpler. The complexity of life can only be understood when you approach it very simply, really very, very simply. Life is not merely your daily existence—going to the office, the quarrels with your wife or husband, the nagging, the misery, the conflict of everyday existence. Life includes not only the past, which projects itself into the future, but also death, happiness, and also something beyond time, beyond thought, beyond feeling. And you have to comprehend this immense totality of life—not your little corner of existence, not the little place on the earth which you call your country, not the little temple built by hand, which has no meaning. Life is an extraordinary thing, a total thing in which all this is included. And without understanding the immensity of life in which is included everything—every cry, every tear, every song of every bird, the anguish, the misery, the travail of existence—without understanding the totality of it, you will never have a flash of that immensity.

To understand this extraordinary thing called life—with its sexual demands, with its ambitions, drives, its frustrations, old age, decline, and deterioration—you must come to it very simply. And that is our difficulty because we are such complex human beings, we have so many ideas. We are so clever. But we are all secondhand people; there is nothing original in us, and it is originality that makes for simplicity—not eccentricity, not the capacity to invent. But this simplicity is the simplicity of a mind that has understood all the facets of life—not the technical life, not the life of accumulated knowledge, because knowledge and technical knowledge can expand indefinitely. You will know more and more about things—about Venus, about Mars, about the Moon, how to get to the Moon—but less and less about yourself, about what you are. What you are is the totality of life. Because you are miserable, unhappy with all the anguish, the guilt and the agony that you go through silently or openly, to understand life, you have first to understand yourself.

You can understand yourself, who are a complex entity, by looking at yourself very, very simply. And out of that perception, out of that seeing, out of that listening to yourself, you understand. You have to listen to yourself, not to your higher self; there is no higher self, there is no atma;

that is an invention of the mind, the result of thought—thought being the response of the mind, of the things that have been. So when you look at yourself every day, in every word, when you feel your way into the depth of your own heart and mind, then out of that looking, seeing, listening, and hearing there comes simplicity; and out of that simplicity there is joy—and that is virtue.

The religious mind has really no experience. This is important to understand because we all want experiences, more and more. And every experience, as I pointed out the other day, is the response to a challenge according to your background, according to your conditioning; and so every experience strengthens that conditioning, it does not liberate the mind. But you have to understand the nature of your own thought, the way of your action, the way you look—if you do look ever—at the face of a bus driver. Have you ever looked at the bus driver, have you ever looked at the bus driver's face? I doubt it. Watch it sometimes, see how haggard it is, how weary, how worn out it is! Going up and down the same route day after day, month after month, as you go to your office—there is no joy, there is nothing but mechanical habit, and never being aware of the things about oneself. All that indictates, surely, does it not, a mind grown callous, a mind grown dull. Yet such a mind talks about God, truth, wanting to understand, but it is not aware of the things about itself—the way one dresses, the way one talks, the way one regards the important people and the unimportant people. Without knowing all this, without laying the foundation through all this, you cannot go very far. And virtue is the awareness of the present.

You see, we are always living either in the past or in the future. Especially as you get older, the past becomes extraordinarily significant, and the future is only what you call death. So you go to the past and avoid the future—how happy you were, what a lovely youth you had, or what a miserable existence you had. So we live between the past and the future. If you are still young, you have still the future to make something of, and you shape it according to the past. So you are caught between the past and the future. Observe your own minds, your own life. Do not merely hear what I am saying, but actually observe your own existence. You will see how divided it is between the past and the future, and if it is not divided, you are merely living in the immediate, from day to day, making the very best of that. Because, there may be a war, there may be a revolution, an economic revolution, a social upheaval; anything may happen tomorrow; tomorrow is uncertain. Therefore, if you don't live between the past and the future, you live just for today. There are many who live for today, and they call themselves by many names. And when you make the best of today, consciously or unconsciously, you are bound to be in despair.

Do please listen to what I am talking about. You are in despair if you are living in the past or in the future; you are also in despair if you are living only for today—and that is what most people are doing; that is the political world. This unfortunate country is ruled by politicians. Before, it was the priest and the book, and now it is the politicians' turn. And the politicians are concerned only with the immediate, and that immediate may be extended for a while, but still it has its source in the immediate. Most people are wanting to be happy immediately, are wanting success immediately. When we are concerned with the immediate, all the indications of our existence are in terms of the immediate. When you pursue the immediate, you will come upon untold despair, and out of that despair you invent philosophies; you make a virtue out of that despair. And the more intellectual, the more learned and erudite you are, the more shallow becomes the immediate. So, whether you live in the past or in the future or just live for today, you are all caught in misery, in travail, in a life that is utterly superficial. I mean by that word *superficial* not food, clothes, and shelter—that every one must have—but the psychological superficiality of existence.

Now, if you understand the time past, the time present, and the time future—which breed sorrow and despair, anxiety and guilt—not little by little, not by examining or analyzing the past, but by seeing the thing as a whole, then you see the totality of time divided as the past and the future and the now. If you see it, if you really comprehend it that way as a total thing, then you will see that out of that comprehension, the mind is made free from the past, the present, and from the future. And the mind must be free. It is out of that freedom that the individual comes into being.

It is immensely important that you must be an individual, because governments, education, society, and religion are making you conform, making you into a machine which believes or does not believe. It is essential that you emerge as an individual, that is, with a mind that is free, that has lived in society and society has not left a mark upon it—and it can be done; it is not something vain, ideological, or theoretical. You can have a mind unspotted, clear, precise, living in this world, in a corrupt society. But it can come about only when you understand the structure, the psychological state of society, which is the past, the present, and the future—that is society, and you can comprehend the totality of it.

So, the religious mind is the revolutionary mind. We have thought of revolution only in terms of economic, social, or structural upheaval. But every upheaval is a reflex of the past, and therefore it throws up a similar pattern, but with a different set of people, with a different set of ideas—but it is still the same pattern. But we are talking of a religious mind that has really understood the whole structure of itself, the state of itself, and therefore denies. You must deny; you must always be a no-sayer, not a yes-sayer. And you know how difficult it is to say no, not to your wife or your husband—that is comparatively easy—but to say no to society, to say no to your ambition, to say no to your fears, to say no to authority. When you say no, you mean no—completely no. If you will say no, you will discover how extraordinarily complex it is.

But by saying no, you will find out about yourself: what you are made of, how your thought functions, the deep corners, the deep untrodden space in your mind which you have never looked into. It is only when you discover yourself, you will emerge out of society, you become an individual. When you say no, you will find that out of that comes energy. You must have energy. You do have energy when you go to the office day after day—there is the boredom of it, but you go. When you do your business, when you talk, when you ride in the bus, when you ride in your car—everything is a form of energy. Life is energy. Every thought, every feeling is a form of energy. But the energy that we breed, cultivate, comes into being through resistance—resisting, fighting, contradicting, complying, imitating. Through resistance, through suppression, you have energy, and that is all we know—when I push, you push in resistance, but that energy is entirely different from the energy of which we are talking.

The energy of which we are talking is not the outcome of resistance. Resistance implies a motive, either of fear or of loneliness or of guilt or of despair or some form of attachment. Please look into your own mind and your heart; you will see. You have energy through a motive, and therefore such energy meets resistance, and so the battle begins in life—that is the only form of energy that we know. The so-called religious people—those people who are everlastingly seeking God but who never find God—cultivate energy by a denying which has a motive; they think this energy will come into being by becoming bachelors, by denying life—the natural process of life—by withdrawing into a monastery and devoting themselves to good works, by controlling themselves. This does give energy, but that energy is born of resistance, born of conflict, born of suppression. You do have an extraordinary energy when you do suppress, like steam suppressed; only that suppression becomes religious, and it is married to Jesus or to Krishna or to somebody; and inwardly, such energy creates untold misery.

If you listen to what I am talking about, you will see how your energy comes into being. When you discover, uncover, your motives and are free of them, then out of that freedom comes a different kind of energy. This energy is born without any motive because this energy is the very essence of a mind that is completely empty—not blank. A mind that is empty has no resistance, for all thought is resistance. It is that energy that you must have, not the energy born of motive, of conflict, of contradiction, of tension. Motive, conflict, contradiction, tension—they do breed certain forms of energy, and that energy brings, as you can see about you, extraordinary conflict, sorrow. That is your life, that is your everyday existence. You have to understand it—not try to seek that energy which has no motive; you can't find it. You must be free of resistance. And you can only be free of resistance when you can look at life very simply, look at yourself totally without idea, without concept, without formulas, without comparing—when you just look. Then out of that you will see, if you go thus far, a mind that is free—which is not the result of search.

You know, we are all seeking, every one of us. We are seeking truth, happiness, the purpose of life. What does seeking imply? You can only seek something which you have lost or something which you already know; you want to find it. When you say you are a seeker after truth—it is utter nonsense. When you say that, you already must have had the flavor of truth, you must have already comprehended what truth is. And if you are seeking it, you must have lost it—truth is not a thing to be lost, and you can't come to it through searching. All search must cease completely. And that is the beauty of truth. The moment you seek, you are in conflict; the moment you seek, you are setting into motion the energy of escape—escape from the fact, escape from what you are.

So, a mind that is seeking will never find because that immensity is not recognizable. What you can recognize is what you have already known—you recognize your wife, your children, your town, because you already know them. But what you already know about truth is not truth. Truth is beyond time. Search implies distance—from this to that, and so, time is begotten. A mind that is seeking truth will never find it. Please do listen, please understand this once and for all. If you do, you will never seek truth.

If you seek, then the search becomes a problem. Don't have problems in life—not a single problem, even the problem of God or the problem of truth or the problem of happiness. Don't have a problem, because a problem implies struggle, conflict. And a mind in conflict can never understand what is truth. Resolve the problem by understanding what is implied in the problem, the root of the problem. Don't try to resolve it, don't try to break it up, don't try to find an answer to it. But study, go into it, don't escape, look at it with all your being. A mind that has problems can never understand, and therefore is never free. Not how to avoid problems, because every day is a problem. If you are alive, really alive every minute, then it does not become a problem; but there is a constant regard, a constant look—which is the response, not of memory, but of something much more, much wider, deeper.

So the religious mind is not a seeking mind. The religious mind is free of all problems and therefore can meet problems freely, and never gives soil to any problem to take its root in the mind. All this may sound extraordinarily difficult. But your life is difficult. It is a most difficult life you have—the going and the coming, the dying and the living from day to day without certainty, with desire for security, with despair. It is a very difficult life you lead.

But there is a life which is not difficult at all. We really mean what we are saying. It is not at all difficult. Only you must give attention to it, you must give attention to what you are doing. Attention is virtue, attention is order, attention brings efficiency. Whether you are a cook or a bureaucrat or a government official, what you will, when you give your attention completely, with all your being, that is virtue. Virtue is not the tawdry thing which society helps you to cultivate.

As I said, it is love that binds all action for a religious mind. Because the religious mind sees every truth in a flash, from moment to moment, it has the quality of that love which binds all action together. I do not know if you have ever loved somebody—loved with all your being, with your heart, with your mind, with your body, with your thought, with your feeling, with everything that you have. If you have loved so completely, totally, then you will know from that state that in every action, do what you will, there is no conflict, there is no problem. Every action is tied together; it is not born of an idea, it is not born according to your principle, because it is only the religious mind which understands the totality of existence, which we have so terribly broken up. It is only the religious mind that has this extraordinary quality of love, and therefore it can live in this world.

And it is love that is capable of destruction. You know, you must destroy, you must destroy society—not the building, not throw bombs at the governors and politicians; they have their own fate, you leave them to it. But destruction, the psychological destruction of what society has made you into, is necessary. And you can only destroy it completely when there is this quality of compassion. Compassion comes into being only when there is the total comprehension of life. Otherwise you are all very kind, very good, tender; but tenderness, kindness, being good, being considerate is not love; it is a part of love but is not love. A mind has no love when it is not considerate, when it does not look about itself and around where it lives. Love is not a word but an actual state. If there is no love, you cannot destroy; then you merely become a reformer.

Love and destruction always go together as creation. The three—that is, creation, an ending or death, and love—are always together, they are inseparable. That creation—not painting pictures or breeding children—is energy which has no motive. That death is beyond time. And love comes with this. It is only then that you can see that which is beyond time, beyond all thought. Then only is the mind capable of seeing in a flash the unnameable. And there is the everlasting which is not the invention of the mind, the invention of the Gita or the Bible. You have to put aside all the books, all ideas, all ideals, all traditions; you must be completely naked, empty, alone. Then only can that reality be seen.

March 13, 1962

London, England, 1962

First Talk in London

To understand what we are going to consider this evening, and on succeeding evenings, needs a clear mind, a mind that is capable of direct perception. Understanding is not something mysterious, but it requires, I think, a mind that is capable of looking at things directly, without prejudices, without personal inclinations, without opinions. Unfortunately, most of us are so heavily conditioned that we find it very difficult to understand directly, to see what is true immediately. I want to talk about something which is not easily explainable. But one has to use words, and words introduce a difficulty because they can be twisted in so many ways, and also the word is not the thing. The word is never the thing itself; it is only a means. It is or should be like looking through an open door. But if we merely stick to words, then we cannot proceed further, especially in matters which are not technical. It is fairly easy to explain a certain technique by using the corresponding set of technical words, but here we need a mind that is free to see things as they are, a mind that is capable of examining everything without the coloration of its own conditioning.

What I want to say this evening concerns an inward revolution, a destruction of the psychological structure of society, which we are. We are in ourselves the psychological structure of society. Society—with its ambitions, its envies, its pursuit of success—isn't merely the outward show of things. Society is much more inward; it is deeply rooted in each one of us. This psychological structure of society holds us; it shapes our minds, our thoughts, our feelings, and without completely destroying it in ourselves, we cannot possibly be free to discover what is true. But the destruction of this psychological structure of society, which is you and me, does not come about through effort, and I think that is one of the most difficult things for most of us to understand.

I am not using the word *understanding* in any mystical or mysterious sense. You know, when you are relaxed, when you just listen and give your mind to something totally, you understand it fairly easily and quickly. But you are so used to making effort that when I talk about living without effort, you find it very difficult to understand.

The psychological structure of society is what we are, what we think, what we feel—the envy, the ambition, the everlasting struggle of contradiction, both conscious and unconscious—and we are caught in that. To break through it, we think we must make a great deal of effort. But effort always implies conflict, contradiction, does it not? When there is no contradiction, there is no effort—you live. But there is contradiction, brought about by the psychological structure of the society in which we live; there is a conflict, a battle going on within each one of us all the time, consciously or unconsciously; and I feel that until this whole psychological structure is completely understood and broken through, we cannot possibly live a full life or understand that which is beyond the mind.

You see, the world is becoming more and more superficial. There is increasing prosperity throughout the world. There is the welfare state, and great progress is being made in many directions, but inwardly we have remained more or less static, pursuing the same old patterns, the same beliefs. We may alter our dogmas occasionally to suit circumstances, but we are living our lives very superficially. We are always scratching on the surface and never going below. And however superficially clever we are, however much knowledge or information we may have about so many things, until we alter completely, deep down, the whole psychological structure of our being, I don't see how we can be free and so, be creative.

So I would like to consider with you this evening how to bring about a revolution, a psychological revolution, without effort. I am using the word *effort* in the sense of striving, trying to achieve or become something; of a mind that is caught in contradiction, that is struggling to overcome, to discipline, to conform, to adjust, to bring about a change within itself—I am using the word effort to cover all that.

Now, is it possible to bring about a total revolution without effort, not only in the conscious mind, but also deep down, in the unconscious? For when we make an effort to bring about a psychological revolution within ourselves, it implies pressure, influence, a motive, a direction, all of which is the result of our conditioning.

You know, one can listen in many ways. You can listen trying to interpret what another is saying, or comparing what is said with what you already know. You can listen with all the responses of your active memory. But there is only one way of really listening, and that is to listen without the chattering of your own thought.

I don't know if you have ever tried just listening to something, pleasant or unpleasant, without projecting your own process of thinking. It is difficult to do that; it is quite an art because we are always comparing, judging, evaluating, condemning; we never simply listen. We never really see anything because we immediately say it is beautiful or ugly, this or that. So perhaps this evening you will just listen, without agreeing or disagreeing with what is being said, without projecting your own ideas or interpretations—which doesn't mean that you are being mesmerized. On the contrary. To listen demands complete attention. But attention is not concentration. When you concentrate you focus, you exclude, and this exclusion creates a barrier to listening. I am not saying anything extraordinary. You can experiment and find this out for yourself very quickly. When you listen with ease, without exclusion, you are listening to everything, not merely to the words, and you are also aware of your own inner responses. The words are then a means of opening the door through which you look at yourself.

So if during these talks you can listen in that way, then I feel the very act of listening will bring about a deep, fundamental revolution because in that state of complete attention, you will have already broken through your conditioning.

Our conditioning, conscious and unconscious, is very deep and heavy, is it not? We are Christians, Hindus, Englishmen, Frenchmen, Germans, Indians, Russians; we belong to this or that church with all its dogmas, to this or that race with its burden of history. Superficially, our minds are educated. The conscious mind is educated according to the culture we live in, and from that, one can perhaps disentangle oneself fairly easily. It is not too difficult to put aside being an Englishman, an Indian, a Russian, or whatever one happens to be, or to leave a particular church or religion. But it is much more difficult to uncondition the unconscious, which plays a far greater part in our life than the conscious mind. The training of the conscious mind is useful and necessary as a means of earning a livelihood, or to perform a certain function—which is what our education is mostly concerned about. We are trained to do certain things, to function more or less mechanically in a certain way. That is our superficial education. But inwardly, unconsciously, deep down, we are the result of many thousands of years of man's endeavor; we are the sum total of his struggles, his hopes, his despairs, his everlasting search for something beyond, and this piling up of experience is still going on within us. To be aware of that conditioning, and to be free of it, demands a great deal of attention.

It isn't a matter of analysis because you cannot analyze the unconscious. I know there are specialists who attempt to do that, but I don't believe it is possible. The unconscious cannot be approached by the conscious. I will show you why. Through dreams, through hints, through symbols, through various forms of intimation, the unconscious tries to communicate with the conscious mind. These hints and intimations require interpretation, and the conscious mind interprets them according to its conditioning, its peculiar idiosyncrasies. So there is never complete contact between the two, and never complete understanding of the unconscious. It is something that we don't quite know in its entirety. And yet without understanding and being free of the unconscious, with its burden of history, the whole long story of the past, there will always be a contradiction, a conflict, a battle raging within.

So, as I said, analysis is not the way to understand the unconscious. Analysis implies an observer, an analyzer apart from the analyzed. There is a division, and where there is division, there is no understanding.

Now, this is one of our difficulties, perhaps our major difficulty: to be free of the whole content of the unconscious. And is such a thing possible? I do not know if you have ever tried to analyze yourself—to analyze what you think, what you feel, and also the motives, the intentions behind your thoughts and feelings. If you have, I am sure you will have found that analysis cannot penetrate very deeply. It goes to a certain depth, and there it stops. To penetrate very deeply, one has to put an end to this process of the analyzer continually analyzing, and begin instead just to listen, to see, to observe every thought and every feeling without saying, "This is right and that is wrong," without condemnation or justification. When you do so observe, you will find there is no contradiction and therefore no effort, and therefore there is immediate understanding.

But to go very deeply into oneself, one must obviously be free of ambition, of competition, of envy, greed. And that's a very difficult thing to do because envy, greed, and ambition are the very substance of the psychological social structure of which we are a part. Living as we are in a world made up of acquisitiveness, ambition, competition—to be entirely free of these things and yet not be destroyed by the world is really the problem.

If one observes, one is aware of how rapidly knowledge and technology are advancing in the world. Man will soon be able to go to the moon. Computers are taking over, and we ourselves are becoming more and more like machines, more and more automatic. Many of us go to the office day after day and are thoroughly bored with what we are doing, so we seek to escape from that boredom. And religion is a marvelous escape, or we turn to various forms of sensation and to drugs in order to feel more, to see more. This is going on throughout the world. We are in perpetual conflict, not only with ourselves, but with others. All our relationships are based on conflict, on possession, on acquisitiveness, on force. And when the mind is caught in such conflict, in such despair and anxiety, I don't see how one can go very far. But one has to go far. One has to destroy the whole psychological structure of society within oneself—destroy it completely. That is really the crux of our existence. Because, we do lead a most superficial life, and we try to penetrate deeply by reading, by acquiring knowledge, by gaining more and more information. But all knowledge, all information is always on the surface.

So the question really is: How is one to live in this world without bringing about conflict, outwardly and especially inwardly? Because the inward conflict dictates the outward conflict. Only a mind that is really free of conflict, at every level, because it has no psychological problems of any kind—only such a mind can find out if there is something beyond itself.

Essentially our problem is not how to make more money, or how to stop the hydrogen bomb, or whether to join the Common Market—such problems are not very deep. They will be shaped and controlled by economic factors, by historical events, and by the innumerable pressures of sovereign governments, or societies and religions. What matters is to be capable of abstracting oneself from all that—not by withdrawing, not by becoming a monk or a nun, but by actually understanding its whole significance. One has to find out for oneself if it is at all possible to be completely free from the psychological structure of society—which is to be free of ambition. I say it is entirely possible, but it is not easy. It is a very difficult thing to be free of ambition. Ambition implies the 'more'; the 'more' implies time, and time means arriving, achieving. To deny time is to be free of ambition. I am not talking of chronological time—that you can't deny, for then you will miss your bus. But the psychological time, which we have created for ourselves in order to become something inwardly—that you can deny. Which means, really, to die to tomorrow without despair.

You know, there are clever people, intellectuals who have examined the outward processes of man. They have examined society with its endless wars; they have examined the churches with their beliefs, dogmas, saviors, and after doing so, they are in despair. Out of despair they have contrived a philosophy of accepting the immediate, of not thinking about tomorrow but living as completely as possible in the now. I don't mean that at all. That's very easy. Any materialistic, shallow person can do it, and he doesn't have to be very clever. And that's what most of us do, unfortunately. We live for today, and today is extended into many tomorrows. I don't mean that at all. I mean to deny ambition totally and immediately—to die psychologically to the social structure so that the mind is never caught in time, in ambition, in the desire to be or not to be something.

You know, death is a marvelous thing, and to understand death requires a great deal of insight—to die to ambition naturally, without effort, to deny envy. Envy implies comparison, success, the pursuit of the 'more': you have more and I have less, you have a great deal of knowledge and I am ignorant. Can one end this process totally, instantly? One can end it, one can die totally to envy, ambition, competition only when one is capable of looking at it without any distortion. There is distortion as long as there is motive. When you want to die to ambition in order to be something else, you are still ambitious. That's not dying at all. When you renounce with a motive, it is not renunciation. And most renunciations have behind them this motive to be, to achieve, to arrive, to find.

So it seems to me that we are merely becoming more and more clever, better and better informed. We are brought up on words, ideas, theories, knowledge, and there is very little empty space in the mind from which something can be seen clearly. It is only the empty mind that can see clearly, not the mind that's crammed with a lot of information and knowledge, nor the mind that's incessantly active, seeking, achieving, demanding. But a mind that's empty is not just blank. To be aware of an empty mind is extraordinarily difficult. And only in that emptiness is there understanding; only in that emptiness is there creation.

To come to that state of emptiness, one has to deny the whole social structure—the psychological structure of ambition, prestige, power. It is comparatively easy for older people not to be ambitious, to deny power and position, but such denials are very superficial. That's why it is so important to understand the unconscious. To understand the unconscious, that which is hidden and which you don't know, you cannot examine it with a positive, educated, analyzing mind. If you examine the unconscious by the conscious process of analysis, you are bound to create conflict.

Do please understand this; it is not very complicated. Our approach to any deep psychological problem is always a positive one. That is, we want to get at it; we want to control or resolve the problem, so we analyze it, or we pursue a particular system in order to understand it. But you can't understand something which you don't know by means of what you already know; you can't dictate what it should or should not be. You must approach it with empty hands, and to have empty hands, or an empty mind, is one of the most difficult things to do. Our minds are so full of the things that we have known; we are burdened with our memories, and every thought is a response of those memories. With positive thought we approach that which is not positive, the hidden, the unconscious.

Now, if without any idea, without expecting to be told how, you can simply listen to what is being said, then I think you will find that you are able to approach the unconscious—which has such power, such an extraordinary drive, compulsion—without creating contradiction, and therefore without effort.

Sirs, you don't have to accept my word for this, and I hope you won't, for then you would make me your authority, which would be a most ugly thing to do.

There is the unknowable, something far beyond the mind, beyond all thought. But you cannot possibly approach it with all your knowledge and memories, with the scars of experience, the weight of anxiety, guilt, fear. And you cannot get rid of these things by any effort whatsoever. You can be free of them only by listening to every thought and every feeling without trying to interpret what you hear; just listen, just observe and be attentive out of emptiness. Then you can live in this world untouched by its hatred, its ugliness, its brutality. You can function as a clerk, as a bus driver, as a bank manager, or what you will, without being caught in status. But the moment you bring to that function the psychological factors of ambition, authority, power, prestige, you cannot live in this world without everlasting sorrow.

Most of us really know all this. One doesn't need at all to listen to a talk of this kind. We know well enough that this is a terrible, brutal, ugly world, where every religion, every political faction is trying to shape man's thought; where the welfare state is making us more and more comfortable, dull, stupid, because we have used conflict as a means of becoming outwardly clever, bright. But inwardly we have not changed at all; we are carrying on as we have been for centuries: fearful, anxious, guilty, seeking power, seeking sex. We are perpetuating what is animalistic, which means that we are still functioning within the psychological structure of society.

The question is how to break that structure totally, how to destroy it completely and be out of it, without going insane and without becoming a monk, a nun, or a hermit. That structure can only be broken immediately; there is no time in which to do it. Either you do it immediately or never. I am not using the word *never* to imply hell in the religious sense, but if you cannot understand, if you cannot pay complete attention now, will you be able to pay complete attention tomorrow? If you wait until tomorrow, you will still be unable to pay complete attention.

So attention is not a matter of time. Understanding is not a process of gradual growth until you arrive at understanding. That's why it is very important to know how to listen, how to see things as they are, how to look at a fact without opinion, without judgment, without condemnation; to see the fact that you are ambitious—just to see it as a fact without saying it is right or wrong, or asking what would happen to you in this world if you were not ambitious, and so on and so on. If you can simply look at the fact without distorting it, you will find this very observation of the fact not only removes the duality of the observer and the observed, which creates conflict, but also releases a great deal of energy. And you need energy. I do not mean the energy derived from conflict. Such energy is destructive. I am talking of the energy that comes into being when you see a fact totally, completely: that you are sensual, that you are ambitious, that you are envious, that you are afraid. And you cannot see the fact in this way if you are caught in words. Words are ideas; ideas are thought. To look at a fact totally, without distortion, there must be an empty space in the mind that looks.

Please don't misunderstand the word *empty*. You know, our minds are never quiet; they are always chattering; they are always theorizing, building, destroying, and picking up again. But when the mind is very still, there is no time, no space; time and space disappear. There is no tomorrow, or the next second. That stillness of mind is total attention, and that attention is all virtue. That is real virtue; there is no other virtue, no other morality. Every other form of virtue or morality is brought about by the mind, by ambition, envy, which is the psychological structure of society.

To see the fact as it is, is the ending of every problem. When the mind is completely empty of every problem—and it can be so empty—when it has denied every problem, when it no longer gives soil to any problem, then you will find, if you have gone so deeply, that there is something far beyond, something which the mind cannot measure and no religion can capture. And, living in this chaotic, confused world, it is essential to have such a mind—a mind that is capable of looking at everything clearly, sanely, seeing every fact as it is. Only such a mind is quiet, still, and it is only to such a mind that the immeasurable can come.

June 5, 1962

Second Talk in London

This evening I would like to talk about fear, sorrow, and innocency.

We all have many experiences, and every experience leaves a mark; every thought, every influence shapes our minds in a certain way. And it is essential to die to everything we have known so that the mind is young, fresh, and innocent. Only an innocent mind, a mind which, though it has lived through a thousand experiences, is dead to the past—only such a mind can perceive what is true and go beyond the things put together by man. And fear, it seems to me, is one of the corruptive and destructive forces that make this innocency impossible.

Fear is psychological time. There is no fear if you have no psychological time at all. If there is no tomorrow into which you are moving, and no looking back, every form of fear ceases. Fear comes into being when thought projects itself into the future, or compares itself with what it has been in the past. Psychologically, time is thought, both conscious and unconscious, and it is thought that creates fear.

We have every kind of fear: fear of death, fear of being ill, fear of old age, fear of losing the satisfactions we have known, fear of public opinion, of not fulfilling, of not being a success, of being a nobody. Being afraid, we seek various escapes, outwardly as well as inwardly, and for most of us, religion has become an extraordinary escape from fear. To understand fear, one must understand the whole process of thinking, the whole mechanism of thought.

As I pointed out the other day, it is important to listen to what is being said without either agreeing or disagreeing, because we are dealing not with ideas but with facts. We are dealing with facts, regardless of whether those facts are agreeable or unpleasant. And if we are able to look at the fact of fear, listen to the whole content of it, see the structure of it, then I am quite certain that the mind will instantly be free of fear.

But we do not know how to listen because we are always trying to run away from fear; we want to resolve it, we want to discover a way out of it, we want to find its cause. We name the fact "fear," and then the word becomes all-important, so we never listen to the fact.

Finding the cause of fear is not freedom from fear. After a great deal of analysis, inquiry, one may know the cause of fear, but at the end of it, one is still afraid. And without really being free of fear, every form of search, every form of inquiry only brings about further illusion or distortion. A truly religious man, if I may use that word, has no fear psychologically, inwardly. By a religious man I mean a total man, not one who is merely sentimental or escapes from the world by drugging himself with ideas, illusions, visions. The mind of a religious man is very quiet, sane, rational, logical—and one needs such a mind, not a mind that is sentimental, emotional, fearful, caught in its own peculiar conditioning.

Now, if I can, I would like to go into the question of fear in such a way that, in the very act of listening, the listener is free of fear. You know, we want to be free of fear always, for ever and ever. There is no such thing as being free for ever and ever. To understand this, one has to understand continuity. What gives continuity to something, pleasant or unpleasant, is thinking about it. When we think about something, we give it a continuity. We give continuity to fear by thinking about it—which doesn't mean that we mustn't inquire into the whole process of fear.

As I said, fear is time, in the psychological sense, and time is thought. Time is the process of becoming, avoiding, fulfilling—"I am this and I want to be that." So time is the factor of fear. When you are immediately faced with something, whatever it be, at that moment there is no fear. But thinking about it causes fear.

Thought is the reaction of memory. Memory in the ordinary sense is necessary;

otherwise, we would walk in front of a moving bus or take a poisonous snake in our hands. But when memory creates thought as a reaction, it becomes an impediment and creates fear. This is a psychological fact.

Death is the unknown, but when we say we are afraid of death, we are not really afraid of the unknown but of leaving the known, leaving the things that we have experienced, enjoyed, built up. Thought is this memory of the known and its response, so thought can never be free. There is no such thing as freedom of thought because thought is always conditioned, it is always the response of memory. And to be totally free of fear, this building up of memory as a continuity has to be understood.

As a mechanic, as a scientist, as an engineer, and so on, you need the continuity of memory; otherwise, you could not function. But the continuity of thought as a bundle of memories concerning 'me' and 'mine', and the responses of that conditioned thought, is psychological time, which is fear. Thinking about death—the sudden ending of everything one has known—creates fear and gives it continuity. So, to really end fear, there must be the ending of thought. You may say, "That is completely crazy. How can I possibly end thought? If I end all thinking, how can I earn a livelihood? How can I go on with my job tomorrow morning?"

There are two different kinds of thinking: thinking in performing a function, and thinking in the sense of using that function to acquire status. The psychological continuity of thought that is built up in the use of function to acquire authority, position, prestige—it is this that brings about fear.

Please just listen to what is being said. Not that you must accept what I am saying, but just listen. I am not telling fables; I am not saying anything extraordinary. I am merely pointing out the fact that time, in the psychological sense, breeds fear. Time is the way of thought, and a man who would be totally free of fear, right through, has to end thought. That requires attention—not concentration, but total attention to every thought. If you can give total attention to every thought, whether important or unimportant, whether deeply significant or without great meaning, then you will find that in this state of total attention, there is an ending of thought.

Fear breeds guilt, anxiety; and anxiety in every form is the beginning of sorrow. There is the sorrow of not being loved; there is sorrow when someone to whom we are deeply attached is suffering or dying. And we have worshiped sorrow. This is especially true in Christianity, which has always regarded sorrow as a most extraordinary thing. Go into a church, and you will see the Man of Sorrows. There is no ending of sorrow as far as most of us are concerned because we have enthroned sorrow and live in its shadow throughout our days. Sorrow has become very respectable. It is a thing that every cultured man knows and keeps locked up in his heart, and when he goes to church, he worships it there, or he tries in various ways to escape from it.

But there *is* an ending to sorrow. Sorrow must come to an end completely; otherwise, there can never be the religious mind of which I am speaking. Sorrow doesn't lead us to truth, but sorrow is of great significance because it indicates something. Unfortunately, most of us avoid that indication, that hint, and live with sorrow. If you examine it deeply, you will see that sorrow is self-pity, although you may call it something else. You have lost someone—a husband, a wife, a son—and your sorrow is self-pity at being left alone. We all know this self-pity that arises out of loneliness, and self-pity in every form, the concern about oneself, is the beginning of sorrow. The feeling of inferiority and the struggle to become superior, the conflict and the triumph of achievement, attainment, the misery of frustration—all these engender sorrow.

You see, very few of us ever face sorrow. We have probably never experienced sorrow directly. I will explain what I mean. We have directly experienced hunger, sex; but I wonder if we have directly experienced sorrow. We remain with that which is pleasurable; we want to continue in it, but sorrow we try to avoid; we never look at it. The desire to find a way out, to escape through words, through ideation, through belief, through drink, or what you will—all this prevents us from actually looking at the fact of sorrow.

My son dies, my wife or husband leaves me, and I am in sorrow. What actually has taken place? I am left alone, I am lonely; I have nobody to rely on anymore. I had identified myself with that person completely, and now that he is gone, I feel lost. The fact is that I am psychologically dependent, and this fact brings about other facts, various forms of escape that only perpetuate fear and sorrow.

So it becomes very difficult to look at and directly experience the fact of sorrow. The word *sorrow* has certain overtones of meaning, and to experience anything directly, totally, there must be freedom from the word. But you are slaves to words—to words like *British, French, Indian, Christian, Hindu.* Similarly, the word sorrow has an extraordinary hold on you. The word, the symbol has centuries of religious propaganda behind it—that you must bear sorrow, that through sorrow you will find redemption, that through sorrow there will be peace, and so on. All this has conditioned the mind, and you never break through that conditioning. But to be free of sorrow, you must shatter all the symbols, discard all the words and look directly at the fact. And you cannot look at the fact of your self-pity if the picture on the piano or on the mantelpiece becomes all-important, for then you have identified yourself with an idea, with a memory, with a thing that is dead, gone, and you are living in the past. To break away from the past completely, to destroy it totally, with all its story, with all its memories, is the ending of sorrow.

Just as fear distorts the mind, bringing about various forms of illusion and corruption, so sorrow makes the mind dull, insensitive, because in sorrow the mind is concerned with its own darkness, with its own self-pity, with its own loneliness. And I assure you—not that you must believe, but I assure you—there is an ending of sorrow, and then one sees everything afresh, every incident, every movement of life anew. It is only when the mind is free from sorrow and from all fear that there is innocency. And the mind needs to be innocent, though it has lived a thousand years, because it is only the fresh, innocent mind, the young mind, that is capable of seeing that which is beyond the measure of man.

But all this requires a great deal of attention, real seriousness—not a long face and all the rest of the absurdities, but the capacity swiftly to follow a particular thought right through to the very end, letting it unfold completely without hindering it, and this is not possible if you have moorings in the past.

You may come to these meetings and listen seriously, or casually, with half-attention, but words and speeches will not alter the fact that one is afraid, and that there is sorrow. Most of us have never experienced a state of innocency, though we will argue, discuss, write, split hairs about all this, about who is right and who is wrong, what to do and what not to do. If you are rich or fairly well-to-do, you may go to an analyst, but no outside agency, no effort can free you from sorrow or fear. What brings freedom is attention, which is to face the fact out of emptiness and see things as they are without distortion. In that state of attention there comes an innocency which is virtue, which is humility.

Now perhaps you will ask some questions. And may I suggest that your question be to the point of what I have been talking about. Don't ask, for example, how to stop war. We can discuss that another time. Don't ask what to do about the atom bomb, or whether it is right or wrong to enter the common market. You see, each one of us has problems; we are ridden with problems. Everything we touch with the hand, the mind, or the heart becomes a problem. And when you ask a question about a problem, I am quite sure you are expecting an answer. But there is no answer apart from the problem itself. What is important is not the finding of an answer to the problem but preventing problems from arising. A man who is ill wants to get well, and there are doctors who will treat him. But there are also doctors who will work to prevent disease, and that is much more important than the curing of symptoms. Unfortunately, most of us merely want to be cured of symptoms. We don't know how to prevent the problem from arising in the first place. There is great beauty, great sensitivity in being aware of every problem as it arises and dealing with it immediately, ending it on the spot, so that it is not carried over to the next day. This can be done, not by taking a drug, or trying to forget or escape from the problem, but simply by seeing that the problem, whatever it be, has no answer apart from itself. I am talking of psychological problems, not mechanical ones. In looking at a problem with total attention, there is the ending of that problem.

Question: Is total attention essential with regard to pleasurable things, as it is with regard to unpleasant or painful ones?

KRISHNAMURTI: You see, we want to give continuity to pleasurable things. We go back in memory to the joys of childhood, to the pleasures we experienced long ago, or we cling to that which we are enjoying now, and we want to put an end to the things that are not pleasurable. But when one gives total attention, one gives it to the pleasurable as well as to the painful. The desire for the continuity of pleasure is the beginning of sorrow. Why shouldn't pleasure end? You want pain to end, but pleasure you want to continue; and to be dependent on pleasure dulls the mind, it makes the mind insensitive, just as pain does. Avoiding what we call sorrow, and seeking pleasure—both bring about that peculiar inattention of a lazy mind. The mind that has had lots of pleasure, that seeks pleasure and lives in pleasure, is a stupid mind; and it is also a stupid mind that avoids or continues in sorrow. But, you see, to understand total attention is quite a—I was going to use the word *problem.*

To be attentive is to enter a room and see the people, the proportions of the room, the color of the carpet, the pictures on the wall—everything. But you can't do that if you say, "I don't like that picture; there is my friend; I don't like the color of the carpet; the room is not in right proportion," and so on and so on. If your mind is chattering, dividing itself into like and dislike, then you are not attentive.

You know, you can look at a flower either botanically or nonbotanically. If you look at it botanically, even then there is a certain quality of attention. But you can also look at a flower nonbotanically, which is to look at it without knowledge. Please don't translate "without knowledge" as being a state of ignorance. To be without knowledge is to have wisdom, for knowledge has continuity, and wisdom has no continuity. To be attentive implies a state of attention which has no border, no limit, no boundary. You observe everything, take in everything. But you cannot do that if there is a motive behind your attention, however worthy that motive may be. If you say, "I will attend in order to end my sorrow," then you are not attentive.

Try sometime, if you will, to look totally at a flower or a tree or a human being. Look without knowledge, without thinking—which is not to be in a condition of amnesia or blankness. You will find, when you do so look at something, that there is an extraordinary state of attention which is not concentration. Concentration is exclusion. A mind that is attentive can concentrate effortlessly, without exclusion. But a mind that has acquired concentration through effort, through training, discipline—such a mind can never be attentive.

Question: One finds that the mind can actually be quiet for only about thirty seconds. What then do you mean by quietness of the mind?

KRISHNAMURTI: First of all, quietness of the mind is not a state to be achieved. You can't take various steps to it; you can't practice a system in order to become quiet because such disciplinary action only makes the mind dull. A conforming mind is a dead mind. That is the first thing to realize. A conforming mind, whether it conforms to the dictates of society, to a neighbor's opinion, to the dogmas of the church, or to any other structure of authority can never be sensitive—which doesn't mean that you are going to disobey the policeman. That is quite a different matter. I am talking of conformity in the sense of obeying the authority of tradition, of a book, of a system, of a belief. The mind that conforms to a pattern, which is a form of discipline—such a mind is not quiet, it is merely insensitive. That is the first thing to comprehend deeply. Behind our conformity is the desire to be psychologically secure. A mind that is seeking security can never be free, and it is only in freedom, complete psychological freedom, that there can be stillness of the mind.

So there are no steps to a still mind. Moreover, you really don't know what stillness of the mind is. All that you are concerned with is to experience that state and hold it; therefore, you say it doesn't last more than thirty seconds. Why should it last? You see, what is important to you is not the thing itself but what it gives you. Therefore you want to know how to come to it and whether it is enduring, so you bring in the element of time: it must have continuity, it must last more than thirty seconds. Silence that has continuity is not silence. If you come to it through time, it is not stillness of the mind.

Then there is this question of the observer and the observed. If there is a 'you' who experiences silence, it is not silence. The moment you are aware that you are happy, it is no longer happiness. The moment you say, "I am in an extraordinary state of humility," it is gone. For you, silence is a state which you experience, as you experience hunger, and you want to hold that experience, you want it to continue. So there is a duality: you, and the thing to be experienced. If you go into this very deeply, you will find that the silence you have experienced and want to continue is merely the recognition of a thing that is over; therefore, it is no longer silence.

Please, this is perhaps a little bit complicated, and it requires attention on your part. What I am saying is this: Silence is not to be "experienced." To experience silence is a terrible thing. What is involved in that experience? There is a recognition of the thing you have experienced as silence, which is the response of your memory. Thought recognizes silence. And the moment thought recognizes silence, it is no longer silence; it is something of the past to which you have given the name silence in the present.

So, to understand what silence is, you must be free of conformity and imitation, free of authority, free of the experiences of yesterday which you have accumulated. For all the experiences that you have accumulated are conditioned as well as conditioning; they are of the past and strengthen the past. Also there must be an ending of the thinker and the thought as two separate things, for this division gives rise to the conflict of duality. Then, if you are not seeking silence, if there is no demand for any experience whatsoever because you have understood the whole significance of experience—then perchance, when you are not looking, silence may come. It is only the innocent mind that is silent. And if one has gone so far, then in that silence there is an extraordinary movement without an observer watching the movement; there is only a movement; there is no experiencer and therefore no experiencing. Time is not.

For most of us that is merely hearsay and therefore has no value. What has value is to see the fact that authority of any kind is destructive, whether it be the authority of tradition, of the savior, of the Master, or of the present speaker. We seek authority because we want security; we don't want to go wrong; we want to do the right, the safe, the respectable thing. And a mind that is respectable is not only a bourgeois, mediocre mind, but it is insensitive and utterly incapable of being totally attentive. When there is total attention, there is a virtue—which is not the imitation of virtue as practiced by a respectable society. Then virtue is something new, fresh, to be picked up every day, round every corner. Then you will find there is a silence, and in this silence there is a creation which is immeasurable.

Question: If we see things as they are with total attention, with choiceless awareness, what happens to the various forms of art, and in particular to those forms concerned with words?

KRISHNAMURTI: Is beauty something put together by man? Is beauty a matter of capacity or personal taste? Or is beauty something beyond thought and feeling, something which has nothing whatsoever to do with capacity, with inclination, with like and dislike or personal taste?

And what is the need of expression? You may express something in words, in the form of a poem, or you may express it on canvas or in marble; you may express it in your kitchen, or by holding another's hand. But what is the need of expression? I am not saying that you should not express. You may express something; you may put it into words, but the word is not the thing. The symbol is never the real. But you have expressed it, and because you have capacity or talent, the expression becomes significant; it has value, it brings a profit, and then begins all the circus around it.

Now, as I was saying, in total attention there is a creation which cannot be expressed in words, in symbols, in ideas. It is total energy. I may have the gift of writing poetry, but how can I express in words that total energy, that extraordinary thing called creation? If you don't like the word *creation,* give it any other name; *God* or *dog* will do just as well. One feels, perhaps, that there is such a thing—a movement of creation, an immensity, a timelessness. But how can you express in words the immeasurable? And even when it is expressed, the expression is not the thing itself. So of what value is poetry in relation to that? What significance, what importance, what meaning has poetry to a man or a woman who has understood this total attention? Has such a person any need to go out and look at works of art, visit museums, attend concerts? Do you understand? When you have drunk at the fountain of creation, what need have you of anything more?

You see, for most of us, art, poetry, or music has become very important. We are like the people at a football match who are watching the players. A few are playing, and thousands are only watching. But when you have extricated yourself from the whole psychological structure of society, what significance has the word, the shape, the sound, the symbol?

I am afraid you are listening to the speaker, expecting to be put in that state by some miracle, or hoping to be led to it by him, but you can't be. You have to work tremendously hard. It requires immense energy to listen rightly. It requires all your attention to destroy inattention, and then there is no distraction of any kind. There is no such thing as distraction, ever, to a man who is attending. But to the man who is concentrated there is always a distraction.

Art has its own place, obviously, but that is not the end of the matter. Only when you can go beyond art, beyond the beauty that man has put together—only then will you know for yourself that beauty which is incapable of being expressed. And when there is that beauty, there is no need to seek any more.

June 7, 1962

Third Talk in London

This morning we are going to discuss, and we ought to be very clear what we mean by discussion. I feel it will be worthwhile if we can, in exchanging words, see clearly the pattern of our own thinking; that is, if we can expose ourselves, not to another, but to ourselves, and see what we actually are and what is inwardly taking place. To be worthwhile, a discussion should serve as a mirror in which we see ourselves clearly, in detail, without distortion, taking in the whole picture and not merely looking at one particular fragment. This is quite an arduous task because most of us distort what we see either through seeking pleasure or avoiding pain, but in this discussion, and in the one to follow, next Sunday, I hope we can see ourselves in full measure. It would be a pity, I think, if we were merely to remain at the verbal or intellectual level and not go very deeply—which most of us are apt to do. Because we do tend to think in fragments, we rarely do anything totally, with our whole being. We function at different levels, not as a total human being who is inwardly aware of all the implications of his own thought and feeling. So let us see if we cannot go beyond the verbal level, the mere intellectual exchange, and penetrate deeply into the unconscious. If we can do that, then I think this kind of gathering will be eminently useful.

Question: You speak of seeing or hearing a fact without distortion, regardless of whether that fact is pleasant or unpleasant. Is this a gradual process of investigation and therefore a matter of time, or is it an immediate perception?

KRISHNAMURTI: You know, the more civilization seems to advance outwardly—increasing prosperity, going to the moon, exploring Venus or Mars, and so on—the more complex our human problems are becoming. I do not mean the problems of outward living: where one should live, what kind of job one should have, how much money one should earn, and all the rest of it. Those things are fairly easy to manipulate or work out. I am talking about our psychological problems, which are much more acute and much deeper—or perhaps they have always been acute and deep, but now one is becoming more aware of them. Some of us, having arranged our outward circumstances more or less conveniently, are perhaps turning inward, but I doubt it. Nevertheless, there are these psychological problems. And, if I may say so, to the problems we already have, we shouldn't add yet another problem by making an extraordinary issue out of what it means to see or hear something without distortion.

To listen is not only to listen to the speaker but also to your neighbor, to your wife or husband, to a bird. To see a flower is to see it both botanically and nonbotanically. To listen is to be aware of the incessant propaganda of the church, of the state, of the newspaper, of the advertiser—to hear all this without being influenced one way or another. Most of us are very easily influenced; our whole psychological structure is based on influence, on propaganda. We are British, Catholic, Protestant, American, Hindu, and so on—the result of thousands of years of propaganda. We are influenced by the food we eat, the climate we live in, the clothes we wear, the books and newspapers we read. The radio, the television—everything influences us incredibly, and this influence is either conscious or unconscious. In America I believe they have tried various experiments in subliminal propaganda, which is aimed directly at the unconscious without the conscious mind being aware of it. For a fraction of a second they flash, repeatedly, on the cinema or television screen an advertisement which the conscious mind doesn't take in, but which the unconscious sees and remembers, and the next time you go into a shop, you tend to buy what they have advertised.

Actually, we are the result of many influences, and intelligence, it seems to me, is that quality which enables the mind to be aware of every influence, or as many as possible, and to walk through them all without becoming entangled in them, without being twisted or impregnated by them. To be constantly aware of influence and throw it off—this, I feel, is the very essence of intelligence.

What is important is to listen to propaganda, to what is being said now, and see directly for yourself what is true and what is false, but this you cannot do according to your evaluations, your likes and dislikes, which are merely the response of your cultural conditioning. Surely, to see truly is to see the fact as it is, and this seeing is an immediate thing; it is not a question of time.

Most of us think that understanding comes about slowly, through comparative evaluation, do we not? But is understanding comparative, gradual? Or is it immediate? Surely, I understand something now, or I don't understand it at all. I may say to myself, "I will gradually understand what is being said; understanding of it will come at some future time." But will the future bring understanding? Unless there is now a radical change in my outlook, in my approach, in my listening, the future will not help me. If I don't throw off immediately my conditioning, my prejudices, my evaluations, my likes and dislikes, they will still be there tomorrow.

If I may say so, I think it is a lazy mind that has this idea of gradualism, that says, "Eventually I will understand, but not now." I am not talking about the acquisition of knowledge. That does take time. To master a language, to study mathematics, to learn about machinery, and so on—all that will take time. But to see the fact that one is acquisitive—this perception is immediate. And to listen to something without distortion is also immediate—to listen, not just to the speaker, but to everything, without interpretation, without the interference of the mechanical process of thought. If you have tried this you will know that it is very—I was going to use the word *difficult*. But it isn't difficult in the accepted sense of the word. It requires tremendous energy.

You know, to live with something very ugly, to live in an ugly street without a tree, to go by bus to your office every day through the noise, the smell, the filth of a big city—to live with all that and not be corrupted or made insensitive by it, one must have a great deal of energy. Equally, to live with something very beautiful, with a mountain, with a tree, with a beautiful face, and not get used to it—that also requires a great deal of energy.

In the same way, to listen, to see without distortion, you need great energy of attention, but attention isn't a process of concentration—controlling the mind and bringing it back when it wanders off. It isn't that at all. And I hope all my talking about it isn't making it into a problem. If it becomes a problem, then please just drop it. God knows, we have enough problems without adding this to all the existing ones.

Comment: By seeing and listening to facts as they are, one may succeed in disentangling oneself from various problems and complications. But behind all this there is still the desire for that permanency which may be called God.

KRISHNAMURTI: I wonder why we want permanency? Surely, the desire for permanency is a reaction to conflict. We are in a constant state of wanting and not wanting, coming and going, hope and despair. A battle is going on within us all the time, and we want some peace, a place of refuge, a god who will give us complete rest from this battle of longing to fulfill and not fulfilling, of loving and not being loved in return, and so on. So our desire for permanency is a reaction to conflict. We will discuss presently whether there is such a thing as permanency, but first we must be clear that we want permanency, an enduring peace, only because we are in conflict. If there were no conflict in us at all, then we wouldn't seek a state of permanent peace.

Now, the question is whether or not the mind can be free from conflict of every kind. Is it possible for you and me to be totally free from conflict? Or is life inevitably a perpetual struggle from the moment we are born until we die? Struggle, contradiction, the conflict of the opposites—if we accept all this as inevitable, then the problem is how to make the conflict as mild and refined as possible. This is what most cultures try to do. So we must be very clear as to whether we are merely trying to refine the conflict or whether we want to eliminate conflict altogether. We are talking of the psychological conflict in each one of us, which later projects itself as conflict in the world between groups, races, and nations.

To me, mere refinement of the conflict within does not solve the problem because conflict continues, and conflict is always very destructive. However subtle and refined it may be, however learned, sophisticated, analyzed or reasoned away, conflict makes the mind dull, stupid. It makes the mind incapable of going beyond itself. I think that is fairly clear without further explanation.

So the question is: How are you to be totally free from conflict? Not that you should seek a method or a system, for then you get caught in the system, and again begins the conflict between what you are and what you should be.

Is it possible to eliminate conflict altogether? That is the question. To me, the elimination of conflict is absolutely essential. Not that I am a lazy person, or temperamentally inactive, but I see what conflict does. Outwardly one can see very well what conflict does: the competition between the various commercial and political groups, leading to devastating wars between this country and that country. And inwardly it is much worse because it is the inner conflict that projects the outer. Where there is inner conflict, there is a tension which may produce certain artistic activities. It may express itself as surrealism or objectivism or nonobjectivism, or you may write a book—or end up in an asylum.

Now, we have been educated from childhood to compete. Our examinations are competitive, and in school we try to get better marks than somebody else—you know the whole process. We have been brought up on all that: psychologically always wanting more, using function to acquire status. And one can see what it does to the mind. It really makes the mind old, insensitive, dull. An ambitious man is everlastingly in conflict; he doesn't know a moment of peace; he can never know what love is. And we are encouraged to be ambitious from the start. Conflict is firmly rooted in us at different levels, superficial and very deep.

So, is it possible to live in this world, psychologically and therefore outwardly, without any conflict at all? Please don't say it is possible or impossible; you don't know. I say it is possible; for me it is a fact, but it isn't a fact for you; therefore, you have to find out.

Is it possible to eliminate conflict, not partially or in small fragments, but totally? That is, can the mind be free of the past and not say, "I am going to be something tomorrow"? To end conflict implies the complete cessation of this whole motive or intention of arriving somewhere, achieving something: achieving fame, virtue, pursuing the ideal, putting away anger in order to be more peaceful, and so on.

All this is not just child's play. It requires a great deal of understanding, perception.

Psychologically to end conflict is to be nothing, and most of us cannot face being nothing, literally being nothing. But after all, what are you? What are all the VIPs, the very important people? Strip them of their titles, their positions, their decorations and all that rubbish, and they are nothing. And I am afraid we ordinary people also are trying in various ways to become something, but inwardly we are absolutely nothing. And why not be nothing? Be nothing—which does not mean trying to become nothing, because that only creates another problem.

You know, this is a very serious thing; it is not just a matter of exchanging a few words and listening to a few ideas. To be really nothing implies tremendous inward meditation—real meditation. But we won't discuss that for the moment.

What matters is to be nothing immediately, and not try to maintain that state, because if you are nothing, you are nothing. You don't have to maintain it. It is the idea that you must achieve or maintain a certain state that creates conflict, for then you are back again in the struggle to become something.

Then there is the question of whether there is anything permanent. Is there anything permanent? What do we mean by permanency? This building will last perhaps a hundred years unless it is destroyed by fire, by a bomb, by this or that. Do we want such permanence psychologically? Do we want the perpetuation of what we are, with all our struggles, with our mediocrity, our pettiness, our despairs, anguish, guilt? You say, "That is only on the surface; we must go beyond it, and going beyond it is to find something permanent." So you project the idea of the soul as being something permanent; you have ideas about heaven, about Jesus, and you believe in God. But is there anything permanent? As one looks into the matter, investigates it, understands it, does one not find that there is nothing permanent, outwardly or inwardly? Biologically you are changing every day, every minute; every seven years your blood undergoes a change. But psychologically, intellectually, you cling to certain ideas, and no bomb can destroy those ideas. You are British, Catholic, or what you will, and that you remain for the rest of your life; nothing can shake it. So that is permanency, is it not? And if that permanency is merely a reaction to contradiction, to conflict, as in fact it is, then what? If everything is actually in flux, in movement, if life is flowing ceaselessly, then how can a mind which has been nurtured on time, on recognition, and which clings to permanency—how can such a mind know the timeless, that which has no limits, no borders, and cannot be recognized?

You see, for those of us who are religious in the conventional sense, God is a permanent entity who exists from everlasting to everlasting. And if we are not religiously inclined, we invent substitutes: the state, an ideology, a utopian something or other. Whether in Moscow or in Rome, it is essentially the same thing.

Now, is it not possible psychologically to step out of time and not think at all in terms of permanency or impermanency? Can one not live in the sense of being so completely attentive, so completely out of time as tomorrow and yesterday, that all the agonies of longing, all the memories and anticipations are dead?

You see, to a very serious problem like this there is no answer as yes or no. There is only a process of inquiry, which reveals what is true and what is false. That revolution, that perception is much more important than finding an answer. There is no answer to any psychological problem. There are answers to mechanical problems. But a psychological problem you have to investigate, you have to go into it very deeply for yourself; and as you look, as you investigate, as you perceive, the problem disappears. It is no longer a burden; you are out of it. The whole process of thinking as we know it comes to an end, and then, perhaps, there is something totally new.

Comment: After all this talk about permanency and conflict, I have nothing to take away with me.

KRISHNAMURTI: Sir, this isn't merchandise; it is not something you can buy. We are looking together at the same problem, trying to see it as totally as possible. You are not listening to me in order to learn from me. You are listening to find out about yourself. Self-knowledge, self-knowing is far more important than carrying home the idea of another and living with that idea. If what we just now discussed about conflict and permanency was not a self-revelatory, self-understanding process, if the explanation remained merely verbal, then you have discovered nothing, and naturally you go away saying, "What was that man talking about?" But if, in listening, you have been observing the whole process of your own thinking, your own feeling, your own effort, then you will have opened the door to something immense.

Question: Supposing one were to achieve this freedom from all conflict of which you speak, if one did not devote oneself to social work, animal welfare, and so on, what would one do with one's spare time and energy?

KRISHNAMURTI: You know, one must put the right question to get the right answer. If one puts a wrong question, it will bring about a wrong answer. Now, is this the right question?

If I have no conflict at all, I will have an astonishing amount of energy. That is a fact, is it not? Most of our energy is dissipated in conflict, in the ceaseless battle with ourselves and with our neighbors. If that conflict comes to an end, what happens to one's greatly increased energy? Obviously, one will find out for oneself when conflict comes to an end—if it ever does.

Now, what do we mean by energy? We know the energy created by conflict. An ambitious man drives himself; he keeps on struggling to achieve this goal, and that brings a certain quality of energy, a ruthlessness—you all know the sort of thing involved in ambition. But when ambition totally ceases—which is not a state of apathy or indifference—there is an energy that has nothing to do with the energy of conflict. The energy of conflict, of competition, of hate, is obviously not comparable to the energy of affection, for affection or love is not the opposite of hate. When there is the abundant energy that comes with freedom from all conflict, one may still go to the office and attend to business affairs, or one may expend that energy in a totally different way.

I will tell you something: Most of us are insensitive, or we are sensitive to beauty and struggle to put away ugliness. But if there is no conflict between beauty and ugliness, if there is just the state of being sensitive—which is also an expression of energy—then everything becomes alive. Every color is a burning, furious color; it is not just red, blue, or white. Every thought, every feeling is burned out. And if this energy is not tied to any particular form or demand, as energy generally is—my wife, my house, my children, my job, my country, my belief—then energy is total stillness. In this stillness there is a tremendous movement which is not from here to there. It is not a movement of time; and that, I feel, is creation, that is God, or whatever name you like to give to it. But for total stillness to come into being, every form of struggle, every form of conflict, every desire to become something, every demand for more experience—all that must come to an end.

But what is the good of my talking about it? You see, for me this is not a speculative thing, but if I talk about something of which you do not know, it will naturally become speculative for you, and therefore unreal.

Question: It seems to me that the moment the 'I' enters the picture, there is a problem. This 'I' then gets to work to try to solve the problem—which is nonsense. Is not the 'I' the only problem?

KRISHNAMURTI: Yes, sir, obviously it is. As long as there is a center, there is a circumference, which is psychological time. And the question is: Seeing all the chaotic demands created by the 'I'—my country, my religion, my family, my insurance, my mortgage, my this and my that—in which every human being is caught, is it possible to live in this world and wipe out the 'I', not theoretically but actually, like operating on a cancer? Is it possible to live in a particular country, to hold a job, to have a wife or husband and children, to have a house, and at the same time have no center? To dance through life without pain—is such a thing possible?

Question: Is not habit part of the problem? One tends to perpetuate all these demands through habit.

KRISHNAMURTI: Obviously. Habit is mechanical, and our thinking is habitual. If we are British, we will be British for the rest of our lives. If we are Catholics, we habitually think in terms of the Savior, the Mass, the confession. If we are Hindus, for the rest of our lives we will be slaves to Hinduism. Going to the office day after day, looking habitually at the same faces, repeating the same pleasures, smoking, drinking, sex—the terrible tyranny of habit. Habit is in essence a bundle of memories, which is the 'I'.

Now, living in this world, is it possible to drop that bundle completely? Again, please don't say it is, or it is not. You have to investigate, you have to be aware of it, you have to go into it—not with despair, and not in the hope of ending it, but simply to uncover it. I say it can be done, and it must be done; otherwise, life is so sordid. You may be able to write poems, you may be a famous man; you may have a good job, a nice house, a lovely wife, talented children, and all the rest of the business; but until there is freedom from the 'I', you are still within the man-made prison and are not capable of going beyond.

Sir, you may put any number of questions, but we come back to the same thing over and over again, which is your own capacity to look, to listen, to find out. And this capacity is not something to be nurtured, developed, because the moment you set about developing something, it becomes a habit; it becomes a form of knowledge to which you will always refer. So the thing is really very subtle; it demands total attention all the time.

Now, wait a minute. When I say, "all the time," I do not mean that total attention must be a continuous process without a break. It doesn't matter if you drop it; if you do, then pick it up from time to time and find out why you dropped it, so that your mind is active, alert, alive.

Question: When there is no 'I', what is it that looks and listens?

KRISHNAMURTI: You see, this becomes a theoretical question. When you die to everything you have known, when all your yesterdays and all your tomorrows are gone, and also the present in the sense of psychological time, then what is there? How can I answer you? Verbally I can say there is something immense, something tremendously alive, but that will have no meaning at all. I think the question really is: Is it possible to eliminate the 'I'? If you go deeply into that, you will answer your own question.

Question: I am contaminated by society. How am I to be free of that contamination?

KRISHNAMURTI: Surely, the question is not how to be free of that contamination, for then you merely create another conflict, another problem. The 'I' is not contaminated by society; it is the contamination. The 'I' is a thing that has been put together through conflict, through envy, through ambition and the desire for power, through agony, guilt, despair. And is it possible for that 'I' to dissolve itself without conflict?

These are not theoretical or theological questions. If one is at all serious about understanding oneself, one sees that any effort to dissolve the 'I' has a motive; it is the result of a reaction, and therefore still part of the 'I'. So what is to be done? One can see the fact and not do a thing about it. The fact is that every thought, every feeling is the result of society with its ambitions, its envies, its greeds; and this whole process is the 'I'. The very act of seeing this process in its entirety is its dissipation; you do not have to make an effort to dissipate it. To see something poisonous is to leave it alone.

Question: Would you then say that effort is destructive?

KRISHNAMURTI: That is what I have been saying all morning. I wonder why it is so difficult to understand something very simple. If two people insist upon quarreling, there can obviously be no peace between them. Similarly, the nations of the world may sign peace treaties and all the rest of it, but they can't live together in peace as long as they are nationalistic and bent upon maintaining their sovereign governments, or as long as they take pride in being Frenchmen, Englishmen, and all that nonsense. To wipe all that away doesn't require effort. It is just a matter of seeing how stupid it is, and how absurdly limited and petty our minds are. Pettiness may try to alter, to bring about a tremendous revolution in itself, but how can it? Any "revolution" it brings about will be as shallow and stupid as itself. But when you just see your own pettiness, your own stupidity, there is then a totally different action which is not instigated by any demand or urge on your part. That is why a negative approach is so important. I am speaking of a negative approach which is not the opposite of the positive. It is negation. Do you understand? When we say no, that no is a reaction; it is the opposite of yes. But there is a denial, a saying no which is not a reaction at all.

I hope you also are working, and are not merely listening to the speaker.

Comment: I find it impossible to be aware all the time.

KRISHNAMURTI: Don't be aware all the time. Just be aware in little bits. Please, there is no being aware all the time—that is a dreadful idea. It is a nightmare, this terrible desire for continuity. Just be aware for one minute, for one second, and in that one second of awareness you can see the whole universe. That is not a poetic phrase. We see things in a flash, in a single moment; but having seen something, we want to capture, to hold it, give it continuity. That is not being aware at all. When you say, "I must be aware all the time," you have made a problem of it, and then you should really find out why you want to be aware all the time—see the greed it implies, the desire to acquire. And to say, "Well, I am aware all the time," means nothing.

Is love, like marriage, for ever and ever? Are marriages for ever and ever? You know better than I do. Is love for ever and ever, or is it something totally stripped of time?

It is quarter past twelve. Perhaps we can discuss this on another occasion.

Question: As you say, it is quarter past twelve, and that chronological time binds us. Wouldn't it be possible to have an organization where we could meet every day and carry on?

KRISHNAMURTI: If you want to, sir, have an organization. I am out of it. If you want to meet with several others, meet. You don't have to ask my permission. But it is true that we are bound by chronological time. You have to catch a bus, go to lunch, you have to keep an appointment this afternoon, you have to see people, and so on. I have to leave this country on such and such a date. We are bound by the watch, by chronological time. That is obvious. But I am not talking about that, as I explained very carefully at the beginning. I am talking about being free of psychological time.

June 10, 1962

Fourth Talk in London

This evening I would like to talk about time and death, and I would also like to talk about what we call love.

In these talks we are not dealing with ideas. Ideas are organized thought, and thought does not solve our deep psychological problems. What really wipes away our problems is facing them, not through the screen of thought, but coming directly and vitally into contact with them, actually seeing and feeling the fact. If I may use the word, one has to be emotionally—not sentimentally, but emotionally—in contact with the fact. If we rely on thought, however clever, however well-organized, however learned, logical, sane, rational it may be, our psychological problems will never be solved. Because, as I was pointing out the other day, it is thought that creates all our problems, and a man who would really go into this whole question of death and not run away from it must find out for himself how thought creates time, and how thought also prevents us from understanding the meaning, the significance, and the profundity of death.

Most of us are frightened of death, and we try to escape from that fear by rationalizing death, or we cling to various beliefs, rational or irrational, again manufactured by thought. Now, to go into this question of death demands, it seems to me, a mind that is not only rational, logical, sane, but which is also able to look directly at the fact, to see death as it is and not be overwhelmed by fear.

To understand fear, we must understand time. I do not mean time by the watch, chronological time; that is fairly simple, that is mechanical; there is nothing much to understand. I am talking about psychological time—the looking back to many yesterdays, to all the things that we have known, felt, enjoyed, gathered, and stored up in memory. Remembrance of the past shapes our present, which in turn is projected into the future. This whole process is psychological time, in which thought is caught. Thought is the result of yesterday passing through today to tomorrow. The thought of the future is conditioned by the present, which again is conditioned by the past.

The past is made up of the things that the conscious mind learned at school, the jobs it has held, the technical knowledge it has acquired, and so on, all of which is part of the mechanical process of remembering; but it is also made up of psychological knowledge, that is, the things that one has experienced and stored away, the memories which are hidden deep in the unconscious. Most of us have not the time to inquire into the unconscious; we are too busy, too occupied with our daily activities, so the unconscious gives various hints and intimations in the form of dreams, and these dreams then require interpretation.

All this, both the conscious and the unconscious process, is psychological time—time as knowledge, time as experience, time as distance between *what is* and 'what should be', time as a means to arrive, to succeed, to fulfill, to become. The conscious mind is shaped by the unconscious, and it is very difficult to understand the hidden motives, purposes, and compulsions of the unconscious because we cannot feel our way into the unconscious through conscious effort. It must be approached negatively, not by the positive process of analysis. The analyzer is conditioned by his memories, and his positive approach to something which he does not know, and of which he is not fully aware, is of very little significance.

Similarly, we must approach death negatively because we don't know what it is. We have seen others die. We know there is death through disease, old age, and decay, death through accident, and death with a purpose, but we don't really know what it means to die. We may rationalize death. Seeing old age coming upon us—gradual senility, losing our memory, and so on—we may say, "Well, life is a process of birth, growth, and decay, and the ending of the physical mechanism is inevitable." But that doesn't bring deep understanding of what death is.

Death must be something extraordinary, as life is. Life is a total thing. Sorrow, pain, anguish, joy, absurd ideas, possession, envy, love, the aching misery of loneliness—all that is life. And to understand death, we must understand the whole of life, not take just one fragment of it and live with that fragment, as most of us do. In the very understanding of life there is the understanding of death because the two are not separate.

As I said, we are not dealing with ideas or beliefs because they solve nothing. A man who would know what it means to die, who would actually experience and know the full significance of it, must be aware of death in living; that is, he must die every day. Physically you can't die every day, although there is a physiological change going on every moment. I am talking about dying psychologically, inwardly. The things that we have gathered as experience, as knowledge, the pleasures and pains we have known—dying to all that.

But you see, most of us don't want to die because we are content with our living. And our living is very ugly; it is mean, envious, a constant strife. Our living is a misery, with occasional flashes of joy which soon become only a memory, and our death is also a misery. But real death is to die psychologically to everything we know—which means being able to face tomorrow without knowing what tomorrow is. This is not a theory or a fanciful belief. Most people are afraid of death and therefore believe in reincarnation, in resurrection, or cling to some other form of belief. But a man who really wants to find out what death is, is not concerned with belief. Merely to believe is immature. To find out what death is, you must know how to die psychologically.

I don't know if you have ever tried to die to something which is very close to you and which gives you immense pleasure—to die to it, not with reason, not with conviction or a purpose, but just to die to it as a leaf falls from the tree. If you can die in this way every day, every minute, then you will know the ending of psychological time. And it seems to me that for a mature mind, for a mind that would really inquire, death in this sense is very important. Because to inquire is not to seek with a motive. You cannot find out what is true if you have a motive, or if you are conditioned by a belief, by a dogma. You must die to all that—die to society, to organized religion, to the various forms of security that the mind clings to.

After all, beliefs and dogmas offer psychological security. We see that the world is in a mess; there is universal confusion, and everything is changing very rapidly. Seeing all this, we want something lasting, enduring, so we cling to a belief, to an ideal, to a dogma, to some form of psychological security; and this prevents us from really finding out what is true.

To discover something new, you must come to it with an innocent mind, a mind that is fresh, young, uncontaminated by society. Society is the psychological structure of envy, greed, ambition, power, prestige; and to find out what is true, one has to die to that whole structure, not theoretically, not abstractly, but actually to die to envy, to the pursuit of the 'more'. As long as there is the pursuit of the 'more' in any form, there can be no comprehension of the enormous implication of death. We all know that sooner or later we shall die physically, that time is passing and death will catch up with us; and being afraid, we invent theories, we put together ideas about death, we rationalize it. But that is not the understanding of death.

After all, with physical death you can't argue; you can't ask death to let you live another day. It is absolutely final. And is it not possible to die to envy in the same way, without argument, without asking what will happen to you tomorrow if you die to envy, or to ambition? This means, really, understanding the whole process of psychological time.

We are always thinking in terms of the future, planning for tomorrow psychologically. I am not talking about practical planning; that is a different matter altogether. But psychologically we want to be something tomorrow. The cunning mind pursues what it has been and what it will be, and our lives are built on that pursuit. We are the result of our memories—memory being psychological time. And is it possible effortlessly, easily to die to that whole process?

You all want to die to something which is painful, and that is comparatively easy. But I am talking of dying to something which gives you great pleasure, a great sense of inward richness. If you die to the memory of a stimulating experience, to your visions, to your hopes and fulfillments, then you are confronted with an extraordinary sense of loneliness, and you have nothing to rely on. The churches, the books, the teachers, the systems of philosophy—you can't trust any of them anymore, which is just as well because if you put your trust in any of them, then you are still afraid, you are still envious, greedy, ambitious, seeking power.

Unfortunately, when we don't trust anything, we generally become bitter, cynical, superficial, and then we just live from day to day, saying that is enough. But, however cunning or philosophical the mind may be, that makes for a very shallow, petty life.

I do not know if you have ever tried this, if you have ever experimented with it—to die effortlessly to everything that you know, not superficially, but actually, without asking what will happen tomorrow. If you can do this, you will come to an extraordinary sense of loneliness, a state of nothingness where there is no tomorrow, and if you go through it, it is not bleak despair—on the contrary.

After all, most of us are terribly lonely. You may have an interesting occupation, you may have a family and plenty of money, you may have the wide knowledge of a learned mind; but if you push all that aside when you are by yourself, you will know this extraordinary sense of loneliness.

But you see, at such a moment we become very frightened. We never face that loneliness; we never go through that emptiness to find out what it is. We turn on the radio, read a book, chatter with friends, go to church, go to the cinema, take a drink—all of which are on the same level because they all offer an escape. God is a cheerful escape, just as drink is. When the mind is escaping, there is not much difference between God and drink. Sociologically, perhaps, drink is not so good, but the escape to God also has its detriment.

So, to understand death, not verbally or theoretically, but actually to experience it, one must die to yesterday, to all one's memories, one's psychological wounds, the flattery, the insults, the pettiness, the envy—one must die to all that, which is to die to oneself. Because all that is oneself. And then you will find, if you have gone so far, that there is an aloneness which is not loneliness. Loneliness and aloneness are two different things. But you cannot come to aloneness without going through and understanding that state of loneliness in which relationship means nothing anymore. Your relationship with your wife, with your husband, with your son, your daughter, your friends, your job—none of these relationships has meaning any more when you are completely lonely. I am sure some of you have experienced that state. And when you can go through it and beyond it, when you are no longer frightened by that word *lonely,* when you are dead to all the things that you have known, and society has ceased to influence you, then you will know the other. Society influences you only as long as you belong to it psychologically. Society can have no influence on you whatsoever from the moment you cut the psychological knot that binds you to it. Then you are out of the clutches of social morality and respectability. But to go through that loneliness without escaping, without verbalizing, which is to be with it completely, requires a great deal of energy. You need energy to live with something ugly and not let it corrupt you, just as you need energy to live with something beautiful and not get used to it. That uncontaminated energy is the aloneness to which you must come, and out of that negation, out of that total emptiness, there is creation.

Surely, all creation takes place in emptiness, not when your mind is full. Death has meaning only when you die to all your vanities, your superficialities, to all your innumerable remembrances. Then there is something which is beyond time, something to which you cannot come if you have fear, if you cling to beliefs, if you are caught in sorrow.

Question: What are the implications of being aware without choice?

KRISHNAMURTI: We must not give too great a significance to that word *aware.* Awareness isn't something mysterious that you must practice; it isn't something that can be learned only from the speaker, or from some bearded gentleman or other. All that kind of fanciful stuff is too absurd. Just to be aware—what does it mean? To be aware that you are sitting there and I am sitting here; that I am talking to you and you are listening to me; to be aware of this hall, its shape, its lighting, its acoustics; to observe the various colors that people wear, their attitudes, their effort to listen, their scratching, yawning, boredom, their dissatisfaction at not being able to get from what they hear something to carry home with them; their agreement or disagreement with what is being said—all that is part of awareness, a very superficial part.

Behind that superficial observation there is the response of our conditioning: I like and I don't like, I am British and you are not British, I am a Catholic and you are a Protestant. And our conditioning is really very deep. It requires a great deal of investigation, understanding. To be conscious of our reactions, of our hidden motives and conditioned responses—this also is part of awareness.

You can't be totally aware if you are choosing. If you say, "This is right and that is wrong," the "right" and the "wrong" depend on your conditioning. What is right to you may be wrong in the Far East. You believe in a savior, in the Christ, but they don't—and you think they will go to hell unless they believe as you do. You have the means to build marvelous cathedrals, while they may worship a stone image, a tree, a bird, or a rock, and you say, "How silly, how pagan." To be aware is to be conscious of all this, choicelessly; it is to be aware totally of all your conscious and unconscious reactions. And you can't be aware totally if you are condemning, if you are justifying, or if you say, "I will keep my beliefs, my experiences, my knowledge." Then you are only partially aware, and partial awareness is really blindness.

Seeing or understanding is not a matter of time, it is not a matter of gradations. Either you see or you don't see. And you can't see if you are not deeply aware of your own reactions, of your own conditioning. Being aware of your conditioning, you must watch it choicelessly; you must see the fact and not give an opinion or judgment about the fact. In other words, you must look at the fact without thought. Then there is an awareness, a state of attention without a center, without frontiers, where the known doesn't interfere, and it is in this state of total attention that the mind can comprehend the unknowable. A petty mind, a mind that is crippled with neurotic ideas, with fear, greed, envy—such a mind may think about the unknowable, about God, about this or that, but it will have very little meaning. Such a mind is not a religious mind at all.

Question: Is it not important to get rid of negative emotions, while keeping the positive ones?

KRISHNAMURTI: What do we mean by emotion? Is it a sensation, a reaction, a response of the senses? Hate, devotion, the feeling of love or sympathy for another—they are all emotions. Some, like love and sympathy, we call positive, while others, like hate, we call negative and want to get rid of. Is love the opposite of hate? And is love an emotion, a sensation, a feeling that is stretched out through memory?

Do we know what it means to love? Do we? We talk of loving God, of loving our wives, our husbands; we say we love our animals, and on the posters we read, "Lovely beer." Is that love? Do we love our families? A most extraordinary thing, the family. The family has become a dreadful thing because we cling to it, we invest in it, we immolate ourselves to it, we continue ourselves through the family name; it is ourselves extended and perpetuated. But one can have a family without all that mess and ugliness.

So, what do we mean by love? Surely, love is not memory. That is very difficult for us to understand because for most of us, love is memory. When you say that you love your wife or your husband, what do you mean by that? Do you love that which gives you pleasure? Do you love that with which you have identified yourself and which you recognize as belonging to you? Please, these are facts; I am not inventing anything, so don't look horrified.

When we say we love, what do we mean by that? Is love a matter of time? Can love exist when there is attachment, or when you possess another? When you say, "She is my wife," "He is my husband," is there love in that relationship? Is there love when you are jealous? When you feel lonely, miserable, agonized because your wife or husband has turned away from you, is that love? And is it love of God when you attend a church service every day, or once a week, and go through all the business of it?

To love something you must be with it completely; your heart, your mind, your whole being must be with it so that there is not the observer and the thing observed. This doesn't mean identification, which is merely another trick. When you identify yourself with your family, that is not love at all. It is yourself extended that you love.

It is the image, the symbol of "my wife" or "my husband" that we love, or think we love, not the living individual. I don't know my wife or my husband at all, and I can never know that person as long as knowing means recognition. For recognition is based on memory—memory of pleasure and pain, memory of the things I have lived for, agonized over, the things I possess and to which I am attached. How can I love when there is fear, sorrow, loneliness, the shadow of despair? How can an ambitious man love? And we are all very ambitious, however honorably.

So, really to find out what love is, we must die to the past, to all our emotions, the good and the bad—die effortlessly, as we would to a poisonous thing because we understand it.

Question: Is not life in the West more artificial than life in the East?

KRISHNAMURTI: I am afraid they are about the same; there is not much to choose between them. We have got romantic ideas about the East.

Question: I would have thought it more primitive there. Is there not a more primitive virtue?

KRISHNAMURTI: A primitive life is not a spiritual life. The primitive is just as frightened as the so-called civilized man, only his fears are more crude, more superficial. But there is a sense in which the sophisticated, the highly educated, the very knowledgeable person must become primitive. He must become young, innocent; he must die to all the knowledge he has gathered. And that primitiveness can be found in the West just as well as in the East. This division between the East and West is so utterly immature; apart from the natural geographical division, it is completely artificial. Men suffer there as much as they do here, and they are just as materialistic, only they spin out a lot of words about God, about wisdom, and do a few cunning tricks with their minds.

Question: Can one arrive at the state of which you speak without first training the mind?

KRISHNAMURTI: Sir, after you have trained your mind, you must die to the trained mind. You see, this is one of our peculiar ideas: that we must go through a certain training or discipline in order to "arrive" at freedom. I didn't use the word arrive. I said just die to the things that you experience every day; just watch your own misery, your attachments. Surely, that doesn't need training.

Attachment is obviously not love. You are attached to your wife or husband. Why? First of all, because you are lonely, and you find pleasure in the companionship of another; it gives you joy, comfort, a sense of security, and all the rest of it. Being attached, you say you love that person, and if that person turns to somebody else, you are jealous, envious, you suffer. Does love bring suffering?

So, being aware of one's attachment and to die to it immediately—does that require training? You say it does because you don't want to give up your attachment, and you think you will free yourself from it gradually.

Have I answered your question, sir?

Comment: Not quite. I don't see how a person who isn't first educated and trained to think can understand your answers.

KRISHNAMURTI: You are all educated, you all speak English. What is there so difficult to understand in what I am saying? I am saying that attachment is not love, and that to find out what love is, you must die to attachment. Does that require training? Must you go through a system of discipline to die to attachment? Psychologically to uncover why you believe in certain things, and after uncovering, looking at that belief, to die to it—does that need training? Must you go through various forms of training to find out what love is?

Comment: We have to pay close attention to everything.

KRISHNAMURTI: Does that mean you must follow a system? You see, I am afraid most of us are rather sluggish; we don't really want to look immediately; therefore, we say it will take time.

Comment: We don't seem to be able to apply what you are talking about; we haven't the energy.

KRISHNAMURTI: We have plenty of energy when it comes to the things we really want to do. It took a lot of energy for you to come here. It takes a great deal of energy to believe, to be jealous, to be envious, to be ambitious. The ambitious man—you know how energetic he is. But we say we have not the energy to get rid of ambition. Why? The answer is very simple; we have only to look at ourselves, to examine our own minds and hearts.

Question: You have described to us a nothingness, a state of emptiness. Can you tell us something of the great truth that might fill this emptiness?

KRISHNAMURTI: First of all, the nothingness is not something mysterious. It is the denial, without motive, of everything, of the whole psychological structure of society. If you deny without motive, without ambition, you are left with an emptiness, aren't you? If you are no longer ambitious, no longer driven by the desire for fame, success, no longer escaping from fear—if you have died to all that, cut through it, then, as I pointed out, there is an emptiness, a state of negation. And the questioner asks: "What great truth will fill this emptiness?"

Now, are we merely exchanging words, talking theoretically, or have you—without any influence, urging, or compulsion—completely broken away from the psychological structure of society? You may have given up one ambition and are keeping another ambition going; you may have partially got rid of fear and are still clinging to certain beliefs. But when you are completely free from the psychological social structure, then there is an emptiness; there is neither tomorrow nor yesterday, nor is there an observer who is observing. If you have not come to that point, then any verbal communication about what is beyond is merely theoretical; it has no value because the word is not the thing. So, if you don't mind, we won't discuss what lies beyond that state of emptiness. It becomes merely a speculative amusement.

Comment: You have not mentioned the imminent destruction of the world through the hydrogen bomb.

KRISHNAMURTI: I am afraid historical events must take their course. If in the meantime we are constantly threatened with being blasted out, vaporized, what are we going to do about it? Do you mean to say we are going to stop the politicians from cultivating this marvelous mushroom? Just see what is invested in it; look at the private and governmental interest in it. The army, the navy, the air force, the captains, the generals—they are all interested in it, and that interest cannot be dissolved overnight. They are going to resist any attempt to outlaw the bomb, just as you would resist if your particular racket were attacked. But we—not the world, not somebody else, but you and I—can die psychologically to our greed and envy, to our hatred and nationalism. To all that we can die immediately, and not wait for the hydrogen bomb to blast us out.

Question: Wouldn't it be better to use the words psychological serenity, tranquillity, *instead of* psychological death?

KRISHNAMURTI: If the words *serenity, tranquillity* mean psychological ending or death, then they will do just as well. You see, we can easily enough substitute one set of words for another, but the fact remains that psychologically we don't die. If there is such a thing as God, truth, or what name you will, it can be found only when there is freedom from the known. To die to the known is an extraordinary thing—the known being your experience of yesterday, the things that you cherish and look back to with longing. In using the word *die* I do not mean being tranquil about it. To die to the known is to put an end to it. Such dying brings tranquillity, but tranquillity is a minor affair because out of this immense death there is an innocency which in itself is stillness of the mind. The innocent mind is a still mind, and only the still mind can discover what there is in that stillness.

June 12, 1962

Fifth Talk in London

This evening I would like to talk about something which for most of us will be a little foreign, a little outside our everyday life, but I think it is important to understand it. I am going to talk about meditation. That word has many connotations. In the Orient they are supposed to do a great deal of meditating, but I doubt it. Serious people do meditate. And in the West, if you are a religious person, you are supposed to do what is called contemplation, or you offer up a prayer occasionally when you are in difficulties. But to me meditation is something entirely different.

As you know, I have been talking about fear, sorrow, time, death, and about the things with which we are faced every day of our life. There is the office routine with its boredom, and the constant effort we make to maintain a certain outward standard of life; and inwardly also we seek to maintain some degree of dignity and freedom by following a set course from which we rarely deviate. These things are not something fantastic, mystical; they are part of our very existence, and we have to deal with them in the course of our everyday living.

Now, without laying the right foundation, one cannot possibly meditate. The foundation essential for meditation is self-knowledge—knowing oneself. Without knowing oneself, all meditation, all contemplation, all prayer, however profitable or seemingly beneficial, leads inevitably to various forms of illusion. Unless one has begun to be aware of oneself, of the unconscious as well as the conscious, unless one perceives one's own motives, conflicts, miseries, one's sense of guilt, one's anxieties and despairs, any form of meditation, contemplation, or prayer can only lead to self-hypnosis. One may have visions, but they are merely the projection of one's conditioning. The Christian will see the Christ, and the Hindu his own particular God. People who have such experiences get very excited about them. But what they experience, what they see in their visions is really the response of their background, of their education, their culture; and to meditate rightly one must be free of this conditioning. Otherwise "meditation" is like going round and round in a circle: one's conditioning projects visions, which in turn strengthen the conditioning.

So, not only for meditating, but also for living fully—which is to throw off the burden of anxiety, the ceaseless battle of hope and despair—it is absolutely essential to know oneself. And to know oneself requires a peculiar attention—an attention in which you observe without evaluation. That is, you see what is actually going on without condemning or judging. You see yourself, as it were, in a mirror, without thought—if I may use that word, which I shall presently explain.

We know what a flower is in the botanical sense, its name, its species, and so on, but we rarely look at a flower nonbotanically. Most of us have neither the interest, the patience nor the capacity to look and to listen without all the misery and travail of the past, without projecting the things we have known, which interrupts perception. To know ourselves we need attention without choice; we have to be able to look and to listen without interpretation.

As this is going to be a rather difficult subject, may I suggest that you simply listen without making an effort to understand. Not that I am mesmerizing you, but just listen as you would listen to the song of a bird, or as you would see a leaf fluttering in the wind, or a cloud floating by, full of light and delight. Just listen, don't try to capture with reason the significance of what is being said. Not that we should not use reason. Without reasoning we shall not be able to go very far—and this evening I would like, if I can, to go very far. But to go very far, we must begin very near, and the nearest thing is yourself. Without understanding yourself, not partially but totally, you may talk about God and be able to quote the Bible or some other sacred book, but you are not a religious person at all; you are merely a slave to the propaganda of the particular culture or society in which you live.

What is needed is this extraordinary state of attention in which you look and listen without decision, without motive, without purpose, which is really to attend without choice. And knowing yourself is not an additive process. You see yourself being angry, jealous, sexual, envious—you merely observe the fact, and that observation without analysis unfolds all the implications of the fact; you don't have to make an effort to uncover them. The moment you make an effort to analyze, to understand, you are distorting the facts; you are bringing in your conditioning as an analyst, as a Christian, as a this or a that.

As I said, knowing oneself is not an additive or accumulative process. The moment you accumulate knowledge about yourself, that knowledge interferes with perception. When you look at yourself through a screen of knowledge which you have accumulated about yourself, there is a distortion in what you see.

I hope I am making this clear, because it is a very important point. Most of us accumulate; we accumulate virtue, wealth, desires, experiences, ideas, and burdened with this accumulation, we have further experience. Thus whatever we experience is conditioned by the knowledge or experience we have previously acquired. All experience has already been tasted, known; therefore, there is nothing new.

I was talking the other day about death. You must die to all knowledge about yourself, not go on accumulating knowledge about yourself, because the self is never static, it is always changing, not only physically but also psychologically. You are not what you were yesterday, though you would like to be; a change has been going on, of which you may not be conscious.

To know yourself—and you must know yourself completely, right through—the accumulative process of knowledge about yourself must come to an end, and there can be that coming to an end only when you cease to judge, to evaluate, to condemn, to justify. This sounds very simple, but for most of us it is not because we are trained to condemn, to judge, to evaluate, to compare, to justify. That is our conditioning. And to see things clearly as they are, without the distortion introduced by our conditioning, is not a matter of time; it is a matter of immediate necessity. You obviously cannot see what is actually the fact as long as you bring all your memories and opinions into it. If that is clear, not just verbally or intellectually, but factually, then we can proceed with an investigation of the unconscious.

The unconscious plays a very great part in our life. Most of us don't know the unconscious except through dreams, through an occasional hint or intimation of things that are concealed. I don't think it is necessary to dream at all; it is a waste of energy. If you are awake, choicelessly aware from moment to moment and therefore not adding to what you have already known; if you are watching everything about you as well as every movement of thought within yourself, then you will find that dreaming ceases altogether—however much psychologists say that you cannot help dreaming, though you may not always remember it. This is not a matter of dispute or argumentation. You can test it out for yourself. If you are not half asleep during the day but wide awake, watching everything around you and inside yourself—every movement of thought, every feeling, every reaction—then you will find that when you go to sleep, you do not dream.

The unconscious, which is hidden and of which one is so little aware, can be approached negatively. That is what I am trying to indicate in saying that there is no need to dream.

I don't know how far you have gone into all this for yourself. Probably you feel it is too bothersome to talk about the unconscious; it is too Jungian, or Freudian, or whatever it is. But you must know the unconscious because it is the unconscious that guides most of our life, that shapes our thoughts, our feelings, and brings about various kinds of conflict. Without knowing the unconscious, you may talk about God, about prayer, war, peace, the atom bomb, but it will have very little meaning.

In the unconscious are rooted not only the everyday responses of the individual but also the collective responses of the race to which you belong, of the culture in which you have been brought up—not just the immediate culture of a few years, but the tremendous accumulation of man's endeavor throughout the ages. It is all there. To uncover the whole of the unconscious through analysis, through investigating it step by step, is absolutely impossible because if at some point in the process you analyze incorrectly, as you are sure to do, the rest of your analysis will also be wrong. If you see the futility of such analysis, if you see that it cannot go very far into and certainly not beyond the unconscious, then you have to approach the unconscious negatively—that is, totally. I shall explain what I mean.

I hope all this is not too much. I am not being patronizing, clever, or superior—nothing of the kind. But most of you have probably not thought about this matter at all, and logically, sanely to follow what is being said without getting confused or worried, you have just to listen. Perhaps much of it you won't understand, but you will understand if the seed falls into soil which is prepared through right listening.

If one's approach in the process of examination or observation is negative, then there is in that process no separation between the thinker and the thought. But for most of us there is a separation, a conflict between the thinker and the thought, between the observer and the observed, between the part of the mind which says, "I must," and another part which says, "I must not." One desire is pulling in a particular direction, and another desire in the opposite direction. We all know this duality of the censor who is always watching, judging, evaluating thought.

Now, is there in fact a separation between the observer and the observed, between the thinker and the thought? We assume there is, but is there? This is very important to find out because if there is no censor, no thinker, no center from which there is judgment, evaluation, then conflict ceases altogether.

Surely, there is only thought—thought as the machine-like response of accumulated memory. This thought has created the thinker as a permanent entity, the 'me', which it then calls the ego, the soul, the higher self; but it is still the result of thought because it can be conditioned to think whatever society wants it to think. The communists do not believe in God at all, but you do because you have been brought up in that belief. It is a matter of propaganda. To understand this whole process, the totality of the unconscious, you have to watch it negatively—and that is the only way you can watch it because any positive watching of the unconscious brings about a division between the observer and the observed.

I wonder if you have noticed that in the moment of seeing something without thought, there is no observer; there is just observation. If you look at a cloud without the accumulated memory of clouds, you are just watching. In the same way one has to observe the unconscious, and when you do so observe, negatively, is there the unconscious? Have you not wiped away the unconscious with all its content? So there is an immediate perception of the totality of consciousness. But you cannot see the totality of consciousness as long as you are looking through your conditioning, through the accumulated experience of the past.

When you have gone that far, as you must, then you will have laid the foundation for meditation because then you will have altogether eliminated sorrow. This does not mean that there is no compassion. But you will have eliminated sorrow, which dulls the mind and makes it insensitive—sorrow being self-pity, self-concern, which has nothing whatsoever to do with compassion.

Now, what is meditation? There are those who say that in meditation you must control your thought. What does such control imply? It implies contradiction, which is a form of conflict. You try to concentrate on something, and other thoughts creep in which you keep pushing away, so concentration gradually becomes a process of exclusion. It is like the schoolboy who wants to look out of the window, but the teacher tells him to look at his book, and the effort to look at his book is called concentration. But such concentration is exclusion.

I think there is a state of attention in which concentration is not exclusion. When the mind concentrates through discipline, through control, through suppression, through various forms of punishment and reward, that concentration divides the mind against itself and brings about conflict. In attention there is no conflict. Attention can be understood only when you see the significance of trying to concentrate through control—which means that the effort to concentrate ceases. As long as you are making an effort to concentrate, there is contradiction, conflict; therefore, there is no attention, and you must have attention.

Meditation is not prayer. Prayer implies supplication, begging, and that is utterly immature. You pray only when you are in difficulties. A happy man doesn't pray. It is only the sorrowful man who prays, the man who is asking for something, or who is afraid of losing something. And contemplation as practiced by Westerners—that also is not meditation.

Please, I have used the word *Westerners* merely as a means of communication. To me there is no division of East and West. That is all too absurdly nationalistic and prejudicial.

What is generally called contemplation implies a center from which to contemplate; it means being in a state to receive, to accept, and again that is not meditation. To lay the foundation for meditation, one has to understand all this, so that there is no fear, no sorrow, no motive, no effort of any kind. If you cease to make effort merely because someone has told you that you mustn't make effort, you are trying to achieve that effortless state, and it cannot be achieved. You have to understand the whole structure of effort, and only then will you have laid the foundation for meditation. That foundation is not fragmentary; it is not a thing to be gradually put together by thought, by the desire for success, achievement, or in the hope of experiencing something much wider and greater. All that has to stop. And when the foundation has been laid, then the brain becomes completely quiet. It is no longer responding to any form of influence or suggestion; it has ceased to have visions; it is no longer caught in or conditioned by the past. To be in that state of quietness is absolutely essential. The brain is the result of centuries of time. It is the biological, the animalistic result of influence, of culture, of the whole psychological structure of society. And it is only when the brain is completely quiet, without a movement, but alive, not made dead by discipline, by control, by suppression—it is only then that the mind can begin to operate. But this absolute quietness of the brain is not a state to be achieved. It comes about naturally, easily, when you have laid the foundation, when there is no longer a division as the thinker and the thought.

All this is part of meditation; meditation is not just at the end of it. Laying the foundation is being free of fear, sorrow, effort, envy, greed, ambition—free of the whole psychological structure of society. When through self-knowledge the brain is no longer an accumulative machine, then it is quiet, still, silent. You must come to that state of silence; otherwise, you are really not a religious person; you are merely playing with things that have no meaning at all. You may call yourself a Christian, a Hindu, a Buddhist, or what you will, but those words are merely the result of propaganda, and they have no value for a man who is really religious. But when there is that state of silence, then there is the coming into being of that immensity, that unnameable. There is then neither acceptance nor denial; there is no entity who experiences the immensity. There is no experiencer—and that is the most marvelous part of it. There is only that immense, timeless movement, and if you have gone that far, you will know what creation is.

Perhaps you would like to ask some questions.

Question: What is the purpose of man's life on this planet?

KRISHNAMURTI: I wonder why we want a purpose? Isn't living in itself the purpose of life? But our life is so sordid, so mean, so ugly, so mediocre. Our life is a battlefield, and therefore we want a superior purpose, something for which we can live—an ideal, a utopia, a marvelous heaven. If you could free yourself from all this turmoil, I wonder if you would still ask what is the purpose of life? I am afraid you would not, for then you would live a full, rich life, not a life of sorrow, misery, and confusion. It is because we are confused that we want clarity, but we don't find out how to free ourselves from confusion. We want something beyond, and so again we are caught in the dualistic battle of *what is* and 'what should be'.

I am afraid there is no purpose to life—which doesn't mean that you must accept the sordid life that you are now living. On the contrary, you must tear through it, destroy completely the psychological structure of society. Then you will find out for yourself what an extraordinary thing life is.

Question: You said that the thinker and the thought are one. Would you be so kind as to go more into detail about this?

KRISHNAMURTI: What is thought? Thought is the response of memory. I ask you where you live, and your response is immediate because that is something with which you are very familiar. The thinking process is instantaneous, like the functioning of a computer, the electronic brain. But if one asks a more difficult question, there is a time interval, a lag between the question and the answer, between the challenge and the response. In that time interval, thought is going on; memory begins to inquire; it goes back into itself looking for the answer, and presently the answer comes. If one then asks you a much more difficult question, you say, "I don't know." But when you say that, you actually want to know, you are waiting to find the answer, and either you go and look it up in an encyclopedia or you ask somebody. The "I don't know" is merely temporary.

But there is an "I don't know," a state of not-knowing which has a completely different significance. Up to now there has always been the thinker and the thought. You say, "I don't know," but you are actually waiting to know. When at last you do know, what you know will be added to the knowledge you have already accumulated, and you will then be able to reply very quickly next time that question is asked. So your "I don't know" is really a process of accumulation.

Now, there is an entirely different "I don't know" in which there is no thinker and no accumulation of thought. It is a fact: You don't know. And for most of us that state of not-knowing is rather terrifying. We never really say, "I don't know"; there is always the vanity of knowing, the feeling of the superior and the inferior, and all the rest of it. But when one says, "I don't know," without any sense of wanting or waiting to know, then there is neither the thinker nor thought. It is a state of complete negation. In that state of negation, one can look negatively at the unconscious, at the whole content of consciousness. Then there is no conditioning, no conflict between the thinker and the thought; therefore, the mind is fresh, young, new, alive.

Question: When one gets to the point of realizing that mere verbalization is static, where does one go from there?

KRISHNAMURTI: First of all, you are assuming that you can be free of verbalization. Is it possible to see the limitation of the word and be free of the word? All verbalization is a process of thinking. Can we think without the word, without a symbol, without an image? And how is the word to come to an end? Most of us are slaves to words. You are British, and that word means a great deal to you. When you say that you believe in God, you are a believer in the word, not in God. You don't know anything about God, and how can you believe in something you don't know? Which doesn't mean you are an atheist—that is equally absurd.

Most of us are lonely; we know what the word means. We know—at least we think we know—what that state of loneliness is. Do we recognize it by the word? And if the word were not there, when we have a certain feeling, would we recognize it as loneliness? Most of us are such slaves to words that we are incapable of looking at the fact.

There is a state of loneliness, and can you look at that state without the word? Take a much closer thing. Can you look at the fact of your anger or your jealousy without the word, without the symbol? The word has associations, memories; through the word there is recognition, and all the rest of it. To look at the fact, one must be free of the word. And when one does look at the fact without the word, is the fact what one thought it was?

Sir, naming, or verbalization, is a very complex process. When you understand that the word is not the thing, you are then in contact with the thing, not through the word, but directly and vitally. And what happens then?

Take jealousy. Becoming aware that you are experiencing a certain feeling, you recognize it through the word *jealousy*. You have had the same feeling before, and the memory of that feeling which you have named jealousy pops up every time the feeling recurs, and you say, "I am jealous." So you never look at the fact but merely recognize what you think is the fact.

Now, what happens when you look at the feeling without the word jealousy—that is, without the whole business of verbalization, recognition, association, memory? When without the word you look directly at that which you have called jealousy, is there jealousy?

As long as you are merely going through the process of recognizing, which is looking at the new thing in terms of what has been, conflict is inevitable; therefore, there is no renewing, there is nothing new. This is a psychological fact. If you go deeply into yourself, you will see it all in a flash; you don't have to listen to me or to anyone else. In throwing off the burden of words, in being free of the whole structure of symbols, ideas, and looking directly at the thing itself, there is a rejuvenation, a freshness; something totally new is taking place.

But just see how difficult it is for a Christian to throw off the symbol of the cross, or for you to throw off the word *British*. And you must throw off the symbol, you must be free of the word. You must be free of the word *God* to find out what there is.

Comment: One gets to the point of inwardly realizing the truth of what you say, but one has to live in the outside world, and the great difficulty is the application of these things.

KRISHNAMURTI: There is no application because there is no contradiction; the world outside and the world inside are not two separate things. The world outside is mechanical, and one has to apply to it the mechanical process of thought. Naming, which implies the whole accumulative process of knowledge, is really very detrimental. Not that you must not have mechanical knowledge—we are not discussing that. You must have mechanical knowledge; otherwise, you wouldn't know what to do the next minute. That is not the problem. Knowledge or experience becomes a detriment when there is merely recognition in terms of that background. It is only when the process of recognizing ceases that there is observation, and from that observation there comes a movement of life.

Question: How can stillness of the mind be prolonged?

KRISHNAMURTI: Oh, I am afraid you have got it all wrong! You like the state of stillness, so you want it to continue. But that which continues is not stillness; it is your memory of the thing that has been. Stillness or silence has no continuity. If ever you come to that silence—and you cannot come to it without laying the right foundation—you will never ask this question. Never. In that silence there is no time, no continuity, no sense of perpetuating something that you have already experienced. Love has no continuity, has it? If it has continuity, it is no longer love. Oh, you don't see the beauty of it, unfortunately!

Question: You said that life is sordid. Is it good to assume that life is sordid?

KRISHNAMURTI: I don't assume it. I don't take it for granted. I see it. I see sorrow, fear, anxiety, guilt; I see the insults, the public houses, the drinking, the smoking—not that they are right or wrong. I see the routine of life, going to the office day after day, the utter boredom of it. If you don't like to call it sordid, call it something else, but that is the fact. I used the word *sordid* just to describe what is taking place. And shouldn't we intelligent people break away from all that, die to all that? Have you ever tried dying to the habit of smoking? Not fighting it with reason, not finding a substitute for it, not going through all the misery of resisting something which gives you pleasure, but just dropping it?

Question: Having emptied ourselves of the 'I', what is there to fill the mind?

KRISHNAMURTI: How can I answer you? First empty the mind, and then you will find out. Not you personally, sir—all of us. This is a general question. We have such fear of being nothing. We have such fear of emptiness, we want to fill it. We are afraid of our own exhausting loneliness, and we try to run away from it. It is the running away that breeds fear, but it makes us active, and in running away we think we are being very positive. When you have understood that loneliness, gone through it and beyond it, you will find out for yourself what there is when the 'I' is not. As in everything else, sir, you must begin with emptiness. The cup is useful because it is empty. But to understand that emptiness, one must go through it in a flash, as it were, and lay the right foundation. Then you will know, and you will never ask another what there is beyond that emptiness.

Comment: Surely, the meaning of life is that the cup should be useful.

KRISHNAMURTI: The cup is useful only when it is empty. You can then fill it with what you like. But if your cup is already full—full of pain, misery, conflict—of what use is it? Sir, of what use is our life as it is: competition, wars, nationalistic conflicts, the division between East and West, between this religion and that? What is the use of it?

Comment: You misunderstand me. By saying that the cup should be useful, I mean that the purpose of life is to do the will of God.

KRISHNAMURTI: Every politician, every businessman, every general who is preparing for war talks about the will of God. The communist also talks about the will of God, only in his case it is the will of the state, and so on and so on. What is the will of God? You can find out only when you are empty, when you are not seeking, when you are not asking, when you don't belong to any particular group of people, when you have no fear, when you are in a state of complete uncertainty—which is not insanity. In that state of uncertainty, thought is no longer seeking an abode in which to be secure. Then perhaps that which may be called God, or what you like, will function.

June 14, 1962

Sixth Talk in London

To ask the right question is not easy, but in the very asking of the right question, if you know how to face it, you have already the answer. The difficulty with most of us is, I think, that we are not very clear what we want to ask. We are very confused, and in our confusion we fumble, we try to put a question or two, hoping for clarity. But I don't think a confused mind can find clarity. Being confused, it cannot find light; it cannot find understanding, but what it can do is to find out why it is confused, what is the source of its confusion, and grapple with that. We must start with confusion, not with the desire to find understanding or clarity. How can a confused mind find clarity? Whatever it finds will still be confused.

So it seems to me that merely to try to find an answer to a problem is an avoidance of the understanding of the problem itself. If I have a problem, my instinctive response is to find an answer, to stumble my way somehow or other out of that problem, and generally I do find some kind of answer that momentarily satisfies me. But the problem comes back again in a different way. Now, if instead of seeking an answer to the problem,

I begin to understand, to unravel the problem itself, then in that very process, the answer is there. I don't have to seek an answer outside the problem.

With that in mind, let us proceed.

Question: Sir, am I right in understanding you to say that attention is in time, and awareness is in eternity? And that by laying the foundation of attention in time, we are led to glimpses of an awareness which is timeless?

KRISHNAMURTI: First of all, may I point out that you are not here merely to understand what I am talking about. You are trying to understand yourself, not what I am saying to you. We are trying to see ourselves as we are, to know ourselves, if possible, totally. We are trying to understand the extraordinarily complex entity that each one of us is, with all its subtle changes, conflicts, urges, compulsions.

I have said that to understand ourselves completely, a certain kind of awareness is necessary, an awareness of ourselves as we are, and we cannot be so aware if we condemn or justify what we see in ourselves. Surely, that is fairly simple. If I condemn myself, there is no understanding. I am not aware of the implications of what I see; I just condemn it. If I condemn another or compare him with someone else, I don't understand that person.

So, to understand ourselves—however noble or ignoble we may be, however sensitive or unfeeling—requires awareness. That awareness implies no justification, no condemnation, no comparison. Justification, condemnation, and comparison are within the field of time; they are dictated by our conditioning. We look at things as an Englishman, as an Indian, as a Christian, as a communist. Our observation and our thinking are conditioned by our particular cultural, educational, environmental influences; and if we are not aware of this conditioning, we cannot see *what is,* we cannot see the fact. That is fairly simple in itself, isn't it? It is not something you are trying to learn from me. To see and to understand the extraordinarily complex entity that you are, you must look at yourself without this background of condemnation, justification, and comparison. And when you do look at yourself without this background, you will see yourself totally.

I think it is very important to understand this question of awareness and not make of it something very mysterious. There is no mystery at all about awareness. It is infinitely practical and applicable to everyday existence. If one is aware that one is comparing, judging, evaluating, aware of one's likes and dislikes, aware of one's contradictions without condemning or trying to get out of those contradictions—if one is aware of all this, just aware of the fact, what happens? What happens if I am aware of the fact that I am a liar—aware of the fact without condemning it, without saying how terrible it is, how evil, how unrighteous and all the rest of that nonsense? If you are simply aware of that fact that you lie, then what is taking place?

Please, you are not learning anything from me. I refuse to be your teacher, I refuse to be followed. That is detrimental, that is a hindrance; it destroys all capacity to find out for yourself. But if you observe, you will see that when you are simply aware of the fact, you come to it without opinion. You look at it afresh, not with all the memories and associations connected with the fact.

I hope I am making this clear. The difficulty is that you never look directly at the fact; you look only at the values and opinions associated with the fact, and this prevents you from seeing the fact.

Now, what takes place when I see the fact that I lie or that I am ambitious or that I am envious or that I am greedy? When I look at the fact without opinion, without past remembrances about the fact, then there is no longer any hindrance in my perception of that fact. I can look at it without any deviation or distortion, and then that fact itself creates energy so that I can deal with it. I can find out why I lie and what I can do about it. Do you understand? If I have no opinion, judgment, or evaluation concerning the fact, then the fact itself creates the energy with which it can be faced.

All this is part of awareness, it is part of time. Don't, please, speculate about the timeless. To discover what is beyond time, you can't just spin a lot of words, nor can you find out from me. You have to work hard at this to find out.

Awareness implies being fully conscious of your reactions when you are confronted with a fact. It implies watching all your responses to challenge—not to some supreme challenge, but to the challenges of every day, the little challenges which occur when you are riding in a bus, when you are talking to the boss, and so on. You have to be aware, not only of your conscious, educated, modern responses, but also of the unconscious motives, compulsions, urges, because both the conscious and the unconscious are within the field of conditioning and therefore of time. The unconscious is the past; it is the accumulated racial inheritance, and one has to be aware of all that.

Now, to be choicelessly aware of this total process of the unconscious as well as the conscious, there must be a negative state of mind, and I think it is fairly clear by now what I mean by a negative state of mind. The positive state is that of condemning, judging, evaluating, approving, denying, agreeing or disagreeing, and it is the result of your particular conditioning. But the negative approach is not the opposite of the positive.

If you wish to understand what the speaker is saying, you have to listen negatively, have you not? To listen negatively is not to accept or reject what he is saying, or compare it with what is said in the Bible, or with what your analyst says. You just listen. In that state of negative listening, you are aware of your own reactions without judging them; therefore, you begin to understand yourself, not just what the speaker is saying. What the speaker is saying is only a mirror in which you are looking at yourself.

Now, this awareness implies attention, does it not? And in the state of attention there is no effort to concentrate. The moment you say, "I must concentrate," you have engendered conflict because such concentration implies contradiction. You want to concentrate on something, but your thought wanders away, so you try to pull it back and you keep this battle going. And when this battle is going on, you are not listening. If you go into it a little, I think you will find that what is being said is an actual fact. It is not a thing to be applied to yourself because you have heard somebody say something about it.

So, awareness is a state of choiceless attention. And without this awareness, this choiceless attention, to talk about what is beyond, what is the timeless, and so on, has no meaning whatsoever. That is mere speculation. It is like sitting at the foot of a hill and asking somebody what is beyond it. To find out, you have to climb the hill. But nobody wants to climb the hill, at least very few want to. Most of us are satisfied with explanations, with concepts, with ideas, with symbols. We try to understand merely verbally what is attention, what is awareness. But this understanding of oneself is quite an arduous task. I am using that word *arduous*, not in the sense of a conflict or an effort to achieve something. One has to be really interested in all this. If you are not interested, it is all right; you can just leave it alone. But if you are interested, you will find it arduous to pursue the understanding of yourself to the very end. All human problems arise from this extraordinarily complex, living center which is the 'me', and a man who would uncover its subtle ways has to be negatively aware, choicelessly observant. Any effort to see, any form of compulsion, distorts what is seen, and therefore there is no seeing at all.

Question: What do you mean when you say that to free oneself from sorrow, one must shatter totally all memory? I have recently lost my wife. When she was dying she said, "Death is the spark to life." How can I ever forget this?

KRISHNAMURTI: I hope we can look at it factually and not personally.

We have all had death in the family, or we have seen it passing in the street. Here the lifeless body is placed in a coffin and covered with flowers; it is transported to the cemetery in a hearse, with Rolls Royces following. In the East it is carried naked with a cloth over it and burned at the most convenient place. And how is one to meet without sorrow this extraordinary thing called death? That is the first point. How is one to understand it? We are all growing old, and it is going to happen to all of us. How am I to meet it? I have seen it; it has happened in my family, but I don't know anything about it. My son is dead and I am in tears; there is loneliness, misery. Being unhappy, I run away; I want to be comforted. Wanting comfort, the mind finds an easy way out; it believes in life after death, in reincarnation, in resurrection. Those are all escapes from the fact of death.

Death seems to be an absolute end to everything one has known: to all the conversations, the experiences, the relationships one has had, to the pleasures and remembrances one has stored up; and there are the last words, the loss of companionship, the agony of loneliness and separation.

Now, all this implies sorrow. And how am I to understand death while living? I can't understand it at the last moment because I am too weak, too ill, too upset, too fearful of the whole process called death. I have to understand death while I have vitality, energy, the capacity to think clearly. That is so, is it not?

What am I to think about the fact of death? How am I to approach it? Death is the unknown. Though a lot of literature has been written about it and many people have said there is life hereafter—that they have proofs and are convinced—death is still the unknown. Now, how do I approach it? What am I to think about it? I may have a feeling about death, but such feelings can be very deceptive. If I have what is called an intuition about life after death, which many people say they have, it may be my desire for comfort, or my urge to continue, which I call "intuition."

So there is the fact of death, and how do I approach it? I seek an answer, an explanation, or I try to forget it, or I cling to the memory of the last words of the friend who is gone, the memory of all the things we once did together. Death is a challenge, and I respond to it with thought as memory, or out of my desire for comfort I believe in reincarnation, in this or in that. We are not discussing whether there is reincarnation or not. We are looking at the fact of death and how we approach it. Our approach to the fact is important, not whether there is reincarnation, whether there is continuity after death, and so on.

When I look at the fact of death, I think about it, and my thinking is the result of my fears, my remembrances, my hopes, my despairs, my loneliness. That is the background from which I think. Now, in looking at the fact, can I die to that background? Do you follow what I mean? Surely, to understand the fact, to live with the fact so that the fact itself gives me the intensity, the vitality, the energy to go into it, I must die to my background of fear, hope, despair, remembrance. I have to be aware of the fact without fear, without saying, "I can't forget her, I can't forget him. How disloyal that would be!" I have to be free of the photograph, the picture, the image that is on the mantelpiece or in my mind. I must be free of everything I have known to understand something which cannot be met with the known. Isn't that so?

We are afraid, not of the unknown, but of losing or giving up the known. If my brother dies, am I really so concerned about my brother? Or am I concerned with my own loneliness, my own emptiness, my own anxiety at having to live alone in this dreadful, isolated world? Isn't it this that is so disturbing to me, and not the unknown? That comes much later.

So, can I give up the known completely, give up the remembrance of pleasure, the remembrance of the things we did together—just die to it easily, without effort? Can I simply drop all that without any compulsion, without any demand, without any motive? Because if I give it up with a motive, I am still within the field of the known.

If you die to the known, to the image of your wife, your husband, your son, to the memories of everything that you did together, what have you left? You are left with nothing, are you not? And it is the conscious or unconscious knowledge of this fact that makes you afraid. To be left with nothing is a brutal state, and most of us don't want to go through it—but that is death. Very few can go through that state because the mind is so frightened, so conditioned by its own fear, by its own anxieties. But if one has gone that far, then there is the unknown, a movement which is beyond the measure of time, beyond thought and the conceptual pattern of existence. It is very difficult to describe that state. But if you come to it, you will find out for yourself that you are living from moment to moment—not accepting the moment with all its illusions, pleasures, and despairs, but living without knowing the next moment, and therefore living with an astonishing sense of immensity.

Question: Why is it so difficult to live without the hunger to be?

KRISHNAMURTI: Sir, you would not ask this question if you had listened to what was said previously. We are doing this all the time. Somebody asks a question, and we are so wrapped up in our own problems that we don't listen. If you had listened to the question about death, you would have answered this question for yourself.

The question is: "Why is it so difficult to live without the hunger to be or to become?"

There is the hunger to be, the hunger for publicity or fame, the hunger to become somebody in this world or in the so-called spiritual world, the hunger of compulsive eating, or compulsive sexuality, and so on. And have you ever tried giving up any of these hungers? Have you ever tried giving up something which affords you pleasure, or which has become a habit—just dropping it? So many of you smoke. It is a common habit. Have you ever tried dropping that habit, just dying to it without effort, without compulsion, without the battle that is engendered by saying, "I must not"? How do you meet that habit—if you do?

I don't smoke, but I see many people smoking for whom it has become a gripping habit. If they don't want to give it up, that is perfectly all right. There is no problem. But if I want to give up a habit which has been going on for years, what am I to do? Can I give it up without effort, just let it drop away from me? If I introduce effort by resisting a habit, you know what happens: there is a perpetual battle with that habit. One day I give it up, the next day I am a slave to it again, and I keep up this game for years.

So I must first understand the futility of resistance or effort in breaking a habit. If that is clear, what happens? I become aware of the habit—fully aware of it. If I smoke, I observe myself doing it. I am aware of putting my hand in my pocket, bringing out the cigarettes, drawing one from the package, tapping it on my thumbnail or other hard surface, putting it in my mouth, lighting it, extinguishing the match, and puffing. I am aware of every movement, of every gesture, without condemning or justifying the habit, without saying it is right or wrong, without thinking, "How dreadful, I must be free of it," and so on. I am aware without choice, step by step, as I smoke. You try it next time—that is, if you want to break the habit. And in understanding and breaking one habit, however superficial, you can go into the whole enormous problem of habit: habit of thought, habit of feeling, the habit of imitation—and the habit of hungering to be something, for this too is a habit. When you fight a habit, you give life to that habit, and then the fighting becomes another habit in which most of us are caught. We only know resistance, which has become a habit. All our thinking is habitual, but to understand one habit is to open the door to understanding the whole machinery of habit. You find out where habit is necessary, as in speech, and where habit is completely corruptive.

Most of us function in a series of habits. In the turmoil, the anxiety, the tremendous agony of our existence, we seek comfort by turning to what we call God, and we function in that habit. We have habits of food, habits of thought, habits of feeling, and we say, "If I don't function in habit, what will I do? How am I to live?"—which is really the fear of being uncertain. Most of us don't know what it is to live in a state of uncertainty without going off the deep end. When we feel intensely uncertain, we become neurotic, which is merely a reaction born of wanting to be certain. Thought has always functioned in habit; therefore, it is afraid of being uncertain, insecure. To live in uncertainty is a healthy, not a neurotic state, but we don't know what it means. So, to understand the hunger to be or to become, you have to be concerned with and understand the whole process of habit.

Question: As we grow older, the mind seems to harden into layers. Is this process natural and inevitable?

KRISHNAMURTI: Physically, as we grow older, we become more rigid, less supple. That is a fact which we can observe very easily. Of course, by eating rightly, doing certain exercises, and so on, you can keep the body fairly supple, but that is not the entire problem. How is one to keep inwardly young, supple, alive, without growing rigid mentally and functioning in fixed patterns? That is really the issue.

You know, it is one of the most difficult things to be free of an idea. Take the idea of God. So-called religious people are terribly burdened with this idea. It is an idea to which you have been conditioned and in which you have grown rigid. The Christian believes in the Savior, in Jesus with his cross. That is the result of two thousand years of propaganda. It is propaganda that makes you believe or not believe that there is only one savior. Certain ideas have been dinned into each one of us from infancy, and most of us continue to function in those ideas. You may become an atheist, but your mind is still held by an idea, a belief. There is the idea of nationalism, the idea of right and wrong—we are not discussing whether there is right and wrong; that is not the point. We are examining idea, belief, and how it takes hold of us. As long as one is living in patterns of thought, in fixed ways of thinking and feeling, the mind is bound to grow rigid, hard.

Take the question of relationship—relationship with one's husband, wife, son, mother, father, and so on. One of the most difficult things in relationship is never to be certain of that relationship. The moment you have a husband, a wife, a child, that person is yours. You have set the pattern of possession, and this possession—in which there is jealousy, anxiety, fear—is called love; it becomes that hardened and respectable thing, the morality of society.

So, as you see, all our acting, thinking, living is in patterns, and naturally our minds grow hard. And the mind grows hard also because there is conflict. To be aware of all this in oneself is to have a mind that is neither hard nor supple—it is something entirely different. But to experience that state one must understand and be free of habit.

Virtue cannot be practiced. Virtue that is born of constant practice is not virtue. It is not humility that practices humility. It is not love that says, "I must love." The moment one is aware that one is virtuous, virtue is destroyed. Virtue comes without discipline, without effort, without imitation, without practice, when there is no accumulation but only a state of learning.

Question: Would it not be valuable to look with awareness into the historical past?

KRISHNAMURTI: I wonder what we mean by the word *valuable?* It is like that word *useful.* Most of us want to be useful, God knows why, and we want to do the valuable thing; we want to look into the past so that it will have some value. I think it is fairly simple to find out about the historical past. You can read the history books. But I am not talking of history books. I am talking of the past that is you and me. You and I are the residue of all human beings, whether they live in the East or in the West. The 'me' is the psychological summation of the historical process. And when you examine the 'me', when you are aware of it, what do you find? You don't find God, you don't find the soul, you don't find the eternal, and all that. What you find is untold memory. We have been conditioned to believe that we are the soul, that in us there is God, or that there is no God and that we exist for the state. We have had it dinned into us that we must do the right thing, we must be useful, we must be good, we must be this and not that. Surely, to find out if there is God, you have to destroy this terrible respectability; you have to strip yourself of the character which you have built up as being somebody in the pattern of virtue, in the morality of society—break it up completely. That is the only real revolution. The crisis is not at the economic or social level but at the psychological level; it is a crisis in consciousness, and that is where the challenge has to be met. And when you have gone into the whole psychological structure of society, which is the 'me', when you have observed it, understood it, and broken it up, you are left with nothing; you are lonely, completely isolated.

Sir, what relation has truth, love, or the unknowable, with this world of jealousy, envy, passing pleasures, beliefs, dogmas, passion? I am sorry to use the word *passion.* Passion is a lovely thing, it is a good thing. I do not mean the passion of ambition, of lust, and all that sort of thing. The passion I am talking of is something entirely different. But what relation has that immensity—if there really is such a thing—with our pettiness? None whatsoever. But we always want to establish a relationship between the known and something unknowable.

Truth is not to be sought after. There is no seeking. How can a petty mind seek truth? A petty mind, a mind that is ambitious, envious, psychologically confused, may imagine, conceive, or formulate what truth is, but what it formulates will still be petty, small, narrow. What is important is not to seek truth but to be free of pettiness, for then you leave the window open, you leave a space in which that immensity—if there is such a thing—may come.

June 17, 1962

Seventh Talk in London

It seems to me that it would be a great pity if we went away after these talks with mere ideas, concepts, or conclusions because, as I have pointed out, ideas, concepts, conclusions do not fundamentally change the human mind. Although politically, economically, socially, and commercially, things are changing very rapidly, the rapidity of these changes is more significant than the changes themselves. What we need is a tremendous psychological revolution, but apparently we cannot keep up psychologically with the swift outward changes. Individually we are still caught in conflict, as we have been for centuries.

To discover what is true, all conclusions, every form of comparison and condemnation must be put aside, and that is a very difficult thing for most of us to do because we are educated, conditioned to condemn, to justify. When we have a problem, we try to find an answer instead of understanding the problem itself, and the answer is in the problem, not away from the problem. For most of us, change is merely a change of pattern, and if you consider it, you will see that a change of pattern is no change at all. Any change within the field of time is the same movement modified and continued.

Now, I am talking not about a change of pattern but about a deep psychological revolution—which means breaking away completely from the psychological structure of society. Change within the pattern of society is a movement from the known to the known, is it not? I am this and I want to become that, which is my ideal, so I struggle to change. But the ideal is a projection of the known, and the pursuit of the ideal is still no change at all.

Revolution implies, surely, a total awareness of the whole psychological structure of the 'me', conscious and unconscious, and being completely free of it without thinking of becoming something else. Whether we are aware of it or not, most of us have established a pattern of thought and activity, a patterned way of life. In trying to bring about a change in our life, consciously or unconsciously we accept a certain pattern, and we think we have changed, but actually there has been no change at all.

As I was saying the other day, without understanding the unconscious, any psychological "change" is merely conformity to a pattern established by the unconscious. And the present crisis—not only the outward crisis, but also the crisis in consciousness—demands a revolution. I am not talking of social or economic revolution, which is very superficial, but of a revolution in the unconscious—a complete breaking away from the psychological structure of society, a total abandonment of ambition, envy, greed, of the desire for power, position, prestige, and so on. This is the only revolution because without it, no new thing can be; without it, we merely indulge in ideas, in concepts, and therefore there is always sorrow. There is an ending to sorrow only when there is this total revolution.

So the question is: How is this inward change, this total revolution to be brought about? If we make a deliberate, conscious effort to change, we engender conflict, struggle, and change that is born of conflict, struggle, is productive only of further misery.

Now, is it possible to bring about a revolution in the psyche without conscious effort? I have carefully explained that the unconscious is the storehouse of the past. In the unconscious are stored, not only the experiences of the individual, but also those of the race. It is the storehouse of the whole endeavor of man throughout the ages: his search for God, his denial of God, his worship of the state, his identification with the nation, with an idea, and so on. The totality of all that is the past; it is the unconscious background of each one of us, according to which we respond. We may try to understand the unconscious through examination and analysis, but that will obviously not bring about a revolution. You can modify, reform, but your reform will need further reform; it is not a revolution, a complete breaking away from the past. One needs a young, fresh, innocent mind, and that can be only when one breaks away psychologically from the past.

So, how is this revolution to take place without endeavor, without trying to do something about it? Any effort or struggle to bring about a change involves a contradiction, and that contradiction emphasizes the conflict that already exists; therefore, it is not a change at all. You can perceive something new only in a state of innocency, that is, only when the past has ceased to have any psychological significance.

You know, innocency is one of the demands of modern society, but its demand is still very superficial. To people who have lived through a great deal of suffering, who are burdened with guilt, anxiety, fear—to them, innocency is a great thing. But the innocency they talk about is the opposite of complexity, the opposite of sorrow, misery, strife, confusion. Real innocency, like love, is not an opposite. Love is not the opposite of hate. Love comes into being only when hate in every form has ceased. Similarly, the mind must be innocent though it has gone through every form of experience. For the mind to realize that state of innocency, the accumulations of experience—which are still the past, still part of the unconscious background—must come to an end.

Now, how is this to be done? The religious people say you must turn to God and be in a state of receptivity so that the grace of God can come into being. And there is every form of religious practice—I was going to use the word *chicanery*—to persuade, influence, or control the human mind to the end that it may in one form or another achieve this innocency. There are also those who try various drugs and experience a heightened sensitivity of perception, an extraordinary state of bliss. But innocency cannot be brought about by any drug, by any form of yoga, by any belief or rejection of belief, or by waiting for the grace of God. All these things imply effort, seeking, the urge to escape from the fact of *what is.* And innocency can come into being only when there is a total freedom from the known—that is, a dying to the known, a dying to the past, to pleasurable memories, to ideas, to all the things that one has cherished, built up, put together as character.

Unfortunately, most of us do not want to die to anything, particularly to that which gives us pleasure, to the memory of things that we have known and cherished. We would rather find an escape, live in an illusion. But one must die to the known for innocency to be. This is not a mere verbal statement or conclusion. There must be an actual dying to the known, to the past. And one cannot die to the known if one has a motive to die, for motive is rooted in time, in thought, and thought is the response of the background of consciousness, which is the known.

We are all conditioned, whether as Englishmen, Russians, Hindus, Christians, Buddhists, or what you will. We are shaped by society, by environment—we are the environment. Most of you undoubtedly believe in God and in Jesus because you have been brought up in that belief, whereas in Russia they are conditioned not to accept any of that. The totality of the mind's conditioning is the known, and that conditioning can be broken, but not through analysis. It can be broken only when it is approached negatively, and this negative is not the opposite of the positive. As love is not the opposite of hate, so this negative is not the opposite of the positive—the positive being examination, analysis, trying to change the existing pattern, or trying to conform to a different pattern. All this we consider to be positive, and the negative we are talking about is not the opposite of that. Nor is it a synthesis. A synthesis implies the coming together of the opposites, but this is productive of a further set of opposites. The negative we are talking about is a denial of the opposites altogether. When one denies totally the approach—which is part of our conditioning—that seeks to change the psyche through effort, through analysis, then one's approach is negative, and it is only in this state of negation that the mind is innocent. Such a mind is really the religious mind.

The religious mind isn't the mind that believes, that goes to church every day, or once a week; it isn't the mind that has a creed, that is bound by dogmas and superstitions. The religious mind is really a scientific mind—scientific in the sense that it is able to observe facts without distortion, to see itself as it is. To be free of one's conditioning requires, not a believing or an accepting mind, but a mind that is capable of observing itself rationally, sanely, and seeing the fact that unless there is a total breaking up of the psychological structure of society—which is the 'me'—there can be no innocency, and that without innocency, the mind can never be religious.

The religious mind is not fragmentary; it does not divide life into compartments. It comprehends the totality of life—the life of sorrow and pain, the life of joy and passing satisfactions. Being totally free from the psychological structure of ambition, greed, envy, competition, from all demand for the 'more', the religious mind is in a state of innocency; and it is only such a mind that can go beyond itself, not the mind that merely believes in a beyond, or that has some hypothesis about God.

The word *God* is not God; the concept you have of God is not God. To find out if there is that which may be called God, all verbal concepts and formulations, all ideas, all thought, which is the response of memory, must come totally to an end. Only then is there that state of innocency in which there is no self-deception, no wanting, no desire for a result; and then you will find out for yourself what is true.

Such a mind is no longer seeking experience. A mind that seeks experience is immature. The innocent mind has ceased to be concerned with experience. It is free of the word—the word being the capacity to recognize from the background of the known. Recognition implies association, either verbal or through actual experience, and without that association you cannot recognize anything. The religious or innocent mind is free of the word, free of concepts, patterns, formulations, and such a mind alone can find out for itself whether there is or is not the immeasurable.

Perhaps you will now ask some questions relevant to what we have been considering together.

Question: What is the essence or mainspring of your teaching?

KRISHNAMURTI: That would be rather difficult to put in a few words. As I have tried to explain, listening is an art. Most of us don't listen because what we hear, we translate according to our pleasure and pain, according to our likes and dislikes, according to our conflicts and the formulations of what we already know. Nor do we generally see anything because what we actually or visually see is interpreted in this way or in that. We may look at a flower botanically, but very few ever look at a flower nonbotanically—which is the only way one can see the essence, the beauty, the whole loveliness of the flower.

In the same way, your perception of the significance of what is being said depends on how you have listened to all these talks. You can't possibly understand by merely picking up a few ideas, a few concepts or opinions. If that is what you have done, then I am afraid these talks will have very little meaning. Either you listen to the whole or you hear nothing at all. And if you have listened to the whole of what we have been talking about, then you will see for yourself the essence of it; you will never ask me what is the essence. This is not just a clever way of turning the tables on you, sir. It is an actual fact. You cannot hold the waters of the sea in a garment or capture the wind in your fist. But you can listen to the deep murmurings of the storm, to the violence of the sea; you can feel the enormous power of the wind, its beauty and its destructiveness. For you must destroy totally the old for something new to be.

Question: What is the still, small voice of conscience? Is it not the voice of God speaking within each one of us?

KRISHNAMURTI: I am afraid that the still, small voice of conscience must be utterly distrusted, just as one must utterly distrust and doubt the voice of God within one. That voice speaks to all the saints, to all the generals, to all the warmongers, as well as to you and to me. Such voices must be totally denied because they lead us disastrously astray. For most people the voice of God is their own desire, their own longing, their own identification with a particular country, belief, or idea. It is easy to produce a voice of God in yourself—too terribly easy. And if you happen to be an organizer with a certain capacity of speech, you will become a leader, and you will lead people to destruction, to greater misery.

Question: Why do you keep talking about the known? Why don't you talk to us about the unknown?

KRISHNAMURTI: First of all, why do I talk at all? What is communication? We can communicate with each other verbally, or we can silently commune. Most of us prefer silent communion because then one can preserve all one's pet ideas and beliefs, one can remain in one's ivory tower. But when we try to communicate verbally, then the trouble begins because then we have to establish a certain relationship, we have to understand each other through the meaning of words and we can understand each other only when we meet at the same level, at the same time.

I am talking, not to persuade you to change, or to push you to any form of psychological revolution, but because one can't help talking about something which is so imminent, so real, so actual. When you yourself see the extraordinary beauty and light of a cloud, you want to tell others to look at it too—at least I do. That's all. That's why I talk.

And the other question is: "Why do I always come back to the known? Why don't I stay with the unknown and talk from there?"

You cannot know the unknown. You can know only that which you have already experienced and are therefore able to recognize. The unknown is not recognizable, and for the coming into being of that immensity, the known must end. There must be freedom from the known. That's why one is constantly talking about the known—to break it down.

You cannot possibly talk about the unknown. No word, no concept can ever bring it within the framework of the known. The word is not the thing, and the thing must be seen directly without the word. And that is extraordinarily difficult: to see something out of innocency. To see something out of love—love which has never been contaminated by jealousy, by hate, by anger, by attachment, possession. One must die to attachment, to possession, to jealousy, to envy—die without reason, without cause, without motive. And it is only then, in this freedom from the known, that the other thing may be.

Question: Do you believe that a repetition of words, however holy, is meditation?

KRISHNAMURTI: Meditation cannot come about through any repetition of words, through what the Hindus call mantras and you call prayer. Prayers and mantras only put the mind to sleep. By droning a series of words over and over again, you can put yourself to sleep very nicely—which is what many of us do. In that soporific condition we feel we have achieved a most extraordinary state, but that is not meditation. That is merely drugging yourself with words. You can also drug yourself by taking certain chemicals, or by drinking, and in various other ways; but that is obviously not meditation.

Meditation is really extraordinary, and it is something you must do every day. But meditation is not separate from living. It is not something to be done in the morning and forgotten for the rest of the day—or remembered and used as a guide in your life. That is not meditation.

Meditation is an awareness of every thought, of every feeling, of every act, and that awareness can come into being only when there is no condemnation, no judgment, no comparison. You just see everything as it is, which means that you are aware of your own conditioning, conscious as well as unconscious, without distorting or trying to alter it. You see all the responses, reactions, opinions, motives, urges within yourself. But that is only the beginning.

If you would have a religious mind, you must meditate. You must be aware of your own feelings, sensitive to every movement of your own thought—which is not concentration. Concentration is very easy. Every schoolboy learns it. But meditation is not being absorbed in something. When a small child is absorbed in a toy, he is very quiet, he is completely with the toy. And that is what most of us want; we want to be absorbed in something, identified with a toy, with an idea, with a belief, with a concept. But that is not meditation.

Meditation is something far beyond all this immature thinking. Meditation is that state of awareness in which there is attention to every thought and every feeling; and out of that attention there is silence—which is not the silence of discipline, control. Silence that is brought about through discipline, through control, is the silence of decay, of death. But there is a silence that comes into being naturally, effortlessly, without your even being conscious of it, when there is this attention in which there is no experiencer, no observer, no thinker. That silence is really innocency, and in that silence—without being invited, without your seeking or asking—the unknown may come.

Question: You have said that in order to be free from the past, free from thought, one must die, and that this was not merely a verbal statement—there must be an actual dying. Do you mean we must die physically?

KRISHNAMURTI: It is rather difficult to die even physically because we so cling to the physical. But I am not talking about physical death. That, I am afraid, is inevitable for all of us. If the scientists discover some new chemical, it may enable us to live for another fifty or more years, but we will still be the same at the end of it, with our pettiness, our worries, our problems, our jealousies, with our longing to be sensitive, to be beautiful, and all the rest of it. I am talking of dying in terms of the psychological structure of the 'me', which is what we are. To die in this sense is to die to one's envy, sir. Most of us are envious. Society is based on envy, on comparison, on the pursuit of the 'more': more knowledge, more influence, more power, more wealth, more, more, more. That is the very essence of envy. And to die to that, to die to envy without argument, without persuasion, without knowing what there will be when you do die to envy—that is real death because out of that death there is innocency. Thought—which in essence is the result of continuity, of the past—can be modified, changed; it can create a new series of ideas, formulas, concepts. But that which has continuity can never know an ending, and through that ending, an innocency. However reasonable, however logical, thought can never know what innocency is because thought can never be free.

Comment: I believe you said that the avoidance of a problem was preferable to the finding of a solution.

KRISHNAMURTI: No, sir, I am sorry, but I did not say that.

You see, most of us have problems, inward and outward, and we are always seeking an answer. All outward, mechanical problems have an answer, but inward, psychological problems have no answer. They have to be understood, and a mind that is seeking an answer to a psychological problem is incapable of understanding the problem. If I have a psychological problem, say, in relationship, and I try to find an answer to that problem, then I am avoiding the problem because my concern with finding an answer prevents me from looking at the fact of the problem itself. To understand the problem, I have to look at the fact without opinion, without demanding an answer.

Question: If time permits, may we sit quietly and experience together a few moments of complete silence?

KRISHNAMURTI: You know, that is one of the most dangerous things to do. (Laughter) You have been sitting here together for an hour, listening, and while listening, you were supposed to have been silent. If you have not been silent during that hour, or even for a few minutes, in the act of listening, then sitting quietly together and trying to experience silence will only lead to various forms of illusion. Silence is difficult and arduous; it is not to be played with. It isn't something that you can experience by reading a book, or by listening to a talk, or by sitting together, or by retiring into a wood or a monastery. I am afraid none of those things will bring about this silence. This silence demands intense psychological work. You have to be burningly aware—aware of your speech, aware of your snobbishness, aware of your fears, your anxieties, your sense of guilt. And when you die to all that, then out of that dying comes the beauty of silence.

Question: What is the difference between meditation and contemplation?

KRISHNAMURTI: First of all, what do you mean by the word *contemplation?* If contemplation implies an entity who is endeavoring to contemplate, to bring his mind into focus, then contemplation is the same as the so-called meditation in which there is a meditator who is trying to achieve a result. A person may "meditate" regularly in order to be quiet, in order to realize God, but that is not meditation, it is not contemplation. As long as there is an observer, a thinker, an experiencer, there cannot possibly be meditation. Meditation is not a thing that you can just pick up from a book and practice for a few years; it is not a matter of discipline. Most of us have disciplined our minds so much that we are dead, and within that pattern we try to meditate. What matters is the breaking down of the pattern, and the breaking down of the pattern is the beginning of meditation.

Question: How is it possible to be intensely aware while one is occupied with a particular job?

KRISHNAMURTI: I do not see the difficulty. Why can't one be intensely aware while doing the job? Whether the job is mechanical, scientific, or bureaucratic, in being intensely aware while you are doing that job, you will not only do it more efficiently but you will also begin to be aware of why you are doing it, what are the motives behind your work. You will find out if you are afraid of your boss; you will observe how you talk to your underlings and to those above you. Being intensely aware in your relationship with others, you will know whether you are creating enmity, jealousy, hatred; you will see all your own responses in relationship, whether you are here, in a bus, in your office, or in the factory. All this is implied in intense awareness.

Also, if you are intensely aware, you might give up your job. Therefore most of us don't want to be intensely aware; it is too disturbing; we would rather continue with what we are doing, even if it is very boring. At best we break away from that which bores us and find a job which is less boring, but this too soon becomes routine.

So we are caught in habit: the habit of going to the office every morning, the habit of smoking, the sexual habit, the habit of ideas, concepts, the habit of being an Englishman, and so on. We function in habit. To be intensely aware of habit has its own danger, and we are afraid of danger. We are afraid of not knowing, of not being certain. There is great beauty, there is great vitality in not being certain. It is not insanity to be completely insecure; it doesn't mean that one becomes psychotic. But none of us want that. We would rather break one habit and create a more pleasant habit.

Question: Can we not learn something from the innocence of a child?

KRISHNAMURTI: The child is not innocent. The child is ignorant. The child is craving for more experience as he grows, matures. We are not talking about childhood innocency; that is for the poets. We are talking about the innocency of a mature mind—a mind that has gone through agony, travail, suffering, intense anxieties, doubts, and has left all that behind, has died to all that.

June 19, 1962

Saanen, Switzerland, 1962

First Talk in Saanen

From the very beginning I think we should be quite clear what is the intention of these gatherings. Many outward changes are taking place in the world; there are many pressures, many demands, innumerable problems, and it seems to me that to meet this situation, there must be a complete transformation of the psyche. I mean by that word *psyche* the mind, the whole process of our thinking—our attitudes, our values, our habits, the many beliefs and dogmas that we have cultivated for centuries. All this, I feel, must be completely transformed if we are to meet the urgent problems of life, and that is what I propose to talk about during these meetings—how to bring about this radical change, this transformation of the mind.

So these talks are very serious; they are not merely an amusement for a Sunday morning or any other morning. If you are at all serious, and I hope you are, then you will listen completely, not just taking in a little part here and there; you will listen to the totality of what is being said, and then you and I will be able to explore together how to bring about this radical revolution in ourselves. By that word *serious* I mean the intention to pursue a particular subject to the very end whether you like it or not, to explore totally a particular aspect of life. We are not going to discuss outward problems such as the common market, how to stop the atom bomb, whether we should go to the moon, and so on; but I think those outward problems will be understood if we can understand the inward problems.

It seems to me also that the outward problem is not so very different from the inward problem. When one comes to think of it, there is really no difference, at least no line of demarcation between the outer and the inner. Living is like a tide that goes out and comes in. To concentrate on the inward process of one's own being will have very little meaning if we do not understand the outward process as well. The outward activities of the mind correspond to the inward activities, and to concentrate on one while neglecting the other will not lead us very far.

As I said, these talks are very serious; they are not a form of entertainment, and certainly it is not our purpose merely to exchange ideas. Ideas, concepts, are organized thought, and they have very little significance in bringing about a radical revolution in the mind. Ideas don't change a human being; they merely alter the pattern of existence. Most of us indulge in ideas, accepting new ideas and discarding old ones, or exchanging one belief for another; but such exchange, such substitution, is merely a superficial adjustment, it does not bring about radical transformation.

Therefore we are not going to indulge in ideas, in formulas, in concepts. We are going to deal, not with myths, but with psychological facts, with our own fears, hopes, despairs. And we are capable of meeting these psychological facts only when we know how to listen to them, how to observe them without condemnation or interpretation. So I think it is important to understand what we mean by listening, by observing, and I would like to go into that a little bit this morning.

Transformation is not brought about by the action of will, or by desire, which is another form of will; it cannot come about through effort, which is again the outcome of an urge, of a motive, of a compulsion. Nor can this transformation, this inner revolution, take place as the result of any influence or pressure, or by mere adjustment. It can only come about effortlessly—and I will go into that later on. But as this is the first talk, it must obviously be an introductory affair, and it is important to begin by understanding what we mean by listening.

I do not know if you have ever actually listened to anything. Try listening to that stream that is flowing by without giving it a name, without giving it a significance, without letting it interfere with your attention—merely listen to it. You can listen only when there is no motive which makes you listen. If you have a motive, then the motive is important, not the act of listening. You are listening in order to get or to achieve something, in order to arrive somewhere, so your attention is divided; therefore, you are not listening.

Do please pay a little attention to this issue, because if you don't fully comprehend it, I am afraid you will totally miss the whole meaning of these talks.

To me, any form of effort to bring about an inner revolution perverts or denies that very revolution. Transformation can come about only when there is no effort of any kind, and that is why it is very important to understand what it means to listen.

You cannot listen if you are comparing what you hear with what you already know. Then you are merely interpreting, and where there is interpretation, there is no listening. If you are condemning what you hear because you think it should be different, or because you hold certain opinions, then you are not listening. And you are certainly not listening if you are merely following an established authority or substituting one authority for another.

So the act of listening is extraordinarily difficult because we are conditioned to accept or to deny what we hear, to condemn it, or to compare it with what we already know. There is almost no unconditioned listening. When I say something, your natural or rather your conditioned response is to accept or to deny it, or to say that you know it already, or that it is in such and such a book, or that such and such a person has said it. In other words, your mind is occupied with its own activity, and when that activity is going on, you are not listening.

Surely, this is all very logical, rational, and sane, isn't it? We are not talking about something mysterious.

Now, the act of listening completely to something that is factual—to listen to it without opinion, without judgment, without condemnation, without any interference of the word—is extremely arduous. It requires total attention, and so also does the act of seeing. I wonder if we ever see anything at all—a tree, a mountain, a river, the face of one's wife or husband, of a child, or of a passerby? I question it because words, ideas, formulas, interfere with what we are seeing. You say, "What a lovely mountain!" and that very expression prevents you from looking—which is again a psychological fact. To see something completely, your mind must be quiet, without the interference of ideas. The next time you observe a flower, notice how difficult it is to look at it non-botanically—particularly if you happen to know something about botany. You know the species, you know all the varieties of that flower, and to look at it without any interference of the word, without the intrusion of your knowledge, of your likes and dislikes, is again very arduous. The mind is always so busy, so distracted; it is constantly chattering, never seeing, never listening. But when the mind is quiet, to listen and to see does not require effort. If you are actually listening to what is being said now, and therefore understanding what is being said, you will find that your listening is without effort.

Inward or psychological revolution implies a complete transformation, not only of the conscious mind, but of the unconscious as well. You can easily change the outward pattern of your existence, or the way you think. You may cease to belong to any church at all, or you may leave one church and join another. You may or may not belong to a particular political or religious group. All that can be changed very easily by circumstances, by your fear, by your wanting greater reward, and so on. The superficial mind can easily be changed, but it is much more difficult to bring about a change in the unconscious—and that is where our difficulty lies. And the unconscious cannot be changed through volition, through desire, through will. It must be approached negatively.

To approach the total consciousness negatively implies the act of listening; it implies seeing facts without the interference of opinion, judgment, or condemnation. In other words, there must be negative thinking. Most of us are accustomed through training and experience to conform, to obey, to follow established moral, ethical, ideological authorities. But what we are discussing here demands that there be no authority of any kind, because the moment you begin to explore, there is no authority. Each moment is a discovery. And how can a mind discover if it is bound by authority, by its own previous experiences? So negative thinking implies the uncovering of one's own assertive, dogmatic beliefs and experiences, one's own anxieties, hopes, and fears; it implies seeing all these things negatively, that is, not with the desire to alter or to go beyond them, but merely observing them without evaluation.

To observe without evaluation is to observe without the word. I do not know if you have ever tried looking at something without the word, the symbol. The relationship of words to what they describe constitutes thought, which is the response of memory; and to look at a fact without words is to look at it without the intervention of thought.

You try it sometime. As you go out this morning, look at the green valley, at those snowcapped mountains, or listen to that river without a thought—which doesn't mean that you are asleep. It doesn't mean that you look at them with a blank mind. On the contrary, to look at something without the intervention of thought, you have to be totally aware. And this is an arduous task because we are so conditioned from childhood to judge, to evaluate. We are conditioned by words. We say of a person that he is a communist or a Catholic or an Englishman or an American or a Swiss, and through that screen of words we look and listen; so we never see, we never hear.

That is why it is so important to be free of our slavery to words. Take the word *God*. We have to be completely free of that word, especially when we consider ourselves to be religious or spiritual, for the word is not the thing. The word *God* is obviously not God, and to understand what that extraordinary something is, one must be free of the word—which means being inwardly free of all the influences and associations of that word. This in turn implies neither believing nor disbelieving; it implies not belonging to any religion, to any organized system of thought.

Only then is there a possibility of finding out for ourselves whether there is something beyond the word, beyond the measure of the mind.

So these talks are a grave matter; they require your whole attention in the discovery of yourself, not tomorrow, not the next minute, but at the moment you are listening, in the immediate present. Without understanding the mechanism, the whole process of one's own mind, one cannot go very far; and we have to take a journey into the timeless. To do this we must begin very near—with ourselves. That is why it is so important to be aware of the operations of one's own mind, which is the beginning of self-knowledge. Without knowing yourself, you have no basis for further inquiry, and to know yourself demands, not an accumulative process of knowledge, but the knowing of yourself from moment to moment. You have to see yourself as you are from moment to moment without interpreting what you see and without accumulating knowledge about yourself; you have to observe with choiceless awareness.

That is why I say that these talks demand a gravity of purpose on your part. They demand that you come regularly or not at all because you cannot understand the whole thing by casually listening to one talk. You wouldn't go to a mathematician and ask him to teach you the whole universe of mathematics in a few minutes. That would be too absurd, utterly immature. Similarly, if you are at all serious in this matter, you will attend the talks regularly, and you will pay attention—effortless attention. By effortless attention I mean a state of attention in which you do not merely listen to what the speaker is saying, but through the words of the speaker, you discover your own process of thinking, which is to come upon the facts within yourself.

The increase of prosperity and scientific knowledge in the world is not going to bring greater happiness. It may bring more of the physical necessities, and I hope it will. It may bring greater comfort and convenience, more bathrooms, better clothes, more refrigerators, more cars. But those things do not solve our fundamental human problems, which are much deeper, much more imminent and within ourselves. And the purpose of these talks is to explore our problems together, because here there is no authority. I am not trying to influence you to think in a particular way, which would be childish, immature, because then it becomes merely a matter of propaganda.

May I suggest that while you are listening you do not take notes but actually listen, and that you remain fairly quiet immediately before and after these talks. At the first meeting, we naturally greet each other and talk, but do not let us sit here afterwards everlastingly talking, which merely indicates the restlessness of one's own mind. What matters is to be aware of all this without effort: to observe effortlessly the fact that you chatter, the fact that you are jealous, the fact that you are frustrated and want fame through expressing yourself in poetry, in pictures, in music, in thought. To be factually and choicelessly aware of all that in yourself, to observe it without effort—it is in this state of effortless awareness that there is a total revolution. And only the mind that is in total revolution from moment to moment, not achieving a total revolution—only such a mind can discover whether there is or is not something immeasurable.

Perhaps some of you wish to ask questions, and we shall see what comes out of it. It is very easy to ask wrong questions, but to put the right question is one of the most difficult things to do. It demands a perceptive mind. The question must reflect an actual problem which you have, something with which you are battling. If you put the right question, then we two can join together in finding the right answer. But a human problem really has no answer. Mechanical problems have answers. When a car goes wrong, when an engine misfires, there is a mechanical answer to the problem, whereas most of our human problems have no answers at all. But unfortunately, when we have a problem, most of us want an answer—that is, we want to escape from the problem, and so we ask a question.

Now, if you merely want to escape from your problem, whatever it is, please don't put a question. But if you really want to understand any human, psychological problem, then we can study it together; we can explore together its subtleties and variations, its nuances and complexities. In the exploration of the problem, you will begin to understand the problem, and that is the only way to resolve it.

I am afraid I have made it rather difficult for you to put a question. That was not my intention. But really to explore any human problem, we must meet at the same level, at the same time—which is, after all, what may be called love. Surely, there is love only when you meet another at the same level, at the same time—that is, when you meet that person totally, completely. To explore our human problems, we must psychologically meet in that way. If you are expecting an answer from me, and I feel there is no answer except in understanding the problem, we won't meet, and you will go away saying, "That man is silly; he can't answer a straight question, he avoids it."

So it seems to me that what is important during these talks is to look at the problem together—which doesn't mean agreement or disagreement. Merely to agree or disagree is too utterly schoolboyish. This is not a political meeting. We are trying to see things as they actually are within ourselves, and this demands observation, not agreement or disagreement.

Question: How can this mental exploration of a problem bring about an understanding which cannot be based on mere intellection?

KRISHNAMURTI: Let us find out what we mean by exploration and what we mean by understanding. Will mental exploration bring about understanding? Please don't agree or disagree. We are examining the question. The exchange of ideas, opinions, formulas—will that bring about understanding? What do we mean by understanding? How does the state of understanding come into being? I will go into it a little bit, and perhaps we may meet.

In the state of understanding, surely, there is no barrier between the fact and yourself. When you understand something, your whole attention is given to it. Attention is not fragmentary as the mental process is. When you examine something mentally, it is a fragmentary process, a separative process; but when you understand, in that understanding, your mind, your emotions, your body, your whole being is involved. You are quiet, and out of that quietness you say, "I understand."

Understanding obviously does not come through fragmentation, and most of us think in terms of fragmentation; all our relationships in life are fragmentary. With one part of ourselves we are politicians, with another part we are religious, with a third part we are businesspeople, and so on. Psychologically we are all broken up, and with these fragments of ourselves we look at life. And then we say, "Intellectually I understand, but I cannot act."

So, mental examination or exploration is fragmentary, superficial, and it does not bring about understanding. Intellectually we agree, for example, that it is immature to have the world broken up into conflicting nationalities and religious groups, but at heart we are still English, German, Hindu, Christian, and so on. Our difficulty is to bring about a direct emotional contact with the fact, and this demands that we approach the fact negatively, that is, without any obsession of opinion.

There is a vast difference, then, between the mental examination of a fact and the understanding of that fact. Mental examination of the fact leads nowhere. But the understanding born of approaching the fact negatively, without opinion or interpretation—this understanding of the fact gives tremendous energy to deal with the fact. I will go much more into it during the coming talks because probably most of us do lack this energy. We have plenty of physical energy—at least I hope so. But to deal with a psychological fact requires astonishing energy of a different kind, and that energy is denied when you approach the fact through habit—the habit of association, the habit of words, the habit of thought. So the fact remains, and the intellect is separated from the fact. This naturally creates a contradiction, a conflict, and therefore a dissipation of energy.

July 22, 1962

Second Talk in Saanen

It is such an enchanting day, and perhaps it is part of that enchantment to talk about serious things.

This morning I would like to begin by considering with you how very superficial most of us are. And behind this superficiality of our existence, behind the everyday routine of work, marriage, sex, children, there is a deep sense of despair and anguish. I think most of us are consciously or unconsciously aware of this. Though we may have a little property, position, prestige, behind all this superficiality there is for most of us a sense of anxiety which is not caused by anything in particular; but when we are not busily occupied with the immediate activities of life, there it is, deeply penetrating into our thoughts and feelings. This anxiety, this sense of despair is not restricted to those who are growing old, but is experienced also, I think, by the young, by those who have still to make their way in the world, who are concerned with their future, with making a success of their life, concerned with marriage, sex, children, housekeeping. For most of us there is this underlying sense of utter hopelessness, the feeling: What is the use of it all? This is especially so now that the world is haunted by the specter of impending catastrophe. I think it is important to talk about this because, being very superficial, we turn to various forms of escape, or we try to find ways and means of deepening the significance of life.

Life embraces both the outer and the inner, and can the significance of life be deepened? I don't mean "deepened" by going to church, by believing or disbelieving in God, by doing social work, or by being interested in paintings and music, all of which is actually very superficial. But a mind which is superficial by its very nature, by its own conditioning, by its education and the influences of society—can such a mind go really deeply within itself? I don't know whether you have ever asked yourself this question.

Most of us seem to think that going very deeply within oneself is an extraordinarily difficult problem and probably not worth it. Even though we may be utterly dissatisfied with the superficiality of our existence, we feel that we haven't got the necessary technique, the modus operandi, to enter very deeply into that vast, extraordinary world—if such a world exists—which is not made up of mere words and symbols, of emotional ideas and the imaginative creations of intellection.

Now, I think we ought to try to find out together what it is that brings about a depth of insight, a clarity of perception in which there is no confusion, no striving after fulfillment, an existence which is not an escape from life. In this modern world, the widening of knowledge is proceeding very swiftly. Through an ever-expanding technology, more and more things are being done by machines. There are electronic brains that can translate, paint, write poems, and solve extremely complex mathematical problems. Knowledge has become extraordinarily important, and in a world where knowledge is given supreme importance, is not knowledge itself a source of despair? Please, I am going to expand it, and don't reject or accept what is said; just listen to it.

Superficially clever minds all over the world, with their capacity to write and to express themselves, influence vast numbers of people to give increasing significance to information or knowledge, thereby making them more and more dependent on external things. Though useful and necessary at certain levels of existence, knowledge is not an end in itself, and when given undue importance, it becomes a source of anxiety, a source of guilt, a source of despair.

The mind has been trained in knowledge, and it has been through many troubles, many experiences, subject to innumerable influences; and can such a mind free itself of that whole background and be innocent? Surely, it is only the innocent mind that has no anxiety, no fear, no despair. But in the modern world, we are enclosed in fear, in despair, in a vast sense of uncertainty.

Now, knowledge is obviously essential; otherwise, we couldn't function at all. In very big, complicated things like building a jet plane, and in small, everyday things like knowing where one lives, we must have knowledge. Knowledge of mathematics, knowledge of biology, technological knowledge of various kinds—it all has its place. But knowledge also impedes clarity of perception. Whether you are a scientist, a musician, an artist, a writer, it is only in the intervals when your mind is free from what it has known that there is a creative movement. The interval may be very brief, or it may be vast and extensive, but in that interval there is no knowing, if I may use that word, no impingement of the past as knowledge. The things you have learned, the mistakes you have made, your successes and failures, your hopes and despairs—it is only when your mind is free of this whole burden of the past that there is a sense of the new; and that sense of the new can then be expressed in composing if you are a musician, or in painting if you are an artist, and so on.

I think it is very important to understand this because for most of us, experience is the way of life. The more experience we have accumulated, the wiser we think we are; but I question that wisdom. Experience is really a response to challenge, whether superficial or very deep, and when that experience is accumulated as knowledge or memory, it conditions the next response.

Please follow this a little bit. I am not a schoolteacher, but since you have taken the trouble to come here, perhaps you will also take a journey with me into this extraordinarily complex problem of experience or knowledge. What I am talking about is not a philosophy; it is not a theory or system of ideas. It is related to your daily existence, which is so full of routine and habit; it is related to the day that you spend at the office, the day that you spend with your wife and children in a relationship of conflict or pleasure. We are dealing directly and deeply with life itself, with our everyday actions, with our thinking and feeling, with our hopes and fears.

As I said, for most of us experience is the way of life, and the more experiences we have been through, the more we want; or we want some ultimate experience, an experience of something immeasurable that will give a deeper, wider significance to life. For most of us there is no end to experience. But when one looks at experience, one sees that it is accumulative, and that the background of accumulated experience conditions our further response to challenge. Whether one is a mathematician, a housewife, or whatever one is, the response of the past as accumulated knowledge or experience is further experience, which in turn strengthens the past.

So we have this accumulative burden of past experience, both individual and collective. In whatever particular society we may live, it is there; it is our background, it is our tradition, it is our knowledge, it is our culture. This background is always dictating our further experiences, shaping our thoughts, and so there is no ending to experience. We do not see how there can be such an ending, for we say to ourselves, "What would life be without experience?" But it is the background of experience that breeds anxiety, the sense of despair, the fear of not arriving, not achieving. There is always the feeling of incompleteness, insufficiency, and so we look to more and more knowledge or experience as a means of giving us greater depth. But knowledge or experience—if you will not misunderstand what I am saying—has to come to an end if one is to inquire into the whole question of despair.

We have various forms of despair: the despair of not being able to fulfill ourselves, of not achieving a goal, of not being somebody in this world, and so on. There is also the despair of loneliness, and the despair of never-ending confusion. Not knowing what to do, we look to somebody—a political leader, a religious leader, or a scientific leader—to tell us what to do, and sooner or later we know the utter futility of merely being told what to do. Being uncertain and in despair, we pile up experience as knowledge, but knowledge doesn't wipe away despair; experience doesn't dispel the sense of anxiety in life.

So, what is the significance of experience, not only of the little, everyday experiences, but also of the deep experiences that we have? An orthodox Christian who has been brought up with certain beliefs and dogmas may see a vision of the Christ, and to him that is an astonishing thing; but it is fairly obvious psychologically that such experiences are a projection of his own background, his own conditioning. When a Hindu has visions, he sees his own gods, not the Christ.

Now, is it possible to live without experience? To me, the background of knowledge or experience, with its ceaseless demand for yet more experience, is the source of despair because there is no innocency in this conditioned state. It is only the fresh, innocent mind that has no despair. But you see, most of us would go to sleep if there were no outward challenge. If we did not have to earn a livelihood, to compete with our neighbor, to get along with our boss; if there were not the urgings of propaganda, the magazine articles telling us how to make a success, how a bootblack can become a millionaire, a president, or whatever it is—if there were not these outward spurs, demands, and challenges, most of us would have a dull, stagnant, stupid life. Not that we haven't got it now—it is there, but this constant pressure from the outside keeps us going.

If one sees all that is implied in this response to outward pressure, one rejects it—and that is not a very easy thing to do. It is difficult not to respond to the stupidities of propaganda and to the psychological demands of the social structure, but if one is able to put all that aside, then one creates one's own challenges and responses. I do not know if you have observed this fact. When you are all the time questioning, asking, doubting, that becomes your own challenge—

a challenge which is much more strict and vital than the outward demands of society.

But this constant questioning, this constant inquiry, this doubting and tearing things to pieces, is still the outcome of discontent, is it not? It is still the outcome of the desire to know, the desire to find out what is the purpose of life, whether it is this or whether it is that. So, though one has rejected the outward challenges, one is still a slave to experience, to challenge and response. There is a state of inward conflict, and that also keeps one alive—much more alive than the outward conflict does.

Please, I am not saying anything outrageous. This is what actually takes place with all of us. The more intellectual and subtle you are, the more you will reject the obvious propaganda of religions and politicians. But then you have your own challenges, your own demands and standards, your own vitality to find out; and this indicates, surely, that you are still dependent on the stimulus of asking a question and demanding an answer. Both the inward and the outward challenges, with their responses, indicate a conditioned mind that is still seeking an answer, still groping to find out, and therefore still within the field of will, which is the realm of despair.

Now, when one has deeply understood and therefore rejected both the outer and the inner challenges, then experience has very little meaning because then the mind is intensely awake and a mind that is intensely awake does not need experience. It is only the dull mind that seeks experience, that depends on the stimulus of challenge and response. Being caught in its own conflicts and confusion, such a mind depends on the acquisition of knowledge, and in depending it becomes more and more dull.

I am not advocating ignorance. To me, ignorance is not the lack of book knowledge. If you haven't read the latest novels, if you are unfamiliar with the philosophy of the dialectical materialists and all the rest of it, that in itself doesn't mean that you are ignorant. To me, ignorance is unawareness of the operations of one's own mind. The lack of self-knowledge is the essence of ignorance. I am not saying that we must throw away all book knowledge. We can't. I am pointing out that a mind that is awake does not need the stimulus of challenge and response. Because it is awake, it is not demanding any experience. It is a light unto itself. And such a mind, surely, can live in this world of guilt without anxiety and without despair. It is the unawakened, dependent mind, the mind ignorant of itself, that is in a state of conflict and misery.

Now that you have listened to all this, don't say, "How am I to have a mind that is so completely awake? How am I to get it?" You can't get it. It isn't something you buy; it isn't a thing to be acquired through practice. You can't seek it out. There is no method, no system that will give it to you. What is important is just to listen without wanting, without seeking, for such listening is a state of mind when there is no impingement of knowledge, no activity of thought; and in that silence of the mind there is creation, which is understanding.

If you have really listened in that sense of the word, then you will be out of this conflict, this misery and despair. For there is a miracle in listening—and that is the only real miracle.

You see, we are all growing old, even the young are growing old, and the older we get, the more rigidly fixed we become in our conditioning. Our habits of thought become heavier, our days become more and more routine, and anything that threatens the habitual, the routine, breeds anxiety and fear. And inevitably, at the end of it all, there is death—which becomes another tremendous horror. So it is not the clever mind, not the informed mind, not the mind that has become philosophical, rationalizing everything away in order not to be disturbed—it is none of these, but only the innocent mind that can understand, that can know or be aware of that extraordinary something which may be called the nameless, the immeasurable, or what you will.

I think one can live in this world with that innocency. You can have a family, read the ugly newspapers, or not read them, listen to concerts, go every day to the office—you can do all this in that state of innocency. You can live a full life, and it will have much greater significance. And I have talked about it this morning because most of us obviously spend our lives in varying degrees of shallowness. The question really is whether it is possible by effort to make the shallow mind deep. I don't think it is possible. The shallow mind may try to be deep by making an effort to dig into itself, but it is still a shallow mind. Whereas, if one understands this whole process of experience, of challenge and response, both the outer and the inner, then one is immediately out of it. Then one's mind is young though one may have an old body; the mind is clear, sharp, fresh, and it is only in that state of innocency that the real can be.

Shall we discuss what I have been talking about this morning?

Comment: It seems to me that there can be no feeling of having had experience unless there is a storing up of experience, which creates a sense of time as past and future.

KRISHNAMURTI: I think that is what I was saying. The past is knowledge, is it not? What you were yesterday, your aspirations, your demands, your jealousies, your vanities—that is the past, that is time in the psychological sense, and without the past, without that psychological yesterday, is there a psychological tomorrow? If I deny all yesterdays, die to them, cut them off as if by a surgical operation—which is absolutely essential—can there be a tomorrow? And can there be experience for a man who is living completely? Surely, you cannot live completely if you are looking back to the past and forward to the future. But when there is complete awareness in the sense of living totally from moment to moment, is there experience?

Please, this is a factual, not a rhetorical or an ideological question. If I actually don't care what happened yesterday, whether I was hurt or jealous or insulted, if I have cut it away completely, then is there a sense of time, a sense of past and future?

You see, time is experience. The memory of the pleasure and pain we have had, the demand to fulfill, to achieve, to become somebody—all this implies time. And it is really a complex question because to most of us time is very important. I am not talking of chronological time, time by the watch, but of the time structure built by the psyche, by thought; and this implies the whole question of cultivating memory.

As that gentleman's question suggests, there must be time as long as there is a center from which you are experiencing. As long as there is that center—a conditioned center which responds to every challenge, conscious or unconscious—there is no moment in which creation can take place. Whether you are a musician, a painter, a scientist, a chemist, or just a person without any particular skill or training, I wonder if you have ever observed a strange thing in yourself: that when your mind is completely quiet, when all thought has ceased, when there is no sense of going or coming, no looking to the past or the future, in that moment of quietness you know something totally new.

But that newness is not to be recognized as the new. The moment you recognize the new, it is already the old, it is no longer the new. One has to remain—not "remain," that is the wrong word—one has to be in that moment without going backward or forward, without having any sense of time. Try it sometime—no, not "try," that again is the wrong word. To try implies "in the meantime," which is absurd. You can't try, for there is no "in the meantime." Either the new is there, or it is not. And it is there with an extraordinary vitality, an astonishing potency, the moment you understand this whole process of experience, knowledge, seeking.

I hope you are working as hard as I am!

Question: Is this energy you speak of limited by physical health?

KRISHNAMURTI: Somewhat, but not entirely. You obviously need good physical health. If you are in constant, agonizing pain, naturally your energy is dissipated by that. Having had pain, one knows how to dissociate oneself from pain, not by escaping from it, but by being completely with pain. When we say to ourselves, "I wish the pain would stop; when will it be over?"—that is, when thought is operating on pain—it increases and sustains pain. But it is possible to be completely with pain—unless, of course, one becomes unconscious, which is quite a different matter. I know what I am talking about, so don't think, "Oh, you don't know what pain is." We all have pain. If you live with pain completely and don't resist it, if you are totally aware of it, then you will find that in spite of the pain and however severe it may be, you have a different sense of vitality. But again, you see, pain becomes a problem of time because you are comparing pain with your memory of freedom from pain.

You know, to live with something is an extraordinary thing. I have been living with the noise of that stream all morning; I have been listening to it while I was talking, and not resisting it, not wanting to push it away. Then the stream with its noise and its beauty, and your own talking, are all part of the awareness which we are discussing.

Question: What about our responsibilities and our mistakes of yesterday?

KRISHNAMURTI: We all have certain responsibilities, and there are the mistakes of yesterday, but why do we carry over those mistakes to today? That is one question. And what do we mean by responsibility? It is an ugly thing to feel responsible. Please don't misunderstand me. I am not saying that you must become irresponsible. I am not talking about irresponsibility—to do so is a cheap way of avoiding the issue. Do you feel responsible if you love somebody?

Comment: If one has children one feels responsible for them.

KRISHNAMURTI: First of all, we are trying to understand what we mean by responsibility. Don't immediately say, "Am I not to feel responsible for my children?" That is such a futile way of discussing. Besides children we have husbands, wives, grandmothers, mothers-in-law, houses, property, jobs, and all this makes us feel very responsible. But what do we mean by that word *responsibility?* The soldier says, "I am responsible for maintaining peace." What nonsense! The police say they are responsible for upholding the proper conduct of society. So we must examine the meaning, the deep significance of that word.

When I love somebody, do I feel "responsible"? What do I mean by love? Is love a matter of attachment? You see, that is just it. When I am attached to somebody, I feel responsible for that person, and my attachment I call love. Please don't agree or disagree. This is a very difficult issue. Let us go further into the meaning of that word responsibility. I think we use words like *duty* and *responsibility* when we have no love.

You are silent!

Comment: We are trying to understand you.

KRISHNAMURTI: No, sir, you are not trying to understand me. I am only saying, look at yourself, go into yourself, and all these things are revealed.

Please, let us remain with that word responsibility, because we are all so weighted down by it. We say, "I have got to go to the office every day, whether I like it or not, because I have a family to maintain, and it is my responsibility to earn the money"; or, "It is my responsibility to educate my children"; or, "It is my responsibility to be a good citizen, to become a soldier," and so on and so on and so on. Why do we feel responsible? When do we use that word?

Comment: When we give importance to the self.

KRISHNAMURTI: If I may suggest it, please look at yourself. When do you use that word responsibility?

Comment: When there is a sense of obligation.

KRISHNAMURTI: Yes, sir, a sense of obligation. When you feel that you are obliged, that you have got to do something. You may not like it, but you feel that you have got to do it. Go behind the word and look at the feeling—look at it as a father, as a mother, as a husband, as a wife. Surely, you talk about responsibility only when you feel that you have got to do something; you say it is your duty, that everything depends on you, and so on.

Now, can one live in this world without the feeling of responsibility—that is, without feeling that what one is doing is a burden? Look, sir, I came here this morning to talk. I didn't feel it to be a burden, a responsibility. There was no saying to myself that I must talk because so many people have come to listen. It is not my duty to talk—I wouldn't do it on that basis. It would be terribly boring to me. I never use that phrase: I am responsible—it is too hideous. What I am doing, I love to do—which doesn't mean that I get a satisfaction out of it, or that I fulfill myself in talking. That is all utterly immature and childish. But if one loves, then the words responsibility and duty disappear altogether. If one loves, there is no country, there are no priests and no soldiers, no gods and no wars.

July 25, 1962

Third Talk in Saanen

We were talking the other day about the significance of knowledge, and how knowledge impedes clarity of perception. I think we went into that matter fairly deeply, and this morning I would like, if I may, to discuss what is virtue. To inquire into this question, one has to consider the influence of society, the social significance of virtue and authority, and the state of aloneness. All these factors are implied in that word *virtue.*

There is, first of all, this whole question of social influence, how we are shaped by the sociological as well as by the psychological structure of society. The way we think, the way we act, our sense of responsibility, if I may use that word which we talked about the other day—all this is the result of social influence. Psychologically we are not separate from society. Our reactions, our thoughts are the result of our conditioning, which is determined by the psychological structure of society. Though we are educated in schools and colleges and acquire a certain amount of technical knowledge in various fields in order to earn a good living, most of us are left at the mercy of society. Our character is shaped by society. Our religious ideas are conditioned by society, by the culture in which we are born. The influence of society shapes our whole being. We are Catholics, Protestants, Jews, Hindus, this or that, with a corresponding set of dogmas, beliefs, and superstitions. Within that pattern we cultivate what we call our own values, but in this also we are consciously or unconsciously influenced by many things—by the food we eat, by the climate we live in, by the clothes we wear, by the newspapers, magazines, and books we read, by radio and television. Without understanding all these influences, which are quite imminent, penetrating, and constant, without being totally aware of influence from moment to moment, virtue loses its meaning. When there is no understanding of influence, we merely follow a pattern which has become respectable, and respectability is not virtue. On the contrary, respectability is a horror; it has nothing whatsoever to do with that which may be called virtue, and into which I shall go presently.

So, if one really wants to understand the extraordinary virility, the vitality and the strength of virtue, one has first to be aware of influence—not only of the influence that we receive consciously, but also of the unconscious influence to which most of us are so receptive and of which it is much more difficult to be aware.

Now, is it at all possible to be free of influence—the influence of one's wife or husband, of one's children, of society, of everything about us? Is it possible to be free of that extraordinarily insistent influence which is going on all the time in the form of propaganda through newspapers and books? If we say it is not possible to be free of influence, then obviously the matter ends there. Then there is no need for further inquiry, and all virtue becomes mere imitation, conformity to a pattern. Society, with its code of ethics, its responsibilities, its traditional values, is insistent in its demand that the individual shall conform to the established pattern, and this conformity it calls morality; and an immoral person is he who deviates from the pattern. But surely one has to be totally free of the pattern, one has to break away completely from the psychological structure of society—which means that one has to be aware of this whole structure in oneself, in the unconscious as well as in the conscious mind. And it's very difficult to be aware of one's unconscious conditioning. Consciously one may reject the moral structure of society, and many people do; they shrug their shoulders and put it aside. But the influence of society is not limited to the present century; it includes also the immense past with all its propaganda, its tradition, and this pattern is deeply embedded in the unconscious; and to be aware of the unconscious pattern demands a certain quality of negation.

Please, I hope you are not merely listening to the words and agreeing or disagreeing but are actually experimenting to see how deeply you can go into yourself, into the unconscious. These gatherings will be utterly useless, they will have no meaning at all if you casually listen to a few talks and go away. And don't say, "I can't do this," because nobody else can do it for you. Each one of us has to do it for himself.

The unconscious is the hidden storehouse of the past, both individual and collective. It is the repository of centuries of propaganda, of all the experience and knowledge, the traditions and complexities of the race. Now, however clever you or the analyst may be, the conscious mind cannot approach the unconscious by way of analysis. Through analysis you can only scratch on the surface of the unconscious; you cannot go into it very deeply—as I think most analysts and psychologists would now agree. The conscious mind has been educated, trained, in a particular direction; it has acquired technical knowledge along certain lines so that one may gain a livelihood, which is called the positive approach to life; but such an approach to the unconscious is not possible.

I hope I am making myself clear. If not, please ask questions afterwards and we shall discuss the matter further.

The unconscious, which is the hidden, must be approached negatively. Do you understand what I mean by the negative and the positive approach? When we have a problem, most of us approach it positively, which means that we try to change *what is* according to a certain pattern. Being so-called positive people, our approach to the unconscious is equally positive. Actually we are not positive people at all because our positive approach is a reaction to the negative. I hope you understand all this.

To be aware of something negatively—of the flapping of that curtain, or the noise of that stream—is to look and to listen without resistance, without condemnation, without denial. In the same way, it is possible to be choicelessly aware of the totality of the unconscious, which is negative perception. But this state of negation is not the opposite of the positive; it has nothing whatever to do with the positive because it is not a reaction.

If you would understand something, your mind must be in a state of negation; and it is not in a state of negation when you deny or condemn what you see. The state of negation is not blankness. On the contrary, you are aware of everything, you see and hear with the totality of your being—which means there is no resistance, no denying, no comparing, no judging. And I think it is possible to listen in the same way to all the responses of the unconscious, which is to be negatively aware of the unconscious. If you can do this—and this is really the only way to approach the unconscious—then the unconscious reveals itself totally, immediately. Of course, you can go step by step, analyzing every form of conditioning, every tradition, every value as it comes up, which is a very long and tedious affair; and in that way your approach can never be total.

Now, through this negative or choiceless awareness, you can completely break through the conditioning of the unconscious. Your conditioning of nationality, of traditional values, of racial inheritance, the conditioning imposed upon you by the present society—you can break through all that immediately, and then you begin to understand the significance, the truth or the falseness of influence.

Most of us have divided influence into good and bad. We consider that there is such a thing as good influence, and that it is right to have good influence. But to me, all influence is the same: it perverts, it distorts. A mind that is influenced in any direction cannot see clearly; it is incapable of direct perception. If one understands this, not just intellectually or verbally, but totally, with one's whole being, then one is no longer a slave to any form of influence.

Please don't regard what is being said as something theoretical, or as something not applicable to you because you are too old or too young or too conditioned, or because you have too many responsibilities. All that is sheer nonsense; it is merely an escape from the fact that you don't really want to understand this whole process of influence. And it is very important to understand the process of influence because it is influence that makes us conform to respectable morality, which has behind it the authority of tradition, the authority of society, the authority of a job; and so authority becomes very dominant in our life. Society demands obedience, the obedience which a mother expects of her child, and because we are slaves to influence, we instinctively accept the authority of society, the authority of the priest, the authority of the symbol, the authority of tradition. In matters like keeping to the right of the road, paying taxes, and so on, one must naturally accept the authority of the law, but we are not talking about that. We are talking about the psychological urge to obey, which implies slavery to influence.

You know, I am not just making a speech for you to listen to. We are doing something together—at least I hope we are doing it together—which is this: we are going into the whole question of virtue. If we understand virtue rightly, it releases an enormous vitality, and it is this vitality, this energy that is needed to bring about the complete transformation of which we were talking at our first meeting. So, in listening to what is being said, it should be you yourself who are working, and not I working for you. Most of us are content to go to a tennis match and watch the players; we never take part in a game; we just watch, listen, and enjoy the playing of others. I am afraid, here, it is not at all like that. Here you have to work as hard as the speaker; otherwise, it has no value at all. By work I mean listening to what is being said and finding out if it applies to you—which means seeing for yourself the fact, the truth or the falseness of what is being said. To see the fact is neither to accept nor to deny what is being said, but to be so vitally aware that, if it is true, you capture and apply every nuance of every word by digging into yourself. That is what I mean by work. If you do that, when you leave this tent you will be virtuous, and I really mean it: you will be virtuous.

So one has to understand the acceptance of authority, which is really the psychological demand to be secure, to be certain, to be assured that one is following the right path. Most of us hate to be uncertain about anything, especially about ourselves. But you see, we have to be uncertain to find out what is true. One has to free oneself from all authority, from all following, from all obedience, and that is a very difficult thing to do because freedom is not a reaction to the fact that you are a prisoner. It is only when you understand for yourself your own bondage to words, to influence, to authority—understand it, not react against it—that there is freedom.

So authority has to be understood, whether it is the authority of the priest, of the politician, of the book, of the specialist, of your next-door neighbor, or the authority of your own experience. And, as we have seen, to understand something, the mind must be in a state of negation. To understand your child, you must watch him while he is playing, crying, eating, sleeping; and when you compare him with another child, you are not watching him. In the same way, one has to observe the instinctual desire to obey, to follow, to conform, to imitate; one has to go into it very deeply within oneself. Conformity is obviously necessary in certain things. The language that one uses in speaking is based on conformity to an established linguistic pattern, and to reject that pattern would be absurd, for there would then be no way of communicating with each other. I am not talking of conformity in the sense of accepting certain obvious and necessary facts to which we all agree; I am talking of the psychological conformity, acceptance, or imitation, which is essentially the desire to be secure.

Most of us are afraid of going wrong; we are always seeking success in this world, or psychologically we want to arrive somewhere; therefore, obedience, which means accepting the psychological structure of society, becomes extraordinarily important. If you understand the whole significance of this, then you will find that the very essence of virtue is aloneness. If you are not completely alone, you are not virtuous. The mind is alone only when it has understood influence and is not affected, not captured by it. Such a mind is no longer seeking position or power, and therefore it is free of authority, obedience, following. The state of aloneness is not a reaction; it is not an escape from the crowd; it does not mean withdrawing, becoming a hermit, living in isolation, all of which is a reaction. And by that word *aloneness,* I mean something entirely different from loneliness.

It is very difficult to communicate to another the significance or the quality of being alone. Most of us are never alone. You may withdraw into the mountains and live as a recluse, but when you are physically by yourself, you still have with you all your ideas, your experiences, your traditions, your knowledge of what has been. The Christian monk in a monastery cell is not alone; he is with his conceptual Jesus, with his theology, with the beliefs and dogmas of his particular conditioning. Similarly, the sannyasi in India who withdraws from the world and lives in isolation is not alone, for he too lives with his memories.

I am talking of an aloneness in which the mind is totally free from the past, and only such a mind is virtuous, for only in this aloneness is there innocence. Perhaps you will say, "That is too much to ask. One cannot live like that in this chaotic world, where one has to go to the office every day, earn a livelihood, bear children, endure the nagging of one's wife or husband, and all the rest of it." But I think what is being said is directly related to everyday life and action; otherwise, it has no value at all. You see, out of this aloneness comes a virtue which is virile and which brings an extraordinary sense of purity and gentleness. It doesn't matter if one makes mistakes; that is of very little importance. What matters is to have this feeling of being completely alone, uncontaminated, for it is only such a mind that can know or be aware of that which is beyond the word, beyond the name, beyond all the projections of imagination.

Perhaps you will ask questions about this particular thing that we have been considering together this morning.

Question: If in the very act of listening there is no experiencing, then listening remains at the verbal level, which is of little or no value. But to experience, one needs great sensitivity, and how is one to have this sensitivity?

KRISHNAMURTI: Sir, listening is not an act of experiencing. I will explain what I mean. If you listen in the way I have been attempting to make clear, then there is no entity or center which experiences. You just listen with all your being—and your being has no limits, it is not confined to the words of Krishnamurti. But in listening to the speaker, to that river, to the birds, to the wind among the trees, or in looking at the mountains, if you hear and see from a center, then you are experiencing, and that experience is added to your past experiences and only further conditions the mind. Whereas, in listening and looking without the center, without verbally translating what is heard and seen, the idea of experiencing ceases completely; there is only the fact, not you who are experiencing the fact. Perhaps this requires a little further explanation.

You know, you can look at a flower in two different ways. You can look at it botanically, that is, with knowledge, with all the information about flowers that you have gathered from books, and so on. You look at the flower through your knowledge, and therefore experience through that knowledge the peculiar quality or state of being of the flower. That is one way. The other way is to look at the flower nonbotanically, to look at it without knowledge—if you understand what I mean by looking at something without knowledge. To look at your wife, at your children, at the facts of relationship without knowledge is to see them without all the previous hurts, enmities, cruelties, insults, impositions. All that, which is part of knowledge, has dropped away, and you look directly at *what is.* That very looking, in which there is no new experiencing, is the highest form of sensitivity.

A person who "experiences" a sunset is not sensitive. He may say, "How lovely, how marvelous it is!" and go into an ecstasy over it, but he is not sensitive. To be sensitive implies a state of mind in which there is only the fact, and not all your memories about that fact. Such perception, such seeing, such listening at every moment has an extraordinary action in life. Please don't be carried away by the speaker's intensity or enthusiasm. Don't get mesmerized, but watch, listen, and find out for yourself.

Question: Even without your becoming an authority to us, are you not influencing us through your words, through your manner, through your gestures, and so on?

KRISHNAMURTI: I have been saying that every form of influence, including the influence of the speaker, is destructive. If you are influenced you are destroyed, you become a soldier, a follower, an automaton. But if—without comparing, judging, evaluating—you listen to discover for yourself what the actual fact is, whether what is being said is true or false, then you are beyond all authority, beyond all influence; it doesn't matter whose it is.

Sir, when I talk of influence I am talking of all kinds of influence, and not of one particular influence. In listening, one has to be intensely aware not to be influenced, pushed around. Here there is no form of propaganda. I am not trying to convert you to something, which would be a terrible thing to do. I am only pointing out what seem to me to be psychological facts, and you can take it or leave it. If they are facts, surely, you have to listen to them, not because I say so, but simply because they are facts. But it is tremendously important how you listen to a fact. It's a fact, for example, that a train is going by. What is important is to listen to the noise and the rattle of that train without resisting it, because the moment you resist it, you are being influenced. But if you can be aware of that noise as you are aware of the murmuring of a stream, or of the wind among the leaves; if you can listen to a fact without resistance, whether it is spoken by your wife, by your child, by the porter, or by the present speaker, then you will find out for yourself that you can go beyond all influence; you can step completely out of this destructive influence of society.

Question: When there is total integration of one's mind, emotions, and body, in that state is there not love?

KRISHNAMURTI: What does that word *integration* imply? It implies bringing about unification or harmony by putting together the different parts. Now, you cannot integrate the body, the mind, and the feelings because they are always broken up. Nothing can be brought together which is broken up by conflict within itself.

Please do listen to this a little bit. We are all very fond of that word integration. Politicians use it, psychologists use it, and we also rattle along, spinning out that word in various ways. "To integrate" implies an entity who is bringing the various parts together—an outsider, or an insider, who is placing the fragments in harmonious juxtaposition. As long as there is an entity who is making an effort to integrate, there can be no integration because there is a contradiction, a division, between the entity and the parts that are separate, between the idea and the fact. There is a conflict created by the effort to bring together the various fragments, and any such "integration" has no meaning. However much we may talk about it, the fact of integration is not possible. But if you have gone deeply into this question and have understood the impossibility of integration as long as there is an entity who is trying to bring the fragments together—if you have understood this completely, then you will find that there is a totally different operation taking place. There is then no entity at all; therefore, there is no contradiction, and therefore there is harmony. And only in this effortless state, when there are no fragments to be brought together, when there is total, sensitive awareness—only then is there a possibility of that which may be called love.

Question: Technique implies effort, conformity, discipline, achievement; and what you are talking about seems to deny all that. Is this so?

KRISHNAMURTI: Please, this is an immense question, and I don't want to go into it now. We will discuss it another time. But to understand, one must really be free of effort, of all techniques, methods, systems, and not just say, "Well, I will go and live effortlessly," which doesn't mean a thing.

Before concluding I would like to go back to what I was talking about earlier this morning. You know, to be alone without withdrawing from society, without becoming a hermit, is an extraordinary state. One is alone because one has understood influence, authority. One has understood the whole question of memory, conditioning, and out of this understanding there is an aloneness which can never be touched by influence. And you have no idea what an astonishing beauty there is in it, what a tremendous sense of virtue, which is vitality, virility, and strength. But that requires an immense understanding of all our conditioning.

July 26, 1962

Fourth Talk in Saanen

We were talking the other day about the vitality and the virility of virtue, and I would like to go much more into this question of energy—the necessity of an energy that is not brought about through conflict or resistance. Such energy is of the highest importance because one needs such energy to penetrate very deeply into that state which is beyond all experience and which is not a matter of faith.

But first of all I think one ought to clarify once more what it is we are trying to do in these meetings. The speaker is not indulging in any form of propaganda; he is not trying to convert you to a particular manner of thinking or course of action, nor is he attempting to create a special atmosphere or environment in which the individual can bring about this total energy. But there is beyond all question of doubt, beyond reason and intellection, an energy which comes into being when conflict of every kind is removed. Conflict itself creates a certain form of energy, which is the energy born of reaction, resistance, suppression, contradiction; but conflict must totally and utterly disappear for this other energy to come into being.

Now, before we go into the question of emptying the mind of all conflict, of all ideas, of all concepts, I think we must be very clear what is the function—if I may so use that word—of you who are listening. Are you listening merely in order to adjust yourself to what is being said? Are you listening to find the flaws and contradictions in the words of the speaker? Are you trying to create from what is being said a pattern of your own from which action can take place? What is it that is actually going on in your mind as you listen? I would like to talk about something which is desperately serious and which, if understood, can totally and immediately bring about a revolution in the mind. I would like to go into it rather extensively and deeply, if it is not presumptuous of me to say so, and that is why it is important to find out for yourself what is the state of your own mind as you are listening.

Are you merely listening to the words and trying to correlate or adjust what you already know to what is being said? Are you lazily listening on this rather pleasant morning to pass the time of day, hoping to be entertained in the so-called spiritual or religious sense? Or are you observing your own mind and becoming aware of all its hidden corners, its dark recesses and untrodden space? If you are really observing your own mind, then you and I, as two individuals, can work out together this thing of which I am going to speak. But to do that, one has to be in a state of complete awareness, attention.

You know, there is no attention if there is any form of resistance. There is no attention if there is any grasping or struggling to understand. If you would understand something, you must give to it your complete attention. To be aware of all that is implied in what is going to be said, your body, your mind, your emotions, your whole being must be given to it. And then you will discover for yourself that in emptying the mind totally of its content, there comes an extraordinary energy. This may sound absurd or impossible, or it may seem to be just a fanciful idea, but we are not dealing with ideas. We are dealing with facts—the facts of what exactly is taking place in one's own mind. To perceive the significance of these facts, one has to be aware of them; one has to be conscious of every movement of thought without trying to correct or to alter it in any way. And if we are so aware, then we can proceed to investigate the conflict which exists within each one of us. Conflict in any form, outward or inward, destroys clarity; and it is only out of clarity that there can be this energy of which I am speaking.

There are two types of energy. There is the energy that is brought about through resistance, contradiction, conflict in our daily relationships, and this energy produces certain activities with which we are all familiar. Then there is another type of energy which is not at all the outcome of resistance, contradiction, conflict; but you cannot jump from one to the other without understanding conflict, because as long as conflict exists in any form, however subtle, this other type of energy cannot be. This other type of energy can come into being only when there is a total cessation of conflict, and you cannot bring conflict to an end with a motive in order to arrive at the other.

Obviously, we all have both physical and mental energy in varying degrees. As most people in the West are physically comfortable and well-fed, with a certain amount of leisure, they generally have much more physical energy than people in the East, where there is less food and more discomfort, and where the land is overpopulated. Physical energy is of course necessary, but we are now talking of mental energy, without which you cannot have a sharp, clear mind—a mind capable of thinking sanely, without bias or equivocation, without any fanciful, romantic, or illusory ideas. And there can be this energy, this clarity of mind only when there is no conflict of any kind.

As you know, conflict wears out the mind. Conflict implies a human problem, and any human problem, at whatever level—whether it be a sexual problem, an economic problem, a problem of relationship, a problem of virtue, the problem of death, or what you will—wastes mental energy and blocks clarity of perception. And is it possible to live in this world without a problem? We can find that out for ourselves only if we understand the essence of conflict.

Let me say here that you are not listening in order to realize a particular state of mind or to capture a certain vitality with which to approach your daily living. You are listening in order to discover your own problems, which means being aware of your own activities, your own contradictions.

Now, what do we mean by contradiction? There is inward contradiction, conflict, as long as we have an idea, a concept, a pattern of action, a goal, or an ideal, because that is unreal; it is not factual. The fact is one thing and the idea about the fact is another, and this division creates conflict. Without understanding the fact of what we actually are, we create an idea, a pattern of how to be good, of what our inward state should be; we create the prototype, the hero, the example, the perfect state, and we struggle to approximate our living to that ideal. And I feel quite sure that you are now going to create the idea of "no conflict," which will again become the pattern.

So, why do we create the pattern? We create the pattern because we want to escape from the fact, whatever that fact may be. Being dissatisfied with and not understanding the fact of what we are, we create the idea of what we should be, and so there is a division, a contradiction. Throughout the world this process is going on, this escape from *what is* through the ideational pursuit of 'what should be'. And surely, as long as we struggle to bring about an approximation between the fact and the idea, conflict is inevitable.

Most of our actions are based on ideas, are they not? We are motivated by the thought "I should" or "I should not," which means that our action is rooted in an idea, and we are always trying to approximate the two. What I am going to talk about is the total elimination of idea, and therefore the complete cessation of conflict—which does not mean going to sleep in your own comfortable, nonideational world. On the contrary, it demands complete awareness.

I hope I am making myself clear.

To me, any form of conflict—in relationship, in study, in love, in thought—is detrimental; it dulls and makes the mind insensitive, and to have this astonishing energy which enables the mind to meet and resolve every problem, there must be the highest sensitivity. All the senses, every part of your being must be totally alive, and that can happen only when you understand the whole process of conflict—that is, when conflict has come to an end.

When I stop from time to time, it is because I do not know how far you have gone with me—not that you are following me, not that I am your authority, but I wonder how far you have understood, because this is a very complicated issue. To live without idea is something entirely different from what most of us are accustomed to. We live habitually with ideas; we live with our thoughts, our concepts, our formulations; but to me, that is not the way to live because it only creates conflict, misery, confusion. To live totally, completely, the mind must be empty of all ideation so that it is capable of facing the fact of *what is* from moment to moment without interpreting that fact. But we are heavily and deeply conditioned to this concept of struggle. We live in the world ideologically; we live with ideas, with heroes, with examples, with patterns, we pursue the 'what should be'.

Now, I am proposing the wiping away of all that. And what I am talking about is factual; it is not just a fanciful idea. One can see for oneself, if one observes, that where there is conflict there is confusion, there is a lack of clarity, there is suffering, misery, every form of travail. And is it possible to live and act without conflict? One has to act, not only in the outer world, but inwardly. One has to go to the office; one has to do so many things, and is it possible to live in this world without idea and therefore without conflict? Can there be an activity in which the mind is not approximating itself to an idea? You don't know whether that is possible or not. I say it is possible and that it is the only way to live, but it requires a great deal of understanding, and to understand you must have tremendous energy, not just vague aspirational hope.

The idea, the concept, the pattern, is born of our thinking, which in turn is based upon our conditioning. All our thinking, however noble, refined, or subtle, is the outcome of our experience, of our knowledge. There is no thinking without the past. Our thought is merely the reaction of memory. And what I am talking about is action without reaction, which means living without thought as the reaction of memory.

In this world there is war, there is the atom bomb, and there are the so-called pacifists, the people who do not want war and who talk about banning the bomb; to them that is the ideal. The bomb is only a result; it is the outcome of historical process shaped by our nationalism, our greed, our ambition, our prejudices, our class distinctions, our conflicting religious inclinations. All these things have produced the bomb, and it is no good fiddling with bombs—we have to change totally our way of life, our way of thinking. But nobody wants to do that. Nobody wants a total revolution, and that is what I am talking about: a total revolution, which is not a reaction. Communism is merely a reaction to capitalism; therefore, it is not a revolution at all. As long as there is nationalism, as long as there are class distinctions, as long as there is patriotism, the identification of oneself with a particular group or sect, whether political, economic, or religious, there is bound to be war. To end war, one must uproot all this conditioned thinking.

So, what I am talking about is not a reaction. Do you understand what I mean by a reaction? You insult me, you say something which I don't like, and I react; or I like what you say, and again I react. But is it not possible to listen to what another says without reacting? Surely, if I listen to find out the truth or the falseness of what you are saying, then from that listening, from that perception, there is an action which is not reaction.

All reaction is based on an idea, on a pattern of thought; so, if one is to be totally free from conflict, one must go into this question of thought. Thought is really quite mechanical, and it can never be free. Thought can aspire, it can create, it can imagine, but it can never be free because it is the outcome of our conditioning, of our memory, of our knowledge of the past. To look at facts without reaction, inwardly as well as outwardly, implies looking at them without thought.

You may say, "What nonsense are you talking?" It is nonsense only if you have not followed from the beginning what we have been considering together. If you just pick up a phrase like "to live without thought," it obviously sounds moronic, absurd. But if you have observed in yourself every movement of thought and feeling, whether pleasant or unpleasant, if you have watched without reaction the complexities of your own mind and have understood the implications of thought, then you will have discovered for yourself what it means to live, to function, to do things without thought. But this requires an enormous awareness.

Do you know what I mean by being aware? To be aware is to see the fluttering of those leaves in the wind and hear that stream rushing by; it is to observe the lighting of clouds and the deepening of shadow; it is to be conscious of all these people sitting here dressed in different colors and holding different opinions, with different expressions on their faces. You are aware of all that, and also of your own reactions to all that—reactions of prejudice, of like and dislike. You observe and listen to everything without choosing, without interpreting, without comparing, without condemning or justifying; and to do this implies that you have understood your own background, your own conditioning.

After all, we are educated to condemn, to agree or disagree, to compare, to justify, to resist. That is all we know; it is our background—the background created by our education both at school and at the hands of society. We look upon ourselves as German, English, French, as Catholic, Protestant, Hindu. We believe or don't believe. That is our background, and when our background reacts, we say we are thinking. Now, to be aware is to perceive and to understand the whole process of that background, not only the conscious background, but the unconscious as well. Because it is our background that becomes the authority and creates the conflict.

A person who is concerned with the understanding of conflict has no goal and therefore no frustration. Most of us are in a state of frustration. We want to be a famous musician, a great politician; we want to be this or that, but we are not sufficiently capable, cunning, or whatever it is. We want to fulfill ourselves, but we are prevented by circumstances, by ideas, by our own lack of capacity, by our desire to be secure, so we are frustrated. And even if we do fulfill ourselves, there is always in fulfillment the shadow of frustration.

I hope you are not merely following my words but are watching yourself.

To live without a goal, to live without wanting to fulfill oneself, demands a great deal of understanding. It means dealing with facts, with what is actually taking place in the mind. And when the mind knows itself, when it has observed and understood itself, then you will find that all conflict has been emptied from the mind. And out of that emptiness there comes the energy which is absolutely necessary if one is to proceed further.

Most of us, being torn by conflict, are in misery, confusion, and therefore we have very little mental energy. But when the mind has emptied itself of all conflict because it has understood the whole process of thinking, of ideation, of pursuing concepts, ideals, prototypes, and all the rest of it, then out of that emptiness there comes an energy which lives from moment to moment, from day to day, and then the mind does everything without frustration, without fear. It is only then that there is real peace within oneself. It is not an induced peace. Peace that is induced, a disciplined peace, is a lifeless thing, and that is why most so-called religious people are inwardly dead.

When there is no conflict of any kind in the mind because it has understood itself, then you will find that there comes this energy which is no longer seeking experience; it is beyond all experience. Being totally empty, the mind is completely aware; it has no dark corners, no untrodden space; it is wholly alive, awake. If you have gone that far, you will discover for yourself that time has lost its meaning; and only such a mind can understand that which is beyond words, beyond names, beyond symbols, beyond all thought.

Shall we discuss what has been said this morning?

Question: I find that I have left behind all forms of preference. I have no likes or dislikes any more. Is that surprising?

KRISHNAMURTI: Not at all, sir. But isn't there a great danger—I am not saying this with regard to you personally—of withdrawing from life and therefore becoming utterly insensitive? Do you understand what I mean by sensitivity? Most of us want to be sensitive to the beautiful—to lovely music, to fine pictures—but we don't want to be sensitive to the ugly, to the noisy, to the dirty, to the foul things in the streets. To be sensitive in one direction, you must be sensitive in both directions. There is no real sensitivity if you are sensitive in one direction and callous with regard to the other. If one is callous towards anything in life, one is not totally sensitive, and it seems to me there is a danger of this in saying, "I have no preferences any more; I am rather indifferent to what is taking place, indifferent to my own quarrels and anxieties, to my guilts and conflicts."

Question: My very wish to understand what you are saying—is that not in itself a contradiction?

KRISHNAMURTI: Surely you are understanding yourself, not the speaker, and therefore there cannot be a contradiction. But if in listening you are trying to shape your thoughts, your feelings, your aspirations, in accordance with what the speaker is saying, then there is bound to be a contradiction. Sir, I thought I had made it clear from the very beginning that I am not marketing ideas. I am not propagating a new system of thought or a new way of activity. I am only pointing out how essential it is to be totally aware of yourself, and I am explaining what it means to be aware. That explanation is reasonable, logical, sane, healthy, as you will find out for yourself if you are at all aware of your own ways and activities. You are not following anyone because here there is no authority. The moment there is an authority whom you are trying to understand, you are in a state of contradiction, conflict, and all the wretchedness begins.

Question: Will you please repeat what you have just said?

KRISHNAMURTI: I am afraid I cannot repeat, but I will put it in different words.

You see, sir, we are accustomed to having somebody tell us what to do. We are used to following somebody. It is our habit to approximate ourselves to what is being said by the preacher, the teacher, the savior, who is supposed to know what he is talking about. We say, "I must look up to him, I must follow him"; so we set up an authority, an ideal, and inevitably there is a contradiction between that ideal and what we actually are. But here there is no ideal and no authority. On the contrary, we are concerned with the understanding of ourselves. And we are complex entities; we are the totality of life, the result of centuries of human endeavor, the repository of all thought, of all conflict. You are not here to understand the speaker but to use the speaker as a mirror in which to watch yourself.

One moment, sir, I haven't finished. I know you have questions, but you see, the difficulty is that you are already so concerned with your own question that you are not listening to the previous question. Do please pay a little attention.

The world is bound by authority—by the authority of the priest, of the politician, of the specialist. But authorities do not help you to understand yourself, and without understanding yourself, there can be no freedom from conflict, though you may go to the temple, meditate, or stand on your head for the rest of your life. You are society, you are the world; you are the result of centuries of the historical process, and you are also the result of your immediate environment; and without understanding and breaking through all that, shattering it completely, you cannot go very far. To go very far, you must begin very near, which is to understand yourself. To take this far journey, there must be a total ending of all conflict.

Question: When I observe a particular feeling, that feeling comes to an end, and then there is a state of attention which brings with it a new kind of energy. Is this what you mean?

KRISHNAMURTI: When you observe a particular feeling, what is important is to find out how you observe it. Please follow this. Do you see the feeling as something separate from yourself? Obviously you do.

I do not know if you have experimented and have found out that when you observe a feeling, that feeling comes to an end. But even though the feeling comes to an end, if there is an observer, a spectator, a censor, a thinker who remains apart from the feeling, then there is still a contradiction. So it is very important to understand how we look at a feeling.

Take, for instance, a very common feeling: jealousy. We all know what it is to be jealous. Now, how do you look at your jealousy? When you look at that feeling, you are the observer of jealousy as something apart from yourself. You try to change jealousy, to modify it, or you try to explain why you are justified in being jealous, and so on and so forth. So there is a being, a censor, an entity apart from jealousy who observes it. For the moment jealousy may disappear, but it comes back again, and it comes back because you do not really see that jealousy is part of you. You are jealousy, that feeling is not something outside of you. When you are jealous, your whole being is jealous, as your whole being is envious, acquisitive, or what you will. Don't say, "Is there not a part of me which is heavenly, spiritual, and therefore not jealous?" When you are actually in a state of jealousy, there is nothing else but that.

So it is very important to find out how to look, how to listen. I will go into it a little bit more.

When one is jealous, observe what is taking place. My wife or my husband looks at somebody else, and I have a certain feeling which goes with all that nonsense we call love. Or perhaps somebody else is cleverer than I, or has a more beautiful figure, and again that feeling arises. The moment that feeling arises, I give it a label, a name. Please see what is taking place; just follow it step by step. It is a fairly simple psychological process, as you will know if you have observed it in yourself.

I have a certain feeling, and I give it a name. I give it a name because I want to know what it is; I call it jealousy, and that word is the outcome of my memory of the past. The feeling itself is something new; it has come into being suddenly, spontaneously, but I have identified it by giving it a name, In giving it a name, I think I have understood it, but I have only strengthened it. So what has happened? The word has interfered with my looking at the fact.

I think I have understood the feeling by calling it jealousy, whereas I have only put it in the framework of words, of memory, with all the old impressions, explanations, condemnations, justifications. But that feeling itself is new; it is not something of yesterday. It becomes something of yesterday only when I give it a name. If I look at it without naming it, there is no center from which I am looking.

Please see this. Are you working as hard as I am?

What I am saying is that the moment you give a name, a label, to that feeling, you have brought it into the framework of the old; and the old is the observer, the separate entity who is made up of words, of ideas, of opinions about what is right and what is wrong. Therefore it is very important to understand the process of naming, and to see how instantaneously the word *jealousy* comes into being. But if you don't name that feeling—which demands tremendous awareness, a great deal of immediate understanding—then you will find that there is no observer, no thinker, no center from which you are judging, and that you are not different from the feeling. There is no 'you' who feels it.

Jealousy has become a habit with most of us, and like any other habit it continues. To break the habit is merely to be aware of the habit. Please listen to this. Do not say, "It is terrible to have this habit, I must change it, I must be free of it," and so on, but just be aware of it. To be aware of a habit is not to condemn it but simply to look at it. You know, when you love a thing, you look at it. It is only when you don't love it that the problem of how to get rid of it begins. When I use the word *love* with regard to the feeling which we call jealousy, I hope you see what I mean. To "love" jealousy is not to deny or condemn that feeling; then there is no separation between the feeling and the observer. In this state of total awareness, if you go into it very deeply without words, you will find you have completely wiped away that feeling which is habitually identified with the word jealousy.

It is time to stop. This morning we have talked about something very serious. We live in a world that is full of ambition, of competition, and the worship of success, in a world crowded with people who want to be famous, who want to be known as writers, as painters, as scientists, as great people. They live in a state of conflict, of contradiction, which is a state of great tension. That tension produces certain activities, and if one has capacity, one may become a successful writer or painter or scientist or politician. But that tension of contradiction does not bring about clarity; it only brings more misery. Driven by that tension, one may go to church, worship God, but it has no meaning whatsoever. God is not found through tension, through contradiction, but only when the mind is totally empty of every form of ideation, imagination, contradiction, conflict. And in that emptiness there is great beauty, an astonishing vitality.

July 29, 1962

Fifth Talk in Saanen

We were talking the day before yesterday about action without idea, because, as I was pointing out, thought is a response of our memory; thought is always limited, conditioned by the past, and it can therefore never bring about freedom.

I think it is very important to understand this fact. Psychologically, there can be no freedom at all if the defensive process of thought is not completely understood. And freedom—which is not a reaction to or the opposite of nonfreedom—is essential because it is only in freedom that one can discover. It is only when the mind is totally free that there can be the perception of what is true.

Truth is not something which has continuity and which can be maintained through practice or discipline, but it is something to be seen in a flash. This perception of truth does not come about through any form of conditioned thinking, and therefore it is not possible for thought to imagine, conceive, or formulate what is true.

To understand totally what is true, there must be freedom. For most of us, freedom is only a word or a reaction or an intellectual idea which serves as an escape from our bondage, from our sorrow, from our boring daily routine; but that is not freedom at all. Freedom does not come by seeking it because you cannot seek freedom; it is not to be found. Freedom comes only when we understand the whole process of the mind which creates its own barriers, its own limitations, its own projections from a conditioned and conditioning background.

It is very important for a really religious mind to understand that which is beyond the word, beyond thought, beyond all experience; and to understand that which is beyond all experience, to be with it, to see it in great depth in a flash, the mind must be free. We were talking about all this the other day, and we saw how idea, concept, pattern, opinion, judgment, or any formulated discipline prevents freedom of the mind. And this freedom brings its own discipline—not the discipline of conformity, of suppression or adjustment, but a discipline which is not the outcome of thought, of a motive.

Surely, in a confused world where there is so much conflict and misery, it is extraordinarily urgent to understand that freedom is the primary requisite of the human mind—not comfort, not a fleeting moment of pleasure or the continuity of that pleasure, but a total freedom, from which alone there can be happiness. For happiness is not an end in itself; like virtue, it is a byproduct of freedom. A person who is free is virtuous, but a man who is merely practicing virtue by conforming to the pattern established by society can never know what freedom is and therefore can never be virtuous.

This morning I would like to talk about the quality of freedom and see if we can together feel our way into it, but I do not know how you listen to what is being said. Do you listen merely to the words? Do you listen in order to understand, in order to experience? If you listen in either of these ways, then what is being said will have very little significance. What is important is to listen, not just to the words, or in the hope of experiencing this extraordinary quality of freedom, but to listen without effort, without striving, with a sense of ease. But this demands a certain quality of attention. By attention I mean being completely there with all your mind and heart. And then you will discover for yourself, if you so listen, that this freedom is not a thing to be pursued; it is not the result of thought or of emotional, hysterical demands. Freedom comes without your seeking it when there is total attention. Total attention is the quality of a mind that has no border, no frontier, and is therefore capable of receiving every single impression, seeing and hearing everything. And this can be done; it is not something enormously difficult. It is difficult only because we are so caught up in habits—and that is one of the things I would like to talk about this morning.

Most of us have innumerable habits. We have physical habits and idiosyncrasies as well as habits of thought. We believe in this and do not believe in that; we are patriotic, nationalistic; we belong to a certain group or party and hold on to its particular pattern of thought. All these things become habits, and the mind likes to live in habits because habits give us certainty, a sense of security, a feeling of having no fear. When established in a series of habits, the mind seems to function a little more easily, but it is really thoughtless, unaware.

Please do not merely listen to my words, but observe as in a mirror your own mind and see how it is caught in habits. Habits, which give a sense of security, only make the mind dull; however subtle they may be, and whether one is conscious of them or not, they invariably darken the mind. This is a psychological fact; whether you like it or not, it is so.

Partly because of our education at school, partly because of the conditioning which society psychologically imposes upon us, and also because of our own laziness, our minds function in a series of habits. If we do not approve of a particular habit of which we are conscious, we struggle to break it, and in breaking one habit, we form another. There seems to be no moment when the mind is free from habit. If you observe yourself, you will see how difficult it is for the mind not to be caught in habit.

Take a simple habit that many people have: the habit of smoking. If you smoke and you want to give it up, the idea of giving it up creates a resistance against smoking; therefore, there is a conflict between the habit and the desire to break that habit. Now, through conflict or resistance, you may break one particular habit but that does not free the mind from the whole process of forming habits; the habit-creating mechanism hasn't come to an end. And what I am talking about is not just getting rid of one particular habit but ceasing to create habits.

I don't know if you have ever observed yourself in the act of smoking. By observing yourself I mean being aware of every movement you make: how your hand goes to your pocket, takes out a cigarette, puts it in your mouth, returns to your pocket for a match, lights the cigarette; and how you then take a few puffs and throw away the match. What is important is to be aware of that whole process without resisting, without denying, without wanting to be free of it—just to be totally aware of every movement involved in that habit.

Similarly, you can be aware of the habit of envy, the habit of acquisitiveness, the habit of fear; and then, as you observe, you will see what is implied in that particular habit. You will see instantly the whole implication of envy, but you cannot see the whole implication of envy if in your observation of envy there is the time element. I will explain what I mean.

We think that we can get rid of envy gradually, and we make an effort to put it away little by little, thereby introducing the idea of time. We say, "I will try to get rid of envy tomorrow, or a little later on"—and in the meantime we are envious. The words *try* and *in the meantime* are the very essence of time, and when you introduce the time factor, there can be no freedom from habit. Either you break a habit immediately or it goes on, gradually dulling the mind and creating further habits.

Please observe your own habits and your own attitude towards those habits.

We have habits of thought, sexual habits—oh, innumerable habits, which may be either conscious or unconscious; and it is especially difficult to be aware of the unconscious habits. Socially and at school and college we are trained in this element of time. Our whole psychology is based on time, the idea that there will eventually be brotherhood and peace, but in the meantime we must go through all the horrors of war.

Now, is it possible for the mind to get rid instantly of this idea of gradually arriving somewhere, gradually transcending something, gradually being free? To me, freedom is not a question of time—there is no tomorrow in which to get rid of envy or to acquire some virtue. And if there is no tomorrow, there is no fear. There is only a complete living in the now; all time has ceased, and therefore there is no formation of habit. I mean by that word *now* the immediate, and this state of immediacy is not a reaction to the past nor an avoidance of the future. There is only the moment of total awareness; all one's attention is here in the now. Surely, all existence is in the now; whether you have immense gladness or great sorrow or whatever it is, it happens only in the immediate. But through memory the mind gathers experience from the past and projects it into the future.

Please be aware of your own mind; in the mirror of these words observe how your own mind operates, and then we can go very far together.

So, is it possible to break totally away from the past? The past is really the essence of habit; it is made up of all the knowledge, the suffering, the insults, the innumerable experiences you have had, not only individually, but racially and collectively. You have to step completely out of this framework of the past psychologically, actually; otherwise, there is no freedom, and you cannot do that if in your mind there exists the idea of continuity. For most of us, continuity is very important, but after all, continuity in relationship is merely habit. Continuity in thought is what sustains the limitations of the mind, and is it possible to explode this idea of continuity and be free from the past?

Without freedom from the past, there is no freedom at all because the mind is never new, fresh, innocent. It is only the fresh, innocent mind that is free. Freedom has nothing to do with age; it has nothing to do with experience, and it seems to me that the very essence of freedom lies in understanding the whole mechanism of habit, both conscious and unconscious. It is not a question of ending habit but of seeing totally the structure of habit. You have to observe how habits are formed and how, by denying or resisting one habit, another habit is created. What matters is to be totally conscious of habit, for then, as you will see for yourself, there is no longer the formation of habit. To resist habit, to fight it, to deny it, only gives continuity to habit. When you fight a particular habit, you give life to that habit, and then the very fighting of it becomes a further habit. But if you are simply aware of the whole structure of habit without resistance, then you will find there is freedom from habit, and in that freedom a new thing takes place.

It is only the dull, sleepy mind that creates and clings to habit. A mind that is attentive from moment to moment—attentive to what it is saying, attentive to the movement of its hands, of its thoughts, of its feelings—will discover that the formation of further habits has come to an end. This is very important to understand because as long as the mind is breaking down one habit and in that very process creating another, it can obviously never be free; and it is only the free mind that can perceive something beyond itself. Such a mind is religious. The mind that merely goes to church, repeats prayers, clings to dogmas, or that leaves one sect and joins another, is not religious; it is just stupid. The religious mind is the free mind, and the free mind is in a state of constant explosion; and in this state of constant explosion, there is the seeing of that truth which is beyond words, beyond thought, beyond all experience.

Perhaps we can now discuss or ask questions about what I have been saying this morning.

Question: For centuries the mind has sought self-preservation, and you say that a mind that is seeking to protect itself is incapable of seeing what is true. Perhaps your mind is different from the minds of those who hear you. If this is so, then what is one to do?

KRISHNAMURTI: Let us go into it. There is the brain, and there is the mind. Please, I am using these two words very carefully. For centuries the brain has been occupied with preserving itself; it is the outcome of time, the result of all man's animalistic endeavors. The human brain is still like the animal which fights to preserve itself, and it is the very center of the 'me': my property, my house, my wife, my religion. This we all know. All of us have this brain which seeks its own preservation; we have inherited it from the past.

Now, according to biologists, the back part of the brain is the animal brain, and it is very active, whereas the forepart of the brain has still to be developed. Not that I read biology, but I have some friends who do, and they tell me the biologists have said that the forepart of the brain is still largely undeveloped, and that the human brain is destined to change from the animalistic into something extraordinarily new. And my point is that to arrive at the totality of the mind, in which the limited brain is included, time is not necessary. The totality of the mind is a state which must be realized; you cannot speculate about it because it is not just a religious idea like the idea of God, or the idea of the soul, or the idea of heaven. And can one jump from the limited state of mind which is the outcome of the past, and which develops through time, directly to the timeless, the complete, the total? Is it possible to jump from the limited to the limitless? That is the issue. I say it can be done—but it requires an explosive breaking away from the past. It demands this tremendous energy of which I have been speaking and which is not the result of conformity, of resistance, of conflict. One has to be totally aware in oneself of the animalistic instincts, aware of fear, of ambition, and the pursuits of desire; one has to be wholly attentive to all that. Then you will find that you have put an end to time as evolution. Not that there is not evolution—there is, but you have gone beyond time. Time is no longer a means of arriving, a means of gradually achieving the sublime, the highest form of creation. Where there is this explosive realization of total attention, the brain, which has always been very active in acquisitive pursuits, becomes quiet—and it must be completely quiet to go beyond the whole process of time.

You know, the quieting of the brain is part of meditation. I don't want to discuss meditation now; we will do that in a few days, but one must see the importance of quieting the brain, which implies being free of the psychological structure of society. The psychological structure of society is still animalistic; it makes the brain ambitious, greedy, envious, jealous, attached, and such a brain does not know love. You may hug a man or a woman, you may marry, you may hold the hand of a friend, or do what you will, but there is no love as long as the brain is still part of the animalistic past, which is the psychological structure of society. The understanding of the psychological structure of society in oneself is part of meditation; and you will find, if you have gone this far, that with that understanding there comes an immensity, a sense of creation which has nothing to do with writing books, poems, or with painting pictures, or with any of the absurdities and childish demands of a society which sets great store by fame. It is a creation that takes place in the immeasurable, which is the ultimate of all existence. But that can come about only when the animalistic, psychological structure of society is completely denied—which means that the mind, the brain, is no longer ambitious, attached, dependent, no longer wanting to fulfill itself, no longer wanting to be somebody, no longer seeking power, position, prestige.

Have I answered your question, sir?

Comment: You have given me something to think about.

KRISHNAMURTI: Don't think about it, sir. To think about it admits time. You say, "I can't see it now, but I will think about it, and later on I will see it." Thought isn't going to make you see; time isn't going to give you understanding. The moment you say that you are going to think about it, you have created the framework of "in the meantime I will try"—and then you are completely lost. What matters is to listen with one's whole being—and that is our real difficulty. To listen with one's whole being is not just to hear the words of the speaker but to see for oneself immediately the truth or the falseness of what is being said, and such listening demands extraordinary energy. So it is not a matter of "in the meantime I will try." You either listen with your whole being or you don't. If you listen with your whole being, you will find that an inner explosion takes place, not tomorrow or at the end of the day, but on the instant. That is what I was talking about earlier: this explosive transformation that must take place in the immediate.

You see, when you merely think about it, all your defensive reactions come in, and then you continue to adjust yourself to the established pattern of your daily existence, conforming to that pattern whenever it is inconvenient to deny it. That is all thought can do: go endlessly round and round. So thought is not the instrument of perception; it is not the dynamite that explodes the past. You have to give your heart to listening, and I really mean it; you have to give your heart to listening and not merely listen to words with the intellect. One may be terribly clever; one may be able to spin a lot of words, quote many books, but that doesn't bring about the miracle. The miracle is in total listening.

Question: What do you mean by the title of your book, "The First and Last Freedom"?

KRISHNAMURTI: I am afraid you must ask the publisher because it is he who wanted that title. (Laughter)

Sir, let us discuss what we have been talking about this morning, because we all have so many habits. When we say, "I will think about it," that is a habitual response, is it not?

Question: Is there no place for habit in anything? Does not technique imply habit?

KRISHNAMURTI: Yes, sir, but why do you ask that question? Technique obviously implies habit. If I want to learn how to drive a car, I have to acquire the technique of operating the clutch, shifting the gears, and all the rest of it; I have to practice until I can do it freely, easily, which implies habit. But we are not talking about the mechanical habits involved in the practice of a technique. We are talking about the whole habit-forming mechanism of the mind.

Question: Could you tell us more about our unconscious habits?

KRISHNAMURTI: Most of us are not aware of our habits at all, so our habits have become unconscious. The moment you are aware of a habit, you have pulled it out of the unconscious, have you not? If whenever I am in doubt about something I scratch my head and don't know that I am doing it, if it is automatic and I am unaware of it, then it has obviously become an unconscious habit. But the moment I am fully aware of that habit and don't resist it but merely watch it, then it has been pulled out of the unconscious.

Now, it is because our habits are mostly unconscious that we don't shatter them, explode them. If we are accustomed to driving a car, we turn on the switch instinctively and shift the gear-lever without giving it any particular thought. That is the habit of technique, but most of us are equally unaware of how we regard our neighbors. In walking down a crowded street, we are unaware of pushing somebody, and so on. So the question is how to be conscious, how to be fully aware of all the habits, animalistic and refined, which have partly been imposed upon us by society or which we have unconsciously cultivated? How would you set about it?

One is a Hindu, a Christian, a German, a Russian, a Swiss, an American, or what you will, with a corresponding set of habits of which one is generally unconscious. And how is one to be aware of this conditioning? How are you to be aware of the unconscious, in which there is this immense series of unrevealed habits? How are you to be aware of the unconscious pattern which is deeply rooted in you? Will you go to an analyst and pay fifty dollars, or one hundred pounds, or whatever it is you pay, to have the pattern pulled out of the unconscious by him? Will that help? Or will you analyze yourself?

What is implied in the process of analyzing yourself? When you analyze yourself, there is a division between the observer and the observed, is there not? And the observer is as conditioned as the observed, so there is a conflict between the two, between the analyzer and the analyzed. The analyzer may misinterpret what he is examining, and if he resists a certain habit or seeks to transform it to suit his own particular idiosyncrasies, and so on, he merely gives strength to habit. So self-analysis is not the way either. Then what will you do?

Please bear in mind that we are talking about how to open the book of the unconscious so that its whole content is exposed to the light. Professional analysis is not the way—unless you have money and leisure and are so dreadfully concerned about adjusting yourself to society that you want to play with it. And as I have explained, introspective analysis is not the way either. If that is clear, then what will you do?

Comment: I will do nothing at all.

KRISHNAMURTI: Which means what, sir? If you are no longer caught in the fallacious idea of analysis, then there is only observation, is there not? There is only a state of seeing and no translating of what is seen. You just see.

But what happens to most of us when we see ourselves as we actually are? When I see that I am brutal, hateful, petty, full of vanity, I get depressed. I say, "How terrible," and I fiddle about trying to change it. Now, this trying to change it, trying to do something about it, is still within the field of analysis. Whereas, if I merely observe without choice, which means that I am negatively watching, then there is no longer a series of analyses of the unconscious; I am completely out of the field of analysis because I have broken the pattern.

What is important is to break through this wall of conditioning, of habit, and most of us think we will break through it by means of analysis, either by ourselves or by another; but it cannot be done. The wall of habit can be broken through only when you are completely and choicelessly aware, negatively watchful.

Sir, when you suddenly see a mountain in all its immensity and beauty, with its shadows, its tremendous heights and great depths, what can you do about it? You can't do a thing. You just look at it, don't you? But what generally happens? You look at the mountain for a fleeting second, and then you say how beautiful it is; and by the very verbalization, you have ceased to look at it, you have already turned away. If you really look at something, your mind becomes very quiet because you are no longer judging, no longer translating what is seen in terms of comparison. You are just looking—which is what I mean by watching negatively. And if you can look at yourself in this way, you will find that all the unconscious habits and conditionings are transformed into a single thing which by direct understanding you have shattered completely. These are not just words. Go at it and you will see for yourself.

Comment: Our daily life is full of contradictions and conflicts; there are so many things we have to do, and all this is in strange contrast to what we feel or sense when we come here and listen to you.

KRISHNAMURTI: Why do we create a division between our daily life and what we are listening to here? Why do we separate the two? Life is everything, is it not? Life is our daily existence with its routine, its boredom, its conflicts, as well as our listening here. Life is also our listening to the trees, to the birds, to the river; it is our fleeting joy, our misery, our sorrow. The whole of that is life, but we divide it into daily life and something else. Why? Why don't we look at life totally instead of in fragments? We talk about the life of Wall Street, the life of the city, the life of the hermit, and all the rest of it. We have been talking like this for the last umpteen years, and isn't this also a habit?

To deal with life, you have to deal with it as a whole, not in fragments; and you can do that only when you know yourself. It is because you do not know the whole process of yourself that you divide life into fragments, thereby perpetuating conflict, misery. You cannot make a harmonious whole by putting the fragments together, but out of self-knowing, there comes a completeness, a sense of totality.

July 31, 1962

Sixth Talk in Saanen

This morning I would like to talk about something with which some of you are perhaps not very familiar, and that is the question of emptying the mind of fear. I would like to go into it rather deeply, but not in great detail because one can supply the details for oneself.

But before we go into that question, one must know what is meant by learning, maturity, and self-knowing. These are not mere words, they are not just concepts, the meaning of which is easily captured. To go behind and see the real significance of the words requires a great deal of understanding. By understanding I mean that effortless state in which the mind is totally aware without any impediments, without any bias, without any struggling to understand what the speaker is saying. What the speaker is saying has very little importance in itself. The really important thing is for the mind to be so effortlessly aware that it is in a state of understanding all the time. If we don't understand and merely listen to words, we invariably go away with a series of concepts or ideas, thereby establishing a pattern to which we then try to adjust ourselves in our daily or so-called spiritual lives.

Now, what I would like us to do this morning is something entirely different. I would like us from the very beginning to be in this state of effortless awareness, so that together we can go very deeply into the feeling, into the meaning that lies behind these words.

There is no movement of learning when there is the acquisition of knowledge; the two are incompatible, they are contradictory. The movement of learning implies a state in which the mind has no previous experience stored up as knowledge. Knowledge is acquired, whereas learning is a constant movement which is not an additive or acquisitive process; therefore, the movement of learning implies a state in which the mind has no authority. All knowledge assumes authority, and a mind that is entrenched in the authority of knowledge cannot possibly learn. The mind can learn only when the additive process has completely ceased.

It is rather difficult for most of us to differentiate between learning and acquiring knowledge. Through experience, through reading, through listening, the mind accumulates knowledge; it is an acquisitive process, a process of adding to what is already known, and from this background of knowledge we function. Now, what we generally call learning is this very same process of acquiring new information and adding it to the store of knowledge we already have. One learns a language, for example, bit by bit, gradually building up one's knowledge of the syntax, the colloquial phrases, and so on—and that is probably what most of you are doing now. In listening to the speaker you are learning in the sense of acquiring knowledge. But I am talking about something entirely different. By learning I do not mean adding to what you already know. You can learn only when there is no attachment to the past as knowledge, that is, when you see something new and do not translate it in terms of the known.

We will discuss this later if you have not understood it, because I think it is important to differentiate between learning and acquiring knowledge. The mind that is learning is an innocent mind, whereas the mind that is merely acquiring knowledge is old, stagnant, corrupted by the past. An innocent mind perceives instantly; it is learning all the time without accumulating, and such a mind alone is mature.

But for most of us maturity is a process of ripening in experience, in knowledge; that is what we call maturity. A mature person, we say, is one who has had a great deal of experience, who is wise in years, who knows how to adjust himself to unforeseen circumstances, and so on. Moving in time, he has gradually arrived at a fully ripened state. We consider that in time, the mind matures by freeing itself from ignorance—ignorance being a lack of knowledge of worldly affairs, a lack of experience and capacity. A young person, we say, needs time to mature. By the time he is sixty, he will have suffered; through all the pressures, the strains, the travails of life, he will have gathered experience, knowledge, and then perhaps he will be mature.

Now, to me maturity is something entirely different. I think it is possible to be mature without going through all the pressures and travails of time. To be completely mature, whatever one's age, implies that one is able to deal immediately with any problem that arises, and not carry it over to the next day. To carry over a problem from one day to the next is the very essence of immaturity. It is the immature mind that continues in problems from day to day. A mature mind can deal immediately with problems whenever they arise; it does not give soil for problems to take root, and such a mind is in a state of innocency.

So, to be mature is to learn and not to acquire knowledge. The acquisition of knowledge is essential at a certain level. You must have knowledge in dealing with mechanical things, as when you are learning to drive a car. You acquire knowledge in learning a language, in studying electrical engineering, and all the rest of it. But to be in the state of maturity of which I am speaking is to see oneself as one actually is from moment to moment without accumulating knowledge about oneself, because that maturity implies breaking away from the past, and the past is essentially the piling up of knowledge.

What is the self? If one really looks at oneself, one sees that it is a mass of accumulated experiences, wounds, pleasures, ideas, concepts, words. That is what we are: a bundle of memories.

Please, this is a rather complex thing we are examining, but if I go into it a little bit more, perhaps it will become clear to each one of us.

We are psychologically the result of our educational and social environment. Society, with its codes of morality, its beliefs and dogmas, its contradictions, its conflicts, its ambitions, greeds, envies, wars, is what we are. We say that in essence we are the spirit, we are the soul, we are part of God, but these are merely ideas given to us by the propaganda of the church or of some religious society; or we have picked them up from books, or from our parents, who reflect the conditioning of a particular culture. So what we are essentially is a bundle of memories, a bundle of words.

Memory identified with property, with family, with name—that is all each one of us is, but we do not like to discover that fact for ourselves; it is too unpleasant. We prefer to think of ourselves as extraordinarily intelligent beings, but we are nothing of the sort. We may have a certain capacity to write poems or to paint pictures; we may be rather cunning in business, or very clever at interpreting a particular theology; but what we actually are is a bundle of things remembered—the wounds, the pains, the vanities, the fulfillments and frustrations of the past. All that is what we are. Some of us may be superficially aware of the fact that we are this residue of the past, but we are not aware of it deeply, and now we are looking at it—which does not mean acquiring knowledge about oneself. Please see the difference.

The moment you acquire knowledge about yourself, you are strengthening yourself in the residue of the past. To see the actual facts about yourself from moment to moment, which is the movement of learning, is to be innocent of all knowledge about yourself. I don't know if I am making myself clear.

What does it mean when I say that I have knowledge about myself? Suppose I have been insulted or flattered. That experience remains in my mind as memory. With the memory of that wound or of that pleasure I look at myself, and I interpret what I see in terms of those past reactions. To interpret what one is in terms of the past merely depresses or elates one, and in that state there is no learning because there is no freshness, no spontaneity of perception. But if one really sees oneself as one is and does not interpret it in terms of the past, if one just observes the fact of *what is* at every minute, then it is possible to learn about oneself without accumulation.

It is really not too difficult to see ourselves as we are, simply and clearly, without resistance. If one is a liar, if one is lustful, greedy, envious, one can fairly easily find that out. But most of us, when we discover what we are, immediately interpret it in terms of what we think we should be, and therefore we don't learn about what we are. I wonder if I have made this clear?

When we judge or interpret what we discover in ourselves, we are adding to what we already know, and therefore we strengthen the background of memory. This process does not bring freedom at all—and one can learn only in freedom. We like to think that the essence of the self is the non-self, but there is no such essence or spiritual center; there is only the memory of things that are past, and this background of memory is always interpreting, judging, condemning that which actually is. Freedom from this background is the state of immediate maturity, and to be mature is to empty the mind of all fear.

Please, I hope you are listening and learning. To learn is not merely to understand the words of the speaker but to see directly for oneself what lies beyond the words.

Now, is it possible for the mind to empty itself totally of fear? Fear of any kind breeds illusion; it makes the mind dull, shallow. Where there is fear there is obviously no freedom, and without freedom there is no love at all. And most of us have some form of fear: fear of darkness, fear of public opinion, fear of snakes, fear of physical pain, fear of old age, fear of death. We have literally dozens of fears. And is it possible to be completely free of fear?

We can see what fear does to each one of us. It makes one tell lies; it corrupts one in various ways; it makes the mind empty, shallow. There are dark corners in the mind which can never be investigated and exposed as long as one is afraid. Physical self-protection, the instinctive urge to keep away from the venomous snake, to draw back from the precipice, to avoid falling under the tramcar, and so on, is sane, normal, healthy. But I am talking about the psychological self-protectiveness which makes one afraid of disease, of death, of an enemy. When we seek fulfillment in any form, whether through painting, through music, through relationship, or what you will, there is always fear. So, what is important is to be aware of this whole process in oneself, to observe, to learn about it, and not ask how to get rid of fear. When you merely want to get rid of fear, you will find ways and means of escaping from it, and so there can never be freedom from fear.

If you consider what fear is and how to approach it, you will see that for most of us the word is much more important than the fact. Take the word *loneliness.* By that word I mean the sense of isolation that suddenly comes upon one for no apparent reason. I don't know if this has ever happened to you. Though you may be surrounded by your family, by your neighbors, though you may be walking with friends or riding in a crowded bus, suddenly you feel completely isolated. From the memory of that experience there is fear of isolation, of being lonely. Or you are attached to someone who dies, and you find yourself left alone, isolated. Feeling that sense of isolation, you escape from it by means of the radio, the cinema, or you turn to sex, to drink, or you go to church, worship God. Whether you go to church or take a pill, it is an escape, and all escapes are essentially the same.

Now, the word loneliness prevents us from entering into a complete understanding of that state. The word, associated with past experience, evokes the feeling of danger and creates fear; therefore, we try to run away. Please watch yourself as in a mirror, do not just listen to me, and you will see that the word has extraordinary significance for most of us. Words like *God, communism, hell, heaven, loneliness, wife, family*—what an astonishing influence they have on us. We are slaves to such words, and the mind that is a slave to words is never free of fear.

To be aware of and learn about fear in oneself is not to interpret that feeling in words, for words are associated with the past, with knowledge; and in the very movement of learning about fear without verbalization, which is not to acquire knowledge about it, you will find there is a total emptying of the mind of all fear. This means that one has to go very deeply into oneself, putting aside all words; and when the mind understands the whole content of fear and is therefore empty of fear, both conscious and unconscious, then there comes a state of innocency. For most Christians that word *innocency* is merely a symbol; but I am talking of actually being in a state of innocency, which means having no fear, and therefore the mind is completely mature, instantly, without going through the passage of time. And that is possible only when there is total attention, an awareness of every thought, of every word, of every gesture. The mind is attentive without the barrier of words, without interpretation, justification, or condemnation. Such a mind is a light unto itself, and a mind that is a light unto itself has no fear.

Question: Is there no motive at all in learning about oneself?

KRISHNAMURTI: There is a motive in the sense that I want to know myself because without knowing myself, I have no foundation for anything I do, no basis for anything I think or feel. The 'myself' is so complex, so swift, so subtle, so cunning, and I must know myself completely, both the conscious and the unconscious, if I want to find out whether or not there is something real beyond my imagination, beyond my longing, beyond my desires, beyond the propaganda of church and society. To find out what is true, my mind must be clear; it must not be in a state of conflict; it must have no fear of any kind and no authority. That is obvious, is it not? There can be no dependency, no longing, no frustration—I must be completely empty of all that.

Now, how do I learn about myself? I cannot assert that I am the result of a particular society or culture, or that I am the soul, an eternal, spiritual entity, because these things are merely what other people have told me. To learn about myself, I have to throw out all the religious nonsense that society has taught me. This means that I can have no fear of public opinion, and I must know what it is to be completely alone. If I merely add to or subtract from what I think I know, saying there is a God, or there is no God, there is this and not that, then I am not learning.

Please do see this very simple fact. You cannot learn about yourself if you are trying to escape, or if you want to become a most extraordinary saint, which is utter nonsense. You can become what is called a saint by conforming to a pattern, by disciplining, denying yourself, by eating only one meal a day, and all the rest of it, but in that way you will never find out what is true. To find out what is true you must be free of the desire to become a saint.

If you love your child, you observe him, you learn about him, don't you? You don't assume anything about him. You don't tell him that he must be like his elder brother, who is so clever. When you compare your child with another, you are destroying that child. In the same way, to learn about yourself there must be no comparison. You cannot be depressed or elated about yourself. You cannot assume anything, for assumption is based on authority, and the denial of authority is the beginning of learning.

What is important is to be curious about oneself. I do not mean mere intellectual curiosity, or being verbally stimulated to examine oneself because at the end of it one hopes to get some ugly result. To be really curious about oneself is to see all the twists and turns, all the stresses and strains, all the subtle and hidden ways of one's own mind; and a mind that is tethered to knowledge cannot swiftly follow the ever-changing movements of itself.

To learn about yourself is to be without motive, and that is the beauty of self-knowing. You don't want to become a great person or a famous saint; you just want to learn about yourself as you would want to learn about a most extraordinary flower that you had found in the desert. We are in a desert, and we are the most extraordinary flowers. To look at the flower, to smell it, to understand it, we must love that flower.

Question: Is not an immature mind one that is caught in habits?

KRISHNAMURTI: I wonder if you are exercising all your attention or are merely waiting for me to awaken your intelligence, your awareness. Are you working intensely in spite of this heat, or are you being rather slack?

The question is: "Is not an immature mind one that is caught in habits?" Now, I wonder why you put this question? Are you aware that you are immature, caught in habits, or are you merely pointing out what has already been explained? Please, I am not speaking derogatorily of the questioner. If you see that you are immature, caught in habits, as most people are, then the further question is how to be mature immediately, that is, how to break through habit completely, not at some future time, but now. Is that the question?

I see that I am caught in habit. Politically, religiously, as a writer, as a painter, as a man or a woman, I am caught in a particular way of thinking. Being an Englishman, I have a certain tradition with a fixed attitude towards life; or I am trained in Catholicism, in this or in that, and it has become a habit. Can that habit be broken immediately, or must it be done away with gradually over the years? If I say it will take time, that it must be done away with gradually over the years, what then is the state of my mind? Obviously my mind is lethargic, dull, thoughtless, unaware.

Nationalism, for example, is a habit, and it can be broken instantly; but it gives us pleasure, it gives us a sense of importance to be identified with a particular country, especially if it is a powerful one. Most of us like being identified with a particular government, with the flag, and all the rest of that nonsense, so we don't want to break the habit of nationalism, and then there is no problem. But if you want to break that habit—and you can only break it instantly, not over the years—then how is it to be done?

Is there a method by which to break a habit? Surely, a method implies time, moving from a beginning to an end. If you see for yourself that time does not free you from habit, and that methods or systems are therefore of no avail, then you are actually faced with the fact that your mind is caught in habit. You are faced with it, not through words, not through ideas, but you directly see the fact that your mind is crippled with habit; it is inescapably so. And then what happens? You are not trying to change the habit; you are not trying to break it down. You are simply faced with the fact that your mind functions in the groove of habit. And what happens when you are directly faced with a fact? What happens if you come face to face with the fact that you are a liar, that you are jealous? If you don't try to change it, then the fact itself gives you enormous energy to break that fact completely. Do you understand? When you are directly faced with the fact, your mind is no longer dissipating itself in escapes, in denials, in trying to change the fact through time, and all the rest of it; therefore, your attention is complete; all your energy has been gathered, and that energy totally shatters the fact.

Question: Can one dissolve fear completely by finding the cause of fear?

KRISHNAMURTI: You know, if you are giving your complete attention, at the end of an hour of this kind of talk, your mind must be tired, and your body must be tired too. To listen with complete attention is something which most of us have never done before, and it is very arduous.

The lady asks: "Is fear dissolved through knowing the cause of fear?" Is it? One generally knows the cause of fear: death, public opinion, the things one has done that one doesn't want to be discovered, and so on. Most people know the cause of their fear, but that obviously doesn't end fear. Through analysis one may discover some hidden cause of fear, but again that does not free the mind from fear. What brings freedom from fear—and I assure you the freedom is complete—is to be aware of fear without the word, without trying to deny or escape from fear, without wanting to be in some other state. If with complete attention you are aware of the fact that there is fear, then you will find that the observer and the observed are one, there is no division between them. There is no observer who says, "I am afraid"; there is only fear without the word which indicates that state. The mind is no longer escaping, no longer seeking to get rid of fear, no longer trying to find the cause, and therefore it is no longer a slave to words. There is only a movement of learning which is the outcome of innocence, and an innocent mind has no fear.

August 2, 1962

Seventh Talk in Saanen

The last time we met here we were talking about fear and whether it is at all possible to be completely free of fear, which is the reaction that occurs when one is aware of danger. And this morning I would like, if I may, to talk about the ending of sorrow, because fear, sorrow, and what we call love always go together. Unless we understand fear we shall not be able to understand sorrow, nor can we know that state of love in which there is no contradiction, no friction.

To end sorrow completely is a most difficult thing to do, for sorrow is always with us in one form or another. So I would like to go into this problem rather deeply; but my words will have very little meaning unless each one of us examines the problem within himself, neither agreeing nor disagreeing, but simply observing the fact. If we can do this, actually and not just theoretically, then perhaps we shall be able to understand the enormous significance of sorrow and thereby put an end to sorrow.

Throughout the centuries, love and sorrow have always gone hand in hand, sometimes one predominating, and sometimes the other. That state which we call love soon passes away, and again we are caught up in our jealousies, our vanities, our fears, our miseries. There has always been this battle between love and sorrow; and before we can go into the question of ending sorrow, I think we must understand what is passion.

May I point out that we are not a privileged group of people who—being fairly well-to-do and having enough money to travel to a place like this—have come here merely to indulge in a form of intellectual amusement. What we are talking about is very serious, and one has to be very serious to go into it. By being serious I mean having the intensity, the drive to go to the very bottom of this thing called sorrow. We are here to find out for ourselves whether it is at all possible to end sorrow completely, so that the mind is without a shadow, clear, sharp, capable of thinking without illusion. And we cannot do this if we merely live at the level of words, as most of us are apt to do. Concepts, patterns, ideals, words, symbols—these have an extraordinary meaning for most of us, and there we stop. We seem unable to break through the verbal level and penetrate beyond it, but to understand sorrow, one has to go beyond words. So, as I go into this problem of sorrow, I hope you also will examine it intensely and clearly, without sentimentality or emotionalism.

Now, unless we understand passion, I don't think we shall be able to understand sorrow. Passion is something which very few of us have really felt. What we may have felt is enthusiasm, which is being caught up in an emotional state over something. Our passion is for something: for music, for painting, for literature, for a country, for a woman or a man; it is always the effect of a cause. When you fall in love with someone, you are in a great state of emotion, which is the effect of that particular cause; and what I am talking about is passion without a cause. It is to be passionate about everything, not just about something, whereas most of us are passionate about a particular person or thing; and I think one must see very clearly this distinction.

In the state of passion without a cause, there is intensity free of all attachment; but when passion has a cause, there is attachment, and attachment is the beginning of sorrow. Most of us are attached; we cling to a person, to a country, to a belief, to an idea, and when the object of our attachment is taken away or otherwise loses its significance, we find ourselves empty, insufficient. This emptiness we try to fill by clinging to something else, which again becomes the object of our passion.

While I am talking, please examine your own heart and mind. I am merely a mirror in which you are looking at yourself. If you don't want to look, that is quite all right, but if you do want to look, then look at yourself clearly, ruthlessly, with intensity—not in the hope of dissolving your miseries, your anxieties, your sense of guilt, but in order to understand this extraordinary passion which always leads to sorrow.

When passion has a cause, it becomes lust. When there is a passion for something—for a person, for an idea, for some kind of fulfillment—then out of that passion there comes contradiction, conflict, effort. You strive to achieve or maintain a particular state, or to recapture one that has been and is gone. But the passion of which I am speaking does not give rise to contradiction, conflict. It is totally unrelated to a cause, and therefore it is not an effect.

Please, may I suggest that you just listen; don't try to achieve this state of intensity, this passion without a cause. If we can listen attentively, with that sense of ease which comes when attention is not forced through discipline but is born of the simple urge to understand, then I think we shall find out for ourselves what this passion is.

In most of us there is very little passion. We may be lustful, we may be longing for something, we may be wanting to escape from something, and all this does give one a certain intensity. But unless we awaken and feel our way into this flame of passion without a cause, we shall not be able to understand that which we call sorrow. To understand something, you must have passion, the intensity of complete attention. Where there is the passion for something—which produces contradiction, conflict—this pure flame of passion cannot be, and this pure flame of passion must exist in order to end sorrow, dissipate it completely.

We know that sorrow is a result; it is the effect of a cause. I love somebody, and that person doesn't love me—that is one kind of sorrow. I want to fulfill myself in a certain direction, but I haven't got the capacity; or if I have the capacity, ill health or some other factor blocks my fulfillment—that is another form of sorrow. There is the sorrow of a petty mind, of a mind that is always in conflict with itself, incessantly struggling, adjusting, groping, conforming. There is the sorrow of conflict in relationship, and the sorrow of losing someone by death. You all know these various forms of sorrow, and they are all the result of a cause.

Now, we never face the fact of sorrow; we are always trying to rationalize it, explain it away; or we cling to a dogma, a pattern of belief which satisfies us, gives us momentary comfort. Some take a drug, others turn to drink, or to prayer—anything to lessen the intensity, the agony of sorrow. Sorrow, and the everlasting attempt to escape from sorrow, is the lot of each one of us. We have never thought of ending sorrow completely so that the mind is not at any time caught in self-pity, in the shadow of despair. Not being able to end sorrow, if we are Christians we worship it in our churches as the agony of Christ. And whether we go to church and worship the symbol of sorrow, or try to rationalize sorrow away, or forget our sorrow by taking a drink, it is all the same: we are escaping from the fact that we suffer. I am not talking about physical pain, which can be dealt with fairly easily by modern medicine. I am talking about sorrow, the psychological pain that prevents clarity, beauty, that destroys love and compassion. And is it possible to bring all sorrow to an end?

I think the ending of sorrow is related to the intensity of passion. There can be passion only when there is total self-abandonment. One is never passionate unless there is a complete absence of what we call thought. As we saw the other day, what we call thought is the response of the various patterns and experiences of memory, and where this conditioned response exists there is no passion, there is no intensity. There can be intensity only when there is a complete absence of the 'me'.

You know, there is a sense of beauty which is not concerned with what is beautiful and what is ugly. Not that the mountain is not beautiful, or that there is not an ugly building; but there is beauty which is not the opposite of ugliness, there is love which is not the opposite of hate. And the self-abandonment of which I am speaking is that state of beauty without cause, and therefore it is a state of passion. And is it possible to go beyond that which is the result of a cause?

Please do listen to this with complete attention. I may not be able to explain it very clearly, but do gather the meaning rather than stay with the words. You see, most of us are always reacting; reaction is the whole pattern of our life. Our response to sorrow is a reaction. We respond by trying to explain the cause of sorrow, or by escaping from sorrow, but our sorrow doesn't end. Sorrow ends only when we face the fact of sorrow, when we understand and go beyond both the cause and the effect. To try to be free of sorrow through a particular practice, or by deliberate thought, or by indulging in any of the various ways of escaping from sorrow, doesn't awaken in the mind the extraordinary beauty, the vitality, the intensity of that passion which includes and transcends sorrow.

What is sorrow? When you hear this question, how do you respond? Your mind immediately tries to explain the cause of sorrow, and this seeking of an explanation awakens the memory of the sorrows you have had. So you are always verbally reverting to the past or going forward to the future in an effort to explain the cause of the effect which we call sorrow. But I think one has to go beyond all that.

We know very well what causes sorrow—poverty, ill-health, frustration, the lack of being loved, and so on. And when we have explained the various causes of sorrow, we haven't ended sorrow; we haven't really grasped the extraordinary depth and significance of sorrow any more than we have understood that state which we call love. I think the two are related—sorrow and love. And to understand what love is, one has to feel the immensity of sorrow.

The ancients talked about the ending of sorrow, and they laid down a way of life that is supposed to end sorrow. Many people have practiced that way of life. Monks in the East and in the West have tried it, but they have only hardened themselves; their minds and their hearts have become enclosed. They live behind the walls of their own thought, or behind walls of brick and stone, but I really do not believe they have gone beyond and felt the immensity of this thing called sorrow.

To end sorrow is to face the fact of one's loneliness, one's attachment, one's petty little demand for fame, one's hunger to be loved; it is to be free of self-concern and the puerility of self-pity. And when one has gone beyond all that and has perhaps ended one's personal sorrow, there is still the immense collective sorrow, the sorrow of the world. One may end one's own sorrow by facing in oneself the fact and the cause of sorrow—and that must take place for a mind that would be completely free. But when one has finished with all that, there is still the sorrow of extraordinary ignorance that exists in the world—not the lack of information, of book-knowledge, but man's ignorance of himself. The lack of understanding of oneself is the essence of ignorance, which brings about this immensity of sorrow that exists throughout the world. And what actually is sorrow?

You see, there are no words to explain sorrow, any more than there are words to explain what love is. Love is not attachment, love is not the opposite of hate, love is not jealousy. And when one has finished with jealousy, with envy, with attachment, with all the conflicts and the agonies one goes through, thinking that one loves—when all that has come to an end, there still remains the question of what is love, and there still remains the question of what is sorrow.

You will find out what love is, and what sorrow is, only when your mind has rejected all explanations and is no longer imagining, no longer seeking the cause, no longer indulging in words or going back in memory to its own pleasures and pains. Your mind must be completely quiet, without a word, without a symbol, without an idea. And then you will discover, or there will come into being that state in which what we have called love and what we have called sorrow and what we have called death are the same. There is no longer any division between love and sorrow and death; and there being no division, there is beauty. But to comprehend, to be in this state of ecstasy, there must be that passion which comes with the total abandonment of oneself.

Sir, please don't take photographs. You ought to know better than that. This is not a political meeting, nor is it a gathering for entertainment, and it's pity to reduce it to that level.

Shall we discuss, or will you ask questions about what I have been saying this morning?

Question: Is passion or intensity a quality?

KRISHNAMURTI: I wonder what we mean by that word *quality?* Is passion or intensity a virtue to be acquired through practice, through discipline, through self-sacrifice, and so on? Is that what you mean?

Question: May I ask a question?

KRISHNAMURTI: Sir, a question has already been asked. You see, we are so occupied with our own questions that we don't listen to anybody else, and that is always happening in life. We are so caught in our own problems, in our own hopes and ambitions, in our own despairs, that we almost never see beyond our little selves. Perhaps some of us have other questions, but if I may respectfully suggest it, don't be so occupied with your own question.

To come back to the question that was asked: "Is passion or intensity a quality?" I don't like to use that word quality. When you are passionate about something, you don't ask whether it's a quality, do you? You are in that state. When you are angry, or lustful, or when you are being verbally brutal about somebody, you don't ask at that moment if what you are feeling is a quality. You are burning with it. But later on you say, "By Jove, that was an ugly moment," and then it becomes something to be avoided in the future. Or, if it was a beautiful moment, you proceed to cultivate it, but what you cultivate is artificial; it is not a pure thing.

So the passion or intensity I have been talking about is not cultivable; it is not on the market for sale; you can't buy it with practice or discipline, but if you have listened and have really gone into yourself, if you have wrestled with it, you will know what it is. That passion has nothing whatsoever to do with enthusiasm. It comes only when there is a complete cessation of the 'me', when all sense of "my house," "my property," "my country," "my wife," "my children," has been left behind. You may say, "Then it is not worth having that passion." Perhaps for you it is not. It is worthwhile only if you really want to find out what is sorrow, what is truth, what is God, what is the meaning of this whole ugly and confusing business of existence. If that is what you are concerned with, then you must go into it with passion—which means that you cannot be tethered to your family. You may have a house, you may have a family, but if you are psychologically tethered to them, you can never go beyond.

Question: Have we all got the same capacity for passion?

KRISHNAMURTI: I don't think passion is a capacity. You may have the capacity to write books, to write poems, or to play the flute, or to do any number of other things; and capacities can be cultivated, maintained, added to. But passion, intensity, is not a capacity. On the contrary, if you have a capacity, you must die to that capacity to be passionate. If you don't die to capacity, then capacity becomes mechanical, though you may build it up and be very clever at it. You see, we are still thinking in terms of acquiring, and protecting that which has been acquired.

Comment: You have said that sorrow is a beautiful thing, and yet you say that we must get rid of sorrow.

KRISHNAMURTI: I did not say that you must get rid of sorrow. I said that you have to look at sorrow; go into it, understand it. You can't get rid of sorrow; you can't just put it away. When does one have sorrow? If you love somebody and that person doesn't love you in return, you suffer. Why? Why should you suffer? What does your suffering mean? It means you are thinking about yourself—that is the actual fact. And as long as you are thinking about your own little self, wanting to be loved and being afraid that you will not be loved, with all the ugliness involved in that, naturally you are going to have what you call sorrow. Similarly, if I want to be a famous man, and I am not, inevitably I suffer; and if I am satisfied to remain in that state, all right. But if I want to understand my suffering and go beyond it, then I begin to look at it; I uncompromisingly examine the psychological urge to be famous, which is so utterly superficial, immature; and then there comes an understanding of sorrow which is the beginning of the end of sorrow. And, as I said, when one has gone beyond all this personal sorrow, one finds that love and sorrow and death are the same. That is a state of great beauty—which is not the beauty put together by man or by nature.

Question: Is passion or intensity the desire to know?

KRISHNAMURTI: I wonder what we mean by the desire to know? The urge to pile up knowledge is still part of becoming, and is therefore a cause of conflict. But I am not talking about piling up knowledge which can be found in any encyclopedia. I want to understand, go to the very end of sorrow and find out for myself its significance, and that doesn't mean that I must know. Knowing, as I very carefully explained the other day, is one thing, and learning is another. Knowing implies the accumulation of knowledge, and when you have accumulated knowledge, from that background you experience. Through experience you acquire still more knowledge, but in this acquisitive process of adding knowledge to knowledge through experience, there is no movement of learning. You can learn only when you are no longer seeking or acquiring knowledge.

Sir, I don't want to know about sorrow. We all have sorrow. Don't you have sorrow in one form or another? And do you want to know about it? If you do, you can analyze it and explain why you suffer. You can read books on the subject, or go to the church, and you will soon know something about sorrow. But I am not talking about that; I am talking about the ending of sorrow. Knowledge does not end sorrow. The ending of sorrow begins with the facing of psychological facts within oneself and being totally aware of all the implications of those facts from moment to moment. This means never escaping from the fact that one is in sorrow, never rationalizing it, never offering an opinion about it, but living with that fact completely.

You know, to live with the beauty of those mountains and not get accustomed to it is very difficult. Most of you have been here now for nearly three weeks. You have beheld those mountains, heard the stream, and seen the shadows creep across the valley, day after day; and have you not noticed how easily you get used to it all? You say, "Yes, it is quite beautiful," and you pass by. To live with beauty, or to live with an ugly thing, and not become habituated to it requires enormous energy—an awareness that does not allow your mind to grow dull. In the same way, sorrow dulls the mind if you merely get used to it—and most of us do get used to it. But you need not get used to sorrow. You can live with sorrow, understand it, go into it—but not in order to know about it. You know that sorrow is there; it is a fact, and there is nothing more to know. You have to live with sorrow, and to live with it you must love it; and then you will find, as I said earlier, that love and sorrow and death are one.

Question: Is there no love without passion?

KRISHNAMURTI: What do we mean by the word *passion* and by the word *love?* Whether you are a man or a woman, when you fall in love with somebody, don't you have passion, at least for the first two years or whatever it is? And then you become accustomed to each other; you begin to get bored. With that passion, though you call it love, there is lust, attachment, jealousy, ambition, greed, and all the rest of the business. It is like a flame in the midst of smoke. And what happens? Gradually the flame dies, and you have only the smoke left. But if there is a subsiding of attachment, lust, jealousy, and all the other elements that make for the smoke and conflict which we call passion—if there is a dying away of all that, not through time and habit, but because one has gone into it, understood it, seen the depths and the heights of it, then love may be passion without a cause. I do not mean the passion of the missionary who, because he loves Jesus, goes out to convert the heathen—that is not the passion I am talking about. On the contrary, it is the denial of all that without a motive, and out of this denial, the clear flame comes into being.

Question: Is it possible for a human being to be permanently in a state of understanding?

KRISHNAMURTI: It is important to understand what we mean by that word *permanent.* I don't think you can ever be permanently in anything. If you are permanently in something, you are dead. And that is what most of us want: we want certain things—love, passion, understanding, God—to continue permanently. Which means what? That we don't want to be disturbed, we don't want to be sensitive, alive. As I have explained, truth or understanding comes in a flash, and that flash has no continuity; it is not within the field of time. Do see this for yourself. Understanding is fresh, instantaneous; it is not the continuity of something that has been. What has been cannot bring you understanding. As long as one is seeking a continuity—wanting permanency in relationship, in love, longing to find peace everlasting, and all the rest of it—one is pursuing something which is within the field of time and therefore does not belong to the timeless.

August 5, 1962

Eighth Talk in Saanen

We were talking the day before yesterday about sorrow, and I would like to talk this morning about death. For most of us, death is in the frame of fear. We are afraid of death, and therefore we never understand its immense significance. Fear invariably distorts perception and makes us escape from that of which we are afraid; and when we escape from the fact of death, or are overwhelmed with sorrow at the death of a friend, it is impossible to go deeply into and understand the whole problem of death.

We have already discussed to some extent fear and sorrow, and I think we should now be able to consider wisely and deeply this problem of death. As I was saying the other day, love, sorrow, and death go together; they are inseparable. This is not a mere philosophical concept—I am not talking philosophy. But if you go very deeply into yourself, you will see that love cannot be separated from sorrow, and sorrow cannot be separated from death because the three are really one. Nor can the beauty and the immensity of death possibly be understood if there is any vestige of fear.

To understand death, I think we must go into the question of negative thinking and denial. Now, please do not treat this as something theoretical that cannot be put into practice. It is a lazy, indolent mind that dismisses everything as a theory, or reduces it to a system, or to a pattern of activity, thereby missing the real essence, the deep significance of what is being said. So I would most earnestly request that you listen with openness, with friendliness, without agreement or disagreement, without any motive. If we can listen happily, easily, without motive to the problem of death, then perhaps we shall capture the full significance of this immense thing that is always awaiting us.

First of all, I would like to consider with you what may be called negative thinking. Very few of us ever think negatively, and negative thinking is the highest form of thinking; it is to see the false as false, to see what is true in the false, and to see what is true in the truth. We cannot see what is false if we merely consider the false as the opposite of the true; we can see what is false only when there is no contrast, no comparison. Contrast and comparison are born of positive thinking. If I want to understand my son, for example, I must cease to compare; I must look at him as he is. If I consider him in terms of approval or disapproval, both of which are based on my acceptance of a pattern established by tradition, by experience, by opinion, and so on, then there are the so-called positive thinking and positive action which preclude understanding. Understanding is possible only when there is no comparison, no judgment, but merely a perceiving of the actual fact; and such perception is negative thinking.

I would like to explain this negative thinking a little more, because to realize the extraordinary beauty and vitality of it, one must first understand the state of a mind that is free from the known. Please do listen to what is being said, not as a philosophy that is being expounded, or as a system that you have to follow, but listen to find out the truth of the matter for yourself. As you are sitting here, actually experience what is being said. Don't wait and think about it afterwards—"afterwards" has no meaning; to understand, you have to be with it now, at the present moment.

I was talking about negative thinking, and I said it is the highest form of thinking. Most of us are never in a state when we say, "I do not know," except in a very superficial sense. There are two states of not-knowing. In one, the mind says, "I do not know," and it is expecting or looking for an answer. In this state the mind translates what it finds according to its background or conditioning. In listening, please experiment with yourself, and you will see that this is so. But there is another state in which the mind says, "I do not know," and is not expecting or seeking an answer. It is completely empty; its state is one of total negation, and it is only for such a mind that there is the coming into being of this extraordinary thing called creation.

I hope I have made the two states clear: that of the positive mind which says, "I do not know" and tries to find out, and that of the mind which says, "I do not know" and is not seeking an answer. To be in the state of not-knowing without seeking an answer is extremely difficult for most of us because we don't like to be uncertain. But the mind that is certain is still caught in the known, and one has to be completely free of the known to understand the unknowable, which is death. So, let us find out what is implied in the denial of the life of the known.

For most of us life is conflict, pain. There is an incessant striving, a passing joy, a great many stresses and strains, a background of accumulated memory which responds to every challenge and whose response is always inadequate. There is fulfillment and the sorrow of not fulfilling; there is greed, envy, anger, hatred, misery; there is so-called love, which is the flame within the smoke of attachment, dependence, jealousy. The boredom of going to the office every day, the familiarity and contempt in one's relationship with another, the constant undercurrent of fear—that is our life, and we want that life to continue. Our life from day to day has become a habit. It is shallow, empty, and we try to fill this emptiness with religious dogmas and beliefs, with saints, saviors, Masters. Our life—with its sexual appetites, its longing for fame, its desire for comfort, power, position, prestige—is a closed circle of hope and despair. This is all we know, and when death comes we are frightened to leave the known, to leave this petty life of ours, because we are so used to it. That is why there is a conflict between living and dying. The possessions to which we cling, our money, our house, our family, our name, our character, our experience, our memory of the things that we have done and not done—all that is the known, and when death approaches there is fear of leaving it. We want a continuity of all the petty business of that which we have known.

Now, you may have ideas, theories about reincarnation, resurrection, or you may cling to some other belief, but death is the ending of the life of the known; and what matters is to deny the life of the known—to deny it without a motive. By the life of the known I mean the life of our pettiness, of our jealousies, of our ambition, greed. This we have to deny totally; we have to cut it off at the very root, but without a motive because when we have a motive, that very motive gives a continuity to the life of the known, and therefore there is no experiencing of the extraordinary depth of death.

Most of us come to the end of the known bitterly; we come to the end of our tether with anxiety, with fear. We do not die happily, easily, gracefully. At the thought of dying we are in a state of despair, and out of that, if we are very clever, we invent a philosophy of despair—or we turn to a philosophy of hope, which is what most so-called religious people do. Now, what matters is to deny all this because we understand it, which is to deny without a motive the life that we know; and then we shall find that the mind is in a state where it is beginning to free itself from the known. That is one of the things that we must do if we are to understand the immensity and the creativeness of death.

Then there is the question of time. There is chronological time and psychological time. I am not talking about chronological time, the time marked by the ringing of that church bell. I am talking about the ending of psychological time, and this ending takes place only when the mind is not seeking, getting, arriving; it has understood this whole process, and therefore there is no tomorrow as the result of the experiences of yesterday.

The time by which we go to the office, keep an appointment, catch a bus, and so on, is entirely different from the psychological time that we build up through hope: I do not know, but I shall know; I am angry, but eventually I shall be in a state of peace; I am nationalistic, narrow, bigoted, but time will gradually bring freedom from this petty state. Time is used by the mind to move psychologically from here to there, and as long as this psychological time exists in each one of us, we cannot possibly understand what death is.

To understand what death is, the mind must be completely free of fear; it must be in a state when it says to itself, "I do not know" without seeking or wanting an answer, which is the state of freedom from the known. This means that the mind is no longer psychologically building itself up through time in order to become something. Then you will find, if you have gone this far, that all sense of continuity has come to an end. The mind dies to all its petty little anxieties, greeds, envies, vanities, dies to them immediately, and in that dying there is no sense of continuity. It is only when there is an end that there can be a new beginning. When there is an end to the past there is a coming into being of something totally new.

What we call thought gives to the mind a sense of continuity, which is psychological time, because our thought is the result of our conditioning, of our memory, of our experience. Every challenge evokes from that background a response, and this response is thought in action; therefore, there is no spontaneity, there is never a response that is free of the past. But when there is an end to one's thought, to one's greed, to one's envy, to one's ambition and thirst for power, to the whole psychological structure of society which is the 'me'—when all that has come to an end without any motive, then the mind is in a state of not-knowing; it is completely empty, and only then is there death.

What actually takes place when you physically die? You leave everything behind. You can't take anything with you. However many motives you may have for living, you can't argue with death. You can't say to death, "I still have to do this and that, please give me another month, another year." When death comes, it is there, absolutely and finally. You may believe in reincarnation, or in some other form of resurrection in the future, but all beliefs are irrelevant when you are confronted with the fact of death. And if you inwardly die to the psychological structure of society, to all the accumulations of the past, then you will find that death is creation—not the creation of the writer, of the musician, of the painter, of the scientist, but a creation which has no beginning and no end. And without being in this state of creation, which is death, which is love, our life has very little meaning.

So, do not treat all this as some logical or super-logical philosophy, but actually go into yourself, understand yourself completely. Totally deny everything that you have considered to be life—your experiences, your ambition, your greed, your envy—and you will see that in this ending, there is a death which is timeless creation and which, if you want to give it a different name, may be called God, the immeasurable, the unknown.

Do you now want to ask questions about this?

Question: Should we not remain quiet for a few moments?

KRISHNAMURTI: Were you not quiet while you were listening? Were you not very attentive, watchful? And when you are attentive, watchful, there is a peculiar quality of silence. The speaker was explaining something, and though he talked for forty minutes—if you will not misunderstand what I mean—he was not using thought. The speaker was moving from fact to fact, and words were used to explain; but if in listening you moved only as it were horizontally, at the verbal level, then you will not have gone vertically and deeply into yourself. So, quietness is a state of attention, a state of real uncovering. You are not quiet if the mind is made quiet, or if you are merely hypnotized by the words and the feeling of the speaker.

Question: If understanding is not permanent, if it is only to be caught in a flash, then what happens during the interval between flashes?

KRISHNAMURTI: One has to understand the whole inward nature of experience. For most of us, experience is a reaction; it is the response of our memory to a challenge. That memory of things we have known may be very ancient or very modern; it may be superficial or profound, and we experience according to that background. This further experience is accumulated, stored up, and so it strengthens the background.

Now, when there is a flash of understanding, it is not the response of the background. At that moment the background is completely silent. If the background is not silent, there is no understanding, for you are merely interpreting in terms of the old whatever you hear or see. The flash of understanding is not continuous, not permanent. Continuity or permanence belongs entirely to the background of experience and knowledge which is everlastingly responding to challenge. Understanding comes only in a flash, and how does this flash take place? This flash cannot take place in a mind that is lazy, distorted, traditional, dull, stupid, nor in a mind that is seeking power, position, prestige. This flash of understanding occurs only in a mind that is very alert, and when there is no flash, the mind is still alert. Such a mind is completely awake, aware. And to be totally, choicelessly aware, observing every movement of thought and feeling, seeing everything that is going on—this is far more important than to await the flash of understanding.

Question: Can you go further into the question of seeing the true in the false?

KRISHNAMURTI: That is so simple and clear, does it need further explanation? Take any false thing, like nationalism. To see the falseness of nationalism is to see the truth in the false. To see the falseness of authority, the falseness of the church, is to discover what is true. To see the truth in jealousy, in ambition, in the search for power, position, prestige, is to see their complete falseness; and when you see this truth, not just a little bit, but totally, then that very perception frees the mind from the false.

Question: Is there not the danger of merely condemning certain things of which we do not happen to approve?

KRISHNAMURTI: Condemnation is a reaction, a resistance, and what we condemn we obviously do not understand. Suppose I am a Catholic, a communist, or what you will, and because I want to find out the truth of the matter for myself, I begin to look at it, go into it. I then see the falseness of all clinging to dogma and belief, so I reject it. That rejection is not a condemnation of communism or the church. I just see that these things have no meaning for a man who is really serious in wanting to find out what is true.

Question: When the mind is perfectly still, silent, who is aware of that silence?

KRISHNAMURTI: When you are joyous, happy, the moment you are aware that you are happy, you are no longer happy. Have you noticed this? No? The moment you identify yourself with happiness, happiness ceases. Then happiness is only a memory. Similarly, silence is not to be experienced by the 'me'. Perhaps we shall go into this question when I talk about meditation the day after tomorrow.

Comment: One of the causes of conflict within me is the consideration of others and the question of what is the right thing to do.

KRISHNAMURTI: Sir, what is compassion? Is it not a state of sympathy, pity, consideration? And in that state there is surely no feeling that you are helping another. Am I helping all of you who are listening to me? Yes? I hope not. (Laughter) I really mean it. If I feel that I am helping you, then I consider myself a person who knows more than you do, and that makes you the followers. We are not talking about helping each other; we are trying to find out what is true, and to find out what is true requires immense compassion. In that state of compassion one may help, one may give sympathy to another, but there is no conflict within oneself.

Comment: You have said that ambition is false. I do not see how this can be. If I give up my purely materialistic ambitions in order to reach your measureless understanding, that is still a form of ambition. Ambition is necessary if one wants to get somewhere in life.

KRISHNAMURTI: There are so many things involved in ambition. First of all, there is authority—the authority of a pattern which you have established and require yourself to pursue, or the authority of the psychological structure of society. Now, authority implies obedience. The psychological structure of society demands that you be competitive, ambitious, greedy, acquisitive, envious, power-seeking, and all the rest of it. If you see the falseness of all that, must you not deny—in the sense of that word which I tried to explain this morning—the psychological structure of society? It is the psychological structure of society which makes us conform, which makes us dull, utterly stupid; therefore, a religious mind must surely be free from the psychological structure of society.

When you say that one must have ambition to get anywhere in life, what does that mean? It means climbing the heap, struggling to get to the top of this confused and miserable society in which we live. And is it not possible to live in this world without ambition, without a goal?

How do you establish a goal? Either you project it from the background of your own desire, or you follow the example, worship the success of another. So the goal is established by each one of us according to the conditioning which a particular society or culture has imposed upon us. Our projection of a goal is determined by our own reactions, noble or ignoble.

Now, why do we want a goal? To want a goal means that living completely from day to day is not enough. We want to feel that we are getting somewhere, so we establish a goal to give a deeper significance to our living. Our daily life and activities have very little significance for most of us, so we project an ideal which we think will give some meaning to our life, but it does not because that which we project is created out of ourselves. What is important is not to have a goal but to see if our daily existence has a meaning in itself.

August 7, 1962

Ninth Talk in Saanen

This morning I am going to talk about meditation. It is something very complex, and yet very simple. It is not at all the mysterious, oriental affair that many of us imagine it to be, with all kinds of romantic, nonsensical ideas around it. And to go into it very deeply, as I propose to do this morning, certain things are obviously necessary.

First of all, we must understand very clearly that the word is not the thing. The word *meditation* is not meditation, and one has to be extraordinarily aware if one is not merely to remain at the verbal level and regard meditation as something intellectual, or fanciful, and therefore not of great significance in daily life. One also requires a mind that is very subtle and very sensitive. Subtlety and sensitivity go together when the mind is no longer seeking. By that word *seeking* I mean trying to achieve a goal, grasping at visions, being caught in various forms of self-hypnosis. In other words, one must be capable of logical, rational, clear thinking. When one thinks very clearly without any pressure of seeking, one finds that thought comes to an end; and to understand what is meditation, it is essential for thought to end.

Before we go into this question of meditation, we must also understand what is the religious mind. The religious mind is not the confused, stagnant mind which is caught in belief, in dogma, in ritual. It is not a slave to authority. It does not belong to any group, to any organized religion, nor does it look to any savior, Master, or guide. It is a light unto itself.

A religious mind is a mind that is free from all influence. To be swayed by any form of influence distorts the mind. You cannot get rid of influences—you have to be aware of them. You have to be aware, consciously and also unconsciously, of the influence on your mind of all that you have read about meditation—about the various systems of meditation which offer the meditator an opportunity to achieve certain results by conforming to a specified pattern. One has to be aware of all that and put it aside.

A religious mind is very simple, uncomplicated. To me the word *simplicity* means not being caught in conflict. It does not mean taking only one meal a day, or wearing a loincloth, or withdrawing into a monastery. That is not simplicity at all. Such a mind is merely conforming to a pattern, whether laid down by itself or by somebody else, as a reaction to the complexity of life.

So, a religious mind is simple, direct; it is not caught in words and does not create a time interval between *what is* and 'what should be'. It perceives directly the psychological facts of its own nature and therefore does not provide the soil in which problems take root.

Now, let us see if we can go step by step into this question of meditation. I feel that meditation is as important as taking a bath, or having a meal, or seeing the beauty of the mountains and the shallowness of the mind. It is as important as earning a livelihood. If you do not know how to meditate rightly, you have missed a great deal—the enriching, completely beautiful and splendid awakening of life. So, I beg of you, do listen.

Meditation is an extraordinary state that demands no effort. Most of us are conditioned to make effort. We struggle to achieve a result, or to sustain a particular experience, or to gather knowledge, all of which implies various forms of conflict; and without understanding conflict, it is not possible for the mind to be in that effortless state which is meditation.

So, as most of us do not know what right meditation is, it is important that we find out for ourselves. I am not going to teach you a method because any method or system of meditation merely cultivates habit; and a mind that is caught in habit is dull, insensitive, unintelligent. We must understand and be totally free of this idea of conforming to a pattern, regardless of who is supposed to have established that pattern. One has to understand the significance of all patterns, all systems. There are systems which offer a result in meditation, and when you regularly and earnestly practice such a system, it does bring about a certain experience or state; but the system has molded the mind, shaped it according to that particular pattern, and therefore the mind is not free. So, to find out what is real meditation, there must be freedom from this imitative process.

This is such an enormous subject, with such extraordinary nuances and subtleties, that it is really quite difficult to know where to begin.

For most of us, life is turmoil, a constant travail. It is misery, fleeting joy, an ever-changing pattern of shadows and light. Nothing endures; therefore, we consciously or unconsciously seek some form of permanency, and that permanency we variously call peace, happiness, God, enlightenment. Being in conflict, in an unending condition of flux, we want a permanent state, and there is no permanent state. If you achieve a permanent state, your mind is dead.

So meditation is not the achievement of any form of permanency, and it is not prayer. Prayer implies supplication, begging, looking to another for comfort, for psychological security. Meditation is not contemplation. Contemplation implies putting the mind on something and expecting, watching. There is a duality, the watcher and the thing that is watched; so meditation is not contemplation, nor is it the awakening of visions. Visions are merely the reaction, the response of your background. If you are a devout Christian you may see the Christ, and you will regard that as a great spiritual experience, but it is nothing of the sort. It is a conditioned experience, the projection of a most immature, unthoughtful mind. Just as you see the Christ, so the Buddhist will see the Buddha, and the Hindu his own particular deity. They are all projections of the mind's conditioning, and one must be free from that conditioning, and the freeing of the mind from its conditioning is part of meditation.

I have been discussing for the last two or three weeks, among other things, the question of fear and sorrow. When the mind is afraid, or when it is burdened with sorrow, it cannot possibly be in a state of meditation. For a mind that would really understand the depth and the beauty of meditation, fear must cease, and there must be no sorrow of any kind. And when the mind is free from fear, from sorrow, from the whole psychological structure of society which is made up of ambition, greed, envy, the desire for success, the demand for power, position, prestige—when all that has been broken down and understood, then the brain becomes very quiet. But you can understand and be free of all this turmoil only when you are aware of it without effort. If you struggle to change fear into courage, you cannot understand the whole significance of fear. As I have explained, the human brain is the result of centuries of conditioned, animalistic existence. That brain has to be completely quiet, and it cannot be made quiet through discipline, through enforcement. But it is quiet of its own accord, naturally, easily, gracefully, when there is an understanding of all these things that I have been talking about.

So it is now fairly clear that for the mind to be in a state of meditation there must be a total elimination of all conflict. Conflict exists as long as there is a division between the thinker and the thought. For most of us the thinker is separate from thought, the experiencer is different from that which is experienced. As long as this division exists, conflict is inevitable because this division is the origin of conflict. That is why it is absolutely necessary to bring about a complete cessation of this division. The thinker is the censor, the conditioned outcome of centuries of egocentric activity; he is the center of fear, of conflict, of sorrow.

I am going step by step into what is meditation. Please don't wait until the end, hoping to have a complete description of how to meditate. What we are doing now is part of meditation.

Now, what one has to do is to be aware of the thinker, and not try to resolve the contradiction and bring about an integration between thought and the thinker. The thinker is the psychological entity who has accumulated experience as knowledge; he is the time-bound center which is the result of ever-changing environmental influence, and from this center he looks, he listens, he experiences. As long as one does not understand the structure and the anatomy of this center, there must always be conflict, and a mind in conflict cannot possibly understand the depth and the beauty of meditation.

In meditation there can be no thinker, which means that thought must come to an end—the thought which is urged forward by the desire to achieve a result. Meditation has nothing to do with achieving a result. It is not a matter of breathing in a particular way, or looking at your nose, or awakening the power to perform certain tricks, or any of the rest of that immature nonsense. But if you have been listening to these talks with total attention and have more or less grasped the significance of what is being said, I think you will find there is a state of mind which is always meditative. Meditation is not something apart from life. When you are driving a car or sitting in a bus, when you are chatting aimlessly, when you are walking by yourself in a wood or watching a butterfly being carried along by the wind—to be choicelessly aware of all that is part of meditation.

There is another thing I would like to point out, and that is the difference between concentration and attention. When a child is given a new toy, his concentration is complete; he is quiet, he ceases to be mischievous because he becomes wholly absorbed in that toy and loses all interest in everything else. Now, most of us want toys which will absorb us. Whether it is the acquisition of knowledge, or the symbol of the Savior, or a beautiful picture, or the stimulation of the Mass, or the practice of a certain form of discipline such as the control of respiration, and so on—all these are toys which absorb the mind; and being absorbed, limited, taken over by the toy, the mind becomes concentrated. And even when you reject these toys, as most intelligent people do, there is still the urge to be absorbed in your own thought, in your own experience and knowledge. This absorption also brings about a certain concentration, but if you observe it, you will see that such concentration is a process of exclusion.

There is still another form of concentration, which is that of the schoolboy who wants to look out of the window but is told by his teacher that he must read a certain book. The boy knows that if he is to pass the examination, he must not continually gaze out of the window, so he trains himself to study. This does bring about a form of concentration, but like the concentration of absorption, it is based on exclusion, and also on resistance. For a mind that has thus learned to be concentrated, there is always a distraction, and therefore the mind is always fighting that distraction. That is what most of us do when we concentrate, is it not? We resist all so-called distractions in order to concentrate on something to which we think we ought to give our attention.

Now, there is a vast difference between concentration and attention. When you are in the state of attention, you can listen to that stream, hear the train go by, be aware of the rustle of the wind among the leaves and the movements of the people about you, see the various colors people are wearing, notice the shape of this tent, and still be completely attentive to what the speaker is saying. The mind is then without a border, and such a mind can concentrate without exclusion, but a mind that has merely learned to concentrate, cannot be attentive. This state of attention without resistance, without conflict, without forcing the mind into a predetermined groove, is absolutely necessary. And when you have gone that far, you will see for yourself how easily and gently the silence of the mind comes into being.

The silence that most of us are seeking is the silence of decay and death. The so-called peace which is achieved by monks and other people who withdraw from the world is generally a condition of complete insensitivity, a state of dullness. They do experience a certain silence of the mind, but it is the dead silence of exclusion. Whereas, the silence I am speaking of is a state of attention in which every sound, every movement, every nuance of thought and feeling is perceived.

If there is an experiencer or an observer of silence, it is not silence but something projected by the mind. In complete silence there is no experiencer of that silence, and then there is a state of attention in which you hear the airplane flying overhead, the train going by, and yet the mind is completely attentive to what is being said; it is observing, listening to everything. Out of this immense silence and quietude, in which the mind is no longer seeking, expecting, wanting, demanding, there comes a movement which is creation beyond time, beyond all expression. It is not the creation of the writer, of the painter, of the musician—it is something which far transcends all that. This creation is energy—energy as death, energy as love—and in it there is no beginning and no end. It comes about only through self-knowing, and this whole process is meditation.

I hope you are not being mesmerized by my words. If you really go into yourself, ruthlessly putting aside all the pettiness, the envy, the greed, the desire for fame, dying to whatever form of technique or talent you have gathered, so that you are nobody at all—then you will know for yourself what this creation is. But if you are merely influenced by another, that is not meditation.

Question: Is the innocency you have described different from meditation?

KRISHNAMURTI: At some of the meetings we have had here, I have talked about the state of innocency. I have said that an innocent mind is one that is not caught in the psychological structure of society, and is therefore free of conflict; it is not weighed down by remembrances of things past—which is not a state of amnesia; it is no longer held in technique, though technique is necessary. And the questioner wants to know if there is a difference between this state of innocency and the meditation which I have been talking about this morning.

One of our difficulties, it seems to me, is that we get hold of a word like *innocency,* or *immensity,* or *creation,* and then try to relate everything to that particular word. As I have said, the word is not the thing. The word *meditation* is not the state of meditation; the word *innocency* is not the state of innocency. But when there is the state of innocency, it is also the state of meditation. You cannot come to that state of innocency as long as you are ambitious, as long as your mind is petty, as long as you are caught in the psychological structure of society and are nothing but an embodied technique—which is what most of us are. We have a job because we have got to earn a livelihood, and we are little better than machines, however clever, cunning, or subtle we may be. A machine-like mind is not an innocent mind. The computers, the electronic brains are probably very innocent, but they are fashioned out of metals, they are not living beings as we are. Eventually a machine may be invented that will have a kind of life of its own, and perhaps they are very close to it already. But to reduce ourselves to the point where we function like machines in our technological efforts, in our acquisition of knowledge, in our piling up of experience, does not bring about innocency. Innocency is that state in which the mind is always young and fresh. An innocent mind has no fear of death, no fear of any kind, and it is therefore free of time.

Question: Perhaps we can be in this state of attention or meditation while we are awake during the day, but what happens when we go to sleep?

KRISHNAMURTI: Are we awake during the day? We assume that we are. Are we awake when we are caught in habits of thought, in routine activities and behavior? When you constantly condemn, compare, judge, evaluate, or when you think of yourself as belonging to a particular race, nationality, culture, or religion, are you awake? If you are caught in habit and are therefore not awake during the day, then sleep is merely a continuation of that same state of mind. Then it really makes very little difference whether you are physically asleep or awake. You may go to church regularly and repeat a prayer, or you may chant a mantra as they do in India, or you may do any of the other things that so-called religious people do; or you may repeat slogans like the politicians, or look at life from the artist's point of view, but is any of that a state of awakened intelligence? To be in a state of awakened intelligence is to be a light unto oneself. Then one has no nationality, no church, no god; one doesn't depend on music or painting, on the beauty of the mountains; nor does one depend on family, on husband, wife, children. And if one is inwardly so completely awake, what then is sleep? What is the significance of sleep when both the conscious and the unconscious are totally awake?

It is the dull mind, the mind caught in conflict, that dreams. Dreams are merely hints from the unconscious. A mind that is totally awake during the day, observing everything within and around itself, but not from a center of judgment or condemnation—when such a mind sleeps, it does not dream at all. If while you are awake—getting on a bus, listening to a concert, walking alone, talking with friends—you are instantly aware without reaction of every hint or intimation from the unconscious, if all the things that are going on inwardly as well as outwardly are immediately observed, recognized, and understood, then when you go to sleep, the mind is quiet, and because it is quiet, it reaches into great depths. And you will find that that state of deep silence while you are asleep brings a freshness, an innocency, so that the next day is different, there is a newness about it. But all this demands an astonishing, inward awareness.

Question: Are there unconditioned visions?

KRISHNAMURTI: Are not those two words contradictory? Are the implications of the word *visions* and the word *conditioned* essentially different? As I have explained, sir, our minds are conditioned, and we can't help being conditioned. From childhood our minds are shaped by our education, at home as well as at school and college, and later they are further conditioned by society. We are Christians, Jews, Hindus, Buddhists, communists, and God knows what else. Whatever visions we may have will be in terms of our religious conditioning, and the more refined that conditioning is, the more refined will be our visions. We have already discussed what it means for the mind to be unconditioned, so I won't go into that now. A mind that is unconditioned has no visions. God is not a vision.

Comment: I do not see the relationship between death and sorrow and the state of meditation.

KRISHNAMURTI: To see the whole significance of sorrow, not just verbally or intellectually, but to go into it very deeply and be free of its corroding action within oneself, the mind must be in a state of meditation. All real inquiry is a state of meditation. To understand the meaning of death—which is to die every day to one's talents, to one's qualities, to one's work, to one's memories—one has to be choicelessly attentive, fully aware; and this state of choiceless attention is meditation. There is no difference between meditation and the understanding of sorrow, for the understanding of sorrow is the beginning of meditation. To go very far in meditation, the mind must be free of all its psychological entanglements. In this state of freedom there is a movement which is not of distance or of time, and that movement is creation. All this is part of meditation.

Question: Is the creativeness of great artists different from the movement of creation which you are talking about?

KRISHNAMURTI: I am afraid it is, but this is a question I don't want to go into this morning. The movement of creation does not demand any expression; it does not depend on any technique, on any gift or talent. On the contrary, every gift, every talent must come to an end for the mind to find this immense creation. You will ask, "If the movement of creation you are talking about cannot be put on a canvas, if it cannot be expressed in a poem, in architecture, or in music, then what is the value of it?" It has no value whatsoever. It is not marketable. You cannot get any benefit from it. It is something absolute. The mind may dream of translating the movement of creation into action; it may want to express it in words, put it in a frame, but that it can never do. The artist may at rare moments have a feeling of something beyond his own petty little self, but this is not the movement of creation. That immensity can come into being only when the 'me' is completely absent and the mind is therefore truly religious.

August 9, 1962

Tenth Talk in Saanen

I think all of us are aware of the extraordinary outward changes that are taking place in the world, but very few of us change inwardly, deeply. Either we follow a certain pattern of thought established by another, or we create our own ideational frame within which we function, and most of us seem to find it extremely difficult to break out of this conceptual pattern. We live from concept to concept, from idea to idea, and we think that this movement is a change; but, as one can see if one observes it rather closely, it is really no change at all. Thought does not bring about deep changes. Thought can be the cause of certain superficial adjustments; it can create and conform to a new pattern, but inwardly there is no significant change: we are what we have always been and will probably continue to be. These outward adjustments and conformities always correspond to our inward instability, our inward uncertainty, our inward sense of fear and the urge to escape from the dark, unexplored corners of our own minds.

If I may, I would most earnestly request that those who are taking notes cease to take them. You are not here to collect a lot of ideas. We are not dealing with ideas; on the contrary, we are breaking them down. We are shattering the pattern which the petty little mind has established for its own security. So, may I most respectfully suggest that you do not take notes but actually experience or live that which is being said, and to do this you have to listen easily, pleasantly, crisply, without effort. Not that you must agree—we have been through all that, and I won't repeat what has already been said about it.

This morning I would like to go into something which I feel is very important, but first I think we have to realize that the outward movement and the inward movement of life are essentially the same. It is important not to divide this movement as the outward world and the inward world. It is like a tide that goes out very far and comes in very deeply. It is when we divide this movement of life as the outer and the inner, the material and the spiritual, that all the contradictions and conflicts arise. But if we actually experience this movement as a unitary process, which includes both the outer and the inner, then there is no conflict. The inward movement is no longer a reaction to the outer; it is no longer an escape from the world, so one does not withdraw into a monastery or into some ivory tower of isolation. When one has understood the significance of the outer, then the inward movement ceases to be the opposite of the outer; then it is not a reaction and can therefore penetrate much more deeply. So I think this is the first thing to understand: that one cannot divide the outer from the inner. It is a unitary process, and there is great beauty in perceiving its nondivisibility. But to go into this unitary process more extensively, one must understand the nature of humility.

You know, most of us actually do not know what it is to be humble, to have the sense of complete humility. Humility is not a virtue to be cultivated. The moment you cultivate humility, there is no humility. Either you are humble, or you are not. To have the sense of complete humility, you must perceive this outward and inward movement as a unitary process. You have to understand the meaning of life as a whole—the life of sorrow, of pleasure, of pain, the life which is everlastingly seeking a resting place, searching for something which it calls God or by some other name. You have to understand all this, and not reject one part of it and accept another. To understand is to be in a state of choiceless awareness. It means listening choicelessly to your wife, to your husband, to the wind among the trees, to that water rushing by; it means seeing the mountains, being negatively aware of everything. In this state of negative awareness there is an understanding of the outer and the inner as a total, unitary movement, and with that understanding there comes a great sense of humility. And humility is important because a mind that has no humility can never learn. It can accumulate knowledge, gather more and more information, but knowledge and information are superficial. I do not quite see why we take such pride in knowing. It is all in the encyclopedia, and it is silly to accumulate knowledge when it is used for personal pride and arrogance.

So humility is not something to be achieved, but you will come to it naturally, easily, gracefully when this movement of the outer and the inner is perceived to be one total process; and then you will begin to learn. Learning is the state of a mind which never accumulates experience as memory, however pleasant the experience may be; it is the state of a mind which never avoids a sorrow, a frustration. Such a mind is always in a state of learning; such a mind has humility. And you will find that out of humility comes discipline. Most of us are not disciplined. We conform, adjust, imitate, suppress, sublimate, but none of this is discipline. Conformity is not discipline; it is merely the outcome of fear, and therefore it makes the mind narrow, stupid, dull. I am talking of a discipline which comes into being spontaneously when there is this extraordinary sense of humility and the mind is therefore in a state of learning. Then you don't have to impose a discipline on the mind because the state of learning is a discipline in itself.

I hope I am making this very clear. I am not talking about the mechanical discipline of the soldier who is trained to kill or be killed, nor of the discipline of technique. Offices, shops, factories, laboratories, and the various functions of skilled labor all demand efficiency, and in order to function efficiently in a particular job, one disciplines oneself to conform to the required pattern. I don't mean any of that. I am talking of a discipline which is entirely different, a discipline which comes by itself when one understands this extraordinary process of life, not in fragments, but as an undivided whole. When you understand yourself, not departmentalized as a musician, an artist, a speaker, a yogi, and all the rest of it, but as a total human being, then out of your own understanding there is a state of learning, and this very state of learning is itself a discipline in which there is no conformity, no imitation. The mind is not being shaped to fit into a particular pattern, and therefore it is free, and in this freedom there is a spontaneous sense of discipline. I think it is very important to understand this, because for most of us freedom implies doing whatever we desire to do, or obeying our instincts, or following what we unfortunately call our intuition. But none of that is freedom.

Freedom implies totally emptying the mind of the known. I do not know if you have ever tried this for yourself. What matters is to free the mind from the known, or rather for the mind to free itself from the known. This does not mean that the mind must free itself from factual knowledge. In one degree or another you must have such knowledge. You obviously cannot free yourself from the knowledge of where you live, and so on. But the mind can free itself from the background of tradition, of accumulated experiences, and from the various conscious and unconscious urges which are the reactions of that background; and to be completely free from that background is to deny, to put aside, to die to the known. If you do this, you will discover for yourself what a really significant thing freedom is.

What I am talking about is a total inward freedom in which there is no psychological dependence, no attachment of any kind. As long as there is attachment, there is no freedom because attachment implies a sense of inward loneliness, inward vacuity, which demands an outward relationship upon which to depend. A free mind is not attached, though it may have relationships. But freedom cannot come into being if there is not this state of learning which brings with it a deep inward discipline not based on ideation or on any conceptual pattern. When the mind is constantly freeing itself by dying to the known from moment to moment, out of that there comes a spontaneous discipline, an austerity born of comprehension. Real austerity is a marvelous thing; it is not the dry, wretched discipline of destructive self-denial that most of us imagine it to be.

I do not know if you have ever felt this extraordinary sense of being completely austere—which has nothing whatsoever to do with the discipline of control, adjustment, conformity. And there must be this austerity, because in this austerity there is great beauty and intense love. It is this austerity that is passionate, and this austerity comes only when there is an inward aloneness.

Now, I think one must see very clearly the difference between loneliness and aloneness. Most of us are lonely, as we well know if we are at all aware of ourselves. Perhaps you have had the experience of suddenly feeling cut off from everything, of having no relationship with anything. You may be in a crowd, or with your family, or at a party, or you may be walking by yourself beside a river, and suddenly you have a sense of complete isolation. That sense of isolation is essentially a state of fear, and it is always there, lurking in the background of the mind. From this fear we constantly escape by doing all kinds of things: we pick up a book, listen to the radio, watch television, drink, chase after women, turn to the pursuit of God, and all the rest of it. It is out of our loneliness and fear of loneliness that every action and reaction takes place. This loneliness is entirely different from aloneness.

The lonely, fearful mind is swayed by innumerable influence; like a piece of clay, it is malleable, it can be shaped, forced into any mold. But aloneness is complete freedom of the mind from all influence: the influence of your wife, of your husband, of tradition, of the church, of the state. It is freedom from the influence of what you read, and from the influence of your own unconscious demands. In other words, aloneness is complete freedom from the known. It is the state of learning which comes when the mind understands the total process of life, and it brings with it a discipline which is not the discipline of the church, or of the army, or of the specialist, or of the athlete, or of the man who is pursuing knowledge. It is discipline born of a deep sense of humility, and there cannot be humility if the mind is not completely alone.

What has been said up to this point is reasonable, logical, sane, healthy, and if we have understood the words and also gone behind the words, I think we will have had no difficulty in understanding what the speaker is trying to convey. But something else is demanded, something much more is required. What has been described so far is like laying the foundation of a house, and it is only a foundation, nothing more. But that foundation has to be laid, and it must be laid with passion, with intensity, with beauty, and therefore with love. That foundation cannot be laid out of despair, out of conflict, or out of a desire to achieve some stupid result, because then the mind is not in a state of freedom from the known.

I wonder if you have ever been aware of how you gather, of how the mind holds on to innumerable little experiences. The mind provides the soil in which passing experiences take root and further shape the mind. Almost every experience leaves its mark, and therefore experience only perpetuates the mind's limitation. But when, having laid the right foundation by seeing and understanding its own limitation through this process, the mind—easily, without any conflict—frees itself from the known, then there is the coming into being of a movement which is creation.

Most of us are seeking God, and our God is merely a matter of belief. That word spelled the other way round is "dog," which would do just as well for what we call God. But we have been trained from childhood to accept that word, and organized religion, with its two thousand or ten thousand years of propaganda, has conditioned the mind to believe in what that word is supposed to represent. And we accept that belief so easily, just as in the communist world they accept the belief that there is no God because they have been brought up in it. That is another kind of propaganda. The believer and the nonbeliever are the same because they are both slaves to propaganda.

Now, to find out if there is or there is not God, you must destroy everything in yourself which is the outcome of propaganda. What we now call religion has been put together, built up through the centuries by man in his fear, in his greed, in his ambition, in his hope and despair. And to find out if there is or there is not God, the mind must totally destroy, without a motive, all the accumulations of the past; it must wholly erase all belief and disbelief and completely cease to search. The mind must be empty of the known, empty of the savior, empty of all the gods that have been manufactured by thought and carved in wood or in stone. It is only when the mind is free from the known that it can be in a state of complete quietness which is not induced by breathing, by exercise, by tricks, by drugs. And one has to go that far—but it is really not "far," there is no distance. But to abolish distance, time must cease, and time ceases only when there is the knowing of oneself as one actually is from fact to fact. In this extraordinary freedom, which begins with self-knowing, there is a movement—a movement which is immeasurable, beyond all concepts. This movement is creation, and when the mind has come to this movement, it will discover for itself that love, death, and creation are the same.

Question: Is not freedom like the air, and have we not built for ourselves a tent like this one which prevents the air from coming in? We have only to pierce the tent, and then the air will come pouring in.

KRISHNAMURTI: You know, similes and verbal pictures are most dangerous because they give us the feeling that we have understood when we are not actually in that state. It is merely a theory. But here we are not talking theoretically; we are not imagining something. As I explained at the very beginning of these talks, we are dealing with psychological facts. If you do not face the psychological facts of your own mind, then the tent, the air, the soul, and all these similes and theories come tumbling in and you are destroyed.

Sir, when a man is desperately hungry, what is the good of describing to him a tasty dish or a delicate savor? He wants food. Theories and descriptions are meaningless to a man who is hungry to find out for himself what is true. But unfortunately, most of us are not hungry in that sense. We are psychologically well-fed because we are full of our experiences, and we have found shelter in dogma, in belief. We feel secure in belonging to this group or that group, to this church or that. And when we do have a feeling of discontent, which is a very rare thing, we promptly smother it by seeking something which will give us immediate satisfaction. What matters is to be tremendously hungry psychologically, and to remain in that state of hunger without going insane or becoming neurotic. The question is not how to feed that hunger, because the moment you feed it, you are lost. You can feed it very easily with words, with theories, with books, with churches, with—oh—anything. But if you remain in that state of deep psychological hunger without despair, it is like a burning flame that will destroy every false thing until nothing is left but ashes; and out of that emptiness something real can take place.

Question: Does the change of which you are speaking come about through will? Is there a motive behind it?

KRISHNAMURTI: Now, what is will? Please don't theorize; don't quote what somebody has said. Let us find out what that word means. To have the will to do something means that you want to do it. So will is desire, is it not? Many desires, many urges, many resistances, many demands put together give one this sharpened instrument, this extraordinary sense of volition which is the will to do something and to go through with it.

We all know that through will we can force ourselves to do certain things. If I say, "I am not going to be angry tomorrow," and I exercise my will very strongly in that direction, I can prevent myself from being angry tomorrow. But that is not change; as I pointed out earlier, that is merely conforming to a desired pattern. Surely, any change brought about through will is no change at all; it is merely the continuation, in a different framework, of what has been. If I change through a motive—because my mother likes it, or because society wants me to do it, or because there is some profit in it, and so on—that change is the result of persuasion, influence, reward; therefore, it is not really a change but only a modified perpetuation of the past. Now, if I understand the whole process of both the change through will and the change through motive so that these two processes can die and are effortlessly put aside, then out of that understanding there comes a change which is not premeditated, which is not brought about through influence or through various urges, compulsions; and this change is really a total destruction of the known.

Comment: This change you are talking about seems to be a bit of a trick! If I say to myself, "I want to change," I have a motive, so I must change without wanting to change. It's the same problem with ambition: one can't get rid of ambition by wanting to get rid of it. So the whole thing can only be a trick.

KRISHNAMURTI: Sir, you mentioned the word *ambition.* Most of us are ambitious in one degree or another, and we all know the implications of ambition: competition, ruthlessness, an utter lack of love, and all the rest of it. Now, if I am ambitious—ambitious for position, power, ambitious to be somebody in this world or in the so-called spiritual world, and so on—and I have begun to see for myself that it is stupid to be ambitious, how am I to be entirely free of ambition? How is this radical change to be brought about? You may not agree, but just listen to me quietly.

Our education from childhood is built round this idea of becoming somebody, achieving success, and very few of us have ever learned to love what we are doing. You know, when you love what you are doing you work without motive, without the urge to be a success. When you love somebody, you don't think about what you are going to get out of that person. You don't love that person because he or she gives you money, or position, or some other form of satisfaction. You just love—if such a love exists. Now, if I really love what I am doing, there is no ambition. Then I never compare myself with another; I never say that somebody else is doing better or worse than I am. I love my work; therefore, my mind, my heart, my whole being is in it. But we are not educated in that way. Society demands so many scientists, so many engineers, so many technicians, or what you will, and we are shoved through the mill of what is called college so that we can fit into the required pattern.

To love what you are doing implies the total absence of ambition. You do not suppress ambition through will, or try to get rid of it through a motive, a purpose. Ambition falls away from you as a dead leaf falls from the tree. It happens when you love.

Have I answered your question, sir?

Comment: Thanks.

Question: How can one prevent the conditioning of children?

KRISHNAMURTI: First of all, if you are the parent or the educator, you have to be aware of your own conditioning, obviously. But even then, can you prevent the conditioning of the child? Society insists on conditioning the child. Governments with their propaganda, organized religions with their dogmas, beliefs, and codes of morality, the psychological structure of what we call society—the whole of this is constantly impinging, not only on the mind of the child, but on the minds of us all. Modern society being what it is, you can't keep your child away from school, and the school is not interested in leaving the child's mind unconditioned; on the contrary, it wants his mind to be conditioned according to a certain pattern. So there is a battle going on between the desire of the intelligent parent not to condition the child's mind, and the determination of society to condition it. The church wants to train the child to believe certain things; the Protestants, the Catholics, the Hindus, and all the rest of the organized, propagandistic religions are out to condition his mind. And the child wants to conform; he doesn't want to be different because it's much more fun to join the Boy Scouts, or whatever it is, and be just like the rest of the crowd. You know all this well enough. And what are you to do?

At home one can begin to point out to the child the stupidity of merely conforming; one can discuss, argue, constantly explain to him how important it is not to accept everything that society demands, but rather to question, to break through the values that are obviously false, and not become a mere delinquent. To be delinquent is to revolt within the pattern, and that is very easy to do. Real revolt is to understand and not be carried away by the innumerable influences which are constantly impinging upon the mind. You can explain these influences to the child so that when he reads a comic book, or listens to the radio, or watches television, he is aware of them, and does not let them destroy his mind. This demands awareness on your own part; it means that you yourself must work at breaking down your own conditioning, for only then can you help the child.

Question: Is what you are talking about the beginning of a new man? If it is, will that new man go forward, and will his problems be entirely different?

KRISHNAMURTI: I am going to answer your question, but I must hesitate before I do so. You see, I am working, but unfortunately many of you are apparently just listening. If you also were working intensely, furiously, with delight, as I am doing, then your brain would be rather weary too, and you would not be so eager to ask another question.

What do you mean when you talk about going forward? Do you mean making progress? I think there is progress only in the material world. From the bullock cart to the jet plane, to the rocket that will go to the moon—this is progress in technology. But is there progress inwardly? Is there "spiritual" progress, which implies the idea that through time one will become something psychologically? Surely, this very idea of becoming, progressing, arriving, creates a problem. You want to arrive, and you may not, so there is always the shadow of frustration. A mind that is free, a mind that has understood the urge to progress through time, has no problem any more. If there are problems, it meets each problem as it arises, but it does not create or project problems for itself. But most of us are burdened with problems of our own making.

Let me put it differently. When the mind is free from the known, it is a new mind, an innocent mind. It is in a state of creation which is immeasurable, nameless, beyond time. And we have been discussing at these meetings what it is that prevents us from coming naturally, easily, gracefully to that state. It cannot be invited because a petty mind cannot invite the immense. All pettiness has to come to an end, and then the other is. The mind cannot imagine that state of immensity. From its pettiness, from its shallowness it can project something which it thinks is beautiful, but that which it projects is still part of its own ugliness. The psychological structure of society is what we are. When that structure is understood and there is freedom from it, then the nameless, that in which there is no time, no progress, comes into being.

Question: How can a conditioned mind understand what is true?

KRISHNAMURTI: It cannot. Let us make it very simple. Suppose I am nationalistic, bound to my country, to my sovereign, caught up in my petty little identification with a particular race. How can such a mind understand a state which is completely beyond all this? It cannot. So the mind has to understand its own nationalism, break it down, destroy it, completely put it aside; and for most of us that is an extraordinarily difficult thing to do. Nationalism is merely an expansion of our own little selves. You identify yourself with your country because you are small and the country is big. The tribal entity likes to be identified with something bigger—and that is what we are all doing. You may not identify yourself with your country, but you want to commit yourself to some supreme purpose or action; you want to be identified with an idea, or with God. Whether you commit yourself to your country or to your family or become a monk and commit yourself to God, it is exactly the same; it is all conditioning. And to break down this conditioning requires, as we have seen, a choiceless awareness, watching every movement of thought—just playing with it, watching it.

August 12, 1962

Saanen, Switzerland, 1963

First Talk in Saanen

As there are going to be ten talks, I think we should lay the right foundation at the first talk, not only verbally, but also, if possible, in a different and more significant way. This different way will require the active cooperation of all of us, and not just a passive listening to what is being said, which is really not of very great significance. But if as we listen, we can deliberately and seriously examine our own hearts and minds and proceed to lay the right foundation in ourselves, then these meetings will have a great deal of significance.

Now, I would like, if I may, to explain what I mean by that word *serious*. Most of us think we are serious, that is, given to the deliberate consideration of life's problems—and to some extent we are; otherwise, we would not be here. You have spent a lot of money, energy, and time, and have put up with the unpleasantness of travel in order to come here, so you must be somewhat serious; but let us find out together what we mean by that word.

You know, a petty mind, a mind that is shallow, can also become very serious; but when it becomes serious it is rather absurd. I do not know if you have ever noticed that empty-minded people are often very serious. They use a lot of words; they put on a lot of airs, and for such a mind everything becomes a problem to be studied, analyzed, gone into; but it still remains a very shallow mind. Then there is the mind that has read a great deal, that can cleverly argue, analyze, that is able to quote from a great store of information. As you know very well, that type of mind is cunning, sharp, capable, but I would not call it a serious mind any more than I would the shallow mind that attempts to be serious. There is also the mind that is sentimental, emotional, easily stirred to a superficial kind of feeling which is called devotion; but, to me, such a mind is not serious either.

By a serious mind I mean a mind that is deeply religious. A religious mind can be intellectual; it can argue, discuss, but it has its foundation at quite a different level altogether. A religious mind is not one that belongs to any particular society, group, or organized religion. Such people are not serious at all, though they may become monks and nuns and go to church every day, or three times a day, or whatever it is they do. I am not being dogmatic or intolerant, but you will see as we go along how necessary, how imperative it is to have a mind that is not merely seeking, because a mind that is seeking is always in conflict. I will go into all this during these ten talks.

What is important is to have a mind that is trying—or rather, I would prefer not to use the word *try,* because that is a bourgeois word, if I may say so without implying condemnation. I do not give to the word *bourgeois* the meaning that the communists give. I mean only that it is an ordinary, dull mind which says, "I will try." Seriousness is not a question of trying; it is a question of being.

I call that mind serious which is constantly looking, observing, being aware of itself and others, watching its own gestures, words, the way it talks, the way it walks; and which is also aware of the things around it, the pressures, the strains, the influence of environment, of the culture in which it has been brought up, and of all its own conditioning. Such a mind, being totally aware, I call a serious mind. Only such a mind can deliberately consider and give its energy to discover something more than the things which have been put together by man—something which may be called God, or what you will.

So I feel that to be really serious is absolutely necessary during these three weeks if we are to arrive at an understanding of the things we are talking about. As I said, most of us think we are serious, but I'm afraid that the quality we regard as seriousness must be completely changed because in the sense in which I am using the word, we are not serious. Many of you have heard me repeatedly, fortunately or unfortunately, for the last forty years, and had you been serious, you would have been completely transformed. And the world needs such a transformation, a complete mutation of the mind. But that mutation cannot take place by any deliberate practice, or by adhering to a series of cunning theological or practical ideas. The transformation to which I am referring is not brought about by idea—"idea" being a rationalized, logical conclusion, a system of organized words and thoughts. However much one may organize thought and act upon it, through that thought and that action the mutation cannot take place. It is something totally different; it is a completely different quality, and about this I am going to talk during these several meetings.

Now, one of the principal questions which one has to put to oneself is this: How far or to what depth can the mind penetrate into itself? That is the quality of seriousness because it implies being aware of the whole structure of one's own psychological being—with its urges, its compulsions, its desire to fulfill and its frustrations, its miseries, strains and anxieties, its struggles, sorrows, and the innumerable problems that it has. The mind that perpetually has problems is not a serious mind at all, but the mind that understands each problem as it arises and dissolves it immediately so that it is not carried over to the next day—such a mind is serious.

But unfortunately we are educated wrongly. We are never really serious except when some crisis arises, when some dreadful demand is made upon us, or we receive some terrible blow. Then we do try to be serious, we try to do something—but then it is too late. Please believe me, I am not being cynical; I am merely pointing out facts.

What are most of us interested in? If we have money, we turn to so-called spiritual things, or to intellectual amusements, or we discuss art, or take up painting to express ourselves. If we have no money, our time is taken up day after day with earning it, and we are caught in that misery, in the endless routine and boredom of it. Most of us are trained to function mechanically in some job, year in and year out. We have responsibilities, a wife and children to provide for, and caught up in this mad world, we try to be serious, we try to become religious, we go to church, we join this religious organization or that—or perhaps we hear about these meetings and because we have holidays, we turn up here. But none of that will bring about this extraordinary transformation of the mind.

The world is in a state of crisis, and there is disintegration, degeneration. We are caught up in this wave of degeneration, and we seem to be utterly incapable of stepping out of it. Now, if these talks are to be of any value, of any significance whatever, we must discuss what to do, how to step out of this wave of degeneration. Most of us are getting old; those who have heard me, fortunately or unfortunately, for the past thirty or forty years are obviously much older than they were when they first began to listen. They have physically degenerated, and mentally—well, they know whether they have degenerated or not. And during these talks, and during the questions and answers afterwards, I would like us to discover for ourselves, without any shadow of doubt, the extraordinary energy which arises spontaneously and which will naturally and inevitably push us out of this wave of degeneration. Not that we are going to become any younger physically—that is one of those absurd, fanciful, romantic ideas. I am talking of an inward state of mind that does not degenerate.

Degeneration comes when there is conflict of any kind, and it is conflict that makes you a so-called individual. Through conflict you develop character, and within the psychological structure of the present society, you have conflict and so you do have character. There, character is resistance. To leave the world and become a monk, you need character. But we are not talking of character, which is comparatively easy to acquire. We are talking of a mind that is completely free from conflict, and it is only such a mind—a mind that is totally free from conflict of every kind, conscious as well as unconscious—that has no problem. If any problem arises, it can face that problem and dissolve it immediately. Such a mind is individual in the true sense of the word; it is unique. And it seems to me extraordinarily important that we should be such individuals—but we are not.

By individuality I mean a mind that is completely alone. Though it has been through a thousand experiences, known a thousand memories, lived a thousand years, such a mind has faced itself and is no longer a slave to the psychological structure of society. It is alone—by which I do not mean that it is isolated. There is a vast difference between the two. The mind that isolates itself becomes neurotic. The isolated mind has identified itself with a particular idea or belief—that is, with a particular form of psychological comfort—and the more it isolates itself in this way, the more it hopes to be free of conflict. But the very process of isolation is conflict, is resistance. We will discuss this as we go along, but we are talking now about the mind which has become an individual through being aware of its own processes and understanding the structure, the psyche of itself, the conscious as well as the unconscious. It is possible to go beyond the unconscious, but this is not the moment to go into detail as to what the unconscious is, and how to go beyond it. What we are doing this morning is laying the foundation for further inquiry.

Now, only a mind that is completely alone can find reality. And there is a reality—not a theoretical reality, not something invented by the Christians or the Hindus or experienced by a few saints according to their particular conditioning, but a reality, an immensity which can be discovered only by a mind that has seen through its own ways and understood itself.

You know, it is an extraordinary thing to find out for oneself what it means to understand something immediately, without a lot of words—to see a fact as a fact, completely, without argumentation. From that act of seeing, one can argue, discuss, go into detail; but one first has to have that astonishing intensity of seeing because it is the very act of seeing—seeing without thought—that brings about transformation. This may sound rather absurd, but it is not, as you will find when we go into it later.

We look at everything, we listen to everything, as you are listening now. You hear only words, and the words produce certain reactions, conscious or unconscious, and those reactions interpret what you hear. You already know what the speaker is talking about because you have heard him for thirty years, or you have read a great deal, not only about what he is saying, but about other things as well. From that background the words bring forth a response, and that response prevents you from listening, prevents you from seeing. I wonder if you have ever noticed, when you suddenly see something beautiful—a majestic mountain, or a swift-running river, or a lovely smile on a child's face—how you look at it, how you see it. At the first moment of seeing it, there is no thought—the thing is too marvelous for words. But a second later the verbalization takes place, and you begin to interpret, translate; you go back to your memory. All such action prevents seeing, prevents listening.

Now, even though you have heard me umpteen times, can we, as we go along in these talks three times a week, find out for ourselves what is this act of seeing, this act of listening? If we can do that, everything else follows because that very act brings about a transformation. But to see, to listen, the mind must be completely and spontaneously quiet—not forced, not drilled into quietness. It is only a really quiet mind that can listen, that can see, not a mind that has innumerable problems. When the mind realizes that it cannot see because it has many problems, that very knowing that it cannot see brings about the act of seeing.

All this demands an extraordinary attention. When you can pay undivided attention, not just intellectual or verbal attention, but when your whole being—body, mind, and emotion—is attentive, you are then in a state of the highest sensitivity, and it is only such a mind that is virtuous.

Please do listen to this. The man who strives after virtue is not a virtuous man. The man who struggles to be good, kindly, is not good or kindly, because goodness, kindliness, or love comes only when the mind is so completely attentive that it has no conflict.

I hope we are going to understand all these things as we go along together for the next three weeks. Perhaps you will now ask questions relevant to what I have been talking about this morning, and we can discuss some of them.

Question: Is not the deterioration of the mind that is going on in each one of us the result of distraction?

KRISHNAMURTI: Now, sir, why are we distracted? And why shouldn't we be distracted? As I am talking, is it distraction to listen to that stream, to listen to the birds, to see the green leaves shining in the sun? Surely, it becomes a distraction only when you want to put everything aside in order to concentrate on what I am saying. Distraction implies conflict, doesn't it? You want to pay attention to what I am saying, but your mind wanders off to the bird, to the river, to the train, to the leaf. You object to this wandering off; you want to stop it, to bring the mind back, and so it becomes a distraction, a conflict. Whereas, if you can listen to the stream and at the same time listen to what is being said, there is no distraction, no contradiction. Being attentive, you are not fighting off distraction. The moment you fight distraction, you have conflict and therefore deterioration.

So, for a mind that is aware, there is no distraction. Experiment with me as I am talking. Listen to that stream, be aware of the bird that is singing, notice the leaf—if you can see it, as I can from here—that is shining in the sun; see all these people who are wearing different colors, looking in different directions, listening in different ways, and do not fret over the botheration of these flies. Then you will find there is no distraction at all, and so the mind is extraordinarily alert. But a mind that is constantly fighting off distraction because it wants to concentrate on something is in conflict, and therefore in a state of deterioration.

Question: Is it ever possible for the brain to be quiet?

KRISHNAMURTI: This is really quite an enormous problem because the brain is the result of time; it comes into being through association, through nervous responses, and it has accumulated for centuries a background of memory or instinctive knowledge from which it reacts. This is a fact; it is not my speculative explanation. The human brain has grown from that of the monkey, through the primitive to the so-called civilized man. It has learned; it has gathered tremendous experience. It knows when there is danger; it pursues pleasure and tries to avoid pain. It has innumerable desires, ambitions, drives, demands, all pulling in different directions.

Now, the question is: In view of all that, is it possible for the brain, which has accumulated an extraordinary amount of experience as memory, and which is neurologically sensitive, constantly listening, watching, feeling, interpreting—is it possible for such a brain to be completely quiet? Can it be alive, sensitive, yet completely still? I say it can, not theoretically, but actually; and it is only then that the mind, the brain, is capable of meditation. The act of meditation is a most marvelous thing—but I won't go into that this morning.

So the questioner asks, "Is it possible for the brain to be quiet—the brain which is so highly developed, with an enormous background of memory from which it constantly reacts? Being the outcome of association, experience, memory, the result of time, can the brain ever be still?" Most people are in a state of conflict; they are torn apart by innumerable desires: the desire to fulfill themselves through painting, writing, through doing this or that. They want to be known, to become somebody in this monstrous, stupid world. And is such a brain—which is both the conscious and the unconscious—capable of being totally silent? If so, then how is it to jump from one state to the other? We will discuss this problem as we go along.

Question: When one looks at a flower through association and memory, one immediately names it, one says it is a rose or a violet. Since this verbalization takes place so instantaneously, what can one do about it?

KRISHNAMURTI: Have you understood the question? Please, I am not being patronizing, but have you all understood the question? Yes? All right.

Now, doesn't this also happen to you? When you look at a flower, don't you immediately say it is a violet, it is this, it is that? When you look at a woman, at a man, at a friend, you say it is so-and-so, don't you? And when this naming process takes place, it prevents you from listening with a fresh mind to what that person is saying, or you are not really looking at the flower because your mind is caught up in a word, with all its past associations. So what is actually going on? We will analyze it a little bit and you will see.

When you see a certain flower, your immediate reaction is to say that it is a daffodil, because through time, through education, that particular flower has come to be associated in your mind with the word *daffodil*, and your memory responds instantly with that term. So what has happened? You have given to what you see a name; you say it is a daffodil, and through naming it, you have further fixed that image, with all its associations, in your memory. This process of naming prevents you from looking at the flower nonbotanically, that is, without the background of your botanical knowledge. Do you follow?

Now, is it possible to look without naming? Can one look at another human being without saying he is a German, he is a Russian, he is a communist, he is a capitalist, he is a Hindu, he is a Negro, he is this, he is that? Surely, to look without naming, one has to be free of words. Your mind is a slave to words because you cannot think without words. For any form of communication, you must use words, and every word has its associations, its shades of meaning. But you can't just ignore the word and look. You have to be aware in yourself of this extraordinary process of naming, of associating, you have to see the immense value we have given to words through education and memory. To perceive that whole process and to be free of it requires an extraordinary alertness. If you try—not "try," but if you do it, you will find out. It is meaningless to "try" something. Either you do it, or you don't.

Comment: When we see a flower, or a tree, there are generally two states of mind, one following the other. For a second or two we are not conscious of looking, we just look, but a moment later we begin to translate what we see in terms of our established ideas; we want to find out if it can be photographed, and so on.

KRISHNAMURTI: Quite right, sir. You look at that mountain, which is so immense, so magnificent, and the very beauty of it knocks out your consciousness and keeps it quiet for a second. Then you come out of that shock, and the whole process of memory comes into operation.

This question requires a great deal of consideration. During the first second or two, your consciousness is quiet as the result of an influence; the beauty of the tree, of the mountain, has overpowered you and made you quiet. But is that real quietness? Is that not a process which is going on in the world all the time? If you go to church, attend the Mass—the beauty, the pageantry of it makes you feel tremendously holy, awed, inspired, and you are quiet. But is that not a process of drugging the mind? Please follow this.

If something external, through the influence of its beauty, its majesty, its pomp, forces the mind to be quiet, is such a mind alert? Or is the alert mind one that is already silent when it sees the mountain, and not having been made silent by the beauty of what it sees, it does not get caught up in verbalization? Such a mind observes without naming; it is in a state of silence all the time—but I won't use the words "all the time" because you will misunderstand them. That is what you want—you want to achieve this state and be in it all the time, which is so utterly childish.

First see the problem, the beauty of the problem. We are for a moment made silent by an incident: by a motorcar accident, by seeing a majestic mountain or a beautiful tree, by the death of someone we love. And then begins the verbalizing process of naming, associating, of saying, "I am in sorrow; how beautiful; how terrible; what a lovely thing that is." You all know these two states: the state of enforced silence, followed by the state of perpetual verbalization. So the problem arises: How to achieve that state in which the mind can look without naming, that silence which is not brought about by somebody's greatness, or by the overwhelming grandeur of a mountain? I don't know if you have understood the problem.

Question: What is the relationship of the individual to society?

KRISHNAMURTI: "What is the relationship of the individual—the real individual about whom I have been talking—to society?" And what is our present relationship—the relationship of the so-called individual—to society? And what do we mean by relationship?

Let us begin with relationship. What do we mean by that word? To be related is to be in contact, to have communion with another who understands me and whom I understand; it is to have companionship, friendship with another. Whether it is a relationship between wife and husband, between parent and child, or the relationship of the individual to society, we mean by that word a sense of communication, a sense of contact, little or great, superficial or profound. I think that is what we generally mean by relationship.

Now, are we related to anyone? Are you related to your wife or husband? Please question it, don't merely assume that you are. To be related to someone, we must be in contact with that person, not just physically, but emotionally, intellectually—at all levels. And are we? I am afraid we are not. Our attitudes, our activities, our self-expressions, our pride, isolate us; and from that state of isolation we try to establish a relationship with another, with society. This is a fact; it is not my invention. We would like to be related, but we are not. In the process of what we call relationship, which is society, we think we are individuals because we have a name, a family, a bank account; our faces are different, we dress differently, and so on. All this gives us a peculiar sense of individuality. But are we really individuals, or merely the conditioned product of a particular society, of certain environmental influences?

To be an individual is to be unique, inwardly apart, quiet, alone. A mind that is alone has freed itself from all its conditioning. And what is its relationship to the mind which is conditioned? What is the relationship of a mind that is free to a mind that is not? Can there be a relationship between them? If you see and I do not, what is our relationship? You may help me, you may guide me, you may tell me this, that, or the other, but we can have a relationship—in the true sense of the word—only when we both see, that is, when we can communicate immediately on the same level at the same time. Surely, it is only then that there is a possibility of communion—which is love, is it not?

July 7, 1963

Second Talk in Saanen

I feel it is always rather difficult to communicate exactly what one wants to say. One has to use words. There are other forms of communication, but they are apt to be misleading and must be distrusted. Words, too, can be distorted; there are so many shades of meaning to each word, and when one is communicating something which is not purely objective, it demands a certain flexibility on the part of the listener, a certain subtlety of mind, a quality that the words themselves do not possess. Whatever the language that is being used, whether it is French, Italian, or English, it is always difficult, I think, to go beyond the words and really capture the significance of what the speaker wants to convey. It requires a great deal of determined consideration, a penetrative quality, an insight rather than mere argumentation, clever explanation, or subtle analysis.

To me, the most important thing in life is to have a religious mind, because then everything else comes into right relationship—everything: jobs, health, marriage, sex, love—and the innumerable problems and travails of life are understood. The religious mind is not something that you can easily get at by reading a few books, by attending a series of talks, or by drilling yourself into a certain attitude. But I feel one must have such a mind, and perhaps during these talks we may come upon it—not deliberately, not through any form of cultivation, or by developing a certain capacity, but come upon it darkly, unexpectedly, unknowingly.

The mind—which includes both the conscious and the unconscious—is, as we have observed, the field of a great deal of contradiction. It is caught up in an enormous striving, torn by many conflicts, struggles, clashes of desire, and such a mind can never understand what it is to be religious. Do what it will—go to church, read the sacred books, or do any of the other things we do in our juvenile attempts to find out if there is God, if there is a hereafter, and so on—such a mind can never come upon that extraordinary religious state. That is why I feel it is very important, especially during these three weeks, that we should be deeply aware of this inward field of conflict. I think that very few are fully conscious of this ceaseless battle which is going on within each one of us, and as I was pointing out the other day, the important thing is not what to do about it, but rather to see it, because the very act of seeing the thing is freedom from it.

So I want to discuss this morning the fact of conflict and degeneration—for the two go together; they are not separate. Where there is conflict, whether it is conscious or unconscious, deep or superficial, it does destroy the subtlety, the quickness, the sensitivity of the mind. Conflict makes for dullness, insensitivity. By conflict I mean having problems, and to be free of conflict, of contradictions, one has to understand, surely, this thing called consciousness, the mind, the thing which we are.

I am going to go into all this, not theoretically, not abstractly, or merely by way of explanation, but I am going to go into it, I hope, with your cooperation. That is, you and I are going to take the journey together; you are not merely listening to me, but in the very act of listening, you are observing the processes of your own consciousness.

You know, there are two ways of looking at something. Either you look at it because you have been told to look, and what to look for; or you look because you want to find out, and you begin to discover. When you are hungry, you eat; you do not have to be told. But to be told that you should eat and to feel hungry are two quite different matters. So we must be very clear on this point. I am not telling you that you should look, or what to look for, but together we are going to look, and together we are going to discover. It will be a firsthand experience for both of us because neither is directing the other. I hope this is clear.

This is a very complex problem, and to go into it one requires a mind that is able to look, to observe, to consider, without immediately saying, "What I see pleases me, I like it," or, "It does not please me, I don't like it." One requires a scientific mind, a mind that does not distort, that does not give color to what it sees. The important thing is to bring about a transformation in the very process of our thinking, in the very matrix, the very makeup of the mind. A revolution is necessary—not an economic or a sociological revolution, but a revolution in consciousness, at the very center of our being, and such a revolution can take place only if we understand this question of conflict. Conflict at any level of consciousness, superficial or deep down, is the factor of deterioration.

Don't just accept this—don't accept anything the speaker says. But let us examine together this problem of conflict, by which I mean self-contradiction, self-pity, and the urge to fulfill, with its inevitable frustration. There is conformity, imitation, and the contradiction of wanting to change *what is* into something which we call the ideal—the contradiction between what I am and what I think I should be. Contradiction implies competition, the desire to be somebody marvelous, famous, with all the striving that goes with it, the battling, the anxiety, the fear of not being something, the agony of despair—all this and much more is implied in the word *contradiction*, and it is the factor of deterioration.

We are educated to live in perpetual conflict: economically, morally, spiritually, our society is based on conflict; all the religious teachers have told us to discipline ourselves, to struggle to be or to become something. We always have the example, the national or religious hero; we imitate the saint, the savior, the one who has attained; there is always this gulf between the one who knows and the one who does not know, with the one who does not know everlastingly struggling to know—the stupid trying to become clever. That is the psychological structure of our society. We are driven by ambition; we worship success and condemn failure; there is the multiplication of sorrow, and a ceaseless trying to get out of sorrow. This constant battle goes on, whether we are asleep or awake, whether we are going for a walk or sitting still. This is our lot; it is what we have been educated to, what we have accepted; it is the state in which we live. So the mind is never clear; it is always confused, always self-contradictory.

Please observe your own state. Now, how do you observe yourself? Do you observe as a watcher looking at something apart from himself, which means that there is a division, a contradiction between the observer and the observed? Or do you observe without the observer? Please follow this, it is important. When we are looking into the enormously complex process of our own consciousness, whose very essence is conflict, we must understand what we mean by looking, observing. I am sure most of us observe as someone from the outside looking inward. You are aware of your conflicts, and you are watching them as a censor, as a judge, as an observer apart from the observed. That is what most of us do, and that prevents us from understanding this very complex thing called conflict—the enormous weight, the content, the varieties of it. When you observe as an outsider looking in, you actually create conflict, do you not? You are not understanding conflict but only increasing it. Being aware of conflict within himself, the observer says, "I must change that; I do not like conflict, I like pleasure." So the observer always has this attitude of judging, censoring, and when you so observe, you are not understanding conflict; on the contrary, you are multiplying it. Have I made myself clear on that point?

To me, the whole psychoanalytical process is the intensification of conflict, and it cannot bring about freedom from conflict. I wish you would see this fact once and for all, see the truth, the beauty of it, and then you would know what it is to look, not with the eyes of the censor, but just to look. If you look with the eyes of the censor, you are going to increase your conflict; but if you observe, not from a center, then you will begin to understand this extraordinary process called consciousness, which is the very essence of conflict, of struggle, a ceaseless striving to become, to suppress, to achieve.

You observe those snowcapped mountains, those hills and valleys, the green earth; and how do you observe them? Do you see them from an analyzing center? Or do you just see their extraordinary beauty? There is a difference, surely, between perception and analysis. If that difference is somewhat clear, then it will also be clear that analysis does not bring about a revolution. Analysis may help you to adjust yourself to society; it may remove some of your peculiarities, your idiosyncrasies, your neuroses; but we are not talking of that. We are talking of something much more fundamental than mere adjustment to a rotten society. Analysis implies the analyzer and the analyzed. The analyzer is the censor, the judge who examines, interprets, who condemns or approves what is seen, and therefore brings about further conflict. We are not doing that at all; we are doing something entirely different, which is to understand conflict, not only outwardly in the world, but inwardly. I am using the word *understand* in the sense of observing without taking any position. When you do that, you already have a field of observation in which there is no conflict. I do not know if you see the truth of that.

You know as well as I do that there is conflict outwardly. Nation is set against nation, and sovereign governments with their armies are constantly on the verge of war. There is competition, the antagonism of race and class divisions, and the battle that is going on between East and West, between those who are well-fed and the hungry millions of Asia. There is the population explosion with its threat of total starvation, and the overshadowing fear of a nuclear war. All this is obvious; it is on the lips of every politician, of every reformer—the "cold" war that is going on, and that may at any moment become "hot."

Then there is this inward battle that is going on in each one of us: the self-contradictions, the unresolved problems, and the problems that have been temporarily resolved, all of which leave their mark on the mind. We want to be somebody; we want to be famous as a painter, a writer, a speaker, a big businessman, and if we cannot be, we are frustrated—which brings on still another form of conflict.

So there is the outer and the inner conflict, and the outer is not essentially different from the inner. They are both part of the same movement, which is like a tide that goes out and comes in. To separate them is absurd, stupid, because they are one and the same thing. You must deal with the problem as a whole and not divide it as the outer and the inner; otherwise, you will never be able to understand it. The moment you divide the outer from the inner, you have increased the conflict in which you are caught.

Now, seeing this ceaseless battle, this self-contradiction in which one is caught, what is one to do? This inner conflict may produce a certain effort, a certain result. It may and often does produce paintings, poems, literature, so-called religious movements; but they are all within the field of conflict, and a man who produces a book, a poem, a picture out of this tension of conflict, is a factor of degeneration. He helps other people to degenerate. This is very obvious. So, conflict in any form, whether one is conscious of it or not, and any action arising from that conflict, is a factor of degeneration.

Please do not accept what I am saying because if you accept it, it is merely verbal agreement, and we are not here to verbally agree or disagree. This is not a debating society.

You see, for centuries upon centuries we have been brought up on this idea that we must struggle to be or to achieve something. We struggle to be successful in this world, and we also think that through conflict we can arrive at godhead, or create something in the artistic or religious sense. Look at the innumerable saints who have battled with themselves to arrive at a state which they call spiritual, and which is recognized as such by the churches. So conflict is a time-honored institution, a thing that we worship. You see conflict represented in ancient Egyptian pictures and in the caves of Lascaux where man is portrayed as battling with the animals, the good against the evil, with the hope that the good will prevail. Conflict is a historic process; it is like an enormous wave that is always overtaking us, and we are part of that wave.

Now, to see conflict—this historical, sociological process of which we are a part—as a deteriorating factor requires close attention, real intelligence. Most of us do not recognize conflict as a deteriorating factor because we are used to it. At school, in business, in everything that we do, conflict, competition is our way of life, and nobody will admit that it is deeply destructive. A few may admit it theoretically but not factually, so let us go into it.

As I said, there are many varieties of conflict. The so-called religious people have their various disciplines. They control, subjugate themselves; they conform to a pattern which they call spiritual, or imitate some hero; they accept the authority of a savior, a teacher, according to whose dictates they struggle to live. If they are at all serious—like the Christian monks, or like those people in India who have given up the world—their life is a battle to control, to discipline themselves.

And look at our own lives. Perhaps some of you smoke. You may feel it is absurd to be a slave to any habit, but how extraordinarily difficult it is for you to give up a little thing like smoking; what tortures you go through! It becomes a conflict, and, of course, with more emotional things like sex, and so on, it becomes untold misery. But you are used to conflict; it is your habit, your way of life. Conflict has been made holy, respectable; and when a person like me comes along and says that one can live totally without conflict, you either become cynical and say, "Poor chap," or you try to imitate the way he lives, and therefore you are again caught in conflict.

As I said, whether one is aware of it or not, the whole of consciousness, the whole of what we call thought, is conflict—thought as the word, the symbol, thought which is the response of memory, not only the memory of yesterday, but of many thousands of yesterdays. And if you did not think at all, what would happen? Would you vegetate, be satisfied with what you are, like a cow? Or is not to think at all an extraordinarily vital state, because it means that you have understood and are free of this whole mechanical response of memory, which is the brain responding with all its accumulations of experience as knowledge?

Most of us give up the effort to be free of conflict and allow ourselves to drift, thereby making the mind dull; and if the pain of conflict becomes too great, we resort to a belief in God, hoping in this way to find peace, but sooner or later that too becomes a source of conflict. Or, being afraid that if we had no conflict we would vegetate, become dull, satisfied, we maintain the sharpness of conflict by intellectually arguing with others, by reading and being informed about every subject on earth. But there is an approach to this problem which requires the highest form of intelligence, the highest sensitivity, and it is to observe, to be aware of this whole process of conflict, without choice. If you go into it, you will find that in this state of awareness your mind understands immediately every problem as it arises so that conflict has no soil in which to take root.

Now, that is what I am going to talk about: not how to escape from conflict—which you do anyhow by running to your favorite god, or to your favorite analyst—but how to understand negatively this whole process of conflict. By negative understanding I mean the state of a mind that looks at a problem, or at a mountain, without verbalizing—it just looks. It is the state of a mind that doesn't interpret, censor, or choose, but is aware without choice. Such a mind does not say, "I like this and I don't like that," but merely observes with an attention that is total; and in this state of mind you will find that conflict of every kind, at any level of your being, comes to an end. The mind that has no conflict is the only religious mind—but this state you do not yet know. However much you may be enchanted by my description, it will have no value.

For a man or a woman who would really understand the beauty, the extraordinary significance of a life without conflict—and I say that such a life is possible—the first thing is to be totally aware of the whole content of consciousness. To be totally aware is not to analyze but simply to observe. And that is our greatest difficulty because we have been trained through a thousand years of habit to judge, to condemn, to compare, to identify; that is our instinctive response, and therefore we never really observe.

So, living in this world, which is made up of conflict, which maintains conflict through fulfillments and frustrations, and which demands that you also live in conflict, in a state of self-contradiction—living in this world, can you, by understanding, by being sensitive to that whole process, be totally free of conflict? Surely, only the mind that has no problems, no scars of conflict, is innocent, and only an innocent mind can know that which is immeasurable.

Well, let us discuss what I have talked about this morning.

Question: What is the real function of thought?

KRISHNAMURTI: I really do not know, but let us find out. Has thought any importance? If it has, what is its place in our life? We are not offering opinions about it. It is not a question of what you think, or what I think, or what somebody else thinks—that has no value at all. We are going to find out the truth of the matter. To do that, one has to hesitate, one has to wait, to look, to listen, to feel around, and not just repeat a reaction or a memory. Having read some book on philosophy, or on thinking, you may remember and quote from it, but we are not here to quote what others have said. That gentleman has asked a very serious question. I have been saying that thought is conflict, that thought is destructive, and he has picked it up, and he is asking, "What do you mean by that? If thought is destructive, then what is the real function of thought? What is the right place of thought in our life?"

Now, before we answer that question, we must find out what thinking is, must we not? Then we can place it; we can give it right significance. But without understanding the whole process of thinking, just to offer a few words in reply does not answer the question.

So, what is thinking? Please don't answer me—it is very easy to say what thinking is, but that puts an end to our inquiry. I ask you a question: What is thinking? And what then takes place? There is a challenge in the form of a question, and you respond to it. Between my question and your answer there is a lag, a time interval in which your memory is operating. You say to yourself, "What does he mean? Where did I read about that?" and so on, and so on. If the question is very familiar, if I ask you what your name is, your response is immediate because you do not have to think. But if I ask you something which you don't quite know, you hesitate, there is a time interval during which you are searching, looking into your memory to find out. So, your thinking is the response of your memory, is it not? Please go slowly—it is very interesting if you go into it slowly.

When the question is one with which you are familiar, your answer is instantaneous.

When you are not too familiar with the question, you need time, and during that period you are searching your memory for the answer. And when a question is asked on which your memory has gathered no information at all, you look, search, and you say, "I don't know." (a) Your answer is instantaneous. (b) You take time to answer. (c) You say, "I don't know." But when you say, "I don't know," you are waiting to know, waiting to be informed, waiting to go to the library and look it up; you are expecting an answer. So when you say, "I don't know," it is a conditional "I don't know." You expect to know in a few days, or in a few years—which is conditional. There is also (d), which is to say, "I don't know," and which is not conditional; the mind is not waiting, not looking in the hope of finding an answer. It just says, "I don't know."

Now, (a), (b), and (c) are all a process of thinking, are they not? If you ask a Christian if there is a God, he will immediately say, "Of course there is." If you ask a communist the same question, he will say, "What are you talking about? Of course there isn't." His god is the state, but that's a different matter. So our response to any challenge is according to our conditioning; our thinking is according to our conditioning, according to our memory. If memory is sharp, clear, active, vivid, our responses are strong, and that is the whole process of what we call thinking. Whether our thinking is simple or elaborate, whether it is unlearned or very erudite and scientific, it is based on that process.

But there is the point where you say, "I really don't know," and you are not waiting for an answer. No book can tell you. There is no memory that will say, "This is it." Surely, that is entirely different from the other three processes; (a), (b), and (c) are not the same as (d), in which all thinking has stopped because you don't know and are not waiting to be told.

Now, from what point of view are you asking the question, "What is the right value of thought?" Are you asking it in order to receive a reply, as in (a), (b), and (c)? Or are you asking this question in the state of mind represented by (d), in which there is no thought? And what relationship has thought to the state of mind represented by (d)?

Am I explaining myself, or is this becoming too complex?

Thought has value at a certain level, has it not? When you go to the office, when you do something in any field of activity, thought obviously has value; in all such matters there must be thought. But has thought any value when you say, "I don't know," that is, when the mind has gone through (a), (b), and (c) and is completely in a state of not-knowing?

As I have pointed out, if you are a Christian and someone asks you if there is a God, you will answer according to your conditioning; you will say that there is, and your thinking then has a certain value depending on your code of morality, how you behave, whether you go to church, and all the rest of it. But the man who says, "I don't know whether there is a God or not," who neither affirms nor denies that there is a God, and who is really in a state of not-knowing—such a man does not exercise his thought to discover because if he uses his thought to discover, he comes back to the known. Are you getting it?

Now, I must deny the three, (a), (b), and (c), to find out. Do you understand? I must deny the whole structure of knowledge and belief and be in a state of not-knowing. There is then no exercising of thought at all, and therefore my mind gives no value to thought. But thought obviously has value in every other field.

You see, knowledge has been accumulated through experience, through thought; and thought, which is itself the outcome of knowledge, has importance in the field of knowledge. In the field of knowledge you must have thought. But knowledge, which is the known, is not going to help you to find the unknown. So the mind must be free of the known—and that is one of our difficulties.

I hope all this means something to you all.

July 9, 1963

Third Talk in Saanen

For many people religion is probably a hobby. The old turn to religion, and so do people who are somewhat neurotic. I am using that word *religion* to mean not only the organized churches, with all the inward security they offer, but also the various and most extraordinary forms of belief, dogma, and ritual to which so many adhere. Religion, to most people, is not a very serious matter. The government is now allowing organized religion in Russia because politically it is not very important; it does not contain the seed of revolt; it is not a center of revolution, so they let it go on.

And I wonder what part religion plays in the life of those of us who are here? By religion I now mean something entirely different, something that is as important, if not very much more important, than earning a livelihood. To me, religion is something to which you give your whole heart and mind and body, everything that you have. It is not something to turn to as a hobby, or to take up when you are old with one foot in the grave because you have nothing else to do, but something that becomes devastatingly important, something intensely necessary as a whole way of living from the moment you wake up until the moment you go to sleep, so that every thought, every act, every movement of your feeling is observed, considered, weighed. To me, religion encompasses the whole of life. It is not reserved for the specialists, for the rich or the poor, for the elite or the intellectual. It is like bread, something that you must have. And I wonder how many of us take it as seriously as that—which does not mean being cantankerous, bigoted, exclusive, sectarian, or somebody very special. Religion demands, not knowledge or belief, but an extraordinary intelligence, and for the religious man there must be freedom, complete freedom.

Though we talk of freedom, most of us do not want to be free at all. I do not know if you have observed this fact. In the modern world—where society is so highly organized, where there is more and more progress, where the production of things is so vast and so easy—one becomes a slave to possessions, to things, and in them one finds security. And security is all that most of us want—physical and emotional security—therefore, we really do not want to be free. By freedom I mean total freedom, not freedom along one particular line; and I think we ought to demand it of ourselves, insist upon it.

Freedom is different from revolt. Revolt is against something: you revolt against something and are for something. Revolt is a reaction, but freedom is not. In the state of freedom, you are not free from something. The moment you are free from something, you are really in revolt against that something; therefore, you are not free. Freedom is not "from something," but in itself the mind is free. That is an extraordinary feeling—for the mind to be free in itself, to know freedom for its own sake.

Now, unless one is free, I do not see how one can be creative. I am not using that word *creative* in the narrow sense of a man who paints a picture, writes a poem, or invents a machine. To me, such people are not creative at all. They may be inspired for the time being, but creation is entirely different. Creation can be only when there is total freedom. In that state of freedom there is a fullness, and then writing a poem, painting a picture, or carving a stone, has a different meaning altogether. It is then not mere self-expression; it is not the result of frustration; it is no longer seeking a market—it is something entirely different. It seems to me that we should demand to know this complete freedom, not only in ourselves but outwardly, and I shall go into it a little bit this morning.

First, I think we should differentiate between freedom on the one hand, and revolt or revolution on the other. Revolt and revolution are essentially a reaction. There is the revolt of the extreme left against capitalism, and the revolt against the dominance of the church. There is also the revolt against the police state, against the power of organized tyranny—but nowadays that doesn't pay because they very quietly liquidate you, put you away.

To me, freedom is something entirely different. Freedom is not a reaction but rather the state of mind which comes into being when we understand reaction. Reaction is the response to challenge; it is pleasure, anger, fear, psychological pain; and in understanding this very complex structure of response, we shall come upon freedom. Then you will find that freedom is not freedom from anger, from authority, and so on. It is a state per se, to be experienced for itself, and not because you are against something.

Most of us are concerned with our own security. We want a companion and hope to find happiness in a particular relationship; we want to be famous, we want to create; we want to express, expand, fulfill ourselves; we want to have power, position, prestige. In one degree or another, that is really what most of us are concerned with; and freedom, God, truth, love become something to be looked for after that. So, as I said, our religion is a superficial thing, a kind of hobby which does not play a very important part in our life. We are satisfied with trivialities, and therefore there is not the alertness, the perception that is required to understand this complex process which we call living. Our existence is a constant struggle, a fatuous, endless effort—and for what? It is a cage in which we are caught, a cage that we have built out of our own reactions, out of our fears, despairs, anxieties. All our thinking is a reaction—and you will remember that we went into this matter the other day when the question was asked, "What is the right function of thought?" We went into it very carefully, and we discovered that all our thinking is a reaction, the response of memory. The whole structure of our consciousness, of our thought, is the residue, the reservoir of our reactions. Obviously, thought can never bring about freedom because freedom is not the result of a reaction. Freedom is not the rejection of the things that give us pain, nor is it detachment from the things that give us pleasure and to which we have become slaves.

Please, as I said the other day, do not accept anything that the speaker is saying. Look at it neither accepting nor rejecting but trying to see the fact for yourself by observing yourself.

Our consciousness is the whole area of our thought, the whole field of idea and ideation. Organized thought becomes the idea from which action takes place, and consciousness is made up of the many layers of thought, both hidden and open, the conscious as well as the unconscious. It is the field of the known, of tradition, the memory of what has been. It is what we have learned, the past in relation to the present. The past which we have inherited through centuries, the past of the race, of the nation, of the community, of the family; the symbols, the words, the experiences, the clashing of contradictory desires; the innumerable struggles, the pleasures and pains; the things that we have learned from our forefathers, and the modern technologies which have been added—all that is consciousness; it is the field of thought, the field of the known, and we live on the surface of it. We are trained from childhood to acquire knowledge, to compete; we learn a technique; we specialize in a particular direction in order to have a job and earn a livelihood. This is our whole education, so we continue to live on the surface, and below the surface there is this enormous past, time untold. All of that is the known. Even though we are not aware of the unconscious, it is still within the field of the known.

Please follow all this, observing yourself, watching your own consciousness. The more sensitive, the more watchful you are, the more aware you will be of the conflict between the conscious and the unconscious. When this conflict demands action, if you do not find a way to act, you become neurotic or end up in an asylum; and so you have innumerable psychologists, analysts, trying to bridge over this gulf and resolve the conflict.

The unconscious, although that word conveys the idea of something hidden that you are not aware of, is still part of the known; it is the past. You may not know the whole content of the unconscious; you may not have examined it, looked at it, but you have probably had dreams, intimations of that vast underground region of the mind. It is there, and it is the known because it is the past. In it there is nothing new, and we must understand for ourselves what is involved in that state which is not new, because innocency is freedom from the known.

This is one of the major problems of modern life because we are trained, educated, conditioned to remain within the field of the known, and within that field there is endless anxiety, despair, misery, confusion, sorrow. It is only the innocent who can be creative, who can create something new and not just mechanically turn out a picture, a poem, or whatever it may be. The unconscious is part of the known, and most of us remain on the surface of the known because that is our way of life. We go to the office every day, with its routine, its boredom; we are afraid of losing our job; we are subject to the demands, the pressures, the strains of modern living; we are torn by sexual and other appetites—and on that level we live. From that level we try to find something much deeper because we are not satisfied with that level, so we turn to music, to painting, to art, to gods, to innumerable religions. When they fail, we worship the state as the most marvelous thing, or practice community living—you know all the tricks we indulge in, all the gadgets we invent, including rockets for going to the moon. And when we are dissatisfied with all that, we turn inward, or if we are very intellectual, we analyze, tear everything to pieces, but we have our own secret Jesus, our own secret Christ. And that is our life.

Now, the only real freedom is freedom from the known. Please follow this a little bit. It is freedom from the past. The known has its place, obviously. I must know certain things in order to function in everyday life. If I did not know where I lived, I would be lost. And there is the accumulated knowledge of science, of medicine, and the many technologies, to which more and more is being added. All of that is within the field of the known, and it has its place. But the known is always mechanical. Every experience that you have had, whether in the distant past or only yesterday, is within the field of the known, and from that background you recognize all further experience. In the field of the known there is attachment, with its fears, its despairs; and the mind that is held within this field, however extensive, however wide, is not free. It may write very clever books, it may know how to go to the moon, it may invent the most complicated and extraordinary machines—if you have seen some of them, you will know how really extraordinary they are—but it is still held within the field of the known.

Consciousness is of time; thought is built on time, and what thought produces is still within the bondage of time. So a man who would be free of sorrow has to be free of the known—which means that one has to understand this whole structure of consciousness. And can one understand through analysis, which is again a thought process? What does it mean to understand something? What is the state of the mind that understands? I am talking about understanding, not about what is understood. Do you follow what I mean? I am inquiring into the state of the mind that says, "I understand." Is understanding the result of thought and deduction? Do you examine a thing critically, reasonably, sanely, logically, and then say, "I understand it"? Or is understanding something entirely different?

The day before yesterday, when that gentleman asked, "What is the right function of thought?" you will remember that we talked about the mind's response to challenge. When the question is familiar, an immediate response takes place. When the question is a little more complicated, abstruse, the response takes time, and in that lag of time you are thinking, that is, looking into memory and then responding, like the computers, through association. A still more complicated question requires a greater interval. Now, these three responses, which the other day we called (a), (b), and (c), are all part of the process of thought, within the field of the known. Within that field you can produce, you can invent, you can paint pictures, you can do the most extraordinary things, including going to the moon—but that is not creation. This everlasting search for achievement and self-expression is utterly juvenile, at least for me.

Now, freedom from all that is freedom from the known; it is the state of a mind which says, "I do not know," and which is not looking for an answer. Such a mind is completely not seeking, not expecting; and it is only in this state that you can say, "I understand." It is the only state in which the mind is free, and from that state you can look at the things that are known—but not the other way round. From the known you cannot possibly see the unknown, but when once you have understood the state of a mind that is free—which is the mind that says, "I don't know," and remains unknowing and is therefore innocent—from that state you can function, you can be a citizen, you can be married, or what you will. Then what you do has relevance, significance in life. But we remain in the field of the known, with all its conflicts, striving, disputes, agonies, and from that field we try to find that which is unknown; therefore, we are not really seeking freedom. What we want is the continuation, the extension of the same old thing: the known.

So, to me, what is important is to understand for oneself this state in which the mind is free from the known, because it is only such a mind that can discover for itself whether or not there is an immensity. Merely to function within the field of the known—whether that functioning is on the left, on the right, or in the center—is gross materialism, or whatever you may like to call it. It has no answer to anything, for in it there is misery, strife, endless competition, the search for a security that you will never find. That is what most young people are concerned with, is it not? They first want security for themselves, for their family, security in their job, and later on, perhaps, if they have the time and inclination, they will look for something else. When the crisis becomes too intense, you look for a happy, convenient answer, and with that you are satisfied. I am not talking of that search at all. I am talking of something entirely different. I am talking of a mind that has completely understood the whole function of the known, and it cannot possibly understand that enormously complex field without understanding itself, its whole consciousness.

Now, you cannot understand yourself through self-examination, through introspection, through analysis—that much is fairly clear. I do not have to go into it, do I? The mind cannot possibly understand itself through analysis, because in analysis there is a division between the analyzer and the analyzed, and therefore increased and sustained conflict. Any analysis, any striving to probe, to question, to inquire, starts from the center that is already conditioned, burdened with the accumulations of time, which is the known. However much the analyzer tries to penetrate into the unconscious, he is still part of the known. Once you have grasped the truth of that, then—in spite of all the analysts and psychologists—you can see the whole content of the unconscious and understand it at one swift glance. Understanding only takes place in a flash, not in the course of time, through the accumulation of knowledge from books, and so on. You see something immediately, or not at all. Dreams may indicate, symbolize, hint at something, but that is still part of the known, and the mind must totally empty itself of the known. The mind must be free of this process which we call thinking.

If you are now hearing for the first time this statement that you must be free of thought, you may say, "Poor chap, he is crazy." But if you have really listened, not only this time but for the many years during which some of you have perhaps read all about it, you will know that what is being said has an extraordinary vitality, a penetrating truth. Only the mind that has emptied itself of the known is creative. That is creation. What it creates has nothing to do with it. Freedom from the known is the state of a mind that is in creation. How can a mind that is in creation be concerned with itself? Therefore, to understand that state of mind, you have to know yourself; you have to observe the process of your own thinking—observe it, not to alter, not to change it, but just observe it as you see yourself in a mirror. When there is freedom, then you can use knowledge and it will not destroy humanity. But when there is no freedom and you make use of knowledge, you create misery for everybody, whether you are in Russia, in America, in China, or anywhere else. I call that mind serious which is aware of the conflict of the known and is not caught in it, not trying to modify, to improve the known—for on that path there is no end to sorrow and misery.

Shall we discuss?

Question: Would you mind going into the problem of the unconscious? How can one be conscious of the unconscious? How can one examine it, uncover it, roll it out?

KRISHNAMURTI: Do you all see the problem? You do not know the unconscious; you are not aware of it, so how are you going to uncover it? How am I—who am so caught up in the daily activities and routine of the conscious mind—to look into the unconscious?

Now, see what you have already done by putting this question. You have created a contradiction. Do you follow? I will explain what I mean. What is the instrument with which you are going to look at the unconscious? The only instrument you have is the conscious mind, the daily, operative mind that goes to the office, that has sexual and other appetites, fears; and with that conscious mind you are going to look into the unconscious. But it is not possible to do that, and when you have found out that it is not possible, what happens? During so-called sleep, when the conscious brain is somewhat quiet, the unconscious intimates certain things through dreams, through symbols, and then the conscious mind on waking says, "I have dreamed and I must interpret my dreams." Because it is so occupied during the day, the conscious mind can discover the content of the unconscious only through dreams. Therefore the analyst gives tremendous importance to dreams. But just see the complications involved. Dreams need right interpretation, and to give the right interpretation, the analyst must know the background of your consciousness, the whole of it; otherwise, his interpretation will be wrong. It may be Freudian, or Jungian, or reflect the opinions of some other authority, but it will not be right—and that is what generally happens because the analyst does not know your whole background, and he cannot know it. And if you yourself begin to analyze the unconscious, if you write down every dream and interpret it, then your interpretation will have to be extraordinarily free of the unconscious. So you see the difficulty. I am going into the problem negatively, you understand?

This thing that you call the unconscious is unknown—unknown in the sense that you are not acquainted with it, you do not know the content of it. So far, you do not know what it is. You have been trying to understand it with a mind that is trained to accumulate knowledge, and with that knowledge to look. But now you have discovered that this is not the way to fathom the unconscious, that is, through analysis. And when you say, "Analysis is not the way," what has happened to your mind? Do you follow? I wonder if this is clear.

When you say about anything, "This is not the way," what is the state of your mind? Surely, it is in a state of negation. Now, can you remain in that state? It is only in the state of negation that you can observe, so what is important is to approach negatively something which you do not know. That is how inventions come about, is it not? That is how the big rockets have been developed. But it is much more difficult to approach negatively a psychological problem, because we are in torture, we are caught in our own emotional jangles, and we want to find a way out.

So, to uncover the unconscious, one must first see very clearly for oneself the truth that one can really look at something which one does not know only with a mind that is empty. You have been told to analyze, but analysis has led you nowhere except to more and more of nothing at all, so you see for yourself that analysis is not the way. Having realized the futility of analysis, do not immediately try to find out what the unconscious is, but rather inquire to find out what is the state in which the mind says, "That is not the way." Surely, it is a state of negation, and in that state the mind can observe because it is not translating, interpreting, judging, but only watching. That you can do anywhere: sitting in a bus, in your office, when the boss speaks to you, when you talk to your wife, to your children, to your neighbor, when you read the newspaper. With such a mind, every reaction of the unconscious can be observed, and if you do that with intensity—not just casually, one day doing it and forgetting it the next—if you keep tremendously alive, then you will find that you do not dream at all. What need is there for symbolic dreams when every minute of the day the unconscious is showing you its responses, giving up its conditioning, its memories, its anxieties—when everything is being revealed as you are watching? Then the mind is like an empty canvas on which the unconscious is throwing its picture from moment to moment, so when you go to sleep the mind, the brain, rests. And it needs rest because it has been working furiously all day, not only doing its job, but also watching. The brain thus becomes highly sensitive—much more so than through analysis and introspection. A mind, a brain that is completely at rest during sleep renews itself. It has the energy to go further—but I won't go into that now.

We have answered the question, have we not, sir? The uncovering of the unconscious takes place when the mind is in a state of negation, a state of emptiness; that is, it is watching without interpreting.

Question: Do intuitions spring from the unknown?

KRISHNAMURTI: Obviously not. We have intuitions about everything, don't we? Do you really want me to answer this question? I had better because I see that lots of you are saying yes.

Why do you want intuitions or inspirations? When you are intensely watching yourself, observing every movement of the unconscious without choice, do you want to be inspired, to have intuitions? Intuitions about what? It is only when you are caught in self-contradiction, when there is a strain, a denial, a struggle, that you want some release, some hope, a promise of something different. Oh, that is all so juvenile—sweep it all away!

Question: You use the word mind *in so many different ways. What do you mean by the mind?*

KRISHNAMURTI: That is a good old time-honored question. Surely there is a difference between the brain and the mind. We must go into it very hesitantly, tentatively.

The mind is everything, and it is also nothing. The mind encompasses everything, and at the same time it is empty. Please, you don't know what I am talking about, so don't agree. The mind has no frontiers, and therefore it is not a slave to time. The mind has no horizon towards which it is going, and therefore it is completely empty. But there is the brain, which is the result of time; it has grown from the single cell to this complex entity which is the human being. The brain is the result of time, but the mind is not. The brain is the result of a thousand experiences with their scars, with their memories, conscious and unconscious. The brain is the result of association, of the experiences that you remember—the recent experiences, and also the marvelous ones you had when you were a child. The brain is the future, invented by itself in its passage from the past through the present towards that future. All of that is part of the brain. And—because we have so tortured it, misused it, compelled, disciplined, forced, drilled it—the brain has become dull, a dead, mechanical thing. That is what the brain is for most of us—just mechanical. It is not highly sensitive, sharp, eager, alive; and with this mechanical brain we try to understand the mind. All our literature, all our talking and writing about the mind is from the recollections of the brain.

So, if you go into it for yourself, you will find that what is required is a highly sensitive brain capable of sound reasoning, a brain that is healthy and not neurotic, not based on the beliefs and assumptions of the theologians, the communists, or anyone else, for these things only make the brain mechanical, dull, stupid, however cunning it may be. If you go into it, you will find that the brain can be extraordinarily alive, every part of it. But it can be so alive only when there is no conflict, when it has no problem, when it is not in despair, not thinking in terms of the future, when it is free of anxieties, of sorrow. Then the brain can be highly sensitive, alive in the real sense of the word; and only such a brain can find the mind which has no horizon, the mind which is completely empty and functions from that emptiness.

July 11, 1963

Fourth Talk in Saanen

This morning I would like, if I may, to talk about something which may be rather abstruse. Most of us are slaves to words, and words have become extraordinarily important. Words are necessary as a means to communicate, but for most of us the word is the mind, and we are enslaved by words. Until we understand this deep question of verbalization, and the importance of the word, and how slavish we are to words, we shall go on thinking mechanically, like computers. The computer is the word and the problem. Without the problem and the word, there would be no computer; it would have no value. For the majority of human beings too, the word and the problem are tremendously significant, so we should go into this question of words.

I do not know if we are aware of how bound we are to the word, to the symbol, to the idea. We never question the importance or the significance of the word. When I use the term *word*, I mean the symbol, the process of naming, with its extraordinary depth or shallowness, whereby we think we have understood the whole significance of life. I do not think that each one of us realizes to what an extent the mind, our whole being, depends on the word, the symbol, the name, the term; and it seems to me that as long as we are slaves to words and remain at that level, all our activity, both physical and psychological, is bound to be superficial.

There is a great deal of discussion nowadays concerning the philosophy of words, and the building up of a structure, a system of words. I think we should be aware of this question and observe how deeply or superficially it plays a part in our life, and we should inquire to find out whether the mind can ever be free of the word.

Now, I want to go into this matter because it seems to me that the word is the past; it is not the active present. In a world of such violence, of such hatred and brutality as the present one, a word like *compassion* has very little meaning. We are all aware of what is going on in the world: the competition, the ambitions and frustrations, the extraordinary brutality, hatred, and violence arising from the conflict between political parties, the right against the left and the left against the right. Certain words are twisted to fit expediency and have lost all their meaning. There is violence in all of us, conscious or unconscious. There is aggressiveness, the desire to be or to become something, the urge to express oneself at any cost, to fulfill oneself sexually, in relationship, in writing, in painting—which are all forms of violence.

I do not know how deeply each one of us is aware of all this without being told. There is an extraordinary amount of cruelty in a world where a small group of people takes complete charge of millions of others and directs their lives through tyranny, as is going on in the East and in Russia. And I wonder to what depth we are aware of our own cruelty, our own aggressive ambitions, our urge to fulfill ourselves at any cost, so that a word like compassion has very little meaning?

As I was saying the other day, unless there is a complete change, a total mutation in the whole consciousness of the individual, any society built on acquisitive drives and aggression is bound to become more and more cruel, more and more tyrannical, more and more given over to materialistic values—which means that the mind will become constantly more slavish to those values. I do not know if you are aware of all this. Probably most of you read the newspaper every day, and unfortunately you get used to it—used to reading about the cruelties, the murders, the brutalities. Reading it all every day dulls the mind, and so one gets accustomed to these things. So I would like this morning to discuss or talk over with you the question of how to break through the layers of this ugly, stupid, environmental conditioning that has made the mind a slave to words, and also a slave to the social structure in which we live.

As I have been trying to explain, I feel that the crisis that has arisen in the world is not an economic or a social crisis, but a crisis in the mind, in consciousness; and there can be no answer to this crisis unless there is a deep, fundamental mutation in each one of us. This mutation can take place only if we understand the whole process of verbalization, which is the psychological structure of the word. Please do not brush it off by saying, "Is that all?" This is not a matter that can be lightly dismissed, because the word, the symbol, the idea has an extraordinary grip on the mind. We are talking of bringing about a mutation in the mind, and for that there must be the cessation of the word. When you hear a statement of that kind for the first time, you will probably not know what it means, and you will say, "What nonsense!" But I do not quite see how the mind can be totally free as long as we have not understood the influence of the word, and the interpretation of the word—which means that we have to understand the whole process of our own thinking, because it is all based on the word.

Please, this is not an "intellectual" talk. I have a horror of the intellectual mind that just spins words without much meaning. You have gone to a lot of trouble to come here, and it would be rather a pity if you did not take seriously what we are talking about. Surely, we must consider this problem of the word with great determination and depth.

Now, if the word is removed, what have you left? The word represents the past, does it not? The innumerable pictures, images, the layers of experience, are all based on the word, on idea, on memory. From memory comes thought, and we give to thought an extraordinary importance, but I question that importance altogether. Thought cannot, by any means whatsoever, cultivate compassion. I am not using that word compassion to mean the opposite, the antithesis of hate or violence. But unless each one of us has a deep sense of compassion, we shall become more and more brutal, inhuman to each other. We shall have mechanical, computer-like minds which have merely been trained to perform certain functions; we shall go on seeking security, both physical and psychological, and we shall miss the extraordinary depth and beauty, the whole significance of life.

By compassion I do not mean a thing to be acquired. Compassion is not the word, which is merely of the past, but something which is of the active present; it is the verb and not the word, the name, or the noun. There is a difference between the verb and the word. The verb is of the active present, whereas the word is always of the past and therefore static. You may give vitality or movement to the name, to the word, but it is not the same as the verb which is actively present. And I am not using the term *present* in the existentialist sense at all.

Most of us live in an environment of aggression, violence, brutality, and like those around us, we are driven by ambition, by the urge to fulfill ourselves. Whatever talent we may have—some absurd little capacity to paint pictures, to write poems, or what you will—demands expression, and we make of that an enormous thing through which we hope to gain for ourselves glory or renown. In one degree or another, that is our life, with all its satisfactions, frustrations, and despairs.

Now, the mutation must take place in the very seed of thought itself, not in the outward expressions of that seed, and this can happen only if we understand the whole process of thought—which is the word, the idea. Take a word like *God*. The word God is not God and one will come upon that immensity, that immeasurable something, whatever it may be, only when the word is not, when the symbol is not, when there is no belief, no idea—when there is complete freedom from security.

So we are talking of a mutation at the very source, in the very seed of thought. As we found when we went into it the other day, what we call thought is reaction; it is the response of memory, the response of one's background, of one's religious and social conditioning; it reflects the influence of one's environment, and so on, and so on. Until there is the decay of that seed, there is no mutation and therefore no compassion. Compassion is not sentiment; it is not this woolly sympathy or empathy. Compassion is not something which you can cultivate through thought, through discipline, control, suppression, nor by being kind, polite, gentle, and all the rest of it. Compassion comes into being only when thought has come to an end at its very root. If you are hearing this statement for the first time, it will probably have no meaning for you at all. You will say, "How can thought end?" or, "What happens to a mind that is incapable of thinking?" You will have innumerable questions. But we have already talked it over; we have more or less gone into it, though perhaps not in detail.

What I want to go into this morning is the question of observing the self. But first let us understand what it means to observe, and then we can go into what that word *self* means. Take the word *observation.* What does it mean? Most of us observe dead things, the things that are gone, the things that are over. We never observe a thing that is living, moving, active.

Please, as I talk, as I explain, do not be caught in the explanation, in the word, but observe yourself; notice how you see, how you observe. What comes next is very important, and it will be very difficult to understand what comes next if you do not first understand the beauty of observation.

Most of us observe with a sense of concentration, which means there is a detaching of the thing observed from the whole context of which it is a part. There is the observer and the thing observed, and therefore a conflict arises between the observer and the thing observed—the struggle to eliminate it or to modify it, or else one identifies oneself with what has been observed, which will inevitably bring other problems. Such observation is merely a process of analysis, which we went into previously. That is what most of us do—we analyze what we observe. I want to know, I want to understand this extraordinarily complex entity, this consciousness which is myself, and I say, "I will observe myself." And I observe by looking at one thought, separating it from the whole movement of thought. It is as if one were to observe that stream by casually taking up a cup of water and looking at it as a separate thing, away from the full flow, away from the noise and the power of the stream itself. Obviously, that would not convey the full significance of the stream. To observe the stream, one has to watch every wave, however small, and be aware of the curving of that wave before it breaks; one has to move with that extraordinarily rapid water. In observation there is no time to interpret, no time to say this is right, that is wrong, this is beautiful, that is ugly, this must be, that must not be. There is no censor—in observing a living, moving thing, a thing as vital as that stream, you cannot possibly have a censor, a judge. There is a censor, a judge, only when you separate a little of the water from the stream and look at it.

So please understand very clearly that the moment you separate something from its context in order to observe it, you have brought into being the censor, and therefore there is conflict, there is the word, the whole process of verbalization with its fulfillment and the agony of frustration. You separate yourself from the thing you are looking at, and then you say, "I have watched myself, and I know that I am this, I am that, I am the other, but I can't get any further." Obviously, because those are the observations of an outside observer who has separated himself from the flow, from the movement, from the rapidity of thought. If this is not clear, we will discuss it at the end of this talk.

To observe oneself without conflict is like following that stream, being ahead of the waterfall, ahead of the movements of every little wave, seeing every little stone that makes the wave break. This is not a theory. I am dealing with the question scientifically, objectively; I am not being sentimental, ideational, or hypothetical, but factual. When once you have really grasped the deep significance of observation, you will find that the very process of observation, of seeing, is the end of conflict because you have removed this division between the observer and the observed; you have completely wiped it away, and therefore you are looking at thought, not as a separate entity, but as the thing itself. You are that thought, and not a thinker looking at his thought. If you are really following something very alive, very rapid, something that is in tremendous movement, you have no time to judge, to evaluate, to condemn, or to identify yourself with that thing. It is so dynamically vital that you have no time—and this is important—you have no time to verbalize, no time to name it, no time to give it a word, which are all separative functions.

So, if that is understood, let us look at this complex thing called the self, which is the 'me', the field of consciousness. We are looking to find out if it is true, and not just my idea or your idea, that to bring about a complete mutation, a total revolution in consciousness, thought can have no place in it.

Thought is not compassion—to think that it is would be too absurd. You cannot cultivate compassion any more than you can cultivate love. Do what you will, you cannot produce love through the mind; you cannot manufacture it by thought. Now, can one observe the conscious as well as the unconscious movements of this whole entity called the 'me', bearing in mind that there is no time? Time is the word. The moment you say, "That is anger; that is jealousy; that is bad," you have already separated it from yourself and are looking at something that is dead; so you are not observing yourself. And if you do not know yourself, all about yourself, your thought has no raison d'être; in any movement of thought, in any action, you are just functioning blindly, like a machine. Most of us do not think completely but fragmentarily; what we think at one level is contradicted by our thought at another level. We feel something at a certain level and deny it at another, so our daily action is equally contradictory, fragmentary, and such action breeds conflict, misery, confusion.

Please, these are all obvious psychological facts, and to understand them, you don't have to read a single book on psychology or philosophy, because there is the book inside you—the book which has been put together through centuries by man.

So, we are dealing, not only with action; but also with compassion, because action has within it compassion. Compassion is not something separate from action; it is not an idea to which action is approximating itself. Please do look at this, consider it carefully because for most of us, idea is important, and from idea there is action. But idea separated from action creates conflict. Action includes compassion; it is not just at the technological level, or at the level of relationship between husband and wife, or between the individual and the community, but it is a total movement of one's whole being. I am talking about total action, not action in fragmentation. When there is observation and therefore no observer—the observer being the idea, the word—and you begin to understand this whole complex thing called the self, the 'me', then you will know this total action, not the separative, fragmentary action in which there is conflict.

I do not know whether you understand all this.

What is the point of my talking? You are sitting there, and I am talking. What is the point? I am not talking to fulfill myself. This is not my métier; it is not my bread and butter. So why am I talking? Why are you listening, and what are you listening to? You and I are on a journey together to find out what is the fact, what is the truth—not an abstract idea of truth, not a word apart from the fact, but the fact itself. One observes the catastrophic state of the world, and one feels that there must be a tremendous revolution, a complete mutation in the mind, so that the human being really is a human being—one who is free of problems, free of sorrow, one who lives a full, rich, complete existence—and is not the tortured, driven, conditioned entity he is now. That is why I talk, and I hope that is also why you are listening.

Now, what does it mean to observe, let us say, the movement of ambition? I am taking ambition as one of the ugly things in our life—although some of you may call it beautiful. What does it mean to observe the structure, the anatomy of ambition?—not the word, because the word is not the thing. The word *tree* is not the tree. You may say, "Yes, that is so"; but psychologically, when we observe ambition in ourselves, we immediately identify ourselves with that state, with that word, and we are caught in it. It is simple to see that the word tree is not the tree, but to observe in oneself, without the word, that extraordinary state called ambition, is quite another matter. That state is built into you, into your thought, into your very being, by the society, the environment in which you live, by your education, by the church, by countless centuries of man's aggressive endeavor to achieve, to get ahead, to kill, and all the rest of it. And what matters is to observe that state in yourself, not only now as we are talking about it, but to observe it as you go to the office, as you read in the newspaper the praise of some hero or successful man. If you observe without naming it, you will see that it is not a static thing but a movement unidentified with the word, and therefore unidentified with the name, with you; and if you observe it with intensity, with a certain swiftness, you will go beyond ambition. It will have lost its significance—and yet you can be totally in action. But to observe that state in oneself, to look at thinking without an observer, without a thinker who is watching, is extremely arduous.

Observation implies no accumulation of knowledge, even though knowledge is obviously necessary at a certain level: knowledge as a doctor, knowledge as a scientist, knowledge of history, of all the things that have been. After all, that is knowledge: information about the things that have been. There is no knowledge of tomorrow, only conjecture as to what might happen tomorrow, based on your knowledge of what has been. A mind that observes with knowledge is incapable of following swiftly the stream of thought. It is only by observing without the screen of knowledge that you begin to see the whole structure of your own thinking. And as you observe—which is not to condemn or accept, but simply to watch—you will find that thought comes to an end. Casually to observe an occasional thought leads nowhere. But if you observe the process of thinking and do not become an observer apart from the observed, if you see the whole movement of thought without accepting or condemning it, then that very observation puts an end immediately to thought—and therefore the mind is compassionate; it is in a state of constant mutation.

Can we discuss what I have talked about just now?

Question: How are we to be free of influence so that we can see a fact as a fact?

KRISHNAMURTI: First of all, we must be aware of this whole question of influence, must we not? There are influences all around us, and we are influenced. When you pick up a newspaper, read a book, listen to the radio, or watch television, consciously or unconsciously you are being influenced. Your whole education is a series of influences and directives, and with that conditioning, how can you see a fact as a fact? You can't, obviously. So you have to begin by understanding influence.

Now, is it possible to be free of influence? You can put that question only when you are aware of being influenced, not before. Probably you are being influenced by the present speaker. If you are, then you are not looking at the fact. If because the speaker has a certain reputation you are accepting what he says, you are obviously being influenced. That is the nature of propaganda—and we are not doing propaganda here. Either you see for yourself what is true or you do not see it. It is up to you. It is not my intention to influence you, but everything in life is an influence. Your wife and children influence you, as you influence them. Influence may be conscious or unconscious. If it is conscious, you can more or less push it aside—that is comparatively easy. If your wife nags you, you can accept it or do something about it—you can walk out of the house. But if you are influenced unconsciously, if the influence is deep and you are not aware of it, it is much more difficult to be free of—and that is our problem. Influence takes many forms. There is the influence of tradition, the influence of words like *communist, Catholic, Protestant,* the influence of the party you belong to, and so on.

Now, is it possible to be aware of all the influences that are pouring in upon us? Please don't immediately say yes or no, because you don't know. Is it possible? Surely, to be free of influence, you must have an extraordinarily sensitive body, and also a mind, a brain, that has not been made dull by tradition, by society, by the church with its beliefs and dogmas. All these influences, and many more, are making the brain dull. To be aware of and to understand these innumerable influences, and to be free of them, one has to break through the dullness, the lethargy that has settled upon the mind—and most of us don't want to. Most of us are comfortably settled in life. We are Catholics, Protestants, communists—oh, you know the innumerable things we cling to: our nationalities, our class divisions, and all the rest of it. We have settled in a nice comfortable stagnating mind, and we are satisfied. We are "yes-sayers"; we accept, and we never question.

So, one has to be aware of the many influences, just be aware of them, and not say, "I am for this and against that." To be aware, one has to observe. One can be aware of the influences that are pouring into the unconscious—completely aware of them. As we discussed the other day, it is only when the brain is quiet—not resistant, not made dull, but only when the brain is very sensitive, very alert and watchful—that it can perceive all the unconscious influences and therefore be free of influence. Then one can see the fact as a fact, and it's not so very difficult; that is, one can be aware of oneself, with all the complicated twists of ambition. One can observe all of that in oneself, and observe all the unconscious influences. Then one sees the fact as a fact, the truth in the false, and the truth as the truth. It is not divided; it is a total process.

Question: The brain is a dead thing, and how can it come to life?

KRISHNAMURTI: Is the brain a dead thing? Surely, it is dead only when it is paralyzed, when the nerves have no longer any sensitivity. But for most of us the brain is made dull through conflict, through pain, through suffering, through the innumerable securities and sanctions with which we live. It is made dull by fear, by the do's and don'ts of society. If you are specialized exclusively in one direction as a doctor, as a scientist, as an engineer, or whatever it may be, one part of your brain may be extraordinarily bright, but the rest is obviously made dull. Knowing all this, observing all this, and probing into the whole process of thinking, you will find that the brain is not dull; but you have to break through the dullness and not just accept it.

Question: I put the question wrongly. What I meant to ask is this: How can a mechanical thing like the brain become part of the total thing called the mind?

KRISHNAMURTI: Sir, when we say that the brain is mechanical, do we mean that? I don't think we do. If you lose your job, or if your wife turns to somebody else, you don't say, "My brain is mechanical." You are aflame with anxiety, with jealousy. So you see how misleading words can be. You say that the brain is mechanical, and you leave it at that. You don't find out if it really is mechanical. If the brain were a mechanical thing like the computer, it would have no problems. A machine has no problems, but the operator of the machine has problems. So you see how extraordinarily easy it is to fall into the trap of a word and get caught in it.

As we saw the other day, biologically as well as psychologically, the brain is an instrument which can be highly sharpened, made extremely sensitive. But society—by which I mean our relationships on the job, in the family, the whole psychological structure of society—is not going to make it sensitive. On the contrary, it is only when one understands this whole psychological structure of society, of which one is a part, by observing and understanding the process of thought—it is only then that the brain becomes sharp, alive, keen, aware.

July 14, 1963

Fifth Talk in Saanen

I would like this morning to talk about several things, but before I go into them, I think it is important to understand how to listen. I have often talked about listening, and those of you who are hearing it for the tenth time may think that I am merely repeating myself. You know, for me there is no repetition in these matters. If I found myself repeating, it would be dreadfully boring to myself. For me, what is being said is never a repetition. It is something that one discovers anew each time. It is like the spring. One has seen many, many springs, but each time it is different. Each time the new leaf has somehow a different color, a different tenderness, a different movement. In the same way, when I talk about all these things, it is not repetitive at all. Each time one discovers something fresh, totally new.

So, I would like to talk about listening, because it seems to me that in listening there is no effort at all. There is effort only if you don't understand the language, the words that are being used. When you try to listen, try to follow what the speaker is saying; when you try to concentrate, to put your whole mind on it, it prevents you from listening. Listening implies no inward contradiction; there is no attempt to do something, no endeavor to capture or to realize something; you just listen, easily, with an attention that doesn't demand concentration. And what I am going to talk about needs very deep listening—not just hearing through the ears, but listening with an extraordinary profundity. If you can listen in this way, you will find that you have understood for yourself a great many things, and in the very act of listening, the nature of action is changed. Because, listening is an action. It isn't something apart from daily activity. It includes listening to your wife or husband, to your children, to your neighbor, to noises, to all the ugly things that go on in life, to all the brutalities, the words of cruelty, to the words of pleasure and pain. And you will find that in this act of listening a mutation is taking place in the very nature of action itself.

This morning I want to talk about fear and love, and whether it is at all possible to be totally free of fear. If deep down in the unconscious, at the very root of consciousness, there is any element, shadow, or darkness of fear, all our thinking, all our activity becomes perverted, leading to various forms of self-contradiction, a neurotic state of mind.

Now, most of us are seeking fulfillment, whether in the family, in relationship, or in some form of action or self-expression. To fulfill ourselves in something has become extraordinarily important. If there were no fear at all, there would be no demand for fulfillment. It is our constant self-centered activity that separates us and brings about fear, anxiety, an extraordinary loneliness, a sense of isolation, and therefore we demand fulfillment, some form of self-expression. A mind that has no fear of any kind has no need to fulfill. If one understands this fact, basically, there is then not only no demand for self-fulfillment—there is also no frustration. But for most of us life is frustrating, and to understand this whole process of frustration, one must not only be aware of but tear open every activity, every thought, every feeling through which we are seeking fulfillment, trying to express ourselves—tear it open, not in the sense of reacting to it, but unfolding it so completely that we understand it.

You know, knowing is different from knowledge. Knowledge is of the past; it is a thing that one has stored up: scientific knowledge, knowledge of how to read and write, the knowledge that you must have to put a radio together, and so on. That knowledge is constantly being added to through experience, and it is entirely different from knowing. I don't think I am splitting hairs, and I do think one has to understand this. Knowing implies no accumulation. You are attentive all the time, learning from the thing that is actually taking place; you do not know about it from previous knowledge. I think one should understand the difference between the two. To be aware of the self-centered activity of the mind is just to see it, to look at it; but one looks at it with previous knowledge, that is, in terms of what one has already learned, and this knowledge interprets what one is looking at or listening to.

Please follow this, observing yourselves. Observe every movement of your own thought, just watch it, and you will discover how you are watching it: whether you are watching it from the background of what you have already learned about it, or watching it in a state of discovery. To discover is to look at something anew, as though for the first time, and you can't do that if you recognize what you see. I hope I am making myself clear. The moment there is recognition in the process of observing or knowing yourself, you have brought into your observation the background of knowledge—which means that you have already interpreted, you have translated, condemned, or justified what you see; therefore, you are not watching, you are not observing, you are not listening to the whole process of it. The thing that you are observing, which is thought and the whole background of thought, is not static; it is moving, living, and if you observe it with previous knowledge, you are merely interpreting it, you are not discovering it as something new. Therefore you think there is nothing new in all this, there is nothing more to learn. You say, "I know I am jealous," or "I know I am afraid," which means that you have given the emotion a name; you have recognized it, so it becomes part of that which you already know. But to look at it as though you were seeing it for the first time—with a mind that doesn't interpret, that doesn't translate, that doesn't want to alter what it sees—is to be in a state of discovery.

Am I conveying what I want to say?

You see, there is mutation only when the mind, the brain is no longer seeking experience; and when you begin to translate what you see in terms of what you already know, you are only continuing the cycle of experience. I see I am puzzling you.

There is this complex entity called the 'me', with all its travail, its suffering, its anxieties, its desire to fulfill, to become, to dominate, to have a position, to have security, to be somebody, to express itself in different ways. This 'me' has been put together through centuries by the psychological structure of society; it is the outcome of pressures, influences, propaganda, tradition. With this 'me' I go about looking at everything I meet and translating it accordingly, so naturally I think there is nothing new because everything is always being contaminated by the past.

Now, innocency is something uncontaminated, something totally new, fresh; it is a state of discovery in which the mind is always young. To find that out for yourself, you can't go on carrying with you this burden of the past. The past must somehow come to an end if the mind is to discover that new thing, and it must come to an end without effort, without discipline, without control or suppression. The old cannot find the new because whatever the old experiences is a continuation of the old. The old may undergo a variety of changes, but such changes are a modified continuity of the same thing.

Do you understand the problem? This entity, the 'me', is the product of time, the product of a thousand experiences, a thousand contradictions, battles, anxieties, the outcome of guilt, sorrow, misery, pleasure. It is the residue of the past with all its fears, and therefore it cannot possibly discover the new. The new cannot possibly be put into words; it is something immeasurable, an energy which has no cause, no end, no beginning; and for the mind to be in that state of creation, the old, the 'me', must come to an end. Now, how is it to be done?

The organized religions say that you must control, discipline, train yourself, and wait for the grace of God. In India, in Asia, in Europe, this is expressed in different ways, but it comes to the same thing: that you must train yourself, control yourself, be good—you know all the moral things we are told to do, with their various sanctions. We are told to wait, expect, contemplate, pray, and all the rest of it.

Now, to me, all that is utterly illogical, unreasonable; it has no meaning because, first of all, a mind that disciplines itself is conforming to a pattern; it is imitating, restricting its own activity in order to be or become something; like a soldier drilling, it obeys implicitly, immediately, and therefore there is no freedom. Also, discipline implies fear. Please, if you follow all this very, very carefully, really observe it, you will see that when there is freedom from fear, this freedom brings its own discipline, which is not mere conformity and which has nothing to do with the discipline of enforcement, compliance, imitation. And when we talk about waiting for the grace of God to come to us, there is a deep-down expectation, which means that the brain is already caught in a certain belief, in a certain hope. So all this discipline and prayer, this waiting for something to happen from outside of the mind's own activity, seems to me illogical, irrational, it has no meaning; therefore, I put it all aside. Having a belief in God, in something superior, implies that one has not become a light unto oneself; and a mind that is without conflict, without anxiety, without travail, is a light unto itself. Therefore it is no longer seeking.

So, the problem is: There is this 'me', the result of time, the result of experience, of knowledge. This 'me' is a thing of the past—the past that is always moving through the present and shaping the future, which is psychological time. With this time-bound entity, I try to find something which is not within the field of time and cannot be understood in terms of the past. Now, can this be done? Do you understand the question?

Please don't wait for an answer from me—you and I are working together. You are not merely listening to a lot of words from me, and then trying to put what you understand from those words into action. We are going on a journey together.

First, I say that any form of effort to capture the new or to change what has been, only gives vitality to the old and brings about a contradiction. That is fairly obvious, is it not? No? I will go along, and if you don't understand, you can ask me afterwards. As I pointed out the other day, there is no effort involved in understanding; there is no analysis because there is no division between the observer and the thing observed. There is no trying to suppress the thing observed, or to change it. You are that thing. Do you follow?

Now, wait a moment. There is a hum going on in this tent. That electric fan is working, making a noise. How do you listen to it? If that noise is irritating you, if it is something apart from you, then you are consciously or unconsciously resisting it because you are trying to listen. But if that noise, the hum of that electric fan, is part of your attention, there is no resistance. You are that noise. With that same state of mind, you can look at the whole process of your own consciousness, with all its contradictions, its desires, ambitions, drives, compulsions, fulfillments. You are all that. You are not an observer looking at something separate from himself; therefore, there is no resistance, no conflict between you and that something.

I don't know if you are getting what I am talking about.

Take fear, for example. Fear is you who are observing it; therefore, there is no question of getting rid of fear. The moment you try to get rid of fear, you develop courage, or a resistance which is called courage; there is an effort to be or to become something, and therefore you are again caught in fear.

So consciousness, which includes both the conscious and the unconscious, is like a vortex which you are observing, but not as something apart from yourself. You are that vortex. You are the thinker and the thought, the observer and the observed; there are not two different states. Therefore all effort, all analysis has stopped; all struggling to improve yourself, to change, has come to an end. Do you understand what has happened? You are watching yourself, not just listening to me. Your mind, your brain, which has been trained to condemn, to justify, to resist, to make an effort to bring about a mutation, to develop courage, and so on, your brain, which has been conditioned to think of itself as the observer apart from the thing observed is no longer making an effort to be or to do something. Your thought is not trying to conquer or to change itself into something else. So you have removed all resistance; therefore, there is no longer the desire to fulfill, and therefore there is no fear. I am talking of psychological, and not organic, fear. The two things are different, are they not? If I am not attentive, I will be run over by a car, drop over a precipice, and so on. For that reason I need to be watchful, extraordinarily alert; there must be a certain sense of organic self-protection. But I am talking of psychological fear—the many psychological fears that we have developed. As long as there is this thing called the 'me'—with all its trivialities, aspirations, intuitions, with all its drives, its compulsions, its wanting to fulfill—there is bound to be fear, and in that state there can obviously be no love. For most of us, love is a tortured thing. We are caught in jealousy, envy, attachment, sorrow. We are afraid of being left alone, of losing someone, of not being loved—you know what we go through. That is what we call love, but it is all part of fear.

So, when you observe this whole consciousness, not in terms of time; when thought is no longer a slave to time, no longer a reaction, and there is complete quietness of thought; then you will find that—because the brain is completely quiet, no longer experiencing—you can go to the very root of all consciousness, and only then is there real mutation, transformation. Every activity is then entirely free from fear, and therefore there is no demand for self-expression or fulfillment.

Shall we discuss what I have been talking about?

Question: How does the division between thought and the thinker arise?

KRISHNAMURTI: You know there is this division, don't you? Are you aware of it? And how does it arise? We have accepted this division as normal, as inevitable; we have accepted it as naturally as we accept the sun and the clouds, but we have never asked ourselves how it arises. There are those who say that first there is the thinker, who then creates thought, and that the division between them follows. A whole philosophy is built on that. But you and I have not read all the philosophical books on this subject, so we can try to find out for ourselves the truth of the matter. How does this division arise? Please, you work along with me. How does it arise?

Question: Does not the consciousness of time create the division?

KRISHNAMURTI: What do we mean by the consciousness of time? The memory of yesterday, the knowledge, the experiences we have gathered, the things that we have known; and that gentleman suggests it is this consciousness of time that creates the division between the thinker and the thought.

Now, why are we questioning this division? Because as long as there is a division between the thought and the thinker, there must be conflict. Please see that this is the root of it. Do you understand? As long as there is a division between the observer and the observed, between the experiencer and the thing experienced, there must be conflict. And any form of conflict dulls the mind, wears out the brain; it cripples and makes the brain insensitive. So, to bring about freedom from conflict, you have to understand this division.

How does this division arise? Is there any division if there is no thinking at all? Not to think at all is extremely difficult, so don't say, "That's easy, one is just blank." I am not talking of that idiotic state of blankness, nor of taking a drug and numbing the brain. But if there is no thinking, there is no division, obviously. If you were so completely insensitive, paralyzed, that you were incapable of thinking, then there would be no self-contradiction. So it is thinking that produces this division between the thought and the thinker. And how does thinking bring it about? Thinking is a transitory process, is it not? It is all the time changing, moving; it is not what it was; it is in a constant state of flux, and this very process of thinking wants stability, security; it wants to feel itself safe. Thinking is painful; it creates so many problems, and because thinking does not solve the problems it has created, we hope that God, or something, will somehow give us security, peace.

If you are following, you can see for yourself that this is obviously not a theory. Contradictory thoughts, contradictory desires, wants, create conflict, pain, suffering; so the mind says, "There must be something secure, something permanent—God, an idea, or a divine part of me that is untouched by conflict." To the Hindu it is the atma, the Supreme; to the Christian it is something else, and to the communist it is again something else. So thinking demands security, and that is why we have built up a society which is psychologically seeking security all the time. Thought creates the division because it demands security, permanency; and having created the division, thought says, "How am I to reach that permanency?" From this you have all the various systems for reaching that extraordinary state of permanency in which the brain will never be disturbed.

To put it differently, thought projects from itself that which it calls the permanent—heaven, nirvana, God, peace, the perfect state. Then having established the goal, the ideal, thought tries to conform to it. That is what you are all doing. You want perfect peace, an ideal relationship with yourself, with your husband or wife, with society, and so on, and so on. You have an idea, and you are approximating yourself to that idea. So there is the 'you', and the thing apart.

Now, is there anything permanent? Not just verbally, but actually, deep down, is there anything permanent—permanent in the sense of being fixed? Is there anything permanent between you and your wife or husband, between you and your children? Is there permanency in an idea? But you want permanency; therefore, when the existence of permanency is questioned, you get upset or become angry.

So, observing and understanding this whole process, the mind lives not seeking permanency, either in name, in activity, or in relationship. And surely that is love, is it not? If you demand permanency in your relationship with yourself, with your friend, with your wife and children, just see what happens—the tortures you go through, the jealousies, the misery, the confusion and sorrow. Yet that is what we call love.

So we begin to see that thought—which is the response of memory, the result of time, the result of many, many thousands of yesterdays—is constantly seeking to establish for itself a state of certainty. But the mind that is certain can never be free—nor can the mind that is uncertain.

Question: Consciously we are in harmony, in complete agreement with what you are saying, but unconsciously, when we leave here and are again caught up in our daily activities, we act quite contrary to what we have listened to and understood. Why does this happen?

KRISHNAMURTI: It is fairly simple, isn't it? How do you listen? Do you listen only to words? Is what you hear merely a statement with which you intellectually agree or disagree? Or do you listen with your whole being, not only consciously, but also unconsciously? When you so listen, there is neither agreement nor disagreement. You see the fact itself, not the fact as someone else presents it. And you cannot be in harmony with a fact. Do you follow? If you attempt to be in harmony with a fact, you are inevitably brought into conflict. But if you are that fact, there is no conflict; therefore, when you leave this tent, there is no contradiction between what you have heard and what you do. You hear and do—it is a complete, unitary process. That is why it is very important that you listen—listen with your whole being, and not just intellectually or verbally, with your conscious thought alone. Have you ever listened to anything with your whole being? I question it.

Question: Even if one does listen with one's whole being, I wonder if that in itself is sufficient to affect the unconscious?

KRISHNAMURTI: Sir, when you give your attention totally to what is being said, you are listening, not just to the words and the meaning of words, but to the whole content that lies behind the words; and the very giving of your total attention is an act in which the nature of your action is changing. Therefore, when you leave here, there is a total action, and not just an intellectual action contradicting your unconscious.

Now, you will say, "How am I to listen with total attention? I don't know how to listen in that way; I don't really listen to anything, so please give me a method, a way, a system that will help me to listen with my whole being." And what would happen if I gave you a system? Your trying to listen would create a contradiction with your habit of not listening, and therefore you would be caught again in the same old business.

Sir, when suddenly you have a great sorrow, what do you do? At that moment you are completely in a state of shock, are you not? The crisis has forced you to be silent; you are absolutely confronted with something which you don't understand, and you are momentarily paralyzed; you have no words. In that state of shock—if you don't try to find a way out of it, or explain it away—you are looking, observing, listening with total attention. Now, can you listen in the same way to yourself? Your whole being is in a constant state of flux, always active, never still—wanting this, not wanting that, contradicting itself, fulfilling itself, in endless turmoil. And can you listen to that turmoil without becoming neurotic? To become neurotic, slightly off the beam, is very easy. That is what most people do. But if you can listen to yourself without running off, and without trying to change what you hear—just listen to the silent noise that is going on within yourself—that act of listening brings about a vital change in the very nature of action, and then in action there is no contradiction.

July 16, 1963

Sixth Talk in Saanen

This morning I would like to talk about sorrow. It is a very complex problem, and as one cannot go into it in great detail, I shall, if I may, go only into the essentials of it.

Without understanding sorrow, there is no wisdom; the ending of sorrow is the beginning of wisdom. To understand sorrow and to be completely free of it demands an understanding, not only of the particular individualistic sorrows, but also of the enormous sorrow of man. To me, without being totally free of sorrow, there can be no wisdom, nor is the mind capable of really inquiring into that immeasurable something which may be called God, or by any other name.

Most of us have sorrow in different forms—in relationship, in the death of someone, in not fulfilling oneself and withering away to nothing, or in trying to achieve, trying to become something, and meeting with total failure. And there is the whole problem of sorrow on the physical side—illness, blindness, incapacitation, paralysis, and so on. Everywhere there is this extraordinary thing called sorrow—with death waiting round the corner. And we do not know how to meet sorrow, so either we worship it, or rationalize it, or try to run away from it. Go into any Christian church and you will find that sorrow is worshiped; it is made into something extraordinary, holy, and it is said that only through sorrow, through the crucified Christ, can you find God. In the East they have their own forms of evasion, other ways of avoiding sorrow, and it seems to me an extraordinary thing that so very few, whether in the East or in the West, are really free of sorrow.

It would be a marvelous thing if in the process of your listening—unemotionally, not sentimentally—to what is being said this morning, and before you leave this tent, you could really understand sorrow and be totally free of it; because then there would be no self-deception, no illusions, no anxieties, no fear, and the brain could function clearly, sharply, logically. And then, perhaps, one would know what love is.

Now, to understand sorrow, one must inquire into the whole process of time. Time is sorrow, not only the sorrow of the past, but also the sorrow which involves the future—the idea of arriving, the struggle to achieve, the hope that you will someday be something, with its inevitable shadow of frustration. This whole idea of achievement, of becoming something in the future, which is psychological time, is to me the greatest sorrow—not the fact that my son dies, or that my wife or husband leaves me, or that I am not a success. All this, it seems to me, is rather trivial, if I may use that word, which I hope you will not misunderstand. There is a much deeper sorrow, which is psychological time: thinking that I will change in future years, that, given time, I will transform myself, I will break away from habit, I will achieve liberation, acquire wisdom, find God. All this implies time—and that, to me, is the greatest sorrow. But to go deeply into the problem, one has to find out why there is sorrow within oneself—this wave of sorrow in which one is caught and which makes one a prisoner. By first understanding the particular sorrow within ourselves, perhaps we can understand also the collective sorrow of man, the despair of humanity.

Why do we suffer? And is there an end to sorrow? There are so many ways of suffering. Ill health is one type of suffering—the incapacity to think due to feebleness of the brain, and the various kinds of physical pain. Then there is the whole field of psychological suffering—feeling frustrated because one is not able to achieve, or has no capacity, no understanding, no intelligence; and also this constant battle of conflicting desires, of self-contradiction, with its anxieties and despairs. There is furthermore the idea of changing oneself through time, becoming better, nobler, wiser, in which also there is sorrow without end. And ultimately there is the sorrow of death, the sorrow of separation, of isolation, the sorrow of being completely lonely, of being cut off and having no relationship with anything.

We all know these various forms of sorrow. The very learned, the intellectual, the saintly, the religious people all over the world are as tortured as we are by sorrow, and if there is a way out, they have not found it. To inquire very deeply into ourselves is to know that this is the first thing we want—to put an end to sorrow—but we do not know how to set about it. We are well acquainted with sorrow; we see it in others and in ourselves, and it is in the very air we breathe. Go where you will—retire to a monastery, walk in the crowded streets—sorrow is always present, openly, or hidden, waiting, watching.

Now, how does one meet sorrow? What does one do about it? And how is one to be free of it, not just superficially, but totally, so that there is no sorrow at all? To be completely free of sorrow does not mean that one feels no love, no sympathy, that one has no kindliness, no understanding of another. On the contrary, in total freedom from sorrow there is no indifference. It is a freedom which brings great sensitivity, openness; and how does one come to that freedom? You all know sorrow; it is not something to which you are a stranger. It is there. And how do you meet it? Do you meet it only superficially, verbally?

Please do follow this. Step by step let us go together to the very end of it. See if you can listen this morning with complete attention, being aware of your own reactions, and go deeply with me into this problem of sorrow—not that you are going to follow me; that would be too absurd. But if we can understand this thing together, inquire into it widely and deeply, then perhaps, when you leave here, you can look at the sky, and sorrow will never touch you again. Then there will be no fear, and when all fear is gone, that immeasurable something may walk with you.

So, how do you meet sorrow? I'm afraid that most of us meet it very superficially. Our education, our training, our knowledge, the sociological influences to which we are exposed, all make us superficial. A superficial mind is one that escapes to the church, to some conclusion, to some concept, to some belief or idea. Those are all a refuge for the superficial mind that is in sorrow. And if you cannot find a refuge, you build a wall around yourself and become cynical, hard, indifferent, or you escape through some facile, neurotic reaction. All such defenses against suffering prevent further inquiry. I hope you are going along with me, for this is what most of us actually do.

Now, observe a superficial brain or mind—please, whether I use the word *mind* or *brain*, I mean the same thing. The other day we went into the separation of the brain and the mind, but the separation is only verbal and does not matter. I am going to use the word mind, and I hope you will follow and understand what is being said.

The superficial mind cannot solve this problem of sorrow because what it tries is to avoid sorrow. It escapes from the fact of sorrow through an easy and immediate response. If you have a severe toothache, naturally you go immediately to the dentist because you want to be free of that physical pain—which is a normal and right response. But psychological pain is much deeper and more subtle, and no doctor, no psychologist, nothing can dissolve it for you. Yet your instinctive response is to run away from it. You turn on the radio, watch television, go to the cinema—you know all the distractions that modern civilization has invented. Entertainment of every kind, whether it is a church service or a football match, is essentially the same. It is merely a way of escaping from your own misery, your emptiness—and this is what you are all doing everywhere throughout the world: using various forms of the circus to forget yourself.

Similarly, it is the superficial mind that tries to find explanations. It says, "I want to know why I suffer. Why should I suffer and not you?" It feels that it has done nothing particularly wrong in this life, so it accepts the theory of past lives and the idea of what in India is called karma—cause and effect. It says, "I have done something wrong in the past, and now I am paying for it"; or "I am now doing something good, and I shall get the benefit of it in the future." So the superficial mind gets caught in explanations.

Please watch your own mind; observe how you explain your sorrows away, lose yourself in work, in ideas, or cling to a belief in God, or in a future life. And if no explanation, no belief has been satisfactory, you escape through drink, through sex, or by becoming cynical, hard, bitter, brittle. Consciously or unconsciously, this is what is actually taking place with each one of us. But the wound of sorrow is very deep. Generation after generation it has been passed on by parents to their children, and the superficial mind never takes the bandage off that wound; it does not really know, it is not really acquainted with sorrow. It merely has an idea about sorrow. It has a picture, a symbol of sorrow, but it never meets sorrow—it meets only the word *sorrow*. Do you understand? The word sorrow it knows, but I am not at all sure it knows sorrow.

Knowing the word *hunger* and actually being hungry are two very different things, are they not? When you are hungry, you are not satisfied with the word *food*. You want food, the fact. Now, most of us are satisfied with words, symbols, ideas, and with our reaction to those words, and we are never completely with the fact. When we suddenly come face to face with the fact of sorrow, it gives us a shock, and our reaction is to run away from it. I wonder if you have noticed this in yourself? Please follow your own state of mind, and don't merely listen to the words that are being spoken. We never meet sorrow, we never live with it. We live with a picture, with the memory of what has been, and not with the fact. We live with a reaction.

Now, if in facing sorrow the mind has a motive, that is, if it wants to do something about sorrow, there can be no understanding of sorrow any more than there can be love if there is a motive for love. Do you understand? Most of us have a motive when we look at sorrow; we want to do something about it. That is, suppose I have lost somebody by death; deeply, psychologically, I can no longer get what I want from that person, and I am in sorrow. If I have no motive in looking at my sorrow, will it still be sorrow, or will sorrow be something quite different? Are you following all this?

Let us say that my son dies, and I am in sorrow because I am alone. I had invested all my hopes in him, and now my whole world has collapsed. I had wanted to establish for myself a certain immortality, a continuity through my son; he was to have perpetuated my name, inherited my property, carried on my business, and the ending of all that has given me a shock. Now, can I understand the sorrow I am in if there is a motive behind my looking at it? And if there is a motive behind love, is it love? Don't please agree with me; just observe yourselves. Surely, there cannot be a motive if I want to understand sorrow, if I want to discover the full depth and significance of sorrow—or of love, because they always go together. Death, love, and sorrow are inseparable; they are always together, and with them goes also creation; but that is another matter, and we will go into it some other time. If I want to understand deeply, completely, the fact of sorrow, I cannot have a motive which dictates my reaction to that fact. I can live with the fact and understand it only when I have no motive. Do you understand? If not, you can ask questions afterwards about this point.

If I "love" you because you can give me something—your body, your money, your flattery, your companionship, or whatever it is—surely that is not love, is it? Of course, you get something from me also, and that exchange for most of us is love. I know we cover it all up with fine words, but behind the verbal façade there is this pressure to have, to own, to possess.

Now, is not sorrow self-pity? You have been deprived in some way; your relationship with another has been a failure; you have not fulfilled yourself by being recognized as a big man in the name of social reform, in the name of art, in the name of any one of a million things, with all the stupid nonsense it implies—so there is sorrow. To understand sorrow is to live with it, to look at it, to know it for what it really is—and you cannot possibly know it if you look with a motive, which is time. A superficial mind that is everlastingly concerned with bettering itself, pitying itself, torturing itself in a particular relationship, wanting to be free of sorrow and not facing the fact—such a mind will go on suffering indefinitely. The fact is that you are lonely. Through your education, your activities, your thoughts and feelings, you have deeply isolated yourself inside, and you cannot live with that extraordinary sense of loneliness; you do not know what it means because you approach it with a word that evokes fear.

So you see the difficulty—the subtle ways in which the mind has built escapes so that it is incapable of living with that extraordinary something which we call sorrow. To be free of sorrow, this whole process has to be understood, consciously as well as unconsciously, and you can understand it only when you live with the fact, look at it without motive. You have to see the tricks of your own mind—the escapes, the pleasurable things which you hold on to, and the painful things that you want to get rid of quickly. You have to observe the emptiness, the dullness and stupidity of a mind that merely escapes. And it makes little difference whether you escape to God, to sex, or to drink, because all escapes are essentially the same. Do you understand?

What happens when you lose someone by death? The immediate reaction is a sense of paralysis, and when you come out of that state of shock, there is what we call sorrow. Now, what does that word *sorrow* mean? The companionship, the happy words, the walks, the many pleasant things you did and hoped to do together—all this is taken away in a second, and you are left empty, naked, lonely. That is what you are objecting to, that is what the mind rebels against: being suddenly left to itself, utterly lonely, empty, without any support. Now, what matters is to live with that emptiness, just to live with it without any reaction, without rationalizing it, without running away from it to mediums, to the theory of reincarnation, and all that stupid nonsense—to live with it with your whole being. And if you go into it step by step, you will find that there is an ending of sorrow—a real ending, not just a verbal ending, not the superficial ending that comes through escape, through identification with a concept, or commitment to an idea. Then you will find there is nothing to protect because the mind is completely empty and is no longer reacting in the sense of trying to fill that emptiness; and when all sorrow has thus come to an end, you will have started on another journey—a journey that has no ending and no beginning. There is an immensity that is beyond all measure, but you cannot possibly enter into that world without the total ending of sorrow.

Question: Is humor an escape from sorrow?

KRISHNAMURTI: Before you ask a question, please remain silent for a little while and think out, go further into what has just been said. If you pop up immediately with a question, it means that you haven't really gone into it at all. What we have been considering together has great significance. It isn't something cheap that you can buy to end sorrow and then say, "Well, I have ended sorrow." That would be too childish. When we have uncovered the whole field of human experience, which has been enriched through centuries of man's sorrow, you cannot just brush it off with a word, with a symbol, or by running away. To get the right answer, you must ask the right question; and you will ask the right question only when you are really in it, when you have exposed yourself to the problem.

Question: What about the sorrow which is not one's own sorrow, but sorrow for somebody else?

KRISHNAMURTI: Before we go into that question, let us look at the former question: "Is humor an escape from sorrow?" If you can laugh about your sorrow, is that an escape? There is this enormous thing called sorrow, and do you see what you have reduced it to when you ask such a question? When you are in sorrow, you may perhaps laugh it away, but there is still sorrow. There is the suffering, the torture that is going on in the world: the misery of having no food, of being afraid of death, of seeing the rich man in the big car and feeling envious, the brutality, the tyranny that is going on in the East, and all the rest of it. Can you laugh all that away? I am afraid you are not really aware of your own sorrow.

The second question is: "What about the sorrow one feels for somebody else?" When you see somebody else suffering, don't you suffer also? When you see a man who is blind, or a man who has no food, or a man who is not loved, who is caught in misery, strife, confusion, don't you suffer with him? Now, why should one suffer with him? I know it is the accepted, the traditional, the respectable thing to say, "I suffer with you." But why should you suffer? If you have a little, you give of that little. You give your sympathy, your affection, your love. But why should you suffer? Please follow this. If my son contracts polio and is dying, why should I suffer? I know this sounds terribly cruel to you. Having done everything possible, given him my love, my sympathy, brought the doctor, the medicine, and having sacrificed—but is it sacrifice? Is that the right word?—having done everything in my power, why should I suffer? When I suffer for somebody, is that suffering? Do think it out, go into it; don't just accept what I am saying. You know, when you go to India and to other places in the East, you see immense poverty—poverty such as you know not a thing about in the West. When you walk in the streets, you rub shoulders with people who have leprosy and other diseases. You do everything you can, but what is the need to suffer? Does love suffer? Oh, you will have to go into all this. Surely, love never suffers.

Question: Can deep suffering turn to deep joy?

KRISHNAMURTI: Do you put such a question when you are suffering? Please, what are you talking about?

Comment: I mean suffering in itself changes to joy.

KRISHNAMURTI: If suffering changes to joy, where are you at the end of it? Sir, some people, fortunately or unfortunately, have listened to me for forty years, and I know those people quite well. We have met off and on over the years. Do I suffer because they have no understanding? They are still asking about authority, about self-expression, about God—you know all the childish things that are asked. Do I suffer? I would suffer only if I expected something from them; I would be disappointed if I had put myself in a position to be disappointed by feeling that I am somebody who is giving something to somebody else. I hope you understand what I am talking about.

Please, what is important is not how to transform sorrow into joy, or whether sorrow changes into joy, or whether you should suffer when you see others suffering—all those questions have no importance at all. What is important is to understand sorrow for yourself, and thereby to end sorrow. Only then will you find out what lies beyond sorrow. Otherwise it is like sitting on this side of the mountain and speculating about what lies on the other side. You are just talking, guessing. You don't grapple with the problem, you don't face it; you don't go deeply into yourself and look, search, understand; and you don't do it because you know it would mean really letting go of many things—letting go of your pet ideas, of your traditional, respectable responses.

Comment: One suffers if one cannot help somebody.

KRISHNAMURTI: If you can help somebody physically or economically, you do, and that is the end of it. But why do you suffer if you can't? You haven't tackled the basic problem yourself, so who are you to "help" another? The priests all over the world are "helping" somebody—which means what? They are helping to condition others according to their own particular beliefs and dogmas. Disinterestedly feeding the starving, building a better land, a better world—that is a help. But to say to another, "I will give you help psychologically"—what conceit! Who are you psychologically to help another? Leave that to the communists, who think they are providence and can dictate to millions of people what they should do. But why should you suffer if you can't help another? You do everything you can to help, which may not be much, but why go through this torture of suffering? Oh, you don't see, you have not gone into the real problem at all!

Question: I realize that to be completely free of sorrow, one has to be totally aware, fully attentive all the time. I have rare moments of total awareness, but the rest of the time I am caught in a state of inattention. Is this my lot for the rest of my life, and can I therefore never be free of sorrow?

KRISHNAMURTI: As the questioner says, to be free of sorrow is to be completely attentive. Attention is virtue in itself. But unfortunately one is not attentive all the time. I am attentive today, but tomorrow I am not, and I pick it up again the day after tomorrow. In the intervening period I am inattentive, and all kinds of activities go on, of which I am not fully aware. So the questioner says, "I see that I am caught in the state of inattention, and does this mean that I am bound never to be free of sorrow?"

Now, sir, the idea of being free forever implies time, does it not? We say, "I am not free now, but by becoming attentive I shall be free, and I want that freedom to continue for the rest of my days." So we are concerned with the continuity of attention. We say, "Somehow I must be attentive always; otherwise, I shall always be in sorrow." We want this state of attention to continue day after day.

Now, what continues? What is it that has continuity? Don't answer me, please; just listen for two minutes, and you will see something extraordinary. What has continuity? Surely, it is when I think about a thing, whether it is pleasurable or painful, that it has continuity. Do you understand? When I think about a pleasure or a pain, my thinking about it gives it continuity. If I like you, I think about you, and my thinking about you gives continuity to the pleasing image I have formed of you; so through the continuity of thought, association, memory, my response to you becomes a mechanical response, does it not? It is like that of a computer, which responds according to memory, association, on the basis of an immense amount of stored-up information.

Now, with that same mentality we say, "I must have continuity of attention." Do you follow, sir? But if we see what is implied in both attention and continuity, we will never put the two things together. I don't know if you have understood what I am trying to convey. The mistake that we are making is in trying to relate continuity with attention. We want the state of attention to continue, but what will continue is our thought about that state, and therefore it will not be attention. It is thought that gives continuity to what we call attention, but when thought gives continuity to attention, it is not the state of attention. If you give your whole mind to this and understand it, you will find there is a peculiar state of attention without continuity, without time.

Question: To what extent is sorrow attenuated by acceptance?

KRISHNAMURTI: Why should I accept sorrow? That is merely another superficial activity of the mind. I don't want to accept sorrow, or to attenuate it, or to run away from it. I want to understand sorrow, I want to see what it means; I want to know the beauty, the ugliness, the extraordinary vitality it has. I don't want to make it into something it is not. By accepting sorrow, or by running away from it, or by approaching it with a concept, a formula, I am not dealing with it. So a mind that would understand sorrow cannot do anything about it; it cannot transform sorrow or make it gentle. To be free of sorrow, you cannot do a thing about it. It is because we have always done something about it that we are still in sorrow.

July 18, 1963

Seventh Talk in Saanen

We have been exploring many problems which concern our daily life because without understanding these daily problems of conflict, greed, ambition, envy, the travail of love, and so on—without understanding them completely—it is utterly impossible to discover for oneself whether there is something beyond the things that the brain puts together: the everyday respectable morality, the inventions of the various churches throughout the world, the obviously materialistic outlook, and the intellectual attitude towards life.

Now, it seems to me that any human problem which continues to be a problem inevitably dulls the mind and makes it insensitive because the mind merely goes round in circles without ever coming out of its confusion and misery. So it is vitally necessary to understand each problem and be finished with it as it arises. I think very few of us realize that if any human problem is not resolved immediately, it gives to the mind a sense of continuity in which there is unending conflict, and this makes the mind insensitive, dull, stupid. This fact must be clearly understood, and also it must be understood that we are not talking in terms of any particular system of philosophy, or looking at life along any special line of thought. As you know, we have discussed many things, but not from either an Oriental or an Occidental point of view. We have tackled each problem, not as Christians or Hindus or Zen Buddhists or from any other slanted viewpoint, but simply as rational, intelligent human beings, without any bias or neuroticism.

This morning I would like to talk about an important question, which is that of death—death not only of the individual, but death as an idea which exists throughout the world and which has been carried on as a problem for centuries without ever being resolved. There is not only the particular individual's fear of death but also an enormous, collective attitude towards death—in Asia as well as in the Western countries—which has to be understood. So we are going to consider together this whole issue.

In considering such a vast and significant problem, words are only intended to enable us to communicate, to have communion with each other. But the word itself can easily become a hindrance when we are trying to understand this profound question of death, unless we give our complete attention to it, and not just verbally, flippantly or intellectually try to find a reason for its existence.

Before, or perhaps in the process of understanding this extraordinary thing called death, we shall have to understand also the significance of time, which is another great factor in our lives. Thought creates time, and time controls and shapes our thought. I am using the word *time,* not only in the chronological sense of yesterday, today, and tomorrow, but also in the psychological sense—the time which thought has invented as a means to arrive, to achieve, to postpone. Both are factors in our lives, are they not? One has to be aware of chronological time; otherwise, you and I couldn't meet here at eleven o'clock. Chronological time is obviously necessary in the events of our life—that is a simple, clear matter which need not be gone into very deeply. So what we have to explore, discuss, and understand is the whole psychological process which we call time.

Please, as I have been saying at every meeting here, if you merely hear the words and do not see the implications behind the words, I am afraid we cannot go very far. Most of us are enslaved by words and by the concept or formula which the words have put together. Do not just brush this aside because each one of us has a formula, a concept, an idea, an ideal—rational, irrational, or neurotic—according to which he is living. The mind is guiding itself by some pattern, by a particular series of words which have been made into a concept, a formula. This is true of each one of us, and please make no mistake about it—there is an idea, a pattern according to which we are shaping our lives. But if we are to understand this question of death and life, all formulas, patterns, and ideations—which exist because we do not understand living—must entirely go. A man who is living totally, completely, without fear, has no idea about living. His action is thought, and his thought is action; they are not two separate things. But because we are afraid of the thing called death, we have divided it from life; we have put life and death in two separate watertight compartments with a great space between them and live according to the word, according to the formula of the past, the tradition of what has been; and a mind that is caught in this process can never possibly see all the implications of death and of life, nor understand what truth is.

So, when you inquire with me into this whole question, if you inquire as a Christian, a Buddhist, a Hindu, or what you will, you will be completely at a loss. And if you bring to this inquiry the residue of your various experiences, the knowledge which you have acquired from books, from other people, again you will not only be disappointed but rather confused. The man who would really inquire must first be free of all these things which make up his background—and that is our greatest difficulty. One must be free from the past, but not as a reaction, because without this freedom one cannot discover anything new. Understanding is freedom. But, as I said the other day, very few of us want to be free. We would rather live in a secure framework of our own making, or in a framework put together by society. Any disturbance within that pattern is very disquieting, and rather than be disturbed, we live a life of negligence, death, and decay.

To inquire into this enormous question of death, we must not only be choicelessly aware of our slavery to formulas, concepts, but also of our fears, our desire for continuity, and so on. To inquire, we must come to the problem afresh. Please, this is really very important. The mind must be clear and not be caught in a concept or an idea if one would go into something which is quite extraordinary—as death must be. Death must be something extraordinary, not this thing that we try to cheat and are afraid of.

Psychologically we are slaves to time—time being the memory of yesterday, of the past, with all its accumulated experiences; it is not only your memory as that of a particular person but also the memory of the collective, of the race, of man throughout the ages. The past is made up of man's individual and collective sorrows, miseries, joys, his extraordinary struggle with life, with death, with truth, with society. All that is the past, yesterday multiplied by thousands; and for most of us the present is the movement of the past towards the future. There are no such exact divisions as the past, the present, and the future. What has been, modified by the present, is what will be. That is all we know. The future is the past modified by the accidents of the present; tomorrow is yesterday reshaped by the experiences, reactions, and knowledge of today. This is what we call time.

Time is a thing that has been put together by the brain, and the brain in turn is the result of time, of a thousand yesterdays. Every thought is the result of time; it is the response of memory, the reaction of yesterday's longings, frustrations, failures, sorrows, impending dangers; and with that background, we look at life, we consider everything. Whether there is God or no God, what the function of the state is, the nature of relationship, how to overcome or to adjust oneself to jealousy, anxiety, guilt, despair, sorrow—we look at all these questions with that background of time.

Now, whatever we look at with that background is distorted, and when the crisis demanding attention is very great, if we look at it with the eyes of the past, we either act neurotically, which is what most of us do, or we build for ourselves a wall of resistance against it. That is the whole process of our life.

Please, I am verbally exposing these things, but if you merely look at the words and do not observe your own process of thinking, which is to see yourself as you are, then when you leave here this morning, you will not have a complete understanding of death, and there must be that understanding if you are to be free of fear and enter into something quite different.

So, we are everlastingly translating the present in terms of the past, and thereby giving a continuity to what has been. For most of us, the present is the continuation of the past. We meet the everyday happenings of our life—which always have their own newness, their own significance—with the dead weight of the past, thereby creating that which we call the future. If you have observed your own mind, not only the conscious, but also the unconscious, you will know that it is the past, that there is nothing in it which is new, nothing which is not corrupted by the past, by time. And there is what we call the present. Is there a present untouched by the past? Is there a present which does not condition the future?

Probably you have not thought about this before, and we shall have to go into it a little bit. Most of us just want to live in the present because the past is so heavy, so burdensome, so inexhaustible, and the future so uncertain. The modern mind says, "Live completely in the present. Don't bother about what will happen tomorrow, but live for today. Life is such a misery anyhow, and the evil of one day is enough, so live each day completely and forget everything else." That is obviously a philosophy of despair.

Now, is it possible to live in the present without bringing into it time, which is the past? Surely, you can live in that totality of the present only when you understand the whole of the past. To die to time is to live in the present, and you can die to time only if you have understood the past, which is to understand your own mind—not only the conscious mind which goes to the office every day, gathers knowledge and experience, has superficial reactions, and all the rest of it, but also the unconscious mind, in which are buried the accumulated traditions of the family, of the group, of the race. Buried in the unconscious also is the enormous sorrow of man and the fear of death. All that is the past, which is yourself, and you have to understand it. If you do not understand that; if you have not inquired into the ways of your own mind and heart, into your greed and sorrow; if you do not know yourself completely, you cannot live in the present. To live in the present is to die to the past. In the process of understanding yourself, you are made free of the past, which is your conditioning—your conditioning as a communist, a Catholic, a Protestant, a Hindu, a Buddhist, the conditioning imposed upon you by society and by your own greeds, envies, anxieties, despairs, sorrows, and frustrations. It is your conditioning that gives continuity to the 'me', the self.

As I was pointing out the other day, if you do not know yourself, your unconscious as well as your conscious states, all your inquiry will be twisted, given a bias. You will have no foundation for thinking which is rational, clear, logical, sane. Your thinking will be according to a certain pattern, formula, or set of ideas—but that is not really thinking. To think clearly, logically, without becoming neurotic, without being caught in any form of illusion, you have to know this whole process of your own consciousness, which is put together by time, by the past. And is it possible to live without the past? Surely, that is death. Do you understand? We will come back to the question of the present when we have seen for ourselves what death is.

What is death? This is a question for the young and for the old, so please put it to yourself. Is death merely the ending of the physical organism? Is that what we are afraid of? Is it the body that we want to continue? Or is it some other form of continuance that we crave? We all realize that the body, the physical entity, wears out through use, through various pressures, influences, conflicts, urges, demands, sorrows. Some would probably like it if the body could be made to continue for 150 years or more, and perhaps the doctors and scientists together will ultimately find some way of prolonging the agony in which most of us live. But sooner or later the body dies, the physical organism comes to an end. Like any machine, it eventually wears out.

For most of us, death is something much deeper than the ending of the body, and all religions promise some kind of life beyond death. We crave a continuity, we want to be assured that something continues when the body dies. We hope that the psyche, the 'me'—the 'me' which has experienced, struggled, acquired, learned, suffered, enjoyed; the 'me' which in the West is called the soul, and by another name in the East—will continue. So what we are concerned with is continuity, not death. We do not want to know what death is; we do not want to know the extraordinary miracle, the beauty, the depth, the vastness of death. We don't want to inquire into that something which we don't know. All we want is to continue. We say, "I who have lived for forty, sixty, eighty years; I who have a house, a family, children, and grandchildren; I who have gone to the office day after day for so many years; I who have had quarrels, sexual appetites—I want to go on living." That is all we are concerned with. We know that there is death, that the ending of the physical body is inevitable, so we say, "I must feel assured of the continuity of myself after death." So we have beliefs, dogmas, resurrection, reincarnation—a thousand ways of escaping from the reality of death; and when we have a war, we put up crosses for the poor chaps who have been killed off. This sort of thing has been going on for millennia.

Now, we have never really given our whole being to find out what death is. We always approach death with the condition that we must be assured of a continuity hereafter. We say, "I want the known to continue"—the known being our qualities, our capacities, the memory of our experiences, our struggles, fulfillments, frustrations, ambitions; and it is also our name and our property. All that is the known, and we want it all to continue. Once we are granted the certainty of that continuance, then perhaps we may inquire into what death is, and whether there is such a thing as the unknown—which must be something extraordinary to find out.

So you see the difficulty. What we want is continuance, and we have never asked ourselves what it is that makes for continuance, that gives rise to this chain, this movement of continuity. If you observe, you will see that it is thought alone which gives a sense of continuance—nothing else. Through thought you identify yourself with your family, with your house, with your pictures or poems, with your character, with your frustrations, with your joys. The more you think about a problem, the more you give root and continuance to that problem. If you like someone, you think about that person, and this very thought gives a sense of continuity in time. Obviously, you have to think, but can you think for the moment, at the moment—and then drop thinking? If you did not say, "I like this, it is mine—it is my picture, my self-expression, my God, my wife, my virtue—and I am going to keep it," you would have no sense of continuity in time. But you don't think clearly, right through every problem. There is always the pleasure which you want to keep and the pain which you want to get rid of, which means that you think about both, and thought gives continuity to both. What we call thought is the response of memory, of association, which is essentially the same as the response of a computer; and you have to come to the point where you see for yourself the truth of this.

Most of us do not really want to find out for ourselves what death is; on the contrary, we want to continue in the known. If my brother, my son, my wife or husband dies, I am miserable, lonely, self-pitying, which is what I call sorrow, and I live on in that messy, confused, miserable state. I divide death from life—the life of quarrels, bitterness, despair, disappointments, frustrations, humiliations, insults—because this life I know, and death I don't know. Belief and dogma satisfy me until I die, and that is what takes place for most of us.

Now, this sense of continuity which thought gives to consciousness is quite shallow, as you can see. There is nothing mysterious or ennobling about it, and when you understand the whole significance of it, you think—where thought is necessary—clearly, logically, sanely, unsentimentally, without this constant urge to fulfill, to be or to become somebody. Then you will know how to live in the present, and living in the present is dying from moment to moment. You are then able to inquire because your mind, being unafraid, is without any illusion. To be without any illusion is absolutely necessary, and illusion exists only as long as there is fear. When there is no fear, there is no illusion. Illusion arises when fear takes root in security, whether it be in the form of a particular relationship, a house, a belief, or position and prestige. Fear creates illusion. As long as fear continues, the mind will be caught in various forms of illusion, and such a mind cannot possibly understand what death is.

We are now going to inquire into what death is—at least, I will inquire into it, expose it—but you can understand death, live with it completely, know the deep, full significance of it, only when there is no fear and therefore no illusion. To be free of fear is to live completely in the present, which means that you are not functioning mechanically in the habit of memory. Most of us are concerned about reincarnation, or we want to know whether we continue to live after the body dies, which is all so trivial. Have we understood the triviality of this desire for continuity? Do we see that it is merely the process of thinking, the machine of thought that demands to continue? Once you see that fact, you realize the utter shallowness, the stupidity of such a demand. Does the 'I' continue after death? Who cares? And what is this 'I' that you want to continue? Your pleasures and dreams, your hopes, despairs and joys, your property and the name you bear, your petty little character, and the knowledge you have acquired in your cramped, narrow life, which has been added to by professors, by literary people, by artists. That is what you want to continue, and that is all.

Now, whether you are old or young, you have to finish with all that—you have to finish with it completely, surgically, as a surgeon operates with a knife. Then the mind is without illusion and without fear; therefore, it can observe and understand what death is. Fear exists because of the desire to hold on to what is known. The known is the past living in the present and modifying the future. That is our life day after day, year after year, until we die, and how can such a mind understand something which has no time, no motive, something totally unknown?

Do you understand? Death is the unknown, and you have ideas about it. You avoid looking at death, or you rationalize it, saying it is inevitable, or you have a belief that gives you comfort, hope. But it is only a mature mind, a mind that is without fear, without illusion, without this stupid search for self-expression and continuity—it is only such a mind that can observe and find out what death is because it knows how to live in the present.

Please follow this. To live in the present is to be without despair, because there is no hankering after the past and no hope in the future; therefore, the mind says, "Today is enough for me." It does not avoid the past or blind itself to the future, but it has understood the totality of consciousness, which is not only the individual but also the collective, and therefore there is no 'me' separate from the many. In understanding the totality of itself, the mind has understood the particular as well as the universal; therefore, it has cast aside ambition, snobbishness, social prestige. All that is completely gone from a mind that is living wholly in the present, and therefore dying to everything it has known, every minute of the day. Then you will find, if you have gone that far, that death and life are one. You are living totally in the present, completely attentive, without choice, without effort; the mind is always empty, and from that emptiness you look, you observe, you understand, and therefore living is dying. What has continuity can never be creative. Only that which ends can know what it is to create. When life is also death, there is love, there is truth, there is creation—because death is the unknown, as truth and love and creation are.

Do you want to ask any questions and discuss what I have been talking about this morning?

Question: Is dying an act of will, or is it the unknown itself?

KRISHNAMURTI: Sir, have you ever died to your pleasure—just died to it without arguing, without reacting, without trying to create special conditions, without asking how you are to give it up, or why you should give it up? Have you ever done that? You will have to do that when you die physically, won't you? One can't argue with death. One can't say to death, "Give me a few more days to live." There is no effort of will in dying—one just dies. Or have you ever died to any of your despairs, your ambitions—just given it up, put it aside, as a leaf that dies in the autumn, without any battle of will, without anxiety as to what will happen to you if you do? Have you? I am afraid you have not. When you leave this tent, die to something that you cling to—your habit of smoking, your sexual demand, your urge to be famous as an artist, as a poet, as this or that. Just give it up, just brush it aside as you would some stupid thing, without effort, without choice, without decision. If your dying to it is total—and not just the giving up of cigarettes or of drinking, which you make into a tremendous issue—you will know what it means to live in the moment supremely, effortlessly, with all your being; and then, perhaps, a door may open into the unknown.

July 21, 1963

Eighth Talk in Saanen

You may have observed that during the seven meetings we have had here, I have not talked in terms of any theory, belief, or ideal. For a religious man, there are no theories at all, nor are there beliefs or ideals of any kind because he is always living completely in the active present. Any dependence on an idea, any conformity to a pattern, any adjustment to a theory or belief, is utterly foreign to a mind that is seeking what is true.

Now, for most of us, certain words—words like *death, sorrow, conflict, prayer, God*—are weighted with special meaning; they have an extraordinary significance for the mind, and we are burdened with these words. They shape our lives by causing us to conform, to imitate, to discipline ourselves to an established pattern. And this morning I am going to use such a word—a word which to many may be rather foreign, but to others who have probably done a little reading on the subject, it will have some meaning. That word is *meditation.* Meditation, for most people in the West, is something exotic, foreign, Asiatic; and for people everywhere, whether in the East or in the West, it is something one has to do if one wants to find truth or God. I am going to talk about it because, to me, a life without meditation is a wasted life. If one does not know the profound meaning and significance of meditation, one's everyday living becomes very superficial. But to understand the content of this word, and to go beyond the word, requires very clear thinking—a mind that is alert and active.

Before we go into this question of meditation, we must be very clear as to what we mean by discipline. For most of us, discipline implies control, shaping our thought and activity according to a certain ideational pattern. Conforming, adjusting, suppressing, following, imitating—all this is implied in the word *discipline.*

Please do follow this very carefully. It is going to become very difficult, arduous; and unless you exercise your mind tremendously as I go into it, you will be completely lost. To pursue what the speaker is going to talk about will require your total energy.

With most of us, the mind is conditioned through discipline; it is shaped by innumerable influences, thoughts, experiences, actions; and discipline has become almost our second nature. We begin to discipline ourselves at school, and carry on in the same way for the rest of our lives, adjusting to the demands of society, conforming to the established social and moral pattern, suppressing ourselves through fear, adjusting to public opinion, to what we think is right, and so on. Our minds are conditioned to seek security through discipline, yet we think that through discipline we shall find out what truth is. But surely, to find out what truth is, one must be free of all this imposed or self-imposed discipline. There can be the discovery of what is true only when there is freedom from conformity, from all fear—and then there is discipline of quite a different nature. It is no longer discipline in the sense of imitation, suppression, or conformity to a pattern. It is a free movement—not doing something out of the desire for a particular result, or because one is afraid. So it must be clearly understood that every form of discipline as we know it indicates a desire to conform, to be secure, and that behind this desire there is fear—the fear of being insecure, of not getting what we want, of not discovering the ultimate truth, and so on and so on.

Another very necessary thing is to be aware of how conditioned we are by society, by the innumerable experiences we have had—which means that we must be totally aware of our whole consciousness, and not just of certain parts of it. To be aware implies observation through space—that is, having space in your mind so that you are able to observe without opinion, without evaluation, without conclusion. Most of us have no space in our minds because we come to everything we observe with a conclusion, with an idea, with an opinion, with a judgment or evaluation; we condemn, approve, or justify what we see, or we identify ourselves with it, so there is no space at all in which to observe.

Please don't make this into a theory, into something which you have to practice, which would be a terrible thing, because what you practice becomes a habit. Unfortunately, most of us live in a series of habits, whether pleasant or unpleasant—which is utterly destructive of intelligence. You can see the truth or the falseness of this by observing yourself.

Do you know what learning is? Learning, in the true sense of the word, is not additive. You don't pile up knowledge and then, through looking, experiencing, add to what you have previously learned. When you merely gather information and add it to what you already know, there is never freedom to observe; therefore, you are not learning. Do you understand? If not, we will discuss it.

By awareness I mean a state of watchfulness in which there is no choice. You are simply observing *what is.* But you cannot observe *what is* if you have an idea or an opinion about what you see, saying it is good or bad, or otherwise evaluating it. You have to be totally aware of the movements of your own thought, of your own feeling; you have to observe your own activities, both conscious and unconscious, without evaluation.

This demands an extraordinarily alert, active mind. But with most of us, the mind is dull, half asleep; only parts of it are active, the specialized parts, from which we function automatically through association, through memory, like an electronic brain. To be alert, active, sensitive, the mind must have space in which to look at things without the background of what it already knows; and it is one of the functions of meditation to bring tremendous alertness, activity, and sensitivity to the mind.

Are you following all this?

To be aware is to watch your bodily activity, the way you walk, the way you sit, the movements of your hands; it is to hear the words you use, to observe all your thoughts, all your emotions, all your reactions. It includes awareness of the unconscious, with its traditions, its instinctual knowledge, and the immense sorrow it has accumulated—not only personal sorrow, but the sorrow of man. You have to be aware of all that; and you cannot be aware of it if you are merely judging, evaluating, saying, "This is good and that is bad," "This I will keep and that I will reject," all of which only makes the mind dull, insensitive.

From awareness comes attention. Attention flows from awareness when in that awareness there is no choice, no personal choosing, no experiencing—which I will go into presently—but merely observing. And to observe, you must have in the mind a great deal of space. A mind that is caught in ambition, greed, envy, in the pursuit of pleasure and self-fulfillment, with its inevitable sorrow, pain, despair, anguish—such a mind has no space in which to observe, to attend. It is crowded with its own desires, going round and round in its own backwaters of reaction. You cannot attend if your mind is not highly sensitive, sharp, reasonable, logical, sane, healthy, without the slightest shadow of neuroticism. The mind has to explore every corner of itself, leaving no spot uncovered, because if there is a single dark corner of one's mind which one is afraid to explore, from that springs illusion.

When the Christian sees the Christ in his meditation, in his contemplation, he thinks he has achieved something extraordinary, but his visions are merely the projections of his own conditioning. It is the same with the Hindu who sits on the bank of a river and goes into a state of ecstasy. He too has visions born of his own conditioning, and what he sees is therefore not a religious experience at all. But through awareness, through choiceless observation—which is possible only when in the mind there is space to observe—every form of conditioning is dissolved, and then the mind is no longer Hindu, Buddhist, or Christian because all ideas, beliefs, hopes, and fears have completely gone. From this comes attention—not attention given to something, but a state of attention in which there is no experiencer and therefore no experience. This is tremendously important to understand for a man who is really seeking to find out what is truth, what is religion, what is God, what is beyond the things put together by the mind.

In the state of attention, there is no reaction: one is merely attending. The mind has explored and understood all the recesses of itself, all the unconscious motives, demands, fulfillments, urges, sorrows; therefore, in the state of attention, there is space, emptiness; there is no experiencer who is experiencing something. Being empty, the mind is not projecting, seeking, wanting, hoping. It has understood all its own reactions and responses, its depth, its shallowness, and there is nothing left. There is no division between the observer and the thing observed. The moment there is a division between the observer and the observed, there is conflict—the very gap between them is the conflict. We have gone into that, and we have seen how important it is to be completely free of conflict.

Perhaps this is a little more complicated than that to which you are accustomed because I am talking about meditation, which is something beyond all words.

Now, it is only in the state of attention that you can be a light unto yourself, and then every action of your daily life springs from that light—every action, whether you are doing your job, cooking, going for a walk, mending clothes, or what you will. This whole process is meditation, and without it religion has no meaning whatsoever; it becomes merely a superstition exploited by the priests.

For most people who do what they call meditation, it is a form of self-hypnosis. Having taken lessons in meditation or read books about it they sit cross-legged and go through all the tricks they have learned, breathing most regularly, controlling their thoughts, and so on and so on. There are many systems of meditation, but if you understand one of them, you have understood the whole lot because they are all concerned with controlling or hypnotizing oneself in order to have certain experiences which are considered to be marvelous, but which are in fact an illusion. That form of meditation is utterly juvenile; it has no meaning. You can indulge in it for ten thousand years, and you will never find out what is true. You may have visions, you may experience what you think is God, truth, and all the rest of it, but it will all be projected by your own reactions, by your own conditioning, and will therefore have no meaning at all.

What I am talking about is something entirely different: freeing the mind, through intense alertness, from all its reactions, and thereby bringing about—without control, without deliberate will—a state of inward quietness. It is only the very intense, highly sensitive mind that can be really quiet, not a mind that is paralyzed by fear, by sorrow, by joy, or deadened by conformity to innumerable social and psychological demands.

Real meditation is the highest form of intelligence. It is not a matter of sitting cross-legged in a corner with your eyes shut, or standing on your head, or whatever it is you do. To meditate is to be completely aware as you are walking, as you are riding in the bus, as you are working in your office or in your kitchen—completely aware of the words you use, the gestures you make, the manner of your talk, the way you eat, and how you push people around. To be choicelessly aware of everything about you and within yourself is meditation. If you are thus aware of the political and religious propaganda that goes on ceaselessly, aware of the many influences about you, you will see how quickly you understand and are free of every influence as you come into contact with it.

But very few people ever go that far because they are so conditioned by their traditions. This is particularly true if one happens to live in India where people must absolutely do certain things. They must control the body completely and thereby completely control their thought. Through this control they hope to reach the supreme, but what they reach will be the result of their own self-hypnosis. In the Christian world you do the same thing in a different way. But what I am talking about is something that requires the highest form of intelligence.

Now, the mind that wants experience is not intelligent, and if you observe, you will see that most of us want experience. Being tired of the everyday challenge and response which we have known for so long, we turn to so-called meditation, or we go to a church, hoping through this or some other mysterious means to have more and deeper experience. But a mind that is in a state of wanting experience, however exalted, is not innocent;

therefore, there is no such thing as having a "religious" experience. It is the mind that is longing, seeking, groping, the mind that is afraid, anxious, in despair—it is only such a mind that demands experience. A highly sensitive mind, being a light unto itself, does not want or need experience, and therefore it is in a state of innocency; and it is only an innocent, highly sensitive mind that can be completely quiet. When the mind is completely quiet because every part of it is alive, sensitive, it is then in a state of meditation, and from there it can proceed to find out what is truth. But until it is in that state of meditation, every attempt on the part of the mind to find out what is truth, what is God, what is the something beyond itself, is an utter waste of time and only leads to illusion. To be in that state of meditation requires extraordinary energy, and you have very little energy as long as you are in conflict, as long as you have the problems of desire. That is why, as I have said from the very beginning, every conflict, every demand for fulfillment, with its hope and despair, must be understood and dissolved away. Then the mind has no illusion because it has no longer the power to create illusion.

A mind that is caught in problems, in fear, in despair, in the desire to fulfill itself, is always creating illusion and is therefore in a state of neurosis. That is the first thing to realize. But when the mind is highly sensitive and free of all illusion, out of that clarity and sensitivity there is intelligence, and only then can the mind be completely and effortlessly quiet. That state of complete and effortless quietness is the beginning of meditation.

So, first there is an awareness, a choiceless observation of all your thoughts and feelings, of everything that you do. Out of that there comes a state of attention which has no frontier, but in which the mind can concentrate, and from this state of attention there is quietness of the mind. And when the mind is completely quiet, without any illusion, without any kind of self-hypnosis, there is the coming into being of something which is not put together by the mind.

You see, now comes the difficulty of trying to express in words something which is inexpressible—and that something is what we are seeking. We all want to find something beyond this world of agony, of tyranny, of force and subjugation, this world which is so indifferent, callous, brutal. With our ambitions, our nationalisms, our diplomacy, our lies, we are continually precipitating the horrors of war; and being weary of all that, we want peace. We want to find somewhere a state of quietness, of bliss, so we invent a God, a savior, or another world which offers us the peace we want if we will do or believe certain things. But a conditioned mind, however much it may want peace, brings about its own destruction, and that is what is actually going on in the world. All the politicians throughout the world, whether of the right or of the left, use that word *peace*, but it has no meaning at all. What I am talking about is something far beyond all that.

So, meditation is the emptying of the mind of all the things that the mind has put together. If you do that—perhaps you won't, but it doesn't matter, just listen to this—you will find that there is an extraordinary space in the mind, and that space is freedom. So you must demand freedom at the very beginning, and not just wait, hoping to have it at the end. You must seek out the significance of freedom in your work, in your relationships, in everything that you do. Then you will find that meditation is creation.

Creation is a word that we all use so glibly, so easily. A painter puts on canvas a few colors and gets tremendously excited about it. It is his fulfillment, the means through which he expresses himself; it is his market in which to gain money or reputation—and he calls that "creation"! Every writer "creates," and there are schools of "creative" writing, but none of that has anything to do with creation. It is all the conditioned response of a mind that lives in a particular society.

The creation of which I am speaking is something entirely different. It is a mind that is in the state of creation. It may or it may not express that state. Expression has very little value. That state of creation has no cause, and therefore a mind in that state is every moment dying and living and loving and being. The whole of this is meditation.

Do you want to discuss this?

Question: How can the attention which flows from awareness be maintained?

KRISHNAMURTI: If I may say so most respectfully, sir, I think you have asked a rather wrong question. Why should we desire to maintain attention? What lies behind the word *maintain?* I want to maintain a particular relationship with my wife, with my husband, with a friend. I want to keep it going at a certain level, at a certain tension, so that we always love and respond to each other completely. Or I want to maintain a certain feeling. And how will I maintain it? By saying, "I am going to keep it going"—that is, by volition, by will. And what happens when you maintain something by will? It becomes brittle and is destroyed. Can you maintain love by volition, by will? So there must be a different approach to this question.

Let us say that I see in a flash what it means to be aware. I see it fully, not just verbally. I have caught myself being aware without choice, and I have actually understood it. For a second I am aware, and I see the extraordinary freedom, the beauty, and the joy of it. Then I say to myself, "I must maintain it," and the moment I want to maintain that state, it has become a memory. What I am maintaining is not the fact but my memory of the fact, and therefore it is a dead thing. Please do see this.

I remember my brother, my son, my wife, my husband, who is dead, and I live in that memory, I maintain that memory, with all its pleasures, despairs, longings—you know all that one goes through. But I have not found out what it means when someone dies; I am not aware of the whole significance of death. So one has to be aware of the significance of the fact, and not merely live in a memory. Do you understand, sir? Not to live in a memory is never to say of an experience of a relationship, "I want to maintain it, I want it to continue." Then, if someone dies, it doesn't matter. This is not callousness or indifference. Be alive to the present every minute, and you will see.

Have I conveyed something?

Truth has no continuity because it is beyond time, and what has continuity is not truth. Truth must be seen instantly and forgotten—forgotten in the sense that you do not carry with you as memory the truth that has been seen. And because your mind is uncluttered with memory, at any instant—the next minute, the next day, or some time later—the truth will come again.

Truth, having no continuity, can be seen only when the whole mind is free from this process of maintaining, remembering, recognizing. That demands extraordinary attention because it is very easy to slip into saying, "Well, I saw it yesterday, and I am going to live with it." If you live with it, you will be living with a memory, which is a dead thing and has no meaning, and it will prevent you from seeing the truth anew, afresh. To see the truth or the beauty of that mountain, your mind must be extraordinarily sensitive, not made dull by the memory of things that have been; and that requires—as you will know if you watch yourself—acute attention. Therefore, you can't allow your body to become dull, sluggish. You must have a body that is highly alert, sensitive, because the condition of the body does influence the brain, and the brain influences your thought, and so on and so on. Psychosomatically, one has to be fully aware.

Memory is mechanical, and it obviously has its place. Without memory you wouldn't know where you lived, you wouldn't know how to read, and so on. But for most of us, memory, which is the past, interferes with observation. When you have understood that fact, you have space to observe; and in that space, for a split second, for ten minutes, for an hour—the time period doesn't matter—there is a perception. But if you make that perception into a memory, you will never see again.

Most of us live in memories: memories of the pleasant time we had when we were young, the memories of sex, the memories of our joys and despairs, and so on. We live in the past, so our minds are dull, and our technical training therefore helps to make us automatons. What I am talking about is something entirely different: to make the mind astonishingly active and very sensitive by being aware of everything that you do and don't do.

Comment: When I am listening to what is being said here, I feel very alive and sensitive; but when I go away by myself or am in my house, this sensitivity ceases.

KRISHNAMURTI: If you are sensitive only while you are here, you are being influenced, and that has no value whatsoever. It is merely propaganda and therefore should be shunned, put away, destroyed, for in that way you create Masters, teachers, authorities. But if you have observed yourself as you listened when I have talked; if you have been aware of your own reactions at every minute as we have gone along for over an hour; if you have been awake, not only to what was being said by the speaker, but also to the movements of your own thought and feeling—then, when you leave this tent and go away by yourself, you will know your own state of mind and will never be blindly caught in it again.

Question: Do you not think that the desire to free oneself is partly the cause of one's conditioning?

KRISHNAMURTI: Of course, sir, the desire to free oneself from conditioning only furthers conditioning. But if, instead of trying to suppress desire, one understands the whole process of desire, in that very understanding there comes freedom from conditioning. Freedom from conditioning is not a direct result. Do you understand? If I set about deliberately to free myself from my conditioning, that desire creates its own conditioning. I may destroy one form of conditioning, but I am caught in another. Whereas, if there is an understanding of desire itself, which includes the desire to be free, then that very understanding destroys all conditioning. Freedom from conditioning is a byproduct; it is not important. The important thing is to understand what it is that creates conditioning.

July 23, 1963

Ninth Talk in Saanen

One observes that in modern civilization, where everything is being highly organized, there is less and less freedom in action. We are losing spontaneity and passion in action. For most of us, action has become routine. Whether it is going to the office every day, washing dishes in the kitchen, writing, painting, or what you will, our action is becoming more and more canalized, shaped according to a series of patterns; and when everything we do is thus reduced to a routine, there is obviously no questioning of action, no inquiry into action at all. The question of what is the right thing to do does arise when we have problems, but then we merely try to analyze our problems, or we grope about, hoping to find a solution. That is the only action we know. But it seems to me there is a completely different kind of action which is really inaction, and I would like, if I can, to go into it rather deeply this morning.

We never ask ourselves or try to find out what action is, apart from our routine response to the everyday demands of society, or apart from our efforts to solve some particularly urgent problem. Within this narrow field, we do try to find out what is the right thing to do. But I think there is a wider field of inquiry and a greater depth of search to find out what action is; and if we could find that out, then our limited actions in response to the demands of a particular society, whether capitalistic or socialistic, would have a much greater significance.

So, what is action? We are not trying to find out what one should do under a particular set of circumstances—that will be answered a little later. If we restrict ourselves to the question of what to do with regard to a given issue, then action becomes superficial, limited, and not very significant. The question is not what to do, but rather: What is action?

For most of us, action has various motives, or it is an approximation to some ideal. Our behavior is guided by a concept, by a formula, by an idea, so there is a gap between action and the idea. This gap, this division, breeds conflict, and thereby we lose energy, and without energy there is no real action. Action demands the energy of freedom, of spontaneity; and if action is conditioned, limited by an idea, shaped according to a formula or a rationalized system of thought, then action loses its own momentum, its spontaneous drive.

I hope that I shall be able to explain what I mean as we go along. I am not talking theoretically. As I have often pointed out, I am not indulging in theories, in mere ideas. In all these talks we are concerned with facts, with action.

Now, as long as action is limited, confined by an idea, that action not only creates conflict and thereby loses energy, but it lacks the spontaneity that is so productive of energy. We know only the limited energy that is generated in us by conflict, by competition, by friction. Our response to challenge depends upon a concept, an idea, a formulation, which means that our response is limited—and thereby, it seems to me, we lose the extraordinary vitality of action.

To put it differently, if you observe yourself, you will see that there is a concept, an image, an idea according to which you are living. You are always approximating your action to that idea, thereby creating friction, conflict, and losing energy. But to think very clearly, to be highly sensitive, to feel passionately about anything, one needs tremendous energy. So it seems to me that the problem for most of us is that we lack energy inwardly, though outwardly we may be very active—going to the office, doing things at home, and all the rest of it. Inwardly we have not enough energy to tackle a problem directly and resolve it instantly. We carry the problem over from day to day, and thereby we become burdened with problems.

Now, is it possible to act without idea? That is, can one live completely in the present? As we saw the other day, to live completely in the present, to give one's whole attention to the present, is to die to the past. This demands an awareness, not only of the conscious movements of the mind, but also of its unconscious movements. One has to be aware of all one's thoughts and feelings, of all one's actions—not according to an idea or a formula, but be simply aware of them without interpretation—and thereby live so totally in the present that action is immediate and not an approximation to some idea or ideal.

If you are at all aware of the workings of your own mind, you will know that you are constantly observing with a conclusion, and according to that conclusion you approve, condemn, interpret, or try to modify what you see. Now, if there is no conclusion, no interpretation, but pure observation, then that very observation is action without idea. After all, the cultivation of thought, however necessary, is not love. Love, it seems to me, is direct action, not a thought-out, ideational action.

I wonder if I am communicating what I want to convey?

You see, each one of us is in need of a total mutation; there must be a complete transformation deep down, at the very root of our consciousness; otherwise, we are mere automatons living in a shoddy, superficial world with all its conflicts, sorrows, miseries, and responding only to the most superficial demands and urges. To bring about this fundamental inward revolution, one must inquire into action; one must find out if there is an action which is not dictated by circumstances, by ambition, by social demands, by reformatory ideals, by nationalistic or other pressures. To find out if there is such an action, it seems to me that one must go very deeply into oneself—so deeply that the mind is no longer operating according to ideas, conclusions, memories, and is therefore capable of living in that total present which in itself modifies the very nature of action.

I am afraid I am not conveying this at all.

What is communion? I want to convey something to you which I feel is very important; and if it is to be conveyed, there must obviously be cooperation between us, between the listener and the speaker. So, how do you cooperate? How do you listen to what is being said? Do you listen merely to capture the idea, the significance of words? Or are you listening and at the same time observing your own reactions and responses, both conscious and unconscious? That is, are you listening in the active present or merely approximating your thought to what is being said? I want to say something, which is this: One can live completely in the present, without a fixed idea, without any preconceived thought, and this living completely in the present gives the tremendous energy which is necessary to bring about a total revolution in the mind. This is what I want to convey, and not just in words. I want to convey it in such a way that you feel the reality of it, so that when you leave here, a mutation, a tremendous revolution will have taken place.

As I was saying the other day, for most of us thought has become tremendously important—thought being idea, whether rational or irrational, neurotic or so-called normal. Thought guides our lives, shapes our ends, and controls our actions. Now, to the speaker, what we call thought has no importance whatsoever because it is merely the response of memory, the voice of tradition, of the accumulated experiences of the past; and the past cannot meet the ever-changing present. To meet the present, the mind must be totally devoid of thought so that there is observation without idea, and it is this observation without idea which gives the tremendous energy for mutation to take place. That is, the mind must be empty of all the things that memory has put into it. We need memory in order to function, to operate, to do things; we must have the past as knowledge, but without letting it interfere in any way with the present, which is action, which is energy.

Now, you have listened to what has just been said. And how have you listened to it? Have you listened and observed so that you see the fact for yourself? Or have you merely listened with the idea that you must live in the present and capture its significance? Either one sees the fact or one has an idea about the fact and then interprets the fact according to that idea.

You see, in our lives there is very little love; we actually do not know what it means. We know the so-called love that brings with it jealousy, envy, anger, confusion, misery. We all know that well enough. But we do not really know what it means to be in a state of love, do we? We may love somebody in particular, but we do not know that extraordinarily vital, clear state of being which is love. Most of us have very little love in our hearts, and that is why we demand it of another. Being without love, we generally find release along a fixed avenue of self-fulfillment—either sexual or intellectual or in some neurotic way—so our problems increase and become more and more acute.

Now, I am talking of a mind that has no problem at all—or rather, when a problem arises, it understands and deals with it immediately so that there is no residue, and the problem does not leave a mark. That is action; that is living in the present. We are going to have problems all the time, problems of various kinds; and as each problem arises, can we not deal with it so completely that it does not leave a mark—the memory of something we have learned and with which we approach a new problem? If we approach the new problem with a memory, we cannot resolve that problem. What I am trying to convey is that there is an action in which idea is in no way involved, and therefore that action is direct and not the result of a mechanical memory. Such action releases tremendous energy, and you need tremendous energy to find out what is true, to discover what is beyond the measures which man has established for himself, beyond the things built by the mind.

Let me put the question differently. Most of us lead a very shallow life, and for a time we are satisfied to live in this petty, narrow way. Then, realizing that we are living superficially, we feel discontented and try to find a way to become deep. But a shallow mind trying to become deep is still shallow. A petty mind may try to find God, but it will still be petty, and its God will also be petty. Now, how to transform completely the dull, shallow, stupid mind, so that it is totally alive?—that is the question.

The appalling conditions in the world demand that you have a new, fresh mind because otherwise the problems are going to increase. There will be more bloodshed, more wars, more confusion, more competition, more so-called progress and slavery to things. If your mind is not fresh, it is going to be caught by circumstances. Not only that, but you also need a fresh, young mind to find out if there is something beyond the measurable, beyond the things put together by society, beyond the beliefs and dogmas invented by the priests. For that you need tremendous energy—an energy which is not the outcome of conflict, an energy that has no motive. And you can awaken that destructive, liberating, clarifying energy only when you have understood and resolved in yourself every form of conflict. Conflict comes to an end when there is self-knowing—knowing the totality of your own consciousness. We have gone into that—how to inquire into oneself—so I will not repeat it now.

Without love, we live in sorrow and misery, in everlasting conflict. And surely love has no conflict. You may say, "That is merely an idea, an ideal, a theoretically perfect state," but it is not. Love comes into being when we really begin to understand the totality of ourselves. So what is important is to discover for oneself that one is caught in words, in ideas. We are slaves to formulas, to concepts, and the perception of that fact alters the very nature of action. In the mutation of action there is passion, which is energy; and when it has this energy, which is part of love, part of creation, the mind can enter into something which it has not conceived or formulated—something unknown.

Can we perhaps discuss this?

Question: To be aware, one must meditate, and meditation implies complete harmony of thought and feeling. If one is incapable of that complete harmony, how can one be aware?

KRISHNAMURTI: When you speak of being *aware,* what do you mean by that word? I am aware of you, and you are aware of me. I see many faces, many colors; I see the tent, I hear the noise of the river and the song of a bird; through that gap I see the fluttering of a leaf in the wind, and so on. I am aware of all that and of my reactions to all that. I am also aware that these reactions arise according to my conditioning, my memories, my accumulated knowledge. I see that I interpret everything I hear in terms of like or dislike, according to my particular prejudices. I am totally aware of my conscious and unconscious motives, demands, urges. By using the word aware, the speaker means to include all that, but perhaps the questioner does not.

Comment: If one is neurotic or mad, one cannot be aware.

KRISHNAMURTI: Obviously. Now, wait a minute. Are you speaking for someone else who is neurotic, or do you realize that you are yourself neurotic? No, please don't laugh it off. This is a very serious question I have put to you. If one is aware that one is neurotic—and to be aware of it is a very difficult thing to do—then one is already coming out of one's neuroticism. But most of us are not aware of our peculiarities, of our slightly unbalanced states, of our exaggerations, idiosyncrasies, and fixations. To be aware of them requires constant attention, and most of us have neither the energy, the time, nor the inclination to observe ourselves. We would rather go to an analyst, to somebody who will do the job for us, and thereby we complicate our lives still more. So, if you are neurotic, as most of us are, then to bring about a change, you must be aware of yourself, not only superficially, but deeply. You must watch every word, all the things that you feel and think, go into yourself profoundly. Then perhaps, out of that awareness, there comes meditation. But we have gone into that, and I won't go into it again.

Question: When a mother gives birth to a child, she takes care of it immediately. In this action is there not love, even though the woman may not have an innocent mind?

KRISHNAMURTI: Sir, don't you want to find out for yourself what action is? Don't you want to find out what it means to live totally in the present? Don't you want to strip yourself of all the false things that society and environment have imposed upon you and discover what is truth, what is the meaning of this whole business of living? That demands a great deal of inquiry, which most of us are apparently unwilling to undertake, and therefore we ask questions that I am afraid are rather irrelevant.

Sir, you know what is going on in the world: the threats of war, the hectic competition, the senseless brutalities. What is your response to all that? Don't you want to find out how to act in relation to all that? Or are we all so concerned with our own selves that we have no time for the bigger questions? Perhaps you have an answer for all this which you have been given by some authority, and therefore you are able to respond—but only verbally, not profoundly, not from your heart and mind, from your own depth. That is why this morning I have talked about action. A human being has to act; his very living is action, but that action has led us to a great deal of misery, corruption, confusion; therefore, we have to find a completely different way of acting, a different way of living. We cannot merely live according to some definition, according to the ideas of Marx, Lenin, or any other authority. We have to tear all this down and find out for ourselves what is true.

Question: To think clearly, to observe directly, you say we need space in the mind—space between oneself and what one sees. Most of us have no such space; our minds are crowded with ideas, cluttered up with memories. How are we to come by that space?

KRISHNAMURTI: We have already talked about this so much! I wonder with what urgency, with what intensity we live! The world as it is demands the clarifying action of an uncluttered mind, a mind that is not neurotic, a mind that has no fixed point from which it starts to think. First of all, do you see the necessity of such a mind? And if you see the necessity of such a mind, how are you going to get it? Can anybody give it to you? Surely, you have to work furiously; you have to give all your energy to it. But you see, most of us have not that energy because we are so afraid. We are afraid for our own little securities, for our own little back garden, and that fear deprives us of any energy we have. So you have to tackle all that; you have to strip yourself of all fear. We have discussed this during these nine talks, and as I have said, when you see that your mind is clouded, fearful, that very act of seeing brings about an action which will destroy fear.

Question: Is there a difference between observing oneself and observing something outside?

KRISHNAMURTI: When we say *outside* and *inside*, what do we mean by those words? Outside there are the mountains, the trees, the river, the people. Inside are my private thoughts, hopes, fears, reactions; and also, there is the thinker who observes, judges, condemns, evaluates. So there is the psychological division of the thinker and the thought, or the experiencer and the thing experienced, which is one aspect of the inside and the outside; and there is the more obvious division of the objective world outside and the subjective world inside. My wife is outside, and I am inside—the 'I' being my ambition, my greed, my bestiality, my cruelty, my love, and all the rest of it. Now, how do you observe the outside, and how do you observe the inside? Do you observe with a mind which merely reacts, that is, with a mind which says, "That is good, this is bad," "That is a mountain, this is a tree"? Or do you observe without thought, without idea?

Perhaps I can make it a little clearer by putting it differently.

When you see a flower, do you observe it botanically, or nonbotanically? That is, do you give the flower a name, or do you merely observe it without giving it a name? Do you see the difference?

Let us go into it a little bit more. By our circumstances, by our upbringing, by our education and so on, most of us are made dull; we are half asleep, and we need to be challenged; otherwise, we will fall completely asleep. Now, being challenged, I am forced to observe. Generally I observe very little. I observe only the things that are immediately around me, the things with which I am directly concerned. But the challenge of the outside world—society, economic problems, the problems of relationship, death, and so on and so on—shakes me out of my lethargy, my dullness, my laziness, and I become a little more awake, intelligent, sensitive. I begin to question myself, to inquire, to search, to grope, to ask, to demand, so I no longer need an outside challenge; and for the man who does not need an outside challenge, there is no division between the outside and the inside. He is in a state of inquiry, a state of revolution; he is constantly observing, questioning everything around him and within himself. Then, if he goes still further, he becomes a light unto himself; he is completely awake, and therefore needs no challenge at all. But that is far away for most of us.

We say there is the outside and the inside, but is there actually such a division psychologically? Or is it like the tide that goes out and comes in? If you have listened to that question and gone into yourself to find out the truth of the matter, then how do you look at the mountain, at the tree, at your wife, at your children, at your neighbor, at ideas? What is your relationship with the quarreling, the mischief that is going on in the world? Are you a part of it? Are you the result of society, of your environment? Or have you understood and moved away from it? If you have, then you are already something entirely different; there is a mutation taking place that gives you a clarity, an urgency, a sense of love without motive.

Question: Is spontaneous action right action?

KRISHNAMURTI: Do you know how difficult it is to be really spontaneous? When we are so conditioned by society, when we live on memory, on the past, how can we possibly be spontaneous? Surely, to do something spontaneously is to act without motive, without calculation, without any self-interested feeling. It is not self-centered action. You just do it out of the fullness of your being. But to be really spontaneous requires stripping yourself completely of the past. It is only the innocent mind that can be spontaneous.

July 25, 1963

Tenth Talk in Saanen

Perhaps this morning we can inquire together into something which man has been seeking for centuries upon centuries, and which very few, apparently, have found. Through his turmoil and sorrow, through his passing happiness, through all his confusion and misery, man has put together innumerable dogmas and beliefs concerning that something to which, in the West and in the East, he has given different names. Call it God, reality, or what you will, each one of us is seeking it; and if we are to explore and find out for ourselves whether there is or is not something beyond the things put together by the mind, we are going to need a certain skill—the skill that comes in the very movement of exploration itself. It is not that you must first have the skill and then explore, but in the very process of exploring, uncovering, penetrating, there comes the skill, the expertness, the clarity with which to look. But for that you must obviously have a deep skepticism, a certain element of doubt. There must be doubt, not only of the organized religions, but also of everything that you discover within yourself in the movement of exploration. You cannot accept a thing. You cannot accept what society and the organized religions have imposed on the mind, nor can you accept any of the reactions which occur while exploring—the reactions you have because you want something permanent, stable, certain. If through your craving for security, for permanency, you have certain experiences, and with those experiences you are satisfied, contented, inevitably you remain in a state of stagnation. But if from the beginning there is an attitude of questioning, of doubt, of skepticism in all that you see, in all that you feel, then that very skepticism brings about a skill in observation which is absolutely necessary for a mind that would explore or inquire into something which cannot possibly be conceived or formulated.

Organized religions throughout the world have maintained that there is something which is not man-made, something which is not merely mechanical, and they have given a great many attributes to it. For centuries these organized religions, through ceaseless propaganda, have imposed certain concepts on the mind, and each one of us is, consciously or unconsciously, conditioned by this long-continued and subtle propaganda. To put away all that conditioning requires a great deal of energy, and to explore, to inquire into yourself, you need, I assure you, tremendous doubt—doubt of everything you discover.

The organized religions probably had at the beginning a certain usefulness in making man somewhat civilized, but now they no longer have any meaning at all because man has lost all sense of civility. He is prepared to kill thousands and wipe out a whole city in a moment. So you and I have to find out for ourselves—and I am sure this is the intention of most intelligent and even intellectual people—whether there actually is something beyond the creations of the mind. To find out is not to accept or merely to have knowledge of what has been said about it by the various religions, and to find out is also different from wanting to experience that something. The moment you desire to experience it, you cease to doubt, you no longer have any skepticism, and then you are a slave to your experiences.

Please observe your own explorative process as the speaker is talking. Do not just be satisfied with his words, his explanations, because then he alone will be doing the exploring, and you will merely be hearing words which will have very little meaning. But if as you listen, you also take part in the exploration, you will discover in yourself the skill of a mind that is aware, sharp, clear, incisive, and then there is no question of accepting any authority.

But you see, we are bred on authority. Our whole life is based on the authority of the past—the authority of what the various religious teachers have said, and the authority of the priests who have a vested interest in both the teacher and the teaching. We have been brought up, conditioned, shaped by this religious authority, and merely to question it outwardly has very little value. Even in the communist world, where organized religion was once taboo, the priests are now allowed to function because organized religion throughout the world has become politically more or less harmless. You can practice your own particular idiosyncrasies of religious belief, and as long as it is no threat to the political powers that be, they will let you do what you like about religion. It is only when you refuse to be nationalistic, when you refuse to go to war, to kill in the name of the country, and so on, that you become a danger. Organized religion in the Western world has never stood strongly against nationalism, against the butchery of war; on the contrary, it has encouraged war. So now we are tamed human beings, conditioned by fear, by the authority of the church, of the temple, of the priest, and religion has become a dead thing with which we play on Sundays. We turn to it when we are in deep sorrow and want to be comforted. But religion, the real thing, does not give comfort. It is not a tame thing which you can carry about with you. It is drastic, ruthless. It destroys you. And that is what we are now going to explore, to inquire into.

To explore, you cannot look at what you see from the point of view of any particular individual or philosophy. To inquire, to find out, you have to strip yourself completely of the past. To explore, there must be virtue, not custom. Morality has become custom, habit, a superficial thing conditioned by the psychological structure of society—which most of us are. We live in the habitual, in customary morality; and the virtue of which I am talking is something quite different.

Virtue is not authority in action, but in the very process of understanding authority—understanding it intelligently, skillfully, clearly, deeply—virtue comes into being. As you cannot cultivate love, so virtue cannot be cultivated, but if you understand the enormous significance, the depth and brutality of authority, out of that understanding comes the beauty of virtue.

In the beginning man was inquiring, searching, groping, but that original inquiry, that search has become traditional; it is a thing of the past, which is now our custom. The continuation of tradition, the authority of the past, creates the values which society has imposed on the mind and which we have built into ourselves as character. That character becomes the background of authority from which we see, observe, and experience. So, if we would really inquire, explore, there must be freedom from this background of authority.

Please follow this. If we can seriously explore or inquire into this question together, then perhaps, when you leave here and go back to your homes, you will be able to confront your innumerable problems and miseries with a different mind, with a different heart, with a different feeling altogether. After all, that is what we are trying to do here: to bring about a complete revolution, a mutation in consciousness. And that is very important because mere change is degeneration. Change implies only a modification of what has been. It is not a revolution. And we are talking about a revolution, a total mutation in our way of thinking, feeling, being. Such a mutation cannot possibly take place if we remain merely at the verbal or intellectual level. That is why, if you are in earnest about all this, you must explore to the very depths of your being. Out of that exploration you will discover for yourself whether there is or is not something beyond the measure of man.

Psychological authority as memory, as the background that guides you, that shapes your thought and controls your action, must be understood totally and completely. In that understanding, real virtue is born. Virtue is spontaneous; it is not the artificial thing that you have built up as a wall of resistance to help you to remain safely enclosed within your self-centered activity. Exploration implies skill in observation, and for that you must be free of all authority—psychologically, not legalistically. Do you understand the difference? If you disobey the authority of the law, of the policeman in the street, you will be arrested and sent to prison. We are not talking of that. We are talking of freedom from psychological authority—the authority which you have built up through knowledge, through memory, through the experiences which you have had. As long as you are caught in psychological authority, or in any belief that gives comfort, your mind is not swift and subtle enough for real exploration. The mind that is exploring, questioning, inquiring, does not remain at a fixed point; it does not take up a position from which it tries to explore. It is constantly moving, and in that very movement is the exploration.

So, when you begin to explore, you are not exploring something beyond yourself. You are exploring the whole process of your own consciousness, because that is the basis from which you think, from which you feel. You have to begin by examining the very instrument which is going to explore. Do you understand? I hope I am making myself clear.

After all, we have only one instrument, the mind, which is the seat of thought. And if the mind, with its reactions, is not completely questioned, explored, and understood, one has no means of inquiry.

Please follow all this very closely because it is going to be rather difficult. When the mind begins to look at its own reactions, motives, demands, urges, and the experiences it has stored up as memory, there arises a division between the observer and the thing observed, does there not? That is what actually takes place. Now, as long as there is this division between the observer and the thing observed, which creates conflict, there can be no skill in observation, and therefore no real exploration. And it demands a keen awareness, a certain tension of observation if this division between the observer and the thing observed is not to arise. This division only creates conflict—and skill in observation does not come out of conflict. It comes out of your full attention—which means that the observer and the thing observed are one, and not separate. In observing yourself, you will notice that the instrument of thought, of feeling, is overshadowed by the vast experience of centuries which, as instinctual knowledge, has become the authority which tells you what to do and what not to do, and which projects into the future certain pictures or images based on the conditioned reactions of the past. And one has to be free of that whole background if one is to find out whether there is or is not something beyond the measure of man.

When you begin to inquire into yourself, you will find that your mind is divided as the conscious and the unconscious; and to understand right exploration, the whole of your consciousness must be harmoniously one, not separated as two different things. To bring about that harmonious whole, you cannot artificially integrate or bring together the two different things. That harmony, that unity comes into being only when there is an understanding of the process of consciousness, which means that the mind is able to observe itself negatively rather than positively—that is, when the mind can look at its own reactions without guiding, shaping, or otherwise trying to alter what it sees. In other words, your mind must be choicelessly aware of itself. Then you will find that your mind becomes astonishingly quiet, still; and in that stillness it can observe far more profoundly its own thought.

If you would really look at something—a stream, a mountain, a tree—your mind must be steady, quiet, unperturbed. Similarly, to explore the whole range of consciousness, your mind must be completely quiet—but not disciplined into quietness. A mind that is made quiet through discipline is a shallow mind, a dead mind, and inevitably it degenerates. But when the mind explores and understands all its own reactions, when it is aware of every movement of thought and feeling, out of that awareness there comes a spontaneous stillness, an extraordinary sensitivity which is its own discipline.

Most of us are disciplined. The opinion of society, of the neighbor, the newspapers, books, and magazines we read—all these influences shape our thought and feeling, our behavior. As a reaction to all that, we discipline ourselves to conform to some idea or ideal, or to what the teacher, the savior, the Master has sanctioned. All such discipline is mere conformity, repression; it does not bring freedom. But when the mind is totally aware of all the movements of its own thought and feeling, out of that simple, deep awareness there comes a discipline which never conforms. That discipline is skill in observation. You cannot possibly have that skill if there is dependence on authority in any form—the authority of the hero, the example, the priest, or the authority of what you already know—because authority shapes and conditions your mind and therefore limits your inquiry, your subtlety, your skill in observation.

You will find it is only when the mind is completely quiet, empty, that anything can be fully perceived. You need space, you need emptiness to observe. I cannot observe you if there is no space between you and me. Similarly, a mind that is crippled with sorrow, burdened with problems, a mind that is full of its own vanities, its frustrations, its urge to fulfill, a mind that is caught in nationalism and all the other petty things of life—such a mind is not empty; it has no space, and therefore it is utterly incapable of observing. When such a mind says, "I must explore to find out if there is something beyond the mind," it has no meaning. The mind must first explore itself.

When the mind is completely quiet, empty—and that demands astonishing awareness, effortless attention—then, as I have said, there is the beginning of meditation. Then it can see, observe, listen to find out directly for itself if there is something beyond the measures devised by man to discover reality. To the speaker, there is a reality beyond the things which man has put together. But the speaker has no authority for anybody. Each one has to find out for himself. The individual has to be in a state of tremendous revolution, and out of that mutation there is action. In the very process of uncovering yourself, of discovering the whole content of consciousness, there is action, and such a mind in action is explosive. It inevitably affects society, but it is unconcerned with whether it has an effect or not.

Most of us want to change, to reform society; but every reform needs further reform, and every change breeds disintegration because it is a denial of complete mutation. I am talking of psychological revolution, and when there is that revolution, there is total action, not partial action from different levels of our consciousness. It is only the total action from one's whole being that has a tremendous effect on the world.

So, a mind that is seeking reality must be in a state of constant observation—which means that there is no accumulation and no authority. It must also be in a state of questioning, of doubt. There must be a healthy skepticism with regard to everything that it thinks or feels, everything that it considers important or unimportant, so that it strips itself of all its comforting supports and stands completely alone. Only such a mind is innocent, and only such a mind can find out whether or not there is reality.

Do you want to question this, any of you?

Question: May I ask who is it that is aware, and if there is a difference between awareness and the watching of the watcher?

KRISHNAMURTI: When you listen totally to music, or to someone speaking, is there a listener? When you watch something with complete attention, is there a watcher? It is only when our attention is divided, incomplete, that there is a watcher apart from the watching; and then we ask, "Who is the watcher?"

How do you listen to anything? You listen partially, don't you? You do not give your whole attention. You are not deeply interested in what the other fellow is saying, and you pay very little attention; you listen casually, so there is a division between listening and the listener. But if you listen to something with complete attention, there is no such division. You know what we mean by complete attention: to attend without effort. Do not say, "I am distracted, and how am I to attend without effort?" If you pay attention to what you call distraction, then that distraction ceases to be a distraction, does it not?

Generally we do not pay attention, so we are trained in concentration. If in your job you did not concentrate on what you were doing, you would lose your job; so you are trained, conditioned, disciplined to concentrate. Such concentration implies exclusion. In requiring yourself to concentrate on one thing, you are bound to exclude something else. When your thought wanders away from what you want to concentrate on, to that which you are trying to exclude, you call it distraction; so, for you, concentration is a form of conflict, and that is all most of us know.

Now, what I am talking about is something entirely different. It is to attend without conflict. It is to listen without strain, without disturbance, which is to listen with complete attention; and you can listen with complete attention only when in listening there is no profit, no personal motive, no demand, no interpretation. You are simply listening. In that state of total listening there is no entity who listens, no listener separate from the listening. It is a unitary process which takes place when you are interested in something completely.

Have you ever observed a child with a new toy? Until it becomes familiar and he gets bored with it, the toy absorbs him. He is so strongly attracted by the toy that he is temporarily one with it; there is no distraction because the toy has absorbed him completely. We too want to be completely absorbed by something—God, sex, love, a hundred things. We want to be so committed to something that it will completely take us over, but this absorption is not attention. Most of us have something outside or inside the skin to which we are committed and in which we can lose ourselves—a belief, a hope, a relationship, a particular form of work or amusement—and any such commitment is always neurotic. And whatever society you live in, the communist or any other, demands that you be committed to something—to a party, to an ideology, to the defense of the state—because otherwise you are a dangerous human being. But when neither the outer nor the inner absorbs you, and you have understood the whole process of concentration and exclusion, then from that understanding there comes a state of simple awareness, of effortless attention in which your body, your mind, your whole being is alert, completely attentive.

Sir, listen to that train as it is passing by. If you listen to the noise, to the roar of it, without resistance, without any sense of building a wall against it, if you listen to it completely, then you will find that there is no listener.

Question: You speak of the tremendous energy that is required for complete attention. How is one to have such energy?

KRISHNAMURTI: How do we have energy? For one thing, by eating the right kind of food, or whatever kind of food one needs, and by taking sufficient exercise and getting the right amount of sleep. And most of us also derive energy from competition, struggle, conflict, do we not? That is all the energy we know. Being caught in the limited energy and wanting therefore to expand our consciousness, we resort to drugs. There are various drugs that help to expand consciousness, and at the moment of that expansion, induced by a drug, we feel tremendously aware, sensitive. It gives us a different quality, a keen sense of otherness. This effect has been described by various people who have actually taken the drugs.

Now, how do we awaken in ourselves an energy that has its own momentum, that is its own cause and effect, an energy that has no resistance and does not deteriorate? How does one come by it? The organized religions have advocated various methods, and by practicing a particular method one is supposed to get this energy. But methods do not give this energy. The practice of a method implies conformity, resistance, denial, acceptance, adjustment, so that whatever energy one has is merely wearing itself out. If you see the truth of this, you will never practice any method. That is one thing. Secondly, if energy has a motive, an end towards which it is going, that energy is self-destructive. And for most of us, energy does have a motive, does it not? We are moved by a desire to achieve, to become this or that, and therefore our energy defeats itself. Thirdly, energy is made feeble, petty, when it is conforming to the past—and this is perhaps our greatest difficulty. The past is not only the many yesterdays but also every minute that is being accumulated, the memory of the thing that was over a second before. This accumulation in the mind is also destructive of energy.

So, to awaken this energy, the mind must have no resistance, no motive, no end in view, and it must not be caught in time as yesterday, today, and tomorrow. Then energy is constantly renewing itself and therefore not degenerating. Such a mind is not committed; it is completely free, and it is only such a mind that can find the unnameable, that extraordinary something which is beyond words. The mind must free itself from the known to enter into the unknown.

July 28, 1963

Questions

Banaras, 1962

London, 1962

Saanen, 1962

Saanen, 1963

Index

Printed in the USA
CPSIA information can be obtained
at www.ICGtesting.com
CBHW081032280524
9184CB00002B/3

9 781934 989463